Leo Laporte's

PC
Help Desk

Leo Laporte & Mark Edward Soper

que®

800 East 96th Street
Indianapolis, Indiana 46240 USA

Leo Laporte's PC Helpdesk

Copyright © 2006 by Que Publishing

International Standard Book Number: 0-7897-3394-3

Library of Congress Catalog Card Number: 2005924991

Printed in the United States of America

First Printing: September 2005

08   07   06   05   4   3   2   1

Trademarks

Warning and Disclaimer

Bulk Sales

Que Publishing offers excellent discounts on this book when ordered in quantity for bulk purchases or special sales. For more information, please contact

U.S. Corporate and Government Sales
1-800-382-3419
corpsales@pearsontechgroup.com

For sales outside of the U.S., please contact

International Sales
international@pearsoned.com

Associate Publisher
Greg Wiegand

Executive Editor
Rick Kughen

Development Editor
Rick Kughen

Managing Editor
Charlotte Clapp

Project Editor
Dan Knott

Copy Editor
Bart Reed

Indexer
Erika Millen

Proofreader
Tracy Donhardt

Technical Editor
Mark Reddin

Reviewer
Gareth Branwyn

Publishing Coordinator
Sharry Lee Gregory

Book Designer
Ann Jones

Page Layout
Bronkella Publishing

Contents at a Glance

Table of Contents

3 Troubleshooting Storage Devices   163

6 Troubleshooting Multimedia and Imaging Devices   353

About the Authors

Leo Laporte is the former host of two shows on TechTV—*The Screen Savers* and *Call for Help*. Leo is a weekend radio host on Los Angeles radio KFI AM 640 and co-hosts *Call for Help* on Canada's TechTV network. He also appears regularly on many other television and radio programs, including ABC's *World News Now* and *Live with Regis and Kelly* as "The Gadget Guy." He is the author of four recent bestsellers: *Leo Laporte's 2005 Gadget Guide*, *Leo Laporte's Mac Gadget Guide*, *Leo Laporte's Guide to TiVo*, and *Leo Laporte's 2005 Technology Almanac*.

In January 1991, he created and co-hosted *Dvorak On Computers*, the most listened to high-tech talk radio show in the nation, syndicated on more than 60 stations and around the world on the Armed Forces Radio Network. Laporte also hosted *Laporte on Computers* on KSFO and KGO Radio in San Francisco.

On television, Laporte was host of *Internet!*, a weekly half-hour show airing on PBS in 215 cities nationwide. He reported on new media for *Today's First Edition*, on PBS, and did daily product reviews and demos on *New Media News*, broadcast nationally on Jones Computer Network and ME/U, and regionally on San Francisco's Bay TV.

Mark Edward Soper has taught computer troubleshooting and other technical subjects to thousands of students from Maine to Hawaii since 1992.

He is a longtime contributor to *Upgrading and Repairing PCs*, working on the 11th through 16th Editions. He has contributed chapters to *Upgrading and Repairing Networks Second Edition*, *Special Edition Using Microsoft Windows Millennium Edition*, and *Special Edition Using Microsoft Windows XP* (both *Home* and *Pro* editions).

Mark co-authored both the first and second editions of *Upgrading and Repairing PCs, Technician's Portable Reference*, and *Upgrading and Repairing PCs: Field Guide*. He also co-wrote *Upgrading and Repairing PCs: A+ Study Certification Guide, Second Edition* and *TechTV's Upgrading Your PC*.

Mark is the author of *TechTV's Upgrading Your PC, Second Edition* and *Easy Digital Cameras*. Mark also authored *Absolute Beginner's Guide to Home Networking*, *Absolute Beginner's Guide to A+ Certification*, and *Absolute Beginner's Guide to Home Automation*.

Mark has written articles for *MaximumPC* magazine and contributed chapters to *The MaximumPC Ultimate PC Performance Guide* and *The MaximumPC Guide to Building a Dream PC*.

He has also written for Skywire Software's Answer Suite Content Library and developed test questions for ReviewNet. Since 2004, Mark has been teaching classes on digital photography and image archiving for Ivy Tech State College, Evansville, Indiana.

When he's not writing, Mark enjoys spending time with his family and organizing his photography and transportation collection. You can contact him via email at mesoper@selectsystems.com.

Dedication

This book is dedicated to the memory of C.S. Lewis. He taught clear thinking to generations as a professor and tutor, and to many more generations through his books.

Acknowledgments

Above all, I thank God for the opportunity to learn, to share what I know, and to keep learning. He expects each of us to make the most of what He's given us, and with His help, I do my utmost to live up to His gifts.

My family continues to be a source of inspiration, joy, and real-life computer troubleshooting experience. Thanks to Cheryl, who reminds me to take time to enjoy being a grandparent. Thanks to Kate and Hugh and their children, Jarvis and Linus, for reminding me that there's more to life than computers. Thanks to Edward and Erin, Ian, and Jeremy for keeping me up to date on technology and life.

Thanks very much to Leo Laporte for the opportunity to team up with one of the most recognizable faces in technology.

Thanks as always to the terrific team at Que. I've worked with them on book projects since 1999, and it continues to be a pleasure. In particular, my thanks go to:

Greg Wiegand, who has built and maintained a great organization.

Rick Kughen, who conceived the original vision for this book and helped make it even better with his questions and queries.

Charlotte Clapp, who helped keep all of us in line.

Dan Knott, for keeping the author reviews flowing.

Bart Reed, for correcting grammar.

Erika Millen, for helping you find what you need.

Tracy Donhardt, for keeping the cross-references pointing to the right pages.

Mark Reddin, for verifying technical issues and suggesting improvements.

Sharry Lee Gregory, for keeping those advance checks coming.

Ann Jones, for making the cover and interior design attractive and useful.

Gareth Branwyn, for reviewing the text.

And the rest of the team at Que, who pioneered technology publishing over 20 years ago and has kept pioneering ever since.

Tell Us What You Think!

As the reader of this book, *you* are our most important critic and commentator. We value your opinion and want to know what we're doing right, what we could do better, what areas you'd like to see us publish in, and any other words of wisdom you're willing to pass our way.

As an associate publisher for Que Publishing, I welcome your comments. You can email or write me directly to let me know what you did or didn't like about this book— as well as what we can do to make our books better.

Please note that I cannot help you with technical problems related to the topic of this book. We do have a User Services group, however, where I will forward specific technical questions related to the book.

When you write, please be sure to include this book's title and author as well as your name, email address, and phone number. I will carefully review your comments and share them with the author and editors who worked on the book.

Email: feedback@quepublishing.com

Mail: Greg Wiegand
         Associate Publisher
         Que Publishing
         800 East 96th Street
         Indianapolis, IN 46240 USA

For more information about this book or another Que Publishing title, visit our website at www.quepublishing.com. Type the ISBN (excluding hyphens) or the title of a book in the Search field to find the page you're looking for.

Introduction

Why You Need This Book

Whether you use a PC for gaming, creativity, or extending your workday, you're going to have problems with hardware, Windows, applications, networking, the Internet, or peripherals. There's no getting around it—PCs don't always work right. And when they don't work, you want answers that work and you want them fast!

Computer problems can be divided into three categories:

- Hardware problems
- Software problems
- Internet/networking problems

Sometimes, a computer problem involves two or more of these areas, making the solution even tougher. Fortunately, *Leo Laporte's PC Help Desk* is designed to solve the most common problems you'll encounter in all three areas, even if multiple problems are plaguing your system.

This book is designed to give you the answers you need to solve your computer problems—fast! Instead of forcing you to read about the history of computers or stuffing long lists of software and hardware features into your brain and making you figure out which ones hold the answers to your problem, our goal is to take you directly from symptoms to solutions.

You can count on the solutions in this book. They are based on Leo and Mark's over 40 years of combined experience with computers and related technologies and many years of applying their knowledge to solving problems via consulting (Leo and Mark), teaching troubleshooting classes and writing magazine articles (Mark), hosting radio and TV shows (Leo), and writing books (Leo and Mark). Mark's trusty FRANKENPC laboratory computer and its mates were subjected to dozens of configuration changes during the course of research on this book and its predecessor, Mark's *PC Help Desk in a Book*. For this edition, even more problems and solutions have been gathered from discussions with computer users, online research, and suggestions from Que Publishing's editorial and technical staff. This book is based on facts, not fantasy, so you can rely on it.

How to Use This Book

Unlike most computer books, which dump huge numbers of facts into your brain and expect you to sift through them to find the answers to your problem, *Leo Laporte's PC Help Desk* is designed to provide you with fast access to practical solutions you can apply right away. We hope you'll find it fascinating reading, but it's really intended to be a quick reference you'll turn to when your computer has a problem and put aside until you have another problem—or another question.

Some troubleshooting books tell you *what* do to without telling you *why*. *Leo Laporte's PC Help Desk* is different. We love to explain why things are the way they are inside your computer, commiserate with you when things don't make sense, and show you solutions that make sense. We've never believed that treating human beings as robots it a good idea, and we're not about to start. You deserve an explanation of computer problems and their solutions, and we make sure you get what you deserve.

Some books are designed to be read just once; again, *Leo Laporte's PC Help Desk* is different. Because of its broad and deep coverage of computer problems and solutions, you'll turn to it as a valuable reference again and again to solve computer problems at home, at the office, or at the corporate help desk.

Here's how to get the most from this book:

1. Take a look at the chapters; they're discussed in detail later in this introduction. Go to the chapter that most closely matches your general problem area. For example, if you're having a problem getting your digital camera to connect with your PC, go to Chapter 6, "Troubleshooting Multimedia and Imaging Devices."

2. Each chapter starts with a feature we call Fast Track to Solutions, a table of symptoms and solutions. Use this table to point yourself toward underlying problems and their solutions.

Start here when you need help fast. Each table lists symptoms common to the parts of your computer or peripherals discussed in that chapter.

3. As soon as you have located the appropriate Fast Track to Solutions symptoms table, look up the symptom. Each symptom sends you directly to a troubleshooting flowchart or book section that covers your problem and its solution.

4. If you are directed to a flowchart, each flowchart provides step-by-step solutions with ample cross-references to the text that provides detailed information about the problem and how to find the solution.

5. If you are directed to a particular book section, use the text, screen shots, and equipment photos to learn more about how your hardware and software work and to learn the troubleshooting steps needed to solve your problem.

6. Use the special elements in each chapter to find valuable tips and shortcuts, discover useful websites, and avoid potential dangers.

Here's an example of how to use this book to solve a problem:

1. Assume that you can't hear any sound coming from your computer's speakers. Chapter 5, "Troubleshooting Graphics and Sound Problems," covers audio problems, so turn to the start of Chapter 5 to get started. The Fast Track to Solutions symptoms table at the beginning of this chapter offers a flowchart called "Speaker and Volume Control Problems." Go to the flowchart and follow the solutions given in order. For example, in this flowchart, the first question is, "Is your sound hardware working according to Device Manager?" If you are not sure or if you have already used Device Manager to determine the sound hardware is not working, follow the cross-reference to the "Sound Hardware Problems" flowchart for solutions. If Device Manager indicates the sound hardware is working correctly, the next question is, "Did you just attach the speakers to the sound hardware?" If you answer Yes, the flowchart directs you to check the speaker connections. If you answer No, the flowchart directs you to make sure the speakers are turned on. Cross-references to specific sections of the book provide you with illustrations and write-ups to help you answer the questions posed in each flowchart.

Continue through the flowchart until you find the solution that matches your hardware and situation.

2. If you are directed to a particular portion of a chapter by Fast Track to Solutions or a flowchart, read the text and follow the suggestions and cross-references given there until you solve the problem. The pictures and screen shots provided will help you locate and use similar features on your system. For many problems, you will use a combination of one or more flowcharts and particular book sections to find the right solution.

How This Book Is Organized

Leo Laporte's PC Help Desk includes the following sections:

- Ten chapters cover all the important hardware and software components of your computer and peripherals.

- An appendix includes a guide to troubleshooting methods and tools and over 50 flowcharts to help you solve the most common PC and peripheral problems.

The following sections explain the book sections in greater details.

Chapter 1: PC Anatomy 101

The first chapter of this book provides a detailed look at what makes your computer work inside and out, along with coverage of the BIOS setup program, hardware resources, Power-On Self-Test error codes, and coverage of the major I/O port types in typical computers. Because you need to be careful when you work inside your computer, this chapter also provides you with instructions on how to avoid damage from electrostatic discharge (ESD).

Wherever you are on the computer knowledge scale, from novice to expert, be sure to read Chapter 1 for valuable background. If you're in a hurry for particular information about your PC's internal layout or external ports, use the Fast Track to Solutions symptoms table at the beginning of the chapter to go straight to the appropriate section of the book.

Chapter 2: Troubleshooting Windows XP and Windows Applications

Chapter 2 starts with a Fast Track to Solutions symptoms table. Dig into it for fast help with the most common problems with Windows and software (shovel not included).

In this chapter, you learn how to troubleshoot and solve problems with the Windows boot, startup, and shutdown processes. Next, you discover how to use Control Panel to solve problems with your system, how to use Device Manager to fix balky components, and how to use other Windows XP tools such as System Information, Net Diagnostics, CHKDSK, Defrag, and others to solve common problems. This chapter also shows you how to keep Windows up to date with service packs and Windows Update, and how to repair a "broken" Windows installation. If Windows works but programs don't, this chapter also shows you how to fix and update problem programs, how to fix STOP (blue screen) errors, and how to select the best tools to stop viruses and slam spyware. This chapter assumes that you have installed Windows XP Service Pack 2 (because Microsoft says it's good for you, and this is one time they're right!).

Chapter 3: Troubleshooting Storage Devices

If your PC's running out of storage space or can't read some of its drives, forget about passing Go. Instead, proceed directly to the Fast Track to Solutions symptoms table at the start of the chapter.

In this chapter, you learn how to solve problems with floppy drives, ATA/IDE and Serial ATA (SATA) internal hard disks, as well as external drives that connect through USB, IEEE-1394, or CardBus connectors. This chapter also covers drive upgrades for both desktop and portable computers, and wraps up with solutions for rewritable CD and DVD drives, including the latest dual-layer models.

Chapter 4: Troubleshooting Your Printer

No printing? Garbage printing? Wasting paper? Read Fast Track to Solutions at the start of this chapter. (It's preprinted for your troubleshooting convenience!)

Inside this chapter, learn how to diagnose printers that won't print or print gibberish output and solve problems with standard and photo

inkjet printers, dye-sublimation photo printers, or laser and LED printers. Learn how to use printer properties sheets to achieve top-quality
output.

Chapter 5: Troubleshooting Graphics and Sound Problems

Fuzzy monitor? Shaky sound? If you've already cleaned your glasses
and removed your earplugs but things haven't improved, mosey on
over to the Fast Track to Solutions symptom tables at the start of this
chapter for help.

In this chapter, you learn how to troubleshoot monitor and graphics
card problems, tweak your display for best visual quality, set up multiple displays, improve 3D game performance with graphics and audio
settings, reinstall or update a driver, and fix audio problems with applications and music CDs.

Chapter 6: Troubleshooting Multimedia and Imaging Devices

Hit the Fast Track to Solutions symptom tables at the front of the
chapter instead of hitting a balky DV camcorder, bothersome digital
camera, or other multimedia hardware and software.

In this chapter, you learn how to fix DV camcorder or digital camera
connections to your PC, recover data from formatted or erased media,
fix DVD playback problems, solve compatibility issues with digital
music players, make Windows Media Player work *your* way, and
improve the quality and performance of photo scanners.

Chapter 7: Troubleshooting I/O Ports and Input Devices

If your mousing is miserable or your ports are leaning to starboard,
steer for the Fast Track to Solutions symptom tables at the start of
this chapter.

In this chapter, discover the best methods for troubleshooting problems with IEEE-1394, USB, PS/2, serial, and parallel ports. Learn how
to get the most out of USB 2.0 ports and solve problems with standard and wireless keyboards and mice.

Chapter 8: Troubleshooting Your Network and Internet Connections

Got an Internet connection that connects to nothing? Got a "notwork" instead of a network? Get thee to the Fast Track to Solutions symptoms table at the start of this chapter, pronto!

In this chapter, you learn how to fix problems caused by bad web-viewing components, discover the meaning of website error messages and numbers, solve problems with analog and broadband Internet connections, repair broken Ethernet and Wi-Fi networks, and discover TCP/IP configuration and troubleshooting tools and methods.

Chapter 9: Troubleshooting Memory, Processor, and System Performance Problems

If your computer acts as if it's sloth-powered, go to the Fast Track to Solutions symptoms table at the start of the chapter for help.

In this chapter, you learn how to track down the causes of slow system performance and solve them through virtual memory fine-tuning as well as processor or memory upgrades. Discover the best solutions for cooling problems and how to right-size a memory upgrade. Find out how to avoid motherboard and processor failures.

Chapter 10: Troubleshooting Power Problems

If your computer won't boot or reboots whenever it feels like it, power up with the Fast Track to Solutions symptoms table at the start of this chapter.

In this chapter, you discover the signs of power supply overloading and failure, learn how to perform a power supply upgrade, and how to protect your system from poor-quality power or electrical blackouts.

Appendix: Flowcharts and Troubleshooting Methodology

A human appendix is mostly useless. On the other hand, this appendix is one of the most use*ful* sections in the entire book (the rest of the book's pretty good too!).

Whether you've arrived at the flowcharts from a symptoms table or headed straight to the back, you'll find dozens of flowcharts to help you with major PC and peripheral problems. A sample flowchart helps you understand the concept if you're new to flowchart-driven troubleshooting.

If you're an experienced troubleshooter, the flowcharts might be all you need. However, if you're new to solving your own computer problems, be sure to read the section called "Troubleshooting Methodology." We've placed it at the front of this appendix so you won't miss it. This section puts our recommendations for tools, techniques, and general troubleshooting philosophy at your fingertips.

Special Elements in This Book

In addition to extensive cross-referencing, screen shots, and equipment photos, you will also find several special elements in this book to help you with particular troubleshooting issues:

- **On the Web**—Websites that have more information about the current topic
- **Cautions and Warnings**—Information you should read and digest before attempting operations that can be hazardous to you, your data, or your computer
- **Leo Says**—Advice from Leo
- **Shortcut to Success**—Tips for accomplishing a task more easily

A Word from Mark for Fans of *PC Help Desk in a Book*

This book is the long-awaited (at least by some readers) second edition of my *PC Help Desk in a Book*. If you already own that book, you're probably wondering, "Do I need this new edition?" Of course you do!

But seriously, here's what's new and better about this edition:

- Every chapter has been upgraded with updated material, new illustrations, enhanced coverage, and brand-new topics and sidebars.
- Better organization reduces duplication and page flipping and makes finding the right answers faster than ever before.
- Updated and brand-new flowcharts cover additional topics.

To make room for the many improvements in this new edition, a few cuts have been made. Now that Windows XP has been the dominant version of Windows for four years, we felt it was time to do away with legacy Windows coverage. Similarly, coverage of legacy devices no longer in widespread use such as SCSI host adapters and scanners and parallel port scanners has also been eliminated.

We believe that *Leo Laporte's PC Help Desk* is a "must-buy" for every reader of the original edition and is destined to make many thousands of friends in this new and improved edition.

PC Anatomy 101

TROUBLESHOOTING

FAST TRACK TO SOLUTIONS (SYMPTOM TABLE)

Symptom	Flowchart or Book Section	See Page
I want to adjust AGP video settings.	Advanced BIOS and Chipset Features Menus	49
I need to enable my USB ports.	Integrated Peripherals (I/O Devices)	51
I don't know what hardware is inside my system.	Inside a Typical PC	24
I don't know what a parallel or serial port looks like.	Rear Views of Typical Desktop Computers	18
I'm not sure if I have USB or IEEE-1394 ports.	Rear Views of Typical Desktop Computers	18
I'm not sure how to tell if my hard disk is recognized by my system.	Detecting Installed Drives	47
My hard disk is not being recognized; what do I do now?	Points of Failure Inside the Computer	27
I need to disable onboard audio so I can install a sound card.	Integrated Peripherals (I/O Devices)	51
I want to make sure the CPU (processor) fan is running when I start my computer.	PC Health (Hardware Monitor)	54
How can I tell if my processor or memory voltage is correct when I start my computer?	PC Health (Hardware Monitor)	54
My system is wasting time looking for Serial ATA (SATA) drives that are not installed.	Integrated Peripherals (I/O Devices)	51
I can't use my USB mouse or keyboard when the Windows desktop is not running.	Integrated Peripherals (I/O Devices)	51
How can I view IRQ, DMA, memory, or I/O port address usage in Windows?	Viewing Hardware Resources in Use	62
I think I might have a hardware conflict.	Hardware Resources	58
I have replaced my serial or parallel port devices with USB devices and want to disable the serial or parallel ports.	Integrated Peripherals (I/O Devices)	51
My computer is beeping when I start it.	Power-On Self Test and The Computer Doesn't Start	57
My computer won't start.	The Computer Doesn't Start	709
I can hear my computer turn on, but there's nothing on my screen.	The Computer Starts but the Screen Is Blank	658

Subsystems Make the Computer

You can't troubleshoot a computer very well unless you understand what a computer is and how it's put together. Although your "personal confuser" might look like a big (or not-so-big) box on your desk, it's not really a single unit. Instead, it's a collection of hardware subsystems:

- Video
- Storage
- Input devices
- Printers and other output devices
- Audio
- Networking
- Processor
- Memory
- Power

Computer hardware can't do a thing for you (or to you) without software. As it turns out, these subsystems are actually controlled by two types of software:

- **A system BIOS (basic input/output system) chip on the motherboard**—A BIOS chip is an example of "software on a chip," or firmware.

- **The operating system and its device drivers**—These are the files that tell Windows how to use your PC's hardware. In this book, we concentrate on Microsoft Windows XP (Home Edition and Professional, including x64 as well as Service Packs 1 and 2).

Application programs such as Microsoft Office, Adobe Photoshop Elements, Quicken, and innumerable others (we didn't take time to count them) communicate with hardware through the operating system and its device drivers and the system BIOS. The end result? You create, change, store, print, and transmit documents, photos, videos, and other digital masterpieces.

There are plenty of ways the whole process can fail, and with the greater demands we place on our computers today, more is at stake than ever before. A few years ago, a computer failure might have meant that you'd lose your home budget or customer records. Now, a computer failure could also wipe out your digital photo collection or gigabytes of digital music files. That's scary!

We're here to help take the fright out of computer problems and help you keep your PC running right. The first step to handling computer problems is learning what's inside a typical computer. If you don't understand your PC, troubleshooting it is just about impossible.

This chapter introduces you to the major components you will find in typical computers, including those prone to being a "point of failure." Think of this as an anatomy lesson, but without the formaldehyde and nasty smells.

What Is a Point of Failure?

In the following sections, we use the term *point of failure* to refer to a component or BIOS configuration that could cause problems for your system. This term isn't meant to suggest that computers are constantly on the verge of having a problem, but that some parts of the computer are more likely to cause problems than others.

All Around a Desktop PC

Now that external ports such as USB and IEEE-1394 are favorite ways to add additional storage and imaging devices (photo printers, scanners, digital cameras, and DV camcorders), making sure that the external connections on your PC are working properly is more important than ever before.

The outside of the computer is where you'll find the following items:

- Cable connections for external peripherals such as cable modems, printers, monitors, and scanners
- Drive bays for removable-media and optical drives
- The power supply fan and voltage switch
- The power switch, reset button, and signal lights

No matter what you think the source of a computer problem might be, it pays to start with the outside. From systems that won't start to speakers that are "quiet...maybe too quiet," external ports and devices are worth investigating for the answers.

Front Views of Typical Desktop Computers

Most typical "desktop" computers actually use a tower form factor
that is sometimes too bulky for your desk, so they're often placed on
the floor. Figure 1.1 shows the front-mounted drives and ports found
on a typical desktop computer, the Dell Dimension XPS Gen 3.

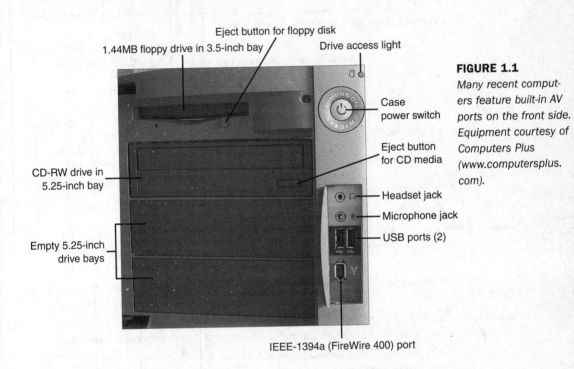

Eject button for floppy disk

1.44MB floppy drive in 3.5-inch bay

Drive access light

Case power switch

Eject button for CD media

CD-RW drive in 5.25-inch bay

Headset jack

Microphone jack

USB ports (2)

Empty 5.25-inch drive bays

IEEE-1394a (FireWire 400) port

FIGURE 1.1

*Many recent comput-
ers feature built-in AV
ports on the front side.
Equipment courtesy of
Computers Plus
(www.computersplus.
com).*

What Makes a "Desktop" Computer a Desktop Computer?

Today, a "desktop computer" (like the one shown in Figure 1.1) is often
found on the floor. Back in the 1980s, though, when the first IBM PCs
were battling the Apple II's for desktop dominance, a PC did sit on the
desk. These days, the term *desktop computer* usually describes computers that have the following features:

- They use standard internal components such as motherboards,
  processors, memory, drives, sound cards, and video cards.
- They can be upgraded and rebuilt by the user without special tools.
- They use separate input devices (keyboard, mouse, or other pointing device).

Most (but not all) desktop computers are multipiece units with a separate keyboard and monitor, although some vendors produce "all-in-one"
PCs that incorporate an LCD display.

The case shown in Figure 1.1 is sometimes referred to as a "mid-tower" case; typical cases in this category have room for six internal drives (three in 5.25-inch bays and three in 3.5-inch bays; two of the 3.5-inch bays are used for hard disks and are not visible in Figure 1.1).

Where Should I Put My Computer?

If you have a desktop PC in a tower case, you might be wondering where to put it. Traditionally, users placed them on the floor, but the problem is that a PC that's on the floor can be kicked, bumped by the vacuum cleaner, might inhale pet fur into its air intakes, and suffer other indignities. If you don't want your PC sitting on your desk, but don't want it resting on the floor, get a computer desk with a shelf for the case, or put wheels on the bottom of the case to raise it above the floor. Just make sure you put it someplace where you can get to the internal drives and front-mounted ports easily. In some cases, you might need to add extension cables to your mouse, keyboard, or video cables to enable them to reach to your system.

The 5.25-inch drive bays are used by CD and DVD optical drives as well as by tape-backup drives (a few now-obsolete removable-media drives also used the 5.25-inch drive bay). You can also install break-out boxes for high-end sound cards (such as the Sound Blaster Audigy series), cooling fans, drive-selection switches, and hubs for IEEE-1394 and USB 2.0 ports into 5.25-inch drive bays. The 3.5-inch drive bays are used by floppy drives, hard drives, and most removable-media drives such as Iomega Zip and Rev. Some IEEE-1394 and USB 2.0 hubs are small enough to fit into 3.5-inch drive bays.

Figure 1.2 illustrates how some systems incorporate flash memory card readers as well as I/O and multimedia ports into their front panels. This trend began with computers built for use with Windows XP Media Center Edition, but it's now very common on computers running Windows XP Home Edition or Professional as well. Some motherboard manufacturers now include front panel ports that mount in a spare 5.25-inch bay and allow you to plug USB and IEEE-1394 into them. You can also retrofit front-mounted USB and IEEE-1394 ports into empty 3.5-inch or 5.25-inch drive bays. Some front-panel ports also include memory card readers and BIOS error code displays for greater versatility and easier troubleshooting.

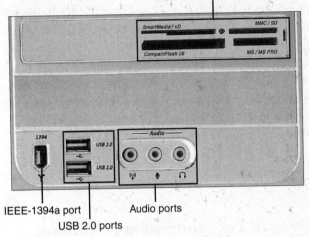

Flash memory card reader

IEEE-1394a port

USB 2.0 ports

Audio ports

FIGURE 1.2
*Some computers
feature front-mounted
flash memory card
readers for use with
digital cameras, PDAs,
and digital music
players.*

Points of Failure on the Front of Your Computer

The front of your computer may provide valuable clues if you're having problems with your system. In case of problems, check the following common points of failure for help:

- **Can't read CD media.** The drive door on the CD or DVD optical drive might not be completely closed or the media might be inserted upside down; press the eject button to open the drive, remove any obstacles, reseat the media, and then close the drive.

- **Can't shut down the computer with the case power switch.** The case power switch is connected to the motherboard on ATX and Micro-ATX systems, not directly to the power supply as with older designs. The wire might be loose or connected to the wrong pins on the motherboard. Keep in mind that most systems require you to hold in the power button for about four seconds before the system will shut down. If the computer crashes, you might need to shut down the computer by unplugging it, using the external power switch built into some power supplies, or by turning off the surge suppressor used by the computer. Check the manual that came with your computer (or with your motherboard if your computer is a home-built PC) to ensure that the case power switch is properly oriented. If your manual isn't clear on how these tiny plugs should be oriented, try contacting the manufacturer's tech support line.

- **Can't see the drive access or power lights.** As with the case power switch, these lights are also connected to the motherboard. These wires might also be loose or connected to the wrong pins on the motherboard.

- **Can't use front-mounted ports.** Front-mounted ports such as the ones shown in Figures 1.1 and 1.2 are connected with extension cables to the motherboard. If the cables inside the case are loose, the ports won't work. If the ports are disabled in the system BIOS, the ports won't work.

→ *See "Inside a Typical PC," this chapter, p. 24, for details.*

As you can see, sometimes it's necessary to open the system to fix a problem with an external port.

Rear Views of Typical Desktop Computers

If you're trying to fix a problem with a balky external peripheral, you need to look for the port to which it's connected. Although more and more PCs have front-mounted ports, many PCs connect some or all external peripherals to rear-mounted ports.

Figure 1.3 shows the rear of the desktop computer shown in Figure 1.1 when common peripheral cables are attached.

FIGURE 1.3
The rear panel of a typical desktop computer with common external peripheral cables attached.

1. Serial (COM) port
2. Parallel (LPT) port
3. PS/2 keyboard cable
4. PS/2 mouse cable
5. USB cable
6. 15-pin VGA display cable
7. DVI-I (digital/analog video) port on graphics card
8. TV-out (S-video) port on graphics card
9. Speaker cable (if you use 5.1 or 7.1 speakers, there will be several speaker cables plugged in here)

Figure 1.4 provides a more detailed view of the rear panel of another desktop system.

FIGURE 1.4
The rear panel of a typical desktop computer with built-in ports (left) and ports on add-in cards (right). Equipment courtesy of ComputersPlus (www.computersplus. com).

1. Rear case fan
2. PS/2 keyboard port
3. PS/2 mouse port
4. USB ports (4)
5. Parallel (LPT) port
6. Serial (COM) ports (2)
7. 10/100 Ethernet port
8. Integrated audio ports
9. DVI-I analog/digital video port (on AGP card)
10. TV-out (S-video)
11. VGA video port
12. Speaker and microphone ports on sound card
13. IEEE-1394a port on sound card (usually found on higher end sound cards, such as the Creative Audigy)

Almost all desktop computers built since the late 1990s use a motherboard design based on the ATX standard. These motherboards use a port cluster, which usually places the mouse and keyboard ports to the left, followed by some USB ports, the serial and parallel ports, and additional I/O or audio ports to the right, as shown in Figure 1.4. Systems that use integrated graphics often replace one of the serial ports shown in Figure 1.4 with a VGA port.

The power supply is located at the top of a typical tower-type desktop computer. If you are looking at a desktop system from the rear, it is to the left of the port cluster shown in Figure 1.4. Figure 1.5 shows the rear of a typical power supply. Power supplies convert high-voltage AC power into the low-voltage DC power used inside the computer. Because conversions of this type create heat, the power supply has a fan to cool itself and also help overall system cooling. The fan is often found on the rear of the unit, as in Figure 1.5, but some use a fan that faces the inside of the PC.

➜ For more details about ATX motherboard variations, see "Troubleshooting Motherboard Upgrades," Chapter 9, p. 602.

➜ For more information about serial, parallel, USB, and IEEE-1394 ports, see Chapter 7, "Troubleshooting I/O Ports and Input Devices."

➜ For more information about 10/100 Ethernet ports, see Chapter 8, "Troubleshooting Your Network and Internet Connections."

Although a few power supplies can switch between 115-volt and 230-volt services automatically, most use a sliding switch for voltage selection, as shown in Figure 1.5.

FIGURE 1.5
A typical power supply mounted in a computer.

→ *For more information about power supplies, see Chapter 10, "Troubleshooting Power Problems."*

Sliding AC voltage selector (set for 115V)
Power supply fan

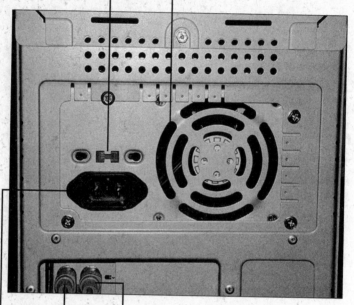

3-prong power connector
PS/2 keyboard cable
PS/2 mouse cable

Points of Failure on the Rear of Your Computer

The most likely point of failure on the rear of your computer is peripheral cabling. Fortunately, more and more devices use the light-weight USB cable shown in Figure 1.6 instead of the bulky, heavy serial and parallel cables (also shown in Figure 1.6). Note that serial, parallel, and VGA cables all use thumbscrews; if you don't fasten the thumbscrews to the connector on the computer, your cables won't connect tightly, and this could cause intermittent or complete failure of your peripherals.

Leo Says

My Favorite Desktop PC Features

As you look over your PC, keep this list of favorite features in mind. It can be helpful as you consider upgrading your "old reliable," or if you're thinking about the ultimate upgrade—a new PC!

- **Lots of USB ports**—I use USB ports for just about everything (printers, scanners, external drives, digital cameras, flash memory card readers, and so on), and I prefer not to use USB hubs until I'm forced to. If you have at least six USB 2.0 ports, you're all set! Note that some systems' front-mounted ports only support USB 1.1 speeds, making them less suitable for storage, printing, and imaging.

- **Some IEEE-1394 ports**—If your system doesn't have an IEEE-1394 port, you can't pull video direct from a DV camcorder. Also, some dual-mode external devices work better with IEEE-1394 than with USB 2.0. If you have a spare PCI slot, it's a worthwhile upgrade.

- **Dual-display (DVI and VGA) graphics**—If you equip your PC with a dual-display graphics card, you'll get so much more work done that you'll have time to play. Having two displays allows you to have your Word or Excel document open on one screen and Outlook on the other—handy! Of course, you could manage your fantasy football league on one monitor and use IM on the other, but that's just a suggestion. We're far too busy, uh, working for such frivolity.

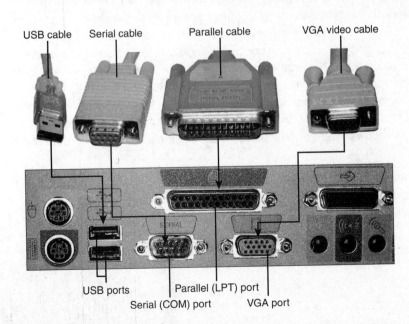

USB cable   Serial cable   Parallel cable   VGA video cable

USB ports   Parallel (LPT) port
Serial (COM) port   VGA port

FIGURE 1.6

USB, serial, parallel, and VGA cables (top) and the ports they connect to (bottom).

Peripheral cables such as the PS/2 mouse and keyboard, audio, as well as newer types of peripheral cables such as USB and IEEE-1394a, are pushed into place and are very lightweight. No thumbscrews or other locking devices are needed. However, these cables can also be pulled out of the socket easily, precisely because they are lightweight. You can disconnect and reconnect USB and IEEE-1394 devices while the power is on because they support hot-swapping.

When you attach cables to the ports at the rear of the computer, avoid tangling them together. Tangled cables could cause electrical interference with each other, leading to erratic performance of external devices such as your printer and monitor. Also, tangled cables put extra stress on ports, which could cause malfunctions or port failures.

The power supply shown previously in Figure 1.5 is another likely point of failure. If the three-prong power cable is not plugged all the way into the computer, the system might not start up at all, or it might shut down unexpectedly. If the voltage selector switch is not set correctly, the computer will not start at all, and if the power supply is set for 115V and is plugged into a 230V supply, the power supply and possibly other parts of the computer will be destroyed.

Stop ESD—Don't Fry Your PC!

ESD (electrostatic discharge) is a hidden danger to your data and your computer hardware, particularly when you open your computer to install new hardware or to troubleshoot a problem inside your system. ESD takes place when two items with different electrical potentials come close to each other or touch each other. ESD can happen even if you don't see a spark or feel a shock, and it takes very little ESD to damage or destroy computer parts. About 800 volts of ESD will give you a tingle or shock, but it takes less than 100 volts (an amount you can't even feel) to ruin a CPU, memory module, or other computer part. Low-power construction makes these parts very vulnerable to ESD.

You can avoid ESD damage when you're working inside your computer by following these tips:

- Use antistatic cleaning wipes to clean cases and monitors.
- Wear cotton or other natural fibers when you work on your PC; if you're working at home, ditch those synthetic-soled shoes and

work in your stocking feet (cotton socks, please!) to avoid generating static electricity.

- Buy and use anti-ESD devices such as a wrist strap with an alligator clip and an antistatic mat. Connect the alligator clip to the computer *after* you disconnect it from power; this equalizes the electrical potential between you and the computer to prevent ESD. Figure 1.7 shows you how a wrist strap works to protect your PC.

- Hold components by the case or card bracket—never by the circuit board or data/power connector.

Metal plate (must touch bare skin on wrist to enable ESD protection)

Snap connector with resistor to protect the wearer

Alligator clip connected to bare metal inside PC

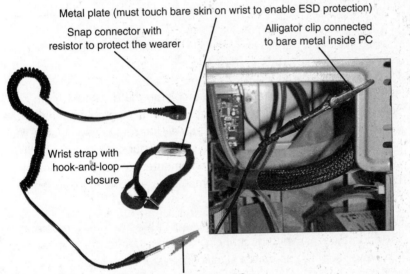

Wrist strap with hook-and-loop closure

Alligator clip connects to PC

FIGURE 1.7
A wrist strap reduces ESD potential when you connect the alligator clip to bare metal inside your PC and wear it properly.

Leo Says

Don't Commit These ESD Goofs

ESD protection is only as good as the user. To make sure a wrist strap works, take off the wristwatch or dangly bracelets on the wrist you want to use for the strap. Adjust the strap so the metal plate is snug against the inside of your wrist (so that hair won't interfere with ESD protection). Make sure you snap the cable with the alligator clip to the wrist strap. Make sure you attach the alligator clip to a metal part of the PC's chassis. You could use the power supply grill or the drive bay frame, as in Figure 1.7.

If you wear your wrist strap over your shirt, sweater or blouse or don't connect it to the alligator clip, you're wasting your time.

If you want to keep parts you remove from the computer safe as well as prevent ESD when you're inside the PC, look for a *field service kit*, which combines a grounding strap for your body with a grounded parts mat for the components you are removing (or installing).

Tracking Down ESD Protection

Try your local computer component store for ESD protection, but if you can't find protective devices locally, try these online sources:

- **e-Mat**—http://www.anti-staticmat.com
- **Radio Shack**—http://www.radioshack.com (search for "anti-static")
- **Static Specialists**—http://www.staticspecialists.com (click "personal grounding")

Inside a Typical PC

As you have already learned, some problems that manifest themselves on the outside of the computer come from problems inside the computer. If you ever add memory, add an internal drive, upgrade your processor or motherboard, or add a card to your computer, you will need to work with the interior of the computer to complete the task. The interior of a typical desktop computer is a crowded place, as Figure 1.8 shows.

Each of the devices highlighted in Figure 1.8, as well as the data, signal, and power cables that connect these devices to the motherboard and power supply, can cause significant system problems if they fail.

Expansion Slots

Typical desktop computers have two or more expansion slots, some of which might already be used for factory-installed devices such as video cards, network cards, or modems. Most computers have several PCI slots, and many also have a single AGP or PCI-Express slot for high-speed video. Although AGP slots are faster than PCI slots, they are configured the same way in the system BIOS. See "PCI Configuration," this chapter, p. 53, for details.

FIGURE 1.8
The interior of a typical PC using an ATX motherboard.

1. Power supply
2. Memory module
3. Empty memory sockets
4. Processor with fan/heatsink
5. nForce 250 chipset with passive heatsink
6. AGP graphics card
7. PCI card
8. SATA hard disk
9. Empty PCI slots
10. Floppy drive (partially hidden)
11. Optical drive (partially hidden)
12. ATX power supply connector
13. SATA cable
14. Floppy drive cable
15. ATA/IDE cable
16. Battery
17. Front panel cables
18. Rear case fan
19. ATA/IDE host adapter

Figure 1.9 compares the AGP and PCI slots in a typical system.

Some systems built since late 2004 have a single PCI-Express x16 slot for high-speed graphics (it's faster than AGP) and one or more PCI-Express x1 slots for general I/O card usage.

FIGURE 1.9
PCI and AGP slots compared.

AGP 4x/8x slot

32-bit PCI slots

Front of Computer

Leo Says

Double Your Graphics Pleasure with SLI

A few high-performance systems for gamers have a pair of PCI-Express x16 slots to enable *scalable link interfacing (SLI)*, a technique invented by NVIDIA that uses a pair of specially designed PCI-Express video cards to more quickly render 3D scenes on a single monitor. If you're really into 3D gaming, SLI rocks!

Figure 1.10 compares PCI-Express slots to PCI slots.

Regardless of the type of expansion slot your add-on card uses, you need to push the card connector all the way into the expansion slot when you install a card, as shown in Figure 1.11.

After the card is properly inserted into the expansion slot, you need to fasten the card bracket to the case with a screw.

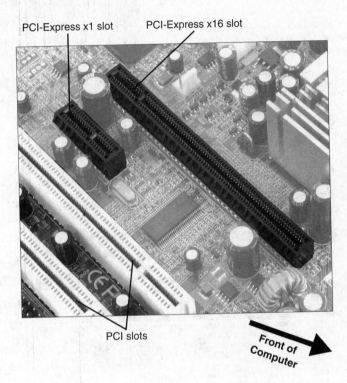

PCI-Express x1 slot   PCI-Express x16 slot

PCI slots

Front of Computer

FIGURE 1.10
PCI-Express and PCI slots compared.

Points of Failure Inside the Computer

Some of the problems you could encounter because of devices inside your computer include the following:

- **Overheating**—Failure of the fans in the power supply or those attached to the processor, North Bridge chip, or video card can cause overheating and can lead to component damage. The CPU fan shown in Figure 1.8 is connected to the motherboard to obtain power. Some case-mounted or older processor fans use a standard four-wire drive power connector instead (shown in Figure 1.14).

- **Loose add-on cards**—See Figure 1.11.

- **Inability to start the computer**—An improperly installed processor or memory module can prevent the computer from starting (see Figures 1.12 and 1.13).

FIGURE 1.11

A video card partly inserted into the slot (top) and fully inserted into the slot (bottom).

Card bracket not flush with rear edge of case

Bracket not flush with rear case wall

Connector not pushed down into slot

Card bracket flush with rear

Bracket flush with rear case wall

Connector pushed completely into slot

- **Drive failures**—If drives are not properly connected to power or data cables, or are not properly configured with jumper blocks, they will not work properly (see Figures 1.14, 1.15, 1.16, and 1.17, later in this chapter).

Fan connector on motherboard   Heatsink not locked into place

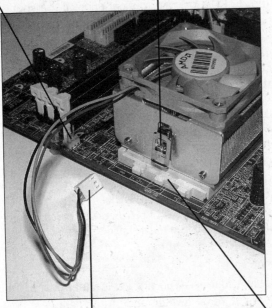

FIGURE 1.12
A Socket A processor that is not properly installed.

Fan not connected to motherboard   Locking tab on processor socket

FIGURE 1.13
A memory module before (top) and after (bottom) being locked into its socket.

1. DIMM memory module
2. Module locks in open position
3. Module locks in closed position
4. Memory module edge connector before module fully inserted
5. Memory module edge connector after module fully inserted

- **Multimedia failures**—If the analog or digital audio cable running from the CD-ROM or other optical drive to the sound card is disconnected, you might not be able to hear CD music through your speakers. Some high-end sound cards also have connections to an external breakout box for additional speaker or I/O options. Be careful when you work inside your computer to avoid disconnecting these cables (see Figure 1.18, later in this chapter).

Audio's Not Broken? Don't "Fix" It

Some systems can transfer CD music through the standard ATA/IDE cable and don't require a separate patch cable. If you can play music CDs through your speakers and your system doesn't use analog or digital audio cables, don't worry about it.

Most CD-ROM and other types of optical drives include analog or digital audio cables, but if you need replacements, most computer stores also stock them.

- **Front panel failures**—The tiny cables that connect the case power switch, reset switch, and status lights are easy to disconnect accidentally if you are working near the edges of the motherboard (see Figures 1.19 and 1.20). For a close-up view of these cables, see Figure 10.3 in Chapter 10.

- **Battery failure**—The battery (see Figure 1.20) maintains the system settings that are configured by the system BIOS. The settings are stored in a part of the computer called the CMOS (more formally known as the *nonvolatile RAM/real-time clock*, or *NVRAM/RTC*). If the battery dies (the average life is about 2 to 3 years), these settings will be lost.

- **BIOS chip failure**—The system BIOS chip (see Figure 1.20) can be destroyed by electrostatic discharge (ESD) or lightning strikes. However, BIOS chips can also become outdated. Whereas some systems use a socketed BIOS chip, like the one shown in Figure 1.20, others use a soldered chip. In both cases, software BIOS upgrades are usually available to provide additional BIOS features such as support for newer processors and hardware.

The ATA/IDE Interface

Virtually every desktop computer built since the mid-1990s has featured two ATA/IDE interfaces on the motherboard. Each ATA/IDE interface can handle one or two drives, including hard disk drives, optical (CD or DVD) drives, and removable-media drives. Therefore, you can install up to four ATA/IDE drives into a typical desktop computer.

The ATA/IDE interface uses a 40-pin connector (see Figure 1.14) that connects to a 40-wire or 80-wire ATA/IDE cable. This cable has three connectors, which go to the following locations:

- ATA/IDE interface on the motherboard
- Master drive
- Slave drive

The 40-wire cables, which are obsolete for hard disk use, support device speeds up to UltraDMA/33 (33MHz). The 80-wire cables support all older devices plus the latest drive speeds up to 133MHz (UltraDMA/133).

Each ATA/IDE interface uses an IRQ: IRQ 14 is used for the primary interface, and IRQ 15 is used for the secondary interface. These IRQs cannot be shared with other devices. For details, see "Hardware Resources," this chapter, p. 58.

Changing Cables Changes Jumpering Standards

The original ATA/IDE drive cable, which contained 40 wires, allowed users to select primary (master) and secondary (slave) drives with *jumper blocks* on the rear or bottom of the drives. Some vendors, such as Western Digital, supported a no-jumper-block configuration for single hard drives. Most drives are labeled with the correct jumper settings as well as with the correct orientation for the power and data cables. If your drive lacks this information, look up the drive model on the vendor's website.

However, in almost all recent systems, hard disk drives are connected with an 80-wire ATA/IDE cable. This cable allows ATA/IDE drives such as hard drives, CD-RW drives, and DVD drives to be jumpered as *Cable Select*, giving control of master/slave settings to the cable. With these cables, the black connector at one end of the cable is used for master, the middle (gray) connector is used for slave, and the blue end of the cable connects to the system board or other ATA/IDE host adapter.

For a close-up comparison of 40-wire and 80-wire cables, see Figure 3.4 in Chapter 3, "Troubleshooting Storage Devices."

FIGURE 1.14

A typical ATA/IDE CD-ROM drive before (top) and after (bottom) typical cabling and configuration problems have been corrected.

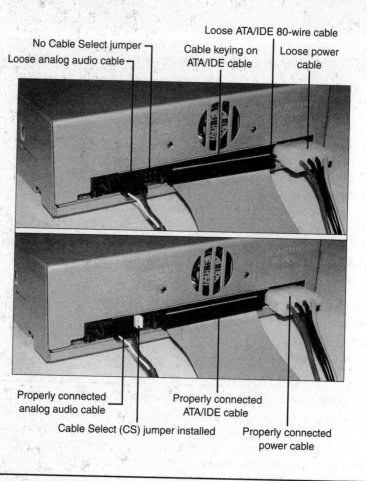

No Cable Select jumper
Loose analog audio cable
Loose ATA/IDE 80-wire cable
Cable keying on ATA/IDE cable
Loose power cable

Properly connected analog audio cable
Cable Select (CS) jumper installed
Properly connected ATA/IDE cable
Properly connected power cable

Beware the Unkeyed ATA/IDE Cable

Most ATA/IDE drives and motherboard host adapters are designed to accept cables only when they are properly connected. The usual method is to match the *key* on one side of the cable plug (refer to Figure 1.14) with a corresponding cutout on the cable connector. However, some low-cost 40-wire cables don't feature keying, making it easy to install them incorrectly. If you use such a cable, note that the colored stripe indicating pin 1 on the cable is usually on the same side of the cable as the power supply connector. Check the motherboard (shown later in Figure 1.15) for markings.

I recommend you use only 80-wire cables (which are always keyed) when you install new ATA/IDE drives.

Even if you aren't installing a new drive, if you move existing ATA/IDE cables around inside your computer to gain access to memory, processor, or other components, you need to recheck those cable connections, both to the drive and to the motherboard. It's very easy to accidentally pull these cables loose, which even if only partially detached will keep your drives from working properly.

Figure 1.15 shows a typical ATA/IDE motherboard connector.

Blue motherboard ATA/IDE drive connector
Colored stripe indicating pin 1 on ATA/IDE cable

Motherboard marking for pin 1 on ATA/IDE connectors

DIP switches for motherboard configuration

FIGURE 1.15
A typical ATA/IDE motherboard drive connector (top) and the DIP switches used on some motherboards for system configuration (left).

The Serial ATA (SATA) Interface

Although most systems still use ATA/IDE interfaces for hard disks and optical drives, Serial ATA (SATA) is an increasingly popular way to add high-performance hard disks to a system. Some systems, such as the one shown earlier in Figure 1.8, use a mixture of SATA and ATA/IDE drives.

The original SATA interface shown in Figures 1.16 and 1.17 does not, unfortunately, have a positive locking mechanism. The power and data cables push into place and can be removed with very little effort. An improved SATA connector that provides for positive locking has been introduced, but it's not yet widespread.

Figure 1.16 shows the SATA power and data cable connectors on the rear of a typical SATA drive.

→ *For more information about ATA/IDE drives, see Chapter 3, "Troubleshooting Storage Devices."*

FIGURE 1.16
Power and data cables on the rear of a typical SATA hard disk drive.

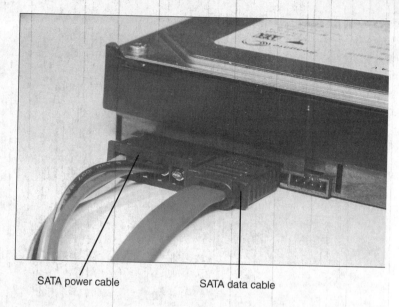

SATA power cable   SATA data cable

Figure 1.17 shows the SATA data cable and host adapter connector on a typical motherboard. Note that some systems with SATA drives use an add-on host adapter card.

SATA data cable

      SATA host adapter   Memory sockets

FIGURE 1.17
SATA host adapters and cable on a typical motherboard.

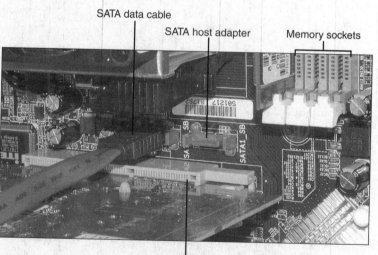

AGP slot

→ *For more information about SATA drives, see Chapter 3, "Troubleshooting Storage Devices."*

Integrated and Add-on Sound Hardware

A few years ago, you couldn't play CD or DVD audio unless your sound card was connected directly to the four-wire analog audio out or two-wire digital audio out jacks on the rear of a CD or DVD drive. Today, most media player applications use digital audio extraction (DAE) to play audio from CDs. However, if you use your modem as part of a voice-answering system or have a drive-bay based breakout box connected to your sound card, you want to make sure that the cables from these devices are connected to your sound card. Figure 1.18 shows typical connections to external devices.

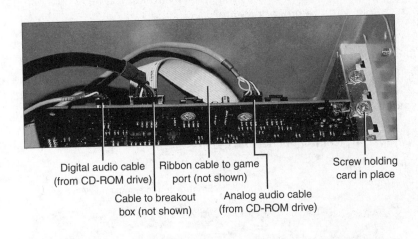

Digital audio cable
(from CD-ROM drive)

Ribbon cable to game
port (not shown)

Cable to breakout
box (not shown)

Analog audio cable
(from CD-ROM drive)

Screw holding
card in place

FIGURE 1.18
The top edge of a typical high-end sound card with multiple cable connections.

If you need to disconnect any cables running to your sound card or motherboard with integrated audio so that you can install another device, be sure to reconnect the cables when you're done.

→ *For more informa-tion about sound cards and integrated audio, see Chapter 5, "Troubleshooting Graphics and Sound Problems."*

Front Panel Connectors

Your motherboard is connected to the front of your PC by several small cables. These cables connect the power switch, power and hard disk access lights, PC speaker, and reset switch on the case to the motherboard. If you don't properly connect these cables to your moth-erboard, you might not be able to start your computer.

Although you might think that these cables would never be disturbed unless you are replacing a motherboard, think again! If you *ever* open a system for any purpose, including cleaning out the gunk that can accumulate over time, you might disturb these wires. We can tell you from experience that front-panel wires are about the easiest to dis-connect accidentally! Some motherboards and wire kits are well marked, whereas others are not. If you need to replace your mother-board, take time to note which cables go where on the old mother-board before you unplug them. This can be tricky because most motherboards use a two-row group of pins for front-panel cables. You must look at the motherboard markings or the system/motherboard manual to determine which cables are plugged in side by side and which are plugged in front of other cables. With some cables, the front-panel light or switch will not work unless you match the cable's pin 1 to pin 1 on the motherboard. If you connect a cable to the correct pins, but the switch or light doesn't work, reverse the connection to the motherboard. When the connection works, you have connected the cable with the proper polarity.

If your system has front-mounted USB, IEEE-1394, or USB-based flash memory card reader or audio ports, each of these ports and device types also uses a header cable. If the cable is disconnected from the motherboard, the port will fail. If the cable is not plugged into the motherboard correctly, the port could be damaged. Figure 1.19 shows a typical header cable installation for front-mounted USB ports compared to typical front-panel cables.

FIGURE 1.19
A USB header cable compared to front-panel cables.

Front-mounted signal and switch cables

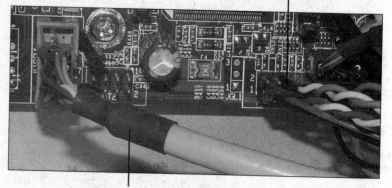

USB header cable

BIOS Chip and CMOS Battery

No matter what integrated ports your computer has—from legacy ports such as the PS/2 mouse, parallel and serial ports, and ATA/IDE host adapters, to newer ports such as IEEE-1394, USB, SATA host adapters, or audio—the system BIOS chip controls them.

The system BIOS chip contains tables of possible settings for each onboard device as well as other motherboard-based devices such as the processor (CPU) and memory. Almost all BIOS chips also contain setup programs, which are used to access the BIOS tables and enable you to choose the appropriate options for each onboard device.

BIOS settings are stored in a chip known officially as the *NVRAM/RTC (nonvolatile RAM/real-time clock) chip*, but often referred to informally as the *CMOS chip*. The name "nonvolatile RAM" is a bit misleading, though. Without the help of a small battery on the motherboard to retain BIOS/CMOS settings, they'd vanish as soon as you shut off the computer.

If your system is unable to store settings or if the onboard clock loses significant amounts of time, the onboard battery should be replaced.

➔ *For more information about battery types, see "What to Do If Your Computer Can't Retain BIOS Setup Information," this chapter, p. 56.*

The BIOS chip on most systems can be reprogrammed with software downloaded from the system or motherboard vendor. A downloadable BIOS upgrade might be necessary before you upgrade to faster memory, a faster processor, or to solve stability or other problems with your system. Before you install any motherboard upgrade, you should check the system or motherboard vendor's website to see if the upgrade you want to install will require a BIOS upgrade.

Figure 1.20 shows a typical socketed BIOS chip and CMOS battery. These items are often found near the front edge of the motherboard, and sometimes close to front-panel cables as in this example.

Battery (maintains CMOS settings)

PCI slots

CMOS clear jumper block

Socketed system BIOS chip

Front-panel cables (signal lights, on/off switch, and so on)

FIGURE 1.20
Front-panel cables, BIOS chip, and CMOS battery on a typical motherboard's front edge.

➔ *For more information about BIOS configuration and upgrades, see "Controlling Your PC's Operation with BIOS Setup," this chapter, p. 41.*

All Around a Notebook Computer

In recent years, notebook computers have gone from being niche items used primarily by travelers, to a mainstay of both offices and homes, outselling desktop computers in many cases. In fact, laptops outsold PCs for the first time in 2003, which is good news for wannabe notebook computer owners because brisk sales means stiff competition, which means lower prices.

Although notebook computers use the same types of peripherals, operating system, and application software as desktop computers use, they differ in several ways from desktop computers:

- Most notebook computers feature integrated ports that are not usually built into desktop computers, including one or more PC Card/CardBus (PCMCIA) slots and a 56Kbps modem.

- Some notebook computers support swappable drives, but less-expensive models require a trip to the service bench for a drive upgrade.

- Low-cost notebook computers typically use combo DVD-ROM/CD-RW drives, whereas mid-range and high-end notebook computers feature rewritable dual-format DVD drives.

- Many notebook computers don't have an internal floppy drive, but rely on rewritable CD, DVD, or removable-media drives on USB connections to transfer or back up data. You can add a floppy drive via USB to both desktop and notebook computers that no longer have a built-in floppy drive.

- Notebook computers have integrated pointing devices built into their keyboards; most use a touchpad, but a few (primarily IBM and a few Toshiba models) have a pointing stick. (Which one is better is a matter of personal preference.)

Figure 1.21 shows you a composite view of the ports on a typical notebook computer, a Dell Inspiron 4100.

This notebook computer, like most recent models, also has a built-in 56Kbps modem (not shown). However, it does not have so-called legacy ports (serial, parallel, and PS/2 mouse and keyboard), because the peripherals that formerly used these ports typically use the USB ports now.

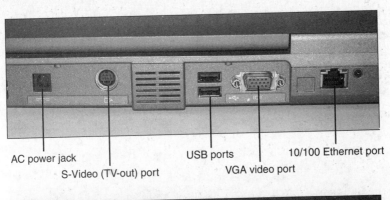

FIGURE 1.21
Rear and left views of a Dell Inspiron 4100 notebook computer.

AC power jack
S-Video (TV-out) port
USB ports
VGA video port
10/100 Ethernet port

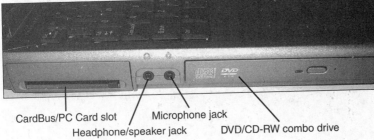

CardBus/PC Card slot
Headphone/speaker jack
Microphone jack
DVD/CD-RW combo drive

Some notebook computers still have some or all of these legacy ports, but you can expect these ports to continue to vanish on new and forthcoming models. Some notebook computers also feature an IEEE-1394a port, but unlike the six-pin version seen in Figures 1.2 and 1.4, notebooks with 1394a ports typically use the four-pin version shown in Figure 1.22.

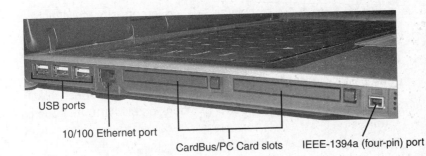

USB ports
10/100 Ethernet port
CardBus/PC Card slots
IEEE-1394a (four-pin) port

FIGURE 1.22
CardBus, USB, and IEEE-1394a ports on an Acer TravelMate 2200 notebook computer. Equipment courtesy of ComputersPlus (www.computersplus. com).

My Favorite Notebook Computer Features

As you look over your notebook computer, look for these features—they'll help your computer keep up with the latest entertainment standards, and also give you the versatility to get more work done:

- **Three or more USB ports**—USB ports work better than hubs for some devices, and most peripherals plug into USB ports these days.

- **One or more IEEE-1394a ports**—IEEE-1394 ports make it easy to pull video from your DV camcorder anywhere.

- **802.11g or dual-band 802.11g/a wireless networking**—Use the Windows Device Manager (Chapter 2, "Troubleshooting Windows XP and Windows Applications") to determine if your notebook computer has integrated Wi-Fi. It's wonderful not to need to fiddle around with a CardBus adapter or worry about losing a USB adapter.

Points of Failure on a Notebook Computer

As with desktop computers, cabling can be a major point of failure on notebook computers. However, notebook computers also have a few unique points of failure. PC Card (PCMCIA card) and CardBus devices represent a significant potential point of failure for the following reasons:

- If a PC Card is not completely pushed into its slot, it will not function.

- If a PC Card is ejected without being stopped by using the Safely Remove Hardware system tray control, it could be damaged.

- Some older PC Cards designed as 10/100 Ethernet network adapters or 56Kbps modems use dongles similar to the one pictured in Figure 1.23. If the dongle is damaged, the card is useless until a replacement dongle is obtained.

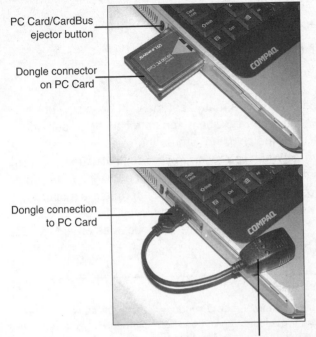

FIGURE 1.23
A 10/100 Ethernet PC Card adapter that uses a dongle being installed into a notebook computer.

PC Card/CardBus ejector button

Dongle connector on PC Card

Dongle connection to PC Card

Dongle connection for RJ-45 Ethernet cable

Although a notebook computer's drives are much more rugged than those found in desktop computers, they are much more expensive to replace if damaged. Whereas some mid-range and high-end notebook computers offer swappable drives, most lower-priced models do not. You can perform an upgrade to a hard disk without special tools on many models, but the replacement of other types of drives on systems that don't support swappable drive bays can be expensive.

Although drives are expensive to replace on notebook computers, the biggest potential expense is the LCD screen.

➔ *For more information on troubleshooting PC Card and CardBus modems, network adapters, and other devices, see "Troubleshooting PC Card/CardBus Devices," Chapter 8, p. 531.*

Controlling Your PC's Operation with BIOS Setup

The system BIOS chip shown earlier in Figure 1.20 is responsible for configuring many parts of your computer, including the following:

- Floppy, optical, and hard drive configuration
- Memory size

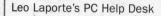

- Drive boot sequence
- Built-in port configuration
- System security
- Power management

Essentially, the BIOS acts as a restaurant menu of possible choices, and the CMOS RAM (which might be a separate chip or be built into the South Bridge on some chipsets) stores the selections made from the menu of choices. When you received your computer from the factory, default selections were already stored in the BIOS, but as you add devices or customize your computer to perform certain operations, you might need to make additional choices. This section is intended to introduce the major BIOS setup options as an aid to troubleshooting your system.

More About the BIOS

Contact your system or motherboard vendor's website for more information about particular configuration options you might see on your system, or check the manufacturer links, discussion groups, and all-around great coverage of BIOS-related issues available at Wim Bervoets's Wim's BIOS website (http://www.wimsbios.com).

How the BIOS Displays Your PC's Components

Whereas some computers display only a system manufacturer's logo at startup, forcing you to read the system manual to determine which key to press to start the BIOS setup program, others, particularly "white box" computers (which use a collection of components from various vendors) or systems that use a replacement motherboard, can provide you with a lot of useful information at startup.

Figure 1.24 shows a typical example of the BIOS chip's POST (Power-On Self-Test) program detecting onboard storage (the memory size is displayed briefly on many systems first). The display also shows which key to press to start the setup program.

Many systems that display information similar to what's shown in Figure 1.24 also display a condensed listing of onboard hardware before starting Windows (see Figure 1.25). Because this information should not change on a day-to-day basis unless you change your system configuration (BIOS changes or hardware upgrades), displaying this information at startup is a valuable aid to troubleshooting a sick system. Note that some systems cut off the top of this menu because of the number of PCI devices onboard.

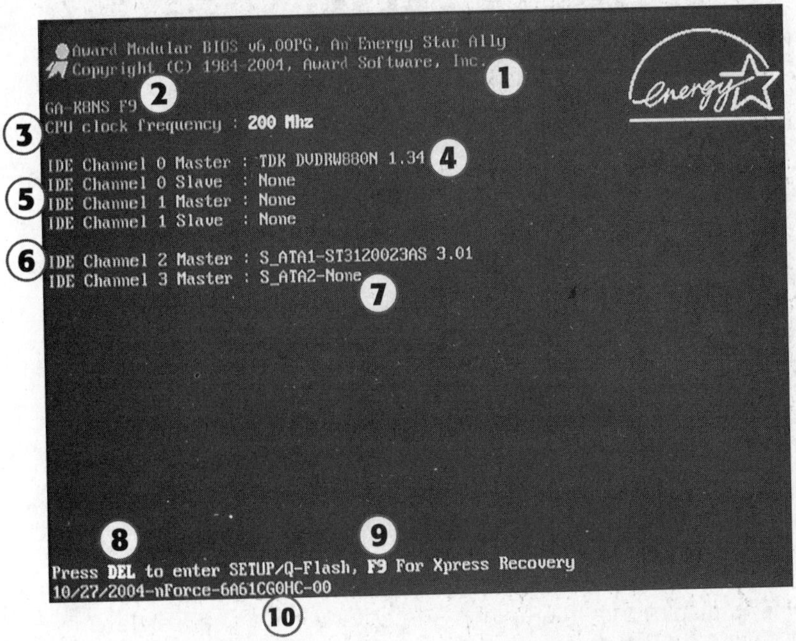

FIGURE 1.24

A typical startup screen displaying detected drives, chipset, and BIOS information.

1. BIOS vendor and release information
2. Motherboard vendor and model number
3. Processor clock frequency
4. Detected ATA/IDE drive
5. Unused ATA/IDE channels
6. Detected SATA drive
7. Unused SATA host adapter
8. Key to press to start BIOS setup
9. Key to press to start system recovery program
10. BIOS release date and version

Encouraging Your System to "Talk" to You

Many computers sold at retail stores do not display the POST and configuration information screens shown in Figures 1.24 and 1.25 as configured from the factory. To display this information, start the computer's BIOS setup program and look for a BIOS option called "Quiet Boot." Disable this option and save your changes. Some systems have an option called "Boot-Time Diagnostic Screen" instead; enable this option and save your changes. When your computer restarts, it should display hardware information.

Note that if your BIOS doesn't have an option such as "Quiet Boot" or "Boot-Time Diagnostic Screen," you might not be able to view your hardware configuration at bootup.

FIGURE 1.25

A typical system configuration screen displayed at system startup.

```
CPU Type          ①  : AMD Athlon(TM) 1400 MHz Processor
Cache Memory         : 256K
                                        Memory Installed  : 512M

Diskette Drive A : 1.44M, 3.5 in.       Serial Port(s)    : 3F8  ③
Diskette Drive B : None                 Parallel Port(s)  : 378
Pri. Master  Disk : 80026MB, UDMA 5     DRAM Type         : 1 - None
Pri. Slave   Disk : None                                    2 - SDRAM  ④
Sec. Master  Disk : CD-ROM, UDMA-2                           3 - SDRAM
Sec. Slave   Disk : CD-ROM, UDMA 2      DRAM Frequency    : PC-133  ⑤


PCI device listing.....
Bus No. Device No. Func No. Vendor ID  Device ID  Device Class          IRQ

    0        4         1      1106       0571      IDE Controller      14/15
    0        4         2      1106       3038      Serial bus controller    5
    0        4         3      1106       3038      Serial bus controller    5
    0       12         0      9004       3060      Mass storage controller 11
    0       17         0      105A       0D30      Mass storage controller 18
    1        0         0      1002       5159      Display controller      11
```

1. Processor type, speed, and memory size information
2. Drive information
3. I/O port addresses for serial & parallel ports
4. Memory slot usage
5. Memory speed
6. Onboard PCI devices

We're information junkies, so that's why we like to configure our systems to display this information at startup whenever possible. Why should you care? One of the reasons it's so important to display this information when you start your computer (if your system permits it) is because you will know immediately if there are any changes in your hardware configuration. If the configuration information displayed some day at startup differs from the normal information you see, it might mean one of the following has occurred:

- Someone has changed your BIOS configuration.

- The computer has reverted to default settings for troubleshooting or other reasons.

- The computer's battery is failing, causing stored setup information to be lost or corrupted.

- The hardware inside your computer has failed or has been removed/replaced.

To determine which of these has taken place, you need to press the key used by your computer to start the BIOS setup program. Popular keys used include:

- F1 or F2 (for various brands that use Phoenix BIOS)
- F10 (Compaq computers)
- Delete (Award or AMI BIOS, as shown in Figure 1.24)

However, your computer or motherboard manual might list a different key or key combination to use for accessing the BIOS.

BIOS Setup Screens and Their Uses in Troubleshooting

Generally, system BIOS setup programs start in one of two ways:

- Some display a menu that allows you to go to any screen you desire.
- Others display a standard configuration screen along with a top-level menu for access to other screens.

BIOSes vary widely, but the screens used in the following sections are representative of the options available on typical recent systems; your system might have similar options but place them on different screens than those shown here. You might find it useful to compare these screens to your computer's BIOS setup screens.

"Don't Touch That BIOS!" Some Vendors Say

The setup screens shown in the following sections are typical of those found on "white box" systems or replacement motherboards. However, if you use a major-brand desktop or notebook computer, don't be surprised if you have far fewer options. To reduce the chances of computer problems caused by incorrect configuration, some system and motherboard makers specify stripped-down BIOS setup programs.

Main Menu

There are two main designs we've seen with BIOS setups: those that open to a menu screen, similar to the one shown in Figure 1.26, and those that open directly to the Standard Setup (see Figure 1.27). If your system has a main menu, follow along with our tour by selecting Standard Setup, Standard CMOS Features, or similar verbiage.

Whichever type of BIOS menu system your computer uses, be sure to note the keys used to select items, quit without saving, and save changes and exit. In most cases, you press the Enter key to open the selected menu, submenu, or menu item you need to view or change.

FIGURE 1.26
A typical Award BIOS CMOS Setup Utility main menu.

When selected, the menus on the left open new sub-menus on right side of screen

Selected submenu

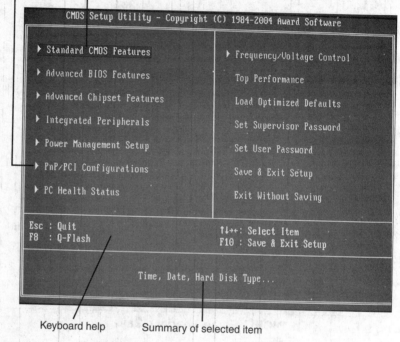

Keyboard help   Summary of selected item

My Favorite BIOS Tweaks

When I get a new system, I like to customize the BIOS so my system works the way I like. Here are some of my favorite BIOS tweaks:

- Adjust the boot order: CD first, then hard disk. This shaves a few seconds off the boot order compared to floppy, CD, and hard disk, but still enables me to start from the Windows CD to perform a repair installation or Recovery Console repair if I need to.

- Disable integrated ports I'm not using, such as serial, parallel, PS/2 mouse, and so on. I'm using USB ports for most external peripherals, so there's no need to clutter up my configuration with ports I don't use anymore.

- Enable USB Legacy mode (USB keyboard, USB mouse) settings so I can use my USB input devices in BIOS configuration and Recovery Console as well as within Windows.

Standard Setup

Most BIOSes have a main or standard setup screen similar to the one shown in Figure 1.27. Generally, this screen is used to set date and time as well as drive configuration options. Some BIOSes also display the installed memory size on this screen.

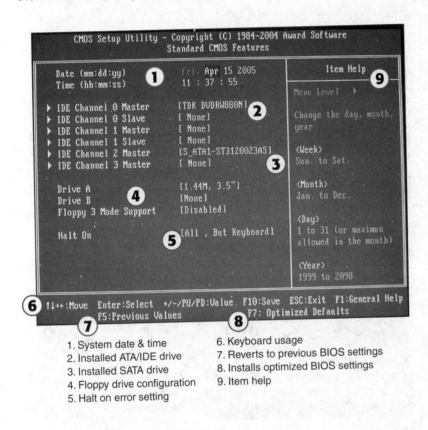

FIGURE 1.27

A typical main or standard BIOS setup screen.

1. System date & time
2. Installed ATA/IDE drive
3. Installed SATA drive
4. Floppy drive configuration
5. Halt on error setting
6. Keyboard usage
7. Reverts to previous BIOS settings
8. Installs optimized BIOS settings
9. Item help

Detecting Installed Drives

Most recent BIOS chips use Auto as the default for each ATA/IDE and SATA drive connection on the motherboard. Auto configuration enables the computer to detect the drive and use the correct settings at startup. If your system displays Auto for each drive, leave this setting as is.

However, if you are installing a new hard disk and want to know if the system can detect it, use the detection option in the system BIOS. In the system shown in Figure 1.27, you detect the drive by highlighting the host adapter or channel the drive is connected to and pressing the Enter key. The submenu (shown in Figure 1.28) should display the hard disk's capacity and configuration. If this information is listed as zeros, press Enter to redetect the hard disk. If the capacity and configuration are still not listed, make sure you have done the following:

- Selected the correct IDE host adapter and channel (master or slave—or Cable Select if you use 80-wire ATA/IDE cables).

- Properly connected the power and data cables to the drive. (Turn off the system first before making this check!)

- Properly jumpered an ATA/IDE drive. (Turn off the system first before making this check!)

FIGURE 1.28

Auto detection of a hard disk.

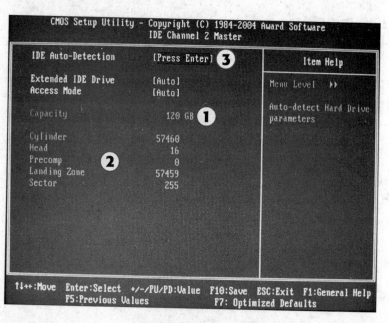

1. Detected hard disk capacity
2. Detected hard disk configuration
3. Press Enter to redetect hard disk

→ **For more information on troubleshooting ATA/IDE and SATA drive installations, see Chapter 3, "Troubleshooting Storage Devices."**

Note that CD and DVD drives as well as removable-media drives connected to SATA or ATA/IDE host adapters should not be detected in this manner. The Auto setting is correct for these drives, and these drives will display capacity and configuration (geometry) settings as zeros.

Advanced BIOS and Chipset Features Menus

No matter how many system BIOSes you've viewed, every time you view a different system you're likely to see yet another variation on how the Advanced BIOS and Chipset Features menus are configured.

Typically, the Advanced BIOS menu (see Figure 1.29) features less "dangerous" options such as boot order, whereas the Advanced Chipset menu usually features options for the CPU clock multiplier and memory speed settings and other chipset-specific options (see Figure 1.30). These functions are mainly used to overclock your PC's processor or memory, a feat you should only attempt if you know what you're getting into.

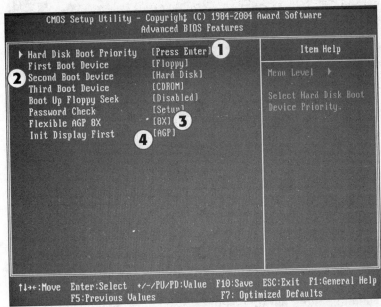

FIGURE 1.29

The Advanced BIOS Features menu can be used to adjust the boot order.

1. Opens submenu to select which hard disk is used as a boot drive
2. Specifies boot order
3. Specifies speed of AGP graphics card
4. Specifies whether to initialize AGP or PCI graphics card if both are installed for multiple-display support

The system shown in Figures 1.29 and 1.30 uses AGP video, but spreads AGP video settings across both the Advanced BIOS and Advanced Chipset menus. Most systems place all AGP video configurations on the Advanced Chipset menu.

→ *To learn more about the recommended boot sequence for your version of Windows, see "Troubleshooting Hard Disk or Optical Drive Bootup Problems," Chapter 3, p. 207.*

FIGURE 1.30

The Advanced Chipset Features menu is used to configure AGP, memory, and processor (CPU) features.

```
         CMOS Setup Utility - Copyright (C) 1984-2004 Award Software
                        Advanced Chipset Features

      AGP Aperture Size (MB)      [128M] ①
   ②  AGP Fast Write              [Auto]                    Item Help
      CPU Thermal-Throttling      [Disabled] ③
   ④  HT Frequency                [4x]                 Menu Level  ▶
      Max Memclock (Mhz)          [Auto] ⑤
      Current Memclock (Mhz)       200                 Driver use selected
      DDR Timing Setting by       [Auto]               sizes of system memory
   x  CAS# latency                 CL = 2.5            for 3D Texturing to
   x  Row cycle time      (tRC)   11 Bus Clocks        increase graphics
   x  Row refresh cyc time(tRFC)  14 Bus Clocks        performace
   x  RAS# to CAS# delay  (tRCD)   4 Bus Clocks
   x  Row to Row delay    (tRRD)   2 Bus Clocks
   x  Min RAS# active time(tRAS)   8 Bus Clocks  ⑥
   x  Row precharge Time  (tRP)    4 Bus Clocks
   x  Write recovery time (tWR)    3 Bus Clocks
   x  Write to Read delay (tWTR)   2 Bus Clocks
   x  Read to Write delay (tRWT)   4 Bus Clocks
   x  Refresh period      (tREF) 2x3120 Cycles
      Enable 2T Timming           [Auto]

 ↑↓←←:Move  Enter:Select  +/-/PU/PD:Value  F10:Save  ESC:Exit  F1:General Help
            F5:Previous Values              F7: Optimized Defaults
```

1. Specifies amount of system memory addresses to use for large AGP 3D textures
2. Configures AGP Fast Write feature
3. Enable this option to slow down the CPU when it gets too hot (useful mainly for notebook computers)
4. Controls speed of HyperTransport bus connection between processor and chipset (Athlon 64-based systems)
5. Change to User-Defined or Manual to permit overclocking of memory
6. Automatic memory settings; can be adjusted manually if DDR Timing option changed

→ **For more information on configuring AGP options, see "Configuring AGP Options in the System BIOS," Chapter 5, p. 337.**

Some systems also place configuration options for USB and PS/2 mouse configuration on one of these menus, but others place these settings on the same menu as other integrated peripherals. These menus often store antivirus settings such as Write-Protect Boot Sector and ChipAway (a BIOS-based antivirus setting that, when enabled, can distinguish between legitimate attempts to access the boot drive's boot sector and virus attacks).

Fixing Chipset Configuration Problems

If you start experimenting with the Advanced menus and foul up your system, use the Setup Defaults (also called Optimal Defaults) option available on most BIOSes to reset all screens to their defaults. Be sure to go through all the screens and make sure that drives and ports are configured as you desire.

Integrated Peripherals (I/O Devices)

Although the Integrated Peripherals menu shown in Figure 1.31 lists all integrated ports, some systems scatter settings such as USB, mouse, IDE, and SATA across multiple BIOS setup menus. The illustration in Figure 1.31 has been edited to show all menu items in a single screen, but the actual menu, as with many other systems, requires you to scroll vertically to see all menu items.

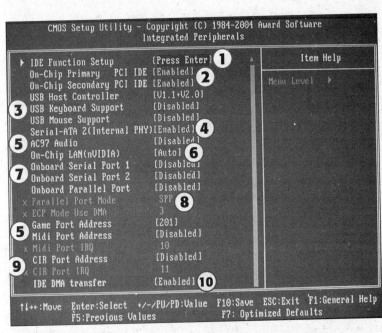

FIGURE 1.31

A typical Integrated Peripherals menu.

1. Configures IDE RAID
2. Configures ATA/IDE host adapters
3. Configures USB ports
4. Configures SATA host adapters
5. Configures onboard audio
6. Configures onboard Ethernet adapte
7. Configures serial (COM) ports
8. Configures parallel (LPT) port
9. Configures Infrared port
10. Configures IDE DMA Transfer

This system has both ATA/IDE (also known as PCI IDE) host adapters enabled as well as both SATA host adapters. If you don't have drives connected to the secondary PCI IDE host adapter, you could disable it. You should disable the SATA host adapters if you don't use SATA drives; this system uses an SATA hard disk as its boot drive. IDE DMA transfers should be enabled as shown here for best IDE performance. Note that bus-mastering drivers must also be installed in Windows when DMA transfers are enabled.

Note that you can configure the USB host adapters to run in USB 1.1 and USB 2.0 modes, run in USB 1.1 mode only, or disabled (no active USB ports). Some systems also permit you to specify the number of active USB ports (2, 4, or 6). If you are unable to run USB 2.0 peripherals at full speed when you connect them to onboard USB ports, make sure your USB ports are configured to run in USB 2.0 mode (if available).

AC97 audio is disabled on this system because a high-performance sound card has been installed. Serial and parallel ports have been disabled because this system uses USB peripherals.

Benefits of Disabling Ports You Don't Use

Each serial and parallel port built into your system (most computers have two serial ports and one parallel port, as in Figure 1.31) gobbles up precious hardware resources, particularly IRQs. Whereas PCI and AGP cards and onboard PCI devices such as USB ports can share IRQs, serial and parallel ports are ISA devices that can't share IRQs. The bottom line is that the rest of your peripherals will have more resources to use and share if you disable the ports you don't use.

If your system supports RAID (redundant array of inexpensive drives) functions and you want to use RAID to create an array of two or more hard disk drives, you need to open the BIOS menu and specify which host adapters will be used for RAID. Then, you need to run the RAID setup option provided in your system BIOS or chipset driver. With two drives, you can specify a striped (RAID 0) array (improves data access performance) or mirrored (RAID 1) array (improves system reliability by making changes to both drives at the same time). With four drives, you can also use RAID 0+1, which combines striping and mirroring for enhanced speed and reliability. To start the RAID configuration process on the system shown in Figure 1.31, open the IDE Function Setup menu.

Power Management

Power management features in the BIOS (see Figure 1.32) can be used to configure how your system operates when it is idle. Some power management menus also incorporate warning systems to alert you to processor fan failures, but these options are often found in the PC Health or Hardware Monitor menu.

```
    CMOS Setup Utility - Copyright (C) 1984-2004 Award Software
                    Power Management Setup
  ┌──────────────────────────────────────┬──────────────────────────┐
  │ ACPI Suspend Type        [S1(POS)]    │      Item Help           │
  │ Soft-Off by PWR-BTTN    [Instant-Off] │                          │
  │ PME Event Wake Up       [Disabled]    │  Menu Level    ▶         │
  │ Modem Ring On           [Disabled]    │                          │
  │ S3 Resume by USB device [Disabled]    │                          │
  │ Resume by Alarm         [Disabled]    │                          │
  │ x Day of Month Alarm      Everyday    │                          │
  │ x Time (hh:mm:ss) Alarm   0 : 0 : 0   │                          │
  │ Power On By Mouse       [Disabled]    │                          │
  │ Power On By Keyboard    [Disabled]    │                          │
  │ x KB Power ON Password    Enter       │                          │
  │ AC BACK Function        [Soft-Off]    │                          │
  │                                       │                          │
  │                                       │                          │
  └──────────────────────────────────────┴──────────────────────────┘
  ↑↓→←:Move  Enter:Select  +/-/PU/PD:Value  F10:Save  ESC:Exit  F1:General Help
            F5:Previous Values            F7: Optimized Defaults
```

FIGURE 1.32

A typical power management setup screen. Enable disabled options to permit you to power on your system with the listed device or event.

PCI Configuration

The PCI slot is the primary slot type used on most recent motherboards for add-in cards (the AGP slot for video cards is considered a PCI slot for configuration purposes).

Although PCI devices can normally share IRQ resources, you might need to manually configure their hardware resource settings in a few cases, such as if Windows can't detect a PCI card you've installed. To do so, use the BIOS's PCI Configuration screen, such as the example shown in Figure 1.33. IRQs are discussed in much greater detail in "Hardware Resources," p.xxx, later in this section.

If two or more PCI/AGP devices are using the same IRQ but they are not working correctly, you have a couple options:

- Manually assign a different IRQ instead of using the Auto setting.
- Move the PCI card to a different expansion slot (if available).

Most recent systems can use virtually any IRQ (3–15). Note that IRQs 3, 4, 5, and 7 can be used by serial and parallel ports. However, if these ports are disabled, those IRQs are available for PCI devices, making it easier to avoid conflicts.

FIGURE 1.33
A typical PCI Configuration screen.

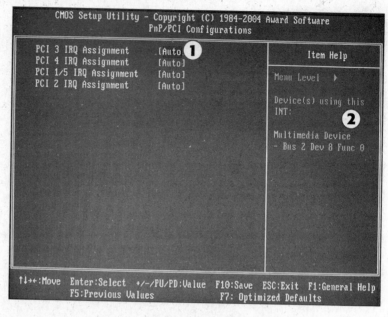

1. Selected PCI slot.
2. Device using this slot.

Discovering Which IRQs Your PCI Cards Can Use

Even if you aren't having any problems with the PCI (and AGP) cards already installed in your system, you might want to examine the Slot x or PCI x IRQ options in your system BIOS to determine which IRQs your PCI cards can use. Originally, PCI cards could be configured to use only IRQs 9, 10, 11, and 12 (and 12 was often unavailable because it was used by the PS/2 mouse port). Newer systems (such as the one shown in Figure 1.33) might also offer IRQs traditionally used by ISA devices such as serial ports (IRQs 3 and 4) and parallel ports (IRQ 7). In such a case, disabling serial and parallel ports you don't use makes it easier for Windows and your BIOS to find resource combinations that work correctly for all cards and motherboard-based devices such as USB and integrated sound.

PC Health (Hardware Monitor)

The PC Health or Hardware Monitor menu has been added to newer systems to help you determine that your computer's temperature and voltage conditions are at safe levels for your computer (see Figure 1.34).

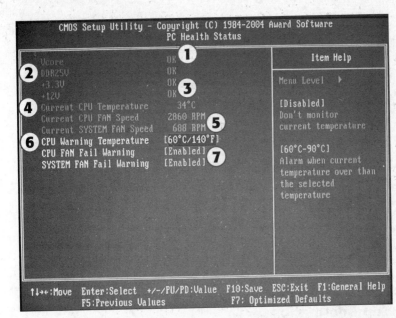

FIGURE 1.34

A typical Hardware Monitor screen.

1. Current processor voltage is within limits
2. Current memory voltage is within limits
3. Current motherboard voltages are within limits
4. Displays current CPU temperature
5. Displays CPU and system fan speeds
6. Specifies CPU warning temperature
7. Fan failure warnings are enabled

Although it is useful to view these settings in the BIOS, temperature values are usually higher after the computer has been working for a while (after you've booted to Windows and no longer have access to this screen). Generally, the major value of this screen is that its information can be detected by motherboard or system monitoring programs that run under Windows and enable you to be warned immediately if there are any heat or fan-related problems with your system.

Use the Right Kinds of Fans for Maximum Benefits

If you need to replace fans that are connected to the motherboard, make sure the replacements use the same type of connectors. This enables you to monitor fan performance. Note that some fan vendors connect the fan to a four-pin Molex power connector used for drives to provide more power to the fan, but also provide a single-wire connector to the motherboard so the fan can still be monitored by the system.

→ *For more information on recommended voltage levels and testing your power supply, see Chapter 10, "Troubleshooting Power Problems."*

Some systems display specific voltages rather than "OK," as in Figure 1.34.

Saving Your Changes and Restarting the Computer

Most BIOSes offer two ways to exit:

- Exit saving changes
- Exit discarding changes

If you didn't intend to make any changes, choose the "exit discarding changes" option. This might require you to return to the starting menu or to press the Esc key several times until you can select this option. Whether you save or discard changes, the computer reboots after you exit the BIOS setup program.

What to Do If Your Computer Can't Retain BIOS Setup Information

If your computer displays "Invalid BIOS Information" messages whenever you start it up or the clock keeps reverting to the same date, you probably need to replace the battery on the motherboard. Most recent systems use a CR-2032 battery sold in the watch battery department of most stores. However, older systems might use any of a wide range of proprietary batteries, and a few use a combined NVRAM/RTC and battery chip made by Dallas Semiconductor or have a soldered-in-place battery. If your computer's battery is soldered in place, your motherboard probably has header pins for an external battery. Most full-line computer stores stock replacement batteries suitable for most models. Typical motherboard batteries last two to three years before you need to replace them.

Hunting for a Motherboard Battery? Try These Sources

If your computer needs an unusual replacement battery, check the following sources:

Baber.com's extensive list is available at http://www.baber.com/baber/computer_clock_battery/generic.htm.

Batteries Plus has retail stores in many areas, and lists its computer battery replacements online at http://www.batteriesplus.com. Select Products, Computer and Laptop. Then choose the manufacturer and model number of your computer.

After you replace the battery, you will need to restart your system and make any BIOS changes necessary to reflect your preferred configuration. Save the changes and exit the BIOS, and your system should restart normally.

Leo Says

Dealing with a Corroded Battery

If you notice your motherboard battery has greenish-white stuff leaking from it, your CMOS settings are not long for this world. As with other types of batteries, a corroded or leaking battery is not reliable, and will damage electrical contacts and electronic components. I get annoyed if leaky batteries ruin a flashlight, but I can always get another one. If a leaky battery wipes out my motherboard, it might take some data with it. My advice? Replace the battery immediately! If the battery is soldered to the motherboard and you can't remove it, make backups of your information and start shopping for a new motherboard!

Power-On Self Test

Every time your computer is turned on, the BIOS performs a Power-On Self Test, also known as the POST. If you see error messages displayed during startup or if the computer beeps during startup, the POST has located problems with your hardware configuration. Technicians can also display additional POST codes with a special add-on card called a POST card, which is installed into an empty expansion slot. However, the most common errors are reported through beep codes or onscreen error messages.

Onscreen error messages are usually fairly easy to understand, but POST beep codes vary by BIOS version. To be able to determine what a particular beep code means, you need to know what BIOS brand and version your computer uses.

The major BIOS vendors include the following:

- AMI (American Megatrends)
- Phoenix
- Award Software (owned by Phoenix)

Most computers use a BIOS developed by one of these companies. IBM also developed its own BIOS which is used for some of its products.

POST Codes

The most common beep codes you're likely to encounter are listed in Table 1.1.

TABLE 1.1
COMMON SYSTEM ERRORS AND THEIR BEEP CODES

Problem	Beep Codes by BIOS Version			
	Phoenix BIOS	Award BIOS	AMI BIOS	IBM BIOS
Memory	Beep sequences: 1-3-4-1 1-3-4-3 1-4-1-1	Beeping (other than 2 long, 1 short)	1 or 3 or 11 beeps 1 long, 3 short beeps	(None)
Video	(none)	2 long, 1 short beep	8 beeps 1 long, 8 short beeps	1 long, 3 short beeps or 1 beep
Processor or motherboard	Beep sequence: 1-2-2-3	(none)	5 beeps or 9 beeps	1 long, 1 short beep

Additional Beep Codes

For additional beep codes, see the following resources:

- **AMI BIOS**—http://www.ami.com/support/doc/AMIBIOS-codes.pdf (requires the free Adobe Reader, which you can download from http://www.adobe.com).
- **Phoenix BIOS**—Go to http://www.phoenix.com and search for "beep code" to find links to Phoenix beep code listings.
- **IBM BIOS**—http://www.computerhope.com/beep.htm.

Hardware Resources

Four types of hardware resources are used by both onboard and add-on card devices:

- IRQ
- I/O port address

- DMA channel
- Memory address

Each device needs its own set of hardware resources, or needs to be a device that can share IRQs (the only one of the four resources that can be shared). Resource conflicts between devices can prevent your system from starting, lock up your system, or can even cause data loss.

IRQs

IRQ is short for *Interrupt Request*. An IRQ is a signaling connection between a device and the processor (CPU). The device uses an IRQ line to "interrupt" the processor when the device needs attention from the processor. At least one IRQ is used by most major add-on cards (network, SCSI, sound, video, modem, IEEE-1394) as well as major built-in system components such as ATA/IDE host adapters, serial, parallel, and USB ports.

Physical IRQs range from 0 to 15, as shown in Table 1.2.

TABLE 1.2
TYPICAL IRQ USAGE

IRQ	Standard Function	Bus Slot	Resource Type	Recommended Use
0	System timer	No	System	—
1	Keyboard controller	No	System	—
2	Second IRQ controller cascade to IRQ 9	No	System	—
8	Real-time clock	No	System	—
9	Available (might appear as IRQ 2)	Yes	PCI	Network Interface Card or VGA
10	Available	Yes	PCI	USB
11	Available	Yes	PCI	SCSI host adapter

TABLE 1.2 (continued)

IRQ	Standard Function	Bus Slot	Resource Type	Recommended Use
12	Motherboard mouse port/ available	Yes	ISA/PCI	Motherboard mouse port
13	Math coprocessor	No	System	—
14	Primary IDE	Yes	PCI	Primary IDE (hard disks)
15	Secondary IDE/ available	Yes	PCI	Secondary IDE (CD-ROM/tape)
3	Serial Port 2 (COM 2:)	Yes	ISA	COM 2:/ internal modem
4	Serial Port 1 (COM 1:)	Yes	ISA	COM 1:
5	Sound/Parallel Port 2 (LPT2:)	Yes	ISA	Sound card
6	Floppy disk controller	Yes	System	Floppy controller
7	Parallel Port 1 (LPT1:)	Yes	ISA	LPT1:

Although Table 1.2 shows you traditional IRQ usage, you should realize that your computer might list much different IRQ usage and still work correctly. Here's why:

- If your computer is a so-called "legacy-free" system without serial, parallel, or PS/2 mouse and keyboard ports, or if you have manually disabled them, IRQs 3, 4, 7, and 12 will also be treated as PCI IRQs. This means they can be used for PCI cards not listed on the chart, such as IEEE-1394a host adapters, SCSI host adapters, video capture cards, add-on multi-I/O (serial/parallel) adapters, and so forth.

- Beginning with late versions of Windows 95 and continuing on to today's Windows XP versions, PCI devices can share IRQs on most systems. Whereas ISA devices such as built-in serial, parallel, and PS/2 mouse ports each need an exclusive IRQ, two or more PCI devices (as well as AGP video cards) can share IRQs, as shown in Figure 1.35. Starting with Windows 2000, Windows might assign PCI devices to virtual IRQs starting at IRQ 16 to avoid conflicts with ISA devices. Figure 1.35 shows the Windows XP Device Manager listing both types of IRQs.

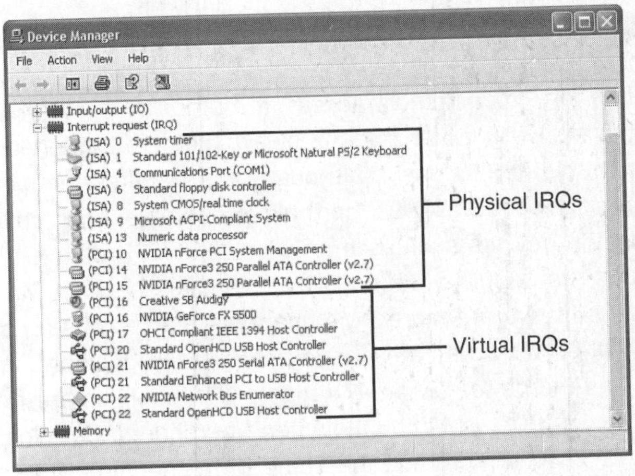

FIGURE 1.35
Physical and virtual IRQs used by a system running Windows XP.

In Figure 1.35, PCI IRQs 16, 21, and 22 are shared between two devices. This is normal, and nothing to be alarmed about. However, if you see an ISA and a PCI device assigned to the same IRQ, or two ISA devices assigned to the same IRQ, you have a hardware conflict. Fortunately, today's smarter systems and Windows versions have made hardware conflicts of this type very rare.

I/O Port Addresses

I/O port addresses are used for the task of moving data to and from a device, and they are used by every device in the computer, including motherboard devices, game ports, and other components that don't need IRQs. Thousands of I/O port addresses are available in today's computers, so resource conflicts are rare unless a user tries to assign two serial ports to the same address (refer ahead to Figure 1.36).

As you look at I/O port address usage in your computer, you might see two different components that are working but are displaying the same I/O port address per the Windows Device Manager. In these cases, the devices listed use the same I/O port address as a way to communicate with each other. For example, the AMD-751 chipset processor to the AGP controller and the TNT2 AGP video card in the computer use the same I/O port addresses to facilitate communication with each other (shown later, in Figure 1.37).

DMA Channels

DMA stands for *Direct Memory Access*, a method of transferring data to and from memory at high speeds by avoiding the bottlenecks of management by the processor. Although DMA transfers are very common today (high-speed ATA/IDE hard disks use a variation called Ultra DMA), only ISA devices such as the ECP or ECP/EPP parallel port and sound cards that emulate Sound Blaster require specific DMA channels. Because there are more DMA channels than any user needs (0–7, with DMA 4 used as a cascade between the original DMA channels 0–3 and the newer DMA 5–7 range), DMA conflicts are rare. However, unlike IRQs, DMA channels can't be shared; data loss could result if two devices try to use the same DMA channel at the same time.

Memory Addresses

Like DMA channels, memory addresses are also abundant in computers. Add-on cards that have their own BIOS chips (some SCSI, some ATA/IDE, and some network cards as well as all VGA and 3D video cards), however, must use unique memory addresses found in the range between 640KB and 1MB. Because there's abundant memory address space and relatively low demand for memory addresses, conflicts are rare unless you manually configured a card to use an address already in use by another device.

Viewing Hardware Resources in Use

→ *For details, see "Using Device Manager," Chapter 2, p. 100, and "Using System Information," Chapter 2, p. 114.*

You can view the current resource usage in your computer with the Windows Device Manager. To see the resource usage for a particular device, open the Device Manager, open the device's properties sheet, and click Resources. You can also use the Windows System Information program to view resource usage.

If you are concerned about installing devices that have limited configuration options, you can also view all the resources currently in use. With Windows XP (and Windows 2000), start the Device Manager, select View, Resources by Type, and click the plus sign (+) next to each category. Figure 1.36 shows the DMA channel, IRQ, and a portion of the memory resource usage in a typical Athlon-based computer running Windows XP. Figure 1.37 shows a portion of the I/O port address usage in the same computer.

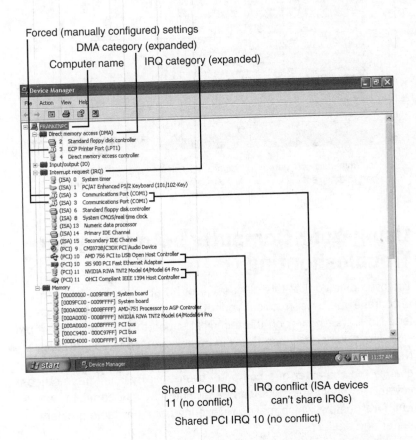

Forced (manually configured) settings
DMA category (expanded)
Computer name   IRQ category (expanded)

FIGURE 1.36
The Windows XP Device Manager configured to display IRQ, DMA, and memory address usage.

Shared PCI IRQ 11 (no conflict)   IRQ conflict (ISA devices can't share IRQs)
Shared PCI IRQ 10 (no conflict)

Note that in these two figures, forced (manually configured) settings are indicated with a white circle containing a blue *i*. Forced settings are seldom a good idea (Plug-and-Play configuration usually works much better, especially with Windows XP). Additionally, if two ISA devices have been forced to use the same hardware resource (such as the COM ports in Figure 1.37), you have a hardware conflict that will prevent the devices from working.

FIGURE 1.37

The Windows XP Device Manager configured to display a portion of the I/O port address usage.

Device Manager

File   Action   View   Help

[00000070 - 00000071] System CMOS/real time clock
[00000072 - 0000007F] PCI bus
[00000080 - 00000090] Direct memory access controller
[00000090 - 00000091] PCI bus
[00000093 - 0000009F] PCI bus
[00000094 - 0000009F] Direct memory access controller
[000000A0 - 000000A1] Programmable interrupt controller
[000000A2 - 000000BF] PCI bus
[000000C0 - 000000DE] Direct memory access controller
[000000E0 - 000000EF] PCI bus
[000000F0 - 000000FF] Numeric data processor
[00000100 - 00000CF7] PCI bus
[00000170 - 00000177] Secondary IDE Channel
[000001F0 - 000001F7] Primary IDE Channel
[00000201 - 00000201] Standard Game Port
[00000274 - 00000277] ISAPNP Read Data Port
[00000279 - 00000279] ISAPNP Read Data Port
[000002F8 - 000002FF] Communications Port (COM1)
[000002F8 - 000002FF] Communications Port (COM1)
[00000376 - 00000376] Secondary IDE Channel
[00000378 - 0000037F] ECP Printer Port (LPT1)
[000003B0 - 000003BB] AMD-751 Processor to AGP Controller
[000003B0 - 000003BB] NVIDIA RIVA TNT2 Model 64/Model 64 Pro
[000003C0 - 000003DF] AMD-751 Processor to AGP Controller
[000003C0 - 000003DF] NVIDIA RIVA TNT2 Model 64/Model 64 Pro
[000003F0 - 000003F5] Standard floppy disk controller
[000003F6 - 000003F6] Primary IDE Channel
[000003F7 - 000003F7] Standard floppy disk controller
[00000778 - 0000077A] ECP Printer Port (LPT1)

start   Device Manager   3:06 PM

Forced (manually configured)   Not a conflict; these   I/O port
I/O port address settings   devices communicate   address conflict
                                 with each other

Using Your Computer's Anatomy for Troubleshooting

The overriding goal of this discussion of PC anatomy has been to encourage you to learn about your computer before you have a problem. No matter how good the technical support your vendor might provide, most computers don't stay in as-delivered condition for long. New hardware, new software, and operating system changes all change the character of a computer over time. By using the methods covered in this chapter, you can determine how your computer works when it's healthy, which makes recovering from inevitable problems faster and easier.

My Favorite System-Exploration Software

If your main gripe with this chapter is that it isn't long enough, you might want to dig even deeper into your system's configuration. My favorite software tools for learning more about hardware include the following:

- SiSoftware Sandra can be downloaded from the SiSoftware Zone at http://www.sisoftware.net/. If you want more features than the free Lite version, get the Professional version.

- Try the free personal version of Belarc Advisor to learn about your system's hardware and software configuration, including Windows hotfixes. Get it from http://www.belarc.com/free_download.html.

- Learn more about your system BIOS with the BIOS Agent, available from http://www.esupport.com/biosagent/index.cfm.

Troubleshooting Windows XP and Windows Applications

TROUBLESHOOTING

FAST TRACK TO SOLUTIONS (SYMPTOM TABLE)

Symptom	Flowchart or Book Section	See Page
Windows will start only in Safe Mode.	Windows Starts Only in Safe Mode	711
I'm getting an error message whenever I try to use a particular program.	A Program Displays an Error When I Use It	713
I can't start a program from its Start menu or Desktop shortcut.	I Cannot Start a Program from a Shortcut	712
When I turn on my computer, it doesn't start up correctly.	I Can't Start the Computer	709
When I turn on my computer, I see an error message.	Computer Displays Error Message at Startup	710
I want to find out what program or process is preventing Windows from starting properly.	Understanding the Boot Log	79
I want to stop some programs from loading at startup.	Using MSConfig	129
I'm having problems shutting down Windows.	Troubleshooting Shutdown Problems with Windows	82
Some of my programs won't run under Windows XP.	Troubleshooting Programs That Won't Run Under Windows XP	136
I'm getting STOP errors on my system.	Troubleshooting Stop Errors with Windows 2000/XP	153
	Preventing and Reducing Occurrences of BSOD Errors in Windows	155
I'm getting "blue screen of death" (BSOD) errors on my Windows XP/ 2000 computer.	Troubleshooting Stop Errors with Windows 2000/XP	153
	Preventing and Reducing Occurrences of BSOD Errors in Windows	155
I'm having problems running game programs.	Troubleshooting Games	151
I'm not sure DirectX is working correctly.	Using DirectX Diagnostics	120

TROUBLESHOOTING

FAST TRACK TO SOLUTIONS, *Continued*

Symptom	Flowchart or Book Section	See Page
I want to test my 3D sound and 3D video drivers.	Using DirectX Diagnostic	120
How can I make sure I have the latest fixes to Windows?	Using Windows Update	132
How do I access the Microsoft Knowledge Base?	Researching Your Program's Compatibility with Windows	142
I can't open some types of files in my favorite programs.	I Can't Open a Particular Type of File	149
Windows XP has displayed an error message, and I need more information about the error.	Troubleshooting with Computer Management	91
I can't see the file extensions in My Computer/Windows Explorer.	Sidebar: Tracking Down the Files You Need	96
I can't install programs or hardware in Windows XP.	User Accounts	99
Windows isn't working correctly since I installed some older software.	Using File Signature Verification	120
A program or feature built into Windows isn't working correctly.	Using System File Checker	122
I need to get help from a Windows XP user located at another computer.	Using Remote Assistance in Windows XP	124
I need to help a Windows XP user located at another computer.	Using Remote Assistance in Windows XP	124
I need to find out which startup program is causing problems.	Using MSConfig	129
I think my system is infected with spyware or adware.	Slamming Spyware	160
I need to check my system for viruses, but I don't have an up-to-date antivirus program.	Stopping Viruses	156
I need to reinstall Windows.	Performing a Repair Installation	134

Microsoft Windows XP is an operating system—but until you have a problem with Windows, the full meaning of that statement might not be clear to you. If Windows stops working, your computer stops working. If your computer stops working, you stop working (or playing). If you feel like a cyborg sometimes (we know we do) when you can't seem to get Windows to work right, you've come to the right place. Let's clean your Windows!

Fixing Startup Problems

If Windows doesn't start properly, you can't get anything done with your computer, because the Windows operating system manages your screen, your peripherals, your drives, your pointing devices—your entire computer life once the computer is turned on and completes its Power-On Self-Test (POST) routine.

Windows might not start properly for a lot of reasons, but the most common ones include the following:

- Corrupted or missing boot files on your startup drive
- Incorrect hard disk configuration settings in the system BIOS
- Loading programs that can't run at the same time because of software conflicts
- Damaged or missing Windows or application files that Windows requires access to at startup
- Hardware resource conflicts

Overview of the Computer Boot and Windows Startup Processes

Although it takes only a couple minutes to go from power-on to seeing the familiar Windows desktop on your screen, many different tasks are performed in that time period to make this possible. The basic sequence of events looks like this:

1. When you turn on the computer, a chip on the motherboard called the system BIOS or ROM BIOS performs a Power-On Self-Test (POST) process to make sure the system hardware is working correctly. Problems detected during the POST might trigger beep codes, onscreen error messages, or might stop the boot process entirely, depending on the problem and the BIOS version used by the computer.

2. The system BIOS checks for Plug and Play devices on the motherboard and expansion slots (such as network adapters, sound adapters, USB ports, video adapters, and so on) and assigns hardware resources to each device.

3. The system BIOS searches for ROM chips on video cards and add-on cards and runs the programs located in those chips to enable those devices.

4. The system BIOS tests the system memory; on some computers, an error message will be generated if the amount of memory detected is different from the last-stored value.

5. The system BIOS searches for operating system boot files on the first bootable drive listed in the BIOS setup. This drive could be a floppy disk, a CD-ROM drive, or an ATA/IDE hard disk.

6. If no boot record is found on the first drive listed, each additional bootable drive is checked until a valid bootable disk is found. If no disk can be found containing a valid boot record, the system will display a message such as "Non-System Disk or Disk Error" or "Disk Boot Failure."

7. If a bootable drive is located by the system BIOS, the instructions it contains are executed to start your operating system.

8. During the operating system (Windows) startup process, Windows loads drivers into memory for each device installed on the computer, runs the programs that are found in the Startup folder or have been set to run at startup by the Windows Registry, and displays a Windows logon screen (if Windows is so configured).

As you can see from this overview, problems with system configuration or Windows configuration can cause the startup process to fail.

---

64 = 32, Feature-Wise, Most of the Time

In May 2005, Microsoft officially introduced Windows XP Professional x64 Edition, the long-awaited 64-bit version of Windows for the AMD Athlon 64, Opteron, Intel Pentium 4 with EM64T, Intel Pentium D, and similar 64-bit processors (and possibly other processors by the time you read this). Generally, Windows XP Professional x64 Edition has the same user interface and features as its 32-bit sibling. However, when there are exceptions or other issues concerning 64-bit Windows you need to know, we'll keep you posted. Just keep your eyes out for more sidebars like this one.

Fixing Hard Disk Configuration Problems

If, following your PC's POST, instead of seeing the normal Windows splash screen when you start your computer, you see an error message such as "No operating system," "Searching for Boot Record from IDE-0," or others, there might be a problem with your hard drive if there are no floppy disks inserted in your floppy drive (a floppy disk that lacks boot files will prevent your system from booting). The master boot record, an area at the beginning of the drive's data storage area that defines the location of operating system files and how the drive is partitioned, might have been erased or corrupted, or the drive might be configured incorrectly in the system BIOS so that it can't read the master boot record properly.

Most hard disk drives are installed using the Auto configuration option found in your PC's BIOS. When using this setting, the hard disk reports its configuration to the computer every time you start the system. Because this is rarely a flawed process, it's more likely that there's a problem with files found in your drive's boot sector than a problem with your drive's BIOS configuration.

Configuring a Hard Disk Drive in the System BIOS

Depending on the version of Windows you use, you could damage your Windows installation if you re-create a master boot record when the real problem is an incorrect BIOS configuration for your drive. To ensure this isn't the case, start your computer and then press the key or keys (usually Delete or F1) specified in your computer's instruction manual or displayed onscreen to start the system BIOS configuration program (see Figure 2.1). Note that many computers display a manufacturer's logo during the boot process, and might not tell you onscreen which key to press to activate the BIOS configuration program. Check your system or motherboard manual to determine the correct key to press in such cases.

Although details can vary from BIOS to BIOS, you should see an option to access the Standard Setup screen. Go to this screen to see how the hard disk is configured. If it is configured as User-Defined with LBA mode enabled or as Auto (see Figure 2.2), the drive should be bootable once you repair the master boot record and restore bootable files. However, if LBA mode is disabled, you won't be able to boot from the drive because your computer won't be able to find the boot sectors.

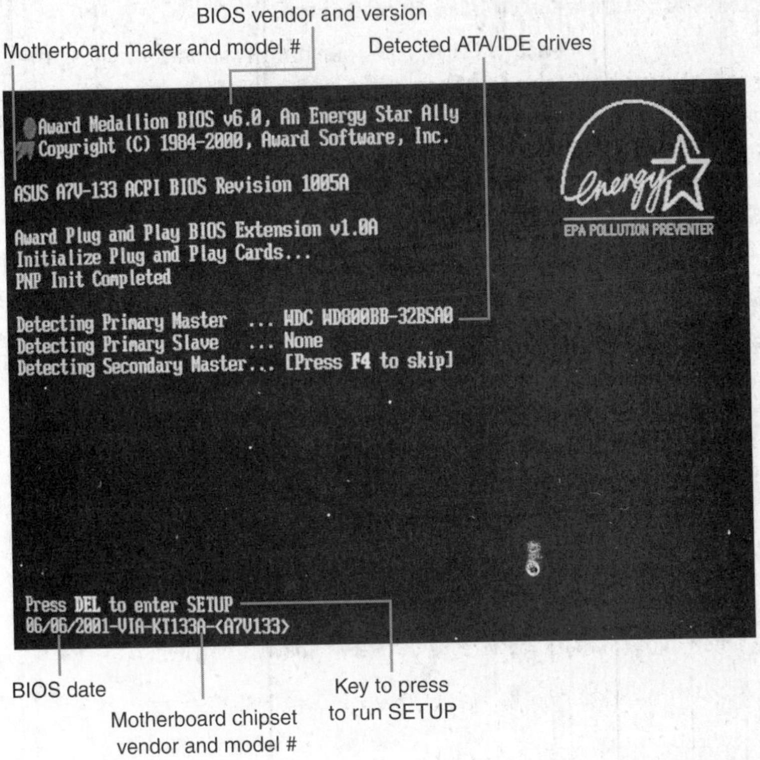

BIOS vendor and version

Motherboard maker and model #   Detected ATA/IDE drives

```
Award Medallion BIOS v6.0, An Energy Star Ally
Copyright (C) 1984-2000, Award Software, Inc.

ASUS A7V-133 ACPI BIOS Revision 1005A

Award Plug and Play BIOS Extension v1.0A
Initialize Plug and Play Cards...
PNP Init Completed

Detecting Primary Master   ... WDC WD800BB-32BSA0
Detecting Primary Slave    ... None
Detecting Secondary Master... [Press F4 to skip]
```

```
Press DEL to enter SETUP
06/06/2001-VIA-KT133A-<A7V133>
```

FIGURE 2.1
A typical PC during startup.

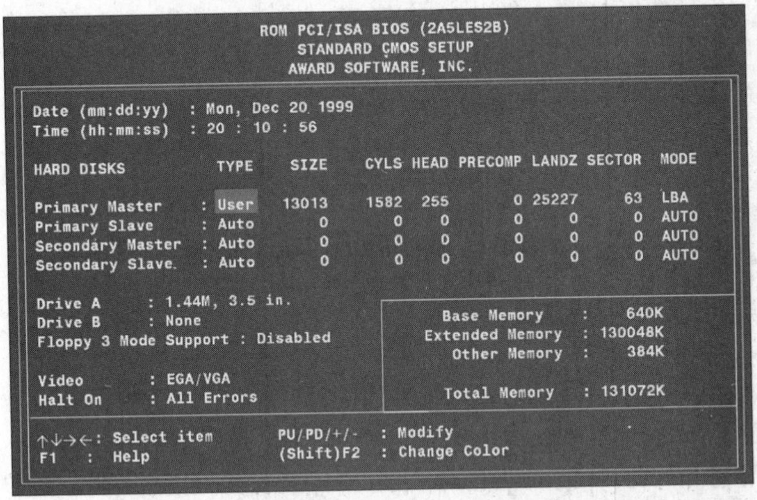

BIOS date

Motherboard chipset
vendor and model #

Key to press
to run SETUP

```
                ROM PCI/ISA BIOS (2A5LES2B)
                    STANDARD CMOS SETUP
                    AWARD SOFTWARE, INC.

Date (mm:dd:yy)  : Mon, Dec 20, 1999
Time (hh:mm:ss)  : 20 : 10 : 56

HARD DISKS        TYPE   SIZE   CYLS HEAD PRECOMP LANDZ SECTOR  MODE

Primary Master   : User  13013  1582  255      0 25227     63  LBA
Primary Slave    : Auto      0     0    0      0     0      0  AUTO
Secondary Master : Auto      0     0    0      0     0      0  AUTO
Secondary Slave  : Auto      0     0    0      0     0      0  AUTO

Drive A    : 1.44M, 3.5 in.
Drive B    : None                   Base Memory     :    640K
Floppy 3 Mode Support : Disabled    Extended Memory : 130048K
                                       Other Memory :    384K
Video      : EGA/VGA
Halt On    : All Errors             Total Memory    : 131072K

↑↓→←: Select item       PU/PD/+/-  : Modify
F1   : Help              (Shift)F2  : Change Color
```

FIGURE 2.2
If your drive is configured with incorrect options for cylinders, heads, sectors, or LBA mode, it won't be bootable. It's safer to use Auto mode when you install a new IDE/ATA hard drive.

Write down the current drive configuration settings, reset the configuration to Auto, save the changes, and restart the computer. If you still can't boot the drive, it's time to target your disk's boot sector.

Repairing a Damaged Master Boot Record

If the master boot record (MBR) on your hard disk is damaged, the computer cannot read it to determine how your drive is partitioned or the location of your operating system boot files. The most typical cause for a damaged MBR is a boot-sector computer virus. You can use the Windows XP CD-ROM or Windows XP boot disks to start your system and fix the problem.

Leo Says

No Windows XP CD-ROM? Boot Disks to the Rescue!

If you use a preinstalled version of Windows XP, odds are very good that you didn't receive a bootable Windows XP CD. Instead, you can download Windows XP boot disks from Microsoft and use them to start your system. Microsoft Knowledge Base Article 310994 gives you the details and the links you need. Go to http://support.microsoft.com and search for 310994 to get started. My advice? If your system uses a recovery CD or recovery files on a hidden disk partition, download the Windows XP boot files and create the boot disks before you have a problem.

Determining Whether the Problem Is the MBR or Missing Boot Files

In addition to a valid MBR, a bootable hard disk also needs to have the correct Windows bootable files installed on it. The error message displayed when a system can't boot will help you determine which problem the drive is having.

If the system displays a message such as "No Boot Sector on Fixed Disk" or "No Boot Device Available," the MBR has been corrupted. If the system displays a message such as "Non-System Disk or Disk Error" or "Invalid System Disk," the MBR is okay but the boot files are missing or corrupted.

Special Procedures for Special Cases

The procedures discussed in the following sections are designed to help you recover from a problem with a damaged MBR or missing boot files if you prepared your hard disk with the standard Windows utilities: the Windows XP Setup program or Disk Management (see Chapter 3 for details). However, if you used a program packaged with your hard disk (or downloaded from your hard disk vendor's website) to prepare your hard disk, you might not have a standard MBR.

Programs such as Maxtor's MaxBlast, Western Digital's Data Lifeguard Tools, Seagate's Disc Wizard, Ontrack Disk Manager, and others serve two purposes:

- They provide an easier-to-use replacement for the Windows XP Disk Management or Setup process.

- Optionally, they can also provide a software-based BIOS replacement for BIOS chips that cannot handle the entire capacity of the drive (typically older BIOS chips found on older boards).

Using the repair procedures in the following section to fix an MBR problem on a drive prepared with a program such as this might overwrite the special MBR created by the hard disk setup program and prevent access to the drive.

If you used a vendor-supplied or third-party disk preparation program *and* your computer displays a startup message such as "EZ-BIOS: Hold the CTRL key down for Status Screen or to boot from floppy" or a message referring to "Dynamic Drive Overlay," your drive is being controlled by a special MBR created by the drive installation program.

To solve bootup problems with a drive that's controlled by EZ-BIOS, contact the drive vendor that supplied the setup software.

For bootup problems with a drive controlled by Dynamic Drive Overlay, contact the drive vendor or the Ontrack website at http://www.ontrack.com/diskmanager/.

Unmasking the "Real" Disk Utility Creator

Hard drive vendors have used both StorageSoft- and Ontrack-produced versions of disk installation programs over the years, sometimes switching between one vendor and the other. The surest way to tell whose product has set up your drive is to watch the startup messages:

- A reference to "EZ-BIOS" indicates that a product created by Phoenix/StorageSoft was used to configure the drive and replace the system BIOS drive support. EZ-BIOS is not compatible with Windows XP, and vendors that used EZ-BIOS now use the Dynamic Drive Overlay software provided by Ontrack. If you want to upgrade an older system using EZ-BIOS with Windows XP, contact the drive vendor for instructions.

- A reference to "Dynamic Drive Overlay" indicates that a product created by Ontrack was used to configure the drive and replace the system BIOS drive support.

Repairing a Missing Boot Sector with Windows XP

If you use Windows XP, boot from the CD-ROM and select the Repair option displayed on the Welcome to Setup menu to fix your installation with the Recovery Console. When prompted, enter the number of the Windows installation you want to fix. Unless you have a dual-boot configuration, your Windows installation will be listed as 1: C:\WINDOWS.

Next, enter the Administrator password to continue; if no Administrator password was set, press Enter.

Enter the command **FIXBOOT** at the Recovery Console prompt that appears. This option installs new bootable files on your hard drive. Answer **Y**(es) when prompted to write a new boot sector. Enter the command **FIXBOOT** to re-create the master boot record.

When this is complete, type **EXIT** and press the Enter key to restart the computer. Remove the CD-ROM so the computer can boot from the hard drive. These commands also work with Windows 2000.

Leo Says

Easy Windows XP Repair with CPR for XP 3.0

You may also want to consider ordering CPR for XP 3.0 from http://www.myezfix.com/ (about $40). This product provides fast rebuilding of unbootable Windows XP installations and also works with the Windows XP System Restore feature to handle problems encountered after Windows begins the boot process.

Getting the Boot Order Right for Fast Repairs

If you need to fix your computer's hard disk or perform other repairs using the Windows XP Recovery Console, you should change the boot order of your drives in your system BIOS so you can boot from the Windows XP CD-ROM:

- First boot device: CD-ROM

  If you do not have a bootable Windows XP CD (you have a preinstalled system with a recovery CD or recovery partition), change the first boot device to Floppy and see the sidebar "No Windows XP CD-ROM? Boot Disks to the Rescue!" to learn how to download Windows XP bootable floppy disk images.

- Second boot device: First hard disk (called hard disk 0 on some systems)
- Third boot device: Floppy

For details, see "Troubleshooting Booting Problems," Chapter 3, p. 206.

You can also add the Recovery Console to the Windows XP startup menu. We recommend this because you won't need to hunt for your Windows XP CD when you need to run Recovery Console.

Online Help for Recovery Console Installation and Use

To learn how to install the Recovery Console as a startup option from the Windows XP CD, see Microsoft Knowledge Base Article 307654. Search for it at http://support.microsoft.com. This article also provides a basic tutorial in using the Recovery Console.

If your system has a preinstalled version of Windows, the i386 folder containing the Winnt32.exe program needed to install the Recovery Console might already be installed on your system. See Gateway's instructions for installing the Recovery Console for a typical example that might also apply to other systems: http://support.gateway.com/s/ SOFTWARE/Medialess/MLXPMC0/MLXPMC0su18.shtml. Contact your computer vendor for help if you don't have the Winnt32.exe program preinstalled on your system.

Fixing Other Startup Problems with Windows XP

If Windows XP starts but can't finish booting properly, or if it displays errors, you'll need to access the Windows Advanced Options menu. To do so, reboot your PC and press the F8 key repeatedly until the menu appears (this might take a couple tries to get the timing down). You can select different options from this menu to get your system back to work in a hurry.

Windows XP also provides the Startup/Shutdown Troubleshooter, available in the Help and Support Center, which can help you determine the reason for startup problems. To use this troubleshooter even if Windows won't start normally, boot your system in Safe Mode or Safe Mode with Networking. Table 2.1 provides a reference to which startup option is best to use depending on your circumstances.

TABLE 2.1
USING THE WINDOWS XP ADVANCED OPTIONS MENU

Problem	XP Startup Option to Select	Notes
Windows won't start after you install new hardware or software.	Last Known Good Configuration	Resets Windows to its last-known working configuration; you will need to reinstall any hardware or software installed after that time.
Windows won't start after you upgrade a device driver.	Safe Mode	After starting the computer in Safe Mode, open the Device Manager, select the device, and use the Rollback feature to restore the previously used device driver. Restart your system. See "Using Device Manager," this chapter, p. 100. Uses 640×480 resolution but retains the color settings normally used.
Windows won't start after you install a different video card or monitor.	Enable VGA Mode	Most video cards should be installed when your system is running in VGA mode (256 colors, 640×480 resolution). Use Display Properties to select a working video mode before you restart. See "Troubleshooting Graphics Cards," Chapter 5, p. 318, and "Display Properties," this chapter, p. 94.
Windows can't start normally, but you need access to the Internet to research the problem or download updates.	Safe Mode with Networking	You can use Windows Update and the Internet, but some devices won't work in this mode. This mode also uses 640×480 resolution, but retains the color settings normally used.

TABLE 2.1 (continued)
USING THE WINDOWS XP ADVANCED OPTIONS MENU

Problem	XP Startup Option to Select	Notes
Windows doesn't finish starting normally, and you want to know what device driver or process is preventing it from working.	Enable Boot Logging	This option starts the computer with all its normal drivers and settings while it also creates a file called ntbtlog.txt in the default Windows folder (usually C:\Windows or C:\WINNT). Restart the computer in Safe Mode and open this file with Notepad or WordPad to determine the last driver file that loaded. You can update the driver or remove the hardware device using that driver to restore your system to working condition. See "Understanding the Boot Log," this page.
Windows is loading programs you don't need during its startup process.	Boot computer in Normal Mode (or Safe Mode if the computer won't start in Normal Mode), click Start, Run, and then type **MSCONFIG**.	Use MSCONFIG to disable one or more startup programs and then restart your computer. You can also use MSCONFIG to restore damaged files, or to start System Restore to reset your computer to an earlier condition. For details, see "Using MSCONFIG," this chapter, p. 129, and "Using System Restore," this chapter, p. 118.
Windows won't start, even in Safe Mode, or has other serious problems that can't be fixed with System Restore.	Boot from the Windows XP CD or boot disks and perform a repair installation.	See "Performing a Repair Installation," this chapter, p. 134, for details.

Understanding the Boot Log

The Windows XP bootlog file (ntbtlog.txt) is a plain-text file that lists the drivers that are loaded or not loaded during the boot process.

Because Windows XP adds entries to the ntbtlog.txt file every time you start the system with boot logging enabled, follow this procedure to make it useful for troubleshooting:

1. Create a bootlog as soon as you have successfully installed Windows XP.

2. Use the Search option to locate ntbtlog.txt and change the name of the file to bootlog.txt.

3. Whenever you install new hardware, delete the ntbtlog.txt and bootlog.txt files and create a new bootlog.txt file as in steps 1 and 2.

4. Press F8 and select Create a Bootlog if you need to restart Windows XP if it failed to start normally to generate a new bootlog.

5. Restart Windows XP in Safe Mode and open bootlog.txt (your original bootlog) and the new ntbtlog.txt (which shows the current status of the computer). Then, compare the entries in each file (see Figure 2.3). If there is more than one section in ntbtlog.txt, scroll down to the section headed by the date and time of the last bootlog creation.

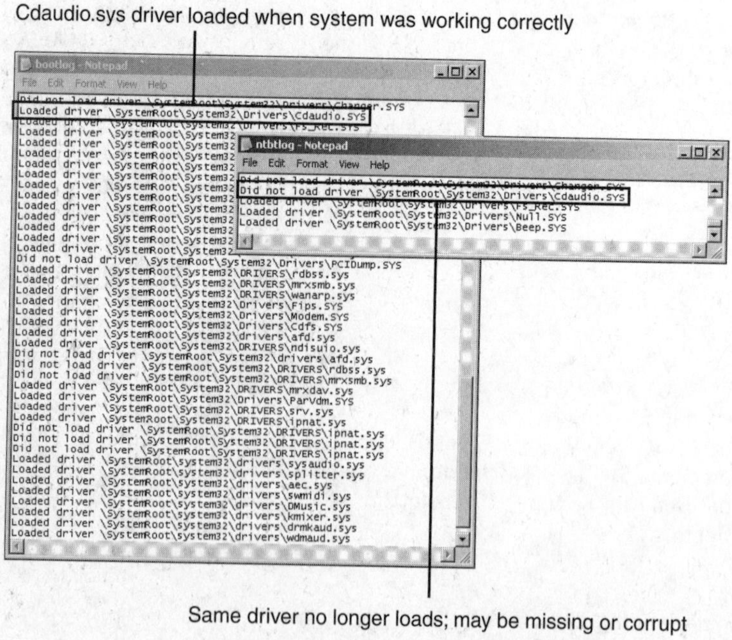

FIGURE 2.3

Comparing the original bootlog (rear) with the latest ntbtlog (front) to find a driver that no longer loads.

Cdaudio.sys driver loaded when system was working correctly

Same driver no longer loads; may be missing or corrupt

To reinstall drivers for a particular device, you can use the Device Manager (see "Using Device Manager," this chapter, p. 100) to reload the driver or to remove the device; it will be reinstalled with a fresh driver when you restart Windows.

Windows Update to the Rescue!

As long as you can get to the Internet (booting up your computer in Safe Mode with Networking will do it for you), you can get updated device drivers and Windows files straight from the source with Microsoft Windows Update. Start your Internet connection after you reboot (if you have a dial-up or other service that requires you to log in), click Start, All Programs, Windows Update, and then let Windows Update scan your system for the features you need.

Fixing Shutdown Problems

Windows doesn't always shut down when you tell it to do so. Sometimes it hangs, or sometimes it restarts instead of shutting down. Windows XP includes a Startup/Shutdown Troubleshooter, available in the Help and Support Center, that may be able to help you isolate the causes. Search for List of Troubleshooters in Windows XP to display the available troubleshooters. To use any of the troubleshooters, answer the question and click Next to go to the next step; the sequence of questions varies according to your answers. The troubleshooters might also direct you to use MSCONFIG, the Device Manager, or other Windows tools.

Leo Says

Don't Expect Windows Troubleshooters to Work Miracles

I'd like to tell you that Windows troubleshooters work most of the time, but I'd be lying. In my experience, they're occasionally useful—and that's mainly if they prompt you to use diagnostic tools such as Device Manager or Net Diagnostics. As far as the standard Q&A troubleshooting process, they're not that useful. It doesn't hurt to try them, but I don't expect they'll help you very often.

Along with the troubleshooters, use the tips shown in Table 2.2 to find the problem and a solution.

TABLE 2.2
TROUBLESHOOTING WINDOWS XP SHUTDOWN PROBLEMS

Problem	Solution	Notes
Computer won't shut down after installing new hardware or software.	First, download and install the latest software patches or device drivers. If the computer still won't shut down, contact the hardware or software vendor for tech support or uninstall the hardware or software.	You can use System Restore in Windows XP to revert the computer back to a point before you installed the hardware or software.
Computer restarts instead of shutting down.	Disable Automatic Restart in the System properties sheet.	Right-click on My Computer, select Properties, select Advanced, click the Settings button in the Startup and Recovery section, and clear the check mark next to Automatically Restart. Click OK.
Computer Displays STOP message at shutdown.	Bad device drivers for one or more devices if STOP 0x9F, STOP 0x8E, or STOP 0x7B is displayed.	Restart, press F8 during boot, and select the Last Known Good Configuration option, or use System Restore to go back to an older working configuration. See also "Troubleshooting STOP Errors with Windows XP," this chapter, p. 153.
Computer won't shut down, but doesn't display an error message.	Programs installed at startup may not be working properly.	Click Start, Run and then enter **MSCONFIG**. Use the Startup tab to selectively disable startup events one at a time until the computer shuts down properly. Try to identify noncritical components first before disabling something more important such as an antivirus program.

On the Web

For additional advice on troubleshooting shutdown problems with any recent Windows version (98 through XP), I recommend James A. Eschelman's Windows Startup and Shutdown Center troubleshooters. The Windows XP version is available at http://aumha.org/win5/a/ shtdwnxp.htm.

Using Control Panel

The Windows Control Panel provides access to most of the diagnostic tools supplied with Windows. In Windows XP, the default view of the Control Panel is the task-oriented Category View (see Figure 2.4).

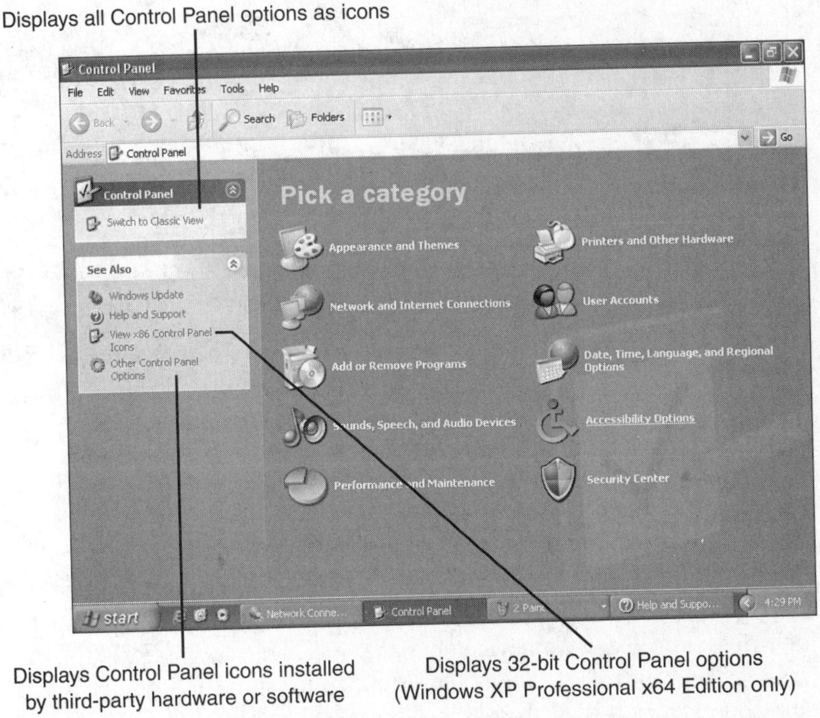

Displays all Control Panel options as icons

FIGURE 2.4
The default Category View of the Control Panel in Windows XP.

Displays Control Panel icons installed by third-party hardware or software

Displays 32-bit Control Panel options (Windows XP Professional x64 Edition only)

What happens when you click a Category View icon? The icon might take you directly to a particular Control Panel icon, such as Add/Remove Programs and User Accounts. Other Category View icons, such as Appearance and Themes, display a submenu of tasks and a list of Control Panel icons (see Figure 2.5) in the main window. Related options and troubleshooters appear in the left window. If you choose one of the tasks, Windows opens up the appropriate Control Panel icon and takes you directly to the menu needed to make the change.

Control Panel icon (not available in Windows XP x64 Edition)

Related Control Panel icons or tasks

Tasks

FIGURE 2.5

The Appearance and Themes category in Control Panel.

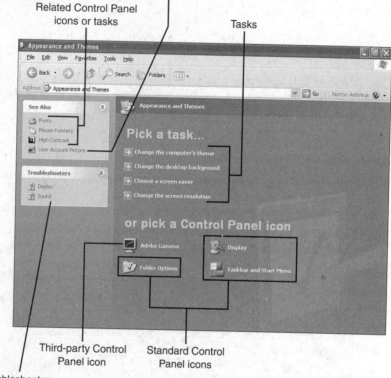

Third-party Control Panel icon

Standard Control Panel icons

Troubleshooters

If you never used a version of Windows before Windows XP, you might prefer the Category View access method shown in Figures 2.4 and 2.5. However, if you prefer direct access to each Control Panel icon (the default in older Windows versions), you can click the Switch to Classic View button shown in Figure 2.4 to toggle to the Classic View shown in Figure 2.6. To switch back to Category View, click the Switch to Category View button shown in Figure 2.6.

Table 2.3 provides a breakdown of the tasks and Control Panel icons available through each Category View icon in Windows XP. You might find additional options available on your system, depending on how Windows XP was installed.

Reverts to the default display of Control Panel categories

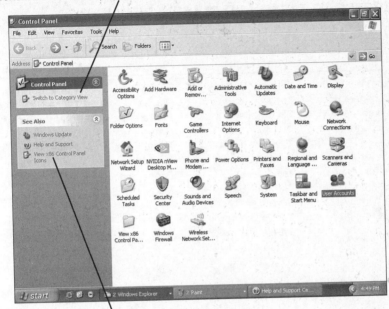

FIGURE 2.6
The optional Classic View of the Control Panel in Windows XP.

Displays x86 Control Panel icons (x64 Edition only)

TABLE 2.3
CATEGORY VIEW ACCESS TO TASKS AND CLASSIC VIEW ICONS

Category View	Tasks	Control Panel Icons	See Also	Troubleshooters
Appearance and Themes	Change or select the computer theme, background, screen saver, or screen resolution.	Display Folder options Taskbar and Start menu	Fonts Mouse Pointers High Contrast User Account Picture[1]	Display Sound
Printers and Other Hardware	View installed printers or fax printers. Add a printer.	Game Controllers Keyboard Mouse Phone and Modem Options Printers and Faxes Scanners and Cameras	Add Hardware Display Sounds, Speech and Audio Devices Power Options System	Hardware Printing Home or Small-Office Networking

1. Not available from this menu in x64 version

TABLE 2.3 (continued)
CATEGORY VIEW ACCESS TO TASKS AND CLASSIC VIEW ICONS

Category View	Tasks	Control Panel Icons	See Also	Troubleshooters
Network and Internet Connections	Set up or change the Internet connection. Create a connection to the network at your workplace (VPN). Set up a wireless network for a home or small office. Change Windows Firewall settings[2].	Internet Options (see Chapter 8 for details) Network Connections (see Chapter 8 for details) Network Setup Wizard Windows Firewall Wireless Network Setup Wizard	My Network Places Printers and Other Hardware Remote Desktop[2] Phone and Modem Options	Home or Small-Office Networking Internet Explorer Network Diagnostics
User Accounts	Change an account. Create a new account. Change the way users log off or log on.	N/A	N/A	N/A
Add or Remove Programs	Change or remove programs. Add new programs. Add/remove windows components. Set program access and defaults.	N/A	N/A	N/A
Date, Time, Language and Regional Options	Change date and time. Change numeric, date, time format. Add other languages.	Date and Time Regional and Language Options	Scheduled Tasks	N/A
Sounds, Speech and Audio Devices	Adjust the system volume. Change the sound scheme. Change the speaker settings.	Sounds and Audio Devices Speech	Accessibility Sound Options Advanced Volume Controls	Sound DVD
Accessibility Options	Adjust the contrast for text and colors. Configure Windows to work for vision, hearing, and mobility needs.	Accessibility Options	Magnifier On-Screen Keyboard	N/A

2. Introduced with Windows XP Service Pack 2

TABLE 2.3 (continued)
CATEGORY VIEW ACCESS TO TASKS AND CLASSIC VIEW ICONS

Category View	Tasks	Control Panel Icons	See Also	Troubleshooters
Performance and Maintenance	See basic computer information. Adjust visual effects. Free up hard disk space. Back up data.[3] Rearrange items on the hard disk for faster performance (defrag).	Administrative Tools Power Options Scheduled Tasks System	File Types System Restore[1]	Startup and Shutdown
Security Center[2]	Configures Firewall and Automatic Updates, checks for antivirus software, and configures Internet security.	N/A	N/A	N/A

1. Not available from this menu in x64 version

2. Introduced with Windows XP Service Pack 2

3. Listed only if XP Backup application is installed

As Table 2.3 demonstrates, if you prefer to work with Control Panel icons directly, you might prefer to configure Control Panel to use the Classic View. Using the Control Panel in Category View might slow you down because of the extra navigation required. However, if you're not an experienced Windows user, you might prefer the default Category View. It's your choice.

The following sections describe how to use the Classic View Control Panel icons in Windows XP to perform troubleshooting tasks.

Accessibility Options

The Accessibility Options properties sheet is designed to help Windows users with physical, sight, or hearing impairments use Windows more easily. If you use the High Contrast display option in Windows, you will need to work with the Display tab.

Display

The Display tab has three functions designed to make using the Windows GUI a bit more comfortable:

- High Contrast
- Cursor Blink Rate
- Cursor Width

→ *For more information about using High Contrast displays, see "The Text Is Too Small or Too Hard to Read," Chapter 5, p. 311.*

The High Contrast option lets you switch back and forth between your normal Windows color scheme and any of about three dozen other normal or high-contrast color schemes, some of which feature large or extra-large text and icons. To switch, press the left Alt, left Shift, and Print Screen keys; if you hit this option accidentally, you can also disable this option from the Settings dialog.

The Cursor Blink Rate and Cursor Width functions use interactive drag controls that provide a real-time preview of your settings.

Rediscovering "Lost" Windows Color Schemes with the High Contrast Dialog

Whereas older versions of Windows let you select color schemes such as "Red, White, and Blue," "Brick," and "Storm" through the normal Display properties sheet, Windows XP offers custom color schemes only through the High Contrast dialog. Use it if you want a fast way to customize your desktop without the effort of selecting all the colors, fonts, and other features manually.

Add Hardware

The Add Hardware Wizard in Windows XP has two functions:

- It detects and installs drivers for new hardware.
- It enables the user to select a particular hardware device for troubleshooting.

To use this wizard to troubleshoot installed hardware, click Next to start the search process. When prompted, click Yes (you have already connected the hardware to your computer), and click Next. Choose the hardware you want to troubleshoot from the list of installed hardware (see Figure 2.7) and click Next to display its current status (see Figure 2.8).

If the device status box displays an error code or problem, as shown in Figure 2.8, or if you are having other difficulties with the device, click Finish to open a troubleshooter. If the device is working properly, click Cancel to close the wizard.

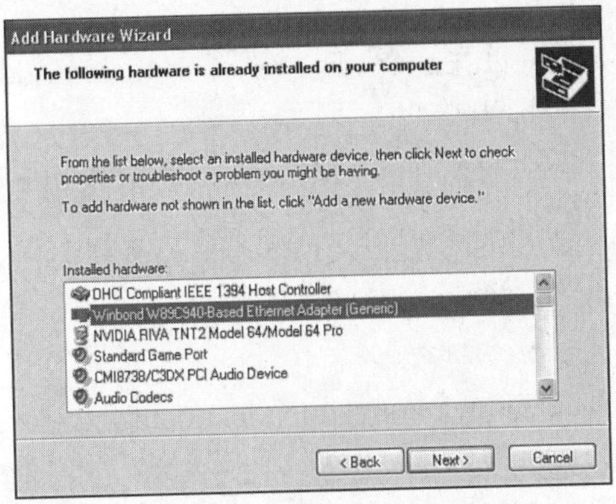

FIGURE 2.7
Selecting an installed hardware device to troubleshoot.

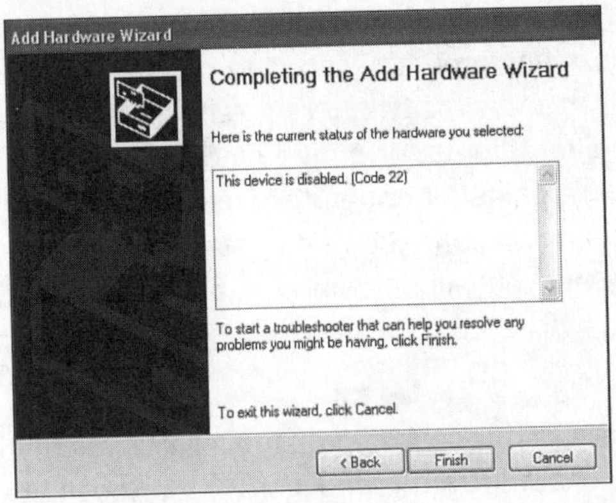

FIGURE 2.8
Displaying the status of an installed hardware device.

When the Remove and Restart Process Works Better Than the Add Hardware Option

Most hardware used with Windows XP supports Plug and Play (PnP), the feature that enables Windows to automatically detect and install drivers for new hardware when you connect it and start your system. If you're having problems with PnP-compliant hardware, you should try removing the device listing in Device Manager, leaving the device connected, restarting your computer, and letting Windows redetect the device and reinstall its drivers. Use Add Hardware to troubleshoot any problems that you might encounter after you use the remove and restart process.

Although Add Hardware works well for non-PnP hardware (hardware that must be manually configured), little of this hardware is still in use.

Add or Remove Programs

If you're having problems with your computer because of a program you just installed, you need to remove it. If you want to use a Windows utility discussed in this book but it's not installed yet, you need a way to install it. Either way, you need to use Add or Remove Programs to get the job done.

Use Add or Remove Programs in Windows XP to do the following:

- Change the installation of an existing program
- Remove an existing program
- Install a new program
- Modify your Windows installation by adding or removing components

Add or Remove Programs works along with the install/uninstall program included in virtually every 32-bit Windows application. To change or remove an existing program, click the program and click Change (to rerun its installer and specify different options, such as additional import/export filters, fonts, or program components) or Remove (to run the program's uninstall option to remove the program from your system). Although you can also add (install) programs with Add or Remove Programs, you will seldom use this feature, because most CD-based programs will automatically run their installation programs when you insert the install CD.

To add or remove Windows Components, click the icon to start the Windows Component Wizard (see Figure 2.9). Check boxes with a white background indicate all components in the category are installed; blank check boxes indicate no components in the category are installed; a gray check box indicates some but not all components are installed. Click the Details button to add or remove programs in a category.

Repairing Applications with Add or Remove Programs

If you have a "broken" program, use Add or Remove Programs to rerun the program's installer. Depending on the program's options, you can reinstall the program completely or run a repair option that checks the installed files against the correct versions and replaces damaged files only.

Note that you might need to insert the original program CD to uninstall or reinstall some applications.

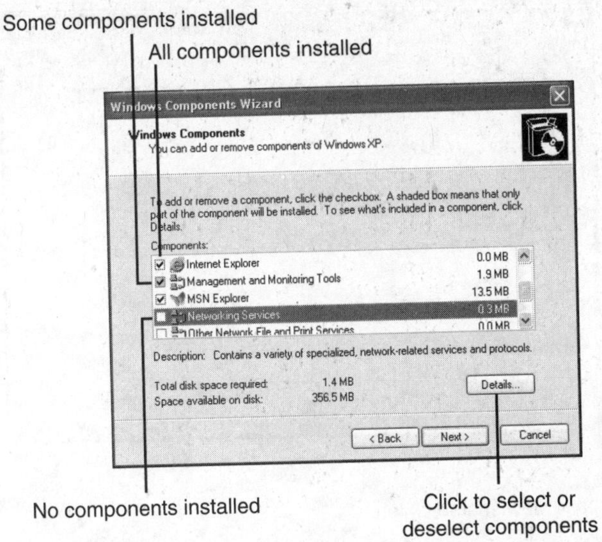

FIGURE 2.9
The Windows Component Wizard.

Some components installed

All components installed

No components installed

Click to select or deselect components

Administrative Tools

Windows XP's ControlPanel provides access to several different administrative tools, which can be used to manage your computer. The most important of these for home and small-office users are the following:

- **Computer Management**—Access to the Device Manager, hard disk preparation, disk management and defragmentation, and network shares management. Equivalent to right-clicking My Computer and selecting Manage.

- **Event Viewer**—Tracks system events and problems.

- **Performance**—Displays system performance.

- **Services**—Displays and manages system services.

Troubleshooting with Computer Management

If you're having problems with network shared resources or network users on your computer, start Computer Management (see Figure 2.10) and click Shared Folders to display information about network shares and users (see Figure 2.11), which network computers and users are accessing shared resources (Sessions), and which files are in use across the network (Open Files).

FIGURE 2.10
The Computer Management display in Windows XP.

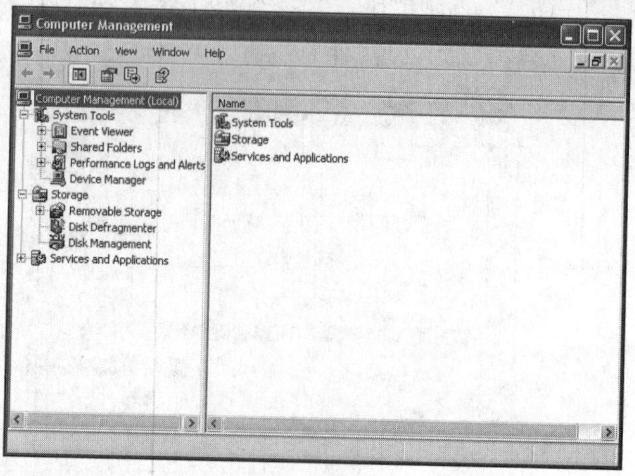

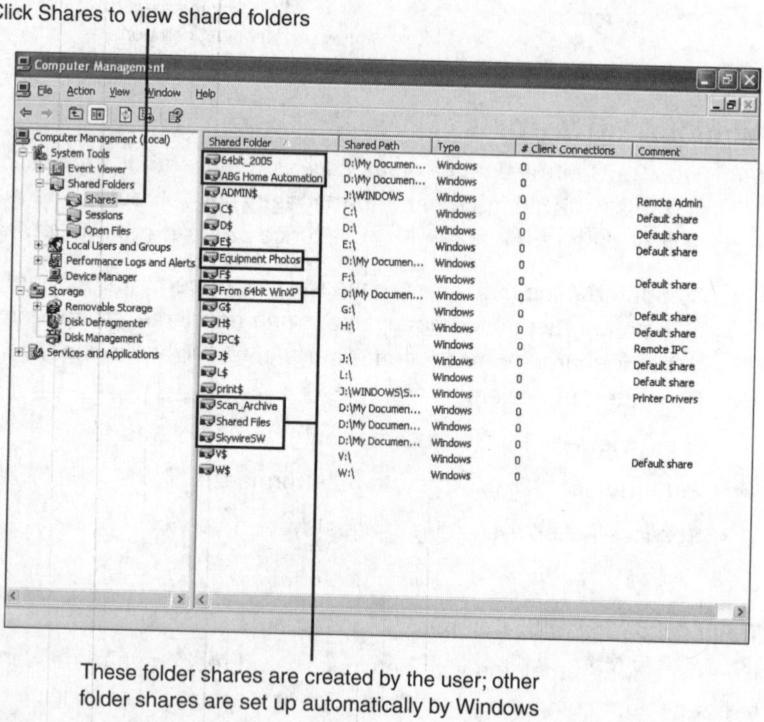

Click Shares to view shared folders

FIGURE 2.11
User-defined shared folders on the co-author's system.

These folder shares are created by the user; other folder shares are set up automatically by Windows

Click Device Manager to troubleshoot hardware problems. This brings up the same Device Manager you can access through the System properties sheet. See "Using Device Manager," this chapter, p. 100, for details.

To learn more about system problems, open Event Viewer and select from Application, Security, or System logs to display their contents. Event Viewer displays three types of events in each category (see Figure 2.12):

- **Information**—Indicates the start or completion of a normal operation, signified by a blue *i* in a white box.

- **Warning**—Indicates an abnormal event has taken place, signified by a yellow triangle containing an exclamation mark (!).

- **Error**—Indicates a hardware, software, or services error has taken place, signified by a red circle containing a white *X*.

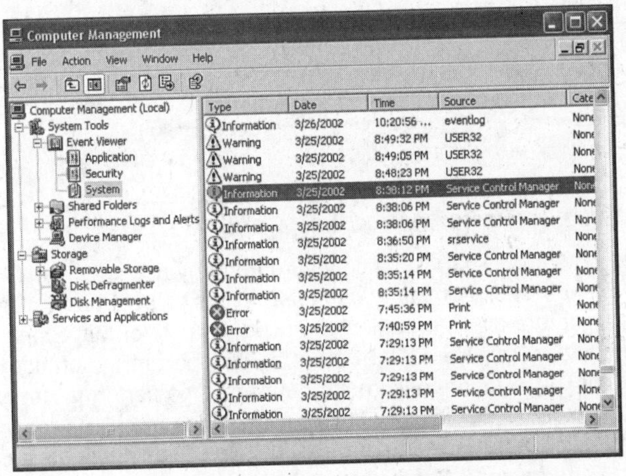

FIGURE 2.12
A system log with information, warning, and error entries.

Double-click an entry to see the details of the computer involved, the date and time, the source of the event, the event type, and a description (see Figure 2.13). Use the scroll buttons shown in Figure 2.13 to move to other events.

Learning More About Event Log Entries

If you'd like to learn more about a particular event, click the hyperlink listed in the description field. If Microsoft doesn't have specific information about the event, you can use the additional Help and Support Center links to perform your own search online.

Use Performance Logs and Alerts to create and monitor logs and alerts you create yourself.

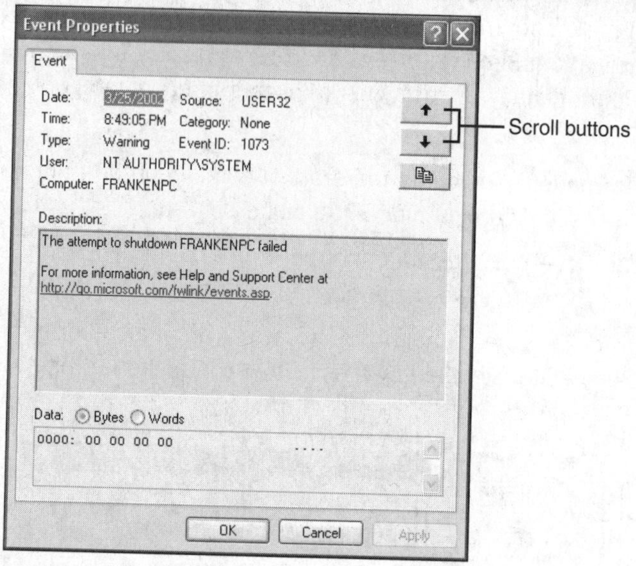

FIGURE 2.13
The properties of a warning event.

Event Properties

Event

Date: 3/25/2005   Source: USER32
Time: 8:49:05 PM   Category: None
Type: Warning   Event ID: 1073
User: NT AUTHORITY\SYSTEM
Computer: FRANKENPC

Description:
The attempt to shutdown FRANKENPC failed

For more information, see Help and Support Center at
http://go.microsoft.com/fwlink/events.asp.

Data: ⦿ Bytes ○ Words

0000: 00 00 00 00   · · · ·

OK   Cancel   Apply

Scroll buttons

Alternatives to Performance Logs and Alerts

It takes time and expertise to configure Performance Logs and Alerts; unlike Event Viewer, nothing is captured unless you set up the logs and alerts to capture the information you need (search for Microsoft Knowledge Base Article 310490 at http://support.microsoft.com to get started). If you're more concerned about real-time performance, press Ctrl+Alt+Delete to display the Windows Task Manager. Click the Performance tab for real-time information. See "Troubleshooting Slow System Performance," Chapter 9, p. 549, for more about Task Manager.

➔ **For details on using Disk Management to configure a new hard disk, see "Preparing an Additional Hard Disk with Windows XP," Chapter 3, p. 195.**

The Storage tool has three components:

- **Removable Storage**—Lists removable-media drives and their contents
- **Disk Defragmenter**—Launches the disk defragmenter tool
- **Disk Management**—Starts the disk management tool for preparing hard drives, managing drive letters, and displaying disk statistics

Display Properties

The Display properties sheet contains the following tabs:

- **Themes**—Your choice of a coordinated desktop, which includes a background image, sounds, icons, and other elements.

- **Desktop**—Lets you specify a background image or web page; click Customize Desktop to select which commonly used icons (My Computer, My Network Places, and others) will be placed on the desktop, whether or not to periodically remove unused icons from the desktop, and whether to use a web page instead of an image on the desktop.

- **Screen Saver**—Specifies a screen saver and the settings to use.

- **Appearance**—Customizes the current desktop's colors, fonts, and spacing. Click Effects to change font smoothing, transition effects, and to enable large icons. Click Advanced if you selected Windows Classic as your theme for additional screen customization.

- **Settings**—Used to adjust color depth, adjust resolution, enable or disable multiple monitors (if available), and troubleshoot display problems. Click Advanced to adjust refresh rate, 3D graphics acceleration options, color management, and other options varying by display adapter or monitor (see Figure 2.14).

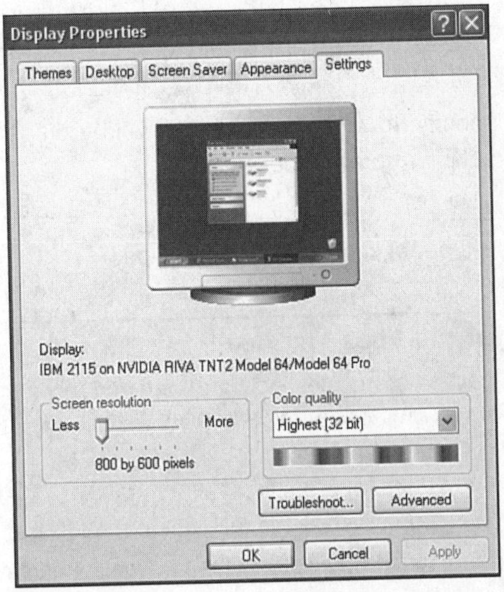

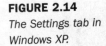

FIGURE 2.14
The Settings tab in Windows XP.

Fast Track to a More Comfortable Display

If you're tired of tiny text and fonts onscreen but don't want to spend a lot of time fiddling with the Appearance tab, use these options to customize your desktop quickly and easily:

- Click Appearance, Effects and then check the box to enable large icons.
- Click Settings, Advanced, General and then select Large Size (120 dpi) or Custom and specify a larger size than the default (96 dpi) to increase the size of text onscreen.

For more information, see "The Text and Icons Onscreen Are Hard to Read," Chapter 5, p. 305.

Folder Options

Folder Options has three or four tabs, depending on the Windows XP Edition you use:

- General
- View
- File Types

- Offline Files (XP Professional and x64 Edition only)

Click General if you want to switch back to the Windows Classic folder view (files and folders only; no tasks), to restore the default task and file/folder view, or to specify folder browsing and file-opening options.

Click View to specify how files and folders will be displayed and to apply current settings to all folders.

Click File Types to view or modify which program is registered to open a particular file type, or to add a new file type.

Tracking Down the Files You Need

If you're maintaining or troubleshooting a system, I recommend you make the following changes to the Advanced settings on the View menu:

- Enable the option Display the contents of system folders.
- Enable the option Display the full path in the title bar.
- Disable the option Hide extensions for known (registered) file types.
- Show hidden files and folders.
- Show Control Panel in My Computer.

Making these changes will help you navigate faster when you're trying to fix a balky system.

Keyboard

The Keyboard dialog has two tabs:

- **General**—Adjusts repeat delay, repeat rate, and cursor blink rate with sliding controls. Use this dialog if you are having problems with repeating keys or with the cursor being hard to see.

- **Hardware**—Displays the currently installed keyboard(s). Click Properties to view the keyboard properties sheet. Click Troubleshoot to start the keyboard troubleshooter.

You might see additional tabs or options if your keyboard uses special software.

Exert Even More Control over the Cursor

You might prefer to use the Accessibility option's Display tab to control the cursor blink rate, because it also offers you the option to adjust the cursor width.

See "Accessibility Options," this chapter, p. 87, for details.

Mouse

The standard mouse dialog (also used for pointing devices such as trackballs and touchpads) contains three tabs:

- **Pointers**—You can select from various standard, large, and extra-large mouse pointers. Use this dialog to make the mouse pointer easier to see.

- **Buttons**—Switches buttons from the default right-hand to left-hand use and adjusts double-click speed. If you find that the mouse buttons are reversed (left-click opens the right-click menu), use this dialog to reset the mouse buttons to their normal behavior.

- **Motion**—Adjusts pointer speed and acceleration, as well as enables cursor trails and SmartMove, which moves the mouse pointer to the default button in the current dialog box. Use this dialog to make the mouse pointer easier to control and see, especially for users of notebook computers and LCD display panels. Older and low-end LCD displays have slower response than CRTs, making it easy for the mouse pointer to be "lost" onscreen.

If you install customized mouse-driver software, additional tabs are added to the mouse dialog. For example, Logitech's MouseWare and Microsoft's IntelliPoint software let you configure your mouse buttons in a variety of ways. For additional mouse troubleshooting, see Chapter 7, "Troubleshooting I/O Ports and Input Devices."

Enhancing Your Mouse

Even if you're not using a brand-new optical mouse, you can benefit from installing the latest mouse software (Microsoft's drivers might also work with some third-party mice). Here are the websites for leading mouse and pointing-device vendors:

- Logitech—http://www.logitech.com.
- Microsoft—http://www.microsoft.com/hardware/mouse/download.asp.
- IBM (now owned by Lenovo)—http://www.pc.ibm.com. Click on Support and Downloads.
- Belkin—http://www.belkin.com.
- Kensington—http://www.kensington.com.

Power Options

If you need to adjust how and when your computer saves power, use the Power Options dialog:

- **Power Schemes**—Configures or disables power savings for monitors and hard drives
- **Advanced**—Configures options such as the use of the computer's sleep button, whether or not to show the Power icon on the taskbar, and whether or not to prompt for a password when the computer comes out of standby
- **Hibernate**—Enables or disables hibernation (which stores current program states on the hard disk)
- **APM**—Enables or disables Advanced Power Management support (not present if the computer isn't configured to use APM)
- **UPS**—Enables or configures battery backup devices

To prevent your computer from going into standby mode when you stop typing or mousing, increase the time settings on the Power Schemes tab.

For computers that will be run in an interactive kiosk or to display a slide show, select Always On as the power scheme.

If the computer can't go into Hibernate mode, check the required versus available disk space information on the Hibernate menu.

Sounds and Audio Devices

The Sounds and Audio Devices dialog has five tabs:

- **Volume**—Sets volume controls and speaker configuration; click the Advanced buttons for additional options.

- **Sounds**—Displays and configures sounds to be played during specified program and system events; your choices can be saved as a sound scheme.

- **Audio**—Displays and configures devices used for sound playback, recording, and MIDI music playback.

- **Voice**—Displays and configures devices used for voice playback and recording. Click Test to verify that your hardware works.

- **Hardware**—Displays hardware devices, drivers, and codecs (compression/decompression) programs. Click Troubleshoot to solve sound problems, and click Properties to view the properties for the selected item.

User Accounts

The User Accounts system folder lets you add or change an account and change logon/logoff settings.

If you share your computer with multiple users, use this folder to configure a separate account for each user; this will help make email and documents more private.

There are two account types in Windows XP Home Edition:

- Administrator
- Guest

An Administrator-level user can install new programs and hardware; make changes that affect all users; access and read nonprivate files; and create, delete, and change user accounts. In other words, if you want to troubleshoot or configure your system, you need to use an Administrator-level account. Guest accounts can change their own passwords and change the picture associated with their own account.

→ *To learn more about using the Sounds and Audio Devices dialog to fix sound problems,* see *"Troubleshooting Audio,"* Chapter 5, p. 339.

→ *For more about the General tab,* see *"Troubleshooting Slow System Performance,"* Chapter 9, p. 547.

→ *For more information about the Computer Name tab,* see *"I'm Not Sure My Network Settings Are Correct,"* Chapter 8, p. 499.

→ *For more information about Device Manager,* see *"Using Device Manager,"* this chapter, p. 100.

→ *For more information about signed and unsigned device drivers,* see *"Signed and Unsigned Device Drivers,"* this chapter, p. 108.

➜ *For more informa-
tion about Add
Hardware, see "Add
Hardware," this
chapter, p. 88.*

➜ *For more informa-
tion about adjusting
Performance settings,
see "Viewing and
Adjusting Page File
(Swapfile)
Configuration,"
Chapter 9, p. 558.*

➜ *For more informa-
tion about adjusting
startup and shutdown
options, see Table 2.2,
"Troubleshooting
Windows XP Shutdown
Problems," this
chapter, p. 82.*

➜ *For more informa-
tion on System
Restore, see "Using
System Restore," this
chapter, p. 118.*

➜ *For more informa-
tion on Automatic
Updates, see "Keeping
Windows Healthy with
Service Packs and
Windows Update," this
chapter, p. 131, for
details.*

➜ *For more informa-
tion on Remote
Assistance, see "Using
Remote Assistance in
Windows XP," this
chapter, p. 124, for
details.*

Let the Administrator Do It!

Guest accounts are very limited, but if you have young children or want to let a friend use your computer for a bit of web surfing, setting up guest-level accounts is a really good idea, because guest-level users can't install programs or hardware and can't make systemwide changes that could clobber your favorite screen display, menus, and so on.

System Properties

The System properties sheet (the same one you see if you right-click My Computer and select Properties) is the single most important hardware troubleshooting tool in Windows, particularly its Device Manager feature.

The Windows XP version has seven tabs:

- **General**—Displays the Windows version, registration information, processor type, speed, and onboard RAM.
- **Computer Name**—Displays and configures the computer name, description, and workgroup.
- **Hardware**—Provides access to the Add Hardware Wizard, Device Manager, and Hardware Profiles features. Driver Signing configures how Windows reacts if you try to install unsigned device drivers.
- **Advanced**—Configures Performance, User Profiles, and Startup and Recovery settings.
- **System Restore**—Configures System Restore.
- **Automatic Updates**—Configures Windows Update's optional automatic updates feature.
- **Remote**—Enables, disables, and configures Remote Assistance. See "Using Remote Assistance in Windows XP," this chapter, p. 124, for details.

Using Device Manager

The Windows Device Manager displays and configures all the hardware built into or connected to your computer. Click the Hardware tab (see Figure 2.15) and then click the Device Manager button to open Device Manager.

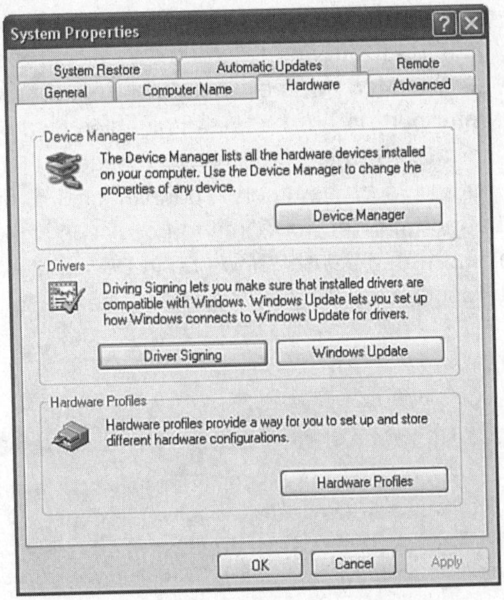

FIGURE 2.15
The Hardware tab in Windows XP SP2/Windows XP Professional x64 Edition. Older releases used a different layout for this tab.

When you open the Device Manager, it displays the device categories found in your computer (computer, disk drives, display, keyboards, and so on), as shown in Figure 2.16.

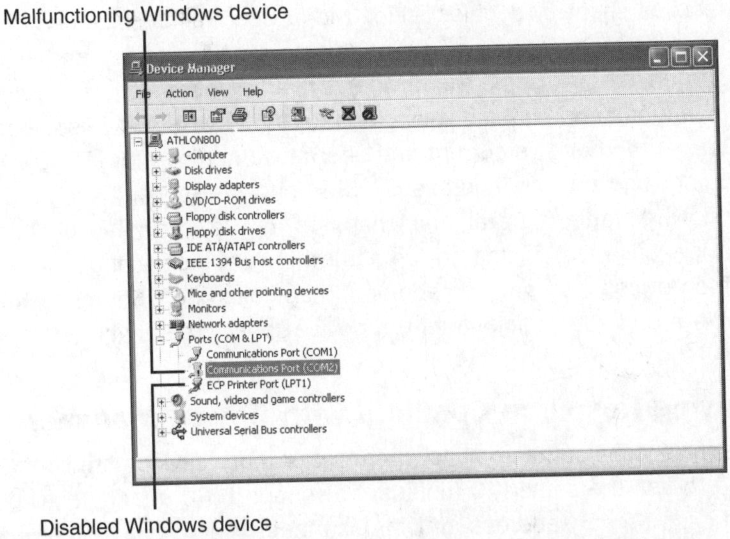

Malfunctioning Windows device

Disabled Windows device

FIGURE 2.16
The Windows XP Device Manager with malfunctioning and disabled devices displayed.

If your computer has devices that are malfunctioning in a way that Device Manager can detect or devices that are disabled, they will be displayed as soon as you open the Device Manager. For example, in Figure 2.16, the Ports (COM and LPT) category displays a malfunctioning port, COM 2, indicated by an exclamation mark (!) in a yellow circle. The parallel printer port, LPT 1, has been disabled by the Device Manager, as indicated by a red X. If the malfunctioning or disabled device is an I/O port, such as a serial, parallel, or USB port, any device attached to that port cannot work until the device is working properly. Not every problem with a device shows up in Device Manager, but most problems with resource conflicts or drivers will be displayed here.

Leo Says

What Happens in the BIOS, Stays in the BIOS

The Windows Device Manager lists disabled devices only if the Device Manager was used to disable the device. For example, if you disabled a built-in parallel (LPT) port in the system BIOS, Device Manager would ignore it because it isn't visible when you start the computer. Consequently, don't depend on Device Manager to report BIOS-disabled ports. Instead, restart your system and enter the BIOS setup program as described in Chapter 1, "PC Anatomy 101."

→ *For more information about hardware resources*, see *"Hardware Resources,"* Chapter 1, p. 58.

To troubleshoot problems with a device in Device Manager, open its properties sheet by double-clicking the device. Each device has at least three tabs, including General (displays device status and allows you to enable or disable the device), Driver (displays device driver files and versions and enables you to update the driver), and Resources (displays the device's current and alternative settings for IRQ, DMA, I/O port, and memory addresses). Starting with Service Pack 2, Windows XP adds a Details tab that lists the Device Instance ID (the PnP identification) for the device and other very technical details. Some devices also have an additional tab called Port Settings, which displays and allows adjustment of device-specific settings.

Solving Resource Conflicts with Device Manager

Resource conflicts take place when two or more devices are configured to use the same IRQ (unless they support IRQ sharing), I/O port address, memory address, or DMA channel.

For example, the General tab for the properties sheet of the malfunctioning COM 2 port (see Figure 2.17) indicates that the port doesn't have correct IRQ or other resources available.

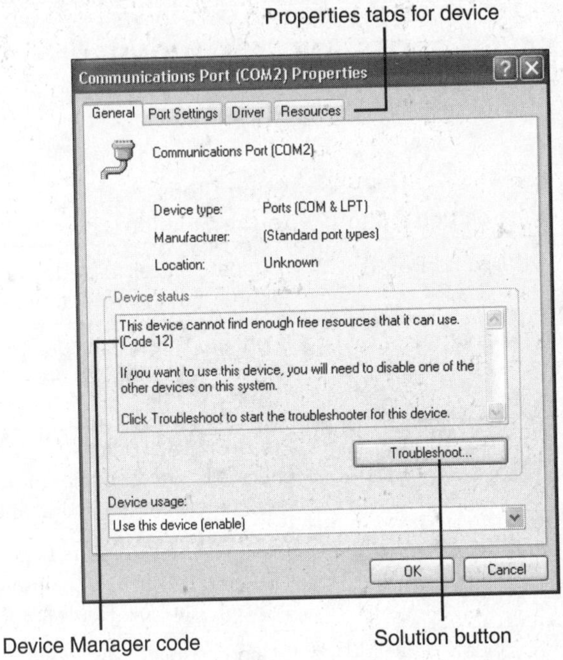

Properties tabs for device

FIGURE 2.17
Windows XP offers a multipurpose solution button that can help you solve the problem with your device.

Device Manager code   Solution button

When you have a malfunctioning device such as the one in Figure 2.17, you have several options for resolving the problem:

- Look up the Device Manager code to determine the problem and its solution (see Table 2.4).

- Click the Solution button (if any) shown on the device's General properties tab; the button's name and usage depends on the problem. Table 2.4 lists the codes, their meanings, and the solution button (if any).

- Manually change resources. If the nature of the problem is a resource conflict, you can click the Resources tab and change the settings and eliminate the conflict if possible. Some recent systems that use ACPI power management don't permit manual resource changes in Device Manager and also override any changes you might make in the system BIOS setup program. On these systems, if resource conflicts take place, you might need to disable ACPI power management before you can solve resource conflicts. Fortunately, such resources conflicts are extremely rare.

TABLE 2.4

WINDOWS XP DEVICE MANAGER CODES AND SOLUTIONS

Device Manager Code Number	Problem	Solution Button	Other Steps to the Solution
1	Incorrect device configuration.	Update Driver	If Update Driver fails, delete device listing and run Add New Hardware Wizard.
2	Can't determine correct device bus type or can't install driver.	Update Driver	If Update Driver fails, delete device listing and run Add New Hardware Wizard.
3	Bad device driver or system resources low.	Update Driver	Press Ctrl+Alt+Delete (Task Manager) to check system resources; if Update Driver fails, delete device listing and run Add New Hardware Wizard.
4	Bad driver or Registry problem.	Update Driver	If Update Driver fails, delete device listing and run Add New Hardware Wizard.
5	Bad driver.	Update Driver	If Update Driver fails, delete device listing and run Add New Hardware Wizard.
6	Resource conflict with another device.	Troubleshoot	If the troubleshooter cannot resolve the conflict, shut down the computer, change the resources used by the device, and restart.
7	Can't configure device.	Reinstall driver	If Reinstall Driver fails, delete device listing and run Add New Hardware Wizard; obtain an updated driver.
8	Various DevLoader (device loader) problems.	(none)	Reinstall Windows to re-create a working VMM32.VXD system file.
		Reinstall Driver	If Reinstall Driver fails, delete device listing and run Add New Hardware Wizard; obtain an updated driver.
		Update Driver	If Update Driver fails, delete device listing and run Add New Hardware Wizard; obtain an updated driver.
9	BIOS enumeration problem.	(none)	Delete device listing and run Add New Hardware Wizard; contact vendor for correct Registry keys or an updated driver if the problem continues.

TABLE 2.4 (continued)
WINDOWS XP DEVICE MANAGER CODES AND SOLUTIONS

Device Manager Code Number	Problem	Solution Button	Other Steps to the Solution
10	Device not present, working properly, or other specified problem.	Update Driver	Check physical connection to system (slot connector, cabling, power); restart system. Run Update Driver if Code 10 reappears. If Update Driver fails, delete device listing and run Add New Hardware Wizard.
11	N/A	N/A	Windows 9x/Me only
12	No free hardware resources.	Troubleshoot	Follow instructions in troubleshooter; might require removal or reconfiguration of other devices.
13	Device not detected by system.	Detect Hardware	If Detect Hardware fails, delete device listing and run Add New Hardware Wizard.
14	Must restart computer before device will work.	Restart Computer	Shut down computer and restart to activate device.
15	Resource conflict with another device.	Troubleshoot	Follow instructions in troubleshooter to find nonconflicting resources.
16	Some device resources aren't known.	(none)	Click Resources tab and manually enter resources required or delete device listing and run Add New Hardware Wizard.
17	Incorrect assignment of resources to multifunctional device.	Update Driver	Delete device listing and run Add New Hardware Wizard.
18	Drivers need to be reinstalled.	Reinstall Driver	If Reinstall Driver fails, delete device listing and run Add New Hardware Wizard.
19	Possibly bad Registry.	Check Registry	Windows will restart and use a previous copy of the Registry; if this fails, start Windows in Safe Mode and use System Restore to return to a working condition.
20	Can't load drivers for device.	Update Driver	If Update Driver fails, delete device listing and run Add New Hardware Wizard.
21	Windows is removing specified device.	Restart Computer	Shut down Windows and computer; wait a few moments, then restart the computer.

TABLE 2.4 (continued)
WINDOWS XP DEVICE MANAGER CODES AND SOLUTIONS

Device Manager Code Number	Problem	Solution Button	Other Steps to the Solution
22	Device is disabled in Device Manager.	Enable Device	Click Solution button.
	Device not started.	Start Device	Click Solution button.
	Device is disabled by driver or program.	(none)	Remove device listing and run Add New Hardware Wizard. If the problem persists, use MSCONFIG to disable startup programs (clean boot) and retry; contact the hardware manufacturer for help if problem continues.
23	Secondary display adapter problems.	Properties	Verify primary display adapter works okay.
	Problem with primary display adapter.	(none)	Correct problems with primary display adapter and retry.
	Other devices.	Update Driver	Click Solution button.
24	Legacy (non-PnP) device was not detected.	Detect Hardware	If device still can't be detected, make sure it is properly connected to the system.
	PnP device was not detected.	Update Drivers	If device still can't be detected, make sure it is properly connected to the system.
25	Device not completely set up by Windows.	Restart Computer	Normally displayed only during first reboots of Windows; if problem persists after Windows is completely installed, you might need to reinstall Windows or remove the device listing and use Add New Hardware.
26	Device not completely set up by Windows.	Restart Computer	If problem persists, remove the device listing and use Add New Hardware.
27	Resources can't be specified.	(none)	Remove the device listing and use Add New Hardware; obtain updated drivers or help from hardware vendor if problem persists.
28	Drivers not installed.	Reinstall Driver	If Reinstall Driver fails, delete device listing and run Add New Hardware Wizard. Obtain updated drivers if necessary.

TABLE 2.4 (continued)
WINDOWS XP DEVICE MANAGER CODES AND SOLUTIONS

Device Manager Code Number	Problem	Solution Button	Other Steps to the Solution
29	No resources provided by BIOS or device disabled in BIOS.	(none)	Restart the computer, start the BIOS setup program, and configure the device in BIOS. Save changes and restart the computer.
30	IRQ conflict.	(none)	Reconfigure the device or conflicting device to use a different IRQ.
31	A specified device is preventing the current device from working.	Properties	Reconfigure the other device's properties (displayed when you click the Solution button) to fix the problem; if the problem persists, delete device listings and run Add New Hardware Wizard. Obtain updated drivers if necessary.
32	Drivers not available.	Restart Computer	Provide the installation CD-ROM or log onto the network after restarting; if the CD-ROM or network doesn't work, resolve its problem so drivers can be accessed.
33	Various hardware errors.	(none)	Hardware has failed; replace the specified hardware.

More About Device Manager Error Codes and Solutions

For more information about the Windows XP Device Manager error codes listed in Table 2.4, go to http://support.microsoft.com and search for Knowledge Base article 310123.

Using Device Manager to Determine Other System Problems

As you saw in Figure 2.16, only devices installed in the system will be displayed in the Windows Device Manager. This can also help you determine why you are having problems with a device. For example, if you cannot use a device attached to a Universal Serial Bus (USB) port, and the Universal Serial Bus category isn't listed in Device Manager, you need to enable the USB ports in your system.

Signed and Unsigned Device Drivers

Microsoft has emphasized the use of digitally signed device drivers for hardware from the days of Windows Me to the present. In a perfect world, using Windows Update would assure you of a constant stream of these MS Hardware Quality Labs–approved, good-as-gold device drivers. In reality, Microsoft doesn't always have the latest drivers at its website.

You may need to get device drivers for urgent fixes, especially involving brand-new hardware, straight from the hardware vendor's website. In such cases, try to avoid beta (pre-release) or test versions of driver software. In general, the latest released versions of a driver are the best to use, but with some older motherboard or video card chipsets, an older driver might work better.

To avoid problems when you install updated drivers, follow these guidelines:

- Download the driver and uncompress it to a known folder location so you can look for Readme files or other information before you install it.

- Uninstall the old driver and use the browse feature of the Detect/Add Hardware Wizard to locate the new driver files when the hardware is redetected. This is often more reliable than installing new drivers over old drivers, particularly with Windows XP if your old drivers were not digitally signed or were made for Windows 2000.

- If you install a new driver over an old driver in Windows XP and the hardware has problems, use the Rollback feature on the device's properties sheet to revert to the old driver.

- Windows XP is configured by default to warn you if you try to install unsigned drivers. However, you can disregard this warning. To adjust the settings used for unsigned device drivers, click the Driver Signing button shown earlier in Figure 2.15. This opens the Driver Signing Options dialog shown in Figure 2.18. By default, Windows XP warns you when you install an unsigned device driver. Depending on the driver, Windows XP might also set up a system restore point if you go ahead and install the unsigned device driver. If you select Ignore, Windows will no longer display a warning message when you use unsigned drivers. If you select Block, you will only be able to install signed drivers.

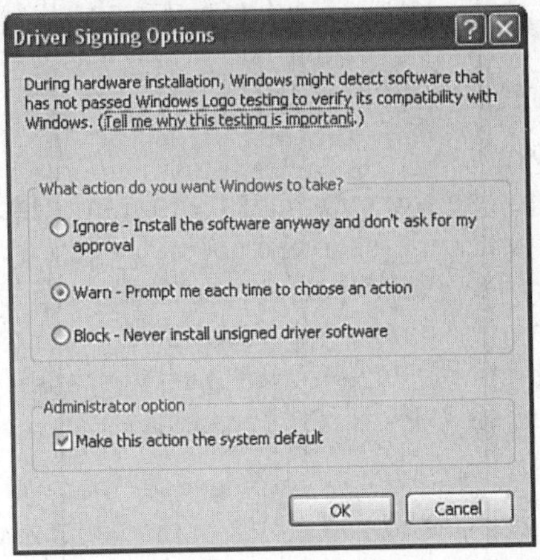

FIGURE 2.18
Use the Driver Signing Options dialog to adjust how Windows XP deals with unsigned device drivers.

Windows Update and Device Drivers

Windows Update has always been used as a method for delivering digitally signed device drivers. However, starting with Windows XP Service Pack 2 and Windows XP Professional x64 Edition, Windows Update can be used to check for device drivers every time you install new hardware. To configure this feature of Windows Update, click the Windows Update button on the Hardware tab shown earlier in Figure 2.15. This opens the Connect to Windows Update dialog shown in Figure 2.19.

FIGURE 2.19
Windows Update can check for drivers automatically, only on request, or never.

In the system shown in Figure 2.19, Windows Update will ask the user each time for permission to use Windows Update to find drivers. We recommend this option because it enables you to choose to use a driver you've downloaded manually or to have Windows help you find one.

Using the Windows XP Hardware Troubleshooter

When you're having problems with a device and you use Device Manager, it might take you automatically to a troubleshooter. Windows troubleshooters ask you a series of questions to help you fix problems with your system. For example, the troubleshooter's first question for a problem such as a malfunctioning serial port would be, "Is your device installed more than once?" As Figure 2.16 indicates, the answer is "No" in this example. Click Next to continue.

In this example, the troubleshooter suggests that you need to configure one or more devices to use different resources, and the text specifically refers to a disabled device displaying error code 12, just as in Figure 2.17. Use the troubleshooter's help to reopen the Device Manager, click the properties sheet for your device, and click the Resources tab. Click the Set Configuration Manually button to change the settings for the disabled device (see Figure 2.20); you might not need to disable another device in spite of the warning listed.

The Set Configuration Manually option is intended for use primarily with ISA devices such as serial and parallel ports which can be configured with Plug and Play. Windows and the system BIOS configure PCI devices for you. PCI devices include cards in PCI slots, ATA/IDE host adapters, USB and IEEE-1394a ports, PCI, AGP and onboard video, and newer integrated sound. Depending on the device and how your computer is configured, you might not be able to alter its configuration settings in Device Manager.

The Resources tab has a Conflicting Devices list that shows the I/O port range used by COM 2 is already in use by COM 1 (see Figure 2.21). There are three ways to solve such a conflict:

- Select a different, nonconflicting resource for the malfunctioning device (COM 2).

- Select a different, nonconflicting resource for the other device (COM 1).

- Disable the other device (COM 1) to prevent the conflict.

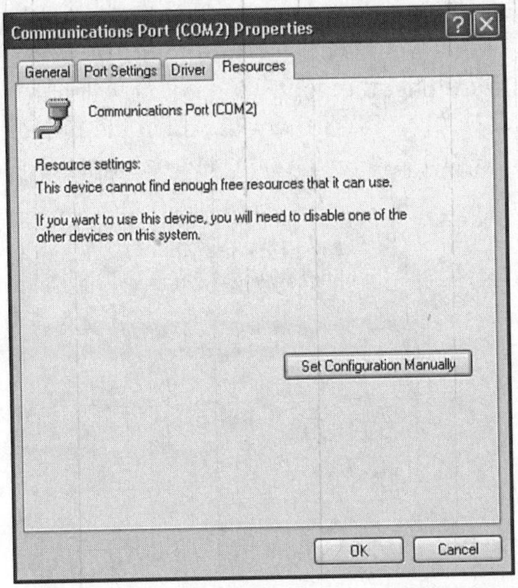

FIGURE 2.20
Click the Set Configuration Manually button to set a working configuration for your device.

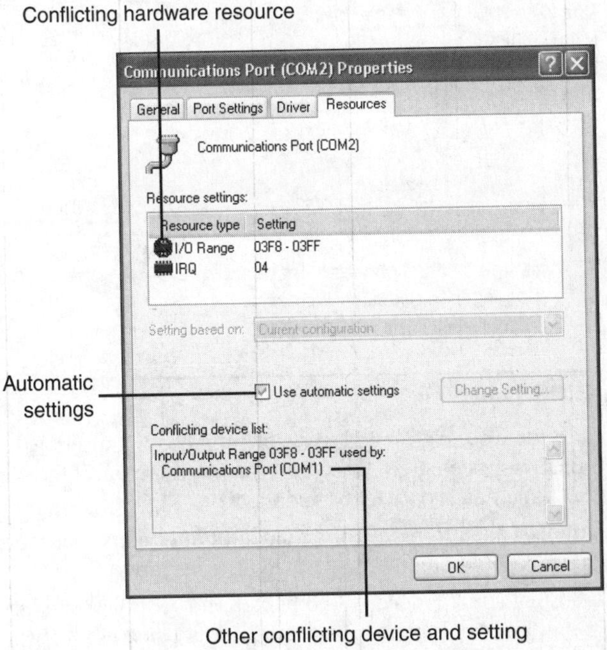

Conflicting hardware resource

FIGURE 2.21
The Conflicting Devices list shows the device and the resource setting that conflicts with the malfunctioning device.

Automatic settings

Other conflicting device and setting

To see if you can use a different setting, clear the Use Automatic Settings box. In a few cases, you might be able to select the conflicting setting and click Change Setting to select a different resource.

However, in most cases, you must click the Setting Based On menu and select a different configuration from those listed. If you can select a nonconflicting setting, the conflicting device will show No Conflicts (see Figure 2.22). Click OK. Otherwise, open the properties sheet for the conflicting device and select different settings for it or disable it.

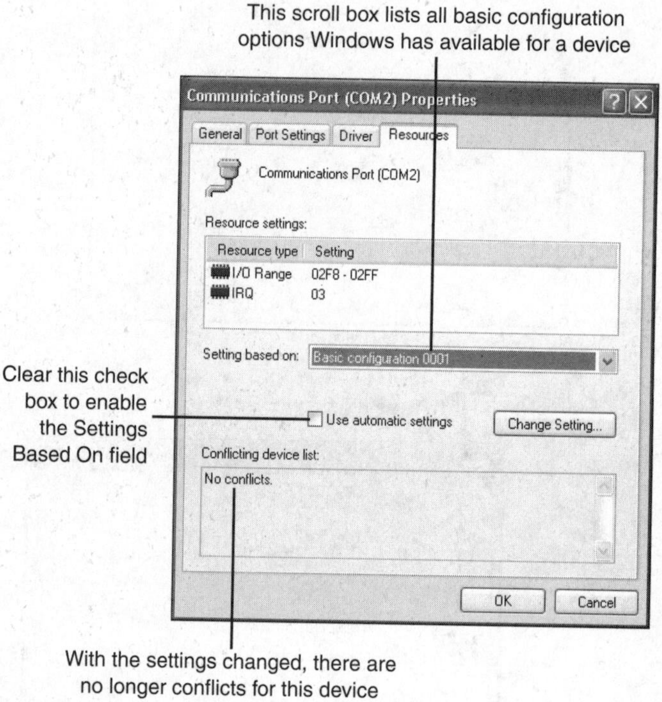

FIGURE 2.22

Choosing a configuration that uses a different I/O port range solves the problem.

This scroll box lists all basic configuration options Windows has available for a device

Clear this check box to enable the Settings Based On field

With the settings changed, there are no longer conflicts for this device

Communications Port (COM2) Properties

General | Port Settings | Driver | Resources

Communications Port (COM2)

Resource settings:

Resource type	Setting
I/O Range	02F8 - 02FF
IRQ	03

Setting based on: Basic configuration 0001

☐ Use automatic settings   Change Setting...

Conflicting device list:

No conflicts.

OK   Cancel

Let the BIOS Do It

In some cases, you might need to restart the computer and use the system BIOS setup program to correct a hardware conflict involving a built-in port such as a parallel or serial port.

You might also need to restart the computer after some hardware changes; you will be prompted to do so if necessary.

If you are running a Windows XP computer and your IRQs are listed as ACPI IRQs in Device Manager, your computer is using ACPI power management, which also is used to control IRQ allocation. If you have IRQ conflicts you cannot resolve, even after updating drivers for the device, installing the latest Windows updates, and installing the latest system BIOS update, you might want to reconfigure your system as a Standard PC instead of an ACPI PC so you can manually change IRQ settings.

To learn more about this process, see the Anandtech.com operating systems FAQ, "Why are all my devices using one IRQ in Win2K or WinXP?" This FAQ is available from the Guides, FAQs and Operating Systems section at http://www.anandtech.com (http://www.anandtech.com/guides/viewfaq.aspx?i=47).

Other Windows Diagnostic, Reporting, and Repair Tools

Windows features a number of other tools you can use to discover and solve system problems, including the following:

- System Information
- File Signature Verification
- DirectX Diagnostics
- Dr. Watson
- Backup
- Defrag
- Error-checking (CHKDSK/ScanDisk)
- System Restore
- Program Compatibility Wizard
- Remote Desktop Connection

Table 2.5 provides a quick reference to these tools and how to access them in Windows XP.

TABLE 2.5
STARTING OTHER WINDOWS DIAGNOSTIC, REPORTING, AND REPAIR TOOLS

Tool	How to Start
System Information	Click Start, Run, type **MSINFO32**, click OK.
File Signature Verification	Click Start, Run, type **SIGVERIF**, click OK. Alternatively, open System Information, click Tools, click File Signature Verification.
DirectX Diagnostics	Click Start, Run, type **DXDIAG**, click OK.

TABLE 2.5 (continued)
STARTING OTHER WINDOWS DIAGNOSTIC, REPORTING, AND REPAIR TOOLS

Tool	How to Start
Dr. Watson	Runs automatically. To view Dr. Watson, open MSINFO32, click Tools, and select from menu. Alternatively, click Start, Run, type **drwtsn32**, and click OK.
Backup	Install from the Windows XP Home Edition CD-ROM.
Defragment	Open Windows Explorer, right-click a drive, click Properties, click Tools, and select Defragment Drive.
CHKDSK	Open Windows Explorer, right-click a drive, click Properties, click Tools, and select Check Now.
System Restore	Click Start, (All) Programs, Accessories, System Tools, System Restore.
Program Compatibility Wizard	Click Start, (All) Programs, Accessories, Program Compatibility Wizard.
Remote Assistance	Click Start, Help and Support Center, Remote Assistance.

The following sections discuss the most important of these tools.

Using System Information

The Windows System Information utility provides you with a powerful way to view the following details about your system:

- Basic hardware configuration
- Installed hardware
- Installed software
- Current software environment, including startup programs and running services
- Internet settings
- System problems

In addition, the Tools menu enables you to run a variety of additional diagnostic programs, including these:

- Net Diagnostics
- System Restore
- File Signature Verification Tool
- DirectX Diagnostic Tool
- Dr. Watson

After you start System Information, the System Summary screen appears (see Figure 2.23). This displays your operating system version, computer name, motherboard brand and model, processor type and speed, Windows folder, boot drive, username, physical and virtual memory, and the location of the page file.

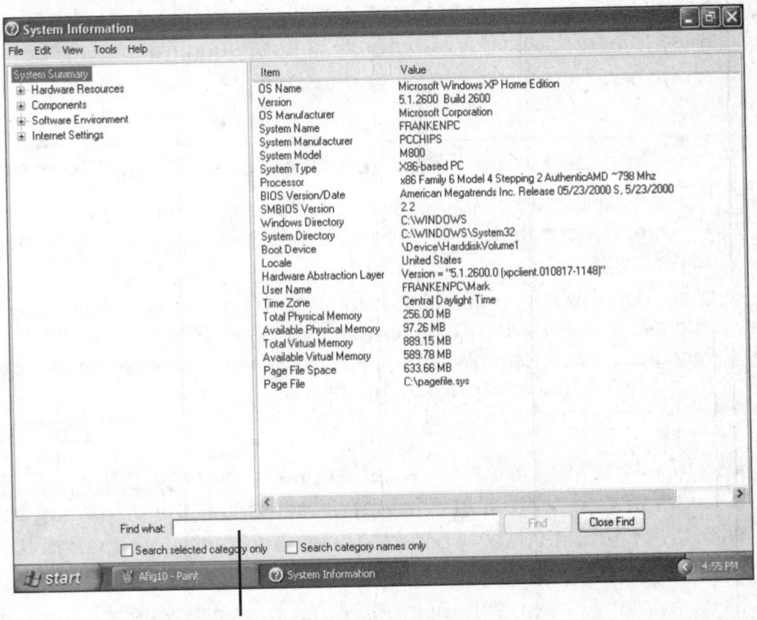

FIGURE 2.23
The System Summary screen in the Windows XP version of System Information.

Use Find What to locate specific information about your system

Click Hardware Resources and select a subcategory to see the resources (IRQ, DMA, I/O port address, memory) that are used by different devices.

➔ *For more information about hardware resources, see "Hardware Resources," Chapter 1, p. 58.*

Watch Out for Forced Hardware

Forced Hardware is Windows's term for devices that have been manually configured to use particular hardware resources instead of using the device's normal Windows Plug and Play settings. Forced Hardware settings are not recommended because they can cause conflicts with other devices.

If you see a device listed in the Forced Hardware category, open Device Manager to confirm that it works correctly. If Device Manager reports problems, open the device's properties sheet, click Resources, and click Use Automatic Settings to allow Windows to configure the device. Restart the computer if necessary.

To learn more about the devices installed on your computer, click Components to open the category, then navigate through the subcategories and device types to see the name of the device, its driver, its features, and the hardware resources it uses. The exact information provided will vary with the device type. For example, network adapters display IP address and MAC address information, whereas modems display the AT commands they use to activate major features.

Faster Access to the Facts You Need from System Information

If you're concerned primarily about devices with problems, go directly to Problem Devices to see the device, its PnP Device ID, and a description of its problem.

If all you know about a problem is a single bit of information (such as IP address or PnP Device ID), enter that information into the Find What window at the bottom of the System Information display and click Find to locate the device or program in question.

Use the Software Environment categories to determine the software running on your system at startup, details about the driver software used to control hardware, current tasks, and other information. Use Internet Settings to learn how IE and other Internet tools are configured. In many cases, you might find that running System Information is faster than navigating through Computer Management, Internet Explorer or Internet properties settings, Device Manager, and other programs to learn about your system.

To access the tools discussed in the following sections, click Tools and select from the tools listed.

Using Net Diagnostics

Net Diagnostics runs a series of tests on your network, broadband, and dial-up Internet connections to determine whether they are working correctly. Net Diagnostics also checks software configurations for mail and news servers to see if they are properly configured (see Figure 2.24). You should start your dial-up or broadband Internet connection before you start Net Diagnostics.

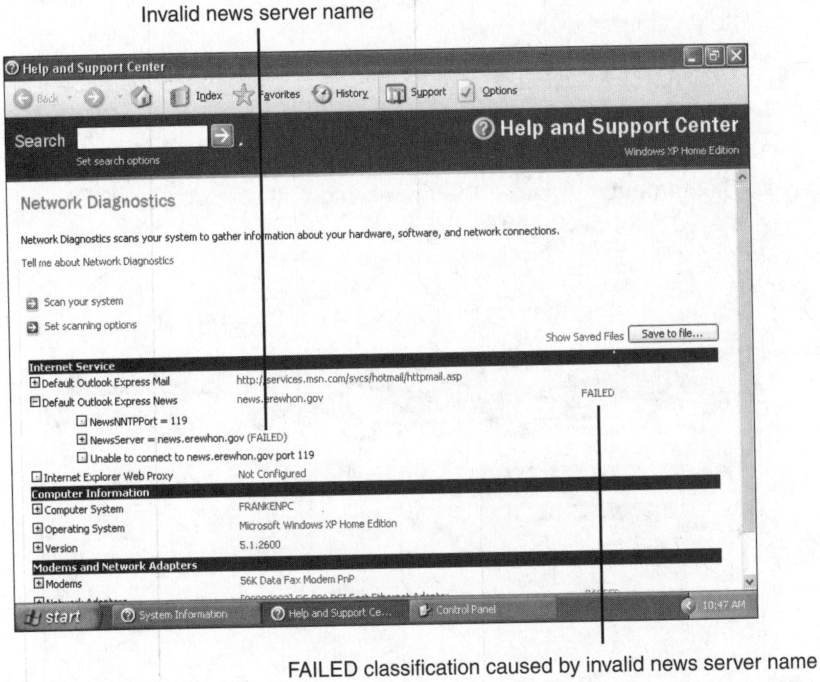

Invalid news server name

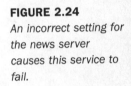

FIGURE 2.24
An incorrect setting for the news server causes this service to fail.

FAILED classification caused by invalid news server name

Click the plus sign (+) next to a category to expand it for more information, particularly if it's marked as FAILED. If a failed message appears next to a mail or news server, check the spelling of the name; if the name is incorrectly spelled, Windows can't find the resource. Open your default mail or news reader software (Outlook Express is included with Windows XP, though you might be running a full version of Outlook or another email client) and correct the· spelling. If the spelling is correct, the remote server might not be responding.

If you see a FAILED message for hardware such as your network adapter or modem, use Device Manager to diagnose the problem.

Using System Restore

System Restore enables you to fix problems caused by a defective hardware or software installation by resetting your computer's configuration to the way it was at a specified earlier time. Restore points can be created by the user with System Restore, and they are also created by the system before new hardware or software is installed.

Here's how to create a restore point:

1. Start System Restore from the System Information Tools menu (see Figure 2.25).

2. Click Create a Restore Point and then click Next.

3. Enter a descriptive name for the restore point, such as "Before I installed DuzItAll Version 1.0," and click Create.

4. The computer's current hardware and software configuration is stored as a new restore point.

Restores computer to a specified restore point

FIGURE 2.25

The main menu of the System Restore program.

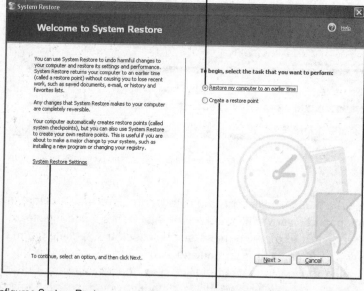

Configures System Restore

Creates a restore point (use before you install new hardware or software)

To restore your system to an earlier condition, follow these steps:

1. Start System Restore.

2. Click Restore My Computer to an Earlier Time and click Next.

3. Select a date from the calendar (dates that have restore points are in bold text).

4. Select a restore point and click Next (see Figure 2.26).

5. Close any open programs and save your work before you click Next to start the process; Windows will shut down and restart.

6. Click OK to close the System Restore program after the computer restarts.

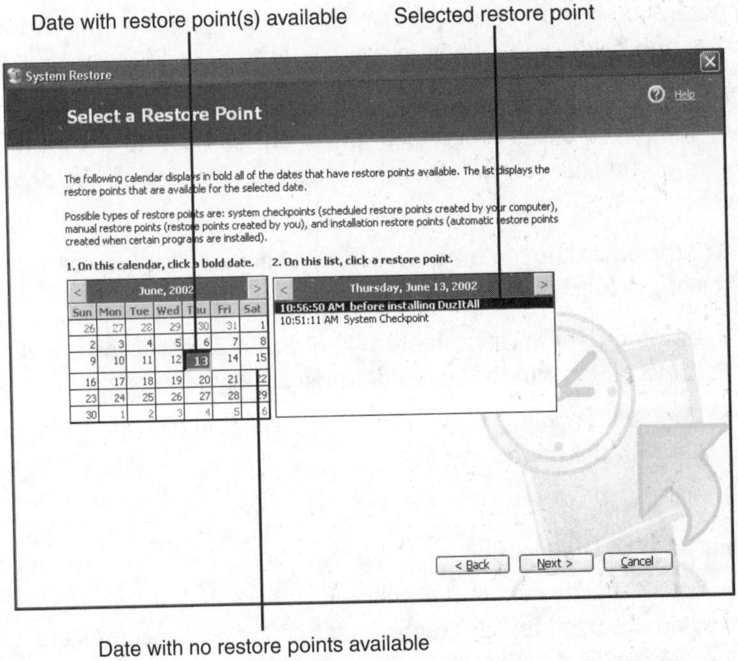

Date with restore point(s) available   Selected restore point

FIGURE 2.26

Choosing a restore point.

Date with no restore points available

What System Restore Keeps—and Takes Away

You can't lose data by using System Restore, but all programs and hardware installed after a specified restore point must be reinstalled if you restore your system to that point. Although the program files remain on the system, Windows can't use the program because the Registry entries and shortcuts have been removed. Be sure to note the location of the program and specify the same location when you reinstall the program so that the new installation will replace the old installation and not use additional disk space.

If System Restore is not available, it might be turned off. You can enable System Restore or change the amount of disk space it uses with the System Restore tab on the System properties sheet; click System Restore Settings from the main menu of System Restore to adjust these settings (refer to Figure 2.25).

➔ See *"Using System File Checker,"* this chapter, p. 122, for details.

Using File Signature Verification

The default setting for File Signature Verification checks for system files that lack digital signatures. Use this feature to determine whether your Windows installation might be corrupted by the use of out-of-date system files that some older programs may have installed. To determine if you are using unsigned driver files, click the Advanced button and select Look for Other Files That Are Not Digitally Signed.

After you configure Advanced options, click OK, then Start. A status bar informs you of the progress of the scan. Click OK to accept the results of the scan. Click Advanced, Logging, View Log to see detailed results.

To fix problems that could be caused by unsigned files, you can do either of the following:

- Use the Update Driver feature in a device's properties sheet (Device Manager) after you download a digitally signed file.
- Run System File Checker (SFC) to replace an unsigned system file with the correct version.

Using DirectX Diagnostics

Use DirectX Diagnostics to determine if DirectX (the software component Windows uses for 3D graphics and sound, game controllers, and multimedia) is working correctly. DirectX Diagnostics has a multiple-tab dialog (see Figure 2.27):

- **System**—A summary of system hardware and Windows version.
- **DirectX Files**—A listing of files and version numbers and a report of any file problems.
- **Display**—Information about your displays (multiple-display systems have a tab for each display), a report of any problems detected, and options to test DirectDraw and Direct3D operations.
- **Sound**—Information about your sound card, a report of any problems found, and an option to test DirectSound.

- **Music**—Information about MIDI and Wave playback features of your sound hardware, a report of any problems found, and an option to test DirectMusic.

- **Input**—Information about all input devices and a report of any problems found.

- **Network**—Information on DirectPlay service providers, a report of any problems found, and an option to test DirectPlay.

- **More Help**—Options to run the DirectX and Sound troubleshooters, to access System Information, and to adjust the DirectDraw screen refresh rate.

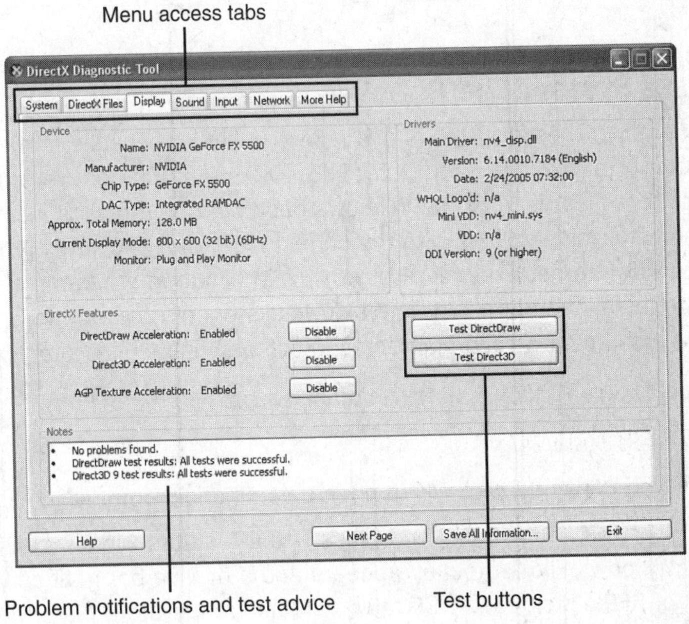

Menu access tabs

FIGURE 2.27
DirectX Diagnostics after testing DirectDraw and Direct3D.

Problem notifications and test advice   Test buttons

DirectX Diagnostics can warn you of driver problems and provides you with a way to test your DirectX features. Replace unsigned or defective drivers if you are having problems in DirectX-compatible software (game and multimedia titles). If your computer fails one or more DirectX tests, download and install the latest version of DirectX from Microsoft.

Two, Two, Two DirectX Diagnostics in One

When you run DirectX Diagnostics on the x64 Edition, it runs the 32-bit version (which supports 32-bit games and 3D applications). To test the 64-bit version, just click the Run 64-bit DxDiag button next to the Help button. The diagnostic tests and user interface are otherwise identical between versions.

Getting the Latest Information on DirectX

Download the latest version of DirectX, get technical help, and learn more about DirectX at the Microsoft DirectX website:

http://www.microsoft.com/windows/directx/default.aspx

Using System File Checker

System File Checker (SFC) is a Windows utility that checks protected system files (files such as .DLL, .SYS, .OCX, and .EXE, as well as some font files used by the Windows desktop) and replaces incorrect versions or missing files with the correct files. Use SFC to fix problems with Internet Explorer or other built-in Windows programs caused by the installation of obsolete Windows system files, user error, deliberate erasure, virus or Trojan horse infections, and similar problems.

To run SFC in Windows XP, follow these steps:

1. Click Start, Run.

2. Type **CMD** and click OK to open a command-prompt window.

3. Type **SFC /SCANNOW** and press Enter. A status window called Windows File Protection appears and a moving bar notifies you of SFC's progress. If SFC finds an incorrect system file or determines that a system file is missing, a dialog appears to notify you. If the system file is available in a backup folder on the system, SFC will replace it for you.

4. If the system file is not available in the backup folder (some systems might not have enough disk space to backup all protected files), SFC will prompt you to insert the Windows XP CD-ROM so that the system file(s) can be restored.

5. To close the command window after running SFC, type **EXIT** and press Enter.

If the computer's backup copy of the system files becomes corrupted, run the command **SFC /PURGECACHE** to rebuild the backup folder on the hard disk with correct system files. You can also configure SFC to run at the next startup with **SFC /SCANONCE**, to run every time the computer is started with **SFC /SCANBOOT**, and to turn off automatic scanning with **SFC /REVERT**.

Using Error-Checking (CHKDSK) and Defrag

Defrag and error-checking can be run from the Tools tab on the hard disk's properties sheet in My Computer or Windows Explorer (see Figure 2.28). Defrag improves the speed at which your computer can retrieve data from the hard disk (by reorganizing where that data is located on the drive), whereas error-checking (CHKDSK) detects and corrects disk errors.

→ See "Using System File Checker," this chapter, p. 122, for details.

You should check drives for errors before you defrag them, or after a system lockup or unexpected power loss during operation.

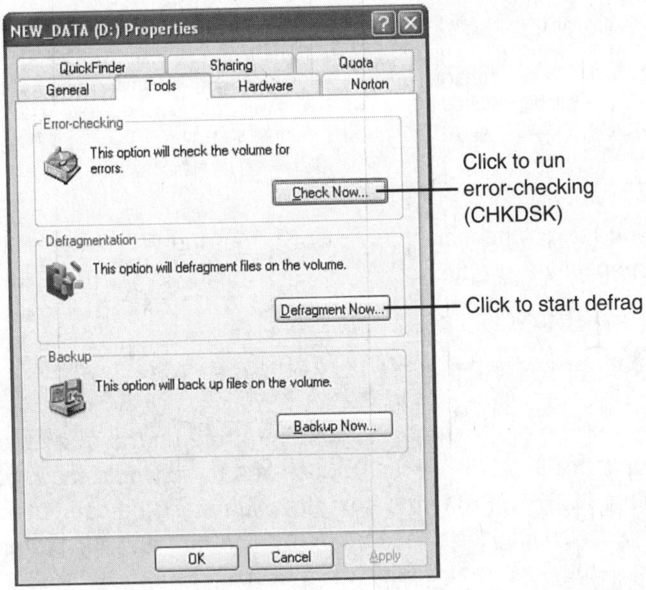

FIGURE 2.28
The Tools tab for a hard disk in Windows XP.

You can also run CHKDSK from the command line, as shown in Figure 2.29. This is useful to determine if you need to repair problems on your hard disk. In this example, CHKDSK was run in read-only mode to determine if the system drive had problems. It stopped before completion because of indexing errors. To repair these errors, you can run CHKDSK with the /F option. If you are trying to fix errors on the system drive, you must schedule these repairs for the next time you start your system.

FIGURE 2.29
Running CHKDSK from the command line.

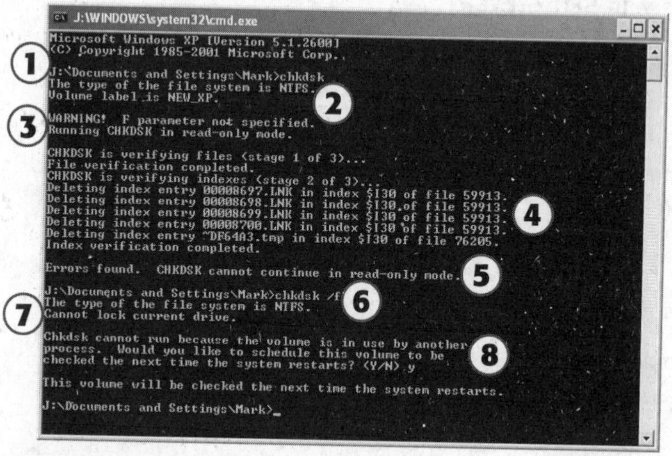

1. Starting CHKDSK in read-only mode (no options)
2. File system in use on target drive
3. No errors will be repaired in read-only mode
4. Errors found on drive
5. CHKDSK stops when errors found
6. To repair errors, use CHKDSK/F
7. Indicates system drive is being checked
8. Answer y(es) to schedule repairs at next startup

When you run error-checking (CHKDSK) from the Windows desktop, you can specify two options:

- Automatically fix file system errors
- Scan for and attempt recovery of bad sectors

If you select the option to fix file system errors on the system drive, a dialog appears as in Figure 2.30. Click Yes to schedule the repair (equivalent to CHKDSK/F) the next time you start the computer. You can use either option to check other drive letters on your system, including floppy and removable-media drives.

Using Remote Assistance in Windows XP

Windows XP's Remote Assistance feature enables you to ask another Windows XP user for help with your computer or to provide help to another user. To request help, you can start Remote Assistance from the Help and Support menu: Click Invite a Friend to Help You with Remote Assistance,, followed by Invite Someone to Help You. Both computers must be running Windows XP and Windows Messenger.

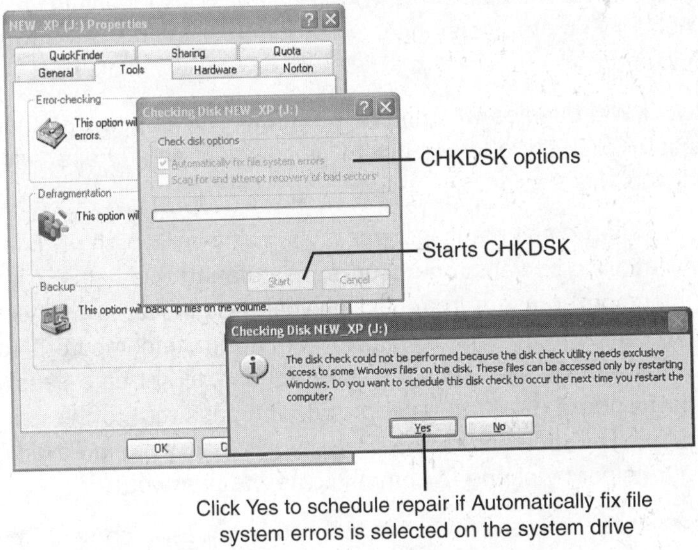

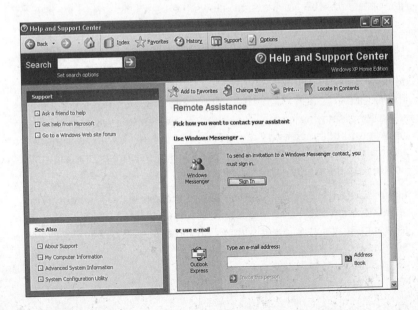

FIGURE 2.30
Running CHKDSK from the Windows desktop.

CHKDSK options

Starts CHKDSK

Click Yes to schedule repair if Automatically fix file system errors is selected on the system drive

You can get help from your Windows Messenger (WM) buddy list or by sending an email to other Windows users (see Figure 2.31).

FIGURE 2.31
Preparing to invite another user to help you with Remote Assistance.

Click Sign In if you want to invite someone on your Windows Messenger (WM) buddy list who is currently online (if you're not already online). If you're already online with WM, click the icon for a buddy list member who can help you, then click Invite This Person. You can even ask for help from the WM interface: Click I Want To…, More, and Ask for Remote Assistance. Select the user from the list to send the invitation.

If all your WM buddies who can help you are offline, type an email address or click the address book icon to select an address, and then click Invite This Person.

If you send an email message, specify a maximum length of time for the invitation to be valid (one hour is the default); this helps to prevent unauthorized users from hacking your system (you are, after all, allowing complete access to your PC from a remote computer). You are strongly encouraged, although not required, to set up a password for your helper to use. You must provide the password to the user separately; I recommend that you agree on a password in advance, or call your helper by phone to communicate the password.

In either case, once the invitation/offer to help has been sent, the WM Conversation box appears on both sides of the connection. The user who requested help is called the Novice, and the helper is called the Expert. The Expert can click Accept (Alt+A) to start the help process, or Decline (Alt+D) to reject the request for assistance. A similar screen on the Novice side allows the user who asked for help to cancel the request if desired.

During the Remote Assistance process, the Novice controls the process; the Novice must specifically grant permission for the Expert to view the screen and use text chat. A two-column toolbar appears on the Novice's screen during the entire help process; the left column is used for displaying both sides' chat messages; the lower-left corner provides a message-entry area. The right column contains controls for file transfer, audio chat and quality settings, disconnecting, and stop control, as shown in Figure 2.32.

Figure 2.33 shows the Expert's view of the requester's screen. The left side shows the chat process, with the lower-left corner used for message entry. The larger window shows a scaled or scrollable actual-size view of the requester's display.

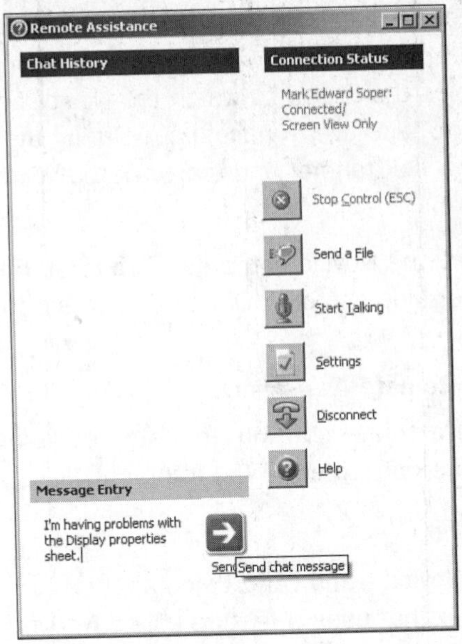

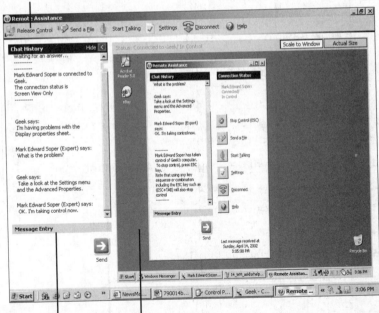

FIGURE 2.32
The Novice's control panel during a typical Remote Assistance session.

Release/Take Control toggle button

FIGURE 2.33
The Expert's control panel during a typical Remote Assistance session. Note the chat window indicates that the Expert has taken control of the system.

Expert's Chat window

Novice's system (in window)

Until the Expert clicks the Take Control button, the Novice controls the system; as before, the Novice must specifically permit this to take place. This enables the Expert to watch the Novice try a process, or allow the Expert to take over if necessary. During the process, either side can initiate a file transfer and start or stop voice chat to help solve the problem.

Whenever desired, the Novice can press Esc to stop remote control of the system. Either side can click Disconnect to stop the process.

Troubleshooting Remote Assistance

If you can't make a connection with Remote Assistance, check to see how both sides are connected to the Internet.

Check the following:

- If both the Novice's and Expert's computers are connected to a type of router that uses a feature called Network Address Translation (NAT) but doesn't support Universal Plug and Play (UPnP), the computers can't connect to each other (check your router's documentation).

- You need to configure your firewall software and your NAT router to allow traffic on TCP port 3389 (the port used by the Remote Desktop Protocol). Check your firewall appliance, firewall software, or router documentation for details.

If your router supports UPnP, but Windows XP doesn't have UPnP installed, and you can't set up a Remote Assistance connection, you need to install UPnP. Follow these steps:

1. Open the Add/Remove Programs icon in Control Panel.
2. Click Add/Remove Windows Components.
3. Scroll down to Networking Services and select it.
4. Click Details.
5. Click Universal Plug and Play.
6. Click OK to install it.

Securing UPnP on Windows XP

Installing UPnP on a Windows XP system that is not running Service Pack 2 or greater creates a significant security risk, described in detail in Microsoft Knowledge Base article 315000.

To prevent UPnP from becoming a way for hostile remote users to take control of your computer, upgrade to Service Pack 2 if your system is still running the original release or Service Pack 1. If this is not possible, install the patch referred to in Microsoft Security Bulletin MS01-059, "Unchecked Buffer in Universal Plug and Play Can Lead to System Compromise." You can download this patch through Windows Update for Windows XP, or directly from this URL:

http://www.microsoft.com/Downloads/Release.asp?ReleaseID=34951

By default, a patched machine will search only the same subnet or a private IP address for UPnP device descriptions, and only up to four router hops.

Using MSConfig

The Microsoft System Configuration Utility, MSConfig, enables you to selectively disable programs and services that run at startup. If your computer is unstable or has problems starting up or shutting down, using MSConfig can help you determine if a program or service run when the system starts is at fault.

The MSConfig dialog has six tabs in its Windows XP version (see Figure 2.34):

- **General**—Select from Normal, Diagnostic (clean boot), or Selective Startup (you choose which items and services to load); can also be used to manually replace a Windows file (Expand) or start System Restore.
- **SYSTEM.INI**—Selectively or completely disables SYSTEM.INI (legacy hardware) statements.
- **WIN.INI**—Selectively or completely disables WIN.INI (legacy software/configuration) statements; WIN.INI might not be present on some systems.
- **BOOT.INI**—Configures advanced Windows XP startup options.
- **Services**—Selectively or completely disables system services.
- **Startup**—Selectively or completely disables startup programs.

To get started with MSConfig, we recommend you click Help from the General tab and read the overview of the utility. Scroll down to the bottom and click Create a Clean Environment for Troubleshooting to Continue.

Help directs you to select the Diagnostic startup option. After you select this option, click Apply, then OK to restart your system.

FIGURE 2.34

MSConfig for Windows XP. Click Selective or Diagnostic Startup to stop loading some or all startup programs, optional settings, and optional services.

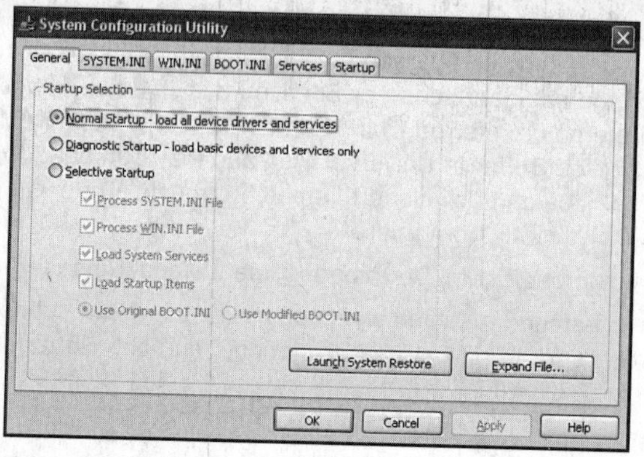

Using the Diagnostic startup option disables all startup programs, services, and special options; essentially, you are performing a clean boot of your system.

When You Can't Select Diagnostic Startup

Most computers running Windows XP don't have a WIN.INI file (a left-over from Windows 3.1!), so if you select Diagnostic startup on a Windows XP system that doesn't have WIN.INI, MSConfig will choose Selective startup instead with Process WIN.INI as its only option. It's strange, but this bug doesn't cause any problems.

If a startup program is causing your computer to malfunction, but the computer works properly after you restart it with the Diagnostic startup option, one or more of your normal startup programs or processes is at fault. After you restart the computer, reopen MSConfig, click Help, and select The Problem Was Not Reproduced for the next step in the process. Use Help to guide you through using Selective startup to reenable one part of the startup process at a time.

Dealing with Startup Error Messages

If you see error messages during startup, open the Help and Support Center, search for Startup Shutdown, and run the Windows XP Startup and Shutdown Troubleshooter. It can also assist you in using MSConfig to find the problem with your system.

Cleaning Up Startup Slowdowns with Paul Collins' Startup Index

Most systems have dozens of programs that run automatically at startup. Unfortunately, most of them are not needed, can slow down your system, and might even be harmful to system stability. Unfortunately, MSConfig doesn't provide much information about startup programs, making it difficult to determine whether you really need a particular startup program.

To get to the bottom of that seemingly endless list of startup programs, we highly recommend Paul "Pacman" Collins' "Start-Up Applications: Do You Really Need All of Them?" website at http://www.pacs-portal.co.uk/startup_index.htm.

This site, updated monthly, provides details about over 8,800 startup items. (How many do *you* have?) You can search it online, or download it with this link: http://www.pacs-portal.co.uk/startup_pages/startups_all.zip.

Paul also provides a variety of ways to prevent unwanted startup programs from running as well as links to dozens of startup managers (many of which display more than MSConfig) and spyware detectors. If you're puzzled about a brand-new startup program not already listed, there's also information about submitting the details for database updates.

Thanks to this site, we've been able to streamline our startup processes.

Limitations of MSConfig

→ See *"Slamming Spyware,"* this chapter, p. 160, *for details.*

If you suspect that spyware and adware programs are clogging up your system, the bad news is that MSConfig can't find most of them. It's designed to work with well-behaved startup programs and tasks. By contrast, most spyware and adware programs hide themselves in places MSConfig doesn't check. The good news is that you can use a variety of anti-spyware programs to find and eradicate these programs.

Keeping Windows Healthy with Service Packs and Windows Update

The best way to solve problems with Windows is to keep them from occurring in the first place. There are several ways you can use a little preventative maintenance to keep a Windows installation healthy:

- Use Windows Update to install the latest Windows components.
- Keep an eye out for patches and updates to your applications.
- Install the latest digitally signed hardware drivers for the components built into or connected to your PC (video card, audio card, motherboard, scanner, printer, and so forth).
- Perform system maintenance tasks such as error-checking disk drives and scanning for viruses.

Performing these four steps, which are detailed in the following sections, can help you postpone the all-too-common fifth way of ensuring reliable Windows usage: installing a new version of Windows to a clean hard disk.

Using Windows Update

Before Windows 98 was released, keeping Windows up to date was a nightmare of downloading all types of patch files, installing them, and trying to remember which files had been installed and in what order. Starting with Windows 98, Microsoft provided a Windows Update feature on the Start menu. Click it to connect with Microsoft's Windows Update website (http://windowsupdate.microsoft.com), which detects your Windows and Internet Explorer version, inventories the software versions on your system, and provides a customized list of files your system needs. These are divided into two categories:

- **Express Install**—High-priority critical updates
- **Custom Install**—Your choice of high-priority critical updates, optional software, and updated hardware drivers

To make Windows Update work effectively for you, I recommend the following:

- Configure your system for automatic updates. Microsoft provides service packs for Windows XP through its automatic update service. See http://www.microsoft.com/windowsxp/sp2/default.mspx for details.
- Use Windows Update to check for updates at least once a week. If you hear of a flaw in Internet Explorer, Outlook Express, or the Media Player, check for updates immediately.

- Even update utilities need to be updated from time to time. Be sure to install updates to Windows Update when Microsoft informs you they need to be installed.

- Download service packs and other high-priority updates and restart your computer before you install less-vital updates. If an update must be installed by itself, Windows Update prevents you from downloading and installing others at the same time.

- Keep in mind that Windows Update doesn't provide updates for applications, so be sure to visit your software vendors' websites for updates.

Fixing a Broken Windows Update

Windows Update is actually a component of Internet Explorer, so a damaged IE installation may keep Windows Update from working. Other causes for Windows Update's failing to work are covered in Microsoft Knowledge Base Article 193385. Look up the step-by-step instructions for fixing a sick Windows Update at http://support.microsoft.com.

If you can't connect to this website because your browser's broken, open the Add/Remove Programs icon in Control Panel, select Internet Explorer from the list of programs, and click Add/Remove. You can uninstall or repair IE with this option.

Ordering and Downloading Service Packs

Microsoft is trying—very hard—to make manual downloading of Windows XP Service Packs a thing of the past by incorporating the downloading of Service Pack 2 into the automatic updates feature of Windows Update. Frankly, we think this is a great idea in theory, but a "not ready for prime time" idea in practice. Here's why:

- Automatic updates with large downloads work very well for broadband Internet users.

- Although broadband is becoming increasingly popular, many users still rely on dial-up modems.

- Automatic updates, especially large files such as service packs, take way too long for dial-up users.

- Dial-up users are therefore the most likely to have outdated Windows installations.

Fortunately, you don't need to use automatic updates with a slow dial-up connection to get Service Pack 2. There are two other ways to get it:

- You can order the Windows XP Service Pack 2 CD from http://www.microsoft.com/windowsxp/downloads/updates/sp2/cdorder/en_us/default.mspx. The CD itself is free (shipping is just a few bucks), and you can give the CD to another user running Service Pack 1 or original Windows XP after you install it.

- Use a friend's broadband connection to download Windows XP Service Pack 2 from the Microsoft Download Center (http://www.microsoft.com/downloads). Enter "Windows XP Service Pack 2 Network Installation Package for IT Professionals and Developers" to get a link to the file (about 270MB). Burn the downloaded file to a CD and install Service Pack 2 from the CD.

After you install Service Pack 2 (which also includes SP1 fixes to Windows XP), you can use automatic updates or Windows Update to keep your system updated.

Performing a Repair Installation

Although Windows XP is designed to be harder to break than previous versions, it's not bulletproof. If you have severe problems with Windows that can't be solved with System Restore, consider performing a repair installation (also referred to as an *in-place upgrade* by Microsoft).

A repair installation, as the name implies, is designed to preserve your existing Windows configuration while replacing corrupt files and repairing incorrect settings. You should make a backup copy of your data files (stored in \Documents and Settings*Username* for each user of your PC) before performing a repair installation in case of problems. However, a properly performed repair installation will preserve data files while (usually) producing a better-running Windows.

Follow this basic outline for performing a repair installation (for details, warnings, and cautions, check the website links provided before performing the repair installation):

1. Remove the Undo_guimode.txt file (if present in the \Windows\ system32 folder) before performing a repair installation. The presence of this file could cause data loss. See Microsoft Knowledge Base Article 312369 at http://support.microsoft.com for details.

2. Copy the Windows Product Activation files wpa.dbl and wpa.bak from the \Windows\system32 folder to a floppy disk for safe-keeping.

3. Disconnect USB devices other than the USB mouse and keyboard. You can reconnect them after completing the repair installation.

4. Back up each user's My Documents files. You should make a backup copy of the data files (stored in \Documents and Settings*Username*) for each user of your PC.

5. Start the system with the Windows XP CD or with Windows XP boot disks.

6. Windows XP Setup asks you if you want to set up Windows, repair Windows, or quit. Press Enter to select the setup option.

7. After you accept the license agreement, the setup program searches for previous Windows installations.

8. When the setup program detects your existing Windows installation, it displays the location (usually C:\Windows) and asks if you want to repair it or install a fresh copy. Select the existing installation and press R to repair it.

9. The installation process continues until completed. See websites listed in the sidebar "Repair Installation Help and How-To" for details.

10. If you performed a repair install of Windows XP original edition or Windows XP Service Pack 1, download and install Windows XP Service Pack 2, either through automatic updates, Windows Explorer, or manually. This step is necessary because changes made by service packs are undone when you perform a repair installation of an earlier revision. This step is not necessary if you are performing a repair install from a CD containing Service Pack 2.

Repair Installation Help and How-To

Many websites provide repair installation tutorials. Some of the most useful include the following:

- **Microsoft Knowledge Base Article 315341**—Available at http://support.microsoft.com.
- http://www.michaelstevenstech.com/XPrepairinstall.htm—Includes very important warnings.
- http://support.gateway.com/s/SOFTWARE/MICROSOF/7509595/ Install/Install06.shtml—Includes illustrations.

Fixing Programs That Won't Run

Most problems that occur after Windows successfully boots involve the applications and programs you use on a day-to-day basis. Typical problems you might encounter include the following:

- Programs that worked with earlier versions of Windows but don't work with Windows XP
- Programs that won't start from their desktop or Start button shortcuts
- Programs you can't open from Windows Explorer
- Programs that trigger a STOP error (Blue Screen of Death, or BSOD)

The following sections will help you solve these problems.

Troubleshooting Programs That Won't Run Under Windows XP

If you've just moved up to Windows XP from an older version of Windows, or you're trying to use programs made for Windows 9x on Windows XP, keep in mind that Windows XP is the first consumer-level operating system to be based on Windows NT and Windows 2000, rather than Windows 95. This means that many programs that ran properly under older versions of Windows might not run properly under Windows XP unless you take advantage of its built-in Program Compatibility Wizard. To start the wizard, click Start, All Programs, Accessories, Program Compatibility Wizard.

Once the wizard is started, you can select from programs already installed on your computer, the current program in the CD-ROM drive, or you can browse to the program manually. After you select a program, you can select the version of Windows the program worked best under (see Figure 2.35).

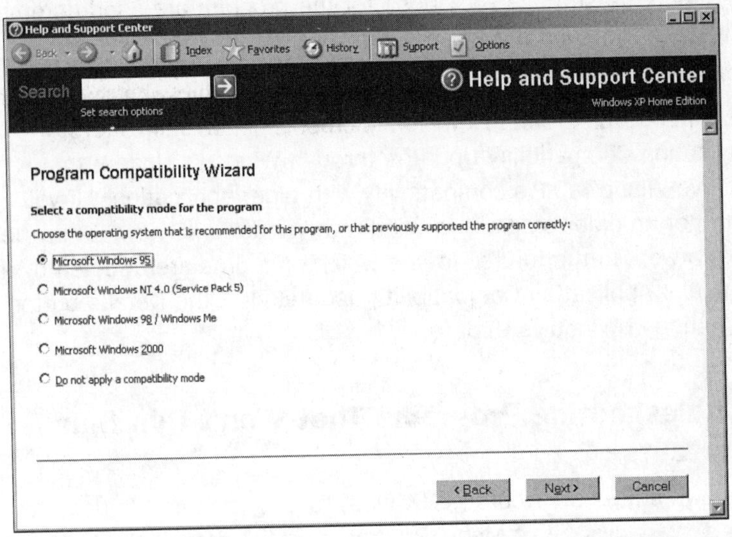

FIGURE 2.35

Using the Program Compatibility Wizard to run an older Windows program under Windows XP as Windows 95 would run it.

On the next screen, you can select one or more of the following options to aid compatibility:

- **256 colors**—Many older Windows programs can't run under 16-bit or higher color depths.

- **640×480 screen resolution**—Many older Windows programs use a fixed screen size and can't run properly on a high-res screen.

- **Disable visual themes**—Many older Windows programs were created before visual themes were common.

Click the box next to each option to select it if desired.

Like an Old Game? Make Windows XP Like It Too!

If you are using the Program Compatibility Wizard to help you run an older game or educational program under Windows XP, you'll probably want to try all three of these options. Setting these options affects only the program you set them for. The rest of Windows will continue to look and function normally.

After you select any visual options you want to try, you can test the program, which will apply the visual options or compatibility mode selected, and then start the program. After you close the program, Windows switches back to its normal screen settings if necessary, and you can decide whether to use these settings for your software or try others. You can choose whether to inform Microsoft of your settings, and the settings you chose for the program are used automatically every time you run the program.

Keep in mind that the Program Compatibility Wizard won't work with all old Windows programs. However, Microsoft periodically offers Application Compatibility Updates through Windows Update that improve Windows XP's compatibility with older applications. If you can't get an older program to work with Windows XP now, it may be able to work in the future. To see which programs are affected by a particular Application Compatibility Update, click the Details button on the listing in Windows Update.

Troubleshooting Programs That Won't Run from Shortcuts

Windows stores shortcuts (.LNK files) to programs in a folder normally called \Windows\Start Menu\Programs on the default system drive (normally C:). The .LNK file points to the correct location for the actual program, so that if you open the .LNK file, it opens the actual program for you. If you open a shortcut but the program doesn't appear to start, check the following:

- **Is there a "Missing Shortcut" error message?** This error means that the file the shortcut is pointing to has been deleted, moved, or renamed. If the shortcut points to a removable-media drive, make sure the program disk or CD-ROM is inserted into the correct drive and that the drive in question is functioning properly.

- **The program you are trying to run may already be started, although it's not visible in the Windows Taskbar.** Press Ctrl+Alt+Delete to display the Task Manager and see if the program you are trying to run appears more than once. Select End Task for each reference to the program (you will need to press Ctrl+Alt+Delete again to redisplay the Task List after you close a program), and try to run the program again after all references to the program have been closed. Some programs can't run properly if you try to start more than one instance at the same time.

When Windows Offers to Fix a Missing Shortcut, Say "Thanks but No Thanks!"

After Windows displays a "Missing Shortcut" error, it will keep searching for a file with the same or similar name as the shortcut's original target. Once it finds a file it believes is close enough to the original shortcut's reference, it will offer to fix the shortcut. Unless you're sure the replacement file reference is the same file, don't let Windows link the shortcut to the file it shows you. Just delete the shortcut and make a new one manually.

For details, see "Adding a Shortcut," this chapter, p. 141.

- **The shortcut isn't broken, but the program won't run correctly. (It might start, but quit immediately, or never start at all.)** The Windows Registry entries for the program may be corrupted, and if the Registry can't find the program, it can't run. You may need to re-register the program's components with the Windows Registry. If the program has a re-registering utility, such as PFREG.EXE, (supplied with some versions of the Corel WordPerfect Office suite), you can run it to re-register program components. Otherwise, uninstall, then reinstall the program.

Troubleshooting Programs That Won't Run from Windows Explorer

If you're having problems with a program's Start menu or desktop shortcut, or the program you want to launch doesn't have a shortcut, you can usually run it directly from the Windows Explorer (also called My Computer) file listing. The only trick is that you'll need to know the folder path to where the program is installed. Most applications install into a folder called Program Files, located on your system hard disk (usually C: drive).

Two Operating Modes, Two Program Files Folders

Windows XP Professional x64 Edition has two Program Files folders. Program Files is used for 64-bit applications, whereas Program Files (x86) is used for 32-bit applications. When you install programs, Windows places programs in the correct folder for you.

Once you've found the folder, you need to double-click the file icon for the application. To save time, use Windows XP's Search tool to track down the folder containing the file, or the file itself. If you can't run the program this way either, the program may already be running, or may need to have its components re-registered into the Windows Registry. See "Troubleshooting Programs That Won't Run from Shortcuts," this chapter, p. 138.

If you still can't run the program from My Computer, check the following list of possible causes:

- **Did you drag and drop the program from another folder or drive location?** If it's possible that you've somehow modified the name or location of the program's folders or files, the Windows Registry listing for the program will be out of date. Put the program back into the correct folder or drive location if possible, and try to run it again. If it cannot run or you don't recall how its files or folders may have been changed, uninstall it (if possible) and reinstall it in the desired location. For details, see "I'm Having Problems Removing My Application," this chapter, p. 144.

- **Have you installed or uninstalled a program recently?** Many Windows programs used shared files that are stored in the \Windows\System folder. If incompatible versions of these files replace other versions during installation of new software, an existing program might stop working. Or, if shared files are deleted when you uninstall a program, other programs that use the same files might also stop working.

- **Have you deleted any files recently?** Deleting files that are found in folders such as \Windows, \WinNT, or \Program Files or their subfolders can break programs if you delete program components instead of data or temporary files (data files should be stored in your personal document folder). Check the Recycle Bin and undelete any files that originated in \Windows or \Program Files or their subfolders and then retry your program.

Don't Break Old Apps with New Apps

When you install a new program, pay attention during the installation process. If the installer asks if you want to replace an existing system file, use the option provided by some install programs to make a backup of the system file being replaced. When you uninstall a file, don't remove files stored in the \Windows\System or \Winnt\System folder if there's any possibility that other programs use the same file. Similarly, if you uninstall one part of a collection of applications from the same vendor, the uninstall program may offer to remove files from a shared folder used by that vendor's programs. Do so only if you're certain that no other program uses those same files.

Adding a Shortcut

If you know the name and location of the application that is missing a shortcut (or never had a shortcut), you can create a shortcut on the Windows desktop or Start menu.

Follow this procedure to create a shortcut on the Start menu:

1. Right-click the Start button and select Explore All Users.
2. Double-click the Programs folder in the right-hand window.
3. If you want to place the shortcut in a subfolder, double-click the folder in which you want to create the shortcut. Otherwise, scroll to the bottom of the list of folders and shortcuts.
4. Right-click empty space in the right-hand window.
5. Select New, Shortcut.
6. Click Browse to navigate to the program you want to run from the shortcut. Highlight the program and click Next to continue.
7. Type a descriptive name for the shortcut. Click Finish.

To create a desktop shortcut, follow this procedure:

1. Right-click on an empty area of the desktop.
2. Select New, Shortcut.
3. Click Browse to navigate to the program you want to run from the shortcut. Highlight the program and click Next to continue.
4. Type a descriptive name for the shortcut. Click Finish.

Leo Says

Love Desktop Shortcuts? Drag and Drop Them!

Although Microsoft is on a mission to get shortcuts off the desktop, lots of folks still use and love desktop shortcuts. Here's an even easier way to make a desktop short if you already have a Program menu shortcut:

1. Click Start, All Programs, and proceed until the program menu shortcut is visible.
2. Right-click the shortcut and drag it to an empty area of the desktop.
3. Select Copy Here from the right-click menu to copy the shortcut.
4. Voila! A fast, easy desktop shortcut.

Why Application Software Can Fail

Software applications, the programs you run to balance your checkbook, write the great American novel, digitize your photographic collection, and surf the Internet, cause computer users a lot of grief when they stop working or don't behave as they're expected to. Some of the most common problems you might encounter with broken programs include the following:

- Not being able to run older programs under a newer version of Windows

- Difficulties in updating software because of uncertainties about version numbers

- Difficulties in reinstalling applications

- Problems with automatic software updates

- Programs that stop working after another program is installed

Use the tips in the following sections to help you get your software back on track.

Researching Your Program's Compatibility with Windows

There are three major sources for information on whether your program will work properly with Windows:

- The Microsoft Knowledge Base

- The program vendor's website

- Internet search engines such as Google

Because the last option (searching the entire Internet) will usually turn up a lot of useless pages unless you construct your search terms very carefully, we recommend starting with the first two options.

To access the Microsoft Knowledge Base, follow these steps:

1. Open your browser (we recommend using Internet Explorer with Microsoft websites).

2. Type http://support.microsoft.com into the address window and press Enter.

3. Enter your search terms. Put quotation marks around phrases. For example, to search for Adobe Photoshop, enter "**Adobe Photoshop**".

Any Microsoft Knowledge Base articles containing the search terms or phrases you entered will be displayed.

If you're having problems getting third-party programs or data to work properly with Microsoft applications, or even problems between Microsoft programs, the Knowledge Base can also help you dig out the answers you need. Just specify both applications in your search.

Using Abbreviations to Speed Your Search

When you view a Microsoft Knowledge Base article about your application, take a moment to scroll down to the bottom to see the keywords and additional query words listed for the article. You can use these terms to save yourself some typing and find answers faster. Here are a few of the most common search terms you might find useful:

- **OFF**—Microsoft Office
- **PPT**—Microsoft PowerPoint
- **WORD**—Microsoft Word
- **PUB**—Microsoft Publisher

To search for a particular version, add 97, 2000, 2002, XP, 2003, and so on. For example, to search for Office 2003, use OFF2003 in your search.

If you are having problems with a third-party (non-Microsoft) program, you should also search the technical information provided at the vendor's website. Depending on the site, you might select the application and version, or you might need to query the website with the site's own search tool.

If you're looking for information regarding a program that is available on multiple platforms and you're getting a lot of answers that don't apply to you, add "Windows" to the search terms you use. This should help screen out Mac or Linux-specific answers that don't apply to Windows systems.

I'm Not Sure What My Exact Program Version Is

In many cases, the solution for compatibility issues between a particular application program and Windows or between two different applications is the installation of a software patch for your application. Some of these patches, also known as *service packs*, can be very large, and if you have a dial-up modem instead of broadband Internet access, you might prefer to order the patch/service pack on CD-ROM rather than trying to download it.

Because a particular version of a program might undergo small changes from its initial release until its final revision, and because some software patches/service packs are designed to work in sequence with previous patches, you might need to determine exactly what revision of a program you have.

Determining this information can be done in two ways:

- You might need to open the program and click Help, About from the menu bar to display the exact version/revision information.

- You might need to search for a particular program file and view its properties sheet in Windows Explorer or My Computer to determine what revision of a program is installed.

The software vendor will inform you on its support website if you need to use either of these methods to determine an exact software version before you install an update.

Here's an example of using Help, About. If you need to install Service Pack 2 for Corel WordPerfect Office 2000, you need to determine whether you have already installed Service Pack 1. If you haven't, you must download and install it first. Start any major application in the suite; click Help, About from the menu bar; and look for the version number. A version number of 9.0.0.528 in WordPerfect, Quattro Pro, Corel Presentations, CorelCENTRAL, or PerfectFit indicates the original release is installed and must be updated with Service Pack 1. Once Service Pack 1 is installed, the release number changes to 9.0.0.588.

I'm Having Problems Removing My Application

If a software patch or service pack doesn't install properly, you might need to remove your application from the system and reinstall it. Normally, this is a simple task:

1. Open the Control Panel.
2. Open the Add/Remove Programs icon.
3. Select the Change or Remove Programs (Windows XP) or Install/Uninstall tab (other versions).
4. Select the program you want to uninstall.
5. Click Change/Remove or Add/Remove and follow the prompts to start the process.

Unfortunately, for various reasons, programs don't always uninstall the way they should when following these steps.

If you have manually deleted or moved the folder that contains the main program, deleted folders created in the default Temporary files location (normally the Temp folder beneath the default Windows folder), or misplaced the original program installation CD, you might not be able to run the uninstall program. If the uninstall program is missing (because you removed the folder containing it) or if it can't find information about the program to be uninstalled, Windows won't be able to uninstall the program without some help from you. There have also been programs that contain bugs that prevent them from properly uninstalling themselves.

You can still uninstall most programs by using one of these methods:

- Reinstall the program using the same file and folder locations you originally used, then uninstall it. This is probably your best option if you don't have a third-party uninstall program on your system.

- Use a third-party uninstall program such as Norton CleanSweep, McAfree Uninstaller, or WinCleaner. These programs are usually part of a utility suite, and they work best if you use them to track the original installation so they know which files were added, updated, or deleted, and which Registry keys were changed. If you install an uninstall utility only after you installed the application you want to remove, it will need to make some educated assumptions on which files can be safely removed; sometimes, files you really need are deleted.

- Check the software vendor's website for manual uninstall instructions or for a downloadable tool you can use to remove the application. In some cases, you might need to manually edit the Windows Registry. This is the most difficult way to uninstall a program, and it should not be attempted unless you understand how the Windows Registry works, have a backup copy of the Windows Registry, and have a list of the Registry keys you must remove or change.

- Use the System Restore feature to revert your computer to the condition it was in before the program was installed. This also undoes any other programs you installed after the restore date you select, but it doesn't remove any data you created (including installed program files, which you must then remove manually from your system).

→ *For details on System Restore*, see *"Using System Restore," this chapter*, p. 118.

I'm Having Problems Reinstalling My Application

As suggested in the previous section, you might need to uninstall and reinstall an application that's stopped working. If you are having problems reinstalling an application, check the following causes and solutions for help.

- **The application won't install because it is an upgrade version.** Depending on the application, you might need to provide the serial number for the original version of the program or the installation CD to prove you're entitled to install an upgrade version. Note that some programs don't display the entire serial number in their Help, About display of program information or might create an encoded version of the serial number that can't be translated back into the original.

- **The application won't install because you don't have sufficient rights.** You need to be the computer administrator (or have administrator status) to install a program on Windows XP. If you logged in as Guest or have a guest-level account, the programs you run aren't authorized to make system-level changes to the computer. You'll need to talk to the person "in charge" of the system to get help with this.

- **The application CD or DVD can't be read.** Clean the CD surface, clean the drive, and try again. To clean the CD or DVD, you can use a variety of CD- and DVD-cleaning products. To clean the drive, use a cleaning CD or DVD (these products have brushes that sweep dust and debris away from the laser in the drive). To use a cleaning CD or DVD, play it as directed in the instructions. If the application CD's data surface is scratched, you need to re-polish the surface to prevent read errors. Check with your favorite computer or electronics store for Skip Doctor, a very popular CD surface repair tool (http://www.digitalinnovations.com/).

Protecting Your Programs

You can spend as much on software as you do on your computer, or even more. To prevent losing CD-based programs to scratches or dust, check out these vendors:

- **CD/DVD Playright**—Manufacturer of Trio Plus, a collection of CD/DVD cleaning and protection products. See its website at http://www.cdplayright.com/.

- **Azuradisc**—Manufactures a line of CD scratch-removal machines designed for use by dealers and rental stores, and also sells a line of optical media cleaners and disc protectors. See its website at http://www.azuradisc.com.

- Many retail stores now carry various brands of CD and DVD protectors.

You should also consider making a backup copy of your application CDs and store the originals in a safe place. Although some application CDs are copy-protected (they can be read but not copied without using special software), most are not.

Upgrading Applications

Although Windows XP uses a side-by-side technology for managing dynamic link library files (.DLL files), files that form the building blocks of Windows applications, using outdated versions of programs can still cause problems. Because older applications in particular like to copy some of their .DLL files into the \Windows\System folder, you could have problems with an older application, or even Windows itself, if you insist on running programs designed for Windows 9x with newer versions of Windows.

Follow these guidelines for painless updates:

- If you are installing an upgrade version, find out what proof of ownership is needed during installation. If the program's CD-ROM or floppy disk #1 is all that's needed to verify you owned the old version, consider removing the old version before you install the new version. Leftover DLL files and Registry entries are prime reasons for Windows and application crashes.

- If the new version of a program must locate the old version's installation on the hard disk, find out if it's acceptable to install the new version to a different folder. This will also avoid mixing up DLL files and Registry entries and make for a more reliable installation; you can remove the old version after you install the new version. You may also be able to remove the old version before you install the new version if you can use the old version's program CD to verify eligibility for the update. This option will save disk space and avoid any problems with data files being opened by the wrong version of the program.

- Before you install the updated version of an application, check the vendor's website for patches and service packs. If possible, download them before you install the main program so you can bring it up to the latest release quickly.

Problems with Applications' Default Settings

You might not have any technical problems with your applications, but if you can't use them the way you'd like to, it's still frustrating to work with them.

Some of the typical annoyances you might encounter include the following:

- Menus that show too many or not enough buttons
- Pull-down menus that don't show you all the options at first glance
- Programs that don't use your preferred default document location
- Programs that can't import or export documents in your preferred formats

Fortunately, these and similar problems can usually be solved by using your software's configuration menu.

I Can't Start My Favorite Commands from Menu Buttons

To add buttons or entire toolbars to the default menu or display in your favorite application, you need to locate the Customize or Options menu. Here are a few examples of where to look:

- **Microsoft Office**—Tools, Customize, Toolbars
- **Corel WordPerfect Suite**—Tools, Settings, Customize, Toolbars
- **CorelDraw**—Tools, Options, Customization, Command Bars
- **Adobe Photoshop**—Window, Show/Hide (various menus)

If you're having problems finding the right menu or understanding how to customize the interface, you should consult the program's Help files or a book dedicated to your specific program.

I Can't See All My Program's Menu Options

Starting with Microsoft Office 2000, and continuing with the latest version of Office, Office 2003, Microsoft has used an adaptive menu system for its pull-down menus. If you're accustomed to seeing all the menu options at a glance, adaptive menus (which hide functions that you seldom use) are disturbing.

To change this behavior in Microsoft Office, click Tools, Customize, and uncheck Menus Show Recently Used Commands First. To make hidden options appear without disabling this feature, you should only have to hover the mouse pointer over the opened menu for a few seconds or click a "down arrow" at the bottom of the menu.

I Need to Configure My Program to Use My Default Document Folder

To make finding your documents easier, you should make sure your applications are configured to use your "My Documents" folder. In Windows XP, this is an alias for the \Documents and Settings*username* folder.

This can be more complicated than simply specifying a folder for your documents. If your application creates periodic automatic backups, if you use style and document templates, or create custom dictionaries, you should also adjust the default locations of these data types as well to make backups easier.

We recommend that you create a folder beneath your default documents folder for each data type you want to store there. For example, we create a Backup folder inside our default document folders for the timed backups created by Microsoft Word and Corel WordPerfect.

To specify the location for documents and other types of custom data, you need to use the customization or option menu offered by your application. The exact menu location varies by program, but here are a few examples:

- **Microsoft Office**—Tools, Options, File Locations.
- **Corel WordPerfect Suite**—Tools, Settings, Files.
- **CorelDraw**—Tools, Options, Workspace, Save (for specifying backup file locations). CorelDraw uses the last folder location you opened for its startup default.
- **Adobe Photoshop**—Tools, Preferences, Plug-ins and Scratch Disks (for plug-ins and temporary files). Photoshop uses the last folder location you opened for its startup default.

I Can't Open a Particular Type of File

Although Microsoft Office is the most popular office suite at present, this popularity conceals the fact that there's only partial file-format compatibility between Office 97, Office 2000, Office XP, and Office

2003. And, by default, Microsoft Office doesn't install the necessary import/export filters needed to send data seamlessly between its apps and other popular products such as Corel WordPerfect Suite, Lotus SmartSuite, and older versions of Word, Excel, and Microsoft Office.

To avoid stumbling into the incompatible file-format trap, follow these guidelines:

- Install *all* the file filters for both text and graphics whenever you install any type of program (office suite, graphics, page layout, and so on), particularly if your computers will be used for service bureau or public access work, or if users with different versions of applications bring work to and from the office. Use the Custom installation option to display this choice.

- If you use Microsoft Word 2000 or later and you share files with users of Word 97, use the Tools, Options Save dialog to disable features not used by Word 97.

- If you need to move data files between different applications, test the roundtrip process with noncritical files before you rely on it for actual work. Despite improvements in import/export filters, trying to export complex files in another program's file format doesn't always result in a perfect product.

- Don't replace the original copy of the file after you edit it with a different version of a program or with a different application altogether. Save the edited file with a different name in case of problems.

- Use a neutral file format such as .RTF (Rich Text Format) to move documents around whenever possible instead of a more-complex, easier-to-break format such as Word.

- If all you need to do is share raw, unformatted text with another user or PC, save the document as a .TXT file. You'll loose any and all formatting, colors, and so on, but the text should make the trip to .TXT format intact. Sometimes, this is easiest way to share documents with people using different versions of Windows, or (gasp!) Mac OS.

The Unworkable Application

Despite your best efforts, you might discover that you simply can't get a particular application to work with your system. This is particularly likely if you are trying to run an older 16-bit or 32-bit Windows program with Windows XP, or if you are trying to use an orphaned program (a program whose vendor no longer supports the product with technical notes or software patches).

Hello 64-bit Applications, Goodbye 16-bit Applications

One of the tradeoffs inherent in moving to the x64 Edition is the loss of support for 16-bit DOS and Windows 3.x applications. This isn't much of a sacrifice for most users, but if you still need to (or want to) run 16-bit software, 64-bit Windows can't do it. That means you'll have to part with some really old custom software, some older email clients, some classic games, and the like, if you want to use x64.

The easiest way to avoid problems with your applications is to do the following:

- Make sure your application is explicitly supported by your version of Windows.

- Install the recommended software patches (if necessary).

- Try the Windows XP Program Compatibility Wizard, specifying the Windows version the program is designed to support.

- Upgrade to a supported version of the application if the version you use won't work.

- Uninstall an application that can't be made to work and replace it with a fully supported product.

Although upgrading or replacing a failed application might seem expensive, the costs of possible data loss through computer crashes and the lost time you spend trying to make an old program work on a new system add up quickly. Avoid the pain by refusing to waste time on an old program if it won't respond to the methods provided in this chapter.

Troubleshooting Games

Problems with Windows-based games come from these sources:

- Problems with the games themselves (bugs and lack of support for new hardware and operating systems)

- Outdated drivers for gaming hardware (sound cards, video, game controllers)

- Problems with DirectX

If you have problems with a particular game, follow these steps to solve them:

- Make sure you have installed the latest patches available for your game. Some of these can be quite large, so if you have a dial-up connection, be very patient or use a friend's broadband connection and CD burner to download patch files.

- Make sure you have installed the latest drivers for your gaming hardware; if Windows Update doesn't have the files you need, go to the vendor's website. Note that the latest drivers might not be digitally signed.

- If you are using Windows XP and the game was designed for older versions of Windows, use the Program Compatibility Wizard to run your game. For details, see "Troubleshooting Programs That Won't Run Under Windows XP", this chapter, p. 136.

If these steps don't solve problems with your game, you might have a problem with DirectX. Most Windows-based 3D games (as well as game-type educational software) depend on the features of DirectX, an application programming interface (API) that provides a convenient way for software coders to access 3D video, 3D sound, game control, and other game features, regardless of the brand of video adapter, sound card, or controllers used. If DirectX components are damaged or missing, you won't be able to play games that depend on DirectX.

To keep DirectX in shape, follow these rules:

- Install the latest version of DirectX for your version of Windows; get it from Microsoft instead of using the outdated versions supplied with some games. Get DirectX from http://www.microsoft.com/windows/directx/default.aspx.

➡ **For details on DirectX Diagnostics, see "Using DirectX Diagnostics," this chapter, p. 120.**

- Run the DirectX Diagnostic tool (DXDIAG) to make sure your DirectX installation is working correctly. You can test, enable, or disable features such as DirectDraw, Direct3D, AGP Texture Acceleration, DirectSound, and DirectMusic with the Display, Sound, and Music tabs. Use the More Help tab to troubleshoot the installation.

Troubleshooting STOP Errors with Windows XP

One of the most vague and frustrating errors any Windows user can encounter is a STOP error. Usually, users refer to this error not-so-affectionately as the Blue Screen of Death (BSOD).

If your program starts, but triggers a crash that locks up your computer and displays a technical error message with white text on a blue background, then you've encountered the dreaded BSOD. The cause might be a problem with a program's files, with its interaction with other software or hardware on your system, or your memory or other hardware. With so many possible causes, BSOD errors can be extremely difficult to troubleshoot.

When you see a BSOD error, be sure to record the numbers listed after the STOP message, such as STOP: 0x0000001E, or 0x1E for short. You should also record the name of the error, such as KMODE_EXCEPTION_NOT_HANDLED. You can then look up the error number and name on the Microsoft Support Site for Windows XP (http://support.microsoft.com/ph/1173/en-us/) to find Microsoft's suggested solutions.

Table 2.6 lists some of the most common STOP errors and possible solutions.

TABLE 2.6
WINDOWS XP STOP ERRORS AND SOLUTIONS

STOP Error Number	STOP Error Name	Suggested Solutions
0xA	IRQL_NOT_LESS_OR_EQUAL	Check device drivers or services used by backup or antivirus utilities.
0xD1	DRIVER_IRQL_NOT_LESS_OR_EQUAL	Check device drivers or services used by backup or antivirus utilities.
0x1E	KMODE_EXCEPTION_NOT HANDLED	Illegal or unknown instruction; check the driver referenced in the error message.

TABLE 2.6 (continued)
WINDOWS XP STOP ERRORS AND SOLUTIONS

STOP Error Number	STOP Error Name	Suggested Solutions
0x24	NTFS_FILE SYSTEM	Test the hard disk for errors.
0x2E	DATA_BUS ERROR	Test memory modules; disable memory caching in system BIOS; check hardware configuration.
0x50	PAGE_FAULT_IN_ NONPAGED AREA	Check printer drivers.
0x7B	INACCESSIBLE_BOOT_DEVICE	Incorrect or missing hard disk device driver; press F6 at startup and supply correct driver on floppy disk.
0x7F	UNEXPECTED_KERNEL_ MODE_TRAP	Test hardware and RAM; check SCSI configuration if in use; make sure CPU is not over-clocked.
0x9F	DRIVER_POWER_STATE_ FAILURE	Check power management and CD-writing software; disable power management temporarily; reinstall or upgrade CD-writing software.
0xC21A	STATUS_SYSTEM_ PROCESS TERMINATED	Reinstall third-party programs; use System File Checker with the Scannow option (SFC/Scannow) to check system files.

In some cases, your computer will reboot immediately after a BSOD, rather than leaving it onscreen. To prevent this from happening, disable Automatic Restart in the System properties sheet. Right-click My Computer, select Properties, select Advanced, click the Settings button in the Startup and Recovery section, and clear the check mark next to Automatically Restart. Then click OK.

Restore CDs and Your Data—Separated at Birth

Unfortunately, most computers shipped with Windows don't come with a "real" version of Windows that works the way the retail upgrade versions do. Instead, they might be supplied with a special "restore" CD that is primarily intended to erase the hard disk, reinstall Windows, and set up the computer in its factory-shipped configuration or with restore files stored in a hidden partition of the hard disk. During the process, any data you have on the system will be deleted, as well as any programs you've installed.

Before you use a system-restore CD or partition, be sure you've backed up all your data. If your computer can't be booted, even in Safe Mode, and you have no backups, consider connecting your drive to another working computer and transferring the data to another drive first.

Preventing and Reducing Occurrences of BSOD Errors in Windows

You can take steps to minimize or eliminate the occurrences of BSOD errors. Consider the following tips to help reduce the likelihood of repeated BSODs:

- If the BSOD occurred directly after you installed new hardware or software, uninstall the hardware or software and check for driver or program updates before you install it again. If the error continues to occur, contact the technical support department for the product in question.

- BSODs that occur only after you've used the computer for a while could be caused by excessive heat in your system, causing corruption to the contents of your system's memory modules. If you have a system monitor program that displays internal case temperature, periodically check the temperature. If you see a temperature rise before the BSOD, install additional case fans and make sure your processor's fan is working properly. For details, see Chapter 1.

- Although a lot of products claim to be compatible with each version of Windows, Microsoft has its own standards for Windows compatibility. Make sure your hardware is included on the Microsoft Catalog list of compatible hardware and software, which is available online at http://www.microsoft.com/windows/catalog/.

- As with hardware, Microsoft also likes to "digitally sign" (certify) device drivers for Windows. Be sure to use digitally signed drivers whenever possible; these drivers have been approved by Microsoft's Hardware Quality Labs.

- If the drivers you use with your hardware are meant for an older version of Windows than what you are using (such as Windows 2000 drivers with Windows XP), attempt to replace these outdated drivers with the correct version as soon as possible. Note that the speed at which OS-specific drivers for your particular device and version of Windows appear is dependent on its manufacturer. Note that you *cannot* use 32-bit device drivers with Windows XP Professional x64 Edition, although most 32-bit applications work correctly.

- You may find that removing the device and installing the correct driver when the device is redetected is more reliable than just updating the driver in Device Manager, because outdated files might still be retained if the drivers are updated instead of being removed and reinstalled.

- If you've overclocked your computer (adjusted its CPU, video, or memory speeds beyond the normal limits for your hardware), reset the component speeds and voltages to their default values. Your processor, memory, or one or more of your components may lose stability when your system is overclocked.

What Does That STOP Error Mean?

For a helpful guide to troubleshooting STOP errors in Windows XP, see the following website:

http://www.microsoft.com/windowsxp/using/setup/getstarted/troubleshoot.mspx

---

Stopping Viruses

Although Windows XP provides a lot of tools for handling various problems you might have with your PC, fighting viruses is completely up to you. Computer viruses are programs that have the following characteristics:

- They carry harmful payloads (erase files, transmit data to other computers, prevent systems from starting, and so on).

- They can spread themselves to other computers via email, instant messaging (IM), infected files, or infected boot sectors.

Computer viruses are usually concealed inside other programs, email attachments, or web-based scripts. Trojan horse programs are similar to viruses, but cannot replicate.

Although Windows XP Service Pack 2 introduced software support for the NX ("no execute") antivirus feature built into the AMD Athlon 64 and Intel EM64T–compatible Pentium 4 processors, this feature stops only one type of threat—the buffer overflow. It's essential that you install high-quality antivirus software and keep it updated.

How critical is updated antivirus software? Many colleges and universities will not permit student computers to connect to campus networks unless the computer is equipped with antivirus software. Administrators of campus networks know that infected PCs can bring down an entire network. Imagine how fast it can happen to your home or small-business network!

Antivirus Strategies

Most home computer users are looking for bargains, and we're no exceptions. There are several ways to save money on virus protection, but some are much better than others. The worst way to save money, other than not using antivirus software at all, is to rely exclusively on free online virus-scanning services.

These services work well at finding viruses already on your system. The trouble is, you don't want an infected PC, especially these days. Virus infections can cripple your PC, might prevent you from getting online, and can infect other PCs you share information with (other PCs at home, PCs at the office if you take work home, and so on).

We recommend using free services for a "second opinion" if you think your primary antivirus program might have missed an infection, or as a stopgap if your regular service has expired, until you can restart it.

A much better option is a standalone antivirus program (some of these might also be free). However, keep in mind that most standalone programs have limited or no protection against spyware and adware and usually don't include a firewall.

The best strategy is to use a suite that includes the following features:

- Antivirus
- Protection against hostile scripts
- Firewall
- Spyware scanner

Alternatively, you can create your own "best of breed" suite by using your favorite products.

Table 2.7 lists some of the major vendors that provide antivirus programs and suites; the table also indicates which vendors provide online scanning.

TABLE 2.7

MAJOR ANTIVIRUS AND SUITE VENDORS

Vendor (URL)	Antivirus Utility	Suite Containing Antivirus	Other Suite Features	Online Scanning
CA (www.ca.com)	eTrust EZ Antivirus	eTrust EZ Armor	1	eTrust Antivirus Web Scanner
		eTrust EZ Armor, Pest Patrol bundle	1, 2	
F-Secure (www.f-secure.com)	F-Secure Anti-Virus 2005	F-Secure Internet Security 2005	1, 2, 6, 7	F-Secure Online Virus Scanner
McAfee (www.mcafee.com)	McAfee VirusScan	McAfee VirusScan Professional	2, 6	McAfee Freescan
		McAfee Internet Security Suite	1, 2, 6, 11	
Panda (www.pandasoftware.com)	Titanium Antivirus 2005	Platinum Internet Security 2005	1, 2, 3, 7	ActiveScan (free), ActiveScan Pro
Trend Micro (www.trendmicro.com)	—	PC-cillin Internet Security	1, 2, 3, 4, 5, 6	HouseCall (free)

TABLE 2.7 (continued)
MAJOR ANTIVIRUS AND SUITE VENDORS

Vendor (URL)	Antivirus Utility	Suite Containing Antivirus	Other Suite Features	Online Scanning
Symantec (www.symantec.com)	Norton AntiVirus 2005	Norton SystemWorks 2005	8, 9, 12, 13	Symantec Security Check (free)
		Norton SystemWorks Premiere 2005	8, 9, 10, 12, 13	
		Norton Internet Security 2005	1, 6, 7, 11	
		Norton Internet Security 2005 Antispyware Edition	1, 2, 6, 7, 11	
Zone Labs (www.zonelabs.com)	—	ZoneAlarm Antivirus	1	
		ZoneAlarm Security Suite	1, 2, 3, 6, 11	

1. Firewall

2. Anti-spyware

3. Anti-phishing (stops fake emails and websites from compromising personal information)

4. Home network control; protects all PCs on the network from a single installation

5. Detects Wi-Fi (wireless Ethernet) intruders

6. Anti-spam

7. Web content filtering

8. Disk management (error-checking, defrag)

9. Data recovery

10. Disk backup

11. Privacy protection

12. System restoration

13. System diagnostics

We recommend security suites that contain a firewall, even if you have Windows XP Service Pack 2. Here's why:

- The Windows XP Service Pack 2 Firewall does a good job of stopping unwanted inbound traffic. However, it does not check outbound traffic.

→ *For details on the Windows XP Firewall, see "Troubleshooting the Windows XP Firewall," Chapter 8, p. 542.*

- It's possible that a Trojan horse or zombie program on your PC could transmit data to an unknown remote user without your knowing it.

- Most commercial firewalls can stop outbound traffic from untrusted programs. Most programs implement this feature by detecting each attempt to access the Internet, flashing up a message, and asking you if the program has permission to access the Internet.

Slamming Spyware

Spyware is a general term for programs that track your web-surfing habits and display pop-up ads based on your interests; these programs are also called *adware*. Pop-up ads might appear even when you're not online, and they can drastically slow down your computer. Although many security suites are designed to detect and delete spyware and adware, infection rates continue to grow (child-oriented websites are notorious sources of spyware) and infection methods are getting more and more clever. Even if you have an anti-spyware security suite, you might want to use additional products to stop spyware and adware from taking over your PC.

Some of the leading anti-spyware programs include the following:

- **Ad-Aware**—www.lavasoftusa.com. The free SE Personal version can detect many types of spyware and adware; upgrade to SE Plus to block infections.

- **Spybot S&D (Search and Destroy)**—http://www.safer-networking.org. This free program detects infections and blocks unauthorized Registry changes to help prevent infections.

- **Microsoft AntiSpyware**—http://www.microsoft.com/athome/security/spyware/software/default.mspx. Microsoft offers its own scanner/infection blocker. Figure 2.36 illustrates some spyware programs detected during a typical scan.

If anything, spyware is sometimes harder to detect than viruses, and most anti-spyware experts recommend using two or more products to protect your system. It can be a pain to maintain multiple programs— although automatic updates make it easier than you'd think! However, the annoyance of scanning for problems is nothing compared to the frustration of watching spyware or adware bring your system to a crawl.

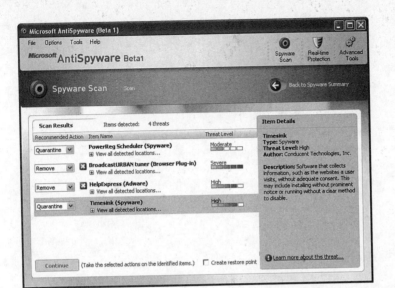

FIGURE 2.36

When Microsoft AntiSpyware detects spyware and adware, you can choose to quarantine, remove, or ignore it.

Troubleshooting Storage Devices

TROUBLESHOOTING

FAST TRACK TO SOLUTIONS (SYMPTOM TABLE)

Symptom	Flowchart or Book Section	See Page
I can't prepare the hard disk for use with any version of Windows.	Can't Prepare ATA/IDE Hard Drive After Installation	**680**
I can't copy files to an ATA/IDE hard drive.	Can't Change Contents of ATA/IDE Hard Drive	**682**
I can't partition an ATA/IDE drive.	Can't Change Contents of ATA/IDE Hard Drive	**682**
I can't delete or change files on an ATA/IDE drive.	Can't Change Contents of ATA/IDE Hard Drive	**680**
I can't format a floppy disk.	Can't Change Contents of Floppy Disk	**695**
I can't erase files from a floppy disk.	Can't Change Contents of Floppy Disk	**695**
I can't read a disk in the floppy drive.	Floppy Drive Problems	**694**
I can't save files to a floppy disk.	Can't Change Contents of Floppy Disk	**695**
I can't boot from the ATA/IDE hard disk.	Hard Drive Doesn't Boot	**681**
I can't access a newly installed ATA/IDE hard drive.	ATA/IDE Disk Drive Installation Troubleshooting	**679**
I can't use any drive connected to the ATA/IDE interface in my computer.	ATA/IDE Disk Drive and Device Troubleshooting	**679**
I can't read optical media.	General Optical Drive Problems	**683**
I can't erase, format, or save files to a removable-media disk (LS-120/240 SuperDisk, Zip Disk, Jaz, Orb, or others).	Removable Media Drive Problems	**693**
I'm having problems writing to CD-R or CD-RW media.	Troubleshooting CD-R and CD-RW Drives and Media	**686**
I can't read recordable (CD-R) media in the target drive.	Can't Read Recordable (CD-R) Media	**690**

TROUBLESHOOTING

FAST TRACK TO SOLUTIONS, *Continued*

Symptom	Flowchart or Book Section	See Page
I'm getting a buffer-underrun error when I try to create a recordable CD (CD-R).	Buffer Underrun Problems	685
I can't copy (drag and drop) files to a CD-R or CD-RW disc.	Can't Copy or Drag and Drop Files to CD-R or CD-RW Media	689
I can't read CD-RW media in the target computer.	Rewriteable (CD-RW) Media Problems	688
I can't delete files from a CD-RW disc.	Can't Delete Files from a CD-RW Disc	691
I can't read a particular recordable or rewriteable DVD disc with my DVD drive.	DVD Media Compatibility	684
I installed Y-splitters to power additional drives, and now I'm having problems.	Checking the Hard Disk Connection to the Power Supply	172
I just installed a new ATA/IDE drive, and the screen is blank when I turn on the computer.	Checking the Drive and Host Adapter Connection to the Data Cable	174
I've lost the documentation for my drive and need information about jumpers and other settings.	Sidebar: Got Questions? Ask the Drive Vendor.	178
I think my hard disk has failed.	Determining Actual Drive Failure Has Occurred	193
My IEEE-1394a or USB drive is detected when I plug it into the rear of the computer, but not when I plug it into a port on the front of the computer.	Sidebar: Connecting Front-Mounted Header Cables Is Trial by Error	429
My PC Card slots work, but a new PC Card drive I just plugged in isn't recognized.	Troubleshooting a PC Card/CardBus Drive	192

TROUBLESHOOTING

FAST TRACK TO SOLUTIONS, *Continued*

Symptom	Flowchart or Book Section	See Page
Windows XP recognizes my new hard disk, but Windows 98 can't read it.	Sidebar: Choosing the Right File System in Windows XP/2000	**196**
I keep running Disk Management but it can't partition the disk.	Troubleshooting Disk Partitioning Problems	**205**
My new CD-mastering program doesn't recognize my writeable drive.	Troubleshooting CD-Mastering Drive Support Problems	**223**
I'm not sure which connectors to use for master and slave ATA/IDE drives.	Table 3.2	**179**
I'm not sure how to jumper my ATA/IDE drives.	Table 3.2	**179**
I keep having buffer underruns with my rewritable CD or DVD drive.	Troubleshooting Buffer Underruns	**234**
I want to reuse CD-RW media written with Windows XP's CD Writing Wizard.	Erasing CD-RW Media Created with Windows XP's CD-Writing Wizard	**231**
I want to upgrade the hard disk in my portable computer to a larger, faster drive.	Upgrading a Portable Hard Disk	**210**
How can I help an existing DVD drive to read DL media?	Troubleshooting Incorrect Media and Media Usage Problems	**219**

Your "personal confuser's" hard disk is one of the most important parts of your PC. If the hard disk built into your system stops working, you can't load your operating system, you can't surf the Web, you can't play a game...well, you get the idea.

You might be using an external hard disk for additional storage or backup. If it stops working, whatever you stored on it isn't accessible. If that happens to be your collection of MP3 or WMA CD rips, it's going to be very quiet at your home or office until you get that hard disk back on line again and working.

Your CPU might be the fastest on your block and your memory might be smokin' fast, but if your hard disk decides not to wake up in the morning, your computer's nothing but a great big paperweight. Frankly, when I need a paperweight, a nicely polished rock works a lot better— and it's easier to lift besides!

Let's be honest—hard disk failures don't happen nearly as often as they did when the IBM PC was a newbie, but they still happen. It's not much consolation to find out that you're the only one in your circle of PC users with a sick hard disk. In this chapter, we'll help you find the reasons for hard disk problems, find the solutions, and show you how to get advance notice of problems before a sick hard disk dies and takes your data away.

If you're reading this book after your old hard disk has been packed off to the manufacturer for replacement, we can still help. You've got to get the new one installed, so let us help you with that process, too.

Troubleshooting Installed Hard Disk Drives

When you turn on your computer, you expect the system to start, load the operating system from the hard disk, and display the usual desktop or sign-on screen. If the screen comes on but the system never displays any activity from the hard disk, your system (boot) hard disk isn't working. If the hard disk that starts your computer isn't working correctly, you'll see an error message referring to a missing "boot device." Although the computer industry likes to use the term *booting* to refer to starting a computer, you're much more likely to want to "boot" your misbehaving PC in the general direction of the trash can!

If the ailing hard disk is an additional drive, such as an external hard disk, it won't show up in My Computer or Windows Explorer and you'll see a "Missing Shortcut" error when you try to access files or programs stored on it.

Instead of getting mad, or getting even, it's time to get smart. What happened? Before you get gloomy and decide that today's the day that your hard disk has really failed, cheer up! There are plenty of other reasons why your computer and your hard disk might not be talking to each other.

A few problems are the leading causes of apparent hard disk failure; they're so common that we like to call them the "usual suspects":

- Nonbootable floppy disk in drive A:
- Loose or missing power or data cables
- Incorrect hardware configuration
- Incorrect BIOS configuration

Whenever we have hard disks that don't want to work, it's useful to look at this list and note that there are many reasons other than actual hard disk failure for your hard disk to seem to "disappear" at startup time or not work properly.

To start your research, check out Table 3.1, where we present, in lineup form, the "usual suspects" that cause hard disks to disappear (as far as your PC is concerned) or not work correctly.

TABLE 3.1
THE USUAL SUSPECTS IN APPARENT HARD DISK FAILURES

Type of Drive	Why Hard Disk Doesn't Work	Solution
IDE/ATA, Serial ATA	Unbootable floppy disk in drive A:.	Remove the floppy disk and reboot.
	System power supply might not be connected to drive.	Shut down the system, attach the power connectors to the drive, and restart.
	Data cable is not connected at all or not connected properly.	Shut down the system and then reconnect the cable to the drive and ATA/IDE or SATA interface.

TABLE 3.1 (continued)

Type of Drive	Why Hard Disk Doesn't Work	Solution
IEEE-1394 (FireWire, i.Link)	Port disabled.	Verify that the port is working by using Device Manager.
	Drive not powered on.	Check the power going to the drive.
	Port can't provide power to drive.	Check that you are using a 6-wire 1394a port. Only 6-wire 1394a ports can power a 1394 drive; 4-wire ports do not provide power.
USB	Port disabled.	Verify that the port is working by using Device Manager.
	Drive not powered on.	Check the power going to the drive.

Table 3.1 gives you an overview of the "usual suspects" and their solutions. If you're an ace hardware detective, Table 3.1 and the cross-references that follow may be all you need to apprehend the culprit.

But if you're a novice at tracking down a troublesome component, keep reading.

Non-Bootable Floppy Disk in Drive A:

When we're on the track of computer troublemakers, we always start with the simplest solutions first. That's not an original idea with us, by the way. It goes back to a medieval philosopher named William of Occam, who developed the notion (known to history as *Occam's razor*) that the simplest solution that fits the facts of a particular case is the favored solution.

What's the simplest reason for a system not to boot? Check for a floppy disk in drive A:.

Hardly any floppy disks are formatted as bootable drives anymore. However, if your computer's BIOS is configured to look at the floppy drive as the first boot device and there are no operating system files on the floppy disk, your computer assumes there are no boot devices anywhere else and stops the startup process.

The simple fix? Eject the floppy disk, restart your computer (you can use the "three-finger salute" of Ctrl+Alt+Del or the reset button), and

→ For more information about the ATA/IDE interface, see "The ATA/IDE Interface," Chapter 1, p. 30.

→ For more information about the Serial ATA (SATA) interface, see "The Serial ATA (SATA) Interface," Chapter 1, p. 33.

→ For more information about USB, see "USB 1.1 and USB 2.0 Ports," Chapter 7, p. 412, and "Troubleshooting USB Ports and Hubs," Chapter 7, p. 418.

→ For more information about IEEE-1394 (Fire/Wire, i.Link), see "IEEE-1394a (FireWire 400) Ports," Chapter 7, p. 413, and "Troubleshooting IEEE-1394 Ports and Hubs," Chapter 7, p. 427.

when your PC restarts, it won't be stopped by an unbootable floppy disk.

The long-term solution? Take the floppy disk out of the boot sequence. Take a trip over to Chapter 1, "PC Anatomy 101," and read "Controlling Your PC's Operation with BIOS Setup," p. 41, to learn how.

If you've already checked out the floppy drive and found it empty, or your computer still can't boot after you remove the floppy disk, it's time to continue to the next suspect in hard disk problems.

To know where to go next, go back to Table 3.1 or the Symptom Table at the start of this chapter, determine the type of hard disk that's not working, and go to the appropriate part of the chapter.

Troubleshooting ATA/IDE Hard Disks

Most computers, whether they're desktop or notebook, use ATA/IDE hard disk drives as their primary storage. Figure 3.1 shows typical examples of both varieties.

FIGURE 3.1
ATA/IDE notebook (left) and desktop (right) hard disk drives.

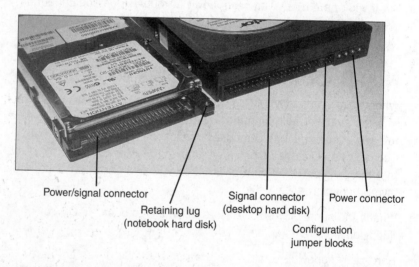

Power/signal connector

Retaining lug
(notebook hard disk)

Signal connector
(desktop hard disk)

Power connector

Configuration
jumper blocks

What causes an existing ATA/IDE hard disk to "disappear" from the system so you can't boot from it or access data on it? Any of the following:

- **The hard disk is not connected to power or the power cable is loose.** If the hard disk doesn't have a reliable connection to power, it never spins up and is never detected by your system. During installation of the drive, be sure to firmly connect the drive to a power cable coming from the power supply. If you use a Y-splitter or power cable extender, be sure the splitter or extender is in good condition and is firmly connected to the power cable and to the drive. Take a good look at Figure 3.2 later in this chapter to see the right way to connect the power cable.

- **The hard disk is not properly connected to the ATA/IDE host adapter on the motherboard or add-on card.** If the hard disk isn't properly connected to the interface, it won't receive the command to spin up when the computer is turned on, and your system won't boot. The 80-wire cables used by recent hard disks are keyed (see Figure 3.4) to prevent reversed connections, but 40-pin cables and some older systems don't support keying, making it possible for the cable to be installed upside down at either the host adapter or drive end.

- **Damage has occurred to the signal cable or power cable.** Replace cables that have creases across the wires, nicks, cuts or tears, or have cracked or loose connectors.

Notebook Hard Disks Are Different

A 2.5-inch ATA/IDE hard disk used in a notebook or laptop computer uses a single 44-pin connection for power and data instead of the 40-pin connection plus 4-pin power connector used by desktop ATA/IDE hard disks (refer to Figure 3.1). In an emergency, you can use an adapter to connect a 2.5-inch drive to a desktop computer to perform data recovery.

If you're installing a new ATA/IDE hard disk but you're unable to prepare it for use, you can also have problems with power and data cables. Plus, two other possible causes join the list:

- The hard disk could be configured as "Not present" or "none" in the system BIOS. The drive should be configured using the Auto setting to enable the drive to report its configuration to the system.

- The drive is not jumpered correctly. The older 40-wire cables require that one drive be jumpered as master and the other as slave; some brands of drives don't use jumpers if only one drive is on the cable. On the other hand, 80-wire cables use cable select jumpers for both drives, using the position of the drive on the cable to determine which drive is the primary (master) and which the secondary (slave) drive. Now that you know what can cause your system to have problems recognizing your existing or newly installed ATA/IDE hard disk, it's time to learn how to fix these problems.

Checking the Hard Disk Connection to the Power Supply

Virtually every ATA/IDE desktop hard disk drive uses a 4-pin Molex power connector. The same power connector, by the way, is also used by ATA/IDE optical drives (CD-RW, DVD-ROM, DVD rewritable, and so forth), and a small version is used by some types of ATA/IDE removable-media drives and by floppy drives. If the power connection is not connected to a matching lead from the system's power supply, the computer will never "see" your hard disk.

Sometimes it's necessary to connect a Y-splitter to the end of a single power cable to provide power to two hard disk drives or a hard disk and an optical drive (see Figure 3.2). A Y-splitter that's not well made (thin-gauge wires, not properly insulated) can prevent one or both drives from receiving power.

Whether you connect the hard disk directly to a power supply lead or use an extender or splitter, it takes a bit of force to make a solid connection with the Molex connectors shown in Figure 3.2; make sure the drive is attached solidly to the power cable.

Don't Overload the Power Supply

If your computer has a power supply with a rating under 400 watts, think twice about using a lot of splitters to power additional drives and case fans. To avoid problems, don't use a split cable to power a processor fan, and don't use a split cable to power two optical drives (the laser and motor mechanisms in an optical drive, such as a CD-RW or DVD rewritable drive, require much more power than a hard drive does). It's acceptable to split power between a hard drive and an optical drive or a drive and a case fan, but it's better to upgrade to a higher-wattage power supply of at least 400 watts that also provides more power connectors for drives and fans.

Remember: If your hard disk doesn't receive enough power, it won't spin, and your computer won't know it's there.

Master/slave/cable
select jumper on drive

ATA/IDE data
cable connector
on drive

Extra power
connector provided
by splitter

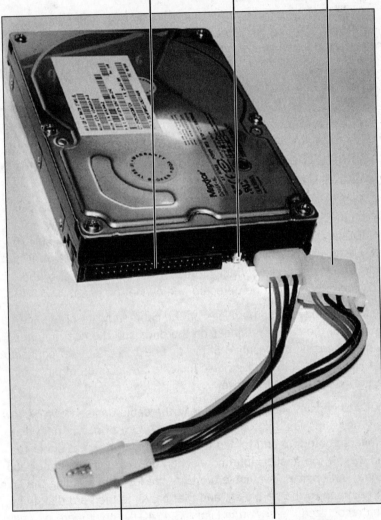

FIGURE 3.2

A typical ATA/IDE hard drive attached to a Y-splitter power cable before installation into a system.

Connection to power
supply (using a Y-splitter cable)

Power connector to hard drive

Been Inside Your PC Lately? Loose Cables Can Happen to You!

No matter how hard I try to keep data and power cables tucked neatly out of the way in my desktop computer, I still find cables all over the place when I open my system for cleaning or hardware upgrades. Sometimes I need to disconnect a drive's data or power cable to make an upgrade. I like to use a sticky note to remind myself to reconnect the cable when I finish the upgrade. Otherwise, it's way too easy to forget.

Checking the Drive and Host Adapter Connection to the Data Cable

The second suspect in the "case of the disappearing hard disk" is the data cable. On a desktop computer, the connection between an ATA/IDE host adapter and the drive is made with a 40-pin cable (the cable itself can have 40 or 80 wires, as shown in Figure 3.4). If the cable is not connected correctly to either the host adapter or the drive, the drive will not be detected and cannot be used.

The contrasting-colored markings on the cable indicate pin 1; line up this side of the cable with pin 1 on the drive and the host adapter. In almost all cases, the location of pin 1 is next to the power connector (see Figure 3.3). Most drives also indicate the location of pin 1 on the bottom or rear of the drive.

What's to prevent you from plugging in the cable upside down? A few years ago, alas, the answer was "nothing!" A lot of novice hard disk installers goofed up and turned the cable upside down at either the hard disk or the host adapter connection on the motherboard or add-on card. An upside-down cable prevents the PC from sending the spin-up command to the hard disk, and that prevents the hard disk from being recognized. As shown in Figure 3.4, 40-pin cables are typically not keyed, making incorrect installation all too easy.

If you use 80-wire cables (as you should with today's hard disks), don't worry. As Figure 3.4 shows, they're keyed with a projection on one side of the cable (and sometimes a blocked hole for pin 20) to prevent incorrect installation.

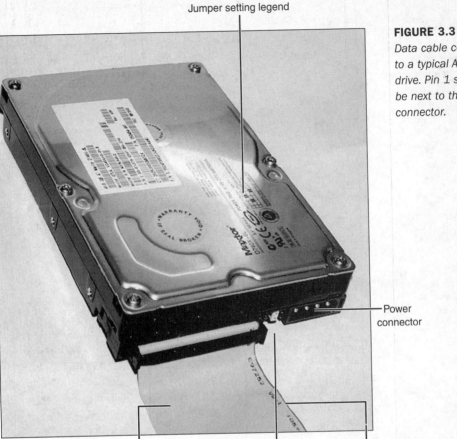

Jumper setting legend

Power connector

Jumper set to cable select

80-wire data cable

Stripe indicating pin 1 (should be on side nearest the power connector)

FIGURE 3.3

Data cable connections to a typical ATA/IDE drive. Pin 1 should be next to the power connector.

Leo Says

Why 40-Wire ATA/IDE Cables Are Off My List

I don't use 40-wire cables anymore, even for optical drives (which are often still packaged with this type of cable for some reason). The additional wires in an 80-wire cable provide a signal ground to support faster transfer rates, making the cable more reliable for any type of hard disk or other ATA/IDE drive.

I probably have a shoebox's worth of these cables in my junk drawers, and that's where they'll stay (unless I just throw them out)!

FIGURE 3.4

An 80-wire keyed ATA/IDE data cable compared to a 40-wire unkeyed ATA/IDE data cable.

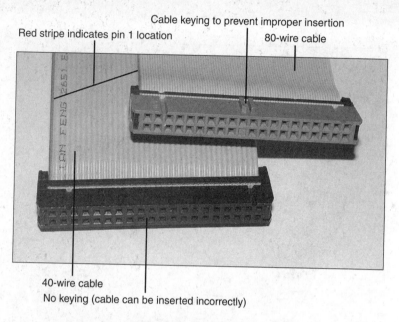

Red stripe indicates pin 1 location

Cable keying to prevent improper insertion

80-wire cable

40-wire cable

No keying (cable can be inserted incorrectly)

A data cable is useless unless it's connected to a host adapter. The ATA/IDE host adapter is usually on the motherboard. Figure 3.5 shows how to attach an 80-wire cable to the host adapter. Note the markings for pin 1 on the motherboard and how the keyed cable prevents incorrect installation. There are usually two ATA/IDE host adapters, and some computers have more. Use the lowest-numbered host adapter for your system hard disk.

Some Motherboards Make It Easy to Install a Cable the Wrong Way

Some motherboards don't surround their ATA/IDE or floppy cable connections with a plastic skirt as shown in Figure 3.5. Whether you're installing a new ATA/IDE hard disk or reconnecting the data cable after removing it temporarily for an upgrade, it's very easy on such motherboards to incorrectly connect the cable to just one row of pins or to miss some pins entirely. These types of cabling faults also prevent the drive from being detected and can lead to bent pins. In such cases, look for a marking on the motherboard or in the instruction manual that indicates the location of pin 1 and connect the end of the cable with the red stripe (refer to Figure 3.4) to pin 1.

Avoid problems with all types of ribbon cables by using a flashlight and a magnifier to help you see the cable and the connector during installation.

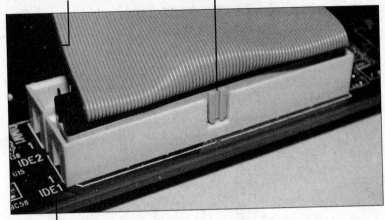

Stripe indicating pin 1
orientation on cable

Keyed cable inserted into
host adapter socket

FIGURE 3.5
*An 80-wire ATA/IDE
cable properly
attached to the host
adapter on the mother-
board.*

Host adapter number and pin 1
markings on motherboard

Configuring ATA/IDE Drive Jumpers

When you took the PC tour that's the highlight of Chapter 1, you might
have been surprised to discover that an ATA/IDE cable can support
two drives. When you install a new ATA/IDE hard disk or other drive,
how does the computer tell which drive is which?

Unlike a floppy drive cable, which uses a twist at the end of the cable
to indicate drive A: and drive B:, an ATA/IDE cable is a straight-through
cable. An ATA/IDE drive is configured as master or slave with jumper
blocks on the rear or bottom of the drive. The position of the jumper
blocks and the type of cable used determines which drive is the primary (master) and which the secondary (slave) drive. These jumpers
are used in the same way on any ATA/IDE device, including optical and
removable-media drives.

ATA/IDE drives have three basic configurations that can be selected
with jumper blocks (see Figure 3.6):

- Master (MA)
- Slave (SL)
- Cable Select (CS, CSEL)

Figure 3.6 shows the most common jumper location and the various
jumpering options supported on a typical hard disk.

FIGURE 3.6

The jumper pins and jumpering options available for Western Digital hard disks.

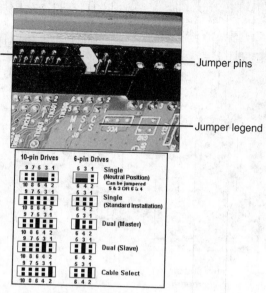

Jumper block set to Master — Jumper pins

Jumper legend

Other brands of hard disks use slightly different jumper block configurations; be sure to follow the labeling or instructions for the particular hard disk you are installing or troubleshooting.

Leo Says

Got Questions? Ask the Drive Vendor!

To learn more about the drives in your system, including performance, jumper settings, and setup utilities, check the manufacturer's website. Major desktop hard disk drive makers include the following:

- **Hitachi**—For Hitachi hard disks (including the former IBM Ultrastar, Deskstar, Travelstar, and Microdrive product lines), see http://www.hitachigst.com.

- **Maxtor**—For Maxtor and Quantum hard disk drives, see http://www.maxtor.com.

- **Samsung**—For Samsung hard disk drives, see http://www.samsung.com.

- **Seagate**—For Seagate and Conner Peripherals hard disk drives, see http://www.seagate.com.

- **Western Digital**—For Western Digital hard disk drives, see http://www.wdc.com.

Different jumper settings are recommended for 40-wire and 80-wire ATA/IDE data cables. Table 3.2 helps you figure it out.

TABLE 3.2
CORRECT JUMPER SETTINGS FOR A NEW ATA DRIVE INSTALLATION

Cable Type	Drive Installed As	How to Jumper	Which Cable Connector to Use	Jumper Original Drive As
80-wire	Slave	Cable Select or Slave[1]	Gray connector (middle of cable)	Cable Select or Master[1]
	Only drive on cable	Cable Select, Master, or single drive[1]	Black connector (end of cable)	N/A
	Master	Cable Select or Master[1]	Black connector (end of cable)	Cable Select or Slave[1]
40-wire	Slave	Slave	Either	Master
	Only drive on cable	Master or single drive (check drive manufacturer recommendation)	Either	N/A
	Master	Master	Either	Slave

1. With 80-wire cables, we recommend you try Cable Select first. If you have problems with drive recognition, use Master or Slave settings as shown in the table. Drive recognition issues are more likely if you are mixing different brands of drives on the same cable.

Before You Change It, Write It Down!

If you need to change the jumpering or cable position of an existing drive when you install a new one, write down the original settings. Note that any drive plugged into an ATA/IDE cable, even if it's an optical or removable-media drive, follows the rules in Table 3.2.

Here's how to apply these settings when you install a new hard disk or other ATA/IDE device:

- **Master/slave**—A drive jumpered as master will be the primary drive on the cable; if you have your hard disk and optical drive on the same cable, the hard drive should be jumpered as master,

and the cable should be plugged into IDE connector number 1 on the motherboard.

- **Slave**—A drive jumpered as slave will be the secondary drive on the cable. If you have your hard disk and optical drive on the same cable, the optical drive should be jumpered as slave.

- **Cable select**—The position of the drive on the cable determines which drive is master and which is slave; Cable Select requires an 80-wire Ultra ATA cable. Some computer vendors use specially designed 40-wire cables that support Cable Select. Note that you can also use Master and Slave settings with 80-wire cables.

Leo Says

Color-Coding for Easier Cable Installation

Almost all 80-wire ATA/IDE cables are color-coded to help you figure out which connector to use for each drive and the host adapter. Use the blue connector for the host adapter on the motherboard or ATA/IDE add-on card. Some motherboards even use blue plastic for some of the ATA/IDE host adapter connectors to make matching the adapter to the cable as easy as possible. The black connector on the other end of the cable is for the primary (master) drive, and the gray connector in the middle of the cable is for the secondary (slave) drive.

Note: Some cables do not use the color-coding described here, but all ATA/IDE cables are made with the primary master connector on one end, the motherboard connector on the other, and the slave connector in the middle.

Checking a Laptop/Notebook's Hard Disk Power/Data Connection

We mentioned earlier in this chapter that a laptop or notebook computer's 2.5-inch hard disk drive uses a single 44-pin connection for power and data. The hard disk might plug into a fixed power/data connector or a flexible cable.

If you actually use your laptop or notebook as a portable computer and move it around frequently, the hard disk's connection to the notebook's motherboard could become loose, causing the hard disk not to be recognized at startup.

If the hard disk is accessed through a removable cover on the bottom of your portable computer, you can follow this procedure to check the connection:

1. Shut down your computer.

2. Unplug it.

3. Turn over your computer.

4. Use a small screwdriver to remove the retaining screw holding the cover and the hard disk in place. Figure 3.7 shows the relationship of the retaining screw and the hard disk as seen from the hard disk drive bay.

Cover over hard disk

Retaining screw

Retaining lug

FIGURE 3.7
Detail view of a 2.5-inch ATA/IDE hard disk and its retaining screw.

5. Slide the hard disk out of the computer.

6. Reinsert the hard disk, making sure it connects tightly to the host adapter power/signal connector in the drive bay. Figure 3.8 shows a top view of the hard disk, retaining lug, and host adapter connector.

7. Close the access cover.

8. Reinsert the retaining screw.

If the hard disk cannot be accessed from the bottom or side of your portable computer, check the manual or the manufacturer's website to learn how to check the hard disk connection. You might need to remove the keyboard or other components to get to the hard disk.

➔ *If you need to install a replacement hard disk in a portable computer, see "Upgrading a Portable Hard Disk," this chapter, p. 210, for complete instructions.*

FIGURE 3.8
Reinserting a portable computer's hard disk into the drive bay and host adapter.

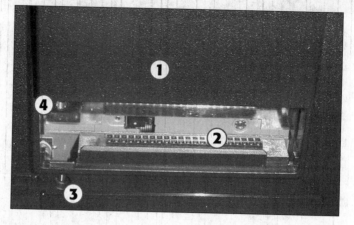

1. Cover over hard disk
2. Signal/power connector in drive bay
3. Hole for retaining screw
4. Retaining lug (positioned under hole for retaining screw when hard disk is completely inserted in drive bay)

Troubleshooting Serial ATA (SATA) Hard Disk Drives

Serial ATA (SATA) hard disks are slowly starting to replace ATA/IDE hard disks in new desktop computer systems, primarily mid-range and high-end models. Figure 3.9 shows a typical SATA hard disk.

Compared to an ATA/IDE hard disk, an SATA hard disk has a much smaller data cable and a wider, thinner power cable connection.

What causes an existing SATA hard disk to "disappear" from the system so you can't boot from it or access data on it? Any of the following might take the blame:

- **The hard disk is not connected to power or the power cable is loose.** If the hard disk doesn't have a reliable connection to power, it never spins up and is never detected by your system. During installation of the drive, be sure to firmly connect the drive to a power cable coming from the power supply. If you use an adapter to convert a 4-wire Molex connector to SATA, make sure the adapter is in good condition and is firmly connected to the power cable and to the hard disk.

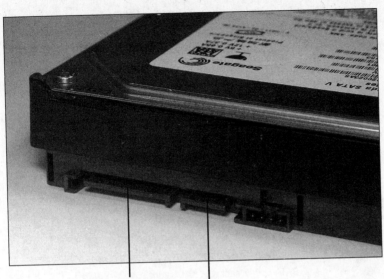

FIGURE 3.9
The power and data cable connectors at the rear of a Seagate Barracuda SATA V hard disk.

SATA power connector
SATA signal connector

- **The hard disk is not properly connected to the SATA host adapter on the motherboard or add-on card.** If the hard disk isn't properly connected to the interface, it won't receive the command to spin up when the computer is turned on, and your system won't boot. The SATA cable and cable connector are keyed, preventing reversed connections, but it's possible, particularly with the original SATA connector shown in Figure 3.9, for the SATA signal cable (see Figure 3.10) to fall off the hard disk.

- **Damage to the signal or power cable can also cause an SATA hard disk to appear to fail.** Replace SATA signal cables that have been creased or folded. Replace SATA signal or power cables that have cracked or torn wires or insulation as well as those that have cracked connectors. Note that an SATA data cable should *never* be folded; folding can damage the small data and signal wires inside the outer jacket.

Figure 3.10 illustrates correct connections between the SATA drive and its data and power cables.

As we noted previously in this chapter, you can cause problems with an existing SATA hard disk if you need to open your system, remove a cable or two to perform a different upgrade, and forget to plug the cables back in. What about a brand-new SATA hard disk installation?

FIGURE 3.10

Power and data cables connected to a Seagate Barracuda SATA V hard disk.

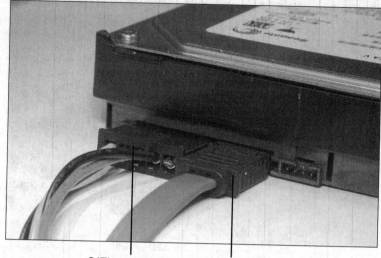

SATA power cable　　SATA signal cable

You can have problems with a loose SATA signal cable or power cable during a new drive installation, but don't overlook these possibilities:

- The SATA host adapter on the motherboard might be disabled in the system BIOS. Although many recent systems include two or more SATA host adapters, many vendors disable them by default, as shown in Figure 3.11.

- You forgot to install drivers for an add-on SATA host adapter during Windows installation. Restart Windows, watch for the prompt to press F6 to install a third-party SCSI or RAID driver, and provide the SATA host adapter or chipset driver disk.

Check out Chapter 1 to learn how to give your BIOS some help in detecting your SATA hard disk.

Now it's time to learn how to fix problems with recognizing your SATA hard disk.

Checking the SATA Hard Disk Power Connector

SATA hard disks use an edge connector (refer to Figure 3.9) to connect to the computer's power supply, although a few might also support a Molex connector. Although many new power supplies include leads with SATA power connectors, the power supply in your PC might not. For that reason, many SATA hard disks and motherboards with onboard SATA host adapters include a Molex-to-SATA power cable adapter (see Figure 3.12).

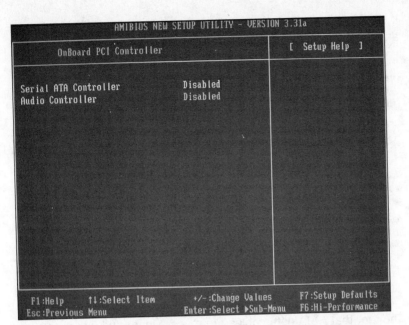

FIGURE 3.11
If the onboard Serial ATA host adapter isn't enabled, your SATA drive is not going to work.

Although the SATA power cable slides easily over the SATA power connector at the rear of an SATA hard disk, it takes some force to plug the Molex connector end into the Molex connector from the power supply. Make sure the power cable adapter is plugged tightly into the Molex power lead. Whether you use a built-in SATA power cable or an adapter, make sure the SATA power cable is plugged securely into the hard disk.

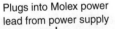

Plugs into Molex power
lead from power supply

Plugs into SATA hard disk

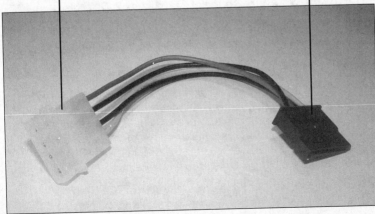

FIGURE 3.12
A typical Molex-to-SATA power adapter.

If somebody (hopefully not you!) steps on an SATA power connector and cracks it, get a replacement. A cracked power connector is not going to be reliable.

Leo Says

Damaged Cables Belong in the Trash, Not in Your PC

Installing a cable with a damaged connector is like installing a kind of hardware virus with an unknown trigger. You know your system's going to crash sooner or later, it's just a question of when. Murphy's Law—whatever *can* go wrong, *will* go wrong—applies double when you install a broken piece of hardware. Don't do it!

Checking the SATA Data Cable

The fact that SATA data cables are much thinner and use a much smaller connector than ATA/IDE cables can sometimes be a mixed blessing. They're so small and thin that it's easy to break them!

An SATA host adapter uses the same L-shaped connector as an SATA hard disk. The L-shaped keying makes it impossible to reverse the cable, which is a definite advantage over its ATA/IDE ancestors. Figure 3.13 shows you how much smaller the SATA motherboard connector is than an ATA/IDE motherboard connector.

Leo Says

Got a SecureConnect Hard Disk? Get SecureConnect Cables!

Some of Western Digital's recent SATA hard disks feature a better way to secure the SATA data cable. WD calls this feature *SecureConnect*.

SecureConnect uses the same power and data connectors as standard Serial ATA, but it adds plug-in mounts on both sides of the standard connectors that are designed to mate with a wide one-piece connector. If you use Western Digital SATA hard disks that feature SecureConnect, I suggest you seriously consider ordering the special SecureConnect cables from the Western Digital online store; see http://www.wdc.com for details.

ATA/IDE host adapter

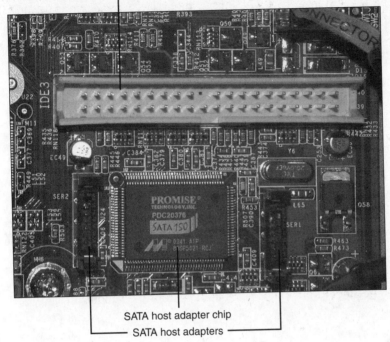

FIGURE 3.13

An ATA/IDE mother-board-based host adapter (top) compared to a pair of SATA host adapters (bottom).

SATA host adapter chip

SATA host adapters

Troubleshooting IEEE-1394 Drives

If you're out of space on your built-in hard disk, don't want to struggle with a hard disk upgrade, and want to share a hard disk between two or more PCs, consider an external IEEE-1394 or a USB 2.0 drive. IEEE-1394 and USB 2.0 hard disks offer Plug-and-Play installation, hot-swap capabilities, capacities rivaling desktop drives, and relatively high data-transfer rates. Although these drives are good choices for expanding data capacity (they can hold tens of thousands of digital photos or music downloads!), keep in mind that these drives should not be used as bootable system drives. They are slower than ATA/IDE and SATA drives, and many systems are not designed to boot from an external drive.

However, none of that matters if you have a problem with your drive or with the IEEE-1394 ports on your PC.

Any of the following can spoil the instant "plug it in and it's ready" joy of a fast external hard disk (or any other 1394 device, for that matter):

- You have a disabled or improperly cabled IEEE-1394 port on your computer.

- Resource conflict exists between IEEE-1394 port and another device.

- The drive is not powered on.

- You haven't installed the correct drivers for your version of Windows and your drive.

→ To learn how to use the Device Manager to diagnose your ports or other system problems, see "Using the Device Manager," Chapter 2, p. 100.

Before you connect an IEEE-1394 drive to your system, make sure the port is enabled and supported by your version of Windows. To do this, open the Device Manager and verify that the port is listed and that it is not reporting any problems.

Make sure you have drivers for your drive and version of Windows. You can get them from Windows Update or from the vendor.

Leo Says

Sorting Out the Flavors of IEEE-1394

I don't know whether to be amused or annoyed at how many names there are for IEEE-1394. Properly speaking, the 6-pin or 4-pin IEEE-1394 port we see on most systems is IEEE-1394a, also known to Mac fans as FireWire 400. Sony calls the 4-pin 1394a port an "i.Link" port.

Some new systems and add-on cards support a 9-pin port known as IEEE-1394b, which runs twice as fast (800Mbps versus 400Mbps) as IEEE-1394a. A bilingual 1394b port can connect to 1394a devices with an adapter cable. Oh, did I mention that 1394b is also called FireWire 800?

If you have the appropriate drivers for your 1394-based hard disk and 1394 host adapter but your drive is not recognized, you might be having problems with your system's 1394 ports. See "Troubleshooting IEEE-1394 Ports and Hubs," Chapter 7, p. 427, for help.

Troubleshooting Other Problems with an IEEE-1394 Drive

If the port is working but the drive is not detected when you attach it to the system, check these issues:

- If the drive's instructions require you to install driver or configuration software before you attach the drive, disconnect the drive from the system, install the software, and reconnect the drive.

- Unplug the device cable from the IEEE-1394 port on the computer and reattach it.

- Make sure the drive is connected to AC power (if it isn't powered by the port) and turned on. Remember that 6-pin 1394a cables and bilingual 1394b ports using 6-pin 1394a adapters can provide power to a device, but a 4-pin DV camcorder or i.Link-style cable can't. See Figure 3.14 for examples of cable connectors.

- Make sure that the IEEE-1394 cable is attached securely to the drive.

- If, after you've reconnected the power and IEEE-1394 cables, Windows does not automatically detect the device, run the Add Hardware Wizard. Open the Control Panel through the Start menu, click Add Hardware (called Add New Hardware on some Windows versions), and follow the prompts to detect and install your new drive.

- Replace the IEEE-1394 cable if the drive still can't be detected and retry.

Don't Run Out of Power with a CardBus IEEE-1394 Card

If you attach devices to an IEEE-1394 CardBus (32-bit PC Card) adapter in a notebook computer, make sure the devices are self-powered or connect an AC adapter to the IEEE-1394 card. The CardBusslot can't provide enough power to support bus-powered IEEE-1394 devices. If your IEEE-1394 CardBus wasn't shipped with an AC adapter, contact the vendor for details about compatible units.

FIGURE 3.14

1394a and 1394b cables compared.

Four-pin (i.Link-type)
1394a cable

Six-pin 1394a cable

1394b beta cable

1394b bilingual cable
(port can be adapted to
1394a devices)

➔ For more details about using the system BIOS setup program to troubleshoot USB devices, see "Using the System BIOS to Solve Problems with USB Devices," Chapter 7, p. 435.

➔ To learn how to diagnose problems with USB 2.0 support, see "Troubleshooting USB 2.0 (Hi-Speed USB) Support," Chapter 7, p. 418.

➔ To learn how to diagnose resource conflict or driver problems with USB 1.1 and USB 2.0 ports, see "Installing the Right Device Drivers for Your USB Device," Chapter 7, p. 423, and "Diagnosing Port and Driver Problems with Device Manager," Chapter 7, p. 416.

Troubleshooting a USB Drive

If you've used a computer for several years, you're probably astounded at how many different types of devices can be connected to a USB port. It truly is a *Universal* Serial Bus! Portable hard disks, flash memory drives, and flash memory card readers all find the USB port a popular way to expand storage.

However, if your USB ports have problems, USB storage (and any other USB device) will just sit there until you get the ports working again. Here are some of the most common problems with USB ports:

- USB ports on your computer are disabled; a device connected to a disabled port cannot be detected until the port is enabled.

- Your USB 2.0 drive is operating slowly because you have connected it to USB 1.1 ports, or the USB 2.0 ports are not configured properly.

- The USB data cable is too long or is defective. Use a cable no longer than 5 meters (about 16.5 feet). If you need a longer connection between the drive and the system, you can use a self-powered hub or an active (self-powered) cable.

- A USB port on the front of the system is not properly connected to the motherboard.

- A resource conflict exists between the USB port and another device.

- The drive is not powered on or is not configured for the correct power source. Select AC power if the drive is using an AC adapter, and select DC power if the drive is receiving power from the USB port or the PS/2 keyboard port.

- You haven't installed the correct drivers for your version of Windows and your drive. You should install drivers included with your drive before connecting your drive to the system.

- Your drive requires more power than the USB port can provide (see Figure 3.15).

➔ *To learn how to check USB front-panel connectors for proper installation, see "Front Panel Connectors," Chapter 1, p. 35.*

➔ *To learn how to diagnose power problems with USB ports and hubs, see "Troubleshooting USB Hub Power Problems," Chapter 7, p. 425.*

How hub is powered

Hub type   Power available per port

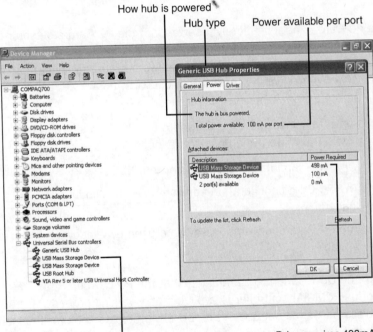

USB drive with problems

Drive requires 498mA (more than hub can provide)

FIGURE 3.15
The USB Mass Storage Device (drive) isn't working because it draws more power than a bus-powered hub can provide.

Troubleshooting a PC Card/CardBus Drive

PC Cards (also called *PCMCIA cards*) provide a wide variety of I/O services to portable computers. Some external drives can be connected to a PC Card or CardBus (32-bit PC Card) interface. A PC Card or CardBus interface drive is useless, however, if any of the following problems are lurking about:

- The PC Card is not completely inserted.
- PC Card handlers are not installed in the operating system.
- The drive attached to the PC Card is not connected to a power source (if it requires external power) or turned on. Although most PC Card devices are powered by the PC Card slot, some devices that can be connected to multiple interface types have an on/off switch.

If a PC Card is not completely inserted into the PC Card slot, you need to eject it and slide it in all the way. When it is installed, you should see a PC Card icon appear in the Windows system tray, by default, at the bottom of the screen (next to the clock). Windows XP refers to this icon as the Safely Remove Hardware icon.

If you have fully inserted a PC Card into the PC Card slot and it is not recognized, there are three possible reasons:

- Windows cannot locate drivers for the PC Card.
- The PC Card configuration software used by Windows is not loaded.
- The PC Card configuration software used by Windows might have a problem.

Open the Device Manager and verify that the PC Card or CardBus(PCMCIA) controller is available and working properly. If the controller is visible but doesn't report any problems, look for the icon for the device you installed. If it was recognized as a PC Card or CardBus device, it will be listed in the PCMCIA category in Device Manager. If you don't see the device listed in the PCMCIA category, it might be listed in the Other Devices category (see Figure 3.16). Open the device's properties sheet to verify that the device is installed in the PCMCIA slot. Follow the troubleshooting instructions listed; normally, you will need to install the correct driver for the device to enable Windows to recognize it.

Problem with device

Device is connected to the CardBus slot

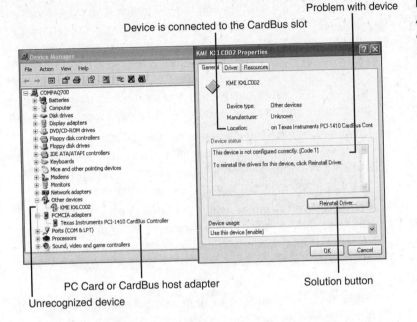

FIGURE 3.16
An unrecognized device installed in a PCMCIA (PC Card or CardBus) slot.

PC Card or CardBus host adapter

Solution button

Unrecognized device

→ **For more information on using the Solution button shown in Figure 3.16, see "Solving Resource Conflicts with Device Manager," Chapter 2, p. 102.**

If the controller is not visible, run Add New Hardware and install or troubleshoot it. A PC Card or CardBus controller is a very resource-hungry beast, using an IRQ, several memory ranges, and several I/O port address ranges. However, it should work correctly unless its drivers have been corrupted or another device is using one or more of the same memory or I/O port address ranges. If the controller is displayed but has problems, use the status listed in the controller's properties sheet to determine the problem and solve it.

→ **See "Using the Device Manager," Chapter 2, p. 100, for details on troubleshooting hardware devices.**

If the drive attached to the PC Card is not connected to a power source (if it has one) or turned on, the card might be recognized, but the drive will not work. Turn the drive on. If the drive won't power up, check the power connection to the drive.

→ **See "Hardware Resources," Chapter 1, p. 58, for details on how IRQs, I/O port addresses, and memory addresses are used by hardware.**

Determining Actual Drive Failure Has Occurred

Although today's hard disk drives are extremely reliable, it's still possible the drive itself has failed. Look for these indications of drive failure:

- **Drive will not power up**. To determine if an internal hard disk has failed, shut down the computer, place your hand on the top of the drive case, and turn on the computer. If you can't feel any vibration through the case (or you can't hear the drive turning) and the drive is connected to a working power supply, it's probably dead. With an external hard disk, make sure the drive is connected to a working power source (USB or IEEE-1394 port, AC adapter, or PS/2 keyboard port) and then hold your head next to the case; if you can't hear the drive running, it's probably dead.

- **Drive makes excessive noise when the system is turned on**. If the drive sounds like it has a marble loose inside or makes scraping or coffee-grinder noises as soon as you turn it on, it has sustained physical damage and is probably dead.

- **Computer won't turn on when the drive is attached to the power supply**. If your computer appears to be dead when you start it with the drive attached but powers up normally when you disconnect the power supply from the drive, the drive has a short-circuit and is probably dead.

- **Other devices connected to the same port work properly**. This is the classic method for discovering whether the port or the device is at fault. A faulty port can't use anything connected to it. But, a bad device is bad no matter where you connect it.

If optical and removable-media drives don't display any power lights at any time and won't spin up when you insert media, check their power, data cable, and jumper configuration as described earlier. If the drive's configuration checks out OK, and another drive works when connected to the same cable, the original drive is certainly damaged or dead and should be replaced.

Preparing a Hard Disk for Use

Preparing a hard disk for use in your PC is the process by which you set up the drive so that it can hold your data (everything from Windows to programs and documents files). Usually you'll only need to go through this process when installing a new drive. Occasionally, however, you might decide it's time to give your PC a fresh start, by erasing everything on your drives, re-preparing them, and installing fresh copies of your software. (If you ever decide to do this, be very sure that you've backed up any essential data to another storage medium.)

Leo Says

Understand Your Restore Options or Pay the Price in Lost Data

If you have a PC made by one of the big PC producers, such as HP/Compaq, Dell, IBM, and so on, you probably received a restore CD or two (or sometimes instructions on how to make them using files stored in a hidden partition on your hard disk). A restore CD or restore partition can work in one of two ways:

- Most restore CDs restore the computer's original software, *wiping out your data and other personal information in the process.*
- Some restore CDs can also repair Windows and applications without wiping out your data.

If you have serious enough problems to justify using a restore CD, make sure you know how yours works or else watch your data vanish!

In most PCs, the system BIOS handles configuration duties for ATA/IDE hard disk drives (the standard type of hard drive found in most systems). Many recent systems also support SATA hard disk drives through the system BIOS.

Preparing either of these types of hard disks requires the use of your operating system's disk preparation utilities (Disk Management in Windows XP or Windows 2000; FDISK and FORMAT in Windows 9x/Me). These programs process the disk according to what the system or SCSI BIOS report. If the system BIOS is not configured properly, an ATA/IDE drive will not be recognized at its full capacity.

Most systems are set to auto-detect the capacity of ATA/IDE or SATA hard disks when you install them and turn on the computer; this type of hard disk configuration is the most common type. You can determine if your version of Windows can view the entire capacity of the drive during the disk preparation process.

Preparing an Additional Hard Disk with Windows XP

The process of installing a hard disk varies according to whether the drive is being added to your computer or is being installed as a replacement. The process described in this section assumes that you are adding an additional hard disk to your existing computer.

Leo Says

It's All About the Gigabytes!

There's no such thing as too much hard disk space. I love the Western Digital "Filling Up!" animation that shows how quickly a 40GB hard disk (a common size in systems just a couple of years old) can become stuffed with data thanks to huge office suites, digital music downloads, and digital photographs. Try it yourself at http://www.wdc.com/en/products/fillrup/fillingup.asp.

If you need a new hard disk to store more data and downloads, adding an additional hard disk is the way to go. Buy the biggest one your system can handle. Keep in mind that internal hard disks are cheaper per gigabyte, but external hard disks can be shuttled from system to system.

If Windows has run out of space (you can tell this is happening if the Disk Cleanup utility keeps running and asking you to get rid of files), you need to replace your system hard disk instead. See "Preparing a Bootable Hard Disk with Windows XP," this chapter, p. 201.

Before you start this process, follow these steps:

1. You need to make sure your hard disk is recognized by your computer.

2. You should decide whether you want to prepare the new drive as a single drive letter or subdivide it into two or more logical drives.

3. You should decide which file system you want to use for your new drive.

Leo Says

Choosing the Right File System in Windows XP

If all you use is Windows XP, you should use the NTFS (New Technology File System) option to format your disk. NTFS lets you use advanced features such as encryption (which can be used to "hide" files on your system from other users) and compression (which uses less disk space). However, if you installed Windows XP to work in a dual-boot configuration with Windows 98 or Windows Me (you select the Windows version you want to work with when you boot), you might prefer to choose FAT32 for your new drive. Both NTFS and FAT32 can work with large drives, but FAT32 drives can be read by Windows 98 and Windows Me.

What if you want to share your files over a network? Use NTFS, no matter what version of Windows other users have. The network software will take care of recognizing the drive's contents, and NTFS lets you apply better security to each shared folder.

Here's how to prepare an additional hard drive for use with Windows XP (these directions also work with Windows 2000, by the way):

1. Open the Start menu, right-click My Computer, and select Manage.

2. Click the Storage icon in the left window of the Computer Management screen.

3. Double-click Disk Management (local) in the right window. The new drive will appear as "Unallocated" in the display window (see Figure 3.17) if the drive is brand new. If the drive has already been partitioned, the display will indicate what type of a partition is on the drive. You can right-click the additional drive's partition to remove it, but this will delete its contents. You should use My Computer to view the drive's contents first and copy any files you want to keep to another drive before you continue.

The drive's listed capacity should be similar to the capacity listed on the drive's faceplate or box. If not, see "Troubleshooting Problems with Recognizing Full Drive Capacity," this chapter, p. 203.

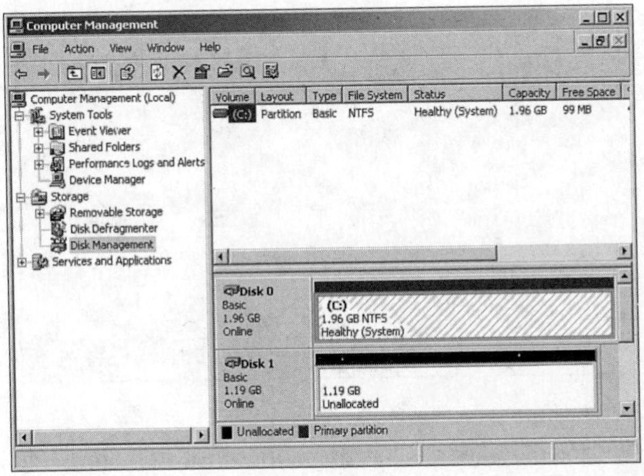

FIGURE 3.17
A hard disk (Disk 1) before partitioning and formatting (which assigns drive letters to the drive) as displayed by the Windows XP Disk Management tool.

4. Right-click the "Unallocated" drive and select New Partition to start the New Partition Wizard.

5. Click Next after reading the introduction to the wizard.

6. Select Extended partition and click Next to create an extended partition (which will be divided into one or more logical, non-bootable drive letters).

Want to Use a Boot Manager? Follow Its Instructions

If you want to boot from a drive you add to your system as well as from your normal drive, you will need to install a boot manager program such as Boot Magic (provided as part of Symantec's Norton Partition Magic) or V-com's System Commander (which includes Partition Commander) and prepare the drive as directed by the vendor. See the documentation for the boot manager program you prefer for details.

Learn more about Partition Magic and Boot Magic at http://www.symantec.com/partitionmagic/features.html.

Learn more about System Commander and Partition Commander at http://www.v-com.com/product/System_Commander_Home.html and http://www.v-com.com/product/Partition_Commander_Home.html.

7. If you want to use the entire hard disk for one or more logical drives, click Next. To leave some empty space on the drive for use by another operating system, adjust the partition size (see Figure 3.18) and click Next.

FIGURE 3.18

Configuring a hard disk as an extended partition with Windows XP's New Partition Wizard.

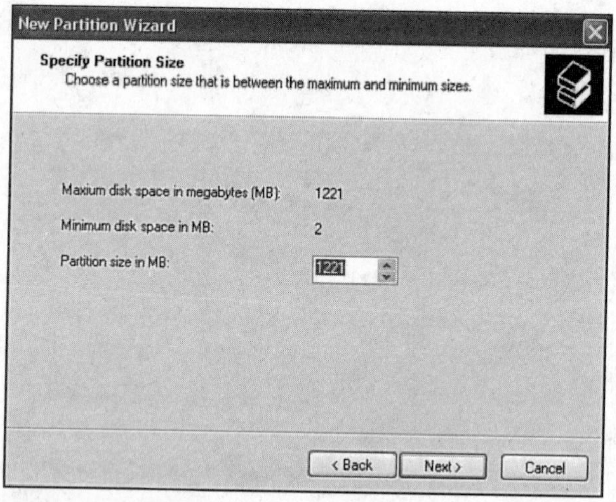

8. The wizard displays the settings you have selected; click Finish to perform the listed operations and convert the drive to an extended partition containing free space.

9. Right-click the free space and select New Logical Drive to set up drive letter(s) to use the free space inside the extended partition (see Figure 3.19). Click Next.

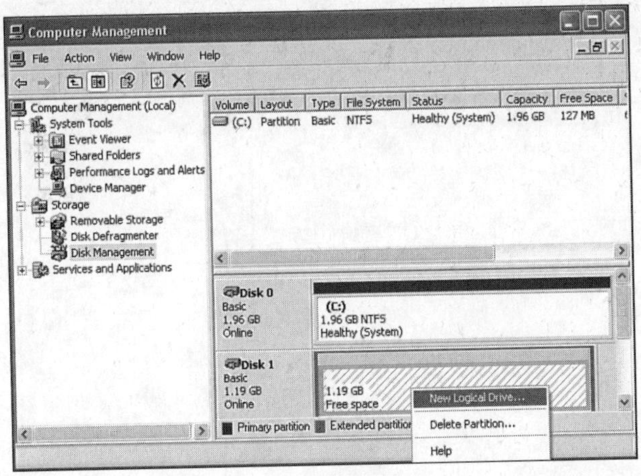

FIGURE 3.19
Preparing to create a logical drive in Windows XP.

10. Click Next to create a logical drive.

11. Specify the size of the logical drive if you want to create more than one logical drive; if you click Next without specifying a size, the entire free space will be converted into a single drive letter.

12. By default, Windows assigns the next available drive letter; click Next to accept it, or use the pull-down menu to choose a different drive letter and then click Next. Other options listed (Mount in Empty NTFS Folder and Do Not Assign a Drive Letter) are for advanced users.

13. Select a format option (see Figure 3.20). We recommend you use the defaults (NTFS and default allocation unit size) unless you need to access the drive by booting the computer with Windows 98 or Me. Change New Volume to a descriptive name you prefer. Select Enable File and Folder Compression if you want the option to try it later. Click Next.

14. The wizard displays the settings you have selected (see Figure 3.21). Click Finish to perform the listed operations and convert the free space into a drive letter, or click Back to make changes. The format operation takes a few minutes to complete.

Change to FAT32 only if Windows 98/Me will be
used to boot the system and access this drive.

FIGURE 3.20

*Selecting format
options for the new
logical drive.*

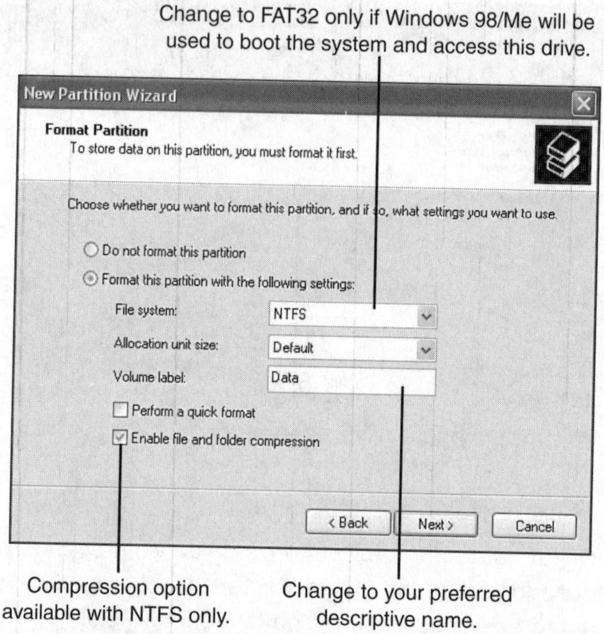

New Partition Wizard

Format Partition
To store data on this partition, you must format it first.

Choose whether you want to format this partition, and if so, what settings you want to use.

○ Do not format this partition
◉ Format this partition with the following settings:

File system: NTFS

Allocation unit size: Default

Volume label: Data

☐ Perform a quick format
☑ Enable file and folder compression

< Back   Next >   Cancel

Compression option
available with NTFS only.

Change to your preferred
descriptive name.

FIGURE 3.21

*The New Partition
Wizard displays the
settings selected for
preparing the new
drive.*

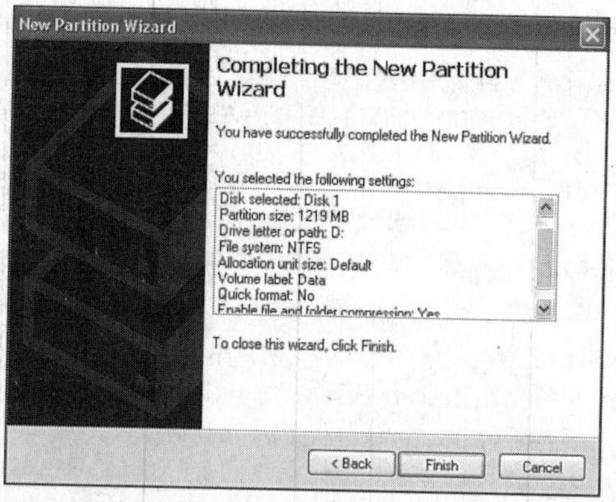

New Partition Wizard

**Completing the New Partition
Wizard**

You have successfully completed the New Partition Wizard.

You selected the following settings:

Disk selected: Disk 1
Partition size: 1219 MB
Drive letter or path: D:
File system: NTFS
Allocation unit size: Default
Volume label: Data
Quick format: No
Enable file and folder compression: Yes

To close this wizard, click Finish.

< Back   Finish   Cancel

15. When the format process is completed, the drive is identified
with a drive letter and its status should be displayed as Healthy
(contact the drive vendor if the drive is not identified as Healthy).
Click File, Exit to close Computer Management. You can use the
newly prepared drive immediately.

Leo Says

Drive Installation Wizards at Your Service, If You Prefer

I started working with hard disk drives long before manufacturers included easy-to-use software in the package. If you don't like fiddling with Windows to prepare your hard disk, use the tools provided by most hard disk vendors to do the job for you. If you didn't get a setup CD or floppy disk with your hard disk, visit the manufacturer's website and download an installation program.

I definitely recommend using a vendor-supplied installation tool if you're still using Windows 98 or Windows Me on some of your older computers. I know how to use FDISK and FORMAT to prepare hard disks in these systems, but those tools are not Windows based, are not user friendly, and frankly make it way too easy to fry your data by mistake.

Installation tools are also the way to go if you're replacing an undersized system (bootable) drive with a bigger, faster model. These programs can copy the contents of your old drive to your new drive during the installation process.

Preparing a Bootable Hard Disk with Windows XP

You can prepare a drive with a primary partition (primary partitions are bootable) with the Disk Management tool described in the previous section. Simply select Primary Partition when prompted and follow the general outline given previously. Generally, you will select this option if you are planning to install a boot manager program and another operating system on your computer.

If you need to replace your existing ATA/IDE or SATA hard disk with a larger hard disk, use the installation program provided with the hard disk or available from the hard disk vendor's website. These utilities can copy the data from the old hard disk to the new hard disk and make the process fairly painless.

However, if you want to prepare a new hard drive on a brand-new system (one that doesn't have Windows XP already installed), you can perform this task as part of the Windows installation process:

1. Verify that your CD-ROM drive is listed before your hard disk in the boot sequence of your computer's BIOS setup (see Figure 3.22).

➔ *To learn more about accessing your BIOS and changing its settings, see "Controlling Your PC's Operation with BIOS Setup," Chapter 1, p. 41.*

CD-ROM (#3 in boot sequence)

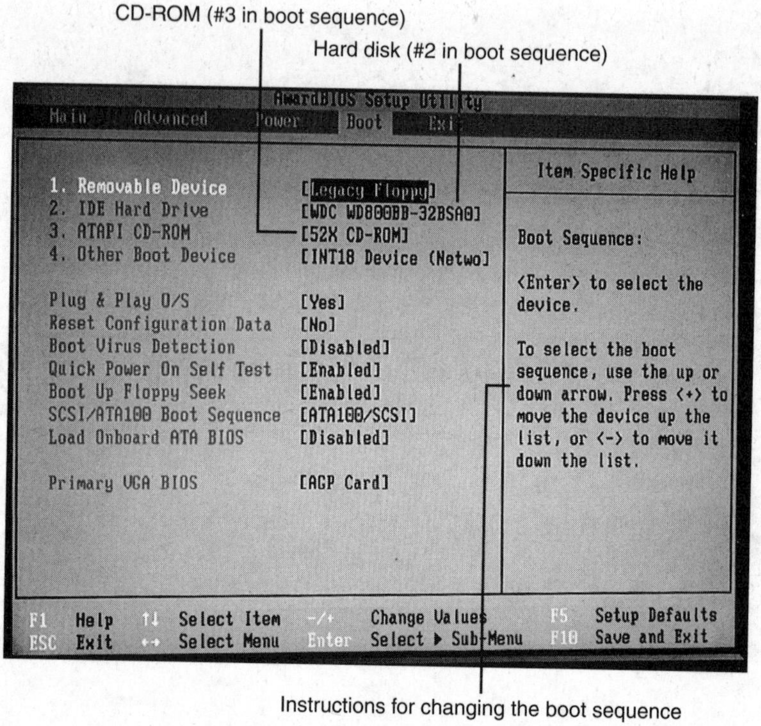

Hard disk (#2 in boot sequence)

FIGURE 3.22

This computer needs to have the CD-ROM moved before the hard disk in the boot sequence to enable the computer to boot from the Windows XP CD-ROM.

```
                        AwardBIOS Setup Utility
     Main    Advanced    Power    Boot    Exit

                                              Item Specific Help
    1. Removable Device      [Legacy Floppy]
    2. IDE Hard Drive        [WDC WD800BB-32BSA0]
    3. ATAPI CD-ROM          [52X CD-ROM]          Boot Sequence:
    4. Other Boot Device     [INT18 Device (Netwo]
                                                   <Enter> to select the
    Plug & Play O/S          [Yes]                 device.
    Reset Configuration Data [No]
    Boot Virus Detection     [Disabled]            To select the boot
    Quick Power On Self Test [Enabled]             sequence, use the up or
    Boot Up Floppy Seek      [Enabled]             down arrow. Press <+> to
    SCSI/ATA100 Boot Sequence [ATA100/SCSI]        move the device up the
    Load Onboard ATA BIOS    [Disabled]            list, or <-> to move it
                                                   down the list.
    Primary VGA BIOS         [AGP Card]


    F1   Help    ↑↓  Select Item   -/+    Change Values    F5   Setup Defaults
    ESC  Exit    ↔   Select Menu   Enter  Select ▶ Sub-Menu F10  Save and Exit
```

Instructions for changing the boot sequence

2. Insert the Windows XP CD-ROM into your CD-ROM drive.

3. Start your computer.

4. The Windows XP installation program starts after the CD-ROM boots the computer.

5. When prompted, select the type of file system (NTFS or FAT32) you want for the hard disk and whether you want to use the hard disk as a single drive letter or subdivide it into two or more logical drives. Windows XP will prepare each drive letter you specify during its setup process.

The drive's listed capacity should be similar to the capacity listed on the drive's faceplate or box. If not, see "Troubleshooting Problems with Recognizing Full Drive Capacity," this chapter, p. 203.

Windows XP Disk Preparation the Microsoft Way

Read Microsoft Knowledge Base articles "How to install or upgrade to Windows XP" (#316941) and "How to partition and format a hard disk in Windows XP" (#313348) to learn more about the process of preparing a hard disk with the Windows XP setup program or Disk Management. Set your browser to

http://support.microsoft.com

and enter **316941** or **313348** in the Search the Knowledge Base box.

Troubleshooting Problems with Recognizing Full Drive Capacity

If Disk Management or a vendor-supplied disk installation tool doesn't report the full capacity of the drive during the preparation process, make sure you are using Auto-configure in the system BIOS setup for the hard disk (see Figure 3.23); this enables LBA (logical block addressing) mode, which allows the entire capacity of the drive to be available in Windows up to the limits of the system BIOS.

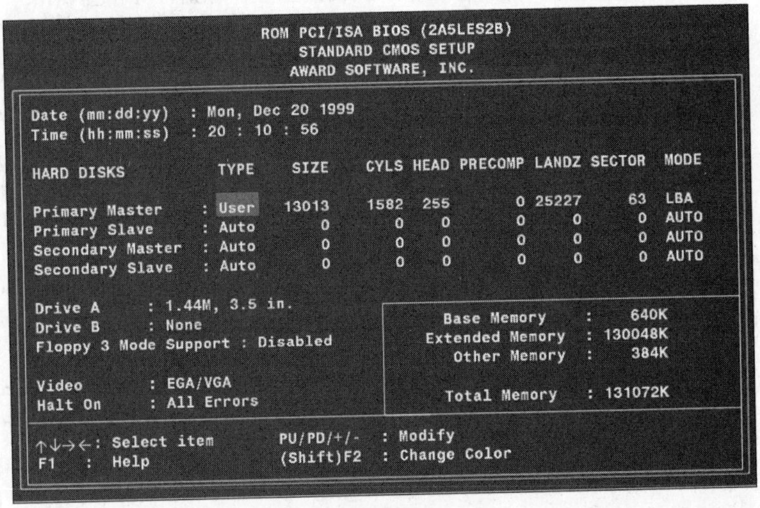

FIGURE 3.23
A typical system BIOS hard disk setup screen with both user-defined and auto-configured drives listed.

If the hard disk is over 128GB in size (such as a 160GB or larger hard disk), but Windows Disk Management only recognizes 128GB, the system BIOS does not support a feature called 48-bit LBA. For a system hard disk, you should update the system BIOS if possible or connect the hard disk to a host adapter card with a 48-bit LBA BIOS onboard. If the hard disk is to be used as additional storage, you could use a USB or IEEE-1394 external hard disk instead.

To enable the computer to work with the entire capacity of the drive, use one of the following options, listed in order from the best to worst option:

- **Best option**—Upgrade the system BIOS if an upgrade is available to handle the larger hard disk; download and install the BIOS upgrade from the system or motherboard maker's website and retry the drive installation. With Windows XP, you also need to upgrade to Service Pack 1 or greater.

- **May also need to...**—Install any chipset-specific drivers required for 48-bit LBA support. Check with your system or motherboard maker for details.

- **Next-best option**—Install an ATA 48-bit LBA BIOS support card; these cards have onboard BIOS chips that override the limitations of your system BIOS and enable your computer to use the larger drive. Your computer must have an open PCI slot on its motherboard to use this option (refer to Chapter 1 for more details on PCI slots).

- **Least desirable option**—Hard disk setup programs provided by hard disk drive makers usually include a utility program that also includes a BIOS override software option. If one is included, you may need to install it to allow your PC to recognize your drive's full capacity. Examples of these types of programs include Disc Wizard, EZ-BIOS, and Disk Manager. As a general rule, I don't recommend going this route. It prevents you from using standard boot sector repair programs if your drive becomes unbootable, thus limiting your recovery options in an emergency. On the other hand, these programs don't cost any money; they either should be included on a utility disk packaged with the drive or are made available for download from the drive manufacturer's website.

BIOS Upgrade Cards to the Rescue

If your computer can't handle your ATA/IDE hard disk at full capacity and a BIOS upgrade isn't available or doesn't solve the problem, your best option is to install a BIOS override card. Some drives, such as certain Maxtor 120GB and 160GB drives, include a high-speed PCI interface card that enables the drives to be used at full capacity; the card is also available separately. Get more information about the Maxtor ATA/133 PCI Adapter Card from http://www.maxtor.com.

Other cards from different vendors include the following:

- Promise Technology's Ultra100 TX2 and Ultra133 TX2 (these use a PCI slot). Go to http://www.promise.com.
- SIIG's UltraATA 133 PCI (uses a PCI slot). Go to http://www.siig.com.

The PCI cards also have onboard ATA/IDE controllers, enabling you to connect up to four additional drives to your system.

Troubleshooting Disk Partitioning Problems

If you run the Disk Management disk preparation wizard or another disk-partitioning utility and find that you are unable to partition your drive, or that the drive you partitioned has reverted to an unpartitioned state after you restart your system, you might have the write-protect hard disk feature enabled in your system BIOS.

Many systems have this feature, which is designed to prevent boot sector viruses from attacking your computer. However, this feature also prevents the boot sector from being changed during the disk preparation process. To disable this feature, follow these steps:

1. Restart the computer.
2. Press the key or key combination that starts the BIOS setup program when prompted.
3. Check the BIOS Features and Advanced BIOS setup menus for an option such as "Write-Protect Boot Sector" or "Anti-Virus Boot Sector." Disable this option.
4. Save the changes and exit to restart your computer.
5. Retry disk preparation.

Trend ChipAway—Intelligent Antivirus Protection

The Trend ChipAway antivirus feature used by some motherboards does not need to be disabled to enable you to prepare a new hard disk. Your motherboard might display Trend ChipAway if it's active during system startup, or you would see this option in your system BIOS setup.

If your BIOS doesn't have write-protect or antivirus boot sector protection enabled but still you can't prepare the hard disk, check the following:

- Disable antivirus software during the hard disk preparation process; some programs of this type can interfere with disk preparation.

- Shut down the computer, open the case, and inspect the data cable running between the drive and the host adapter. Remove and reattach the data cable where it connects to the drive and host adapter; a loose data cable can prevent successful disk preparation.

- Replace any data cables that are damaged (cut, scuffed, or excessively creased).

Troubleshooting Booting Problems

Once you've prepared a drive as a bootable drive, your computer can use it to start your system. However, the drive and your computer must be properly configured to enable this to take place.

Before you can use any type of hard, floppy, removable-media, or optical disk as a bootable drive (a drive that can start your system), the following must be true about the disk:

- The drive must be selected as a bootable device in the system BIOS (see Figure 3.24).

- The drive must be properly prepared to be bootable. A hard disk must be prepared with a primary partition, be formatted, and have system files transferred to it. Other types of media must be formatted and have system files transferred to the media.

- The drive must be properly identified in the system BIOS.

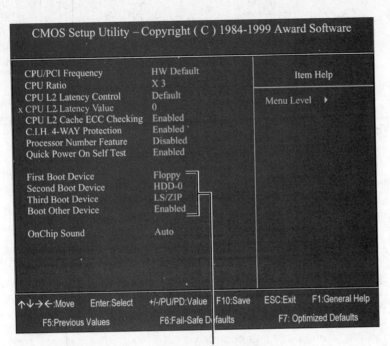

FIGURE 3.24
A typical advanced BIOS setup screen featuring a bootable drive selection option.

Bootable drive options

Troubleshooting Hard Disk or Optical Drive Bootup Problems

If you cannot start your system from a hard disk you were previously able to boot from, or you can't boot your system from a bootable Windows CD-ROM, check the following:

- **Drive A: for a floppy disk**—A nonbootable floppy disk can't be used to start a system and also stops the entire system boot process if the floppy drive is listed before the CD-ROM and hard disk drives in the BIOS boot sequence. Remove the disk and try to restart the system.

- **The BIOS setup for the drive**—Most drives use Auto as the setup type. If your drive is configured as User-Defined, check with the drive vendor's website to see if the values listed are correct for the drive. If they are not, reset the drive to Auto or enter the correct values, save the changes, and restart your system.

- **The boot order**—Your hard disk should be listed somewhere in the boot order. In Windows 2000 and XP, I recommend that the order be CD-ROM, first hard disk, and then any other bootable device you may have.

- **Whether the drive has an active partition**—A hard disk must be prepared as a primary partition and must be set as active before it can be used to start (boot) the system. You can fix this problem using the Windows XP Recovery Console (which can be started from the Windows XP CD-ROM).

Windows XP Boot Troubleshooting

If your computer can't boot from a CD-ROM drive, you might want to create a boot floppy disk that enables you to start Windows XP or Windows 2000 in an emergency. Go to http://search.microsoft.com and search for the following articles:

- Article 305595 for the procedure for creating a Windows XP boot floppy disk
- Article 119467 for the procedure for creating a Windows 2000 boot floppy disk

See article 315261 to learn how to reset the active partition with Windows XP.

➡ See "Fixing Startup Problems," Chapter 2, p. 70, for other types of startup problems and solutions.

If you are having problems booting your system and your drives and boot sequence are configured correctly, you might be having Windows-related startup problems.

Preparing Other Drives to Act as Bootable Devices

Having a bootable storage device other than your hard disk drive in case your hard drive fails for some unforeseen reason can be critical in recovering from a PC disaster. In cases where you cannot boot your PC from its hard disk, you could be helpless if you don't have some other means to boot up. Although having bootable media for a floppy, CD-ROM, or other device won't fix the source problem, it can allow you to keep troubleshooting tools and utilities accessible in case of emergency. If you want to boot from other types of drives, check the following:

- The drive type you want to use must be listed as a bootable device in your system BIOS.
- You must make sure the drive appears in the boot order before the hard disk.
- You must prepare the media to act as a bootable device.

Most recent computers can use optical drives (CD-ROM, CD-RW, DVD-ROM), floppy drives, and SCSI drives as bootable devices. Some can also use removable-media drives such as USB keychain drives, LS-120/LS-240 SuperDisk drives, and Zip drives as bootable devices.

Windows 2000 and Windows XP can be started from the hard disk, from high-capacity removable media that is prepared as a fixed disk, or from the Windows 2000 or Windows XP upgrade or OEM CD-ROM. See the previous section for information on how to make a bootable floppy disk.

If you want to prepare a CD-R, CD-RW, or recordable/rewriteable DVD disc as a startup disc with Windows, see the instructions for your CD mastering program.

Solving UDMA Mode Problems with ATA/IDE Drives

Originally, all ATA/IDE drives used an access method called *PIO (programmable input/output)*. Today, ATA/IDE hard drives (and some types of ATAPI drives) support faster access modes known as *UDMA* (also called *Ultra DMA* or *Ultra ATA*), which range from 33MHz to 66MHZ, 100MHz, and the latest 133MHz speed. If you notice the following problems, your system probably doesn't have UDMA configured correctly:

- Very slow hard disk and optical drive performance
- Inability to use disk-mastering software with your CD-RW or writeable DVD drive

To achieve a particular UDMA speed, all of the following must be present:

- The correct cable must be used. Whereas UDMA/33 drives can use the older 40-wire IDE cable, UDMA/66 and faster drives must use the 80-wire UDMA cable.
- The drive must be configured for the fastest UDMA speed supported by both the drive and the host adapter.
- The host adapter (motherboard or slot based) must have its Windows device drivers installed for maximum performance. View the ATA/IDE host adapters in Device Manager to determine if you need to install device drivers; if the host adapter listing in Device Manager indicates that the correct drivers are not installed,

download them from the motherboard or system builder's website and install them. See "Using Device Manager," Chapter 2, p. 100, for details.

- The correct UDMA speed must be selected in the system BIOS setup for the drive if User-Defined, rather than Auto, is used to configure the drive.

Because drives with fast UDMA modes are frequently used on motherboards that support slower UDMA modes, some drives are shipped with their faster UDMA modes disabled. Use the utility disk supplied with the drive, or download a utility from the drive maker's website, to view and change the UDMA support for your drive.

Upgrading a Portable Hard Disk

If you use a laptop or notebook computer, the method used for upgrading to a larger hard disk is quite a bit different from the one used for upgrading a desktop computer. Here's why:

- Most portable computers have only one internal connector for a hard disk.

- Portable computers use 2.5-inch ATA/IDE hard disks with integrated 44-pin power/data connectors rather than 3.5-inch ATA/IDE hard disks with separate data and power connectors.

- To transfer data from your existing hard disk to a new hard disk, you must use the USB port or PC Card slot to connect your new hard disk, unless you want to connect both old and new hard disks to a desktop computer with desktop ATA/IDE to laptop ATA/IDE adapters.

- You also will need a hard disk preparation and copy utility designed for portable hard disk upgrades.

No matter how large the hard disk in your portable computer, sooner or later you might want to replace it. When you do so, consider the following issues:

- **Size**—You should purchase a hard disk that's at least three times larger than your current drive if possible. For example, if your system has a 20GB hard disk, upgrade to a 60GB or larger drive. If your system has a 30GB hard disk, upgrade to a 100GB or larger drive.

- **Speed**—Until recently, most laptop hard disks had relatively low 4200RPM spin rates. Newer drives spin at 5400RPM or 7200RPM, enabling faster data access and transfer rates.

- **Onboard cache**—Most portable hard disks have 2MB cache, but some high-performance models feature 8MB cache, helping to improve data transfer rates.

- **BIOS compatibility**—As long as the new hard disk is under 130GB, your system should be able to use it without needing a system BIOS upgrade. However, to make sure you buy a hard disk that is not too large for your portable computer, you can check the buying guides listed in the sidebar "Checking Portable Hard Disk Compatibility."

You can purchase a replacement hard disk as a bare drive or as part of an installation kit. Installation kits are available from various vendors, including Apricorn, CMS Products, and SimpleTech among others.

Checking Portable Hard Disk Compatibility

Before you plunk down good money for a bigger laptop hard disk, make sure your system can handle a bigger hard disk. Here are some websites where you can check compatibility and get help with your upgrade:

- **Apricorn Hard Drive Selector**—http://www.apricornproducts.com/config.php?reseller_id=98
- **CMS Products Upgrade Finder**—http://www.cmsproducts.com/guide/index.cfm
- **SimpleTech Upgrade Navigator**—http://www.simpletech.com/upgNav/

Using EZ Upgrade Universal and EZ Gig II

Figure 3.25 shows the contents of Apricorn's EZ Upgrade Universal hard disk upgrade kit and a Toshiba 80GB hard disk (purchased separately). Although some vendors offer data transfer kits that plug into the PC Card or CardBus slot on a laptop computer or connect to a bare drive, we prefer this type of upgrade kit because it can convert the drive you replace into an external hard disk after the upgrade process is complete.

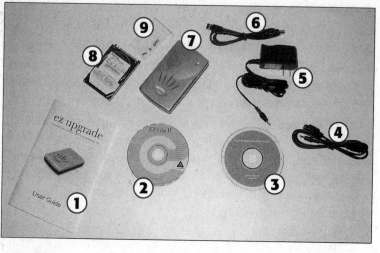

1. User guide
2. EZ Gig II hard disk installation software
3. USB 2.0 driver
4. PS/2 keyboard power adapter for drive enclosure
5. AC adapter for drive enclosure
6. USB cable for drive enclosure
7. Drive enclosure
8. 2.5-inch ATA/IDE portable hard disk
9. Mounting screws

The EZ Gig II program shown in Figure 3.25 is used to do the following:

- Partition the new hard disk.
- Prepare the partition(s) on the new hard disk.
- Copy the contents of the old hard disk partition(s) to the new hard disk partition(s).

Before these processes can take place, you need to follow these steps:

1. Back up important information on your existing system (use your CD-RW or rewritable DVD drive or a network connection to copy each user's My Documents folder).

2. Install the EZ Gig II software.

3. Connect the new drive to your system using the upgrade kit.

Connecting the New Hard Disk to Your Portable Computer

The enclosure shown in Figure 3.25 contains a mounting tray for the hard disk. The mounting tray (see Figure 3.26) features a 44-pin power/data connector. Slide the new hard disk into place until the 44-pin hard disk interface (refer to Figure 3.1) plugs into the connector.

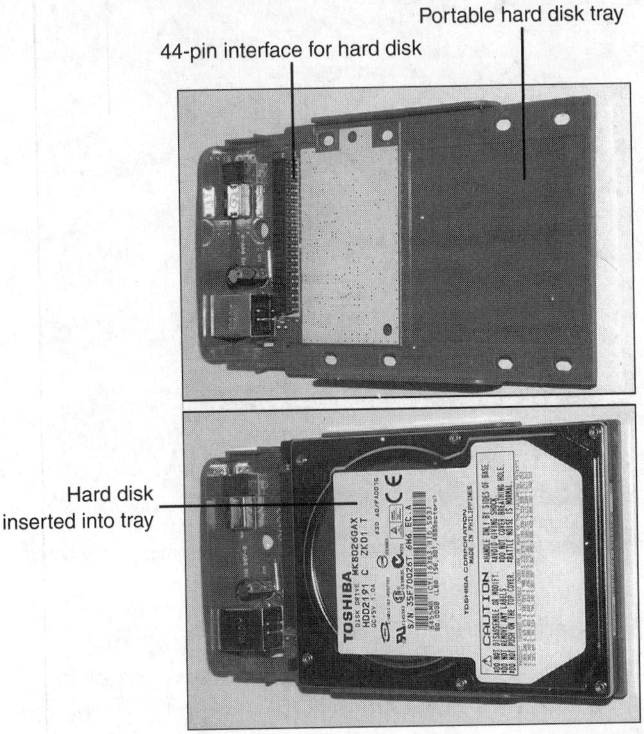

44-pin interface for hard disk

Portable hard disk tray

Hard disk inserted into tray

FIGURE 3.26

Installing the new hard disk into the hard disk enclosure's mounting tray for preparation and copying.

It is not necessary to use the screws provided in the mounting kit (refer to Figure 3.25) to secure the new hard disk. This is only a temporary installation.

After the new hard disk is inserted into the mounting tray (refer to Figure 3.26), connect it to the computer using the USB cable supplied. Connect the AC adapter to the power connector on the rear of the tray, and select DC as the power source (see Figure 3.27).

If you use a USB-based data transfer solution, the hard disk should be detected by Windows as soon as it is connected; you can verify this by using Device Manager. Note that if you use a PC Card or CardBus-based data transfer kit, the card must be detected and have its drivers installed before the hard disk can be detected. After the hard disk is detected and drivers have been installed for the hard disk and the data transfer device (if necessary), you can prepare the new hard disk using the software supplied with your data transfer program.

FIGURE 3.27

Connecting the new hard disk to power and USB cables.

New hard disk inserted in mounting tray

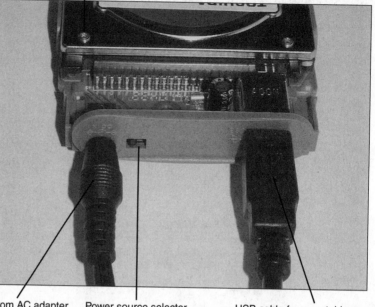

Cable from AC adapter   Power source selector   USB cable from portable computer

Preparing the New Hard Disk with EZ Gig II

Portable hard disk data transfer kits usually include drive installation software that can prepare the new hard disk for use and copy the contents of the old hard disk to it. Apricorn's EZ Upgrade Universal kit includes EZ Gig II software, which can also be used as an image backup and disaster recovery program. If you want to use it exclusively for drive preparation and data transfer, you can boot from the CD. However, if you have problems using it as a bootable CD or want to use its image backup features, you can install it and run it from within Windows. From the main menu (see Figure 3.28), select Disk Clone to start the disk preparation and copying process.

The Disk Clone Wizard analyzes the partitions on your existing hard disk and copies them to the new hard disk connected via USB or PC Card interfaces. Because the new hard disk is usually larger than the original drive it is replacing, you have the option to run the program in Automatic mode, which partitions the new hard disk in the same proportions as the original drive, or Expert mode, which enables you to adjust the size(s) of partition(s) on the new drive.

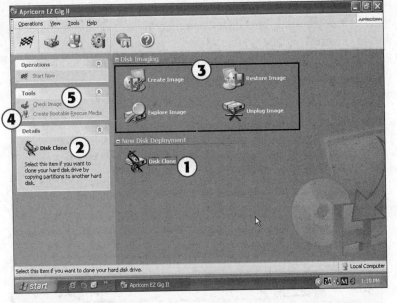

FIGURE 3.28
Starting Apricorn EZ Gig II's Disk Clone Wizard.

1. Starts Disk Clone
2. Description of selected program
3. Disk Imaging programs
4. Click to create a bootable CD for operating EZ Gig II
5. Click to check an existing image file

If your existing hard disk has only one drive letter (C:) and you want to use only one drive letter on the new hard disk, choose Automatic. However, if you want to create an additional drive letter on the new hard disk for your data files, or have two or more drive letters on your existing hard disk, you should choose Expert.

Moving My Documents to a New Drive Letter the Microsoft Way

By default, Windows XP uses the alias "My Documents" to refer to a folder called \Documents and Settings*user name*\My Documents on the system drive (usually C:). You can move this folder to a different folder or a different drive after you create a new drive letter on your new hard disk. After your new hard disk is up and running, go to http://support.microsoft.com/?id=310147 to read "How to Change the Default Location of the My Documents Folder."

In the example shown in Figure 3.29, the original notebook hard disk had a drive letter used by Windows XP Home Edition (C:), a drive letter used for data (D:), and a drive letter used for Windows XP Professional

(F:). We wanted to increase the data storage drive (D:) to occupy more than half of the new hard disk while also increasing the sizes of the C: and F: drives. The Disk Clone Wizard's manual re-layout option enabled us to fine-tune the sizes of the new hard disk's drive letters until we were satisfied (see Figure 3.29).

FIGURE 3.29

Using Disk Clone Wizard to customize the layout of the new hard disk.

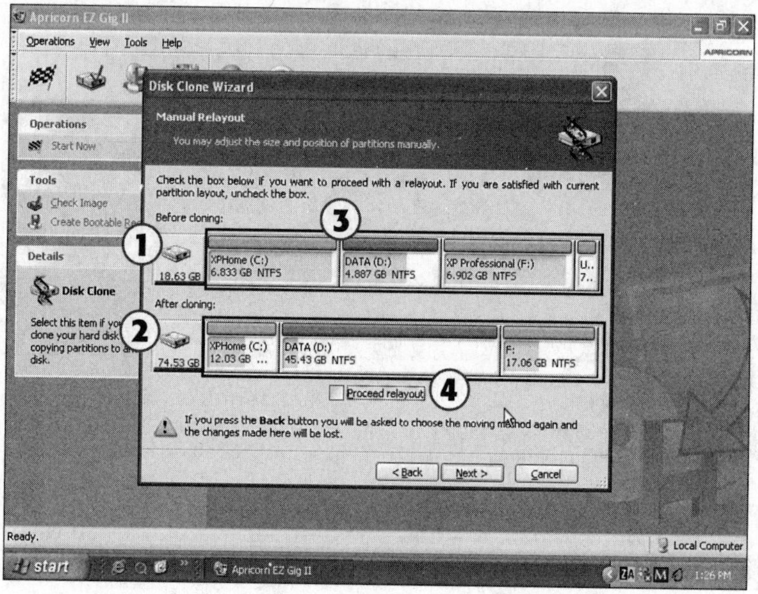

1. Original hard disk size   3. Original hard disk layout
2. New hard disk size   4. New hard disk layout

At the end of the layout process, some drive partition and copying programs list the operations they will perform. You can confirm the operations or go back and make changes. In the example shown in Figure 3.30, click Proceed to make the changes to the new hard disk (the original hard disk will not be changed). Click Reboot when prompted to start or continue the process.

After the disk partitioning and copying program has finished, disconnect the USB cable connected to the new hard disk from the USB port on your computer.

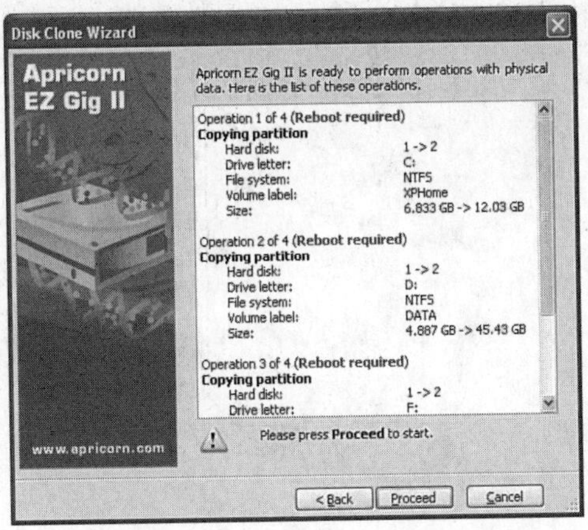

FIGURE 3.30
Preparing to confirm disk copy/partition creation operations on the new hard disk.

Installing the New Hard Disk in Your Portable Computer

To replace the existing hard disk with the new hard disk, follow this procedure:

1. Shut down your portable computer and unplug it.

2. Remove the existing hard disk from the computer. Depending on the computer, the hard disk might be accessible from the bottom of the computer, the side of the computer, or might require you to remove the keyboard. See the specific installation instructions provided by the hard disk or data transfer vendor for your computer.

3. Remove the existing hard disk from its mounting frame (see Figure 3.31).

4. Place the existing hard disk on antistatic material.

5. Disconnect the AC power adapter from the new hard disk.

6. Remove the new hard disk from the drive tray you used for data transfer.

7. Place the new hard disk into the mounting frame used by the original hard disk.

8. Use the screws removed from the original hard disk to attach the new hard disk to the mounting frame used by your portable computer.

FIGURE 3.31

Removing the new hard disk from the external drive tray (top) and fastening it to the internal mounting frame (bottom).

9. After the new hard disk is fastened securely to the mounting frame, install the mounting frame back into your portable computer.

10. Plug in your portable computer and restart it. Your new hard disk should start your computer and be recognized by Windows. In some cases, you might need to restart your computer once.

Using Your Existing Hard Disk as an External Hard Disk

→ See "Preparing an Additional Hard Disk with Windows XP," this chapter, p. 195, for details of Disk Management's operations.

After you are satisfied the new hard disk is working properly, you can use the original hard disk as an external hard disk drive. If your data transfer kit can be used as an external drive enclosure (the EZ Upgrade Universal kit can be), install the original drive into the enclosure and fasten it into place with the mounting screws provided. Connect the enclosure to a working USB port, use Windows XP's Disk Management to erase existing partitions on the original hard disk, and create one or more new partitions. There's no need to hurry: We suggest waiting a day or two to make sure you can browse the Web, read email, and so forth with your new hard disk before you clear out your original drive for reuse.

Solving Problems with Writeable CD and DVD Media

One of the most popular add-ons for computers (and an increasingly popular standard feature) is a writeable DVD drive. Some of the problems you might encounter with such drives include the following:

- Inability to write to the media
- Inability to read written media on another system
- Buffer underruns

The following sections will help you solve these problems.

Figure 3.32 displays the Record CD Setup and Project screens used by the Creator Classic module of Roxio's Easy CD and DVD Creator 6.x, a popular CD- and DVD-mastering program often bundled with rewritable CD and DVD drives. This figure will be referred to frequently in the following sections.

Solving Can't-Write-to-Media Problems

If your drive can't write to writeable media, check the following issues:

- You are trying to use the wrong type of media for your drive.
- Your CD-mastering program doesn't support the drive.
- You are trying to use media that has been closed (write-protected).
- You aren't running packet-writing (drag-and-drop) software.
- You haven't formatted your media for packet-writing (drag-and-drop) file copying.
- Your drive is damaged.
- Windows XP doesn't support your writeable drive.

Troubleshooting Incorrect Media and Media Usage Problems

There are more types of writeable media at your local electronics and computer store than ever before, which means that the chances are increasing that you could buy the wrong type of media for your drive or for the task you want to perform.

FIGURE 3.32

The Record CD Setup dialog in Roxio's Creator Classic.

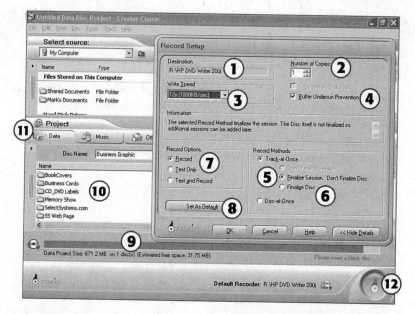

1. Destination drive
2. Number of CD/DVD copies to make
3. Select the write speed that matches your media
4. Enable to avoid creating a useless "coaster" due to a buffer underrun (requires a writeable drive with this feature)
5. Select to allow more data to be written later
6. Closes CD/DVD; no more files can be written

7. Select Test and Record the first time you use your drive to make sure your CD/DVD can be created without any problems
8. Sets the current selections as the default
9. Size of project (files) and estimated space left on media
10. Files and folders to be written to CD/DVD
11. Project type selected
12. Click to start creating (burning) CD/DVD

If you have a CD-RW drive, you can use the following:

- **CD-R media**—CD-R media is designed to be used with CD-mastering programs; you can write to it and add files to nonclosed media, but you can't delete files from it. Some packet-writing programs can also use it for drag-and-drop file copying. CD-R media has a colored recording surface that might appear gold, light green, or light blue, depending on the reflective surface and dye layer.

- **CD-RW media**—CD-RW media is designed to be used with packet-writing programs. Like conventional removable-media drives (USB flash, floppy, Zip, SuperDisk, and others), you can erase CD-RW media and use it again. CD-RW media's recordable surface looks like a mirror.

Both types of media are single-sided; you can write on the printed surface with soft-tip markers.

Both CD-R and CD-RW media are speed rated. If you use slower CD-R media with a faster drive, you can reduce the write speed of the drive (see Figure 3.32) or you can try to write at top speed and then try the completed media on other drives to see if it's readable. However, CD-RW media is sold in four speed ranges, and you can't cheat when you use it. High-speed CD-RW media (4-12×) can be used only in CD-RW drives with rewrite speeds of 4× or faster. If you want to transfer data stored on CD-RW media from a 12× drive to a drive with the slower 2× rewrite speed, you must use standard speed (2×/4×) CD-RW media in your fast drive. CD-RW media is also available in Ultra Speed, supporting rewrite speeds from 16× to 24×, and Ultra Speed Plus, supporting rewrite speeds of 32×.

Leo Says

For Easy Reading, Stick to CD-R

If you're not sure what type of optical drive will be used to read your information, play it safe: Burn a CD and close it (finalize it). CD-RW media is great for making backup copies of your own work in progress, but with four speed ranges, you can have problems reading fast media in older, slower drives. DVD drives are increasingly common, but with different media standards, it can be hard to choose a media type that works with every DVD drive. Fortunately, both CD and DVD drives can read CD-R. Therefore, to make sure everybody can read your stuff, use CD-R!

A number of manufacturers now make various types of writeable DVD drives. There are actually at least seven types of writeable DVD media, and because many drives can use only one or two types, it's essential that you buy the correct type(s) for your drive:

- **DVD-RAM**—A rewriteable/erasable media similar to CD-RW, but can be single- or double-sided. DVD-RAM is usually kept in a closed disc caddy to protect its surfaces. Very few drives use DVD-RAM.

- **DVD-R**—A writeable/non-erasable media similar to CD-R; some DVD-RAM and all DVD-RW drives can use DVD-R media.

- **DVD-RW**—A single-sided rewriteable/erasable media similar to CD-RW. DVD-RW drives can also write to DVD-R media.

- **DVD+RW**—A rewriteable/erasable media. Also similar to CD-RW, but not interchangeable with DVD-RW or DVD-RAM.

- **DVD+R**—A writeable/non-erasable media. Also similar to CD-R, but not interchangeable with DVD-R.

- **DVD+R DL**—The first dual-layer DVD media. Stores up to 8.5GB.

- **DVD-R DL**—A dual-layer version of DVD-R. Stores up to 8.5GB.

DVD media is speed rated. You can use media rated for high-speed (8× and faster) drives with most older drives with no problems. However, some early DVD-RW and DVD+RW drives need firmware upgrades to use 2× or faster (DVD-R/RW) or 4× or faster (DVD+R/RW) media safely; drives using old firmware can be damaged by trying to write to faster media. If you're using a first- or second-generation DVD rewritable drive, make sure your drive can use today's media! Install the latest firmware made for your drive.

Most DVD+RW and DVD-RW drives, along with some DVD-RAM drives, can also use CD-RW and CD-R media. Most drives today support both – and + media.

All rewritable media (CD-RW, DVD-RAM, DVD-RW, and DVD+RW) must be formatted before it can be used for drag-and-drop file copying. Depending on the media type, this process can take as much as a half-hour or longer.

The latest rewritable DVD drives can use DVD+R DL media, and some can also use DVD-R DL media. Keep in mind that most single-layer rewritable DVD drives, even with firmware updates, cannot read DL media. If you write DL media and read it in your DL-compatible drive, but another DVD drive prompts you to insert a disc after you insert the DL media, the DVD drive cannot read the DL media. Check with the vendor of both the DL drive and the target DVD drive for firmware updates.

Although CD-mastering programs can also use rewriteable media, you should not use such media with these programs because the media might not be erasable after being mastered. Use CD-R, DVD-R, or DVD+R media for CD- or DVD-mastering tasks.

Troubleshooting CD-Mastering Drive Support Problems

Originally, the only way to write to CD-R media was with a mastering program such as Roxio Easy Media Creator (originally developed by Adaptec) or Nero Burning ROM. These and similar programs typically feature a Windows Explorer–style interface that you use to create a list of files and folders you want to write to a CD.

Unfortunately, if your particular brand and model of writeable drive isn't supported by the mastering program you want to use, you can't use the program to write to your media.

Here are some indications your mastering program doesn't work with your drive:

- The program doesn't detect your drive at all.
- The program doesn't list your drive as a target drive for writing files.
- The program detects your drive, but displays an error message when you try to write files to the drive.

To solve problems like these, try the following:

- Before you install a new CD or DVD recording program, check the vendor's website for compatibility with your drive.
- Download the latest CD and DVD recorder support files from the vendor's website. Most vendors provide a database of supported recorders and software versions you can query. If your recorder appears on the list of supported recorders, but the version of software listed is more recent than the one you use, download the recommended update. Keep checking the software vendor's website for further updates if your recorder isn't listed yet.
- Upgrade to the latest version of your preferred software. If you use a no-longer current version of CD-mastering software and your recorder isn't listed as supported, see if the latest version will support it and purchase the upgrade if a free update isn't available.
- Use the recording software provided with the drive instead of a third-party product. Although many writeable drives come with bare-bones software that might lack some of the features of a commercial product, the program packaged with the drive will work.
- Change to a different brand of software.

Troubleshooting Problems with Closed Media

All but the earliest CD-ROM drives are designed to read media that can be added to (multiple session) or media that has been closed (write-protected).

If your CD-mastering program displays an error message indicating that you need to insert media that has enough room for the files you want to write, and the media has more than enough space, the media was closed when it was created and no more files can be placed on the media. You can determine how much space is used on a writeable CD with Windows Explorer/My Computer. Right-click the drive and select Properties to see the amount of space used: 74-minute media can hold about 650MB, whereas 80-minute media can hold about 700MB of information. Single-layer DVD media can hold about 4.5GB of information, whereas dual-layer DVD media can hold over 8GB of information. The properties sheet for the drive will also say the media has 0 bytes free, but this is misleading. Most mastering programs will also list the amount of space used by the files you want to transfer to CD or DVD.

If you want to write files to the media more than once, be sure that you select the option that doesn't close (finalize) the CD or DVD when you create it (refer to Figure 3.32). Some programs choose this option for you by default, whereas others might close (finalize) the CD unless you choose otherwise.

Troubleshooting Drag-and-Drop (Packet-Writing) Problems

CD or DVD mastering is an excellent way to copy a large number of files to a CD or DVD all at once, but it's not designed to allow files to be dragged from their original location and dropped (copied) to a CD or DVD. Hence, most CD- and DVD-mastering programs come with separate packet-writing programs to allow drag-and-drop file copying. For example, older versions of Easy CD Creator included DirectCD, newer versions (including the latest Easy Media Creator) include Drag-to-Disc, and Nero Burning ROM comes with InCD (or you can download a copy if your version of Nero didn't include it). Packet-writing software writes files that correspond to a standard called Universal Disk Format (UDF).

Floppy disks, Zip disks, SuperDisk (LS-120/LS-240), and other types of magnetic removable-media storage are preformatted; you can copy files to them as soon as you insert them into the drive. However, optical media must be formatted before you can use it for drag-and-drop copying.

The packet-writing software supplied with your drive (or as part of a CD- or DVD-creation program you bought at the store) is used to perform this task (see Figure 3.33). After you start the program, insert your media and click the Format button.

You should provide a label (descriptive name) for your media to make it easy to distinguish among different CD-RW or rewritable DVD discs (the label is displayed in Windows Explorer/My Computer). Use compression to save space.

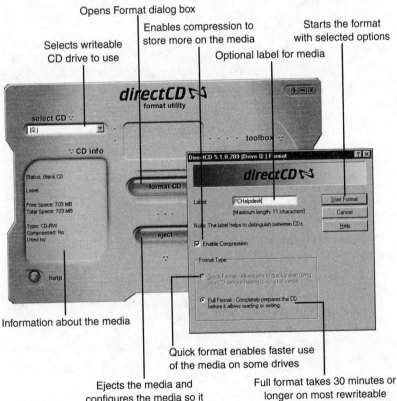

FIGURE 3.33
The Roxio DirectCD formatting program preparing a blank CD-RW disc for use.

Opens Format dialog box

Enables compression to store more on the media

Starts the format with selected options

Selects writeable CD drive to use

Optional label for media

Information about the media

Quick format enables faster use of the media on some drives

Ejects the media and configures the media so it can be read on other computers

Full format takes 30 minutes or longer on most rewriteable drives to prepare the media, but only a few moments on CD-R media

If you are unable to start the formatting process, check the following:

- If you have another writeable drive installed, close any resident software used by the other drive (check the system tray). You should use only one UDF writing program.

- Use the correct type of media for your recorder and packet-writing program. For example, drives that rewrite at 10× or faster can use 4×–12× media, but drives that rewrite at only 4× can't use faster media. If your packet-writing program doesn't support CD-R media, you must use rewritable media.

- If you use rewritable DVD media, use DVD+RW media if your drive supports this type. DVD+RW media is formatted as you work after just a brief preparation process. DVD-RW media takes much longer to format.

At the end of the formatting process, be sure to properly eject the media. Use the Eject option provided by your packet-writing software to make sure the media is properly set for use in other systems (see Figure 3.34).

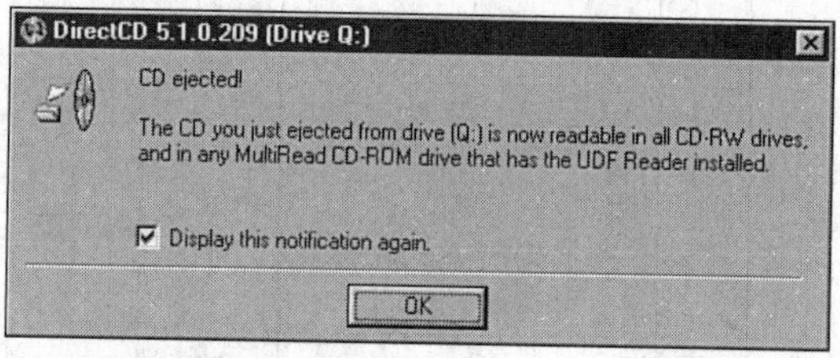

FIGURE 3.34

The Roxio DirectCD program after ejecting formatted CD-RW media. The media must be read with a CD-RW or a CD-ROM drive with UDF Reader.

DirectCD 5.1.0.209 [Drive Q:]

CD ejected!

The CD you just ejected from drive (Q:) is now readable in all CD-RW drives, and in any MultiRead CD-ROM drive that has the UDF Reader installed.

☑ Display this notification again.

[OK]

If the drive reports an error during the formatting process, try another CD-RW or rewritable disc and retry the process. If the problem repeats itself, contact the drive vendor for help.

When you insert the media into your drive for copying files, make sure the packet-writing program recognizes the media before you try to use it.

When you want to remove the media, use the Eject command built into your packet-writing software to close the media so it can be read. Unlike closing the media on a CD-R-mastering program, closing CD-RW or rewritable DVD media doesn't prevent reuse of the media by the packet-writing program. By default, the media is closed so it can be read on any CD-ROM or DVD-ROM drive equipped with compatible UDF

(Universal Disk Format) reading software (some programs, such as DirectCD, copy the reader to the media for you) and by other CD-RW drives.

If you are unable to read a CD-RW disc on another drive, check the following:

- The drive must be MultiRead or MultiRead2 compliant. Almost all CD-ROM drives that are 24× or faster are MultiRead compliant, and most recent DVD drives are MultiRead2 compliant (MultiRead/MultiRead2 drives use different types of lasers to read rewriteable media because it has lower reflectivity than ordinary pressed or CD-R media).

- Return the media to the original computer and use the packet-writing program's Eject feature to properly close the media.

- Install a UDF reader program compatible with the media. If the media didn't include such a reader, download one from the CD-mastering program's vendor.

UDF Readers? Surf This Way!

If you want to read media created with Roxio DirectCD or Drag-to-Disc on systems that don't have this program, you need the latest UDF Reader. Go to the Roxio website (http://www.roxio.com), click Downloads, and look for the UDF Volume Reader (works with Windows 95 through XP).

Ahead Software offers InCD4 Reader for users who want to read InCD-created media. Go to http://ww2.nero.com/us/InCD_4_Reader.html.

For other UDF reader solutions, contact the vendor of your drive or packet-writing software.

Some packet-writing programs, notably Roxio Easy Media Creator, support CD-R, DVD-R and DVD+R media as well as CD-RW and rewritable DVD media. Recordable CD and DVD media is less expensive and more durable than rewritable media, but you need to make sure you select the most suitable option for closing it; you might be prompted for a closing method, or need to select one in the packet-writing program's options menu. If you choose Close to UDF Reader, the target computer needs to use a UDF Reader program to recognize the information on the CD. I recommend you select the Close to Read on Any Computer option so that most CD-ROM and other optical drives can read the files on the CD without using special software. Note that if you use DVD-R or DVD+R media, you must use a DVD-ROM or other DVD drive to read the media.

Troubleshooting Problems with the Writeable Drive Hardware

If your writeable drive has any of the following symptoms, it might be defective and need to be serviced:

- You must remove and insert media a couple of times before the packet-writing or mastering program will recognize it.
- Your drive is no longer recognized as a writeable drive by your mastering or packet-writing program.
- Your drive isn't displayed in My Computer or Windows Explorer.
- Your drive ejects and retracts its media tray when you didn't press the Eject button or use the Eject option in your software.
- A CD or DVD shattered inside the drive.

Before you contact your vendor for help, try the following:

- Review the troubleshooting sections earlier in this chapter for the drive interface your writeable CD uses. Most internal drives are ATA/IDE, whereas external drives usually connect to the USB or IEEE-1394 ports.
- Check the settings for the drive in Device Manager. Check the vendor's documentation for the correct DMA setting (Enable or Disable). If the drive's settings tab indicates the drive is not using DMA and the drive manufacturer recommends it, enable it. If DMA is already enabled, disable it (the drive will create CDs more slowly).
- Install the latest bus-mastering drivers available for your motherboard's chipset. Check your system or motherboard vendor's website for details and files to download.
- Check the data cable and make sure it's tightly connected to both the drive and the host adapter. Replace a defective cable.
- Use an 80-wire UDMA cable instead of a 40-wire cable on an ATA/IDE drive. You might need to change the jumpering from Master/Slave to Cable Select.

→ See "Configuring ATA/IDE Drive Jumpers," this chapter, p. 177.

- Download the latest drivers for your writeable drive and the latest software updates for your CD-mastering and packet-writing programs.
- Check with the drive vendor for a list of recommended media. Substandard media or media that uses a different dye layer than what the drive is optimized for can cause major problems with reliable writing.

Who Made Your Media?

You can download the freeware CD-R Identifier program from the following website:

http://www.afterdawn.com/software/cdr_software/cdr_tools/cdridentifier.cfm

You can use it to determine important information about any CD-R media you have, including the actual manufacturer (which is often *not* the name on the package) and the type of dye it uses (some colors work better with some recorders than others).

A similar program for DVDs, DVD Identifier, is available from http://dvd.identifier.cdfreaks.com/my_site/my_home.htm.

- Check your drive vendor's website for a firmware upgrade. A firmware upgrade changes the instructions inside the drive similar to the way a system BIOS upgrade changes the instructions built into your computer's BIOS chip. Install the firmware upgrade if you don't have the latest one. The Settings tab on the drive's properties sheet in Device Manager indicates the firmware release installed.

➔ *For details on using Device Manager, see "Using Device Manager," Chapter 2, p. 100.*

Troubleshooting Problems with Windows XP and Writeable Drives

Some vendors of computers running Windows XP have not included any CD-mastering software with systems that include CD-RW drives. Yet, it's possible to create CDs with these computers without buying any software. Should you?

Windows XP supports writeable drives...badly. Instead of providing CD-mastering and packet-writing software, Windows XP uses a very slow and inefficient way of copying files to a CD-R or CD-RW disc. The process works this way:

1. Select the files you want to transfer to the writeable drive in My Computer.

2. Select Copy the Selected Items and then select the writeable drive as the destination. The files are copied to a temporary folder.

3. Click the CD icon in the system tray to view the files waiting to be copied to the CD (see Figure 3.35).

4. Click Write These Items to CD to start the CD Writing Wizard.

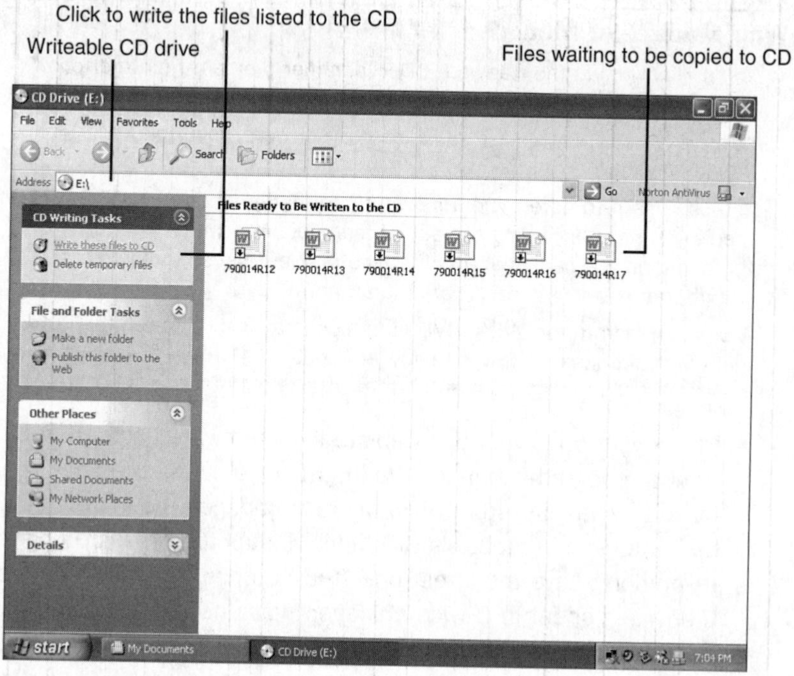

FIGURE 3.35

The Windows XP CD-writing program prepares to write files to the CD.

Click to write the files listed to the CD
Writeable CD drive

Files waiting to be copied to CD

5. By default, the CD Writing Wizard uses the current date for the name of the CD it creates; change this if desired. You can also select Close the Wizard After the Files Have Been Written; do this if you want to create only one copy. Click Next to continue.

6. Windows XP creates a CD image and writes the files to the CD. The process is fairly quick if you select only a few files, but it's very slow if you want to fill a CD with your files. You can add more files to the CD at a later time if you want.

7. Click Finish to exit the wizard.

To see how much space is left on the CD, right-click it in My Computer. One advantage of Windows XP over earlier versions of Windows is that it can display used and free space on a writeable drive; earlier versions treat both CD-ROM and writeable drives as having 0 bytes free.

Here are some of the problems you might have with Windows XP's writeable CD support:

- Doesn't recognize some CD-RW or rewritable DVD drives. Note that Windows XP does not support writing to DVD media; you must use a third-party program.

- Ignores DVD-writing capabilities of rewriteable DVD drives; these drives are used as CD-RW drives only when recognized.

- Writes files to CD-RW media, which can be erased only by Windows XP.

- Prevents your packet-writing software from writing to CD-RW media.

- Automatically prompts you to write files to the media when you insert a blank writeable CD.

Troubleshooting Drives That Windows XP Doesn't Recognize

By default, Windows XP is designed to work with most CD-RW drives on the market (including DVD drives that support CD-RW media). Windows XP features a built-in driver called the Advanced SCSI Programming Interface (ASPI) layer. The Generic layer supplied with Windows XP supports most drives, but if your drive is not supported by the standard Windows ASPI driver, Windows XP will treat it as a CD-ROM or DVD-ROM drive.

If your drive isn't recognized by Windows XP as a writeable drive and you want to use Windows XP's own CD-writing feature instead of third-party software, try the following:

- Go to Windows Update (http://windowsupdate.microsoft.com) or to http://support.microsoft.com and download the update to the Windows XP CD-writing feature discussed in document 320174. This fix also helps solve other CD-writing problems. Look for document 324129 for additional troubleshooting tips for Windows XP's CD-writing wizard.

- Download and install the Adaptec Windows ASPI Package (you don't need an Adaptec or any other SCSI host adapter to use it); it frequently solves the problem. Go to the Adaptec website (http://www.adaptec.com).

  Click Support, Downloads, SCSI Software to locate the link for the program.

Erasing CD-RW Media Created with Windows XP's CD-Writing Wizard

The Windows XP CD-writing feature creates CDFS (CD File System) CDs, which can't be erased by any other application other than Windows, regardless of whether you use CD-R or CD-RW media.

If you want to erase CD-RWs written with Windows XP, you must insert the CD-RW media into a CD-RW drive connected to a Windows XP system and use the CD-writing wizard to erase the files.

If you use UDF-compatible drag-and-drop programs to write files to CD-RW (or rewritable DVD) media, you can erase files using Windows Explorer.

Adjusting and Disabling the Windows XP CD-Writing Feature

It's very likely that you will replace Windows XP's built-in CD-writing software with a third-party product that offers true CD and DVD mastering and packet-writing capabilities. However, even after you install the program you prefer, XP's built-in CD writing features could interfere with your third-party software. Even if you are content with XP's CD-writing feature, you might want to fine-tune it.

To adjust how the Windows XP CD-writing feature works, or to disable it, right-click the drive in My Computer, select Properties, and click the Recording tab (see Figure 3.36).

FIGURE 3.36

The Recording tab for a writeable CD drive in Windows XP.

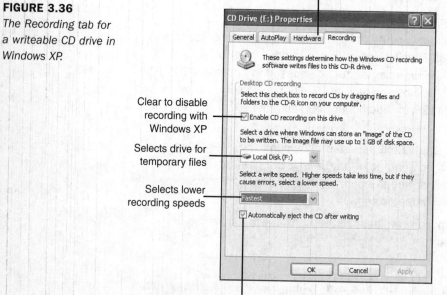

Recording tab

Clear to disable recording with Windows XP

Selects drive for temporary files

Selects lower recording speeds

Clear to keep the media in the drive

If you want to use third-party software to record CDs, clear the check box next to Enable CD Recording. This will prevent Windows XP from trying to run its own wizard when you insert a blank CD and stops Windows XP from interfering with your packet-writing software.

If you can't read the media you wrote with Windows XP with any drive, including the drive that created it, your drive might have experienced a buffer underrun. A buffer underrun takes place when a recordable drive runs out of data to transfer to the media. Because CDs must be recorded in a continuous spiral of data from the center to the edge, a disc with a buffer underrun is unreadable; such a disc is called a "coaster" by some users. You can select a slower record speed than Fastest if you have problems reading the CDs you create.

If your default drive for temporary files is short of space, it could slow down the CD creation process and might cause a buffer underrun (resulting in a useless coaster). Use My Computer to determine which hard disk has the most empty space if you have more than one hard disk drive letter, and use the pull-down menu to select that drive as the location for temporary files.

If you prefer to remove a disc you write from the drive, enable the Eject feature, but if you prefer to view it with My Computer to make sure it's readable, clear the Automatically Eject option.

What Happened to the Recording Tab?

If your computer doesn't display the Recording tab for your writeable drive, it could mean either of the following:

- Windows XP doesn't recognize your drive as a recordable drive; follow the tips given in the section "Troubleshooting Drives That Windows XP Doesn't Recognize," this chapter, p. 231.
- Your third-party CD-mastering or packet-writing software has disabled this tab for you to prevent problems.

Troubleshooting Recorded Media You Can't Read on Another System

Even if you create CDs or DVDs primarily as backups of your own data or music, you should be concerned about whether other systems can read the media you create. This is definitely a concern if you regularly create media for use by others. If other users can't read the CDs or DVDs you create, check the following:

- Make sure you are using a type of media the target system can use. The safest type of media to use is a high-quality CD-R used with a CD-mastering program. Unless you choose the Close to Read on Any Computer option in your packet-writing software, packet-written CD-R media relies on UDF reader software to be readable on CD-ROM drives. CD-RW must be read in another CD-RW drive or by CD-ROM drives with a compatible UDF reader program installed. CD-RWs also don't work in most older portable stereo systems and non-MultiRead CD-ROM drives. DVDs can be read only in DVD drives, and some older DVD-ROM drives have problems reading rewriteable DVD media. Dual-layer DVDs can be read by dual-layer DVD drives and a few late-model single-layer DVD rewritable drives. Had enough of worrying? CD-R is inexpensive and works virtually everywhere.

- Record all the data you want to put on the CD in a single session and close the CD. Some very early CD-ROM drives can read only single-session discs, and by creating a single-session disc you avoid compatibility problems.

- If you need the read/write/erase capability of CD-RW media, make sure you eject it correctly; don't shut off the computer until the media is ejected. The ejection process closes the media so it can be read on other systems.

- Try the media on your own system. If the drive that created the media can read it, but others cannot, you can try reducing the recording speed, closing the CD, or try a different type of CD media with a different combination of dye and reflective layers. However, if even the original drive can't read the media, you might have a defective drive or a buffer underrun.

Troubleshooting Buffer Underruns

Ever since the first recordable CD drive was introduced, users have created untold numbers of useless coasters because of buffer underruns. A buffer underrun takes place when the writeable CD drive transfers data to the disc faster than the computer can provide it to the drive. Because the flow of data is interrupted, the recording stops and the media is useless. Why are the resulting CDs called "coasters"? That's all they're good for! With early CD-R and CD-RW drives, we had so many problems with buffer underruns we could have created some real coasters by putting cork on one side of the media!

Depending on the CD-recording/mastering software you use, you might get immediate notification of a buffer underrun or discover it only after you can't read the disc you created in any drive.

All current writeable CD drives include some type of buffer underrun prevention technology, such as BURN-Proof, SmartBurn, and others. These technologies work by suspending the CD creation process whenever the buffer memory in the CD runs out of information, and they continue the process when more data is available. Upgrading from a drive that lacks this feature to a drive that supports this feature is the easiest way to avoid buffer underruns and enjoy much faster disc creation times.

Here are some other ways to avoid creating a coaster with your drive:

- If your drive supports buffer underrun prevention, make sure your CD or DVD-mastering software also supports this feature and make sure you leave it enabled (refer to Figure 3.32). Generally, the CD and DVD-mastering programs supplied with drives with buffer underrun prevention include this feature, as do recent versions of retail CD/DVD-mastering programs.

- If your preferred CD/DVD-mastering program doesn't offer a buffer underrun prevention feature, upgrade to a version that does if your drive also has this feature.

- If your drive or CD/DVD-mastering program doesn't support buffer underrun protection, use the fastest mastering speed that is reliable. We don't recommend recording speeds above 8× when buffer underrun prevention isn't available.

- If your CD-mastering software offers a Test option (refer to Figure 3.32), use it to simulate CD or DVD recording at various speeds. If the program reports an error at 8× recording speed, reduce the speed and try the test again.

- Copy your data files to a fast, unfragmented hard disk. If your files are scattered across multiple drives, are located on another optical drive, or are on a different computer on a network or a serial or parallel direct connection, the likelihood of a buffer underrun is very high. Copy the files you want to transfer to CD into a single folder and defragment the drive containing that folder.

→ See "Using Error-Checking (CHKDSK) and Defrag," Chapter 2, p. 123, to learn more about checking drives for errors and defragmenting files.

- Leave your computer alone while the CD or DVD-mastering task is running. Don't play Solitaire, read email, or surf the Web; any activity on the system other than CD or DVD mastering can cause a buffer underrun. You should also disable screensavers, prevent antivirus programs from scanning the system, and turn off all other unnecessary programs.

If you continue to burn coasters, even after enabling the buffer under-run features, check for a new firmware update for your rewritable CD or DVD drive.

Get a More Reliable Rewriteable DVD Drive and Avoid the Pain

Buffer underrun prevention features are now universal, and almost every vendor sells rewritable dual-layer dual-format DVD drives that also include buffer underrun prevention features for less than $125! These drives are much faster, more reliable, and a whole lot more flexible and fun than their predecessors. Check the latest reviews at *PC World* (http://www.pcworld.com) and *PC Magazine* (http://www.pcmagazine. com) to find a new writeable DVD drive (remember, they can also write CDs).

Troubleshooting Your Printer

TROUBLESHOOTING

FAST TRACK TO SOLUTIONS (SYMPTOM TABLE)

Symptom	Flowchart or Book Section	See Page
My printer can't print.	Printer Can't Print	**674**
I'm having problems with my scanner.	Scanner Problems	**677**
My printer is producing poor-quality output.	Print Quality Problems	**676**
My USB printer works great on my Windows XP computer, but doesn't work with Windows 98.	USB Printing Issues	**247**
My printer won't display status messages when I use it with a switchbox.	Switchbox Issues	**249**
I'm not sure what the best resolution is to use for scanning photos I want to print.	Choosing Print-Worthy Images	**257**
When I print pages with a lot of graphics on my laser printer, they have to be ejected, and the page isn't completely printed.	Can't Print a Full Page	**272**
Other users on the network can't see my printer.	The Sharing Tab	**280**
My inkjet printer has gaps in its output.	Cleaning an Inkjet Printer	**252**
My inkjet printer's vertical lines are out of alignment.	Correcting Misaligned Printheads	**260**
I'm not sure if Windows can communicate with my printer.	Table 4.2	**287**
My document layout doesn't match the printer layout.	Table 4.2	**287**
The print ejects pages in reverse order.	Table 4.2	**287**
I want to put multiple pages on a single sheet of paper.	Table 4.2	**287**
I'm almost out of color ink but I need to print pages anyway.	Table 4.2	**287**
I need to print my document on a printer I can't connect to over the network or locally.	Table 4.2	**287**
I don't want to waste paper by printing documents that don't match my printer's configuration.	Table 4.2	**287**
I cannot select all the features of my printer.	Table 4.2	**287**
I want to put different paper/media sizes in the different paper trays of my printer.	Table 4.2	**287**
I added additional memory to my laser or LED printer to fix out-of-memory problems, but I'm not sure Windows has detected the additional memory.	Table 4.2	**287**
The printer is producing gibberish output.	Troubleshooting Gibberish Output	**290**

Printer Types and Technologies

Virtually every PC used at home is connected to (or can connect via a network to) one of two major document printer types:

- Inkjet
- Laser/LED

What are the differences? Inkjet printers use one or more ink cartridges and a printhead, which sprays tiny drops of ink onto the paper to make the image. Laser and LED printers use a laser beam or LED array to transfer an electrically charged image of the page stored in the printer's memory onto a rotating drum, which attracts toner that is transferred to the paper to make the printout; a fusing mechanism bonds toner to the paper to complete the process.

If you have an all-in-one unit on your desk (you know, the type of multi-purpose device that combines printing, scanning, copying—and maybe even faxing), it still fits into one of these categories.

Although laser/LED printers don't print very good photos (color models are better than monochrome, but still aren't all that good), many people get very good-looking color prints from their inkjet printers. However, with the rise of digital photography and scanning, specialized photo printers have become very common. Photo printers fall into one of two major categories:

- Inkjet
- Dye sublimation

Inkjet photo printers work in a fashion similar to standard inkjet printers, but are optimized for printing photos. Inkjet photo printers often use six or more ink colors, as opposed to the standard cyan, yellow, magenta, and black inks used by standard inkjet printers. Most inkjet photo printers use standard paper sizes, but a few are designed to print 4×6-inch snapshot prints only. Most recent photo printers also feature flash memory card slots for direct printing from your digital camera's flash memory cards, and some also support direct printing via a USB cable from the camera. Some all-in-one units based on inkjet printers can be considered photo printers, too; they also feature six or more colors and flash memory card slots.

Dye-sublimation printers (often called *photo printers* or *dye-sub printers*) use a special three-colored (cyan, magenta, yellow) ribbon and a heated printhead. The printhead turns the dyes in the ribbon into a gas, which permeates the photo paper to create a true continuous-tone photographic print. Each color is printed separately, and most dye-sub printers add a protective overcoat at the end of the printing process.

Some dye-sub printers can print on multiple paper sizes, but most print 4×6-inch snapshot prints only. Some include flash memory card readers for direct printing, whereas others connect to digital cameras with USB cables or include a proprietary interface for direct connection to a digital camera. The latter are often called *camera docks*. Camera docks can print index prints and snapshots directly from the camera's flash memory card or internal memory, and they can also be used to transfer photos from the camera to the computer's hard disk. You can also use a camera dock to print photos already on your hard disk, just as you would use any other photo printer.

Just as printers fall into separate categories, so do printer interfaces. These include the following:

- Parallel (LPT) ports (primarily on older printers)
- USB 1.1 and USB 2.0 ports
- Network printing via a host PC
- Direct wired or wireless network printing

With so many combinations of printer and interface technologies, printers can be almost as confusing as the "personal confuser" they're usually connected to. When they work well, the results are stunning. But when they stop working—well, that's why you're reading this chapter, isn't it?

Troubleshooting Common Printer Problems

No matter the specifics of your printer problem, the problem is usually found in one of these three areas:

- The printer can't print at all.
- The printer can print, but the print quality is poor.

- The printer prints gibberish instead of the text or photos you expected.

If the printer can't print at all, what should you check? Our checklist includes the following:

- The printer is offline.
- No power to the printer.
- Loose, damaged, or incorrect cabling.
- Problems with the parallel or USB ports.
- A paper jam.
- Printer is out of ink or toner.
- Printer is not configured correctly.
- Network problems (with a network printer).
- Printer is damaged (mechanically or electronically).

If your printer is producing a recognizable document or photo but the print quality isn't what you had in mind, check the following:

- Dirty printer components such as the printhead or paper rollers
- Wrong print-quality or paper-type settings with an inkjet or photo printer
- Not enough installed laser/LED printer memory
- Wrong settings in the printer properties sheet
- Printing a low-resolution or small-sized photo at too large a size

If your printer is wasting massive amounts of paper by printing gibberish, check the following:

- Using the wrong printer driver with a printer (such as an HP LaserJet printer driver with an Epson inkjet printer)
- Damaged printer port or printer cable
- Corrupted printer driver files

Some of these lists of possible solutions are pretty long. But, before you run off wondering if you'll ever be able to figure out the problem, take a closer look at each list. In each situation, we've listed the easy stuff first (an approach we take throughout the book). Here's why: In

our many years of experience with wrestling with computer and peripheral problems, in the vast majority of cases, there's a simple solution
to most problems. Keep that in mind.

Our goal is to help you find the solution (simple or not-so-simple) to
your printer problems.

Leo Says

Got an All-in-One Device? You Might Need to Check Multiple Chapters for a Solution.

The troubleshooting tips and methods in this chapter apply
equally well to standalone printers and the printer portion of an all-in-
one (multifunction) device. If you're having problems with the scanner
part of an all-in-one device, be sure to head over to Chapter 6,
"Troubleshooting Multimedia and Imaging Devices," for help.

Troubleshooting a Printer That Doesn't Print

Regardless of the type of printer you have (laser/LED, inkjet, or dye
sublimation), all printers can suffer from common problems, which
can cause them to fail to print.

If you're trying to print from Windows, you need to understand how
Windows handles print jobs. Normally, Windows sends print jobs to a
print queue (a temporary file that holds the print jobs until the printer
is ready for them). Consequently, you might not see an error message
right away when the printer can't print. You can view the contents of
the print queue by opening the printer icon in the Windows system
tray (see Figure 4.1). However, eventually Windows will display an
error message similar to the one shown at the bottom of Figure 4.1.

As you can see from Figure 4.1, Windows XP offers the Printer
Troubleshooter. If you're totally lost at sea about why you can't print,
give it a click. However, we think you'll spend your time better in most
cases if you give our troubleshooting tips a try first.

For quick solutions for a printer that can't print, see the "Printer Can't
Print" flowchart, p. 674. For details, keep reading!

Printer Is Offline

A printer has two basic conditions in relation to the computer it's connected to:

Click Help, Troubleshooter in
Windows XP to activate the
Printer Troubleshooter   Print queue window

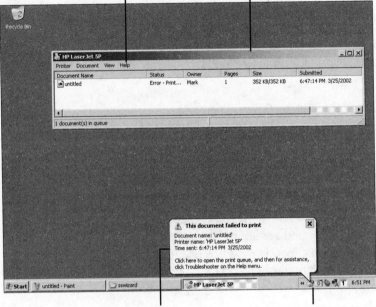

FIGURE 4.1
Windows XP's print queue (top) will try to send a print job to a local printer for several minutes. If it cannot do so, it will eventually display an error message (bottom).

Print queue error message   Printer icon in system tray

- Online (ready to receive data)
- Offline (can't receive data)

When you turn on a printer, it goes online by default. You take the printer offline if you need to perform one of the following tasks:

- Change the toner or ink cartridge
- Add paper
- Eject a partially printed sheet of paper
- Fix a paper jam or other problem

A printer will also go offline if the printer cable is loose or if the printer runs out of paper.

If the printer is offline because it's out of paper, turned off, or for some other reason, you can't print. See "Troubleshooting an Inkjet Printer with Its Status Lights," p. 251 (this chapter), or "Laser/LED Printer Status Lights and Messages," p. 270 (this chapter), to determine whether your printer is online.

If there is nothing wrong with the printer when you set it to online mode, it should begin printing immediately. If it still cannot print, check the following:

- Cable connections
- Port problems
- Paper supply and paper jams
- Ink and toner levels
- Power connections

See the following sections for details.

Printer Cable Is Loose or Detached

Printers are normally connected to the computer through either the parallel (LPT) port or the USB port. Parallel port cables and connectors are heavy and should be screwed securely into place at the computer end and clipped into place at the printer end (see Figure 4.2). If you need to tighten or reconnect a parallel cable, shut down the computer and printer to avoid damaging the ports.

FIGURE 4.2
Attaching the parallel (LPT) cable to the printer (top) and computer (bottom).

Parallel port (called DB25F)

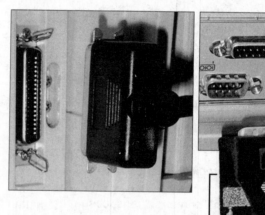

Parallel connector (called DB25M)

Unlike their parallel equivalents, USB cables and connectors are very lightweight and are easily pushed into place without the need for screws or clips. USB cables are also hot-swappable, so you can attach them while the computer and printer are turned on without having to worry about doing damage to the ports (see Figure 4.3).

USB Type B cable connector   USB Type B port (on printer)

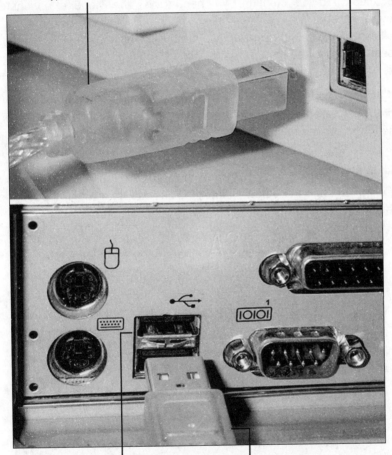

FIGURE 4.3
Attaching the USB cable to the printer (top) and computer (bottom).

USB Type A ports (on computer)   USB Type A cable connector

By the way, USB 1.1 and Hi-Speed USB (also known as USB 2.0) connectors are identical. Most recent USB cables are rated for either version of USB.

Wrong Printer Is Selected in Windows

If you have more than one printer, Windows automatically uses whichever one is set as the default printer. This is the printer that will be used if you select the Print icon from the top-level toolbar in web browsers or other applications. If you want to use a different printer connected to your computer, you need to use the File, Print options on the application's menu bar. This will open a Print dialog box that allows you to select any available printer for this job. Usually you must select the desired printer from a drop-down menu or an icon-based list, as shown in Figure 4.4.

If the selected printer still does not print, there must be some other problem at work. Use the "Printer Can't Print" flowchart on p. 674 or scan the other sections in this chapter to find a solution.

Changing the Default Printer in Windows

You can change the default printer in Windows from within the Printers folder. Here are the steps to follow:

1. Open the Printers folder. In Windows XP, click Start, Control Panel, Printers and Other Hardware, View Installed Printers. In other Windows versions, click Start, Settings, Printers.

FIGURE 4.4

Selecting a different printer than the default in Windows XP.

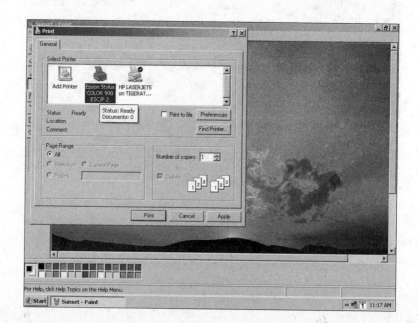

2. Right-click the printer you want to make the default printer and select Set as Default.

Port Problems

A printer cannot work properly if the port it's connected to isn't working properly, isn't configured properly, or isn't present. You can use the Windows Device Manager to view the current configuration of the ports your printer uses and to correct any conflicts.

→ See "Using Device Manager", Chapter 2, p. 100, for details.

Virtually all computers have parallel and USB 1.1 ports built in; many recent computers also have Hi-Speed USB (USB 2.0) ports built in. These ports are enabled, disabled, and configured through the system BIOS.

→ See "Using Device Manager to Troubleshoot USB Input Devices", Chapter 7, p. 433, for details about USB port configuration. See "Parallel Ports Troubleshooting," Chapter 7, p. 453, for details about parallel port configuration.

USB Printing Issues

Windows XP has built-in drivers for most USB devices, including some printers. However, even if the printer you use is listed in Windows XP's printer database, you should go ahead and install the enhanced printer driver CD provided by the printer vendor. Windows XP's built-in printer drivers don't have as many features as the drivers supplied by the printer vendors.

If you plug in your printer before installing the enhanced printer driver and Windows XP doesn't recognize it, it might be installed as a "USB printer" or an "unknown device." Either way, it isn't going to work properly. Remember: First install the driver, then connect the printer!

Hi-Speed USB Support Issues

Some recent printers are especially designed to work with the faster Hi-Speed USB (USB 2.0) ports found on most recent systems. Although these printers will work when plugged into USB 1.1 ports, you will see an error message indicating that they should be plugged into USB 2.0 ports for best performance. Figure 4.5 shows a typical error message generated with Windows XP.

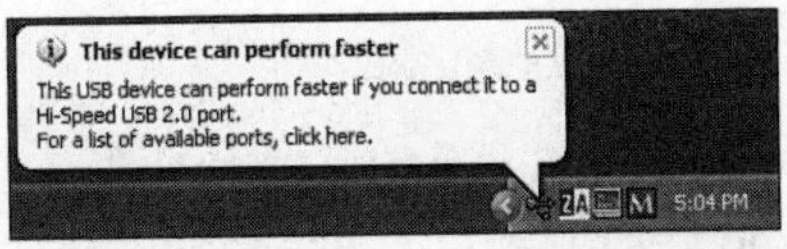

FIGURE 4.5

An error message generated by Windows XP when you plug a Hi-Speed USB device (such as a printer) into a USB 1.1 port.

➔ *See*
"Troubleshooting USB 2.0 (Hi-Speed USB) Support," Chapter 7, p. 418, for details.

If you're positive your computer has built-in or add-on Hi-Speed USB ports but they're only being recognized as USB 1.1 ports, you might need to enable Hi-Speed USB support, install the appropriate drivers, or install the appropriate updates to Windows.

Parallel Port Modes

If you are still using a printer that plugs into the parallel port, you need to understand that parallel ports can be configured in many ways:

- **Standard**—This mode (also called *compatible mode*) is designed for output only, and sends data very slowly; it is the default setting on many computers, but should be changed to one of the other modes to support modern printers or other parallel port devices.

- **Bi-directional**—This mode (also called *PS/2 mode*) can send and receive data at the same rate, and requires a bi-directional cable. It is not as fast as EPP or ECP, but it will allow you to receive information such as ink or toner levels from your printer.

- **Enhanced Parallel Port (EPP)**—This mode is much faster than either bi-directional or compatible, and it supports printers and storage devices you might want to attach to your parallel port.

- **Enhanced Capabilities Port (ECP)**—This mode is designed for use with printers and scanners.

- **ECP/EPP**—This mode combines the features of EPP and ECP; an excellent choice if you are trying to connect devices that prefer different modes on the same port.

EPP and ECP are parts of the IEEE-1284 parallel port specification, which also requires that an IEEE-1284-compliant parallel cable (also compatible with earlier modes) be used with the port.

If you can print, but you cannot receive ink levels or other information back from your printer, or you can't use the port for devices other than a printer, you probably have the wrong parallel port mode set in the BIOS. To change the parallel port setting, follow these steps:

1. Shut down all running programs.

2. Click Start, Shut Down, Restart.

3. When the computer restarts, press the key(s) used to access your computer's BIOS setup program.

4. Navigate to the screen where parallel port configuration is performed.

5. Select the port setting recommended for your printer and any other hardware attached to the parallel port; if you're not sure what to use, use EPP/ECP if available.

6. Save the changes and restart the computer.

For details, see "Controlling Your PC's Operation with BIOS Setup," Chapter 1, p. 41.

Switchbox Issues

Switchboxes allow multiple computers to share a printer, or multiple printers to share a single parallel or USB port. If you use a switchbox to allow two or more printers to share a single parallel port and you fail to switch to the correct printer before printing, you could send a print job intended for one printer to another printer. Because different brands and models of printers use different printer languages, garbage output will usually result.

If you use a switchbox with IEEE-1284 parallel ports (EPP, ECP, and EPP/ECP), you need to make sure the switchbox and the special cable that connects the switchbox to the computer are also IEEE-1284 compliant. Otherwise, slower printing will result and you won't be able to receive status messages from the printer.

The solutions to other types of printer problems vary with the type of printer you have.

Troubleshooting Inkjet Printers

Inkjet printers are far-and-away the most common type of printer found in homes and home offices. Many businesses also find that the quiet printing and ability to print great color pages make inkjet printers very popular at the office as well.

Although most printing problems with inkjet printers are caused by trouble with the cartridge or printhead, mechanical problems with the drive mechanism or paper feed can also lead to print failures.

Figure 4.6 shows the major features of a typical inkjet printer when the cover is opened.

FIGURE 4.6
A typical inkjet printer with a rear-mounted paper feed.

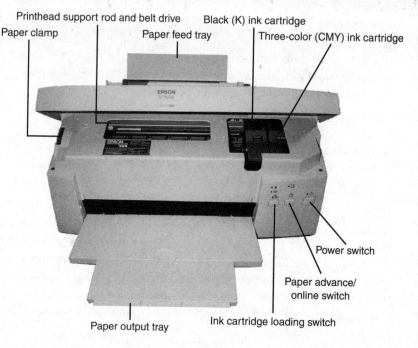

Printhead support rod and belt drive | Black (K) ink cartridge
Paper clamp | Paper feed tray | Three-color (CMY) ink cartridge
Power switch
Paper advance/online switch
Paper output tray | Ink cartridge loading switch

Printers that use a single ink cartridge for cyan, magenta, and yellow force you to replace the cartridge if a single ink color runs out. However, most recent models use separate ink cartridges for each color:

- Cyan (C)
- Magenta (M)
- Yellow (Y)
- Black (K)

Some photo printers also feature light (photo) cyan, light magenta cartridges, and sometimes photo black for a total of six or seven colors.

When the print command is sent to an inkjet printer, a ribbon cable (not visible in Figure 4.6) carries print signals from the computer to the printheads, which spray droplets of ink onto the surface of the paper to form the image.

If the printhead control cable is damaged, you won't be able to print, but this is a very rare problem. However, it's not unheard of. A while back, a colleague of mine made a house call to check out a printer whose LEDs were blinking erratically and wouldn't print. He opened the cover to find that the client's pet ferret had gnawed on the flex ribbon cable attached to the printhead. Don't let your pets eat your printer!

You might think that a house pet's appetite is a pretty unlikely way to damage a printer—and you'd be right! It's more likely that damage could occur to the drivetrain, which moves the printhead back and forth, or to the latches that hold the ink cartridges in place on some models. If you don't park the printhead correctly before you try to remove the ink cartridges, the printhead could actuate and not be able to move because the latches are blocked by the printer enclosure. This could crack the latches or damage the drivetrain if allowed to continue. To avoid damage to these moving parts, always be sure to shut down the printer with its own power switch before you remove any paper jams.

Most inkjet printing problems can be diagnosed through using the printer's status lights or its properties sheets.

Troubleshooting an Inkjet Printer with Its Status Lights

The power light on most inkjet printers glows steadily when the printer is resting. When the printer is receiving data or performing a task such as cleaning its printheads, the light blinks. Other typical status lights are used to indicate the status of the ink cartridges and paper tray. In many cases, these lights stay off unless there's a problem.

Figure 4.7 shows the status lights on a typical inkjet photo printer, the Hewlett-Packard DeskJet 6540.

In this example, if the Resume light flashes, there is a paper-feed problem; add paper or remove the paper jam. If one of the ink status lights blinks, wait until the print cartridge cradle is no longer moving and is silent, then lift the cartridge latch to open it for cartridge replacement.

Note that some printers require you to press a button to move the ink cartridges to a special reload position. Most recent printers include an ink-status-monitoring tool installed as part of the printer driver. Use this onscreen status indicator, which is often displayed during printing, to determine which color(s) will soon need to be replaced. See "Tracking Ink Consumption," p. 259 (this chapter), for more information.

FIGURE 4.7

Status lights and controls on a typical color inkjet printer, the Hewlett-Packard DeskJet 6540.

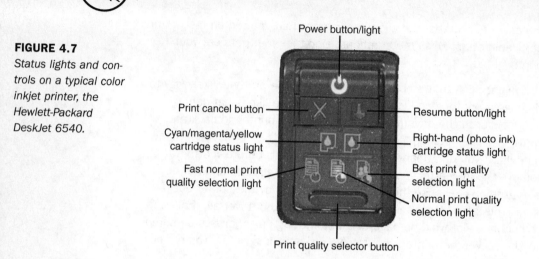

Power button/light

Print cancel button

Resume button/light

Cyan/magenta/yellow cartridge status light

Right-hand (photo ink) cartridge status light

Fast normal print quality selection light

Best print quality selection light

Normal print quality selection light

Print quality selector button

Solving the "Inkjet Printer Blues"

Inkjet printers, no matter how little you pay for them, are amazingly complex devices. It shouldn't be surprising that there are a lot of issues to check when they don't print or don't print as well as they should. Check out our list of typical problems:

- Dirty printer components
- Incorrect print quality/media selections
- Paper jams
- Failure to make use of the options available in the printer properties sheets
- Trying to print an image or document of too low a quality for satisfactory reproduction
- Running out of ink
- Misaligned printhead

Now that you know what can go wrong, let's look at how to fix each of these problems.

Cleaning an Inkjet Printer

Is your inkjet printer dirty? We're not talking about the smudges near the power button or a bit of dust on the top cover (although we'd suggest an occasional wipedown with an antistatic cleaner such as

Endust for Electronics to keep your printer looking its best). No, what we're talking about is gunk on the inside of your printer. A gunked-up printer produces results like these:

- Random ink smudges on the front and rear of printed pages
- Breaks and gaps in printed output

Either one of these problems can turn an expensive piece of heavy-weight glossy photo paper, a sheet of mailing labels, or a page of business cards into instant trash. The good news is that you don't need a screwdriver or an electronics degree to clean your inkjet printer. Instead, use one of the following methods.

To get rid of ink smudges and to help clean off the printheads, start by purchasing a set of inkjet cleaning sheets from your office supply dealer and using one or two in your printer. These sheets might be pre-moistened or might include a spray cleaner that is applied to one side of the sheet before it is run through the printer. This removes most of the ink residue from rollers and printheads. The Staples #569277 Inkjet Printer Cleaning Kit (about $11) also includes swabs you can use to clean up areas the cleaning sheet cannot access.

If you have an HP, Lexmark, Dell, or Canon inkjet printer, you can remove the printheads from the printer (HP, Lexmark, and Dell print-heads are part of the ink cartridge, whereas Canon's ink cartridges and printheads can be changed separately or as a unit). After removing the printheads, you can wipe them off with a standalone inkjet cartridge cleaning kit before inserting them back into your printer. Epson printheads are built into the printer, and you should not remove the ink cartridges until they are exhausted.

Finally, you can use a damp cloth to wipe off the rollers visible below the printhead while you work the paper-feed button to move the rollers. To avoid ink smears or clogs, be sure to shut down the printer with its own power switch instead of with a surge protector. By using the printer's own power switch, you cause the ink cartridges to self-cap to prevent them from drying out or leaking ink onto the rollers.

If breaks and gaps in printed output remain after you clean the printer, you need to use the printer's built-in head-cleaning routine to clean the printheads. With most printers, you can activate this routine and test the effectiveness of cleaning through the Utilities menu of the printer's properties sheet. The test feature makes a printout using each color separately, so you can determine which ink cartridge is causing the problem. Figure 4.8 shows you the Nozzle Check cleaning utility used by the Epson Stylus Photo 925.

FIGURE 4.8

The Epson Stylus Photo 925 Nozzle Check head-cleaning utility.

Click Nozzle Check from the Utility tab to start the utility

Good print quality has no gaps in any color; click Finish

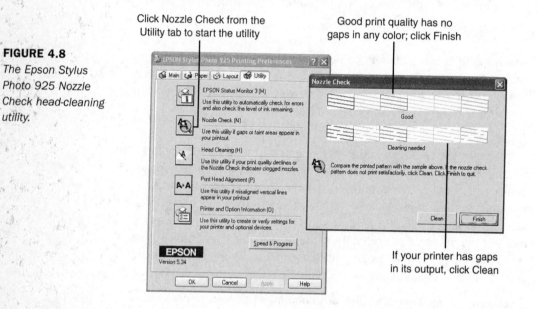

If your printer has gaps in its output, click Clean

➜ See "Enhanced Printing Preferences," this chapter, p. 279, for details.

Some printers also allow you to run the same routine by pressing buttons on the printer itself. If the print quality doesn't improve after you run the printhead-cleaning utility three or four times, you should replace the ink cartridge, which is producing poor-quality printing.

Leo Says

Clean the Printhead Before You Print Your Masterpiece

Before you spend 10 or 15 minutes (and a couple of bucks!) printing a high-resolution photo-quality enlargement onto glossy photo paper, take a few moments to test the output with plain paper and to clean the printheads if they're clogged. Many inkjet printers will develop minor clogs if they're left on for protracted periods of time, and cleaning the printheads will help prevent a spoiled print. Keep in mind that running the printer's cleaning utility uses up ink, so try to avoid the need to run it.

Choosing the Right Print Settings for Your Media

Even if your inkjet printer is capable of printing brilliant photos, it's likely to default to plain-paper printing at a relatively low print resolution of somewhere between 300 and 600 dpi. The results are passable if you do, in fact, use plain paper.

However, the results are cringingly awful if you use glossy heavyweight photo paper or another photo-quality paper stock with the plain-paper setting. Likewise, if you select a glossy photo paper setting but use plain paper, the results are also ghastly.

For results you'll be proud to share or frame, instead of results fit only to throw in the trash, the paper type and output quality selections you make in the printer properties sheet are critical to the quality of your output (see Figures 4.9 and 4.10). They're even more critical if you're printing on decals, overhead transparency film, or other special media.

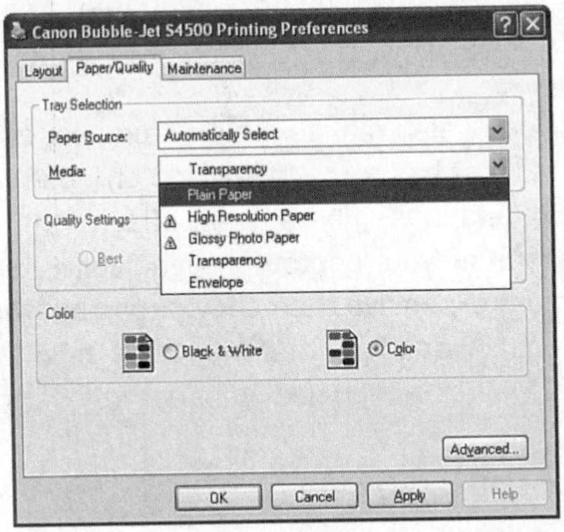

FIGURE 4.9

The media choices available for a typical inkjet printer (Canon Bubble-Jet S4500), as shown in the Windows XP Printing Preferences dialog.

FIGURE 4.10

When Glossy Photo Paper is selected with some printers, the Best quality setting is automatically selected. Plain Paper offers a variety of settings.

Why are media and quality settings so important when you use an inkjet printer? Inkjet printers vary the amount of ink used and how the printhead moves to create the printout based on the media choice you make and the print quality you select. If you mismatch the media option in the Printing Preferences dialog with the actual media used for the printout, you might soak your printout with excessive ink or cause gaps in the printed output.

If you're not happy with the print quality at "Best" output, you have two options you can try:

- Install a custom printer driver made by the printer vendor for your version of Windows. Custom printer drivers often provide more features than the standard Windows printer driver, and might support higher resolutions as well.
- Click Custom in the standard Windows Printing Preferences dialog (refer to Figure 4.10), click the Advanced button, and choose a higher print quality setting or resolution (if available) from the Advanced dialog.

The paper you choose also makes a big difference, even if it's "plain" paper. Avoid paper that has a rough surface or loose fibers. This can cause ink wicking, and loose fibers might stick to the printhead and cause problems with all your printouts. High-quality paper made for inkjets is a bit more expensive than copy paper, but the results are worth the extra cost. We're fond of 24-lb. 100+ brightness paper, which also works well as a high-quality paper in laser printers.

Preventing and Fixing Paper Jams

Paper jams can be painful, both for your media and for you. You'll never know just how tough a standard sheet of paper is until you try to drag it out of the bowels of a printer after a misfeed or jam. You might also be surprised to find out what kind of havoc a tiny torn-off corner piece can have on subsequent printouts. With inkjet printers often being cheaper to replace than to repair, it's best to avoid paper jams, which, if severe enough, could cause your printer to take a trip to the repair shop or the electronics recycler.

How can you avoid paper jams?

- Make sure you install the paper correctly. Be sure to adjust the paper guides correctly and make sure the stack is even before you insert it into the printer. Don't use more than the maximum number of sheets in the feeder. When in doubt, use less paper. If you're printing on heavyweight glossy photo paper, decals, or business card stock, run one sheet at a time to avoid problems.

- Adjust the head gap when you print thick media. If you print on envelopes, labels, transparencies, or card stock, be sure to adjust the head gap wider than normal to avoid smudges and possible paper jams.

- Adjust the head gap back to normal after you switch back to normal (20 to 24 lb.) paper.

If you need to remove a paper jam, turn off the printer with its own power switch and carefully remove all paper residue.

Creating Print-Worthy Images

If you've ever saved a photo from a website and tried to print it out at a larger size, you've probably been disappointed with the results. There's a simple reason: Website pictures are designed to be as small as possible to load quickly and take up minimal space onscreen. They don't have enough pixels to be reproduced properly by a printer if you try to enlarge them, even at the printer's low-quality setting.

The low-quality setting on a typical inkjet printer is 300 to 600 dpi (dots per inch), whereas the resolution of your monitor is about 96 dpi. As a result, a 3-inch-tall image onscreen only has enough dots to make a decent quality printout that's about 1 inch tall (96 is about 1/3 of 300).

What about digital photos? Digital cameras typically store images at 300 dpi. The megapixel (MP) rating, which is calculated from the number of pixels in the image, determines the recommended sizes of prints you can make. If you're as picky about image quality as we are, follow the recommendations in Table 4.1 for matching the MP rating to the maximum print size.

TABLE 4.1
RECOMMENDED MP RATINGS AND PRINT SIZES

MP Rating	Recommended Maximum Print Size
1MP	3×5 inches
2MP	5×7 inches
3MP	8×10 inches
4MP–5MP	11×14 inches
6MP and up	16×20 inches

Leo Says

Lies, Damn Lies, Statistics, and MP Ratings

The MP rating shown in Table 4.1 refers to the actual size of the image sensor in MP. Some vendors use a pair of sensors—one for light areas and one for dark areas—and add the sensor sizes together to claim a higher MP rating. For example, the Fuji FinePix F700 has two 3.1MP sensors (S-pixel and R-pixel) to provide a so-called "6MP" resolution. However, it's really only a 3.1MP camera. Here's the tip-off: If the vendor refers to "interpolated" MP resolution or two different sets of pixels, they're trying to pull a fast one.

Keep in mind that images scale down to smaller sizes very nicely. However, if you try to make prints larger than your camera's recommended print size or set your camera to a lower MP rating to jam more photos on your camera's flash memory card or mini-CD storage and then try to make a print larger than the recommendations, you'll see loss of quality in fine details such as hair, eyes, and so forth.

Similarly, if you're scanning photos you want to print out later, be sure to scan at a resolution of 300 dpi if you want to scan a snapshot (4×6-inch) or larger printout and then print it at the same size. If you want to enlarge a section of your original, scan at 600 dpi. However, if you're using a 35mm slide or negative scanner or a flatbed scanner with a transparency adapter, you will need to use a 2,400 dpi or higher resolution setting without scaling to create a printable image because of the small size of the original slide or negative.

Don't Overdo the Pixels!

The scanning resolutions suggested here might seem too low for the latest crop of inkjet photo printers, which boast of resolutions such as 5,760×1,440 dpi or 2,400×1,200 dpi, even though these settings create excellent, detailed scans that print well. The reason is that printers use their very high output dpi to perform color mixing and halftoning of the image. If you scanned a 4×6-inch photo at 1,200 dpi, you'd chew up hundreds of megabytes of disk space, your printer would take much longer to print the page, and the quality would not be any better than if you had scanned it at 300 dpi.

Tracking Ink Consumption

Most recent inkjet printers are designed to report ink levels back to the user through a dialog that is displayed during the print job or might be available through the Utilities tab on the printer's properties sheet. To receive ink level information from the printer, the printer must be turned on and you must use one of the following:

- A bi-directional printer interface such as EPP, ECP, or EPP/ECP (parallel port) or USB

- An IEEE-1284-compliant parallel cable (if you use the parallel port)

Figure 4.11 shows a typical display of ink levels as reported by the Epson Stylus Photo 925 and Epson Stylus Photo R300 printers.

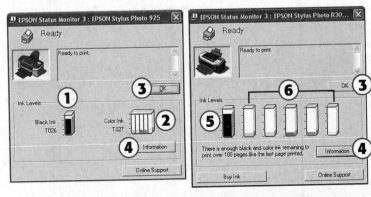

1. Black ink level (925)
2. Color ink level (925)
3. Click to close dialog

4. Click for ink cartridge model numbers
5. Black ink level (R300)
6. Color ink levels (R300)

FIGURE 4.11

The Epson Stylus Photo 925 (left) uses only two ink cartridges (black and photo color), whereas the Epson Style Photo R300 (right) uses six separate ink cartridges.

If any one of the five colored inks used by the single ink cartridge used by the Epson Stylus Photo 925 shown in Figure 4.11 runs out, the entire ink cartridge must be replaced. The waste inherent in this type of design is why most of the newest printers, such as the Epson Stylus R300, feature a separate ink cartridge for each color.

Leo Says

Check the Ink Levels Before You Print Your Masterpiece

Before you spend 10 or 15 minutes printing a high-resolution photo-quality enlargement, take a few moments to check the ink levels in your printer. If you run out of ink partway through the printout, you've just wasted as much as a dollar or two in ink and media.

To avoid using up your colored inks on noncritical printouts (such as web pages), we like to select black ink in the Printing Preferences dialog, as shown in Figure 4.10, before we print the page. The printer will use grayscale shading to reproduce colors with black ink, so you will still see the graphics on the printed result.

Correcting Misaligned Printheads

Did you ever wonder how inkjet printers create large fonts and graphics with a tiny printhead? The printer prints the document in horizontal strips, and the strips must align correctly. A misaligned black printhead can produce an effect similar to Figure 4.12, whereas misaligned color printheads produce grainy output.

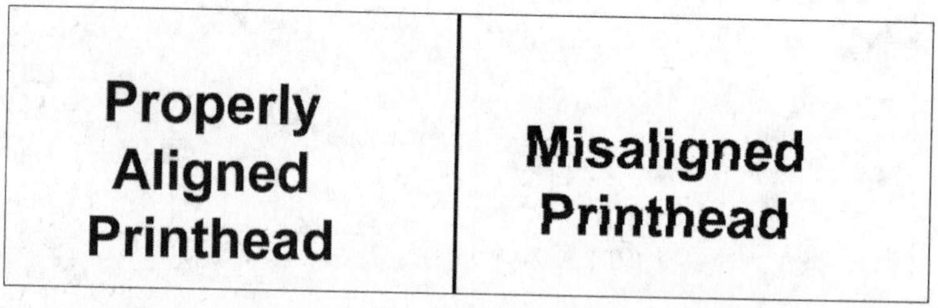

FIGURE 4.12
A simulation of proper printhead alignment (left) and misalignment (right).

Properly Aligned Printhead	Misaligned Printhead

To solve this problem, use the printhead alignment feature in your printer driver. Figure 4.13 shows the Epson Stylus Photo 925's Utility menu and one of the dialogs in the printhead alignment process.

During the process, you will be asked to choose the best-aligned output from your printer for both black and colored inks. Most printers will remember this setting and use it from that point on. However, some printers recommend you realign the printheads after you change ink cartridges. See your printer manual for details.

Click to start process

Click to select best-aligned black print samples

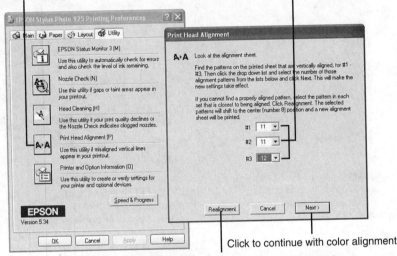

FIGURE 4.13
Using the Print Head Alignment feature in the Epson Stylus Photo 925 printer.

Click to continue with color alignment

Click to realign printhead and reprint black print samples

Troubleshooting Photo Printers

What makes an inkjet printer a photo printer? After all, you can print photos from just about any recent inkjet printer and get passable to terrific results, depending on the printer. Well, at the risk of offending some printer maker, let's take a stab at defining a "photo printer." Inkjet photo printers usually have the following features:

- Special photo inks (often six or more colors)
- Flash memory card slots for direct printing (these can sometimes be used as a card reader for transferring data to your PC)
- The ability to print directly from a camera or, in some cases, an external storage device such as a Zip, CD, or DVD drive

Figure 4.14 illustrates the ink cartridges and control panel of a typical inkjet photo printer, the Epson Stylus Photo R300.

FIGURE 4.14

The control panel and ink cartridges of the Epson Stylus Photo R300, which supports direct printing from flash memory cards and external storage.

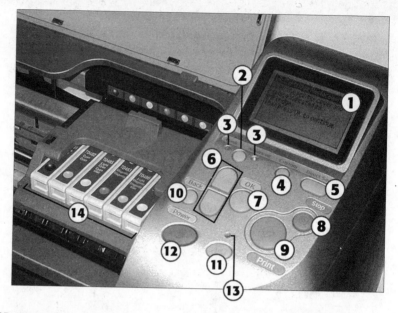

1. LCD control panel
2. Selects Basic (4×6-inch prints) or Advanced (various-sized prints) direct printing
3. Indicator light for Basic or Advanced print modes
4. Press to store user-defined settings for direct printing
5. Press to save photos to external drive
6. Selects options in LCD menu
7. Press to confirm menu selection
8. Press to stop current direct print job or cancel LCD menu settings
9. Press to start direct print job
10. Press to move back one level in LCD menu
11. Press to eject paper or to replace ink cartridges
12. Press to turn on or turn off printer
13. Blinks when ink cartridge(s) need to be replaced
14. Ink cartridges

Another common type of photo printer uses the dye-sublimation (dye-sub) process. Some of these printers are built into a dock—a proprietary device that enables you to print your pictures directly from your digital camera and transfer them to your computer's hard disk. An Eastman Kodak printer dock made for EasyShare digital cameras is shown in Figure 4.15.

As with garden-variety inkjet printers, the first place to learn how to troubleshoot an inkjet photo printer is with its control panel. As you can see from Figures 4.14 and 4.15, the extra features of a photo printer make for a more complex interface than with a regular photo printer (compare Figures 4.14 and 4.15 to Figure 4.7).

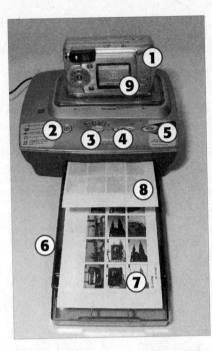

FIGURE 4.15
Creating a multipage index print with an Eastman Kodak EasyShare printer dock.

1. Kodak EasyShare digital camera
2. Press to transfer photos to computer
3. Selects print type
4. Selects photo to print from camera
5. Press to print selected photo or index print
6. Paper tray
7. Completed index print
8. Yellow layer of index print (in process)
9. Camera's LCD display shows selected photo or print process

The next place to look is at the flash memory card slots and external storage or camera connectors. The card slots and USB port used by the Epson Stylus Photo R300 are shown in Figure 4.16.

The proprietary connectors used by a Kodak EasyShare printer dock and EasyShare camera are shown in Figure 4.17.

If you are unable to print directly from your digital camera, check these connections.

Troubleshooting Printing from the PC

Photo printers, except for using additional ink colors, work in the same way as regular inkjet printers do when you print photos or other files from your PC. For troubleshooting procedures, see "Solving the 'Inkjet Printer Blues,'" p. 252 (this chapter).

Compact Flash memory card inserted into slot

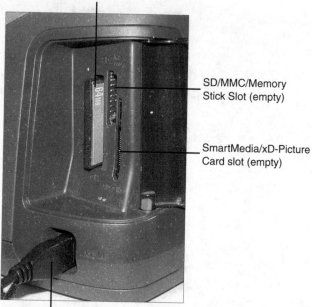

FIGURE 4.16
The Epson Stylus Photo R300, like most recent photo printers, can print directly from flash memory cards, but it can also print from external storage devices and some digital cameras connected via USB.

SD/MMC/Memory Stick Slot (empty)

SmartMedia/xD-Picture Card slot (empty)

USB cable to external drive

Printer/camera dock connector on the bottom of the EasyShare digital camera

Tripod socket on the digital camera

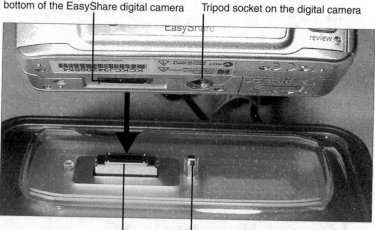

FIGURE 4.17
Digital cameras that work with printer docks, like the Kodak EasyShare camera shown here, use a proprietary connection on the bottom of the camera to connect to the dock. The arrow shows how the camera is connected to the dock.

Camera connector on the dock

Stabilizing post on the dock (inserts into tripod socket)

Got a Printer Dock? You Also Have a PC Printer!

Printer docks aren't just for direct printing from your digital camera. If you prefer to edit your photos for improved cropping, color balance, and contrast, as we often do, you can still make beautiful prints from your digital photos with your printer dock. Select the printer dock from the list of installed printers within your photo editing program or the photo management program supplied with your printer dock and, behold, another PC printer!

Troubleshooting Direct Printing

If you run into trouble printing directly from a flash memory card or from external storage with a photo printer, the problem could be any of the following:

- Can't print from flash memory card
- Can't print from external storage or digital camera connected to the printer
- Poor-quality prints
- Can't start the print job from LCD menu

Want solutions to these problems? Keep reading!

Can't Print from Flash Memory Card

If you don't insert your flash memory card far enough into the printer, the printer won't recognize the card and you won't be able to print from it. Many photo printers have signal lights for the card slots. If the light doesn't come on when you insert the card, remove the card and insert it again. Push on the card until it won't go into the slot any further, and the light should come on. See Figure 4.18 for a typical example of correctly and incorrectly inserted flash memory cards.

The flash memory card reader built into a photo printer will not be able to recognize the card's contents if the card has been erased, reformatted, or has been corrupted by removing it from a camera before shutting down the camera.

FIGURE 4.18

An incompletely inserted Sony Memory Stick (top) is not recognized by the printer; push it in all the way (bottom) until the activity light comes on.

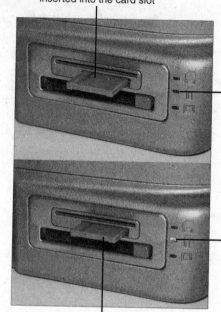

Sony Memory Stick not completely inserted into the card slot

Signal light is dark

Signal light glows to indicate connection

Sony Memory Stick completely inserted into card slot

➜ **For more information about flash memory data recovery, see "Preventing and Troubleshooting Data Loss in Digital Cameras," Chapter 6, p. 374.**

Try reinserting the card into a digital camera. If the card cannot be read by the camera, the card's file system has been corrupted. You will probably need to reformat the card to make it usable. If you reformat the card, you might be able to retrieve photos from the card by using a special flash memory data retrieval program such as MediaRECOVER.

Many different types of flash memory cards are used by digital cameras today. The oldest, bulkiest, and highest-capacity standard is Compact Flash. The bottom slot in Figure 4.18 is for Compact Flash media. If you insert other types of media into this slot, they will not work. However, because other types of media have connectors on the back side instead of on the end, as with Compact Flash, you will not damage your media.

Can't Print from Digital Camera or External Storage

Photo printers with a USB port, such as the Epson Stylus Photo R300 shown in Figure 4.16, are designed to work with specified types of digital cameras or external storage devices. Most recent photo printers and many recent digital cameras support the PictBridge standard, a standard developed by the Camera and Imaging Products Association for enabling direct printing from compatible digital cameras, regardless of brand. Learn more at http://www.cipa.jp/english/pictbridge/. To determine if your photo printer and digital camera support PictBridge, check with the vendors or see the PictBridge website.

What if your printer and digital camera don't support PictBridge? If they are made by Canon, they still might work together. Many Canon digital cameras and photo printers support BubbleJet Direct printing or Direct Print. See the Canon website for details and for firmware updates (required in some cases to enable this feature).

Follow these steps if you believe that your combination of photo printer and camera or external storage device should work for direct printing, but you can't get it to work:

1. Make sure the cable between the external storage device or digital camera and the printer is connected tightly at both ends.

2. Make sure the external storage device or digital camera is turned on. If you see an error message indicating the device is not supported, you cannot use that device as a source for photos.

3. Make sure the digital camera has adequate power. Use an AC adapter, fresh alkaline, or fully charged rechargeable batteries.

4. Make sure the printer is turned on.

5. Make sure your digital camera and printer are PictBridge compatible. Install any required firmware updates.

6. If either device is not PictBridge compatible but both are made by the same vendor, make sure the printer and camera support the same proprietary direct printing solution.

7. Check the printer directions for the proper method of retrieving photos from the digital camera or external storage device. In most cases, you need to print an index print first so you can identify the photos you want to print by number.

8. If all else fails, use the printer's own flash memory card slots or the PC's optical drive to access your photos.

Poor Direct Print Quality

If you are using an inkjet photo printer, you need to make sure you select the correct paper type from the LCD menu on the printer. Also, you need to check the ink levels before you start. Some photo printers, such as the Epson Stylus Photo 925, shown in Figure 4.19, show the paper type selection and the ink levels in the LCD display.

FIGURE 4.19

Setting an inkjet photo printer for glossy photo paper.

Paper Type menu selected   Glossy Photo paper selected

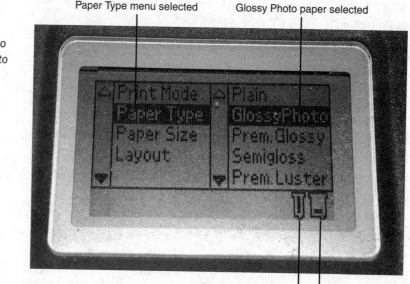

Black ink level (OK)⎦   ⎣Color ink level (low)

If you have the correct paper type selected but the print is streaked, your printer might have one or more clogged printheads or have run out of one or more ink colors. See "Tracking Ink Consumption," p. 259 (this chapter), and "Cleaning an Inkjet Printer," p. 252 (this chapter), for solutions.

Make sure you have loaded the paper correctly, particularly if you are using glossy or satin-finish paper. These types of papers can be printed on only one side.

If you have selected the correct paper type but the print is not as detailed as you would like, the image might have too few pixels for the image size you have selected. Refer to Table 4.1, p. 258, this chapter, for our recommendations for the maximum print size at various megapixel ratings. You might have selected a smaller image size or lower image quality in your digital camera to be able to store more photos than the default high-quality, full-resolution setting. We don't recommend this! Instead, try a smaller print size—for example, a 4×6-inch print instead of an 8×10-inch print.

Troubleshooting Dye-Sublimation Photo Printers

If you are using a dye-sublimation photo printer, check the following if you are experiencing poor print quality:

- **The print ribbon**—Dye-sublimation printers use a special ribbon. If the ribbon is damaged, replace it and replace the paper at the same time. The paper and ribbon are sold as a kit and are matched for best quality.

- **The paper tray**—If the paper is loaded incorrectly, you could be printing on the back side of the paper.

If the printer includes a cleaning cartridge, use it as recommended by the manufacturer.

Troubleshooting Laser/LED Printers

Unlike inkjet printers, in which most moving parts are readily visible to the naked eye, a laser or LED printer's mechanism is concealed within the printer cover. In fact, much of the imaging process is performed within the printer's toner cartridge. Figure 4.20 diagrams a typical laser printer's internal components.

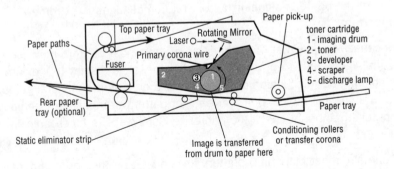

FIGURE 4.20

The components of a typical laser printer based on the Canon/HP laser engine. Some laser printers use a separate toner supply and imaging drum design, but most models use a design similar to the one shown in this figure.

An LED printer is identical to a laser printer, except that a fixed array of light-emitting diodes (LEDs) is used in place of a moving laser beam to place the image on the rotating drum inside the toner cartridge. Because most models of monochrome laser printers use a toner cartridge that contains the imaging drum, replacing the toner cartridge is a fast way to fix many types of printing problems with laser or LED printers.

Color laser printers are becoming increasingly common as prices drop. Traditional color laser printers use a print carousel, which uses four separate toner cartridges to print a color document in four passes. Some newer models use four separate toner cartridges to enable faster single-pass printing. As with monochrome laser printers, many image-quality problems with color laser printers can be solved by replacing the toner cartridge.

Laser/LED Printer Status Lights and Messages

Laser and LED printers work differently than inkjet printers. As soon as an inkjet printer receives data, it starts printing in a line-by-line fashion. Problems are visible right away because the printout starts right away, right in front of your eyes.

By contrast, laser and LED printers are page printers; they must receive an entire page worth of text, graphics, and print commands and transfer them to the imaging mechanism, which transfers them to the paper before the paper emerges from the printer. Because of their more complex operation, more things can go wrong; correct interpretation of the printer's signal lights or status messages is extremely important.

Because every printer brand is different, and most printers now use signal lights instead of an alphanumeric message display to indicate problems, our discussion of laser printer problems is a general guide; for the specific meaning of a given light pattern or message, see your printer's manual or check the printer vendor's website for technical documents.

Generally, most laser/LED printers have a light on their control panel that glows steadily to indicate the printer is online (ready to receive a print job). This same light blinks when the printer is receiving a print job.

Most printers have two or more other lights that will shine or blink in various patterns to indicate problems such as the following:

- Out of memory (the contents of the page are larger than the printer's available memory)
- Paper jam
- Paper out
- Toner cartridge problems
- Imaging drum problems

Although a few printers might use an alphanumeric display panel to provide the error message, you will normally need to look up the light pattern for your printer to determine the problem and its solution.

The bottom line is, learn the difference between normal and abnormal light displays on your printer.

Common Laser/LED Problems and Solutions

Typical problems with laser and LED printers include:

- Poor print quality
- Incomplete page printouts of graphics-heavy pages
- Slow printing of graphics-heavy pages
- Pages printed in reverse order when using the manual feed tray
- Trying to print an image of too low a quality for satisfactory reproduction
- Running out of paper

Use the following sections to solve the most common problems you are likely to encounter with your laser printer.

Troubleshooting Marks and Smudges on the Printout

Because of the different sizes used by the rollers, which are part of a laser or LED printer's paper path, you can often determine the exact cause of repeating or continuous extraneous markings on your printer's output by examining the distance between repeated markings on the output.

For example, with the HP LaserJet 1100 and 1200 series printers, a repetitive print defect that occurs every 1.25 inches indicates that the developing cylinder (part of the toner cartridge) is dirty or defective, whereas a print defect every 1.8 inches indicates a dirty or defective transfer roller. The exact values for your laser printer are normally provided in the documentation for the printer, or they can be viewed online. Follow the instructions for removing the toner cartridge to expose the rollers that need to be cleaned and then wipe the rollers off with a soft cloth. If the damaged or dirty rollers are within the toner cartridge, you might need to replace the toner cartridge. A continuous vertical black streak along all pages of the printout usually indicates a damaged toner cartridge that must be replaced.

It's Hot in There!

There are several potential hazards inside a laser or LED printer, including the following:

- The imaging laser (laser printers only)
- High-voltage electricity (both types)
- Hot fusing assembly (both types)

If you need to clean the printer or remove a paper jam, you should turn off and unplug the printer. If you need to clean the fuser rollers, let the printer cool down for a few minutes before you clean this part of the printer.

If you clean your printer and replace the toner cartridge but still find extraneous marks and smudges on your printouts, the printer might have internal damage, which requires professional service.

Can't Print a Full Page

Even the lowest-cost laser printers should be able to print a page of text, or a page with small graphics. However, if you try to print a page composed mostly of graphics, a page that has several different fonts, or a page with visible gridlines (such as a spreadsheet), you may run out of laser printer memory, causing an out-of-memory error. Because the printer could not finish printing the page, the page will remain in the printer until you eject it. When you eject it, only the part of the page that would fit in the printer's memory will be printed.

Here's how to cure problems with partial-page printouts:

- **Error recovery**—To recover from this error, eject the current page (see your printer's manual); note that the page will not be completely printed but will appear to be cut off at the point where the page contents exceeded the laser printer's memory.

- **Workaround**—If the page uses only one or two fonts but has a lot of graphics, the easiest way to print the page is to decrease the graphics resolution of the printer in the printer's properties sheet. For example, reducing a 1,200 dpi (dots per inch) laser printer's graphics resolution to 600 dpi reduces the amount of required printer memory by a factor of 4. Although graphics won't be as finely detailed, text quality is unaffected. If the printer uses PostScript, reduce the number of fonts in the document.

→ See "Understanding Your Printer's Properties Sheets," this chapter, p. 276, for details.

- **Solution**—Install more memory in the laser printer. The amount of RAM required to print a page varies with the printer's resolution, the size of the graphics, the number of fonts on the page, the size of the page (letter or legal size paper), and the printer's ability to compress graphic data. For a 600 dpi laser printer, your memory upgrade should add at least twice the amount of memory originally installed in the printer. For example, if your printer has 2MB of onboard memory and prints at 600 dpi, you should add at least 4MB (for a total of 6MB of RAM). If you are upgrading a 1,200 dpi laser printer, add at least four times the amount of memory originally found in the printer. This will enable you to print complex pages at their highest resolution, enable you to print two or more pages on a single sheet of paper, and may also speed up printing because the printer doesn't need to spend as much time compressing data.

See your printer's instruction manual for the type of memory module or card needed to upgrade the printer's memory.

Leo Says

Save Money by Buying Printer Memory from Memory Specialists

Although most laser printers use different memory modules than your PC does, you might not need to buy memory from your printer vendor. Check pricing and availability at major third-party memory vendors such as Crucial (http://www.crucial.com), Viking InterWorks (http://www.vikinginterworks.com), and others before you order OEM memory. You may save yourself some money.

Paper Jam

Paper jams can be caused by incorrect paper loading, wrinkled or damaged paper, or damp paper. Here's how to deal with a paper jam, and how to prevent it:

- **Error recovery**—Shut down the printer and open it to locate the paper jam. You might need to remove the toner cartridge on some models to find the paper jam. Remove the misfed sheet(s) and be sure to remove any torn paper or loose labels. Resend the print job after you turn on the printer. If the paper jam is located near the end of the paper path, beware of the hot fusing assembly when you remove the paper jam.

- **Solution**—Be sure to load the paper tray properly and insert it completely into the printer. Use only laser-compatible labels; copier labels aren't designed to handle the heat of laser printing and can come off inside the printer, possibly causing damage. If you can switch to a straight-through paper path (usually an optional rear paper tray) for labels and similar heavy stock, do so to minimize the chances of a paper jam (refer to Figure 4.20). Avoid using paper that is damaged, stuck together, warped, or wrinkled. Don't use media that is thicker or heavier than the printer is rated to accept.

Paper Out

Running out of paper is a normal part of printing, but you can minimize the interruption to your printing task by filling the paper tray before you start printing a long document. Here's how to avoid paper-out interruptions:

- **Error recovery and solution**—Open the paper tray and properly install new paper. Some printers will print normally as soon as you close the paper tray, whereas others require you to press the online/paper feed button to continue printing after you insert paper.

- **Workaround**—If the paper tray is defective or if it isn't completely inserted into the printer, you might continue to get a paper-out signal even after you fill the paper tray and reinsert it. In these cases, use the manual paper tray option (if available), use a replacement paper tray, or service the printer if the paper tray isn't a removable item.

Don't Throw Good Money After Bad

It's long been true that most inkjet printers aren't worth servicing once the warranty period is up; changes in technology and performance along with the throwaway nature of their design make replacement the rule. Laser printers have also dropped in price and improved in resolution and performance, so be sure to determine the servicing cost before authorizing a repair on an out-of-warranty laser printer. You may find that a new laser printer is a better way to spend your money.

I recommend the 50% rule: If a repair costs at least 50% of the cost of a comparable new printer, scrap the old printer and put the money toward a new model.

Toner Cartridge Problems

A damaged toner cartridge will put extraneous marks or smudges on every page it prints, and an empty toner cartridge can't print anything. Sooner or later, you will need to replace the toner cartridge for one reason or the other. Here's how to make sure whether the toner cartridge is the culprit:

- **Error recovery**—Shut down the printer and remove the toner cartridge (refer to your manual for specifics). Verify that the toner cartridge is properly inserted and contains toner. Watch for print quality problems when the first print jobs emerge after you reinstall an existing toner cartridge or install a new one.

- **Solution**—If the new toner cartridge doesn't improve print quality, recheck the printer for other problems; you may need to have it serviced.

If you use a color laser printer, you need to determine which toner cartridge has run out or is damaged. The colors are the same as those used in four-color inkjet printers: cyan, magenta, yellow, and black. Replace the correct color.

Fading or Uneven Text

Laser and LED printers normally produce uniform text. Here's what to do if your printer is producing faded text or text that has different densities in different parts of the page:

- **Error recovery and workaround**—You're probably running out of toner. Remove the toner cartridge and shake it gently, side to side, to redistribute the remaining toner more evenly. Print only necessary documents and check print quality until you can install a new toner cartridge. If you use a color laser printer, check the printer's signal lights to determine which color toner cartridge is low.

- **Solution and prevention**—Install a new toner cartridge immediately. To maximize toner cartridge print life, use the EconoMode (toner saving mode) if available when you print draft copies. Note that some color laser printers also use a separate imaging drum that can also run out and must be replaced periodically.

Understanding Your Printer's Properties Sheets

The Windows properties sheets for your printer enable you to control your printer's print quality, extend the life of consumables such as toner, perform printhead cleaning and other maintenance tasks, and solve various printer performance and output problems.

Whereas specific printers vary in the details of their properties sheets, most laser and LED printers offer similar options. Likewise, most inkjet printers are similar to each other in their properties sheets. Use the examples in this section as a general guide, and see the documentation for your printer for its specific features.

Accessing the Properties Sheets for Your Printer

To display the installed printers on your system in Windows XP, click Start, Control Panel, Printers and Other Hardware, View Installed Printers or Fax Printers. Some Windows XP installations place a Printers and Faxes icon on the Start button's flyout menu.

If you have more than one printer installed, the default printer (the printer automatically selected unless you choose another one) is indicated with a check mark. To view the properties sheet for the printer, right-click the printer's icon and select Properties from the menu (see Figure 4.21).

Virtually all printers of any type supported by Windows XP have the following properties sheets:

- General
- Sharing

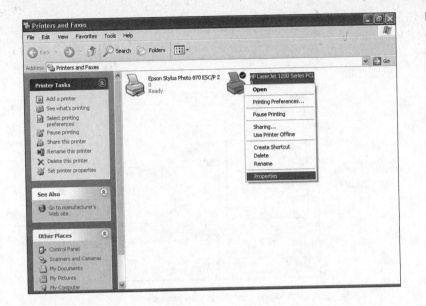

- Ports
- Device Options

To access printer-specific dialogs, click the Printing Preferences button on the General tab.

Each of these properties sheets is described in the following sections. Earlier versions of Windows feature similar options for their printers, although the placement of options on each tab will vary.

The General Tab

The General tab displays the printer name, location, comments, features, and test print option (see Figure 4.22).

Printing Preferences

Clicking the Printing Preferences button opens a new multitabbed window. If the printer uses a standard Windows XP printer driver, the Preferences dialog resembles the one shown in Figure 4.23. Use the Layout tab to select page orientation, number of pages per printed page, and page order. Click the Paper/Quality tab, shown in Figure 4.23, to adjust paper type and tray usage, and, with inkjet printers, to select print quality and media type settings.

FIGURE 4.22

The General tab provides a quick overview of the printer's features and provides access to the most common adjustments through the Printing Preferences button.

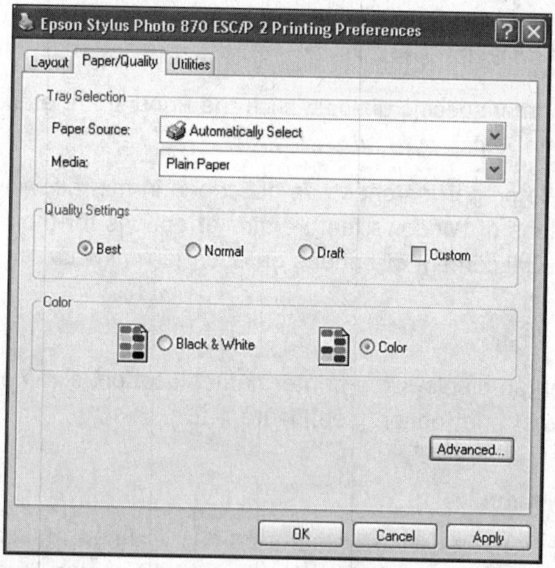

Lists the printer's major features

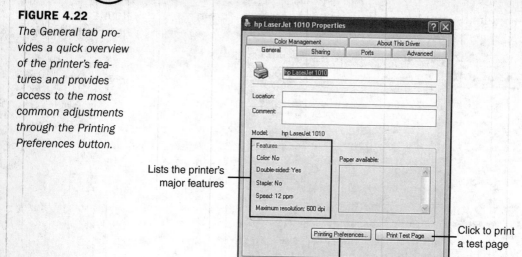

Click to print a test page

Click to open printer preferences dialog

FIGURE 4.23

The Paper/Quality tab of the Printing Preferences dialog for a typical inkjet printer using a standard Windows XP printer driver.

The Advanced button, available from one or more of the tabs in the Printing Preferences properties sheets, typically controls graphics resolution, output options, and printer features (see Figure 4.24).

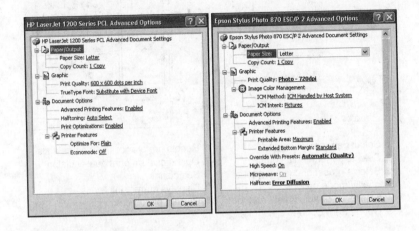

FIGURE 4.24

The Windows XP Advanced Options dialog for a typical laser printer (left) and inkjet printer (right); to change current settings, click the underlined text next to each option.

Enhanced Printing Preferences

Many vendors provide enhanced Printing Preference dialogs as part of their customized printer drivers, particularly for inkjet and photo printers. There are far too many variations to provide comprehensive coverage in this limited space, but some of the options you might see if you install a vendor-supplied printer driver from CD or the Internet include the following:

- **Main**—Sets the paper/media type, print quality, and color adjustments (see Figure 4.25). Click Custom to open up advanced dialogs for adjusting color and image quality (see Figure 4.26).

- **Page Setup (Layout)**—Sets the paper size and type, page orientation, and other options.

- **Maintenance (Utility)**—Used for printhead and component cleaning, print head alignment, and ink status monitoring (see Figure 4.27). Compare Figure 4.27 to Figure 4.13.

FIGURE 4.25

The Main tab of the Printing Preferences pages for Canon and Epson inkjet printers using vendor-supplied printer drivers.

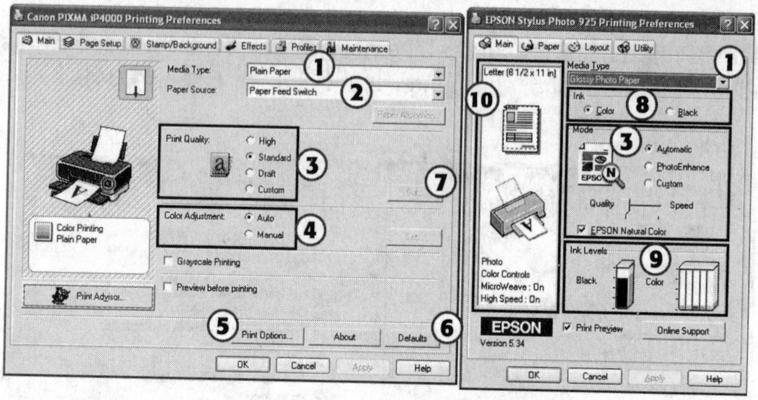

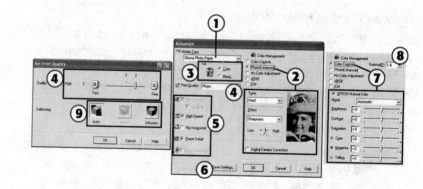

1. Select paper/media type
2. Selects paper/media source
3. Selects preset or custom print quality/mode options
4. Selects color adjustment method
5. Opens Print Options dialog

6. Resets preferences to their defaults
7. Opens custom print quality dialog
8. Selects ink
9. Displays current ink levels
10. Current printer settings

FIGURE 4.26

Custom Print Quality/Mode settings for Canon and Epson inkjet printers using vendor-supplied drivers.

1. Selects paper/media type
2. PhotoEnhanced setting/dialog
3. Selects ink
4. Selects print quality
5. Selects print options

6. Saves custom settings for reuse
7. ColorEnhanced setting/dialog
8. Adjusts gamma (print density)
9. Selects halftoning method

The Sharing Tab

If your computer is on a network, use the Sharing tab to enable or disable printer sharing (see Figure 4.28). If you enable printer sharing, specify a descriptive share name; this can be any name that will help you tell this printer from others, such as "Joe's Inkjet."

Cleaning options

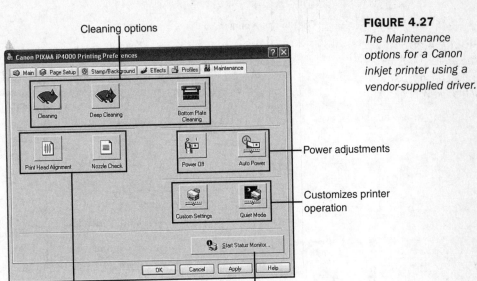

Power adjustments

Customizes printer operation

Nozzle check/alignment — Starts ink and paper status monitor

Use the Additional Drivers button to install printer drivers for other Windows versions so they can be downloaded by other computers on the network if needed. For example, if your network has Windows 9x and Windows Me computers that need to share the printer on your Windows XP computer, use this option to make sure that the correct drivers for those Windows versions will be available on your computer. When Windows 9x or Me computers connect to your computer to use your printer for the first time, they can download and install the drivers from your computer instead of needing to install the driver from their Windows CD or from an Internet download.

Keep in mind that Windows XP doesn't include the actual drivers; it's up to you to track them down and copy them to the system for remote installation. This feature can be more trouble than it's worth unless you're managing a fairly large network with a lot of computers running Windows 2000, Windows 9x, or Windows Me. You can always install the driver on each computer and ask the user to browse to the appropriate network print queue instead of using a local printer port.

FIGURE 4.28

The Sharing tab for a typical printer being shared in Windows XP.

Click to share printer

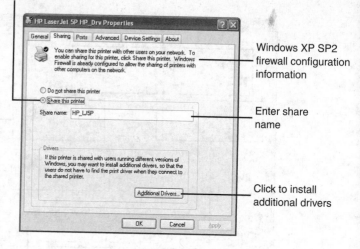

Windows XP SP2 firewall configuration information

Enter share name

Click to install additional drivers

The Ports Tab

Use the Ports tab to select the port (local or network) to be used for this printer. If your printer is Plug and Play, the correct port will be selected automatically for you (see Figure 4.29).

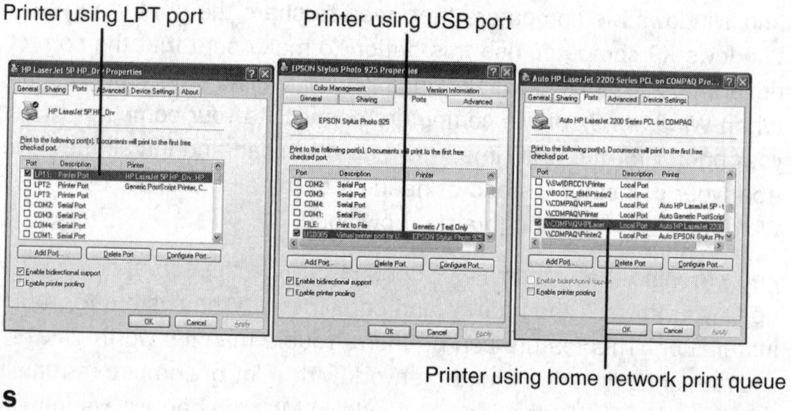

FIGURE 4.29

Printers using LPT (local), USB (local), and a home network print queue.

Printer using LPT port

Printer using USB port

Printer using home network print queue

Leo Says

Don't Mix Up Sharing and Network Printing!

A printer connected to your computer can be shared with others on the network. This type of printer is called a *shared printer*. On your computer, it uses a local printer port, but on other computers on your network, it uses a network print queue. Keep in mind that home networks don't use a dedicated server, and Windows XP describes this type of network print queue as a "local" printer port (see Figure 4.29).

The Advanced Tab

Use the Advanced tab to adjust printer priority, spooling options, separator page options, printer availability, and the data type sent to the printer (via the Print Processor button; see Figure 4.30). By increasing printer priority (default is 1; maximum is 99), you cause documents with a higher priority to be printed before documents with a lower priority. To prevent printer use during certain hours (such as overnight), select the Available From option and adjust the start and end times. The printer shown in Figure 4.30, for example, cannot be used in the morning or early afternoon. You can also elect to keep printed documents in the print queue (the list of documents to be printed) for reprinting later, prevent mismatched documents (documents with incorrect settings such as paper orientation or size) from printing with the Hold Mismatched Documents option, and bypass the print spool entirely if you can't print using print spooling. Changing the data type is not recommended unless the printer vendor specifically recommends it.

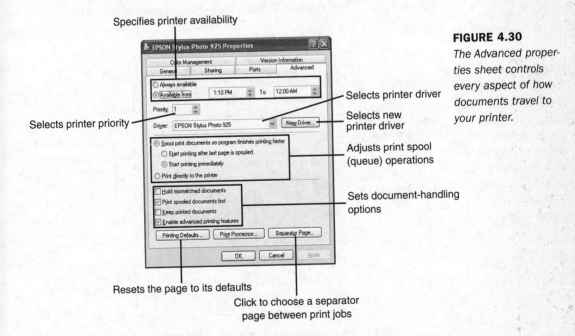

Specifies printer availability

Selects printer priority

Selects printer driver

Selects new printer driver

Adjusts print spool (queue) operations

Sets document-handling options

Resets the page to its defaults

Click to choose a separator page between print jobs

FIGURE 4.30

The Advanced properties sheet controls every aspect of how documents travel to your printer.

Leo Says

Can't Print? Check the Advanced Tab!

If you sent a print job to the printer but nothing happens, the printer might not be available right now. Windows holds the print job until the printer becomes available.

The Device Settings Tab

Although most printer properties sheets are similar from printer to printer, regardless of the printer type, the Device Settings properties sheet will vary a great deal because it controls printer-specific features. Figure 4.31 displays the device settings for a typical laser printer. Inkjet printers that use the standard Windows XP printer driver might use a simplified version of this dialog. However, inkjet printers that use a vendor-supplied driver typically use the Main tab (refer to Figure 4.25) in the Printing Preferences dialog to set paper sizes.

FIGURE 4.31
The Device Settings properties sheet for a typical laser printer lets you specify the default paper type for each tray, control font substitutions, and see (or change) the printer's memory size.

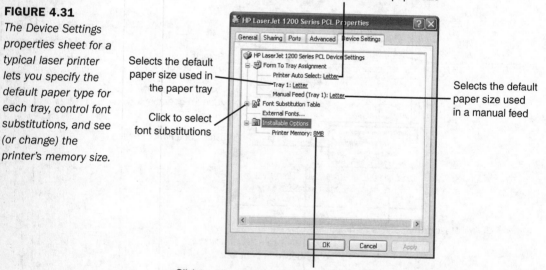

Selects the default auto-select paper size

Selects the default paper size used in the paper tray

Click to select font substitutions

Selects the default paper size used in a manual feed

Click to adjust installed printer memory (if not auto-detected)

The Color Management Tab

A color printer (whether inkjet, laser, or LED) is also likely to have a Color Management tab, which enables you to specify a color profile.

The color profile is used to help you match the colors you see onscreen to the tone and shading of the colors you see in the final printout (see Figure 4.32).

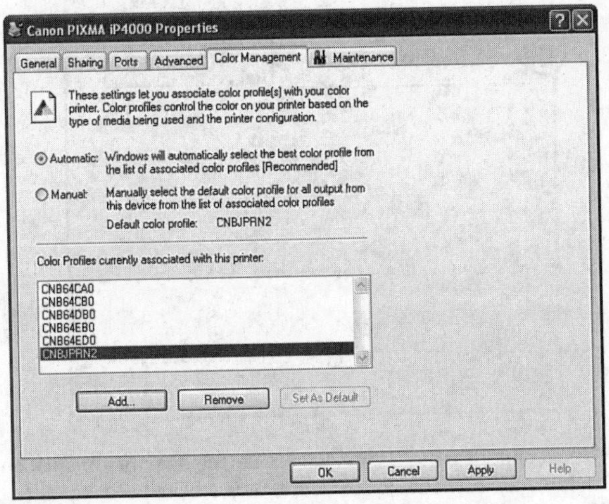

FIGURE 4.32
Color profiles used with the Color Management tab are supplied by the printer vendor.

Generally, the Automatic color profile selection provides the best results. However, if you download or create a different color profile, you should click Manual and select the color profile you want to use from the list of color profiles displayed.

Printer Properties for Dye-Sublimation Printers

Dye-sublimation printers, as you learned earlier in this chapter, work very differently from inkjet or laser/LED printers. Consequently, it should be no surprise that their printer properties sheets might be much different from those you've already seen.

Figure 4.33 shows the Paper properties sheet used by the Olympus P-440 dye-sublimation photo printer. This printer, unlike most other dye-sublimation printers, can use a variety of paper sizes.

Figure 4.34 shows the Color Adjustment properties sheet after making some changes to the default settings.

FIGURE 4.33

The Paper tab for an Olympus P-440 printer using a vendor-supplied printer driver.

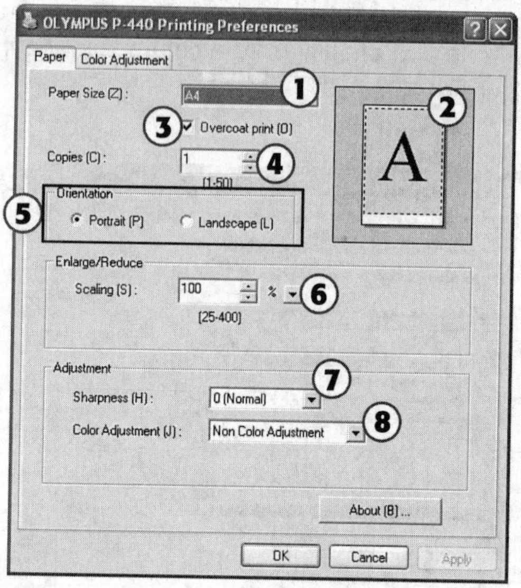

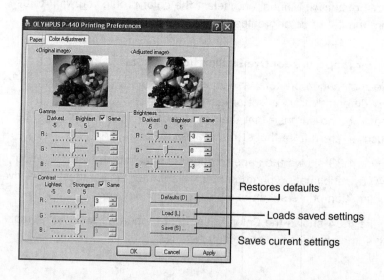

1. Selects paper size
2. Printable area (shaded)
3. Clear check box to disable protective overcoat
4. Selects the number of copies to print
5. Selects the print orientation
6. Adjusts print scaling
7. Adjusts sharpness
8. Enables color adjustment (see Figure 4.34)

FIGURE 4.34

The Color Adjustment tab for an Olympus P-440 printer using a vendor-supplied printer driver.

The Default May Not Be at Fault If You Don't Like Your Prints

Before you fiddle around with the color settings for any photo printer (inkjet or dye sublimation), try using the default settings. You might find they work fine. If not, then try making adjustments.

If your dye-sublimation printer uses a standard-style Windows printer driver, don't expect the level of options visible in Figures 4.33 and 4.34. Keep in mind that a dye-sublimation printer is optimized to print just one thing—photos.

Using Printer Properties to Troubleshoot Your Printer

By using the properties sheets for your printer, you can solve many print problems, including layout, the order in which pages are printed, print quality, and others.

Use Table 4.2 to help you use your printer's properties sheets to solve printing problems. Most of these sheets have appeared in figures in the previous sections.

TABLE 4.2
TROUBLESHOOTING YOUR PRINTER WITH PROPERTIES SHEET OPTIONS

Problem	Properties Sheet	Solution
You're not sure if Windows can communicate with the printer.	General	Use the Test Print button; if the test print doesn't work, applications can't print either. Use the flowchart "My printer can't print," p. 674, to isolate the problem.
Printed document orientation doesn't match document layout.	Layout or Paper	Select the correct paper orientation for the document layout and reprint.
Paper ejects from the printer in reverse order.	Layout or Paper	Select Page Order Back to Front so that the document will emerge from the printer in the correct page order.

TABLE 4.2 (CONTINUED)

Problem	Properties Sheet	Solution
You want to put multiple pages on a single sheet of paper.	Layout or Paper	Select the desired Pages per Sheet setting; for example, to print four pages on a single sheet, select 4.
You are almost out of color ink.	Paper/Quality, Main	Select Black & White to map all colors to grayscale and print with black ink only. Note that some printers will not print if any of the color ink cartridges have run out, even if you select black ink.
You are using special media with your inkjet printer.	Paper/Quality, Main	Select the correct media type to optimize printing.
You want to customize the normal print settings with your inkjet printer.	Paper/Quality and Advanced, Main and Custom	Select Custom on the Paper/Quality menu and then click Advanced. Alternatively, click Main, Custom. Adjust the print quality and other settings as desired.
You need to print your document on a printer you can't connect to over the network or locally.	Ports	Install the printer driver for the printer you want to print to, select Print to File, and specify a drive and filename when you print. A print file will be created in the specified location. Copy the file to a floppy disk or other media and take the file to the computer connected to the printer. Copy the file to the printer port the printer is connected to: COPY MYPRINT.PRN LPT1 Note: This will not work with a USB printer. However, you can use a freeware program called PrintFile to perform this task with USB or other printers. Download it from http://www.lerup.com/printfile/.

TABLE 4.2 (CONTINUED)

Problem	Properties Sheet	Solution
You don't want to waste paper by printing documents that don't match the printer's configuration.	Advanced	Enable the Hold Mismatched Documents option.
You are printing a large document and may need additional copies later.	Advanced	Enable the Keep Printed Documents option and print the document; to reprint the document, open the printer icon and select the document for reprinting.
You cannot select all the features of your printer.	Advanced	Use the New Driver button to install a new driver for your printer, or use Windows Update, Chapter 2, p. 109.
You want to put different paper/media sizes in the different paper trays of your printer.	Device Settings	Select the paper tray or location where you want to use specially sized paper or envelopes and then select the size.
You have added additional memory to your laser/LED printer and want to make sure it's being used.	Device Settings	View the Printer Memory size and adjust it if necessary to reflect the memory upgrade. You should compare its before-upgrade and after-upgrade value to determine if you need to make any adjustments.
There are lines and gaps in the output from your inkjet printer.	Utilities or Maintenance	Use the Head Cleaning option (if available) to clean the printhead; then, use the Nozzle Check option or run a test print to verify proper operation. Repeat the head-cleaning process if needed. If your printer lacks a Head Cleaning option on the Utilities menu, check the manual for the procedure for cleaning the heads. If cleaning the heads doesn't solve the problem, your ink cartridge is almost out of ink and should be replaced.

Troubleshooting Gibberish Output

Gibberish output from a printer is usually caused by one of the following:

- Using the wrong driver for the printer
- A loose or damaged printer cable
- Damage to the printer or the printer port

To determine if the correct driver is being used with Windows XP, follow these steps:

1. Right-click the printer icon and select Properties.
2. Click the Advanced tab and view the driver listed.
3. If the driver listed is incorrect, click New Driver to start the Add Printer Driver Wizard. Select the correct brand and model from the lists displayed. If you have downloaded the correct driver, click Have Disk and browse to the folder containing the correct driver.
4. If the driver listed is correct, check the cable and port. If a switchbox is used, make sure the switchbox is set correctly. Plug the printer directly into the PC, bypassing the switchbox, to determine if the switchbox has failed.
5. To make sure the driver is working correctly, reinstall it and retry the print job. If the printer still outputs gibberish, go to the next test.

To determine if a defective or loose parallel (LPT) cable is causing gibberish output, follow these steps:

1. Shut down the computer and the printer.
2. Remove the cable and examine the cable jacket for nicks, cuts, and exposed wires. Examine the cable connector for bent or broken pins.
3. If the cable appears OK, reconnect it to the computer and the printer. Be sure to secure the cable at both ends.
4. Turn on the printer, then the computer, and retry the print job.

5. If the printer still produces gibberish, or if the cable appears damaged, shut down the printer and computer and replace the cable with a known-working cable. Repeat step 4.

6. If the output is still gibberish, the printer may need servicing.

To determine if the port or the printer is defective, follow these steps:

1. Connect a different printer to the port using the same cable.

2. Install the correct printer driver and retry the print job. If a different printer prints correctly, the original printer is defective. If every printer prints gibberish, the parallel port on the computer is defective. Install an add-in board with a parallel port or replace the motherboard.

Troubleshooting Graphics and Sound Problems

TROUBLESHOOTING

FAST TRACK TO SOLUTIONS (SYMPTOM TABLE)

Symptom	Flowchart or Book Section	See Page
I'm having display quality problems while running 3D games.	3D Gaming Display Quality Problems	663
I'm having display speed problems while playing 3D games.	3D Gaming Display Speed Problems	664
I'm having problems seeing the display when I start my computer.	The Computer Starts, but the Screen Is Blank	658
My CRT display is flickering.	CRT Display Is Flickering	662
Photos and graphics look distorted; there aren't enough colors.	Display Has Too Few Colors	660
My display has wavy lines.	Display Has Wavy Lines	661
My display is too dark.	The Screen Is Too Dim or Too Bright	305
I can't see part of the screen image.	Part of the Screen Image Is Missing There's a Problem with the Size or Position of the Windows Desktop	659 297
The cursor is hard to see.	Keyboard	97
I don't have any tabs for adjusting 3D modes on my display driver.	Sidebar: Where Are My 3D Driver Configuration Tabs?	335
The text and fonts onscreen are too small.	The Text and Icons Are Too Large or Too Small	308
The screen keeps blanking out on a computer I want to keep running all the time.	Power Options Display Properties	98 94
I need to disable the screensaver.	Power Options Display Properties	98 94
The display is blank after I install a new ATA/IDE drive.	Checking the Drive and Host Adapter Connection to the Data Cable	174
Some websites are very hard to read.	Troubleshooting Problems with Viewing Certain Websites	471
The edges of the CRT monitor display are distorted.	The Edges of the Windows Desktop Are Curved	304
The computer starts only if I choose VGA mode or Safe Mode.	Can't Start the Computer Using Normal Display Drivers	318

TROUBLESHOOTING

FAST TRACK TO SOLUTIONS, *Continued*

Symptom	Flowchart or Book Section	See Page
My computer starts, but it locks up frequently.	Computer Locks Up Frequently or Has Display Quality Problems	320
My computer's display gets corrupted when I move the mouse..	Computer Locks Up Frequently or Has Display Quality Problems	320
My computer's display gets corrupted when I play 3D games.	Computer Locks Up Frequently or Has Display Quality Problems	320
My secondary display isn't working.	Troubleshooting Multiple Displays	324
I think my monitor is damaged.	Troubleshooting Damaged or Defective Displays or Display Adapters	317
I can't replace the built-in sound on my motherboard with a sound card.	Troubleshooting Problems with Sound Card Installation and Drivers	340
I can't hear anything coming from my speakers.	Speaker & Volume Control Problems	666
I'm having problems playing music CDs.	Troubleshooting Playback Problems with Music CDs	350
I've replaced my stereo speakers with a set that has additional speakers, but the new speakers don't work.	Can't Hear Sound from Additional Speakers	346
I don't know what volume controls to adjust when I play different types of sounds or music.	Table 5.4	345
I need to update DirectX to fix problems with my sound card.	Sidebar: Gimme a Fresh DirectX!	349
My sound hardware doesn't seem to be working.	Audio Hardware Problems	665
How can I play sounds while I troubleshoot sound hardware?	Sounds and Audio Devices	99
I'm not sure what connectors to use for my speakers and microphone.	Troubleshooting Problems with Speaker and Microphone Connections	342

Troubleshooting the Display Subsystem

You tell your computer what to do with the keyboard and mouse, but how do you know whether the computer got the message? Take a look at the monitor! The monitor is often called the *display* these days, and no wonder:

- It displays the current programs running on your system.
- It doesn't display anything if the system is running in a power-saving mode or is shut down.
- If you use two or more displays on your system, you can comfortably run more programs and get more feedback than with a single display.

Let's face it: The monitor (or display) makes the "personal confuser" a lot less confusing than if you had to wait for a printout. I don't know about you, but I'd rather see an error message than read a printout telling me what an idiot I was for entering the wrong command.

Some of the problems you might encounter include the following:

- Physical problems such as desktop sizing, image distortion, missing portions of the desktop, overly dim or bright text and images, dull text and images, or no picture at all
- Windows configuration problems such as monitor flicker, icon and text sizing issues, text color issues, slow 3D game performance, poor-quality 3D game graphics, multiple-monitor support, and driver problems
- BIOS configuration problems such as correct AGP aperture size, other AGP settings, and primary video BIOS when two or more video cards are being used for multiple-display support

The rise of LCD displays changes the mix of problems you might see, but not the possibility of problems.

When you're trying to solve monitor and display problems, you need to remember that the monitor/display is part of a complex subsystem. What other parts are there to worry about?

- The display adapter (also called the video card)
- System BIOS configuration
- Windows drivers for the monitor and display adapter

It isn't always easy to decide which part of the subsystem is at fault. But, we're here to help. Got a display problem? Let's get started!

Troubleshooting Monitors and Displays

Whether you use the traditional cathode-ray tube (CRT) or newer liquid crystal (LCD) display, a defective or broken display can be a big problem. If you've ever tried typing on a PC with a broken monitor, you know how frustrating it can be to get no feedback from your system. It's vital to keep it working right, but it isn't always easy to tell which problems are caused by the display and which are caused by other parts of the display subsystem.

Display problems typically fall into the following categories:

- Physical problems such as desktop sizing, image distortion, missing portions of the desktop, overly dim or bright text and images, dull text and images, and no picture at all

- Windows configuration problems such as monitor flicker, icon and text sizing issues, text color issues, and driver problems

Other types of problems are usually caused by the graphics adapter (video or display card) or by the video configuration settings in the system BIOS.

There's a Problem with the Size or Position of the Windows Desktop

You stare at the Windows desktop all day and maybe all evening, if you work and play within Windows like we do. You probably know your personal screen layout like the back of your hand. If you see any of the following problems with the Windows desktop, they will affect everything you do on your PC:

- One of the edges of the desktop is cut off.

- There's a black border all around the desktop.

- The edges of the desktop are curved in or out.

Use the following sections to solve these display annoyances.

The Edges of the Windows Desktop Are Cut Off

If one or more of the edges of your Windows desktop isn't visible (see Figure 5.1), the most likely solution is one of the following:

- You might need to adjust the screen position with controls on the monitor.

- You might have a virtual desktop enabled. A virtual desktop uses the screen as a movable window around a larger desktop. For example, if you have enabled a 1280×1024 virtual desktop, but your display's actual resolution is 1024×768, your display will move around the desktop as you scroll vertically or horizontally.

- You are using a screen resolution/refresh rate that has not yet been configured for your monitor/display.

If you see a black border around one or two sides of your display opposite the areas that are cut off, you need to adjust the screen position (see Figure 5.1). If you don't see a black border, but parts of the screen are not visible, you have a virtual desktop enabled (see Figure 5.4, later in the section).

FIGURE 5.1

An LCD display that needs to have its vertical and horizontal screen positions adjusted.

1. Black border at top and left sides of screen
2. Windows toolbar is partially cut off
3. Right edge of screen is partially cut off

To adjust the vertical or horizontal position or size, look at the front of your display. Most displays have controls on the front or under the front edge of the monitor for adjusting vertical and horizontal position, size, and other settings. Press the menu button to activate the onscreen display (OSD) and use the other buttons to move through the menus and make adjustments. These controls are usually fairly easy to operate (see Figures 5.2 and 5.3 for typical examples). However, if you need help, see the instruction manual for your display.

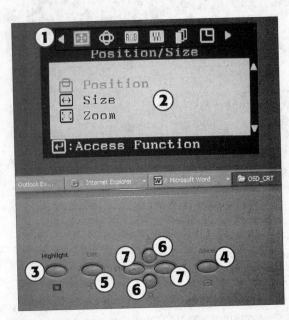

FIGURE 5.2
Adjusting the position and size of a typical CRT display with its OSD.

1. OSD menu items
2. Current OSD menu
3. Press to highlight a selected portion of the display
4. Press to open the OSD menu
5. Press to adjust contrast or move left/right through menu
6. Press to exit current submenu or OSD menu
7. Press to adjust brightness or move up/down through menu

One advantage that LCD displays have over their bulkier CRT siblings is an Auto button (see Figure 5.3). Press Auto to instantly adjust screen position and other settings. Frequently, no other adjustments are needed. However, you can still perform manual tweaking if necessary.

If your CRT screen was properly sized and centered with your normal combination of screen resolution and vertical refresh rate, but you changed the resolution or refresh rate, change back to your previous setting if it is acceptable. If you need to use this new combination, manually adjust the onscreen controls as shown in Figures 5.2 and 5.3. The display will memorize the new settings and use them each time you use a particular combination of resolution and refresh rate.

FIGURE 5.3

Adjusting the position of a typical LCD display with its OSD.

1. OSD menu items
2. Current OSD menu
3. Power button
4. Press to open OSD menu
5. Press to increase brightness or move forward through OSD menu
6. Press to decrease brightness or move back through onscreen menu
7. Press to exit current OSD submenu or OSD menu
8. Auto button – press to automatically adjust LCD display position, brightness, and other settings

To disable the virtual desktop, double-check the resolution you have selected for your monitor against the resolutions supported for that monitor. In the example shown in Figure 5.4, an LCD display with a native resolution of 1024×768 was set to a resolution of 1280×768, causing part of the screen to be cut off. The cut-off area changes as you move your mouse around the screen.

If your display driver specifically supports a virtual desktop, see the display driver's instructions to learn how to disable it. You might have a display driver quick-access tool located in your computer's system tray. However, a virtual desktop can also be created if you accidentally set a resolution higher than your LCD display's native resolution.

Follow these steps to reset an LCD display to its native resolution in Windows:

1. Right-click an empty area on the desktop and select Properties or open the Display icon in Control Panel.

2. Click the Settings tab.

3. If you use a multiple-monitor configuration, click the monitor that is using a virtual desktop.

4. Adjust the screen resolution slider to the display's native resolution (see Figure 5.5).

5. Click Apply and then OK.

Toolbar and top-level menus cut off

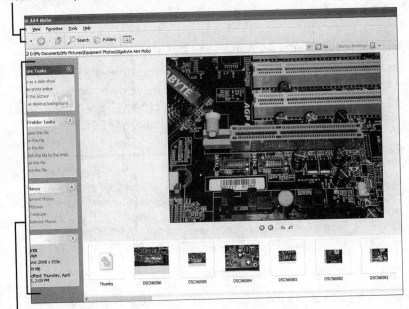

FIGURE 5.4
Setting the resolution to a value higher than an LCD monitor's native resolution results in a virtual desktop.

Task menus cut off

Use the Settings tab to adjust resolution, color quality, and to access advanced menu settings

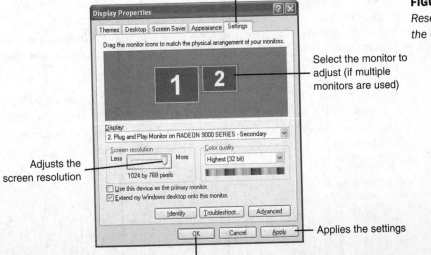

FIGURE 5.5
Resetting a display to the correct resolution.

Select the monitor to adjust (if multiple monitors are used)

Adjusts the screen resolution

Applies the settings

Accepts the settings and closes the dialog

There Are Black Lines or Rectangles Across the Desktop with an LCD Display

If you use an LCD monitor and you see thick black horizontal lines or rectangles across the desktop, the LCD is damaged and should be replaced. The black areas are where the transistors that activate the display have failed.

There's a Black Border All Around the Desktop

If you see a thin black border all around the desktop with a CRT monitor, this is normal; you can increase the actual screen size by using the horizontal and vertical size and position controls. See "The Edges of the Windows Desktop Are Cut Off," this chapter, p. 298, for details.

Speedy Screen Filling

If you want to adjust the size of the visible display on your CRT the fast way, look for a zoom control in the onscreen control functions. This adjusts both vertical and horizontal size at the same time. If you zoom the screen larger and start to cut off one or more edges of the screen, as shown earlier in Figure 5.1, adjust the horizontal or vertical position as needed.

However, if you see a wide black border on an LCD display panel, particularly the type built into a notebook computer, the problem might be that you are not using the native resolution of the panel. LCD panels, unlike CRT monitors, are designed to work at a single resolution (often called the native resolution). Most recent desktop LCD panels automatically handle scaling to lower resolutions, although the results might be much worse than with a CRT, but others, particularly those built into laptops, use only a portion of the screen for a lower resolution (see Figure 5.6) unless you select the scaling adjustment in the laptop display's advanced properties sheet.

If you connect your laptop computer to a projector that uses a lower resolution than the onboard display, you might need to adjust the display resolution to match the projector's resolution. This will enable you to use both the LCD panel and the projector for simultaneous display.

1024×768 display area not used by lower-resolution setting

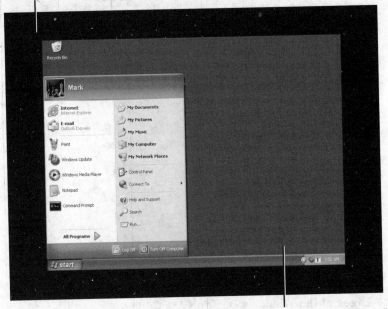

FIGURE 5.6

How a typical 1024×768 LCD notebook display panel will look when configured to use 800×600 resolution if scaling is not used.

800×600 display setting fills only a portion of the display

To adjust how your LCD panel handles lower resolutions than normal, click the Settings tab on the display adapter's properties sheet and click Advanced. Look through the properties sheets to find a setting such as Scale Image to Panel Size or Expand Panel Image (see Figure 5.7). If this option is enabled, setting the resolution lower than normal will cause the display to stretch the image to fill the LCD panel. Depending on the display adapter and panel, the results might be acceptable or might be terrible. If you find the results are not acceptable, but you need to use a lower resolution to enable your system to connect to a lower-resolution display projector or monitor, disable this option.

Liquid View for Easy Desktop Adjustments

If you'd like an easier way to adjust and scale the Windows desktop, check out Portrait Displays, Inc.'s Liquid View program. Learn more about it at

http://personalcomputing.portrait.com/us/products/lv_overview.html.

FIGURE 5.7

Enabling the Expand Panel Image option on this Compaq notebook computer fills the 1024×768 display with an 800×600 image.

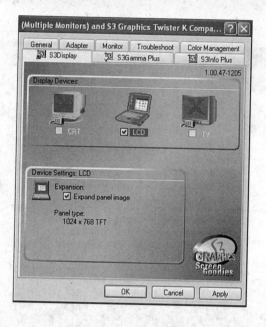

The Edges of the Windows Desktop Are Curved

Because CRT monitors can be adjusted to a wide range of screen sizes, the edges of the Windows desktop (or any other screen display) may become curved, particularly if you increase the size of the desktop to fill the screen. The most common problems include the following:

- **Barrel distortion**—The edges of the screen display are curved outward.

- **Pincushion distortion**—The edges of the screen display are curved inward.

- **Wave distortion**—The edges of the screen display curve back and forth.

To compensate for these display quality problems, use the geometry controls available on most monitors to straighten the edges of the screen (see Figure 5.8).

Changing Settings Can Lead to Geometry Problems

If you change resolutions or refresh rates, you might need to adjust the geometry settings the first time you select a new resolution or refresh rate. However, most monitors will save these settings for you and automatically reuse them when needed.

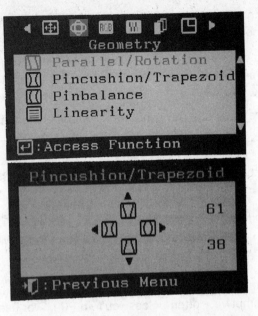

FIGURE 5.8
The Geometry menu (top) and pincushion/ trapezoid adjustment menu (bottom) for a typical CRT OSD.

The Text and Icons Onscreen Are Hard to Read

If you're having problems reading the text or seeing the icons onscreen, these problems can have several causes, including the following:

- Incorrect contrast or brightness settings on the monitor
- Screen resolution set too high or too low
- The color scheme used by Windows
- The refresh rate used by your monitor

The Screen Is Too Dim or Too Bright

Whether you use an LCD or CRT display, it can be annoying to try to use your PC if the display is too dim or too bright. There are several ways to cope with this problem:

- Adjust the display's brightness and contrast.
- Adjust the brightness or gamma with the graphics card's own driver.
- Use a screen-adjustment program provided with a photo-editing program.

Here's how to adjust the brightness and contrast controls on your monitor for command-prompt applications:

1. Open a command-prompt window. Either click Start, Run and then type cmd (Windows XP or Windows 2000) or click Command (Windows 9x/Me).

2. If you can still see the Windows desktop behind the window, press Ctrl+Enter to switch the command-prompt window to full-screen mode.

3. Adjust the brightness display until the text display is at medium brightness.

4. Adjust the contrast display until the background is a solid black.

5. Type exit and press the Enter key to return to the Windows desktop.

The only limitation of this approach is that you probably don't use the command prompt very often unless you're a PC power user/geek. To optimize the display for Windows applications or for 3D gaming, you need to adjust how Windows works with the display. If you are using a vendor-provided video card driver (not the bare-bones drivers used by most Windows versions), you can usually adjust brightness with the driver by opening the Advanced display properties sheet:

1. Right-click the Windows desktop or open the Display icon in Control Panel.

2. Select Properties.

3. Click the Settings tab.

4. Click Advanced.

Figure 5.9 illustrates the Color Correction menu used by an NVIDIA driver. To access this menu from the Advanced dialog, click the GeForce tab and select Color Correction. Note that this menu enables you to adjust gamma, brightness, contrast, and other settings.

Leo Says

Why Gamma Beats Brightness

Although the gamma controls found in some graphics card drivers and applications adjust the brightness of the image, they do it by adjusting the middle tones of the image rather than the entire range of tones the way the brightness control does. For this reason, it's better to adjust gamma than brightness if you can.

Gamma adjustments were originally designed to help cope with the differences between how a monitor displays photographs and how photographs appear when printed, but gamma adjustments can also make video games that use mostly dark graphics and backgrounds playable—especially if you have middle-aged eyes like I do!

Selects nVidia GeForce-specific menu

Selects color-correction menu

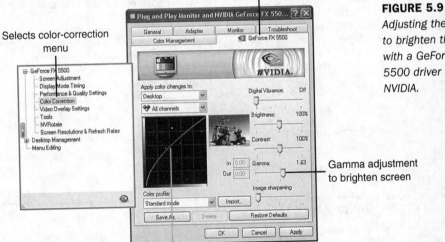

FIGURE 5.9

Adjusting the gamma to brighten the screen with a GeForce FX 5500 driver from NVIDIA.

Gamma adjustment to brighten screen

Screen brightness curve indicating mid-tones (middle of curve) are brighter

ATI's video driver offers a standard desktop brightness control on its Color tab as well as a special Full Screen 3D control for 3D games (which often are very dark). If you install the standard video driver, click Advanced, Color. The ATI CATALYST Control Center, shown in Figure 5.10, offers the same setting options, plus a real-time preview and the ability to save different settings for different games.

→ *For more about ATI video card options, see "Troubleshooting 3D Game Performance and Image Quality,", this chapter, p. 332.*

FIGURE 5.10

The Color dialog in ATI CATALYST is used to adjust the brightness of the Windows desktop and 3D games. The standard ATI Color dialog offers similar options.

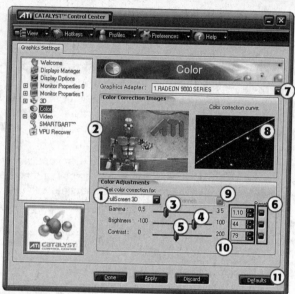

1. Select Desktop or FullScreen 3D (game) settings
2. Preview window displays effects of change
3. Adjusts gamma
4. Adjusts screen brightness
5. Adjusts screen contrast
6. Resets gamma, brightness, and contrast to defaults
7. Select primary or secondary display
8. Tonal curve (changes as settings change)
9. Selects colors to adjust (Desktop mode only)
10. Current values for gamma, brightness, contrast
11. Resets dialog to defaults

Some photo-editing programs, such as Adobe Photoshop, install a gamma control that can be used to help you get matching results from displayed and printed images.

More About Gamma—Much More!

For more technical information about controlling gamma, see the monitor/printer calibration and gamma website at http://www.normankoren.com/makingfineprints1A.html.

The Text and Icons Are Too Large or Too Small

If you switched to a larger display because you got tired of staring at tiny icons and tinier text, you might be disappointed, especially if you let your eagle-eyed kids set up your new display. By default, Windows uses fixed-size icons; the higher the resolution (the number of dots in each direction horizontally and vertically) onscreen, the smaller the icons. Windows also uses fixed-size fonts instead of scalable fonts for its standard windows and menus. PC users under age 30 often tend to crank up the screen resolution as high as they can with a CRT. Newer, larger CRTs can handle higher resolutions and provide better quality than older units. For example, typical 19-inch CRTs offer 1600×1200 and higher resolutions. The end result? Smaller, not larger, icons and text—exactly the opposite of why you upgraded!

Want to improve the odds of having readable text and icons? Upgrade to a 19-inch or larger LCD panel from a CRT. They still cost more than a CRT, but the prices for big LCD displays are comparable to what 15-inch LCDs cost a couple years ago. And, a typical 19-inch LCD has a native resolution of 1280×1024, assuring you of legible text and graphics. By comparison, a high-quality 19-inch CRT can be cranked up to 1600×1200 or even higher.

Because CRTs support many different resolutions, and LCD panels can usually support one resolution lower than their native resolution, you can use a lower-than-optimal resolution. As a result, you get larger-than-normal icons and text. But, you can have too much of a good thing. Some signs that you have your display resolution set too low include the following:

- You need to scroll horizontally to read the contents of many websites.

- You need to scroll vertically to see all your program shortcuts when you click All Programs, even though you only have a few programs installed.

Note

If the desktop icons and text are large, but you don't need to scroll horizontally or vertically to view websites or to see program shortcuts, you might be using the Use Large Icons option. To change this option, see "Display Properties," Chapter 2, p. 94.

Although it's more likely that your display resolution is set too low—resulting in annoyances such as very large icons—if you're experiencing the opposite problem (that text and icons are too small to read comfortably) or if the CRT screen has an annoying flicker, your display resolution might be set too high.

➔ See *"The CRT Monitor Flickers,"* this chapter, p. 315.

To see the current display resolution and color settings your computer uses, right-click the Windows desktop and select Properties or open the Display icon in Control Panel. Click the Settings tab to display this information (see Figure 5.11).

FIGURE 5.11
The Settings properties sheet in Windows XP.

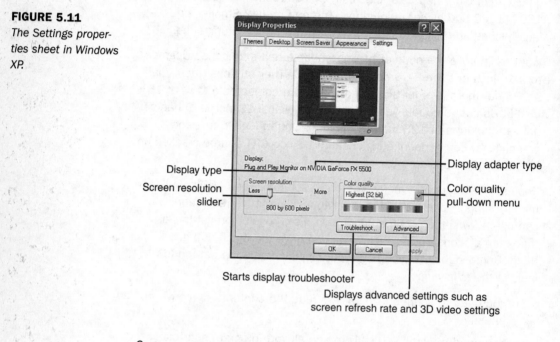

Display type
Screen resolution slider
Display adapter type
Color quality pull-down menu

Starts display troubleshooter

Displays advanced settings such as screen refresh rate and 3D video settings

Compare your computer's current screen resolution setting to the suggestions in Table 5.1. If you are using a different setting than the one recommended for your monitor and you are not comfortable with the screen display, select the recommended resolution with the screen resolution slider and click Apply to preview the results. If you are satisfied, click OK to accept the new setting. If you are not satisfied, the monitor will revert to the old setting in a few seconds.

TABLE 5.1
SUGGESTED SCREEN RESOLUTION SETTINGS BY MONITOR SIZE AND TYPE

Screen Resolution	Resolution Name	CRT Monitor Size	LCD Monitor Size
640×480	VGA	14-inch or less	12-inch or less
800×600	Super VGA	15-inch	13-inch

TABLE 5.1 (continued)

Screen Resolution	Resolution Name	CRT Monitor Size	LCD Monitor Size
1024×768	XGA	17-inch	14-inch, 15-inch
1280×1024	Super XGA	19-inch	17-inch, 19-inch
1600×1200	Ultra XGA	21-inch or higher	20-inch or higher

Note: Windows XP requires 800×600 (SuperVGA) resolution or higher.

The Text Is Too Small or Too Hard to Read

Adjusting the resolution of your display isn't the only way to fight back against text that's too small or too hard to read in Windows. You can also do the following:

- Spend time fiddling with the display properties sheet's Appearance tab, which allows you to customize your color scheme, font sizes, and much more.

- Use the custom DPI setting available under the Settings tab; click Advanced, General, and select normal, large size, or custom settings to enlarge all desktop objects.

- Select a high-contrast display through the Control Panel Accessibility Options icon.

The high-contrast option is particularly well-suited to users with limited vision. To try a high-contrast display, follow these steps:

→ *To learn more about using the Appearance tab, see "Fonts and Icons Overlap on the Windows Desktop," this chapter, p. 313.*

1. Click Start, Control Panel (Windows XP) and open Accessibility Options.

2. Click the Display tab from the Accessibility Options dialog that appears.

3. Enable the Use High Contrast check box.

4. Click the Settings button. To select a high-contrast or other Windows color scheme as your standard color scheme, click the down-arrow next to your current high-contrast scheme and then choose from those listed. True high-contrast schemes include High Contrast #1, High Contrast #2, High Contrast Black, and High Contrast White. All these are available with regular, large, or extra large icons and text. Click OK, Apply, then OK again to activate the high-contrast color scheme.

5. If you want to be able to switch back and forth between your high-contrast and normal Windows color schemes, click the box next to Use Shortcut, then select the high-contrast color scheme you want (see Figure 5.12). Click OK, Apply, then OK again. The screen switches to the high-contrast scheme you selected, but when you press the shortcut combination (Alt+Left Shift+PrintScreen), the screen reverts to the normal Windows color scheme.

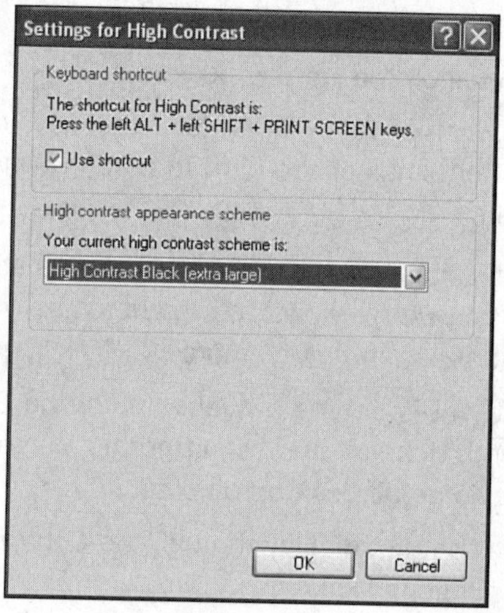

FIGURE 5.12

Enabling switching between standard and the specified high-contrast color scheme in Windows XP.

Settings for High Contrast

Keyboard shortcut

The shortcut for High Contrast is:
Press the left ALT + left SHIFT + PRINT SCREEN keys.

☑ Use shortcut

High contrast appearance scheme

Your current high contrast scheme is:

High Contrast Black (extra large)

OK   Cancel

6. To change back to the high-contrast color scheme after you switch to the normal color scheme, press the shortcut keys again.

Figure 5.13 shows how a typical Windows XP desktop will look after being switched into High Contrast Black (extra large).

As you can see from Figure 5.13, using a large or extra-large color scheme can cause some onscreen icons to overlap each other. You can edit the settings to fix this problem, though. See "Fonts and Icons Overlap on the Windows Desktop," this chapter, p. 313.

If you decide to disable a high-contrast color scheme, follow this procedure:

1. Click Start, Control Panel and open Accessibility Options.

2. Click the Display tab from the Accessibility Options dialog that appears.

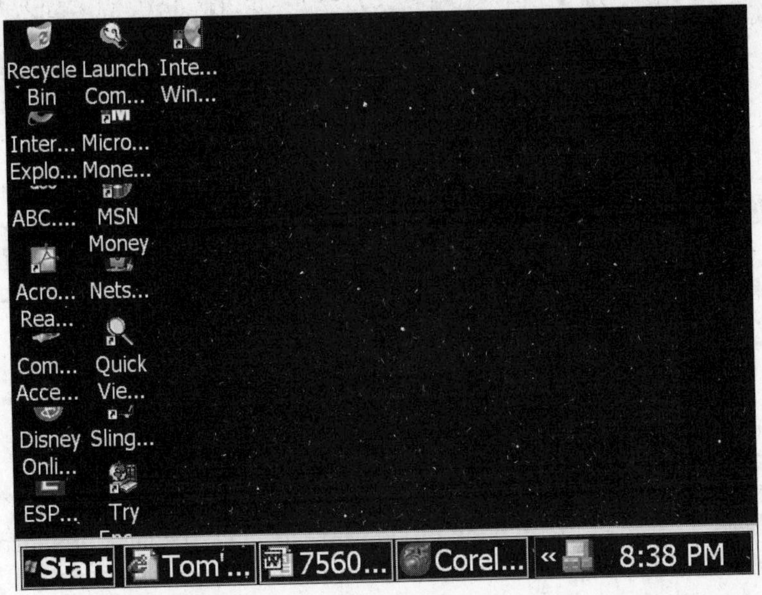

FIGURE 5.13
The Windows XP High Contrast Black (extra large) color scheme.

3. Clear the Use High Contrast check box.

4. Click the Settings button and select the same color scheme you are using as your High Contrast color scheme. Click OK, Apply, then OK again to activate the changes.

Fonts and Icons Overlap on the Windows Desktop

How ironic! You set up a color scheme that uses large or extra-large fonts to make using your PC easier, only to discover that the icons and icon text overlap (refer to Figure 5.13 for a typical example). We don't know why Microsoft hasn't come up with an automatic fix for this annoyance, but we have developed a couple workarounds:

- Adjust the setting for icon spacing in the Appearance tab of the display properties sheet.

- Manually drag icons into position.

Here's how to adjust the setting for icon spacing:

1. Open the display properties sheet and click the Appearance tab; with Windows XP, click Advanced.

2. Click the pull-down menu and select Icon Spacing (Horizontal).

3. Select a number that's about twice the default setting if you are using a large color scheme, or about 2.3 times the default setting if you are using an extra-large setting. For example, if the normal setting is 43, use 86 for a large color scheme or 100 for an extra-large color scheme. Click OK.

4. Click the pull-down menu and select Icon Spacing (Vertical).

5. Select a number that's about 70% larger than the default setting for either large or extra-large color schemes. For example, if the default is 43, use 70. Click OK.

6. Click Apply and OK to finish the process.

The problem with resetting the horizontal and vertical icon spacing is that if you decide to change back to a different color scheme with a different font size, your desktop will still be configured for the old spacing, which will then be too wide. If you decide to change the icon spacing, you should record the original values so you can change them back if you decide to switch back to your previous display.

Here's an easier way to cure overlapping text and icons:

1. Switch to the high-contrast setting you prefer using the steps described in the previous section.

2. Right-click the desktop and select Arrange Icons (By).

3. Deselect Auto Arrange (so that no check mark appears next to it in the menu) and click the desktop to close the menu.

4. Drag the desktop icons around as desired until you can read the descriptions and see the icons.

Your icons will stay put as long as you don't use Auto Arrange, even if you switch back to your normal desktop.

Decluttering Your Desktop Without Losing Your Shortcuts

Windows XP doesn't clutter your desktop with program shortcuts as much as earlier versions of Windows, but if you prefer desktop icons, consider making a folder on your desktop for the shortcuts you use most often. Although it will take an extra double-click to open a desktop folder, it's still faster than navigating through the Start menu to locate your programs.

To relocate desktop shortcuts (icons with the curved arrow) to a folder on the desktop, follow this procedure:

1. Right-click an empty area of the desktop and select New, Folder.
2. Name the folder "Shortcuts."
3. Drag your desktop shortcuts into the folder.

Don't drag the Recycle Bin and other desktop icons that are not shortcuts (My Computer, Network Neighborhood, and so on) into the folder.

The CRT Monitor Flickers

The most common reason why CRT monitors flicker is that the vertical refresh rate is set too low. The vertical refresh rate indicates how quickly the screen is redrawn. By default, most Windows display drivers use low refresh rates (60Hz is typical). Although 60Hz doesn't produce much flicker on traditional 640×480 VGA monitors, higher-resolution monitors running at 800×600, 1024×768, and above will flicker annoyingly if the refresh rate isn't increased. Your ability to adjust the refresh rate is dependent on the capabilities of your display adapter, your CRT monitor, and whether Windows can properly identify them.

Flicker: Bad for Your Eyes—and Your Health!

Screen flicker can be just as annoying as the flickering light emitted by a defective florescent tube. But, screen flicker can be much worse for you. It can cause headaches and eyestrain, making a long day at the computer even longer. And, display flicker (which is also a problem with TV sets) has been known to trigger epileptic seizures in some computer users and TV viewers.

If you never want to worry about flicker again, switch to LCD display panels. They never flicker at any refresh rate.

If you are annoyed by screen flicker, open the display properties sheet, click Settings, click Advanced, and then click the Monitor tab (see Figure 5.14). To reduce or eliminate flicker, choose a refresh rate of 72Hz or higher.

FIGURE 5.14

Adjusting the vertical refresh rate in Windows XP.

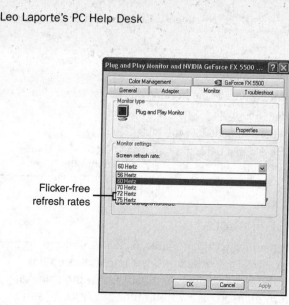

Flicker-free refresh rates

Where Are the *Really* High Refresh Rates?

By default, Windows will not permit you to select a refresh rate that can damage your monitor. The only way to see such refresh rates is to clear the check box Hide Modes That the Monitor Cannot Display (this is concealed by the Screen Refresh Rate pull-down menu in Figure 5.14). With most displays, you can select a wider range of refresh rates at lower resolutions than at higher resolutions.

However, if your display is recognized as "Default Monitor," you will not be able to choose flicker-free refresh rates (72Hz and higher). You need to install the correct driver for your display. Visit your display vendor's website to see if you need a specific driver or if you should use the Plug and Play Monitor driver shown in Figure 5.14.

Looking for a faster way to configure your display? Windows XP enables you to select resolution, color quality, and refresh rate with one mouse click from the Adapter tab. Click List All Modes to see all the available modes that will work with your display (see Figure 5.15).

➔ *If Windows cannot properly identify your display card, see "Reinstalling or Updating Your Display Adapter Driver," this chapter, p. 338.*

How does Windows know what refresh rates are safe? It receives this information from the display driver. If your display uses a custom driver, the name and model number are shown on the Monitor tab of the Advanced display properties sheet. However, many displays are Plug and Play, as in Figure 5.14, reporting their valid range of settings to Windows automatically. After the display adapter is properly configured with the correct driver, Windows can usually identify your monitor. If Windows cannot identify your monitor, contact the monitor vendor for a customized driver file or for technical support.

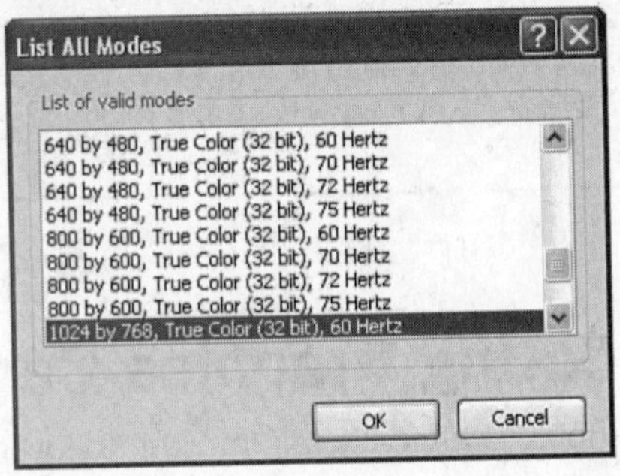

List All Modes ? X

List of valid modes

640 by 480, True Color (32 bit), 60 Hertz
640 by 480, True Color (32 bit), 70 Hertz
640 by 480, True Color (32 bit), 72 Hertz
640 by 480, True Color (32 bit), 75 Hertz
800 by 600, True Color (32 bit), 60 Hertz
800 by 600, True Color (32 bit), 70 Hertz
800 by 600, True Color (32 bit), 72 Hertz
800 by 600, True Color (32 bit), 75 Hertz
1024 by 768, True Color (32 bit), 60 Hertz

OK   Cancel

FIGURE 5.15
Selecting resolution, color quality, and refresh rate with Windows XP's List All Modes option.

Troubleshooting Damaged or Defective Displays or Display Adapters

Damaged or defective displays might have the following symptoms:

- Rectangular blank areas or pixels that are stuck on or off (LCD panels)
- Discolored or extremely dim CRT monitor displays
- Periodic colored flickers
- Buzzing or humming
- Display can't power on

If resetting the display with its onscreen controls (OSD), degaussing a CRT display with the degaussing button available on some models (this option is also sometimes found in the OSD), or tightening the data cable doesn't resolve these problems, you might have a defective monitor. If you can borrow a replacement monitor from another computer, shut down the computer and monitor, attach a different monitor to the computer, and try the operation again. If the problem is solved by using a different monitor, have the monitor serviced professionally. If the problem persists, replace the display adapter.

Keep in mind that if Windows doesn't recognize the new monitor correctly, you will need to install drivers for the monitor. Check the monitor's documentation to determine if the monitor should be configured as a Plug and Play monitor or if it uses special drivers.

Replace the Cable, Remove the Problem?

Be sure to check the data cable running between the monitor and the display adapter for damage. When you remove it, check the connector for bent or broken pins. If you find bent pins, straighten them if possible and retry the monitor. If you can't fix the cable but you can remove it, try a replacement cable for a low-cost fix that won't require a trip to the repair shop. Unfortunately, most low-cost and mid-range monitors use fixed cables.

Troubleshooting Graphics Cards

Display adapter problems typically fall into the following categories:

- Windows configuration problems such as distorted colors, the inability to select the desired color depth and resolution, driver problems, the computer won't start, frequent lockups, and slow 3D game performance

- Physical problems such as BIOS configuration for single- and multiple-display adapters and the inability to install multiple-display adapters

The following sections will help you keep your video card working properly.

Can't Start the Computer Using Normal Display Drivers

→ *For other reasons why Windows won't start, and to learn how to start Windows in Safe or VGA mode, see "Fixing Other Startup Problems with Windows XP," Chapter 2, p. 77.*

If you can't start the computer in normal mode, but you can start it in VGA mode, the problem might be the display drivers. All video chipsets used in Windows-based computers for the last several years use various methods to speed the transfer of video/graphics information to the display. By default, Windows enables all the video acceleration features available for your display adapter. However, if the display drivers aren't working correctly, full video acceleration could cause lockups or display problems or even prevent your computer from starting.

To determine if your display drivers are preventing Windows from starting normally, follow this procedure:

1. Start the computer in VGA mode.

2. If the computer starts normally, disable all video acceleration. Follow this procedure:

   a. Right-click the desktop and select Properties.

   b. Click the Settings tab.

c. Click Advanced.

d. Click the Troubleshoot tab (Windows XP) or Performance (other versions).

e. Adjust the slider all the way to the left to disable all video acceleration. You should also clear the Enable Write Combining check box (see Figure 5.16).

f. Click OK repeatedly to close the Display Properties dialog.

Default (full) acceleration setting

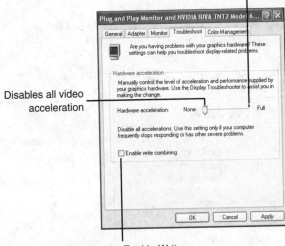

Disables all video acceleration

Disables the Enable Write Combining option when cleared

FIGURE 5.16

Adjusting the acceleration settings to troubleshoot the display adapter in Windows XP.

3. If the computer restarts normally, download updated display adapter drivers and install them if you know what brand and model of chipset your display card uses. To determine this information, allow Windows to install the best driver it has for your display card. You can then view the display adapter information in Device Manager.

4. If you cannot restart Windows after adjusting the acceleration settings, restart Windows in VGA mode, download updated display adapter and motherboard drivers, and install them. If Windows still cannot correctly detect and configure your display adapter, it may be defective; contact the vendor for help.

→ *To learn how to use Device Manager, see "Using Device Manager," Chapter 2, p. 100.*

Computer Locks Up Frequently or Has Display Quality Problems

If your computer starts correctly, but has frequent lockups or screen corruption when you move your mouse, your display, mouse, or DirectX drivers are probably defective and should be upgraded. However, as a workaround, you can reduce the video acceleration using a procedure similar to the one described in the previous section and illustrated in Figure 5.17. Use Table 5.2 to determine the best setting to use for the display problem you're having with Windows XP.

TABLE 5.2
USING GRAPHICS ACCELERATION SETTINGS TO TROUBLESHOOT WINDOWS XP

Acceleration Setting	Left	One Click from Left	Two Clicks from Left	Two Clicks from Right	One Click from Right	Right
Effect of Setting	No acceleration	Disables all but basic acceleration	Disables DirectX, DirectDraw, Direct 3D acceleration (mainly used by 3D games)	Disables cursor and drawing accelerations	Disables mouse and pointer acceleration	Enables full acceleration
Long-term Solution	Update display, DirectX, and mouse drivers	Update display, DirectX, and mouse drivers	Update DirectX drivers	Update display drivers	Update mouse drivers	N/A

Table note: Disable write combining, a method for speeding up screen display, whenever you select any setting other than full acceleration to improve stability. Reenable write combining after you install updated drivers and retry.

If you're not certain which setting is best for your situation, use this procedure:

1. Start the computer.
2. Open the Troubleshooting or Performance dialog as described in the previous section.
3. Slide the acceleration pointer one notch to the left from its current position.
4. Click Apply, OK, and OK again to close the display properties dialog.

5. Use your normal software and perform typical tasks.

6. If the computer now performs acceptably, continue to use this setting until you can obtain and install updated drivers. If the computer continues to have problems, repeat steps 2–5 and move the pointer one step to the left each time until the problems go away or until you can install updated drivers as specified in Table 5.2.

Colors Are Distorted

If you watch movie trailers, play 3D games, or work with digital camera pictures or scanned photos on your computer, your display needs to be configured to display a full range of colors. Typical color quality choices include the following:

- **Low (8-bit color)**—This mode can display up to 256 colors, but does not support 3D graphics; this setting is not available on some video drivers.

- **Medium (16-bit color or High Color)**—This mode can display up to 65,536 colors and supports 3D graphics.

- **Highest (32-bit color or True Color)**—This mode can display up to 16.8 million colors (same as 24-bit color used by older graphics cards without a 3D accelerator) and supports 3D graphics.

Leo Says

Too Many Colors for Old Software? Use the Program Compatibility Wizard!

Windows XP can run most programs made for old 32-bit Windows versions such as Windows NT 4.0 and Windows 95. When these versions were introduced a decade ago, video cards had much lower memory sizes (the size of video memory and the resolution setting controls available color quality settings), and 256-color (8-bit) color settings were common. If you can't run an older Windows program because of color-quality issues, there's no need to adjust the Windows color-quality setting (which would affect all software). Instead, use the Program Compatibility Wizard (also present in Windows XP Professional x64 Edition) to run the program in 256-color mode. For details, see "Troubleshooting Programs That Won't Run Under Windows XP," Chapter 2, p. 136.

If you start Windows XP in VGA mode because of a problem with your video card or drivers, your screen resolution will be only 640×480 and you will use only 256 colors. Believe us, you don't want to see how bad a full-color photo looks when only 256 colors are used! Use VGA mode to help you reconfigure or reload your display drivers. When you restart your computer normally, you'll once again see a full range of colors in websites and photos if you use 32-bit color. We don't recommend 16-bit color settings unless you are using a system that does not have enough video memory for you to use 32-bit (or 24-bit) color at the desired resolution.

As long as your graphics card or built-in display adapter has at least 32MB of RAM, you can use any resolution up to 1600×1200 with 32-bit or lower color-quality settings. To determine how much memory your graphics card or display adapter is using, open the Advanced portion of the Display properties sheet and click Adapter (see Figure 5.17).

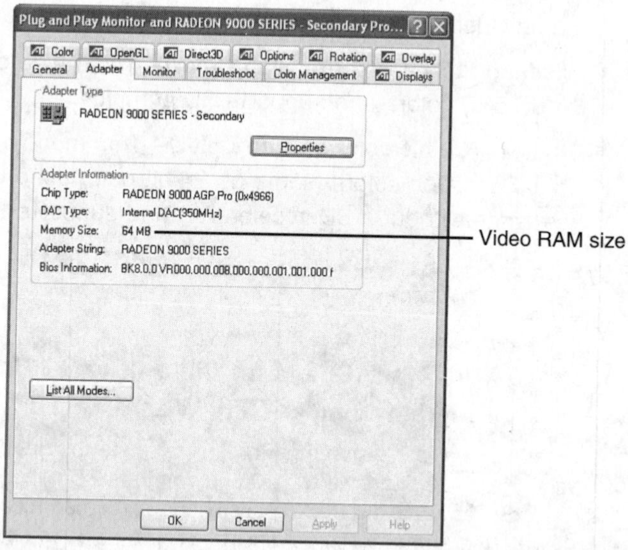

FIGURE 5.17
This ATI graphics card has 64MB of RAM. Newer ATI and NVIDIA graphics cards have as much as 256MB of RAM.

Video RAM size

→ *To learn how to improve 3D performance, see "3D Games Run Too Slowly," this chapter, p. 332.*

If your system supports 32-bit color but you have 32MB of RAM or less for video, you will have very low 3D graphics performance.

If you are unable to select 32-bit color when you set your display for a higher resolution, you don't have enough memory available for graphics. This is most likely to happen if you have a system that uses integrated graphics instead of a graphics card, or if you have a very old AGP or PCI graphics card with less than 16MB of RAM.

You cannot add more memory to a graphics card; instead, replace the card with a model that has a faster 3D graphics chip and more memory (at least 64MB or more). This will also boost 3D performance as well as enable you to display 32-bit color at all resolutions.

However, if your system uses integrated graphics, upgrading available graphics memory can be a bit trickier. See the next section for details.

Increasing Available Display Memory on Systems with Integrated Video

In many notebook and desktop computers, video functions are built into the motherboard, rather than added through a separate adapter card. In these systems, the video memory is actually borrowed from the available system memory. This is sometimes referred to as *unified memory architecture (UMA)*, and this method is also used by some discrete graphics chips built into notebook computers.

With newer designs, particularly those based on the Intel 865 or 915 chipsets, the computer will dynamically adjust video memory as needed: Games need more memory, whereas business applications such as word processors and spreadsheets, need less. The best way to make sure you have plenty of memory for both system and video use is to upgrade system memory to at least 512MB or more.

Systems that use recent VIA Technologies chipsets for Athlon 64, Pentium 4, and Athlon XP Mobile can provide up to 64MB of video memory. Check your system documentation for details.

Older Intel or VIA Technology chipsets made for Intel Pentium III and AMD Athlon and Athlon 4 processors require you to adjust the BIOS settings to increase memory. However, these older systems are not suitable for gaming. Check your system documentation for details.

Getting the Inside Story on Integrated Graphics

If your desktop or laptop system uses an Intel chipset with integrated graphics, go to http://support.intel.com/support/graphics/sb/CS-009481.htm for more information.

If your system uses NVIDIA GeForce Go graphics, go to http://www.nvidia.com/page/mobile.html for more information.

If your system uses ATI Mobility Radeon graphics, go to http://www.ati.com/products/mobile.html for more information.

If your system uses VIA Technology chipsets with integrated graphics, go to http://www.viatech.com for more information.

Troubleshooting Multiple Displays

If you've ever used a system with two or more monitors, it's almost impossible to go back to a single display. Windows XP supports multiple displays both for desktop PCs and, through DualView, for laptop and notebook computers.

There are three ways to add a second display to your desktop system:

- Connect a second display to a dual-display (dual-head) graphics card (see Figure 5.18).
- Install a dual-display video card (if you don't already have one).
- Install a second graphics card.

For best results, we recommend using dual-head graphics cards. They're much easier to work with than two separate cards, and you can choose from a wide range of prices and features. Best of all, you can recycle your old display as a secondary display.

Figure 5.18 shows the rear of a typical dual-head graphics card. Note that this card actually supports three different connections: VGA (works with CRT and most LCD displays), S-video for TV-out (can be adapted for composite inputs), and DVI-I (works with digital LCD displays and can use an adapter for VGA-type displays).

Some video cards, primarily some of ATI's All-in-Wonder cards designed for video production, use a proprietary connector that supports a special cable for two VGA connections and leaves room on the rear of the card for cable TV RG-6 and video I/O cable connectors.

FIGURE 5.18

Video connectors on the rear of a typical dual-head graphics adapter with TV-out.

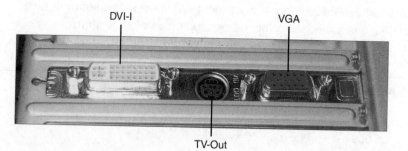

DVI-I   VGA

TV-Out

Watch Out for "TV-Out" Only

Many graphics card vendors claim multiple-display support if the card has only VGA and TV-out (composite or S-video) ports. Sure, you can use the CRT or LCD display and the TV at the same time, but unless you're playing a game, you wouldn't want to. Check the card description very carefully—make sure you're getting all three ports shown in Figure 5.18.

Use the following sections to learn how to enable multiple-monitor support and solve common problems you might encounter.

Enabling Multiple-Monitor Support

The process of enabling multiple-monitor support varies with the type of display adapter you're using. If you have a dual-display adapter, including notebook computers that support DualView, the process works like this:

1. Verify the system works correctly with the current (primary) monitor (this is the built-in LCD display on a notebook computer).

2. Turn off the system and all monitors.

3. Attach the secondary monitor to the other video port on the display adapter, or to the external video port on a notebook computer that supports DualView. If you use a DVI-I-to-VGA adapter to connect the secondary display, make sure the adapter is tightly connected to the DVI port (see Figure 5.19).

4. Turn on both monitors, then the computer. During the boot process, you should see the same information on both monitors. If you don't see anything on the secondary display, check the data cable between the secondary monitor and the data port (and adapter) on the display adapter.

5. When the computer boots to the Windows desktop, open the display properties sheet and click the Settings tab.

6. You should see two icons displayed; your original monitor (the built-in display on a laptop) is displayed as monitor #1, while the new secondary monitor (the display plugged into the VGA port on a laptop) is displayed as monitor #2. To make monitor #2 active, click the icon for monitor #2 and click the box next to Extend My Windows Desktop onto This Monitor (see Figure 5.20). Click Apply. Your Windows desktop background should appear on the second monitor (but with no icons unless you drag them there).

7. Adjust the resolution and color quality for monitor #2 with the sliders shown in Figure 5.20.

FIGURE 5.19
A dual-head graphics card connected to two monitors and a TV or VCR.

VGA cables

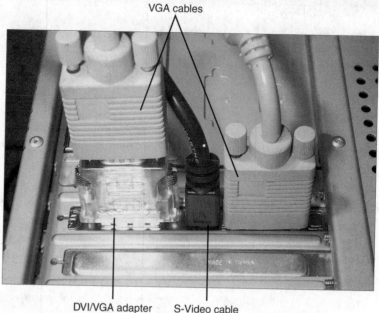

DVI/VGA adapter   S-Video cable

Shortcut to Success

If you're not sure which monitor is which, click Identify, which places a huge number across each monitor for a few seconds.

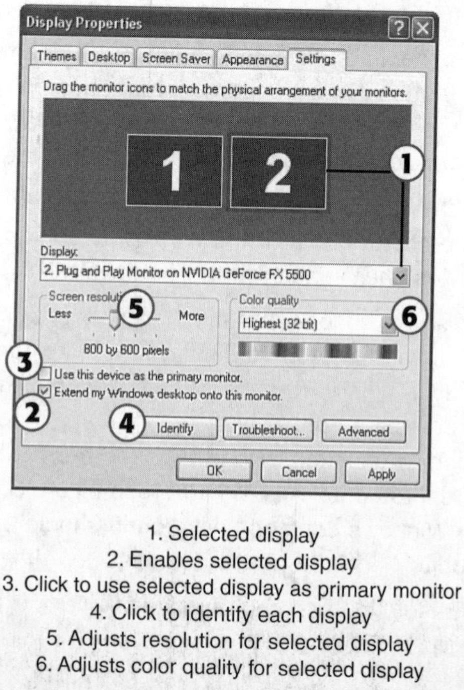

FIGURE 5.20
Enabling multiple monitors in Windows XP.

1. Selected display
2. Enables selected display
3. Click to use selected display as primary monitor
4. Click to identify each display
5. Adjusts resolution for selected display
6. Adjusts color quality for selected display

Each monitor can use a different refresh rate, color depth, and resolution setting. To adjust the settings for each monitor, click it in the display properties dialog and then move through the properties sheets as discussed earlier in this chapter.

Leo Says

Laptops Don't Always Support DualView

Just because your laptop shipped with Windows XP (or has been updated to Windows XP), don't assume it supports DualView. If the laptop's external display only mirrors what you see on the built-in LCD panel and doesn't show two monitor icons in its Settings tab, it doesn't support DualView. Check with the vendor to see if a driver update will help. However, your ability to get DualView depends primarily on how good the graphics hardware is in your laptop. If your laptop uses ATI Radeon Mobility or NVIDIA GeForce Go graphics, it probably supports DualView.

Note that the next time you start Windows, you must have both displays turned on to permit the desktop to be automatically extended to the additional display. If you shut off the secondary display, you will need to turn on the display and follow steps 5 through 7 to reenable the secondary display.

If you're adding a second display adapter to an existing system, the start of the procedure is a bit different and more can go wrong:

1. Shut down the computer and the existing (primary) monitor.

2. Open the computer and locate an empty card slot for the secondary display adapter. You can add a PCI display adapter to systems that have PCI or AGP video. Some recent systems enable you to use an AGP and a PCI-Express video card.

3. Insert the new video card and connect the secondary monitor to the card.

4. Close the computer, turn on the monitors, and start the computer.

5. During the startup process, you should see information on both monitors.

6. Install drivers for the display adapter and monitor as prompted. Use the latest display adapter drivers provided by the vendor, not the one from the Windows CD-ROM, for best results.

7. When the computer boots to the Windows desktop, open the display properties sheet and click the Settings tab.

8. You should see two icons displayed; continue as described in steps 6 and 7 earlier in this section to configure your new display adapter and monitor.

If you are using compatible display adapters, the process of using two (or more) display adapters should go as smoothly as with a multiple-display card. However, if you have problems, see the following sections.

Leo Says

More Power for Multiple Displays

If you want more control over multiple displays than what the standard ATI video driver provides, be sure to download and install ATI's HYDRAVISION. Learn more about the differences between the Basic and Full editions at http://www.ati.com/products/hydravision/features.html.

NVIDIA's ForceWare drivers include the nView multiple-monitor control panel application as a standard feature.

I Can't Get the Second Display to Work

If you're adding a separate video card to support an additional display and you're having problems, make sure that you try the following:

- Check the compatibility of both video cards with each other and with your motherboard or computer. Although Microsoft has some information on multiple-display support available on its website and on the Windows CD-ROM, the chipsets mentioned are not current. We find the best source for researching video chipset and motherboard issues is the Realtime Soft UltraMon website (UltraMon is a terrific low-cost add-on to Windows that enhances multiple-monitor configuration and setup). The website has an enormous database of user-reported configurations; look up the video cards and motherboard/system you have to see if someone has already tried your combination and to learn what happened.

Multiple-Monitor Resources

The Realtime Soft UltraMon website is located at http://www.
realtimesoft.com/multimon/.

- Make sure you have an available slot for the second video card.
  If you want to have dual-display support on a desktop computer
  with built-in video, you will need to install a multiple-display card
  or two separate single-display cards, because built-in video needs
  to be disabled whenever you install add-on display adapters. If
  you don't have room for a second video card, replace your existing card with a multiple-display video card.

Disabling Onboard Video? Methods Differ.

While some computers with built-in video automatically disable the
onboard video adapter when you install another video card, some
require you to adjust a setting in the system BIOS or adjust a jumper
block on the motherboard to disable onboard video. Consult your computer or motherboard documentation for details.

- If Windows can't recognize the secondary display adapter, try
  adjusting the priority of the display cards in your system. Most
  recent system BIOSes with AGP slots have a BIOS setting that
  lets you select either AGP or PCI as the primary display. You
  might need to configure the slower PCI display card as the primary display adapter to enable dual-display support if your system already has an AGP display adapter installed. Because the
  secondary display adapter can't be used for advanced 3D gaming
  or accelerated video, you want to avoid this situation if possible.
  Study the online resources provided earlier to determine which
  combinations of AGP and PCI display adapters will enable you to
  continue to use the faster AGP video card as the primary adapter
  and have dual-display support.

→ *For details about
accessing the BIOS,
see "Controlling Your
PC's Operation with
BIOS Setup,"
Chapter 1, p. 41.*

- Install updated drivers for both video cards. The video drivers
  provided by Microsoft often don't support multiple displays or
  other advanced features. Go to the card manufacturer's website
  and download the latest drivers offered for your card and your
  version of Windows.

→ *For details, see
"Reinstalling or
Updating Your Display
Adapter Driver," this
chapter, p. 338.*

- Make sure the primary display works correctly before you install
  the second video card.

- To verify that the secondary display adapter works if Windows can't detect it, remove the primary display adapter and use the secondary adapter as the only video card in the system. If it works by itself, but not with the original primary adapter in the system, you might not be able to use that particular combination of cards in your system. Try the other fixes listed, try a different card as the secondary display adapter, or upgrade to a dual-display card.

The Second Display Won't Run 3D Graphics

This is a normal limitation of multiple-display setups that use separate graphics cards. The faster graphics card should be used with the primary display. If you are unable to use two separate display cards with the faster AGP card as the primary display, I recommend that you replace your existing AGP card with a dual-display card using an NVIDIA or ATI 3D graphics chip; see the NVIDIA and ATI websites for details about their latest offerings.

The Second Display Shows What's on the First Display

This is normal if you've attached a secondary monitor to a multiple-monitor display adapter. To enable the secondary monitor to display different programs than the primary adapter, open the display properties sheet, click Settings and then click the icon for the secondary monitor (refer to Figure 5.20). Answer Yes to the dialog that asks if you want to enable the monitor. Then click Apply. Adjust the color depth, resolution, and refresh rate as desired.

If you don't see multiple displays listed on the Settings tab, you need to upgrade your display drivers to the enhanced versions available from the display card or chipset vendor; the display drivers supplied with Windows might not support multiple displays. Note that some notebook computers' integrated graphics chips don't support DualView—all you'll get on your external display is a copy (mirror) of the built-in display.

If you're already using up-to-date enhanced display adapter drivers, check the configuration of add-on software. Many vendors provide special software that enables multiple displays to be used as one large desktop, mirrored displays (both displays show the same information), and other features. Disable the mirror feature to enable each display to show different information.

The Secondary Display Doesn't Show Any Programs

To display programs on the secondary display, click the Restore button in the upper-right corner of your program's display to shrink the program into a window. Then, you can drag the window to the secondary display. Click the Restore button again to maximize the program window on the secondary display.

The Secondary Display Is Using the Same Driver as the Primary Display

Windows can't always determine what type of monitor you're using for a secondary display. To select the correct driver in Windows XP, follow these steps:

1. Open the display properties sheet and click the Settings tab.
2. Select the secondary monitor.
3. Click Advanced.
4. Click Monitor.
5. Click Properties, Driver.
6. Click Update Driver.
7. The Hardware Update Wizard starts. If you use Windows XP Service Pack 2 or higher, select Windows Update as a source for drivers this time, every time, or not this time. Click Next.
8. Click Install from a List or Specific Location. Then click Next.
9. If you have downloaded the correct driver or have a driver on CD or floppy disk, keep the default (Search for the Best Driver) and specify the locations to search. If you want to choose the driver from a list, click Don't Search.
10. If you select Search, Windows will locate the correct driver and install it for you. If you select Don't Search and want to see a list of drivers, clear the Show Compatible Hardware check box and scroll through the vendor list to select a vendor. Then scroll through the model list to select the model. Click Next and then Finish.

Troubleshooting 3D Game Performance and Image Quality

3D gaming is one of the major reasons to have a high-powered home computer. If you like to relax after a hard day's work by fragging aliens, racing the hottest cars from around the world, or refighting World War II, you need the best 3D performance you can buy. Use the following sections to help improve how well your computer plays 3D games.

3D Games Run Too Slowly

If your 3D games run too slowly, the causes can vary according to the nature of the game and the hardware in your PC. If you are playing a single-player game or with another human player on a single PC, then the solutions in this section should speed up your game. However, if you are playing a multiplayer game with other players using PCs located on your network or over the Internet, you may also need to adjust the network or Internet options in your game.

The best ways to speed up your visual display also cost money, such as:

- Replacing your older video card with a video card using the latest chipsets made by NVIDIA or ATI.

- Replacing integrated video with an AGP or PCI-Express video card with the latest NVIDIA or ATI chipsets (if your computer has an AGP or PCI-Express x16 slot); you can also use a PCI card if you don't have AGP or PCI-Express slots, but you won't see as big a performance increase. If your computer is a budget system using an Intel Celeron, AMD Sempron, or AMD Duron processor or is more than 2 years old with any processor, your processor isn't powerful enough to provide maximum performance with a high-end graphics card. Consider cards under $200 to get a boost in performance; faster cards will not provide much more performance because your processor acts as a bottleneck.

If you are using a current high-end graphics card with an ATI or NVIDIA chipset, you probably don't need to make customized driver adjustments to improve performance. However, if your game stutters badly as it tries to draw the screen or suffers from other problems, try the following changes to help improve gaming performance:

- **Reduce the color depth (number of colors) used in the game from 32-bit to 16-bit.** Displaying fewer colors can greatly improve performance, though the game's visuals will take a serious hit.

- **Reduce or disable antialiasing.** When enabled, antialiasing smoothes the edges of screen objects, but this can slow down screen rendering.

- **Reduce or disable anisotropic filtering.** When enabled, anisotropic filtering improves the appearance of textured objects, but this can slow down screen rendering.

- **Set image quality for Performance rather than Quality.** This improves overall speed but maintains a reasonable level of image quality.

- **Use only one display unless your game supports multiple displays.** Using a dual-head display can slow down performance. However, if the game enables you to view additional play areas or menus on the secondary display, it might be a worthwhile trade-off.

- **Specify a smaller Z-buffer (the memory used to store 3D scene detail).** Reducing the size of the Z-buffer reduces the amount of data the video card has to manipulate.

Some games allow you to adjust display quality settings within the game setup (see Figure 5.21); if not, you can adjust the 3D effects properties sheets provided as part of a 3D display adapter's properties sheets (see Figures 5.22 and 5.23).

It's important to understand that if you adjust video options from within a game, the interface and options you can choose from vary from game to game. You should check its documentation for more information. Additionally, display quality adjustments made from within a game do not affect settings outside it.

Tweak Your 3D Games to Perfection

For a comprehensive list of tips for improving 3D games and video driver settings, visit the nVnews Tweaks page at http://www.nvnews.net/tweaks/tweaks.shtml.

FIGURE 5.21

Quake III is a popular 3D game that allows you to adjust resolution, 3D lighting, texture detail, and other effects within the game itself.

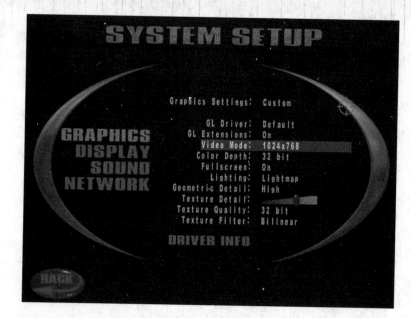

The latest drivers from NVIDIA (Figure 5.22) and ATI (Figure 5.23) enable you to adjust game settings on an individual basis. NVIDIA provides a number of preconfigured profiles for popular games, or you can let the game control the settings.

FIGURE 5.22

NVIDIA's Performance & Quality Settings menu enables you to adjust global settings for all 3D games or choose a game from the Applications menu and customize its performance.

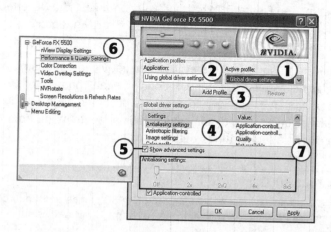

1. Selects active profile
2. Selects application (game)
3. Adds a new application profile
4. Current application settings
5. Enables/disables display of advanced settings
6. Selects Performance and Quality Settings menu
7. Options for current setting

With ATI's CATALYST Control Center, you can create customized profiles for use with games (through the Profiles menu), modify global settings, or directly adjust Direct3D (DirectX) and OpenGL settings, as shown in Figure 5.23.

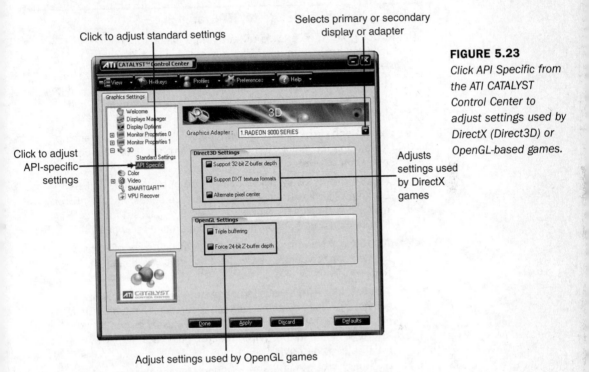

Selects primary or secondary display or adapter

Click to adjust standard settings

Click to adjust API-specific settings

Adjusts settings used by DirectX games

Adjust settings used by OpenGL games

FIGURE 5.23
Click API Specific from the ATI CATALYST Control Center to adjust settings used by DirectX (Direct3D) or OpenGL-based games.

Where Are My 3D Driver Configuration Tabs?

If you don't see options for controlling antialiasing, Z-buffering, or other 3D settings in your graphics driver, you are probably running the bare-bones Windows drivers provided with Windows. You should visit your display adapter vendor's website for card-specific or motherboard video–specific drivers or run Windows Update.

Although you might be able to use generic NVIDIA or ATI display drivers for third-party video cards built with those chipsets, you may be better off with drivers optimized for your particular hardware. The same is true for video drivers for motherboards with integrated video. Some display adapter and motherboard makers customize graphics drivers to match unique features of their hardware.

If you're not familiar with all the options available on your display adapter's 3D configuration options, consult the help function provided in the driver or see the websites in the sidebar "Improving Your Knowledge of 3D Graphics."

Improving Your Knowledge of 3D Graphics

The following websites provide reviews, white papers, and other resources you can use to bolster your knowledge of 3D graphics:

- **Tom's Hardware (http://www.tomshardware.com)**—A website that reviews the latest 3D hardware (and all other major computer subsystems) with incredibly detailed technical information and benchmarks.

- **Anandtech (http://www.anandtech.com)**—Another outstanding review and technology website for 3D hardware and other computer components.

- **NVIDIA (http://www.nvidia.com)**—One of the leading makers of 3D graphics chipsets, such as the GeForce series and the nForce motherboard chipsets with integrated 3D graphics. Products using NVIDIA chips are sold by many vendors around the world.

- **ATI (http://www.ati.com)**—Another leading maker of 3D and motherboard chipsets, as well as graphics cards based on Radeon technology.

- **TweakGuides**—This website offers many guides for optimizing games, operating systems, and other computer features. Check out the ATI CATALYST guide at http://www.tweakguides.com/ATICAT_1.html and the NVIDIA nFORCE guide at http://www.tweakguides.com/NVFORCE_1.html.

- **Upgrading and Repairing PCs**—Scott Mueller, the dean of computer upgrading authors, offers many articles on graphics cards, chipsets, and displays on his book's companion website. Go to http://www.upgradingandrepairingpcs.com, click Articles to review current articles, or click the Articles Archive link to see previous articles.

Improving AGP Video Performance

Although PCI-Express is now the highest-performance PC graphics solution on the market (some motherboards support a pair of matched PCI-Express cards using the NVIDIA SLI technology), most computers sold still rely on the AGP slot for display. If your computer uses an AGP graphics card, you can improve the performance as follows:

- Installing up-to-date motherboard or chipset drivers
- Properly configuring your AGP options in the system BIOS

Finding and Installing AGP Chipset Drivers

If your system uses a motherboard based on a VIA Technologies, SiS (Silicon Integrated Systems), AMD (Advanced Micro Devices), or ULi (formerly Acer Labs) chipset, the proper operation of the AGP slot relies on a driver made for the chipset. Intel chipsets do not require an AGP driver.

Although a version of the appropriate driver for your system is usually provided on the driver CD packaged with your motherboard or system, you will usually have better performance and stability if you install the latest version available for your chipset. After you install the driver, you will need to restart your system.

Better AGP Drivers Are a Click Away!

Get the VIA Technologies Hyperion 4-in-1 driver from http://www. viaarena.com.

Get the SiS AGP GART driver from http://www.sis.com/download.

Get the AMD AGP driver from the AMD Downloads section of the AMD website at http://www.amd.com.

Get the ULi (Acer Labs) unified driver for your motherboard's North Bridge chip from http://www.uli.com.tw.

Configuring AGP Options in the System BIOS

AGP settings in the system BIOS can improve or degrade the stability of your system. Generally, if your system is stable, there's no need to fiddle with these settings. However, if you're having problems with system crashes, especially when you're playing a recent 3D game, it can't hurt to take a look at the settings and see what you have.

→ *To learn more about accessing the system BIOS, see "Controlling Your PC's Operation with BIOS Setup," Chapter 1, p. 41.*

Table 5.3 lists typical AGP settings in the system BIOS and our recommendations. Our recommendations are designed to strike a balance between speed and stability. Remember, it doesn't matter how fast your computer is if you're spending most of your time trying to figure out why it's crashing!

TABLE 5.3
RECOMMENDED AGP BIOS SETTINGS

BIOS Option	What It Does	Recommended Setting	Notes
AGP Mode or AGP Transfer Rate	Sets the speed of the AGP slot	Set to the speed of the card (8x, 4x, 2x)	If an 8x AGP card isn't stable at 8x, use 4x.
AGP Aperture Size	Sets aside system memory addresses for use by the AGP card when it runs out of video memory	128MB	Higher settings can conflict with system memory; lower settings can reduce performance.
AGP Fast Write	Enables transfers to the AGP slot to bypass system memory	Auto or Enabled	Disable if system becomes unstable.
AGP Master 1 WS Read/Write	Uses a single memory wait state (empty cycle) rather than two wait states for reading or writing	Enable	Some systems use zero wait states as the default, so if this slows down the system, disable it.

The settings shown in Table 5.3 are far from the only options available for AGP on some BIOSes. However, these are the most important— and the safest to play with!

Reinstalling or Updating Your Display Adapter Driver

➔ See "Using Device Manager," Chapter 2, p. 100, for general instructions on accessing and using the Device Manager.

One of the best fixes for problems with the display adapter in Windows is to remove the display adapter from the Device Manager and restart the computer. This forces Windows to redetect the display adapter and reinstall the driver. This solves problems caused by damaged Registry entries for the display adapter.

To perform this task, follow these steps:

1. Open the Device Manager.
2. Click the plus sign (+) next to the Display Adapters category.

3. Click the display adapter and press the Delete key.

4. Click OK to remove the display adapter.

5. Click Yes to restart your computer.

6. When the computer restarts, the display adapter will be rede-tected and the driver will be reinstalled.

In some cases, you might also need to update the display adapter to a newer version. Follow these steps:

1. Open the entry for the display adapter in Device Manager, click the Driver tab, and click the Update Driver button.

2. Starting with Service Pack 2, Windows XP can use Windows Update to locate a driver for you. Select the option to run it every time, this time only, or not to use Windows Update.

3. If Windows Update has a new display adapter driver, it can install that driver for you automatically.

4. If Windows Update doesn't have an updated driver, go to the display adapter vendor's website (for an add-on card) or the computer vendor's website (for built-in video) and download the latest driver.

5. The website should provide you with specific directions for driver installation; if the driver doesn't install itself automatically during this process, note the location to which you downloaded it.

6. Follow the vendor's instructions for installing the new video driver with your version of Windows. If you are updating a previous version of a vendor-supplied driver, you might need to uninstall the previous version using Control Panel's Add/Remove Programs icon.

Troubleshooting Audio

If you use your PC as a music player, you're far from alone! A PC without audio is becoming almost as rare as a black-and-white TV. Whether you're a hardcore gamer, a fan of Internet radio or video, or like to watch DVD movies on your computer, you need to fix sound problems quickly. Use the following sections to make sure your sound works the way you need it to work.

Can't Record or Play Back Sounds

Sound recording and sound playback depend on several factors, including the following:

- Correct connection of speakers and microphones
- Correct installation of the sound card and its drivers
- Correct use of sound mixer controls
- Installation of the proper audio codecs

The following sections deal with these issues.

Troubleshooting Problems with Sound Card Installation and Drivers

Generally, sound card installations are simple if...

- The computer doesn't have built-in sound.
- No other sound card has been installed in the computer previously.

However, if you have installed a new sound card in a computer that has built-in sound or you are upgrading from an older sound card, the old hardware could cause you problems. Check the following:

- Disable onboard sound hardware before you install a new sound card. Systems with onboard sound control this feature through the system BIOS setup program (see Figure 5.24).

➔ For tips on using Device Manager, see "Using Device Manager," Chapter 2, p. 100.

- Remove listings for old sound hardware from Device Manager before you install the new sound card. The Sound, Video, and Game Controllers category in Device Manager (see Figure 5.25) lists sound card and onboard sound hardware. Sound card (audio) hardware and drivers should no longer be loaded after you disable onboard sound. If you see the drivers listed, remove them. Similarly, if you are upgrading to a new sound card, remove the sound card from Device Manager before you install the new card.

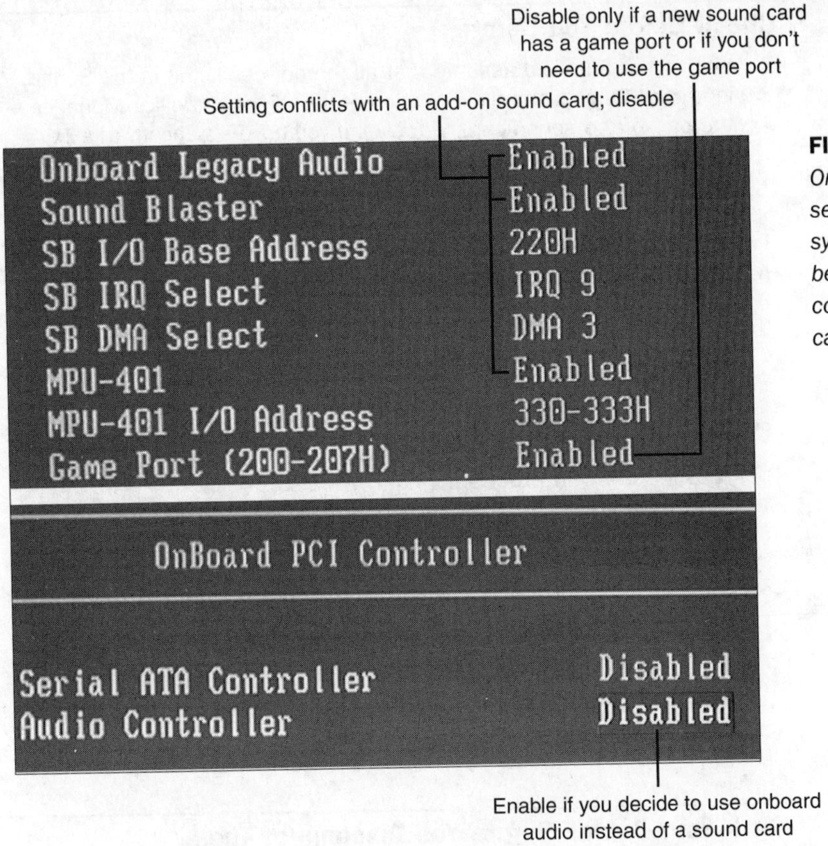

Disable only if a new sound card
has a game port or if you don't
need to use the game port

Setting conflicts with an add-on sound card; disable

Onboard Legacy Audio — Enabled
Sound Blaster — Enabled
SB I/O Base Address — 220H
SB IRQ Select — IRQ 9
SB DMA Select — DMA 3
MPU-401 — Enabled
MPU-401 I/O Address — 330-333H
Game Port (200-207H) — Enabled

OnBoard PCI Controller

Serial ATA Controller — Disabled
Audio Controller — Disabled

Enable if you decide to use onboard
audio instead of a sound card

FIGURE 5.24
Onboard audio settings on typical systems; these must be disabled to avoid conflicts with a sound card.

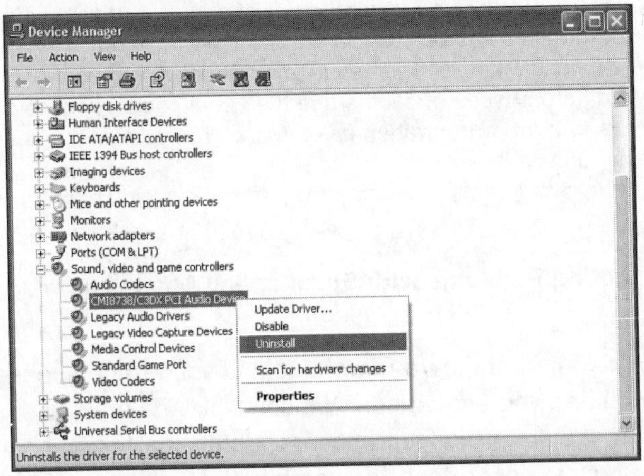

FIGURE 5.25
Preparing to remove existing sound hardware from the Windows XP Device Manager.

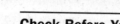

Check Before You Delete

At one time you could assume that all the devices listed in the Sound, Video, and Game Controllers section of the Windows Device Manager were part of the sound card. However, if you have a webcam or a TV tuner, you might also find video-capture tools for those devices in this category. When you delete your old sound hardware from Device Manager, I recommend you delete only the sound card or chipset driver itself; drivers associated with the sound card will also be deleted in the process. If you still use gameport-based controllers and your motherboard has a gameport, but your new sound card doesn't, keep the gameport enabled in the system BIOS settings shown in Figure 5.24, and don't delete the gameport from the Device Manager.

- Download the latest drivers for your sound card before you start the installation process.

- Load the software included with your sound card in the correct order. Depending on the sound card you are installing, you might need to install the driver software before you install the sound card or let the sound card prompt you for drivers when Windows detects it. Generally, software for sound recording, digital audio conversion, and so forth should be installed only after the sound card is installed and tested.

Mark Your Cables Before You Disconnect Them

If you're moving up from built-in sound or an entry-level sound card to a better model, you can save yourself a lot of grief if you label both internal and external cables before you remove them. If you don't have specialized data-cable labels, address labels will do for temporary use. Because different types of cables use the same connectors, you can save yourself a lot of frustration if you mark what each cable does before you unplug it.

Troubleshooting Problems with Speaker and Microphone Connections

Generally, if your sound card is working and you attach speakers to your sound card, you should hear Windows play its startup sound as soon as the Windows desktop appears. Unfortunately, standard sound cards and built-in sound features use identical mini-jacks for speakers, microphones, and other input-output connections.

To make sure you connect the correct devices to the correct jacks, check the following:

- Use the color-coding provided on most sound cards, microphones, and speakers to attach the correct cables to the correct ports. The standard color used for speaker cords and jacks is lime green; line-in jacks use a light blue connector, and the microphone jack is pink. Note that systems with 5.1 or 7.1 integrated surround sound use the same jacks for different tasks, depending on the sound volume and mixer controls. If you have a 5.1 or 7.1 surround sound speaker system, plug in just the stereo speakers to start with, and add the others after you understand the mixer settings and audio jack assignments used for additional speakers. See "Can't Hear Sound from Additional Speakers," this chapter, p. 346, for more information.

- Check the markings on the rear of the sound card or computer if the color-coding systems don't match (some vendors don't follow industry standards) or aren't present.

- Make sure the speakers are turned on and are receiving power.

If the cables are connected correctly, check the volume and mixer controls.

Troubleshooting the Sound Volume Controls

While basic sound cards and integrated audio solutions are limited to the traditional mini-jacks, most mid-range and high-end sound cards as well as better integrated audio solutions offer optical and digital connections to home theater systems and analog or digital connections to 5.1 and 7.1 speaker systems. Whether you use a simple two-speaker hookup, have your system patched into your home theater system, or use 5.1 or 7.1 surround sound speakers, you must configure your sound card's mixer controls to correctly identify which speakers you plan to use. Similarly, if you are recording sound, the mixer controls are also used to determine the source for recorded sound (microphone, line in, and so on).

To access the sound volume control, check the Windows system tray. In most cases, you will find a speaker icon. Click it to open the volume control (see Figure 5.26). If you don't see the volume control in the Windows system tray, open the Control Panel. In Windows XP, select Sounds, Speech and Audio Devices (if using category view) and then Sounds and Audio Devices. Enable the Place Volume Icon in the Taskbar option and click OK.

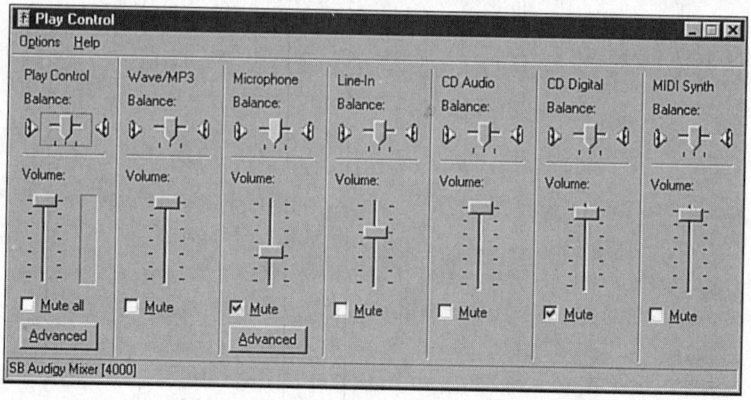

FIGURE 5.26

The volume control for the Creative Labs Sound Blaster Audigy Platinum.

Note that the volume control (also known as the mixer) works with different types of audio sources, but it's not used to specify the number of speakers you use.

If your sound card's default volume control has settings for devices and music types you will never use, you can configure the volume control to display only the controls you need. Click Options, Properties, Playback and clear the check marks from devices you don't use for playing sounds (see Figure 5.27). Click Options, Properties, Record and do the same for devices you don't use for recording.

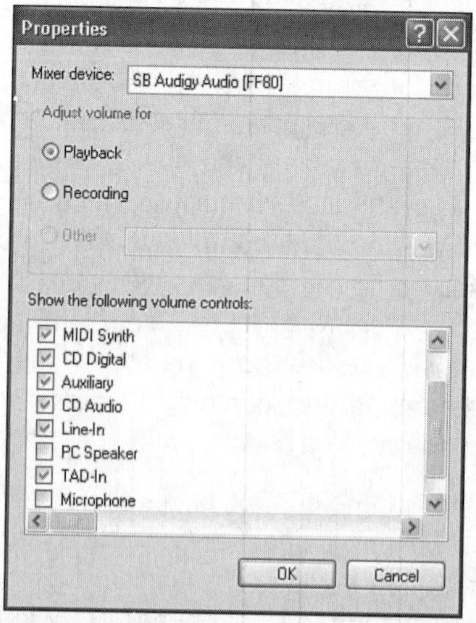

FIGURE 5.27

Customizing the play-back volume control for the Creative Labs Sound Blaster Audigy Platinum.

If you can work with some types of sounds but not others, the volume control for the type of audio source probably has its volume turned down too far or the volume control is muted. For example, in Figure 5.26, you won't be able to record sounds through the microphone until you clear the check mark from the Mute setting. If you don't see a volume control for the sound source you are using, it is probably disabled. Open the Options menu, select Properties, and re-enable the volume control for that sound source.

Table 5.4 lists audio types and their uses. If you are having problems with sound recording or playback, use this table to determine which volume control to adjust.

TABLE 5.4
AUDIO TYPES AND VOLUME CONTROL SETTINGS

Audio Type	Volume Control	Notes
All audio types	Play control	This overrides all other settings if set to a low volume or Mute.
Digital music (WAV, MP3, WMA)	Wave/MP3	
MIDI tracks	MIDI	
Music CDs	CD-Audio or CD-Digital	If you use the standard four-wire cable between the CD-ROM drive and the sound card, use CD-Audio. CD-Digital uses a two-wire cable, which won't work with older CD-ROM drives.
Auxiliary	TV tuner card or additional CD-ROM drive	Uses the same four-wire cable as CD-Audio.
Line-in	Any external sound source, particularly stereo systems, tape players, and so on	Might be the same as the microphone jack on some sound cards.
TAD-in	Works with internal modems that have a telephone-answering device feature	
Microphone	Headset, boom, and handheld microphones	It is muted by default to prevent accidental recording.

Correct adjustment of the volume control is only half the battle. If you want to use more than two speakers, digital speakers, or other nonstandard sound sources or outputs, you need to properly configure the sound-mixing controls provided with the sound card.

Can't Hear Sound from Additional Speakers

Generally, if all you have is the traditional pair of stereo speakers that attach through a mini-jack, you don't need to do anything other than adjust the volume control to have acceptable sound playback. However, most users want more and better speakers, or might be using headphones instead of speakers. If you use analog speakers or headsets, you need to adjust the Sounds and Audio Devices properties in Windows. If you want to use advanced audio features or if you use digital speakers, you also need to adjust settings in the proprietary mixer program provided by the sound card vendor (in this case, consult your audio card's documentation).

If you can't hear anything from the additional speakers you've added to your system, or you've changed your speaker type (even if you have the same number of speakers), you need to adjust your audio configuration to reflect your new speaker setup. Here's how:

1. Open the Control Panel. In Windows XP, select Sounds, Speech and Audio Devices. Then select Sounds and Audio Devices.

2. Click the Advanced button in the Speakers section. An advanced audio properties sheet appears; the Speakers tab is displayed by default.

3. Click the pull-down Speaker Setup menu and select the type of speaker setup you use (see Figure 5.28); the speaker configuration you select is displayed onscreen.

4. After you select the correct speaker configuration, click OK when you're finished.

If you've selected the correct speaker types, but you can't hear any sounds, check the volume control. If you can hear audio through standard stereo speakers or headsets, but can't hear digital audio through the S/PDIF-out port or can't hear surround sound in a 5.1 or 7.1 configuration, you need to enable the appropriate setting in the control software for your audio hardware. Although some audio hardware allows you to enable digital playback through the Windows volume control's Advanced dialog, in most cases you will need to use the proprietary software provided by the audio hardware vendor and configure it properly.

Figure 5.29 shows two possible configurations of the mixer provided by C-Media for its 5.1 and digital audio chipsets (this mixer is accessed through the Audio Rack audio playback program). The jacks in the center of the dialog represent the basic microphone-in, line-in, and speaker/line-out jacks. In a standard two-channel configuration, these are the only jacks needed. However, if you click the S/PDIF Playback option, you can use the coaxial or optical S/PDIF-out jacks on a separate bracket (known as the *S-bracket* in this example) to play the audio through a home theater system via S/PDIF (top view). Keep in mind that some sound cards support up to 7.1 audio through S/PDIF.

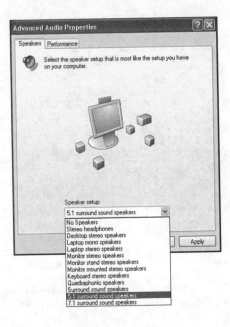

FIGURE 5.28
Selecting the speaker type in Windows XP.

The bottom view shows a six-channel (5.1) configuration. If the Default Phonejack setting is used, the S-bracket must be used to provide rear speaker and center/subwoofer speaker out support. However, if the additional bracket is not available, the mixer can reassign the normal line-in (blue) jack as the rear speaker out jack and the normal microphone in (pink) jack as the center/subwoofer speaker out jack, as shown in Figure 5.29.

As you can see from Figure 5.29, going beyond stereo sound can be complex. Even if you get the mixer set correct, you might also have problems with the speaker cables, or with the speakers themselves. Although some systems now dynamically switch rear audio jack assignments, enabling you to plug stereo speakers or a microphone into any rear-panel jack, you need to use the correct jack for additional speakers. If you use an additional rear-panel bracket for S/PDIF digital audio or surround sound, make sure it is properly connected to the motherboard. Figure 5.30 shows how the S-bracket controlled in Figure 5.29 connects to the motherboard.

FIGURE 5.29

Two possible configurations of a motherboard-based 5.1 surround sound audio mixer.

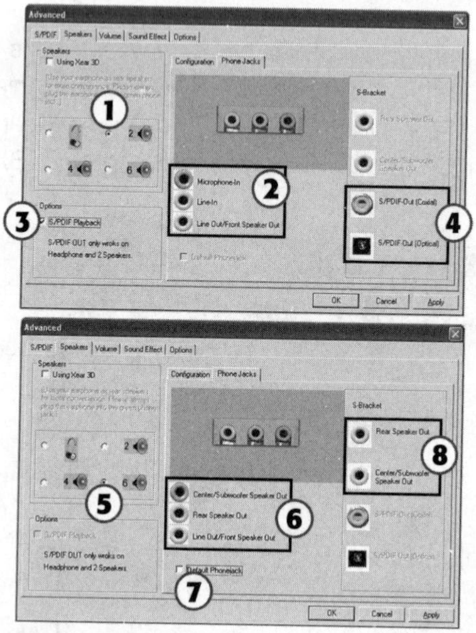

1. Two-channel (stereo) speakers selected
2. Standard assignments for rear-panel audio jacks
3. When checked, enables S/PDIF (digital) audio output
4. Select the appropriate S/PDIF-Out jack based on the S/PDIF connector used by your home theater system
5. Six-channel (5.1 surround) speakers selected
6. Reassigned rear panel jacks enable six-channel output without an additional bracket
7. Check to reenable default assignments for rear-panel audio jacks
8. Surround-sound ports on additional bracket can be used to permit standard assignments of rear panel jacks

If you don't hear any sound from additional speakers after checking the mixer controls, cable connections, motherboard bracket connections, and built-in volume controls, you might have defective speakers.

Troubleshooting Problems with 3D Sound in Games

3D sound makes games sound as realistic as 3D video makes them look. If you're not experiencing directional sound (even if you have just two speakers) or are having other sound quality problems, check the following:

➜ *For configuration details, see "Can't Hear Sound from Additional Speakers," this chapter, p. 346.*

- **The speaker configuration**—Even if you have just two speakers, speakers built into the monitor or headphones need a different configuration than the typical tabletop speakers you might have received with your system.

Bracket connection to motherboard

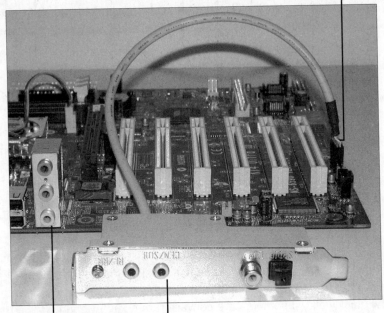

FIGURE 5.30
An additional audio port bracket plugged into the motherboard before the mother-board is installed.

Standard rear-panel audio jacks

Audio port bracket (fits into empty expansion slot on rear of system)

- **The environmental audio settings for your sound card**—If you have a Creative Labs Sound Blaster series card, for example, you should enable the EAX (environmental audio effects) feature through the EAX control panel (part of the Creative Audio HQ program included with the card).

- **The DirectX drivers**—Make sure you have installed the latest DirectX drivers. Most games that use 3D sound use DirectX drivers.

Gimme a Fresh DirectX!

You can download the latest version of DirectX from the Microsoft DirectX website:

http://www.microsoft.com/windows/directx/default.asp.

- **Audio acceleration features**—The default setting for audio acceleration is Full, but you might need to try reduced acceleration for certain games if the default setting produces poor-quality sound.

To adjust the audio acceleration setting, follow these steps:

1. Open the Control Panel. Select Sounds, Speech and Audio Devices (if using category view) and then select Sounds and Audio Devices.

2. Click the Advanced button in the Speakers section; an advanced audio properties sheet appears.

3. Click the Performance tab and adjust the Hardware Acceleration slider one notch to the left from the default Full position (see Figure 5.31).

4. Try your game. If audio performance improves, use that acceleration setting for that game. If audio performance is still poor, repeat steps 1–3 and try each lower setting with your game.

5. Update the audio drivers as soon as possible and retry full audio acceleration after updating them.

A second option for improving game quality is also located on the Performance tab; if you need to adjust acceleration settings downward, also try adjusting sample rate conversion quality (how well and how quickly digital samples are converted to audio). Depending on the speed of your sound card and your system, the default for your system might be set to Good. If it is, slide the control one notch toward the middle; this improves audio conversion quality, but requires a bit more processing power from your computer.

Before You Slow Down Your Sound, Check for Patches

Check with your game vendor for updates and patches for your game before you fiddle around with the acceleration and sample rate conversion sliders. You should also install the latest software drivers and DirectX version and retry your game. Also, be sure to check your game's own menu for sound playback options. Use these controls to customize the right mix of audio quality and game performance for you.

Troubleshooting Playback Problems with Music CDs

Playing music CDs on your computer is an enjoyable way to entertain yourself, but it depends on proper cable connections and volume controls. If you can't hear anything while a music CD is playing, check the following:

- **The volume control on your music player software and the Windows volume control**—Whether you use Windows Media Player or some other playback software, its volume control must be coordinated with the Windows master volume control. Generally, you should set the Windows volume control as high as possible so you can use the application's volume control to reduce the volume (be careful not to damage your speakers by setting the volume too high). If you have your application's volume control turned up full blast but the Windows volume control is set to low levels or is muted, you won't hear your music.

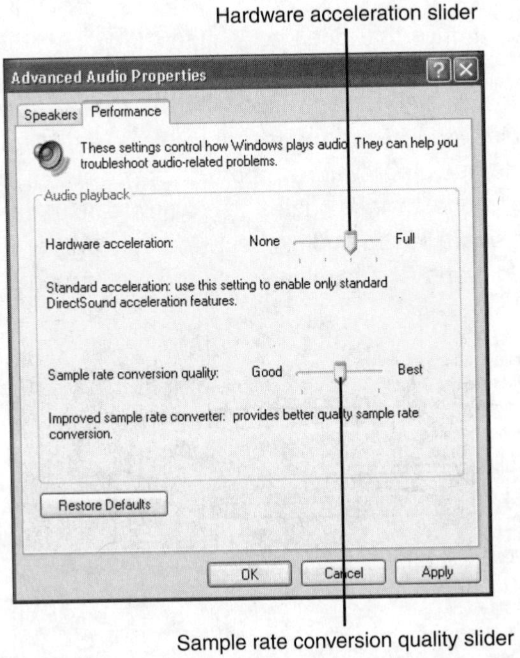

Hardware acceleration slider

FIGURE 5.31

Adjusting the Hardware Acceleration and Sample Rate Conversion Quality settings in Windows XP.

Sample rate conversion quality slider

- **The power and volume controls used by external speakers**—If the external speakers aren't turned on or have their built-in volume control turned down, you can't control the speakers with Windows. Turn them on and adjust their volume controls, then fine-tune the volume with the Windows volume control.

- **Dirt on the CD or in the drive**—If the CD won't play at all or skips, its surface may be dirty. Use a wet-type radial CD cleaner to clean the CD surface, and also use a cleaning CD to clean the lens of the CD-ROM drive. If you have a DVD drive, try to use a DVD-specific cleaning CD for better results.

You might have noticed that your sound card, motherboard with integrated audio, and CD or DVD drive have provisions for two-wire (digital) or four-wire (audio) patch cables. Audio playback programs (including DVD player programs) that support digital audio extraction (DAE) don't need these cables. Virtually all current audio playback programs use DAE.

However, you will need to use a four-wire (analog) cable if...

- You prefer not to use DAE to play back audio (you can choose this option in Windows Media Player and some other applications).

- You use a drive that does not support DAE.

If you want to use DAE but your optical drive does not support it via the data cable, you will need to install the two-wire CD digital cable if your drive and audio hardware support it. Check out Figure 5.32 to learn how to connect these cables to a typical sound card. If you're using motherboard-based audio, check your manual for the locations of the CD-Audio and CD-Digital jacks on the motherboard.

FIGURE 5.32

A typical four-wire analog connection (top) and the newer two-wire S/PDIF connection (middle) between optical drives and sound cards.

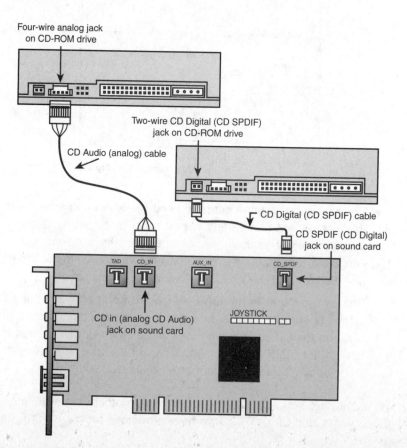

CHAPTER

6

Troubleshooting Multimedia and Imaging Devices

TROUBLESHOOTING

FAST TRACK TO SOLUTIONS (SYMPTOM TABLE)

Symptom	Flowchart or Book Section	See Page
My DV camcorder isn't recognized by my PC.	Troubleshooting Camera and 1394a Port Recognition Issues	**358**
My DV camcorder is recognized by my PC, but it doesn't work with my video-editing program.	Troubleshooting Video-Editing Software Problems	**360**
My DV camcorder capture has been very slow since my system was updated to Windows XP Service Pack 2 (SP2).	Sidebar: Fixing XP's SP2 1394a Slowdown Woes	**361**
I can't use Windows XP Movie Maker 2.1 since I installed other DV-editing or DVD-viewing software.	Troubleshooting Video-Editing Software Problems	**360**
The AutoPlay menu doesn't appear when I connect my DV camcorder, flash memory card, or digital camera.	Troubleshooting AutoPlay Problems	**368**
My digital camera isn't recognized, even as a removable-media drive.	Troubleshooting Digital Camera and USB Port/Hub Problems	**366**
How do I add a program to the AutoPlay list?	Fixing Problems with AutoPlay Handlers	**371**
I accidentally formatted my flash memory card. Can I retrieve my data?	Preventing and Troubleshooting Data Loss in Digital Cameras	**374**
My photos are not stored in My Photos. How can I set the folder to display thumbnails or a filmstrip view?	Troubleshooting File-Viewing Problems	**377**
How do I connect my camera to a camera or printer dock?	Troubleshooting Problems with Camera and Printer Docks	**379**
My images are being cropped when I print them with my printer dock. How can I avoid this?	Troubleshooting Printing Problems with Printer Docks	**380**

TROUBLESHOOTING

 FAST TRACK TO SOLUTIONS, Continued

Increasingly, today's PCs are the hub of family entertainment. They're used to edit videos, play DVDs, scan photos, download or convert digital music, and much more. If you're having problems enjoying the multimedia features of your PC, you've come to the right place. Put down the popcorn and let's get started!

Troubleshooting DV Camcorder Connections

Digital video (DV) camcorders connect to a PC through the IEEE-1394a (FireWire, i.Link) port for video transfer. Some DV camcorders also include flash memory capability for use in still-image capture, and these models use the USB port, just as normal digital cameras do.

Leo Says

1394b On Board? A Bilingual Cable Gets You Connected!

If your PC has the new 800Mbps IEEE-1394b (FireWire 800) port instead of IEEE-1394a, don't fret. Most implementations of 1394b include a bilingual port designed to connect to both 1394b and 1394a. Just use a 1394b to four-pin 1394a cable, and your DV camcorder can "talk" to your new PC.

You'll also need video-capture software, often provided with a DV camcorder, or you can use the Scanner and Camera Wizard and Windows Movie Maker 2 to grab your video. Here's how to connect a typical DV camcorder to your computer through the IEEE-1394a port:

Windows XP and 1394a Cards

If you're using a 1394a card produced before Windows XP, you'll want to make sure it's compatible. We've noticed that Windows XP seems to be fussier than older Windows versions about IEEE-1394a support. If Windows XP doesn't identify your card and install the appropriate driver, download a replacement driver from the card vendor.

Keep in mind that if you can't locate a Windows XP driver for your card, you might be able to use a Windows XP driver from a vendor whose card uses the same IEEE-1394a chipset.

1. Install an IEEE-1394a card (using the instructions provided with the card) if your system doesn't have an IEEE-1394a port. (See Chapter 7, "Troubleshooting I/O Ports and Input Devices," for details.)

2. Turn on the system. Install the drivers for the card and restart the system if necessary.

3. Install the software provided with the camera; with Windows XP, you might be able to use the Camera and Scanner Wizard to transfer pictures from the camera to the computer as an alternative to the software provided with the camera. You can also use a flash memory card reader. See "Troubleshooting Flash Memory Card Readers," this chapter, p. 383, for details.

4. Connect the appropriate type of IEEE-1394a cable to the camera. Cameras use the four-wire connector shown in Chapter 7. Most computers with built-in IEEE-1394a ports and all IEEE-1394a cards use the six-wire connector shown in Chapter 7, except for Sony's computers with i.Link: The i.Link port uses the same four-wire connector as a DV camcorder.

5. Connect the other end of the IEEE-1394a cable to the IEEE-1394a/FireWire/i.Link port on the computer.

6. If the DV camcorder also captures still images to flash memory and you prefer to connect the camcorder directly to the PC instead of using a card reader, connect the USB cable provided with the camcorder to the camcorder's USB port.

7. Plug the Type A (flat) end of the USB cable from the camera into a USB port on the computer or a USB hub attached to the computer.

8. Turn on the camcorder and follow the prompts from the camera's own software or Windows Scanner and Camera Wizard to capture your footage.

9. Follow the camcorder's instructions for transferring still images from the camcorder's flash memory card.

Typical problems with DV camcorders include the following:

- Camera not recognized by system or software.
- Stutters in playback.
- Speed of FireWire ports drops after Windows XP SP2 is installed.

Troubleshooting Camera and 1394a Port Recognition Issues

Normally, when you connect your DV camcorder to an IEEE-1394a port and turn it to VCR mode (see Figure 6.1), you should see an AutoPlay menu appear, similar to the one shown in Figure 6.2.

FIGURE 6.1
Use the VCR mode on your DV camcorder to start the transfer process.

FIGURE 6.2
A typical AutoPlay menu after third-party digital video–editing software has been installed.

➔ To solve problems with AutoPlay, see "Troubleshooting AutoPlay Problems," this chapter, p. 368.

➔ To troubleshoot your computer's 1394 ports, see "Troubleshooting IEEE-1394 Ports and Hubs," Chapter 7, p. 427.

If you do not see this menu, check the following:

• **Is your DV camcorder recognized by Windows?** It should appear in Windows Device Manager as an imaging device, as shown in Figure 6.3. If your camera appears here, AutoPlay might have been configured to take no action. If it does not appear, make sure the computer's IEEE-1394 ports are working.

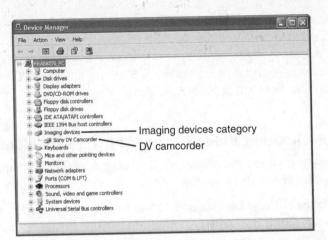

Imaging devices category

DV camcorder

FIGURE 6.3
A DV camcorder is listed in the Windows XP Device Manager when properly detected by the system.

- **Does the camera have a charged battery?** If you left the camera on accidentally, the battery is probably run down. Recharge the battery.

- **Is the camera properly connected to the IEEE-1394a port on the PC?** Check the cable connections at the computer (see Figure 7.3 in Chapter 7) and at the camcorder (see Figure 6.4).

- **If you are using built-in IEEE-1394 ports, make sure the ports are enabled in the system BIOS.** See "Troubleshooting IEEE-1394 Ports and Hubs," Chapter 7, for details.

FIGURE 6.4
Use the DV (IEEE-1394a, i.Link) connection for transferring digital video to/from your DV camcorder.

IEEE-1394a cable   USB port

- **Can you start the capture program manually?** Even if a program appears in the AutoPlay menu, it might not run from that menu. However, it might work just fine if you run the program from a desktop shortcut or the Windows Start menu and start video capture from within the application.

Troubleshooting Video-Editing Software Problems

If Windows recognizes your camera, but you are having problems capturing video, check the following:

- **Make sure your camera and 1394a card are supported by the video-editing application you want to use.** Check the compatibility listings or support forums for your software. Sometimes it might be necessary to use a 1394a card with a different chipset to get some camcorders to work properly. Fortunately, 1394a cards are not very expensive these days.

- **Can you start the capture program manually?** Even if a program appears in the AutoPlay menu, it might not run from that menu. However, it might work just fine if you run the program from a desktop shortcut or the Windows Start menu and start video capture from within the application.

- **Do you have enough disk space for video capture?** Depending on the program you use for capturing video, you can use many megabytes of disk space for just a few seconds of video. No wonder 200GB (and larger) external hard disks are such hot products! You should error-check and defragment any hard disk you want to use for video storage to help prevent dropped frames and poor quality. If you want to buy an external hard disk for use with DV camcorder video, we recommend you buy one with both USB 2.0 and IEEE-1394a ports. They cost a little more, but they enable you to connect the camcorder direct to the drive if you want.

- **Are you using the latest version of video playback applications such as Apple QuickTime and Microsoft DirectX?** Outdated components can cause your video-editing program to fail.

Get Your Fresh Video Components Here!

Download the latest version of Apple QuickTime from http://www.apple.com/quicktime/download/win.html.

Get the latest version of DirectX from http://www.microsoft.com/windows/directx/default.aspx.

If you're having difficulties getting your DV camcorder or other 1394a device to be recognized by your computer, or you experience dropped frames during DV capture, the problem might be that Windows XP has configured your 1394a port as a network port. Windows XP recognizes 1394a ports as network ports by default, although few people use them this way. If you don't use 1394 ports for networking, follow these steps to disable the network features of your 1394 ports:

1. Click Start, My Network Places.

2. Click View Network Connections in the Network Tasks menu.

3. Put your mouse over each connection to see which port it uses. When you find the one using the 1394 port, right-click the port and select Disable.

If you noticed problems with video capture speed and quality after upgrading to Windows XP SP2 and you have FireWire 800 ports, you're not crazy. For some reason, SP2 changed the speed of most 1394b ports from 800Mbps down to 100Mbps, whether you connect 1394a or 1394b devices to your computer. Dropping the port speed makes reliable video capture a really big problem for a lot of people. Fixing the problem isn't so simple, either. It takes a software patch from Microsoft and a bit of digging around in the Windows XP Registry (never for the fainthearted.

Fixing XP's SP2 1394 Slowdown Woes

Get the complete scoop on resetting your 1394 ports to full speed after installing Service Pack 2 from http://support.microsoft.com/kb/885222.

Simply print and follow the directions.

A lot of DV camcorder fans don't like Windows Movie Maker, but let's face it, the latest version (2.1) is still free and it's a lot better than previous versions. It's included in Windows XP Service Pack 2 (no, you can't download it separately), and unlike earlier versions, it can coexist peacefully with third-party multimedia products.

If Movie Maker 2.1 has problems because of third-party video filters, you can disable them through the Compatibility tab of the Options dialog (see Figure 6.5). With previous versions, you had to uninstall conflicting filters.

FIGURE 6.5
Use the Compatibility tab to disable third-party video filters in Windows Movie Maker 2.1.

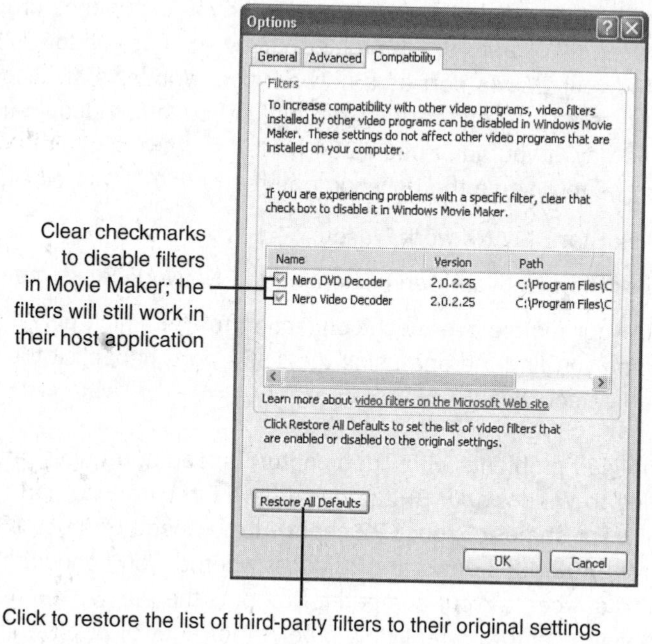

Clear checkmarks to disable filters in Movie Maker; the filters will still work in their host application

Click to restore the list of third-party filters to their original settings

Leo Says

With Video Editing, Try Before You Buy!

I've always been a fan of "try before you buy," but with video editing, it makes even more sense than with other types of programs. Too many users of certain products continue to see weird incompatibilities caused by various combinations of hardware and software that other products shrug off without difficulties. Many vendors offer 30-day trials with few if any limitations, so you can see if you'll fall into the "good luck" or "bad luck" category with the hardware you already have. Just one tip: Be sure to uninstall the first trial product before you try another if the first product doesn't work for you.

The forums at the Camcorder Info website include brand-specific DV camcorder sections to help you focus on problems specific to your brand and model. Check them out at http://www.camcorderinfo.com.

When all else fails, repair or reinstall the application.

Troubleshooting Digital Camera Connections

If you carry the USB–digital camera patch cable included with your digital camera with you, you can transfer your photos to almost any recent PC, making it easy to view your photos on a computer monitor rather than the tiny LCD display on the rear of your camera. You don't need special software to do it, either.

Some of the typical problems that could prevent you from making a successful connection include the following:

- Problems with USB ports and hubs.
- Missing or corrupt drivers.
- AutoPlay doesn't work or has the wrong option selected.
- Data loss.
- Not knowing what folder your photos are stored in.
- Not using the right viewing options to see the information about your files.
- Incorrect date and time settings in your camera.
- Lost or missing USB patch cables.
- Power problems.
- Corrupt flash memory.
- Problems with camera and printer docks.
- Problems with flash memory card readers.

The following sections will help you keep your digital camera and PC talking properly to each other.

Troubleshooting Digital Camera Configuration Problems

Although almost all digital cameras include a USB patch cable for making connections to your PC, you must follow the proper procedure to make a successful connection. The basic procedure works like this:

1. (Optional) Install the driver software provided with the camera. You can skip this step with most digital cameras, but if your camera is not recognized, or you want to use the special features of the software provided with your camera, perform this step.

2. Connect the cable provided with the camera to the camera; the camera might use a mini-USB port or a proprietary port (see Figure 6.6).

FIGURE 6.6

Connecting a digital camera's USB patch cable to the camera and the PC.

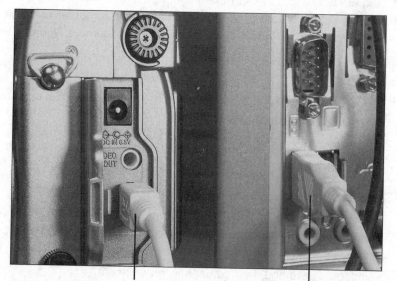

USB connection to camera   USB connection to PC

3. Plug the Type A (flat) end of the USB cable from the camera into a USB port on the computer or a USB hub attached to the computer.

Leo Says

Lost Your Digital Camera Cable? Contact Your Vendor!

If you lose your digital camera's USB patch cable, it can be difficult to find an off-the-shelf replacement at your local electronics emporium. Although some cameras use a standard four-pin or five-pin USB Type Mini-B to USB Type A cable, most use a proprietary connector. Sometimes cables with standard connectors include special circuitry, so you must use a cable made specifically for the camera. The bottom line? If you lose your cable, contact the camera vendor for a replacement, or check with a cable vendor that stocks exact replacements, such as Cables to Go (http://www.cablestogo.com) or dCables (http://www.dcables.com).

4. Turn on the camera and set it to Connect mode if necessary (consult your camera's documentation for exact details). Many cameras use a right-pointing triangle on the mode or power dial for Connect mode.

5. After Windows detects the camera, the software provided with the camera should start automatically after a few moments if you installed it. If not, start the program manually. If you didn't install the camera software, go to step 6.

6. If you didn't install the software provided with the camera, Windows XP detects the camera and adds it to the list of imaging devices.

7. Windows XP features the Scanner and Camera Wizard to transfer pictures from a digital camera to a folder of your choice. You can select this option from a list of programs displayed by the AutoPlay feature (see Figure 6.7). If this menu isn't displayed, see "Troubleshooting AutoPlay Problems," later in this chapter, p. 368.

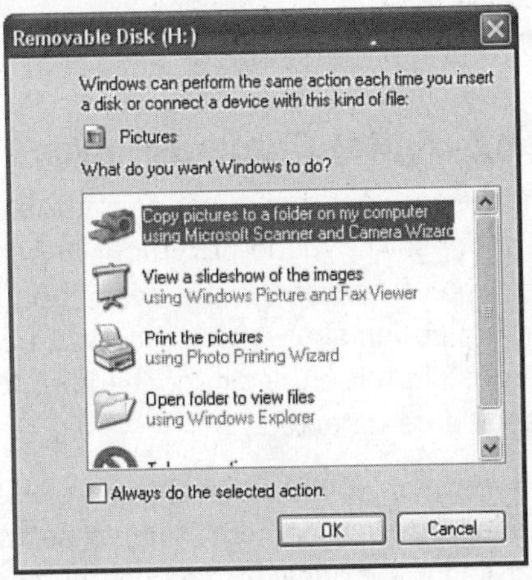

FIGURE 6.7
An AutoPlay menu including Scanner and Camera Wizard is typically displayed when you connect a digital camera.

8. If an AutoPlay menu isn't displayed, the camera might have been detected as a removable-media drive, or AutoPlay might be configured to run a particular program or do nothing. Open My Computer or Windows Explorer to view its contents or to transfer pictures (see Figure 6.8).

→ *To solve problems with AutoPlay, see "Troubleshooting AutoPlay Problems," this chapter, p. 368.*

Folder containing photos on digital camera

FIGURE 6.8

Using My Computer to transfer files from a digital camera.

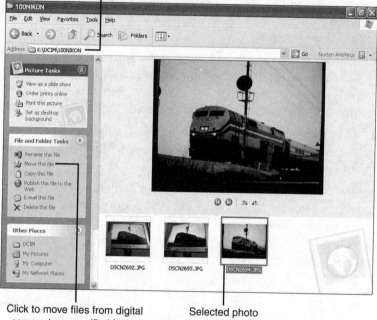

Click to move files from digital camera to a specified folder

Selected photo

Troubleshooting Digital Camera Power Problems

If your camera is detected, but then disappears, the camera might have gone into a power-saving mode or run out of battery power. To wake up the camera, gently press the shutter button. If the camera has run out of battery power, shut it off and insert fresh throwaway or fully charged batteries. Turn it on again, configure it for Connect mode, and the camera should be detected.

To save battery power when you are transferring photos, connect the camera to an AC adapter. Most camera vendors sell AC adapters made for particular camera models, or you can purchase a universal model with interchangeable connectors and variable voltage.

Troubleshooting Digital Camera and USB Port/Hub Problems

If you connect your digital camera to a USB port but it doesn't see your camera as an imaging device or a removable-drive letter, check the following:

- Make sure the camera is turned on, has sufficient battery power, and is set to the correct mode for image transfer.

- Make sure the computer's USB port is enabled and properly configured, particularly if it is a front-mounted port. Front-mounted ports are connected to the motherboard with header cables (small cables that connect the motherboard to the front USB ports; refer to Figure 1.19 in Chapter 1, p. 36). If the header cables are not connected properly, the port won't work. On some computers, you can specify the number of working USB ports in the system BIOS. In such cases, if you specify two ports, only the ports next to the PS/2 keyboard and mouse ports will work. If you specify four ports, only ports on the rear of the system will work. You must specify six ports to enable front-mounted ports to work.

- If you connect the camera to an external hub, make sure the hub is connected to a working USB port and is self-powered, if possible. Self-powered hubs use AC adapters to provide a full 500mA of power to each port. Although digital cameras use less than 100mA in most cases, self-powered hubs are more reliable than bus-powered hubs.

- Be sure to check the Windows Device Manager to see if USB ports and hubs are properly detected and enabled. Ports or hubs marked with a red X are disabled by Device Manager, whereas ports or hubs marked with a yellow exclamation mark have problems that must be resolved before the port or hub can be used.

- If your digital camera and computer support USB 2.0 transfer rates, but your images are transferred very slowly, make sure you have connected your camera to a properly configured USB 2.0 port. Some computers with USB 2.0 ports have them only on the rear of the system, whereas the front ports are compatible with USB 1.1 speeds only. If all ports run at USB 1.1 speeds only, USB 2.0 support might not be enabled in the system BIOS, or the correct USB 2.0 drivers might not be installed. If your camera is plugged into an external hub, make sure the hub supports USB 2.0 speeds and is connected to a properly configured USB 2.0 port.

If your camera is still not detected after you verify that your computer's USB ports are working properly, you might need to install or update the camera's drivers.

→ See "Troubleshooting Digital Camera Configuration Problems," this chapter, p. 363, and "Troubleshooting Digital Camera Power Problems," this chapter, p. 366, for details.

→ For more information about troubleshooting USB ports and hubs, see "Troubleshooting USB Ports and Hubs," Chapter 7, p. 418.

→ For more information about enabling USB 2.0 speeds, see "Troubleshooting USB 2.0 (Hi-Speed USB) Support," Chapter 7, p. 418.

→ For more information about solving driver problems, see "Troubleshooting Digital Camera Configuration Problems," this chapter, p. 363.

Troubleshooting AutoPlay Problems

When you connect a device containing multimedia files, such as digital photos, video, or music, to your Windows XP PC, Windows normally displays an AutoPlay dialog similar to the ones shown in Figure 6.2 and Figure 6.7. The exact programs listed vary according to the device type and media files it contains and the programs loaded on your system that support a particular device and its media files. Digital cameras, DV camcorders, digital music players, CDs, DVDs, flash memory card readers, USB keychain drives, and scanners can all trigger the AutoPlay dialog with appropriate programs for the media type(s) contained on (or supported by) the device or media.

Leo Says

You Don't Need an .INF File to Get AutoPlay

Don't confuse AutoPlay with Autorun. Autorun is a 32-bit Windows feature that's been supported since the days of Windows 95 for CD media. Autorun uses a specially configured .INF file in the root folder of the CD to identify the program that should be run when the CD is opened. You don't need to add anything to your media to get AutoPlay to work—it's an integral part of Windows XP.

Some typical problems with AutoPlay include the following:

- AutoPlay doesn't detect your removable-media drive or digital camera.
- AutoPlay doesn't prompt you to select a program.
- AutoPlay launches a program you don't want to use.
- AutoPlay doesn't offer you the options you'd like to use for your media type.

The following sections can help you keep AutoPlay playing your media the way you'd like.

Fixing AutoPlay with Autofix

AutoPlay sometimes doesn't detect removable-media drives (such as flash memory card readers and USB keychain drives) and digital cameras. You can obtain a free utility from Microsoft called Autofix to find and repair Windows problems that cause this to happen.

Tracking Down Autofix

Learn about the problems that Autofix can solve at
http://support.microsoft.com/default.aspx?scid=kb;en-us;822660. To
download a copy of Autofix, go to http://search.microsoft.com, search
for "AutoPlay Repair Wizard," and click the link Download details:
AutoPlay Repair Wizard.

To use Autofix, you can run it directly from the Microsoft website or
download it to a folder on your computer and run it from there (we recommend saving it to a folder so you can run it as often as desired
without downloading it every time). Make sure your device is plugged
in, turned on, and configured for data transfer.

When you start Autofix, it displays a version number; click Next to continue. First, Autofix checks to see that the Shell Hardware Detection
service is set to "auto start" and that the service is running. If one or
both of these are not true, click the appropriate Repair button to solve
the problem.

Next, Autofix prompts you to choose the drive letter you want AutoPlay
to work with. Click Next. Click Repair next to any problems Autofix
detects (see Figure 6.9).

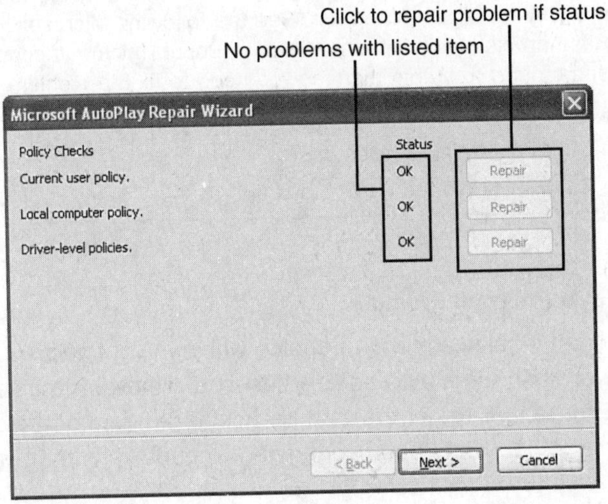

Click to repair problem if status is not OK

No problems with listed item

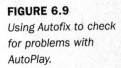

FIGURE 6.9

*Using Autofix to check
for problems with
AutoPlay.*

At the end of the process, Autofix displays the path to a report. If it
repaired a problem, it will direct you to log off and log back onto your
system. Click Finish to close the wizard.

Note that Autofix can repair some, but not all, AutoPlay problems. Some users have reported success with closing down auto-updating features in programs such as RealPlayer to get AutoPlay to work.

No AutoPlay if My Computer Can't "See" the Drive

If you don't get an AutoPlay message from a digital camera or other device, open My Computer to see if the device is listed there. If My Computer can't see the drive, AutoPlay won't work. To get Windows to recognize the drive or device, leave the device or drive connected and shut down Windows and your PC. Restart your PC, and see if the drive or device now shows up in My Computer. Run Autofix if you can't get the drive or device to AutoPlay.

You can also use Tweak UI (a Windows XP PowerToy) to enable AutoPlay for removable-media drives. See "Fixing Problems with AutoPlay Handlers," p. 371, this chapter, for details.

Microsoft Fixes for "Invisible" USB 2.0 Drives

If your computer uses a recent VIA Technologies chipset (see the sidebar "My Favorite System-Exploration Software," Chapter 1, p. 65, for software that can show you your system chipset), Windows XP Service Pack 2 might not properly detect USB devices such as keychain drives or flash memory card readers, thus rendering My Computer unable to display them and AutoPlay unable to run. See the following Microsoft Knowledge Base articles (available from http://support.microsoft.com) for instructions on how to obtain the files you need to fix the problem:

- **Article 892050**—Updated usbehci.sys and updspapi.dll files
- **Article 887173**—Updated usbstor.sys file
- **Article 884868**—Updated usbhub.sys file

Fixing AutoPlay's Program Prompts

If AutoPlay doesn't display a menu of choice when you connect your digital camera or flash memory reader, or insert a removable-media drive or optical drive, but rather starts a particular program or does nothing at all, it probably has been configured to perform in that way.

When AutoPlay Goes Awry

To learn more about this AutoPlay problem, see Microsoft Knowledge Base Article 888022 at http://support.microsoft.com/default.aspx?scid=kb;en-us;888022.

To correct how AutoPlay behaves for a particular drive or device (including digital cameras), follow this procedure:

1. Connect the drive or device to your PC and turn it on (if required). If you are using a digital camera, make sure the camera is set for Connect mode.

2. Open My Computer and select the drive letter of the drive or device.

3. Right-click the drive or device and select AutoPlay.

4. The AutoPlay menu appears. To select a different default action, click the action you want AutoPlay to perform and make sure the check box next to Always Do the Selected Action is selected. To enable AutoPlay to bring up a menu of choices, make sure the Always Do the Selected Action check box is cleared. Click OK.

5. If you selected a default action, it starts immediately. For example, if you selected opening the Scanner and Camera Wizard as a default action for a digital camera, this wizard will run as soon as you click OK. You can permit the action to run, or you can stop it.

6. The next time you use the device, AutoPlay will select the default option or provide you with a list of options, depending on your choices in step 4.

Fixing Problems with AutoPlay Handlers

You might not be satisfied with the default handlers AutoPlay selects for a particular media type (a *handler* is a program designed to work with particular media types). If you'd prefer to see a different mix of programs listed for multimedia files, you can't fix this problem with an "off-the-shelf" version of Windows XP. However, a solution is just a download away: the Windows XP version of Microsoft PowerToys' Tweak UI utility. Tweak UI has many features, including the ability to add, edit, or remove AutoPlay handlers. See the Microsoft PowerToys website for many more downloadable goodies.

Getting Your Hands on Tweak UI and Other PowerToys

Although Microsoft doesn't officially support PowerToys (if they don't work for you, too bad!), you can download the Windows XP versions from the Microsoft website at http://www.microsoft.com/windowsxp/downloads/powertoys/xppowertoys.mspx.

We've had very good luck with PowerToys over the years, so we're not worried about the lack of MS support. Note that there are some updates and additions to the list of PowerToys; be sure to remove old versions before you install the updates. You need Windows XP Service Pack 1 or greater to use Tweak UI. You cannot use the 32-bit or Itanium version of Tweak UI on Windows XP Professional x64 Edition.

After you download and install Tweak UI, it is located in the \Windows\System32 folder. Run it from there to get started. To see settings for AutoPlay, click the plus sign next to My Computer in the menu on the left, then click the plus sign next to AutoPlay.

To enable or disable AutoPlay for particular types of drives, click Types and then check or clear the box next to CD and DVD drives or removable drives (see Figure 6.10).

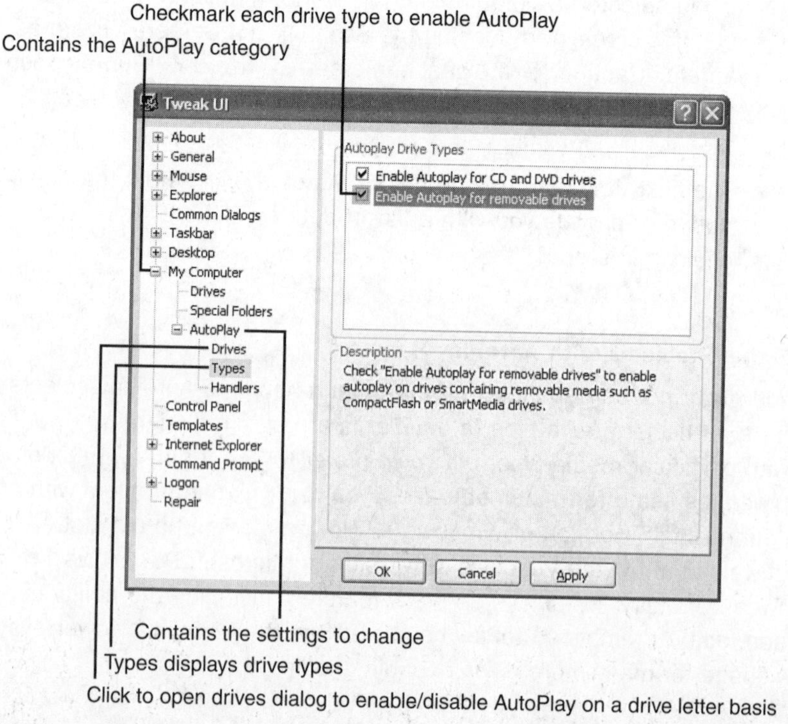

FIGURE 6.10

Using Tweak UI to configure AutoPlay for CD, DVD, and removable-media drives.

Checkmark each drive type to enable AutoPlay

Contains the AutoPlay category

Contains the settings to change

Types displays drive types

Click to open drives dialog to enable/disable AutoPlay on a drive letter basis

To make sure that AutoPlay will work for specific drive letters, click Drives in the AutoPlay menu (refer to Figure 6.10) and enable AutoPlay for each drive letter used by a removable-media or optical (CD or DVD) drive.

To edit, add, or remove AutoPlay handlers, click Handlers in the AutoPlay menu. Current handlers are listed, as shown in Figure 6.11.

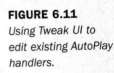

FIGURE 6.11
Using Tweak UI to edit existing AutoPlay handlers.

To edit an existing handler, select the handler and click Edit. For handlers set up by Windows, you can edit the types of media the program can work with, but not other details. You cannot delete handlers set up by Windows.

To create a new handler, click Create. Enter the description, the program name, and select supported media types. Click the Change Program button to browse for the program. Note that most executable programs are stored in subfolders of the Program Files folder in Windows XP. Click OK after completing the fields, then click Apply to accept the changes. Figure 6.12 shows a completed entry for using the QuickView Plus image viewer to view digital photos. You can edit or delete handlers you create with Tweak UI.

Fixing AutoPlay Problems by Uninstalling Your Device

In some cases, you can fix problems with AutoPlay by uninstalling your drive in Device Manager and restarting your system. Windows XP will redetect your drive and reinstall the driver. To determine if AutoPlay is working, insert media containing photo, video, or music files.

→ *For more information on using Device Manager, see "Using Device Manager," Chapter 2, p. 100.*

FIGURE 6.12
Using Tweak UI to create a new AutoPlay handler for digital photos.

Click to select the program

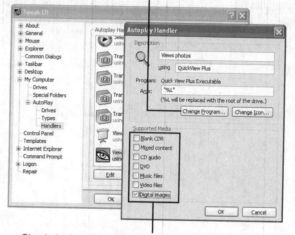

Check the box for each media type the program supports

Preventing and Troubleshooting Data Loss in Digital Cameras

Have you ever opened a 35mm camera without rewinding the film first? The result is a light-struck, ruined roll of film. Although flash memory isn't affected by light, it can be corrupted if you remove it from your camera before shutting down the camera completely. "Completely" doesn't just mean turning the dial to Off, by the way; it means waiting a few seconds after you turn off the camera until the last picture is written to the media and the camera has completely powered down. Here's a good rule of thumb: If you've turned the power dial to Off and you don't see any lights on the camera and the LCD screen is dark (or if you have a camera with a collapsible lens or auto-closing lens cover and it has retracted the lens or closed the lens cover), the camera is really off. Now you can remove the flash memory card from the camera and transfer your pictures via a card reader, or pop in another card and keep shooting.

What if you *did* remove the card from the camera before it finished the last picture? Or, what if you reformatted the flash memory card and didn't realize you hadn't transferred the pictures yet? All is not lost: You can recover "lost" data with utilities made especially for recovering digital photos.

Help for Finding "Lost" Multimedia Files

If you can't find digital photo–recovery programs at your favorite store, check out these products. Many vendors offer free trials, and some programs also work with video and audio files as well as CD/DVD media used by some digital cameras and DV camcorders:

- **Jufsoft BadCopy Pro**—http://www.jufsoft.com/badcopy/bcdigitalphoto.asp
- **mediaRECOVER**—http://www.mediarecover.com
- **DataRescue PhotoRescue**—http://www.datarescue.com/photorescue/
- **LC Technology Photorecovery for Digital Media**—http://www.lc-tech.com/photorecovery.htm
- **Photosrecovery Digital Photo Recovery**—http://www.photosrecovery.com/
- **Recover My Photos**—http://www.recover-my-photos.com/

In the following section, we'll show you how to use mediaRECOVER to retrieve data from a formatted or corrupt flash memory card. The process is fairly similar to those used by other recovery utilities. Note that mediaRECOVER, as well as most photo-recovery applications, is not free. At less than $30, however, the price is nominal when your daughter's first birthday pictures, or similarly irreplaceable photos, are on the line.

Recovering Data from Your Flash Memory Card with mediaRECOVER

To use mediaRECOVER, select the drive containing the files. In this example, drive letter O: is assigned to the SD/MMC/Memory Stick slot on a Lexar Media multi-slot card reader. On the next screen, you specify the location to copy recovered files. On the next screen, click Start to look for deleted files. An Analyze Drive dialog pops up: Select Quick Scan to find deleted files, or select Deep Scan to look for deleted and lost files. We recommend using the Deep Scan option with mediaRECOVER. If you use a different data-recovery program, select the most thorough recovery option available. Click Continue. As mediaRECOVER works though the media, the program displays the number of files recovered and any read errors (see Figure 6.13).

FIGURE 6.13
mediaRECOVER has located over 40 files on this flash memory card and has not encountered any read errors yet.

Progress indicator   Media size and statistics

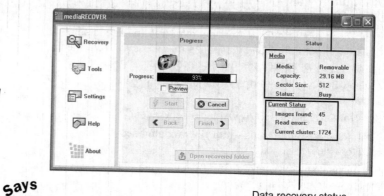

Data recovery status

Leo Says

Get Lost Data Back Faster—Don't Ask for a Preview

mediaRECOVER and many other data-recovery programs made for digital photos offer a preview option you can use during the recovery process. As Figure 6.13 shows, I recommend not using it. You'll see your photos at the end of the process anyway, so there's no need to waste time looking at the pictures during the recovery process.

At the end of the process, a Save File window opens. All files are selected by default; clear the Select check box for any file(s) you don't want to save. Depending on how frequently the card has been used, some recovered files show only a partial image (see Figure 6.14).

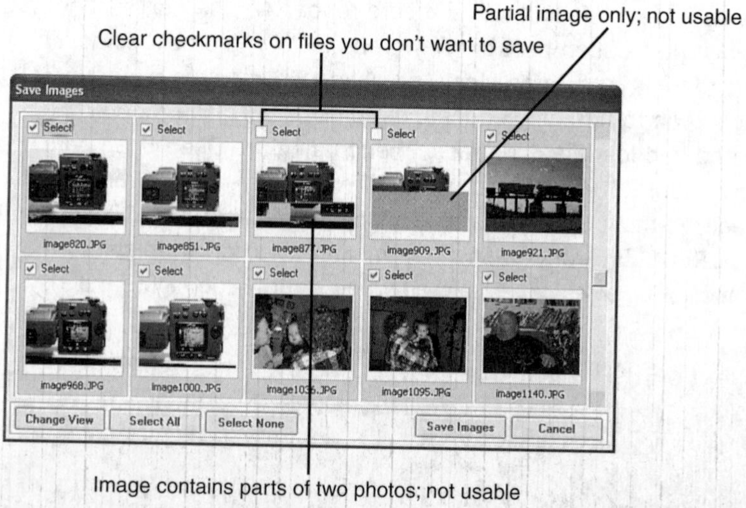

Partial image only; not usable

Clear checkmarks on files you don't want to save

FIGURE 6.14
Depending on how many times the flash memory card has been written to, some images might be unrecoverable.

Select	Select	Select	Select	Select
image820.JPG	image851.JPG	image877.JPG	image909.JPG	image921.JPG
Select	Select	Select	Select	Select
image968.JPG	image1000.JPG	image1055.JPG	image1095.JPG	image1140.JPG

Change View   Select All   Select None   Save Images   Cancel

Image contains parts of two photos; not usable

The original filenames are lost; mediaRECOVER and most other data-recovery programs renumber the files. Click Save Images to save the selected images.

mediaRECOVER can also reformat corrupt flash memory cards so you can use them and recover data from them, and it can wipe data securely.

Troubleshooting File-Viewing Problems

If you store your digital photos in the default My Pictures folder or its subfolders in Windows XP, Windows XP automatically uses the filmstrip or thumbnail view when you open the folder. The filmstrip (photo album) view displays the selected photo in a large window, with a single row of thumbnails below it; it is used when you have a relatively small number of images in a folder (see Figure 6.15).

FIGURE 6.15
The Windows XP film-strip view makes it easy to view a selected photo.

Windows uses the thumbnail view when you have a large number of photos; the thumbnail view displays reduced-size versions of your photos (see Figure 6.16).

However, if you store your pictures in other folders, as often happens if you use the default settings for digital camera management software, Windows might use the default icon view instead. To temporarily switch any folder containing photos to the thumbnail view, click View, Thumbnails. The problem is that as soon as you close My Computer or Windows Explorer, the display will default to the previous view.

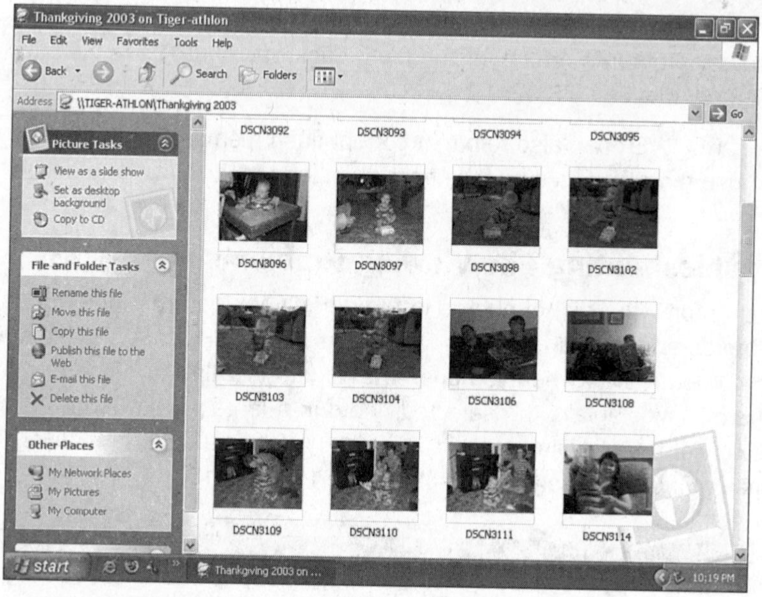

FIGURE 6.16

The Windows XP thumbnail view makes it easy to view a group of photos.

To set the default view for a particular folder, click View, Customize This Folder. Select the folder type to use as a template and click Apply. To use the selected folder type for all subfolders, click the check box Also Apply This Template to All Folders. Figure 6.17 shows this process.

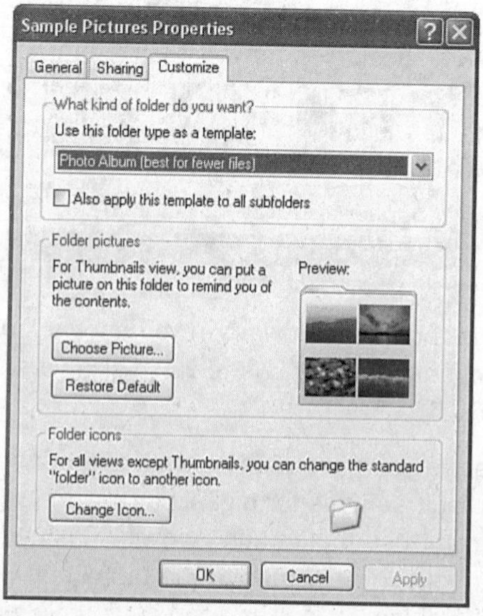

FIGURE 6.17

Customizing a folder to use the photo album (filmstrip) view.

Note that if you move to a different folder that hasn't been customized, the same setting will be applied to that folder, even if it isn't appropriate (for example, a document or spreadsheet folder shouldn't use the thumbnail or photo album view). Follow the same procedure to customize other folders with your preferred views.

If you don't see a thumbnail of a particular photo in photo album or thumbnail view, right-click the photo and select Refresh Thumbnail.

Troubleshooting Problems with Camera and Printer Docks

Some digital cameras use a *camera dock*, a special type of docking station, instead of a direct USB or serial port connection for picture transfer; many camera docks can also recharge batteries in the camera. A *printer dock* performs the same job as a camera dock, but it also functions as a snapshot printer, producing 4×6-inch photos or index prints. Most printer docks use CYM (cyan-yellow-magenta) dye-sublimation technology.

To connect a digital camera to a camera or printer dock, follow this procedure:

1. Install the software provided with the camera or camera dock before you connect the dock. The computer will not know how to handle the dock unless you install the software.

2. Connect the dock to the computer. Plug the Type A (flat) end of the USB cable from the dock into a USB port on the computer. This cable might be the same one provided with the camera or a separate cable provided with the camera dock.

3. Plug the dock into an AC power source with the cable provided.

4. Turn off the camera and attach the camera to the camera or printer dock (see Figure 6.18).

5. Press the connection button on the dock or camera (Kodak refers to this button as the Share button) to begin transferring pictures to the computer. See the instruction manual provided with the camera or camera dock software for details. If the AutoPlay menu appears, select the camera's own transfer program and select the option to use that program every time.

6. Leave the camera in the dock to recharge its batteries.

FIGURE 6.18
Connecting a Kodak EasyShare digital camera to a Kodak printer dock.

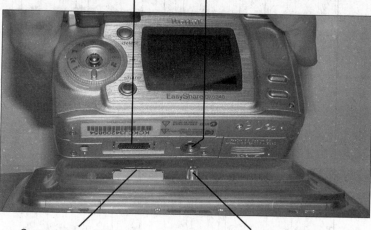

Tripod socket on camera

Connector on camera

Connector on printer dock

Stabilizer on printer dock (slides into tripod socket to stabilize the connection)

If the dock cannot communicate with the computer, check the following:

- Is the dock plugged into a working AC power source?
- Is the AC adapter plugged into the dock?
- Is the USB cable properly connected between the dock and a working USB port on the computer?
- Has the dock software been properly installed?

Leo Says

Get Your Fresh Software Here! (Just Follow the URL.)

If your camera or printer dock is giving you fits and you've tried everything else, get the latest version of the software from the vendor's website. Make sure you specify the correct dock model.

Troubleshooting Printing Problems with Printer Docks

If you're using a printer dock to print direct from the camera, make sure you follow the instructions for selecting the photos you want printed. You might need to print an index print first, or you might select pictures from the LCD display on the rear of the camera.

Some camera docks produce index prints that show the actual area that will be printed from each photo with a red border around the edges of each photo. Edges of the photo beyond the border will not be printed (see Figure 6.19).

Border indicates area that will be printed (4×6-inch)

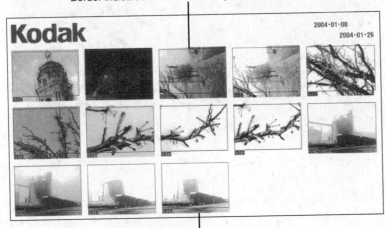

FIGURE 6.19
An index print from a Kodak printer dock.

Area beyond border will not be printed

What's going on? Virtually all digital cameras have image sensors with slightly different proportions than the 2:3 ratio used by 4×6-inch prints made by printer docks and by photofinishers. The solution? Many digital cameras, including those that don't use printer docks, can be configured to produce 2:3 ratio photos (sometimes listed as 3:2 ratio) that don't need to be cropped to produce a 4×6-inch photo. Figure 6.20 shows this setting in the Picture Quality menu of a Kodak EasyShare digital camera.

If you plan to make enlargements (5×7-inch or larger), keep the cropping issue in mind: 4×6, 5×7, 8×10, and 11×14-inch prints all have different proportions.

Leo Says

To Avoid Print Surprises, Crop to Size

You can use popular photo editors such as Adobe Photoshop Elements and Jasc Paint Shop Pro (now owned by Corel) to crop your images to a particular size. After you crop your digital camera or scanned image for a particular paper size, save the cropped image with a different name, such as myphoto_4x6 or myphoto_8x10. You could also save photos cropped for particular paper sizes to separate folders.

FIGURE 6.20

Selecting the 3:2 option for creating 4×6-inch prints without cropping with a Kodak EasyShare digital camera.

Select this option to print 4×6-inch images without cropping

Most printer docks print the photo in four passes because of the dye-sublimation process and the protective overcoat placed on the photo after the colors are printed. If the printer dock stops working before completing the print, you will see a print with distorted colors.

If this happens to you, check the following:

- Make sure the printer is connected to a working AC power source.

- If you are printing from your digital camera, make sure the camera is turned on and is tightly connected to the docking interface.

- If you are printing from your PC, make sure the USB cable is properly connected to the PC and to the dock. Also, make sure the PC is working; if the PC will not respond to commands (the keyboard and mouse appear to be frozen), use the power switch to shut down the PC. Wait about 30 seconds, then restart the system.

- Unplug the printer dock, wait about 30 seconds, and then plug it in again.

If you hear unusual noises coming from the printer dock, check the paper tray. Remove and replace the paper. If you are still unable to print, replace the dye-sublimation printer ribbon or print cartridge. If you are still unable to print, have the unit serviced.

Troubleshooting Flash Memory Card Readers

As an alternative to connecting your digital camera or DV camcorder with removable flash memory to your PC to transfer photos, you might prefer to use a flash memory card reader such as the one shown in Figure 6.21.

Memory Stick inserted in slot

USB cable from computer

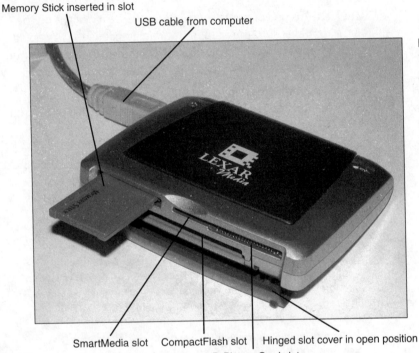

FIGURE 6.21
This Lexar Media multi-slot card reader can work with all popular flash memory cards.

SmartMedia slot   CompactFlash slot   Hinged slot cover in open position
xD-Picture Card slot

Flash memory card readers enable you to transfer pictures while you use your camera or DV camcorder for other tasks. They connect to a computer's USB ports, so they can be used with any recent computer. Many late-model computers now include built-in flash memory card readers for even more convenience.

Some of the most common problems you can have with flash memory card readers are similar to those for digital camera users. They include the following:

- **USB port problems**—If your USB ports are not working, your card reader can't be recognized. If USB 2.0 ports are not properly configured, a USB 2.0–compatible reader will run at USB 1.1 speeds only.

→ For more information about troubleshooting USB ports and hubs, see "Troubleshooting USB Ports and Hubs," Chapter 7, p. 418.

→ For more information about enabling USB 2.0 speeds to support card readers that run at USB 2.0 speeds, see "Troubleshooting USB 2.0 (Hi-Speed USB) Support," Chapter 7, p. 418.

➜ *For more informa-tion about installing drivers, see "Using Device Manager," Chapter 2, p. 100.*

➜ *For more informa-tion about trou-bleshooting AutoPlay, see "Troubleshooting AutoPlay Problems," this chapter, p. 368.*

➜ *For more informa-tion about using Safely Remove Hardware, see "Troubleshooting Safely Remove Hardware," this page.*

➜ *For more information about file-viewing options, see "Troubleshooting File-Viewing Problems," this chapter, p. 377.*

- **Driver problems**—In most cases, flash memory card readers are automatically recognized by Windows XP. However, if you use a reader that is not recognized, install the appropriate driver pro-vided with the unit, or download it from the vendor's website.

- **AutoPlay problems**—These prevent the flash memory card reader from automatically triggering your favorite program or a menu of programs to choose from when you insert media.

- **Data loss**—To prevent data loss, check the activity light on the reader to make sure the card is not being accessed. To unplug the card reader safely, use the Safely Remove Hardware control in the system tray to stop the reader before you disconnect it.

- **File-viewing problems**—If you use the thumbnail or filmstrip option to view files on your flash memory card or digital camera, it can take a long time to view your photos.

Speeding Up Access to Digital Photo Files

Here are a couple of my favorite tricks for making sure I get to work on my digital photos as quickly as possible:

- **Configure My Computer's view as Icons.** Flash memory card read-ers, even those designed to run at USB 2.0 speeds, are slow-pokes compared to hard disks. If you have My Computer configured to use the thumbnail or photo album view, it will seem like forever before you can view the contents of your media. Instead, use the Icons view when you view your flash memory or digital camera storage.

- **Clear your media before you view your photos.** If you use the Scanner and Camera Wizard to transfer your photos, you can select an option to erase the photos after you transfer them. If you prefer to drag and drop your photos, select Move from the task menu, or use Cut and Paste. After your photos are on the hard disk, it's fast and easy to view them with photo album or thumbnail viewing options.

Troubleshooting Safely Remove Hardware

When you connect a device to a USB, FireWire (IEEE-1394), or PC Card/CardBus slot, Windows XP places the Safely Remove Hardware icon in the system tray. This icon, which shows a PC Card with an arrow pointing left, replaces the Eject Hardware icon used in earlier Windows versions.

Safely Remove Hardware enables you to stop a device safely before disconnecting or ejecting it from your system. You should use Safely Remove Hardware to remove storage devices. Here's how it works:

1. Click the Safely Remove Hardware icon in the system tray.

2. The Safely Remove Hardware dialog appears, listing hot-swap storage and other devices.

3. Select a device from the list and click Stop.

4. After the device is stopped, a message balloon is displayed over the system tray, informing you that the device can safely be removed from the system. The device is also removed from the list of devices.

If you want to see more information about the device, use Safely Remove Hardware this way:

1. Double-click the Safely Remove Hardware icon.

2. Choose the device you want to stop from the list and click Stop.

3. Details about the device (such as drive letter and device name) are listed. Click OK to stop the device, or click Cancel (see Figure 6.22).

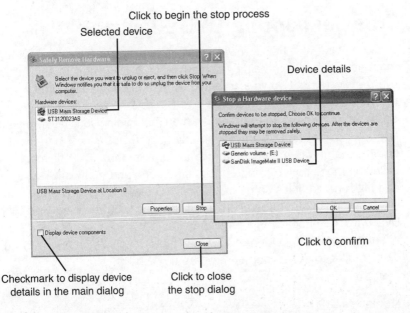

Click to begin the stop process

Selected device

Device details

Click to confirm

Checkmark to display device details in the main dialog

Click to close the stop dialog

FIGURE 6.22

Stopping a flash memory card reader with Safely Remove Hardware.

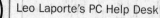
4. After the device is stopped, a message balloon is displayed over the system tray, informing you that the device can safely be removed from the system. The device is also removed from the list of devices.

5. Click Close to close the Safely Remove Hardware dialog.

To use the device again, disconnect it and reconnect it.

If you see a message such as "Cannot stop *device*," try the following:

- Make sure there are no programs accessing the storage device. Close My Computer or any other application (such as a photo editor) that might have been used to view the contents of the device or might have created temporary work files on the device. Retry the process.

- If you are still unable to stop the device, shut down the computer and then disconnect the device.

As an alternative to using Safely Remove Hardware with a flash memory card reader, check the activity light(s) on the reader. If the activity light doesn't indicate the card is in use, and you are not working with files on the card, you can safely remove the card from the reader.

Troubleshooting DVD Playback

If you're using your PC as a DVD movie player, you're not alone. With most new PCs now containing some type of DVD drive, it's easier than ever before to boot up your favorite new release or classic film on your PC. However, if you want to watch a DVD movie on your computer screen, there's more to the process than just sliding your favorite comedy or epic into the DVD drive. You must use a DVD player program to convert the movie into computer-readable form. Most DVD drives, including those built into notebook computers, and many mid-range and high-end graphics cards include a DVD player program. If you think you didn't install the program, dig out the discs you received with your DVD drive, notebook computer with built-in DVD drive, or display adapter and see if you forgot to install the DVD player program. If you did, install it to begin your journey into DVD on PC.

"Free" Spyware on Some DVDs—An Offer You Should Refuse!

Some movie DVDs include DVD player programs you can install if you don't have a DVD player already installed. Unfortunately, virtually all of these "free" DVD players contain some type of spyware (see "Slamming Spyware," Chapter 2, p. 160, to learn more about spyware). *Don't* install a DVD player program included with a DVD movie. Instead, use a player provided by your video card, system, or DVD drive vendor, or purchase a DVD player program separately. You don't need the privacy violations and system performance problems that spyware causes.

Note that Windows Media Player can be used as a DVD movie player only if you install a DVD movie player application on your system; it doesn't include the DVD-decoding software needed to see the movie.

There are a couple of ways to determine if you have a DVD decoder compatible with Windows Media Player installed on your system. Here's the "try it and see if it works" method:

1. Insert your DVD movie into the DVD drive.
2. Start Windows Media Player.
3. Click Play.
4. If the menu lists Audio CD or DVD, you have a compatible DVD decoder installed and Windows Media Player can be used to view your movie; if the menu lists only Audio CD, you need to install a DVD decoder before you can use WMP to view your movie.

The official Microsoft method works like this:

1. Open Windows Media Player.
2. Click Tools, Options.
3. If you see a DVD tab, your system has a DVD player supported by Windows Media Player.

If you didn't receive a software DVD player with your DVD drive or video card, or you're looking for an upgrade, two of the leading products are WinDVD and PowerDVD.

Tracking Down DVD Movie Players

InterVideo, Inc., is the producer of WinDVD Gold and WinDVD Platinum. Get more information or order the latest versions from http://www.intervideo.com.

CyberLink Corp is the producer of PowerDVD. Get more information or order the latest versions from http://www.gocyberlink.com.

Both vendors offer free trial versions you can download.

If you can't play the movie through Windows Media Player, but you can play it through the DVD player's own interface, check the following:

- **Are parental controls enabled in Windows Media Player?** If your children have limited (user) accounts in Windows XP and you have enabled parental controls, they can't watch a movie with a rating higher than the maximum MPAA rating listed on the DVD tab in Windows Media Player (see Figure 6.23).

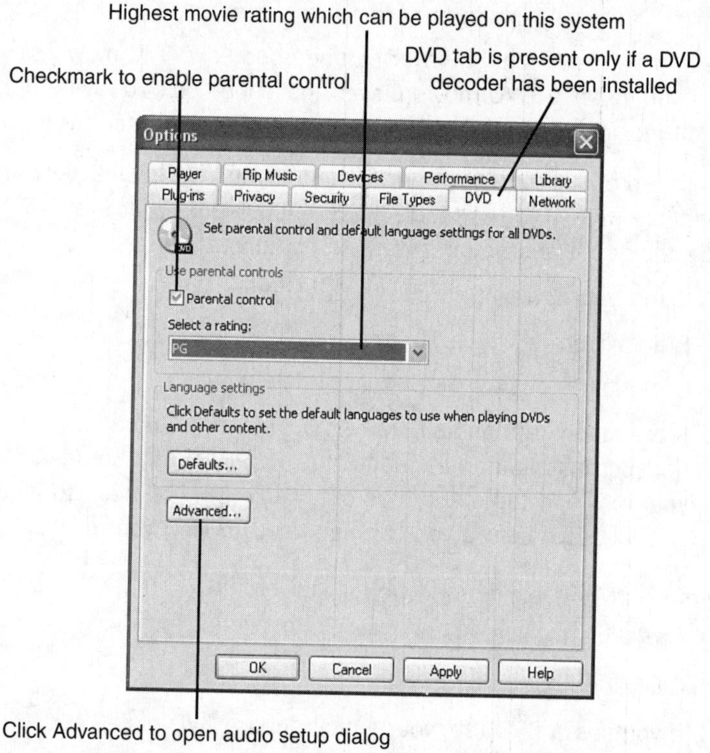

Highest movie rating which can be played on this system

DVD tab is present only if a DVD decoder has been installed

Checkmark to enable parental control

Click Advanced to open audio setup dialog

- **Make sure that DirectShow (the DirectX component used for video playback) is working.** Click Start, Run. Type **Mplayer2** and then click OK (Mplayer2 is an older version of Windows Media Player). Click File, Open and then select a Windows Media Video (.WMV) file to run, such as the Windows Movie Maker 2 Sample File located in the My Videos folder beneath My Documents. Install any codecs the program requires to play the selected file.

If a .WMV file runs, DirectShow is OK. If not, install the latest version of DirectX, available from http://www.microsoft.com/ windows/directx/default.aspx.

- **Reduce video acceleration in Windows Media Player.** Click Tools, Options, Performance. Adjust the slider from Full (right side) to Some (middle). If this fails to improve the situation, try None (left side). See Figure 6.24.

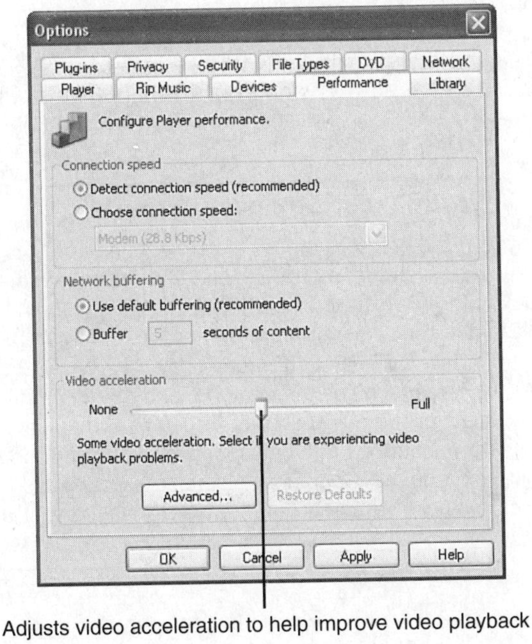

FIGURE 6.24
The Performance tab of the Options dialog in Windows Media Player.

Adjusts video acceleration to help improve video playback

- **Reduce the resolution on the Windows Desktop to 800×600 and the color quality to 16-bit.** Some DVD players aren't designed to work with higher resolutions or color-quality settings. To learn more about adjusting resolution and color quality settings, see Figure 5.11 in Chapter 5, p. 310.

Troubleshooting WMP/DVD Playback the Microsoft Way

See Microsoft Knowledge Base Article 306318, "Troubleshooting DVD playback in Windows Media Player for Windows XP," at http://support.microsoft.com/default.aspx?scid=kb;EN-US;q306318 for more details on these troubleshooting tips and additional links.

Can't Use Advanced Speaker Systems with Your DVD Player

To get the full benefit of watching DVD movies on your computer, there's nothing like connecting your system to a 5.1 or other advanced speaker system. However, some standard DVD movie players (particularly those that are bundled with hardware) might not include support for advanced speaker configurations and sound systems. If you aren't getting the full benefit of your speaker system when you watch a DVD movie on your PC, check the following:

- **Have you connected your speakers correctly?** Check your speaker connections against the wiring diagrams provided with your sound card.

Make Sure Your Breakout Box Isn't "Broken"

To accommodate the greater number of connections needed for advanced speaker systems, many high-end sound cards use external breakout boxes for the extra connections. For example, some models of the Sound Blaster Audigy series from Creative Labs feature the Audigy Drive, which fits into a CD-ROM-sized drive bay and offers extra speaker connections, easy-to-reach volume controls, and other benefits. If you connect your speakers to a breakout box such as the Audigy Drive, make sure the breakout box is properly connected to your sound card. If the breakout box requires a power connector, make sure it's receiving power as well. Without data and power connections, it's just a paperweight.

- **Is your sound card mixer correctly configured for your speaker system?** Some 5.1 and 7.1 speaker systems are analog, whereas others are digital. If you select the wrong setting in your mixer, your speakers won't work. Depending on the sound card or onboard audio solution your computer uses, you might need to access a proprietary audio mixer program to make changes rather than the standard Windows mixer. To learn more, see "Can't Hear Sound from Additional Speakers," Chapter 5, p. 346.

Testing Your Speaker Configuration

If your sound card has a test option, use it to verify that all your speakers are working correctly and that your mixer controls are set correctly. If your speakers work with the test setup, the problem lies with your DVD movie player software.

- **Have you configured your DVD player program to use your speaker configuration?** Until you configure the player program to use your speaker system, it won't work correctly while you're watching movies. If your player program doesn't have an option for your speaker system, contact the vendor to determine if an upgrade has the speaker support you need. You can usually upgrade a bundled player at a reduced price.

- **Have you configured Windows Media Player or your DVD playback program to use your speaker configuration?** If you use Windows Media Player to play back your DVDs, click Tools, Options, DVD, Advanced to view the settings for audio playback. The audio playback options vary with the DVD playback software you use. Figure 6.25 shows a typical example. If your sound card is equipped with S/PDIF output so you can connect to a home theater system or if it connects directly to a 5.1 or 7.1 surround sound speaker system, but your DVD playback software doesn't support your hardware, you need to upgrade to a better DVD playback program. By default, DVD playback programs use stereo sound.

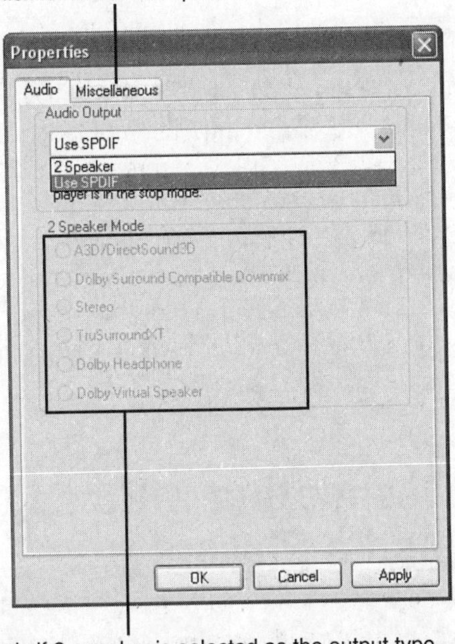

Click for additional options

FIGURE 6.25
Configuring DVD playback to use S/PDIF output to a Dolby Digital decoder on a home theater system.

Options available only if 2-speaker is selected as the output type

Troubleshooting Aspect Ratio and Screen Resolution Settings

DVDs helped launch the letterbox revolution, in which classic movies from the mid-1950s to the present could be viewed in their original widescreen aspect ratios—no more "Three and a Half Brides for Three and a Half Brothers" or "est Side Stor" pan-and-scan atrocities. Instead, you get all seven brothers and see all the grit and glory of the West Side of Manhattan.

If your DVD playback program isn't switching automatically to widescreen playback, check the configuration settings. If your DVD playback program picks up its default setting from the DVD's aspect ratio, you shouldn't change it unless the default doesn't work. If you need to make changes, keep these tips in mind:

- On a conventional 4:3 display (resolutions of 800×600, 1024×768, 1280×1024, and so forth), make sure the Keep Aspect Ratio option is selected. This will provide the familiar black bars at the top and bottom of your display when you watch a VistaVision or Cinemascope epic.

- If you're using one of the new widescreen TV/monitors or laptops (resolutions such as 1280×768 and so forth), you might do better with the Run Full Screen option.

Some DVD playback programs allow you to switch the display to a different refresh rate or resolution combination depending on the movie type you view (4:3 or 16:9 widescreen). Try different combinations of settings if you're not satisfied with the default resolution inherited from the Windows desktop. If you decide to change the resolution, keep in mind that such changes work best if you're planning to use the PC only as a DVD player during the duration of the film. If you plan to watch the movie in a window while getting other work done, don't fiddle with the screen resolution.

Troubleshooting MP3 Digital Music and Media Players

We're not sure what's more amazing: being able to capture high-resolution digital photos with a camera that fits into your shirt pocket, or being able to stuff anything from a Beethoven symphony to a Live Aid concert into an MP3 player no bigger than a large pack of gum.

MP3 players, in some ways, have an even tougher job than digital cameras. Although they don't create content, they must properly handle multiple file formats (MP3, WMA, and AAC are the most common), deal with the increasingly thorny question of digital rights management (DRM), and provide enough storage space for "just one more song." Larger MP3 players (those about the size of a transistor radio) often provide full-blown media playback, adding support for digital photos and videos.

Some of the most common problems with digital music and media players include the following:

- Connecting to your PC
- Balancing audio quality with capacity
- Upgrading capacity
- Working with DRM-protected content
- Determining supported content
- Updating firmware to improve performance, compatibility, and features

Troubleshooting PC Connections to Your MP3 Player

Most digital music players connect to your PC via USB ports, although some models support FireWire (IEEE-1394a) connections instead of, or in addition to, USB.

Unlike digital camera cables, which often use proprietary connectors for the digital camera end of the connection, USB connections are usually made using the Mini-Type B connector, whereas FireWire connections are usually made using the four-wire connector. Consequently, if you lose the patch cable that came with your MP3 player, you can usually purchase an off-the-shelf replacement from your favorite electronic emporium.

Generally, AutoPlay will automatically start when you plug your MP3 player into a USB or FireWire port and turn it on. Note that some MP3 players turn on automatically when you make the connection. AutoPlay displays the disk drive letter used by Windows for your player's built-in flash memory or hard disk storage (see Figure 6.26). If you have inserted additional storage, you will see the drive letter used by additional storage on the Windows task bar.

→ *For more information about troubleshooting USB ports and hubs,* see *"Troubleshooting USB Ports and Hubs," Chapter 7, p. 418.*

→ *For more information about troubleshooting FireWire (IEEE-1394) ports,* see *"Troubleshooting IEEE-1394 Ports and Hubs," Chapter 7, p. 427.*

FIGURE 6.26

A typical AutoPlay menu displayed when an MP3 digital audio player is plugged into a Windows XP–based system.

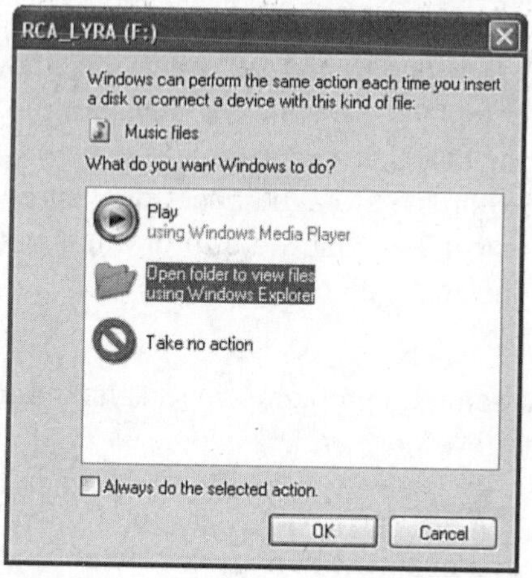

RCA_LYRA (F:)

Windows can perform the same action each time you insert a disk or connect a device with this kind of file:

Music files

What do you want Windows to do?

Play
using Windows Media Player

Open folder to view files
using Windows Explorer

Take no action

Always do the selected action.

OK   Cancel

Leo Says

Got an MP3 Player? Free Portable Storage Inside!

If you read as many electronics flyers as I have, you've probably seen ads for MP3 players that boast the ability to work as a portable drive. Guess what? You don't need a special MP3 player. As long as Windows provides your player with a drive letter and you can drag and drop files between your player and your system with My Computer, you have instant portable storage whenever you plug in your player.

→ For more information about troubleshooting AutoPlay, see "Troubleshooting AutoPlay Problems," this chapter, p. 368.

If AutoPlay doesn't start when you plug in your player and turn it on, open My Computer and make sure the player has been assigned a drive letter. If you don't see it in My Computer, check Disk Management. If you don't see it listed in Disk Management, you might have plugged it into a nonworking USB or FireWire port.

Troubleshooting Capacity Issues with Your MP3 Player

Digital music, whether in MP3 or WMA format, uses lossy compression to use less space than uncompressed audio files such as WAV or CD music tracks. Lossy audio compression discards some of the original audio data to reduce the size of the recorded file (other forms of lossy compression, such as MPEG for video and JPEG for images, work similarly). Lossy compression of all types starts by discarding redundant or unnecessary information. The bitrate used to create a music track affects the size of the resulting compressed file and the quality of the audio. The higher the bitrate, the less data is discarded and the better the music sounds, but higher bitrates also result in larger files.

Originally, digital music players played only MP3 files. However, all recent players also play the WMA file format as well. According to some users, WMA files can be recorded at lower bitrates (resulting in smaller files) than MP3 files and provide equivalent quality. For example, the quality of 64Kbps WMA is often compared to 128Kbps MP3. At the same bitrate, the size of WMA and MP3 files from the same original source is almost identical.

Generally, we favor recording at higher bitrates to improve audio quality. However, if you are trying to squeeze as much music as possible onto your player, you have two options:

- Add additional storage (some flash memory–based MP3 players can use SD or MMC cards).

- Use WMA audio recorded at a 64–96Kbps bitrate instead of MP3 audio at 128–192Kbps.

Watch the Bitrate Limits, or You Might Be Sorry!

Although you can adjust the bitrates you use to record digital music in both MP3 and WMA formats, make sure you stay within the limits of your player. Typical safe limits include 64Kbps to 192Kbps for MP3 and 64Kbps to 128Kbps for WMA. If you want to use a higher bitrate (recommended if you're a classical music fan), check the manual to see what bitrates the player can support. Choose a higher bitrate, record one track at that higher bitrate, and transfer it to your player. If it plays correctly, great! If not, use the maximum bitrate recommended.

Variable bitrate (VBR) recording, available with some MP3-creation software, adjusts the actual bitrate used in real time according to the complexity of the music or audio being recorded to reduce the amount of space required for the final output file. For example, a silent passage will use a very low VBR, whereas a passage played by a solo instrument in the same song will use a higher VBR, and a multiple-instrument passage in the same song will use a very high VBR. Some players can handle VBR recording, whereas others cannot. Try a track recorded with the VBR option on your player to see if it works.

If your player doesn't have any more capacity after you add additional storage, check the following:

- **Has the card been formatted?** The card might have other digital data on it (such as digital photographs). To format the card, you can insert the card into a flash memory card reader and use My Computer to format it, or you might be able to format the card while it is inserted in the player using My Computer. Use My Computer to view the card's contents and to move files you want to keep from the card before you format it. See the instructions for your player to determine which format option to use.

- **Is the card properly inserted into the unit?** Turn off the unit, remove the card, and reinsert the card. Do not remove or insert the card while the player is turned on; you might damage it.

If you cannot format an SD (Secure Digital) card, make sure the write-protect switch on the side of the card is not locked (down position). Slide the write-protect switch upward. Figure 6.27 shows a typical SD card with the write-protect switch in the unlocked position to permit recording of digital music or photos.

FIGURE 6.27

A SanDisk Secure Digital (SD) card configured for recording.

Slide this switch down to write-protect the contents of the card

Note that players treat internal and external memory as separate units, and the card will be displayed as a separate drive letter in My Computer. To play music on the card, you might need to select external memory on your player; see the instructions or menu on the unit for details.

Depending on the program you use to transfer music to your player, you might need to select the drive letter used by additional storage manually when you copy music to your player.

Troubleshooting DRM Problems with Your MP3 Player

Digital rights management, or DRM, has been a thorny problem ever since the introduction of Microsoft's Windows Media Audio (WMA) format. Digital rights management, in spite of the name, isn't about your rights as a consumer to play digital music you have created from your own CD collection or purchased from a source such as iTunes, eMusic, or Rhapsody. Rather, it's about the limitations that the music vendor places on your use of purchased music. In our view, a better name for DRM would have been "Digital Limitations Management." But seriously, if you're having problems moving music tracks you created or paid for to your MP3 player, keep reading.

If you cannot play DRM-protected content on your player, check the following:

- **If you are trying to play purchased tracks, is your player supported by the digital music service?** Before you can use a particular player to play music from some services, you might need to install support software on your system provided by the music vendor or update the firmware in your player. See the player vendor's website for firmware updates.

- **If you use Windows Media Player to transfer your music, is your Windows Media Player license database corrupted?** Install an up-to-date backup copy. If you don't have an up-to-date backup copy of your licenses, contact your music vendor for help. For more information about troubleshooting problems with licenses and backing up and restoring licenses in Windows Media Player, see Articles 891664, 265473, and 810422 at http://support.microsoft.com.

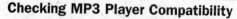

Checking MP3 Player Compatibility

If you're not sure which service(s) to subscribe to, check out MP3.com's compatibility and feature comparison of popular flash and hard-disk players and services: http://www.mp3.com/tech/players_comparison_services.php.

For additional details about the services and devices supported, check with these leading vendors:

- **Audio Lunchbox (http://audiolunchbox.com)**—Uses the MP3 file format; supports all devices that support the MP3 file format.

- **Bleep (http://www.bleep.com/)**—Uses the MP3 file format; supports all devices that support the MP3 file format.

- **BuyMusic (http://www.buy.com)**—See http://www.buy.com/retail/store.asp?loc=41080 for device support.

- **iTunes (http://www.apple.com/itunes)**—Does *not* support third-party MP3 players in its Windows version; see http://docs.info.apple.com/article.html?artnum=93377 for details. Some third-party players can be used with iTunes 4 for Mac OS X; see http://docs.info.apple.com/article.html?artnum=93548 for details.

- **Live Downloads (http://www.livedownloads.com/)**—Uses the MP3 file format; supports all devices that support the MP3 file format.

- **eMusic (http://www.emusic.com)**—Uses the MP3 file format; supports all devices that support the MP3 file format.

- **MusicMatch (http://www.musicmatch.com)**—See http://www.musicmatch.com/info/plug-ins/?plugin=player&version=9.00.0122MMD&os=pc for device support. Alternatively, you can use the following search in Google and click the first link to find the latest information: "support MusicMatch" site:musicmatch.com.

- **Napster (http://www.napster.com)**—See http://www.napster.com/compatible_devices/ for devices that support Napster-to-Go; see http://www.napster.com/compatible_devices/not_ntg_compatible.html for devices that support the basic Napster service.

- **RealPlayer (http://www.real.com)**—See http://music.guide.real.com/realplayerdevices for compatible devices.

- **Rhapsody (http://www.rhapsody.com)**—See http://music.guide.real.com/rhapsodydevices for compatible devices.

- **Wal-Mart (http://musicdownloads.walmart.com)**—Supports any device compatible with Microsoft Windows Media Player 9 or greater and DRM. See http://www.microsoft.com/windows/windowsmedia/devices/.

Troubleshooting Other Types of Media Playback

DRM issues aren't the only reason you might have problems playing back music, photo, or video content on your digital music or media player. If you're having problems, check the following:

- Make sure you are using only supported media types. For example, JPG (JPEG) photos and images are supported on typical media players, but TIFF, GIF, and RAW images are not. If you want to view other image types, you must convert them to JPEG and copy the converted files to your device.

- Make sure videos are stored using the appropriate bitrate and codec. If your media player uses Windows Media Player to convert and upload content, WMP will usually handle conversions for you. If you want to manually transfer data with drag-and-drop or with another program, make sure the source material meets the appropriate standards for your player or is converted during the transfer process. If you want to view video content in a nonsupported format and your transfer software will not convert it for you, convert the content yourself before transferring it.

- Make sure you install the latest firmware updates to your player. These are available from the support section of the vendor's website.

Troubleshooting Scanners

If you're sitting on a pile of photos, slides, and negatives, you can bring them into the twenty-first century with an image scanner. Scanners are terrific for preserving photos, but today's models can also fix faded and color-shifted pictures, and they can scan other fragile family memories ranging from Uncle Joe and Aunt Mabel's love letters during World War II to rare coins and old postcards. Most mid-range and high-end flatbed scanners can also scan slides and negatives.

Typical scanner problems include the following:

- Scanner not recognized by your computer
- Driver problems
- 64-bit Windows support

- Assigning programs to the push buttons on many scanners
- Using the right scanning mode for your images and suggested use
- Using the right repair options for bad photos

Using Device Manager to Troubleshoot Scanner Problems

As with other types of input devices, scanners might have problems caused by two factors:

- Problems with the port
- Problems with the scanner itself

Most scanners today connect through the USB or IEEE-1394 ports, although some older scanners use SCSI or LPT (parallel) ports.

For a scanner to work correctly, the port the scanner is attached to must work properly and the scanner's device drivers must also be installed correctly. See Chapter 7 to learn how to determine if the port used by your scanner is working properly.

Common Problems and Solutions for Scanners

If the scanner is not detected or can't scan, but the port the scanner is connected to is working correctly, try the following:

➜ See *"Using Device Manager to Troubleshoot USB Devices", Chapter 7, p. 433, for details about USB power usage.*

- Turn on the scanner and reboot the system (if the scanner is SCSI or parallel) so the scanner will be recognized. If the scanner doesn't have a power switch, make sure the scanner is plugged into a working AC power source. Some USB scanners are powered by the USB port, so make sure that the scanner is receiving adequate power from the USB hub.

- Make sure the scanner data cable is properly attached to the port on the computer and to the scanner. For USB and IEEE-1394a scanners, you can unplug and reconnect the data cable without shutting down the scanner or system. For other interface types (parallel and SCSI), shut down the system, unplug and reattach the scanner, and restart the system.

- Download and reinstall the latest TWAIN drivers and software for the scanner; use Windows Update to check for updates and then check the scanner vendor's own website. The software or drivers currently installed may be corrupt.

- Check the meaning of any signal lights flashing on the scanner. The lights could be reporting an error; if so, correct the error and retry the scan.

- The scanning head may be locked, particularly if you hear the scanning head trying to move. Unlock the head and try again. Note that moving the scanner with an unlocked scanning head is not recommended, nor is trying to use the scanner while the head is locked; both can damage the scanner.

If you can't use a special feature such as one-button scanning, copying, network scanning, or the automatic document feeder (ADF) or transparency adapter provided with the scanner, try the following:

- Install (or reinstall) the one-button scanning software (if you press the scan button but the scanner won't scan).

- Configure the scanning software to select the correct program or activity to run when you press the email, copying, or another special button.

- Make sure the transparency adapter or ADF is properly installed and that you have selected the correct scanning mode in the scanning software. Note that the Windows built-in Scanner and Camera Wizard does not support transparency adapters or ADFs. You must use the software provided with the scanner.

- To use a network-compatible scanner from a different computer, you must activate the scan server software on the computer connected to the scanner as well as the scan client software on any other computer on the network that will be used for scanning. You may need to rerun the client software after each image is scanned with some programs.

- You must use drivers made for your scanner and your operating system to enable your scanner to work. Drivers for Windows XP are typically provided on a CD packaged with the scanner, or updated versions can be downloaded from the vendor's website.

64-bit Scanning? Surf and Surf Again

If you're using the x64 version of Windows XP Professional, don't expect to find your scanner or all-in-one unit supported with the drivers provided on the install CD. In most cases, you will need to download x64-compatible drivers from the vendor's website. Vendors vary in their commitment to x64 drivers, and delivery times are variable and subject to change. If you don't see drivers the first time you visit the vendor's website, keep checking.

Troubleshooting USB Scanners

The most common scanner interface used today is USB. This section helps you get your USB scanner back into operation in a hurry.

If your scanner is not detected or can't scan and the USB port is OK, check the following:

- The length of your USB cable. Standard USB cables should be no more than 6 feet long; if you need a longer run between your computer and your scanner, attach the scanner to a generic (external) USB self-powered hub.

→ See *"Using Device Manager to Troubleshoot USB Devices,"* Chapter 7, p. 433, *for details about USB power usage.*

- The power required by your USB scanner, particularly if the scanner is bus-powered.

- Make sure you have installed the latest drivers.

- Disconnect and reconnect the scanner data cable.

- Check the power cable if the scanner uses AC power.

- Open the Windows Device Manager and click Refresh or Scan for Hardware Changes to redetect connected devices.

Troubleshooting IEEE-1394a Scanners

The second most common interface for image scanners, particularly for high-end flatbed or transparency scanners, is IEEE-1394a (FireWire 400). Use this section to keep your scanner working reliably.

If your scanner is not detected or can't scan and the IEEE-1394a port is OK, check the following:

- The power switch. Turn on the scanner and reboot system if the scanner isn't detected by Windows.

- The scanner may have gone into a power-saving mode. Turn off the scanner and turn it on again. Contact the host adapter and scanner vendor(s) for updated driver software.

- The scanner might need driver updates. Contact the vendor to obtain the latest drivers.

- Some scanners use a removable IEEE-1394a interface board on the scanner and it might not be connected properly. Disconnect the scanner from the computer, shut down the scanner, and remove the interface board. Reinsert it carefully and restart the scanner. Reconnect the scanner to the computer and retry scanning.

- The data cable may be too long. The maximum length for an IEEE-1394 cable is 4.5 meters (about 14.8 feet); use a high-speed hub or repeater if you need to place your scanner further than 4.5 meters away from your computer.

If the scanner runs slowly when connected to other IEEE-1394a devices, reconfigure the IEEE-1394a daisy-chain to attach low-speed devices such as 200MBps hubs or repeaters at the far end of the daisy-chain, after scanners, DV camcorders, and other high-speed devices. Or, plug the scanner into a separate IEEE-1394 port.

Troubleshooting Scan Quality Problems

Even if a scanner has a working connection to your system, you can still have scan quality problems. Use this section to diagnose and solve typical scanning quality problems you might encounter.

If photos look good onscreen, but the quality of the printed output is poor (jagged edges, unsharp), the photo was scanned at too low a resolution. Use a resolution of 300dpi to scan prints you plan to reproduce at the same or smaller sizes; use 600dpi to scan wallets you plan to print at snapshot (4×6 inches) or larger sizes. Scan 35mm negatives and slides at 1,200dpi for snapshot-sized prints; scan at 2,400dpi or higher for 5×7-inch or larger enlargements. Use higher resolutions if you want to enlarge a portion of a print, slide, or negative.

If color photos have distorted colors when scanned, you probably selected the wrong image type during the scan process. Scan color photographs with a setting such as Photographs, Millions of Colors, or something similar. Don't use the Color Drawing or Thousands of Color setting offered with some scanners. For negative/slide scanners, select the correct film type (positive for slides, negative for negatives). Some high-end scanners enable you to specify the film type, such as Kodachrome, Ektachrome (now known as Elite Chrome), and so on. If your scanner has a color-adjustment setting, use it if your colors are

→ *If the scanner began to run slowly only after you upgraded to Windows XP SP2, see "Troubleshooting Video-Editing Software Problems," this chapter, p. 360, to learn how to reconfigure your IEEE-1394 ports to run at full speed.*

distorted and you are already using the correct Millions of Colors/Photographs scan setting. If the scanner has built-in color restoration, try it, especially when you're scanning faded or off-color originals. You'll be amazed at the amount of work you can save yourself by letting the scanner fix color problems.

Scan Better with Help from Scantips

Wayne Fulton's Scantips website (http://www.scantips.com) provides dozens of useful tips, tutorials, and concepts for anyone wanting to get the most out of a flatbed or slide scanner. Be sure to check out the amazing restoration of a badly color-shifted 40-year old Ektachrome slide to its full glory using manual color adjustments you can do with many scanners or with an image-editing program.

If the scanned image doesn't show all the detail in the original photo, you have used the wrong exposure setting during the scan process. Rescan the image if possible, using correct exposure settings. If the original photo can't be rescanned, adjust the level, brightness, and contrast with a photo-editing program. Note that some scanners offer different operating modes, and the advanced or professional mode might include more powerful exposure settings such as the histogram option. The histogram option, which graphs the distribution of light, medium, and dark tones in an image and allows you to manipulate the proportions of each, can produce excellent scans, even from poorly exposed originals. Figure 6.28 illustrates this option in the Professional Mode setting for the Epson Perfection 3170 scanner.

If the scanned image has a moiré (cross-hatched) pattern, the original image was a halftone print. Rescan the image with the scanner's descreening option if available. If the scanner lacks this feature, you can descreen the image in the photo-editing program (see your program's help file or documentation for details).

If the scanned image has color shifting due to poor storage or lighting issues, use the color restoration feature if available. Depending on the scanner software you use, you might need to use the Advanced or Professional mode or open a special submenu to access this feature. With some scanners, this feature is automatic when scanning print film, but must be enabled manually when scanning slide or negative film. If your scanner software does not offer color restoration, you can adjust colors in your image editor.

Real-time preview shows changes   Histogram shows tonal curve of original image

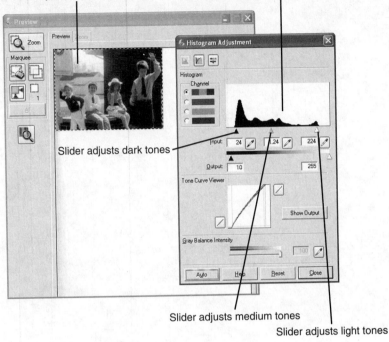

Slider adjusts dark tones

Slider adjusts medium tones

Slider adjusts light tones

FIGURE 6.28
Using the Histogram Adjustment dialog to improve the tonal distribution in a scanned photo.

If you're not satisfied with the level of exposure control or other features available with your current scanner software, check with the vendor for an upgrade. Upgrading scanner software might significantly improve scanning options and scan quality. You can also switch to third-party scanning applications for even greater control, although some of these can be relatively expensive.

Better Scanning from Better Software

Check out these third-party scanning solutions for better scans with your existing scanner. Most vendors offer free trials you can download:

- VueScan (http://www.hamrick.com/index.html)
- SilverFast (http://www.lasersoft.com/)
- Art-Scan (http://www.scanhelp.com/288int/artscan/)

If you want to share a scanner (including scanning features of an all-in-one unit) across a network, try RemoteScan, available from http://www.remote-scan.com/.

To improve image quality after scanning within Photoshop, Photoshop Elements, or Paint Shop Pro, try the plug-ins available from the Kodak Austin Development Center at http://www.appliedsciencefiction.com/.

Troubleshooting I/O Ports and Input Devices

TROUBLESHOOTING

FAST TRACK TO SOLUTIONS (SYMPTOM TABLE)

Symptom	Flowchart or Book Section	See Page
Pointing device pointer won't move.	General Pointing Device Problems	**699**
Pointing device pointer movement is erratic.	Using Other Methods to Diagnose Problems with Input Devices,	**451**
	Using Device Manager to Troubleshoot a PS/2 Mouse or Keyboard	**440**
The basic functions of my pointing device or keyboard work OK, but the extra buttons and scroll wheel don't work.	Using Device Manager to Troubleshoot USB Input Devices	**433**
The pointing device integrated into my portable computer doesn't work.	Pointing Device Problems in a Portable PC	**702**
My PS/2 (6-pin mini-DIN) keyboard or mouse doesn't work.	My PS/2 Keyboard or Mouse Doesn't Work	**696**
None of the keys on my keyboard work.	No Keys on the Keyboard Work	**698**
Some keys don't work on my keyboard.	Some Keys on the Keyboard Don't Work	**697**
I have an IEEE-1394 (FireWire, i.Link) port installed, but my system can't detect it.	Can't Detect Installed IEEE-1394 Port Enabling 1394 Ports	**706** **430**
My wireless input or pointing device doesn't work.	Wireless Input and Pointing Device Problems	**703**
	Troubleshooting Problems with Wireless Input Devices	**438**
I'm having a problem with a device connected to the IEEE-1394 port.	IEEE-1394 Device Troubleshooting	**707**
I'm having problems with an IEEE-1394 port.	Table 7.1	**428**

TROUBLESHOOTING

FAST TRACK TO SOLUTIONS, *Continued*

Symptom	Flowchart or Book Section	See Page
The Device Manager lists an I/O port or device with a problem.	I/O Port Is Detected but Not Working Properly	**704**
I'm having a problem with a device connected to my parallel port.	Parallel Port Troubleshooting	**708**
I'm having a problem with a device connected to the USB port.	USB Device Troubleshooting	**705**
I just bought an adapter to connect my mouse to a different type of port. Why doesn't it work?	Sidebar: When (and Why) Adapters Don't Always Work	**447**
I just connected a bus-powered USB device to a USB hub, and it doesn't work.	Troubleshooting USB Hub Power Problems	**425**
Whenever I move my mouse around the desktop, it drags objects, even if I'm not holding down the left button.	Table 7.4	**449**
I want to switch the mouse buttons around.	Table 7.4	**449**
I'm having problems double-clicking objects.	Table 7.4	**449**
I'm having a hard time seeing the mouse pointer.	Table 7.4	**449**
The mouse pointer is too fast or too slow.	Table 7.4	**449**
The scroll wheel on the mouse scrolls too slowly or too quickly.	Table 7.4	**449**
I plugged a mouse from another computer into the PS/2 port, but it doesn't work.	Using the System BIOS to Solve Problems with PS/2 Pointing Devices	**446**

TROUBLESHOOTING

FAST TRACK TO SOLUTIONS, *Continued*

Symptom	Flowchart or Book Section	See Page
My USB keyboard works fine in Windows, but it doesn't work within the BIOS setup.	Using the System BIOS to Solve Problems with USB Devices	**438**
I'm not sure how to configure my serial ports to avoid conflicts.	Preventing IRQ Conflicts Involving Serial Ports	**460**
How do I re-enable a disabled serial or parallel port?	Troubleshooting a Disabled Parallel or Serial Port	**456**
What's the difference between a USB root hub and a generic hub?	Sidebar: A Fast Introduction to USB Terminology	**422**
My system is supposed to have USB 2.0 ports, but my USB 2.0 device is working at USB 1.1 speeds only.	Troubleshooting USB 2.0 (Hi-Speed USB) Support	**418**
My USB or IEEE-1394a device works fine when I plug it into a rear port, but not when I plug it into a front port.	Troubleshooting IEEE-1394 Ports and Hubs	**427**
	Sidebar: Connecting Front-Mounted Header Cables Is Trial by Error	**429**
I'm having problems with a USB input device (mouse or keyboard).	Table 7.2	**433**
I'm having problems with a PS/2 keyboard or mouse.	Table 7.3	**441**

I/O Port Uses and Types

As desktop computers get smaller and smaller, and more and more PC users are dumping desktop computers for laptop and notebook computers, input/output (I/O) ports are more important than ever before. I/O ports have always been used for connecting input devices such as keyboards and mice and output devices such as printers, but I/O ports can do much more today:

- Expand your computer's built-in storage without your having to open the cover
- Create temporary connections between computers for data transfer
- Add network and Internet capabilities
- Connect to digital cameras, scanners, DV camcorders, and other types of imaging devices

If you're having problems with your computer's I/O ports, you're not going to get much done with your computer.

Common I/O Port Types

Keeping your computer's I/O ports in tip-top shape is vital, but before you start the process, it's useful to understand what types of I/O ports are found on the typical PC and what they are used for. The most common types of built-in I/O ports include:

- USB
- PS/2
- Parallel (LPT)
- Serial (COM)

Desktop computers usually group these ports into the ATX port cluster on the rear of the computer, as shown in Figure 7.1.

Many recent laptops have abandoned serial and parallel ports, and use a single PS/2 port that is designed to work with a mouse or keyboard, as in Figure 7.2.

FIGURE 7.1

Input device ports on the rear of a typical desktop computer.

PS/2 (6-pin mini-DIN) mouse port

Parallel (LPT) port

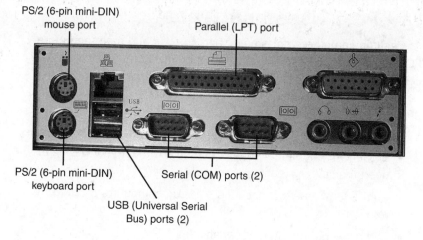

PS/2 (6-pin mini-DIN) keyboard port

Serial (COM) ports (2)

USB (Universal Serial Bus) ports (2)

FIGURE 7.2

Input device ports on a typical notebook computer.

PS/2 (6-pin mini-DIN) mouse/keyboard port

USB (Universal Serial Bus) ports (2)

USB 1.1 and USB 2.0 Ports

Older systems feature USB 1.1 ports, which transfer data at speeds up to 12Mbps. This is more than fast enough for keyboards, mice, and low-end inkjet printers. However, most high-speed USB devices, such as newer types of digital cameras, flash memory card readers, scanners, high-performance inkjet photo printers, and external drives, have been redesigned to use USB 2.0 (also called Hi-Speed USB) ports, which run at up to 480Mbps. USB 1.1 and USB 2.0 ports look identical, and any USB 2.0 device can connect to a USB 1.1 port in a pinch. As Figure 7.3 illustrates, you can add a Hi-Speed USB card to a system to retrofit it for today's USB 2.0–compatible devices.

USB ports support hot-plugging and hot-swapping. You can plug in a USB peripheral while your computer is running, and you can also disconnect it while your computer is running.

IEEE-1394a (FireWire 400) Ports

Another common port on recent systems is the IEEE-1394a (FireWire 400) port. Some recent systems feature one or more built-in FireWire 400 ports, but this port is often found on add-on cards, either by itself or as part of a sound card or multifunction card.

Figure 7.3 illustrates an IEEE-1394a add-on card and cable compared to a USB add-on card and cable.

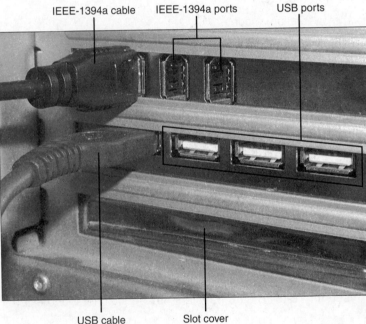

FIGURE 7.3
IEEE-1394a and Hi-Speed USB add-on cards on the rear of a typical desktop computer.

As with USB ports, IEEE-1394a ports also support hot-plugging and hot-swapping.

I/O Port Uses

USB ports can be used for almost any input/output task, replacing PS/2, parallel, and serial ports for tasks as diverse as the following:

- Input devices such as keyboards, pointing devices, and scanners
- Removable-media drives
- Optical drives
- Hard drives
- Tape backups
- Printers
- File-transfer cables
- Network adapters
- Analog (dial-up) modems
- PDA synchronization cradles
- Flash memory card readers

IEEE-1394a ports are used primarily for interfacing DV camcorders, portable hard drives, and high-capacity removable-media drives. They can also be used for direct-connect networking with other computers featuring IEEE-1394a ports.

Compared to USB and IEEE-1394a ports, legacy ports are much more limited in their uses. As their names imply, PS/2 ports are used for mice and keyboards. Serial ports have been used for mice, plotters, old printers of various types, and PC-to-PC data transfer, but are used today primarily for PDA synchronization cradles, label printers, and signaling battery backup units. Parallel ports were originally designed for faster printing than that available with serial ports, and they have also been used for PC-to-PC data transfers, image scanners, and external drives.

Serial, parallel, and PS/2 ports are often referred to as *legacy* ports because the tasks they perform can now be performed by USB ports. Some recent systems no longer feature serial, parallel, and PS/2 ports, so you'll want to use care when purchasing or building new systems if you use devices that are connected via legacy ports (or you can use legacy-to-USB adaptors, as discussed in the next section).

Adapting Legacy Devices to USB Ports

If you need to use a parallel, serial, or PS/2 device on a computer that has only USB ports, you can use adapters to connect these legacy devices to USB ports. Legacy-to-USB adapters feature the legacy port on one end of the adapter and the USB port on the other end.

If you need serial and parallel ports on a system that has a USB 2.0 (Hi-Speed USB) port, you might prefer to plug in a universal port replicator. Some of these can also provide additional USB ports as well as a 10/100 Ethernet port.

You can also install serial, parallel, or multi-I/O cards featuring both serial and parallel ports to add these port types to your existing desktop system.

Leo Says

Add Up the Costs Before Adapting Legacy Devices

Legacy-to-USB adapters can be fairly expensive. It's not uncommon to pay $25 to $30 or more for typical single-port adapters. Adding a universal port replicator to a desktop or laptop system can cost you $90 or more.

Sometimes the money you spend is the least of your worries. For example, parallel-to-USB adapters often don't support status reports from laser or inkjet printers, so you don't know if the toner or ink is low or if you're out of paper. These adapters can make sense if the legacy device you want to use has features you can't match with a USB device or if replacing the legacy device with a comparable USB device would be much more expensive than the adapter. For a desktop computer, it might make more sense to pop in a parallel port card or serial/parallel (multi-I/O) card for anywhere from about $30 to $50 or so if you need to use legacy serial or parallel devices.

However, for most garden-variety legacy devices, it often makes more sense to purchase a native USB device and retire the legacy device or use it on an older system.

Diagnosing Problems with Ports and Input Devices

If you're having problems with a printer, scanner, or other I/O device, it can sometimes be difficult to determine if the device itself is the problem or if the port used by the device is not working. The following sections help you determine where the problem truly lies and provide you with fast solutions.

Diagnosing Port and Driver Problems with Device Manager

→ See "Using Device Manager," Chapter 2, p. 100.

In many cases, the Windows Device Manager provides you a fast, reliable way to figure out if the problem with a device is caused by problems with the port it's attached to or with the port's or device's own device driver.

To access the Device Manager quickly, right-click My Computer and select Properties. In Windows XP, click the Hardware tab, then the Device Manager button (older versions differ slightly).

Figure 7.4 shows the Windows XP Device Manager displaying normal, disabled, and problem devices.

FIGURE 7.4
The Windows XP Device Manager shows normal, disabled, and problem devices.

Standard 101-key keyboard (working normally)

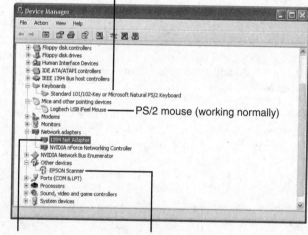

PS/2 mouse (working normally)

Disabled device
(note the red X icon)

Device with problems
(note the yellow ! problem icon)

If you're using Device Manager to figure out a problem with your input device, you need to know two pieces of information: what port it's using (for example, if you use USB input devices, you need to expand the Universal Serial Bus category), and how it's listed in Device

Manager. You also need to understand the symbols that can sometimes appear on a device listed in Device Manager:

- An exclamation point (!) in a yellow circle indicates a problem with the port, device, or driver. Right-click the device or port and choose Properties to get the details.

- A red X indicates that the port or device has been disabled. You might be able to use the properties sheet to re-enable the port or device. However, if the port or device is controlled by the system BIOS, you might need to reboot the computer and use the BIOS setup program to re-enable the port.

- The question mark category is used for devices that are not recognized by Windows because the drivers for the device have not been loaded. Install the drivers, and the device will be recognized.

A device cannot work if you attach it to a port that falls into one of the following categories:

- It's disabled.

- It's not recognized in the Device Manager.

- It has a conflict with another port.

- It has a defective driver.

Even if the port is working properly, the device won't work if you don't have a driver for it, the driver is defective or didn't load, or if the device has a problem that the Device Manger cannot diagnose.

→ For more information about diagnosing problem devices, see "Using Device Manager," Chapter 2, p. 100, and "Using the Windows XP Hardware Troubleshooter," Chapter 2, p. 110.

→ For details about accessing the BIOS, see "Controlling Your PC's Operation with BIOS Setup," Chapter 1, p. 41.

Spare Input Devices Make Troubleshooting Simple

Because Device Manager really looks only at the connection to a device and not the device itself, it's limited in its ability to solve problems with input devices. When it comes time to troubleshoot, it pays to have spare input devices you can use for swapping. This ensures that the problem is the device itself (and not the port it's connected to).

Worried about the expense? Don't be. For very little cash, you purchase a bare-bones mouse or cheapjack keyboard to use as a pinch-hitter when things go wrong, or you can use a mouse or keyboard from a spare system. By swapping a known-working device for one whose condition is unknown, you can get to the bottom of problems in a hurry.

In the case of USB devices, even this is unnecessary. You can use any USB device (even a scanner, webcam, or drive) to confirm that a USB port or hub is working properly—*provided you have the drivers needed for the device and the version of Windows you're using.* Remember, if nothing works when you plug it into a particular port, the port is either disabled or defective. But, if the replacement works, the original device may be defective. If you download updated drivers and the device still won't work, it's defective and should be replaced. Many USB keyboards and mice purchased at retail include PS/2 adapters, enabling you to use the same input device with USB and PS/2 ports.

Troubleshooting USB Ports and Hubs

USB ports present some unique troubleshooting challenges, even if you're familiar with other types of I/O ports. Some of these include:

- Determining if your hardware supports USB 2.0 (Hi-Speed USB)
- Determining if USB 2.0 support has been enabled
- Installing the appropriate drivers for a particular USB device
- Checking the power available for devices from a USB hub

→ *For more information about diagnosing problems with USB keyboards and mice, see "Troubleshooting USB Keyboards and Mice," this chapter, p. 437.*

If you're like most computer users, USB ports are your primary method of interfacing printers, scanners, keyboards, mice, and other devices. If you're having problems with USB ports, keep reading!

Troubleshooting USB 2.0 (Hi-Speed USB) Support

If you use USB ports only for mice, keyboards, and low-end inkjet printers, it doesn't matter whether they support the older USB 1.1 or newer USB 2.0 (Hi-Speed USB) standard. However, if you're tired of seeing a message similar to the one in Figure 7.5 whenever you plug in a newer USB device, use this section to help determine if you have USB 2.0 support that's not enabled or not working properly.

FIGURE 7.5

Windows XP displays a message similar to this if you plug in a USB 2.0–compatible device into a USB 1.1–compatible port or hub.

This device can perform faster

This USB device can perform faster if you connect it to a Hi-Speed USB 2.0 port.
For a list of available ports, click here.

Locating USB 2.0–Compatible Ports

Many recent systems have a mixture of USB 1.1 and USB 2.0–compatible ports. For example, USB ports built into the rear of a system or on an add-on card might be USB 2.0 compatible, but USB ports built into the front of the case might be USB 1.1 compatible. To determine if your system has any available USB 2.0 ports, click the balloon shown in Figure 7.5 to display a dialog similar to one of those shown in Figure 7.6.

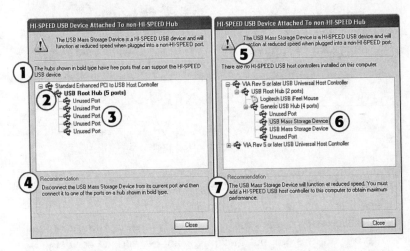

FIGURE 7.6

Typical USB advice dialogs displayed when you connect a USB 2.0 device to a USB 1.1 port or hub.

1. Indicates USB 2.0 hubs available on system
2. Location of available high-speed (USB 2.0) hubs
3. Port usage on high-speed hub
4. Reminder to connect device to available Hi-Speed hub
5. Indicates no USB 2.0 controllers on system
6. The device requesting USB 2.0 support
7. Reminder to add a USB 2.0 controller for maximum device speed

If you see a dialog similar to the one shown on the left in Figure 7.6, you're all set. Just connect your USB 2.0 device to an available port, and you'll enjoy the highest performance. However, if you see a dialog similar to the one shown on the right in Figure 7.6, your USB 2.0 device will run at USB 1.1 speeds until you install a USB 2.0 add-on card similar to the ones shown in Figure 7.7—or until you enable the USB 2.0 support already built into your system.

FIGURE 7.7

Hi-Speed USB (USB 2.0) cards for laptop/notebook computers (left) and desktop computers (right).

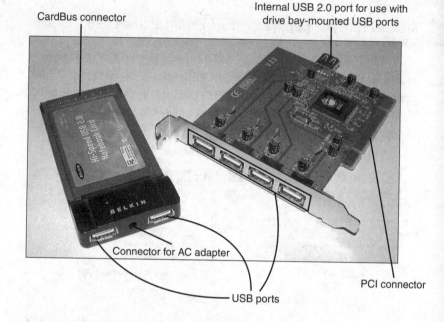

CardBus connector

Internal USB 2.0 port for use with drive bay-mounted USB ports

Connector for AC adapter

USB ports

PCI connector

Checking for Problems with Existing USB 2.0 Ports

If you see the error message shown in Figure 7.6 with a system built in the last two years or so, you might already have USB 2.0–compatible ports on your system, but they might not be working correctly. There are three possible reasons for this:

- Driver problems
- Incorrect BIOS configuration settings
- Using USB 1.1 external hubs with USB 2.0 ports

If you use Windows 98 Second Edition, Windows Me, or Windows 2000, you can use the drivers supplied by the vendor to install your new card. However, the situation is more complex with Windows XP. Some vendors provide Windows XP drivers that work with any release, but many vendors don't provide Windows XP drivers. To get the drivers you need, you must update to Service Pack 1 (SP1) or greater. Service Pack 2 is recommended because it handles USB 2.0 devices and ports better than SP1.

What happens if you don't have USB 2.0 drivers for your device and version of Windows? Your USB 2.0 ports will work as USB 1.1 ports. If you have Windows XP, your best bet is to upgrade to Service Pack 2 or greater if you're still using an older release. Windows XP has been known to have problems if you try to use unsigned device drivers with USB ports. For example, if you have a CardBus USB card for your notebook computer and use unsigned device drivers, it might not recognize the card when you plug it in unless you manually install the card with Add New Hardware (via the Control Panel).

To determine what types of USB ports you have in your system, use Device Manager. Click the plus sign (+) next to the Universal Serial Bus controllers category. If you see only "Universal Host Controller" entries in this category, your system has USB 1.1 ports. If you also see "Enhanced Host Controller," you have USB 2.0 ports. Each Universal Host Controller can control two USB ports, but a single Enhanced Host Controller provides USB 2.0 support for all USB ports on the motherboard or add-on card. See Figure 7.8 for a typical example.

→ *For more information about signed and unsigned device drivers, see "Signed and Unsigned Device Drivers," Chapter 2, p. 108.*

→ *For more information about Add New Hardware, see "Using Add New Hardware," Chapter 2, p. 88.*

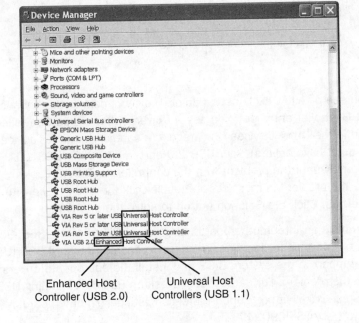

Enhanced Host Controller (USB 2.0)

Universal Host Controllers (USB 1.1)

FIGURE 7.8
This computer has an Enhanced Host Controller to provide USB 2.0 support.

Leo Says

A Fast Introduction to USB Terminology

No matter how much you know about other types of PC hardware, your first view of the Universal Serial Bus controller category in Device Manager is likely to be confusing. Here are some quick definitions of typical terms:

- **Universal Host Controller**—Controls USB 1.1 ports; one controller for each pair of USB ports.

- **Enhanced Host Controller**—Provides USB 2.0 support; only one is needed for all the USB ports on the motherboard or an add-on card.

- **Root hub**—Each root hub corresponds to two (or sometimes more) USB ports.

- **Generic USB hub**—A hub connected to a root hub. A generic hub can be a standalone unit or might be built into a keyboard or monitor base.

- **Composite device**—A USB device that has two or more interfaces in different categories. For example, a USB receiver for a wireless mouse and keyboard is a composite device.

→ *For more information about using the Solution button, see "Solving Resource Conflicts with Device Manager," Chapter 2 p. 102.*

If you see a yellow exclamation point (!) symbol next to the Enhanced Host Controller entry, or if you see a Universal Serial Bus Controller listed in the Other Devices (?) category (a category used for devices that don't have drivers), your USB 2.0 ports will work in USB 1.1 mode only until the problem with the controller has been resolved. To solve the problem in most cases, double-click the entry to view its properties. Click the Solution button to solve the problem.

If you have an Intel motherboard using the 925, 915, 875, 865, 850, 848, or 845 chipset families, you need to enable Hi-Speed USB (USB 2.0) support in the system BIOS and install the appropriate drivers to solve the problem. For details, see "Desktop Boards—Enabling USB 2.0 Support" at http://support.intel.com/support/motherboards/desktop/sb/CS-009024.htm.

You might also need to enable USB 2.0 support in the system BIOS on other motherboards using various chipsets.

If you see a red X symbol next to the Enhanced Host Controller entry, the USB 2.0 controller has been disabled. To enable it, double-click the entry to view its properties and select Enable.

If your USB 2.0 ports are working properly, but you are using USB 1.1 external hubs to provide more ports or more convenient ports, any device connected to these hubs will run at USB 1.1 speeds. To make the most of your USB 2.0 ports, make sure you use USB 2.0–compatible hubs. Some might have the Hi-Speed USB symbol (see Figure 7.9). Some front-mounted ports support only USB 1.1 speeds.

USB 1.1 hub

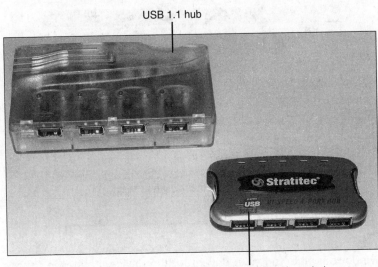

FIGURE 7.9
Typical USB 1.1 and USB 2.0 (Hi-Speed USB) hubs.

Hi-Speed USB (USB 2.0) symbol

Installing the Right Device Drivers for Your USB Device

USB devices are designed to be hot-pluggable, meaning that you can plug them in while your system is running. Naturally, you'd expect the USB device you plug into your system to start working as soon as you plug it in. However, a USB device will work only if the drivers for that device are already installed on the system.

Windows XP provides many more USB drivers than previous versions, so the need to preinstall drivers before connecting the device is not as great. However, we recommend that if your device includes a driver CD with Windows XP drivers, install them. Even if Windows includes a driver, it might be a stripped-down version; this is especially true for USB printers.

What if you plugged in a device and Windows couldn't find a driver for it? Check the Device Manager listing for a category called "Other Devices." Other Devices is a temporary holding tank for devices without drivers. Figure 7.10 shows the results of connecting an Epson photo printer with a built-in card reader to a system without using the driver CD.

FIGURE 7.10
USB devices without drivers are placed in the Other Devices category until drivers are located.

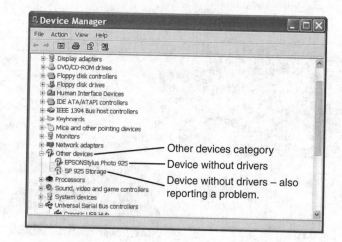

Other devices category
Device without drivers
Device without drivers – also reporting a problem.

→ For more information about using the Found New Hardware Wizard, see "Add Hardware," Chapter 2, p. 88.

If Windows is able to locate drivers for the device, its stay in Other Devices will be a short one. To make the process of finding drivers easier for you, Windows XP, starting in Service Pack 2, will offer to use Windows Update to locate drivers when the New Hardware Wizard starts.

However, there is no guarantee that Windows Update will be able to find a driver. For the devices shown in Figure 7.10, the New Hardware Wizard did locate a driver for the SP 925 Storage (a multi-slot flash memory card reader in the printer), but was unable to find a driver for the printer itself.

The bottom line? Install the drivers yourself! Keep in mind that there's no guarantee that a particular device will work in Windows without installing drivers manually, even if similar devices from other vendors are recognized automatically by the same Windows installation. Even if the device doesn't include a driver CD, you might need to install drivers. That's why we prefer to visit the vendor's website and download the latest drivers before we install a device. Better safe than sorry!

Troubleshooting USB Hub Power Problems

The maximum amount of current that a USB device can draw from a USB port is 500mA. Any root hub (a USB port built into a motherboard or into an add-on card) provides this level of power. This is the major reason why some USB peripheral vendors recommend plugging their devices into the computer's own USB port rather than a USB port on an external hub (known as a *generic hub* in Device Manager).

There are two different types of generic hubs:

- Self-powered
- Bus-powered

External self-powered hubs are plugged into an AC outlet. The multi-port USB hubs you can buy as standalone accessories are almost always self-powered. Many vendors now sell drive bay–mounted USB hubs that connect to the computer's power supply. These are also self-powered hubs.

Self-powered hubs, like root hubs, provide 500mA of current per port. Figure 7.11 illustrates the Power tab on a typical self-powered hub's properties sheet as shown in Device Manager. Note the different power levels required by different types of devices.

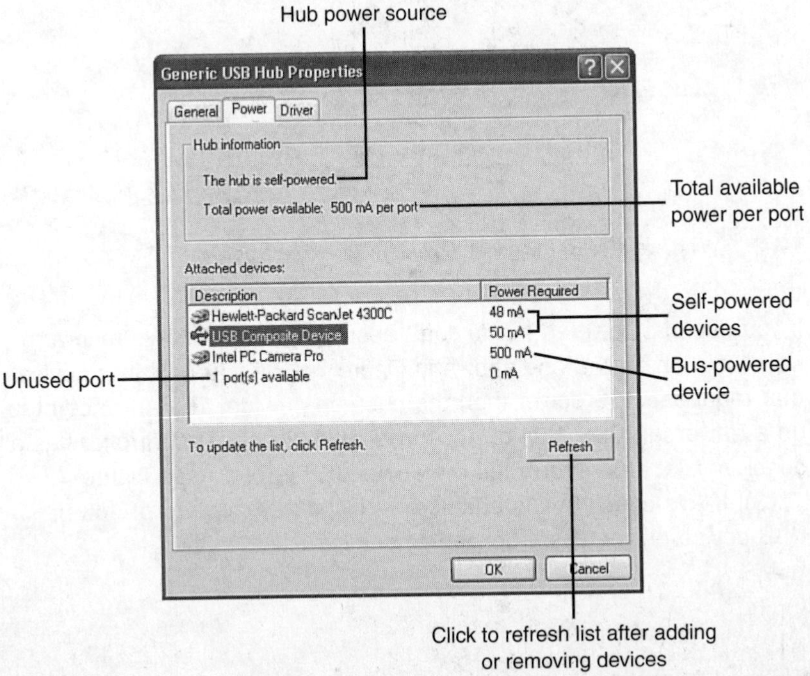

FIGURE 7.11

The Power properties sheet for a generic USB (external) hub that has several devices connected to it.

Bus-powered hubs differ from self-powered hubs in two ways: They are often incorporated into other devices such as keyboards and monitors, and they are powered from the USB port they're attached to. Bus-powered hubs provide only 100mA of current per port. As a result, some USB devices that draw power from the USB port will not work when plugged into a bus-powered hub.

A self-powered hub becomes a bus-powered hub if the external power source is disconnected or fails. If you plug too many bus-powered devices (devices that draw their power from the USB port) into a bus-powered USB hub, they might stop working, as shown in Figure 7.12.

FIGURE 7.12

The Power properties sheet for a bus-powered generic USB (external) hub that has a device requiring more power than is available connected to it. Note the warning on the taskbar.

Hub is getting its power from the PC

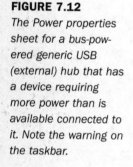

A hub has less available power when drawing from the PC's bus than when self-powered

This Intel PC Camera Pro requires more power than the bus powered hub can provide

Windows XP's warning that the hub requires more power

If you use bus-powered hubs, don't assume you will always receive a warning such as the one shown in Figure 7.12 if you plug in a device that requires more power than the hub can provide. The Advanced tab on a Universal (USB 1.1) or Advanced (USB 2.0) host controller has a check box labeled "Don't tell me about USB errors" (see Figure 7.13). If this check box is enabled, you won't be notified of power, USB device errors, or other problems.

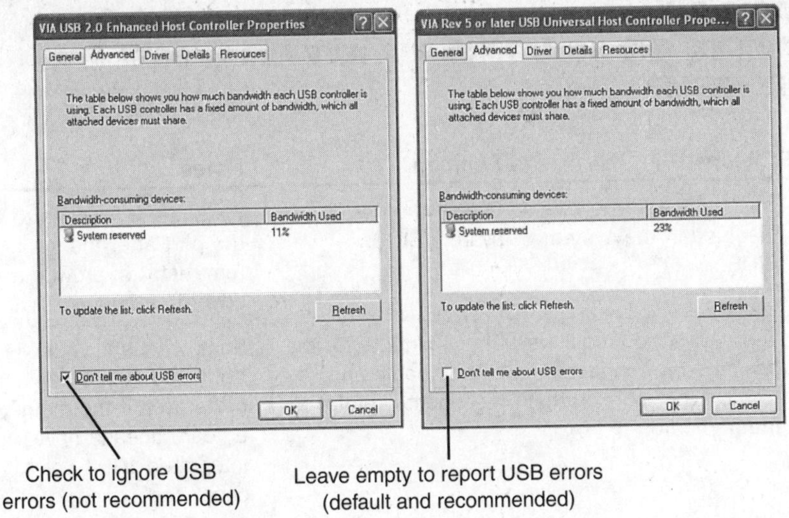

FIGURE 7.13

The Enhanced Host Controller (left) is configured to ignore USB errors, whereas the Universal Host Controller uses the default setting (reports USB errors).

Check to ignore USB errors (not recommended)

Leave empty to report USB errors (default and recommended)

To avoid power problems, follow these guidelines:

- Use self-powered hubs whenever possible.

- If you want to use a bus-powered hub for a device, check its USB power requirements. You can do this by reading the specifications for the device or by plugging it into a USB port on an external or root hub and opening the Power tab for the hub, as shown in Figure 7.12.

Troubleshooting IEEE-1394 Ports and Hubs

IEEE-1394 (FireWire) ports, like USB ports, support hot-plugging and hot-swapping, but they differ in some significant ways from USB ports. Although some systems have integrated 1394 ports, most systems still rely on add-on cards to provide 1394 support. Systems with front-mounted 1394 ports rely on header cables connected to a 1394-enabled motherboard to provide support.

If you plug an IEEE-1394 device into a port on your system and nothing happens, your system probably has a problem with the port. Check out Table 7.1 for the "prime suspects."

TABLE 7.1
CAUSES AND SOLUTIONS FOR IEEE-1394 PORT PROBLEMS

Problem	Solution	Notes
The built-in port is disabled in the system BIOS.	Enable the port in the system BIOS.	Windows will recognize the port after the system restarts; provide a driver if prompted.
The port header cable is not properly connected to the 1394 port on the motherboard.	Check pinouts for the header cable and reconnect it to the port.	Some cases include front-mounted 1394 ports even if the motherboard doesn't have integrated 1394 ports; check the system or motherboard documentation.
The device runs when connected to a six-wire 1394a port, but not to a four-wire port.	Provide an external power source for the device.	Four-wire ports do not provide power to a device; six-wire ports do.
The 1394 add-on card has been disabled.	Enable the card in the Windows Device Manager.	If Device Manager reports problems with a port, use the Troubleshoot button to start the solution process. See Chapter 2 for details.

Tracking Down Integrated and Add-on 1394 Ports

If your computer has 1394 ports, they could be located in three different places:

- Desktop computers' motherboards with integrated 1394 ports usually have one or two ports on the rear panel's port cluster, as shown in Figure 7.14.
- Many recent desktop computers also feature connections for 1394 header cables (see Figure 7.15). The header cables might attach to a card bracket (refer to Figure 7.14) or the front of the case (see Figure 7.16).

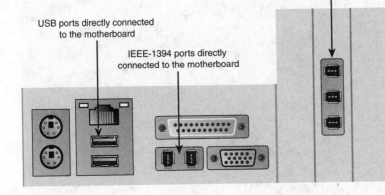

IEEE-1394 ports connected to
the motherboard with header cables
or built into an add-on card

USB ports directly connected
to the motherboard

IEEE-1394 ports directly
connected to the motherboard

FIGURE 7.14
*Two typical locations
for built-in IEEE-1394
and USB ports on the
rear of a desktop
computer.*

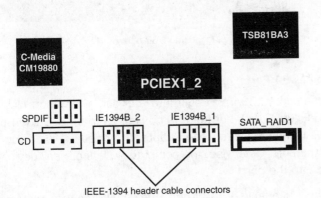

FIGURE 7.15
*Location of 1394
header cable connectors on a typical motherboard.*

IEEE-1394 header cable connectors

Connecting Front-Mounted Header Cables Is Trial by Error

Lots of cases these days feature front-mounted USB and IEEE-1394 ports, just like the ones in Figure 7.16. The trouble is that different motherboard makers use different standards for their header cable connectors. As a result, you might need to connect individual cables to the appropriate header cable pins. If you're like me, you need a magnifying glass, a flashlight, a long pair of tweezers, and a tolerance for starting over a few times before you get it right!

FIGURE 7.16
Front-mounted USB (left) and IEEE-1394a (right) ports.

USB port   six-wire IEEE-1394a port

USB cable plugged into USB port

Enabling 1394 Ports

If you can see a 1394 port built into your computer's port cluster (refer to Figure 7.14), but there is no listing for an IEEE-1394 port in Windows Device Manager (see Chapter 2 for details), then you must enable the port. Otherwise, the computer will ignore any device plugged into the port.

Here's how to enable a 1394 port that's built into your system:

1. Restart the computer.
2. Access the BIOS setup program.
3. Locate the menu that lists the 1394 port.
4. Enable the port.
5. Save the changes and exit.

Take a look at Figure 7.17 for a typical example.

FIGURE 7.17
A disabled IEEE-1394 port that must be enabled with the computer's BIOS setup program.

OnBoard PCI Controller	
Serial ATA Controller	Disabled
Audio Controller	Enabled
1394 Controller	Disabled

If the port is on an add-on card but is not listed in Device Manager, run the Add Hardware Wizard to detect the port and install drivers. Note that some 1394 PCI (desktop) cards require additional power from the computer's power supply, and some CardBus (notebook) cards require additional power from an AC adapter. If your 1394 card requires additional power, like the one shown in Figure 7.18, make sure you connect the appropriate power lead. Otherwise, the card might not be detected by Windows.

➔ *For more details about using the system BIOS setup program, see "Controlling Your PC's Operation with BIOS Setup," Chapter 1, p. 41.*

Power supply lead   PCI slot

1394a port (six-pin)

FIGURE 7.18
A 1394a card, which requires additional power from the power supply.

If the 1394 port is listed in Device Manager but Device Manager reports problems, you must correct these problems before you can expect the port or any device connected to that port to function normally. Some of the problems you might encounter could include the following:

➔ *For more details about using the Add Hardware Wizard, see "Add Hardware," Chapter 2, p. 88.*

- An incorrect driver is loaded for the port's chipset.
- A hardware resource conflict with another port exists.
- A corrupt driver is loaded.
- The device is disabled.

These problems can be detected and resolved with the Windows Device Manager (see Figure 7.19).

To correct these problems, double-click the 1394 port to open its properties sheet. Click the Solution button on the General tab to start the solution process.

➔ *For details, see "Using Device Manager," Chapter 2, p. 100.*

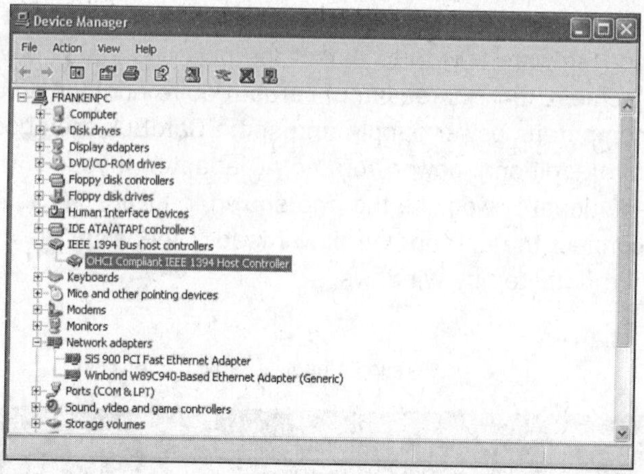

FIGURE 7.19

A disabled IEEE-1394 port (red X) as displayed by the Windows XP Device Manager.

Troubleshooting Keyboards and Mice

When an input device stops working, your ability to use your computer may be crippled or even eliminated. Because input devices are the principal way to interact with the computer and create new information, finding fast, accurate solutions to input device problems is critical.

→ **To determine if USB ports are working properly, see "Troubleshooting USB Ports and Hubs," this chapter, p. 418. To determine if USB keyboards and mice and working properly, see "Troubleshooting USB Keyboards and Mice," this chapter, p. 432. To determine if PS/2 mouse and keyboard ports and input devices are working properly, see "Troubleshooting PS/2 Ports, Keyboards, and Mice," this chapter, p. 440.**

There are four possible sources of trouble with keyboards, mice, and similar pointing devices:

- The port the device is plugged into
- The device itself
- The device driver
- The device configuration in Control Panel

Input devices such as keyboards, mice, and devices that emulate mice (such as trackballs and touch pads) typically connect to the computer through USB ports or the PS/2 mouse and keyboard ports. If the port used by an input device is not working, the input device will not work, and, in the case of USB ports, neither will any other USB device. If the input device itself is not working, swapping input devices will get you back to work. If the input device is not using the correct driver, you might not be able to use the device's advanced features (most input devices can operate with basic functions by using Windows native keyboard and mouse drivers).

Troubleshooting USB Keyboards and Mice

Problems with USB keyboards and mice can result from any of the following:

- Incorrect BIOS configuration of USB ports
- Driver problems
- Hardware problems

The following sections help you solve each type of problem.

Using Device Manager to Troubleshoot USB Input Devices

Table 7.2 provides a quick reference to help you use the Device Manager to fix problems with your USB input devices. The solutions described in Table 7.2 are covered in greater after the table. Table 7.2 assumes that the input device is properly connected to the USB port.

TABLE 7.2
USB INPUT DEVICES AND THE DEVICE MANAGER

Device Manager Display	Problem	Solution
Red X	Device is disabled.	Enable the device with its properties sheet's General tab. If you can't enable the device, remove the listing from Device Manager and restart the computer. It should be detected and reinstalled.
Yellow !	Device has a problem (various codes).	View the device's condition with its properties sheet's General tab; use the codes or Troubleshooter to find a solution. See Table 2.4, Chapter 2, p. 104.
Yellow !	Device cannot start (Code 10).	Check the Power tab on properties sheet for a hub used to connect input device; if not enough power is present, move the input device to a hub with adequate power or supply AC power to the generic hub.

TABLE 7.2 (continued)

Device Manager Display	Problem	Solution
Device not visible in Device Manager; USB Controllers category present in Device Manager.	Device may not be connected to working USB port or hub.	If the USB Controllers category shows problems with controllers or hubs, correct them to enable USB devices to work. Try connecting the device directly to a USB port on your computer; if the device starts working, the hub or port previously used is defective.
Device not visible in Device Manager; USB Controllers category not present in Device Manager.	USB controllers are not enabled.	Restart the computer and enable the USB ports in the system BIOS.
Device visible in Device Manager but properties sheet doesn't indicate location.	Some advanced features (such as programmable buttons on the keyboard) don't work.	Install driver and application software for the input device. If some buttons/features still don't work, download and install updated drivers. If the features still don't work, contact the vendor for a replacement device.
Keyboard visible in Device Manager.	Web buttons don't activate desired features.	Download an updated keyboard setup program, run the setup program, and specify the desired action for each button.

The Universal Serial Bus (USB) category in Device Manager is used for host controllers, root hubs (ports built into your computer), and external hubs (refer to Figure 7.8). However, USB devices are listed under the normal categories. For example, USB mice and pointing devices are listed under "Mice and Other Pointing Devices," and USB keyboards are listed under "Keyboard."

USB keyboards and pointing devices are referred to as *Human Interface Devices (HIDs)*, and each HID-compliant device has at least two listings in Device Manager, as in Figure 7.20. One listing is for the device, and all other listings are for the HID functions of that device.

HID-compliant devices can be plugged into a computer at the same time as older PS/2 or serial input devices, allowing either to be used. Also, HID allows an input device to support additional buttons or features, such as the multimedia or web browser control buttons common on many new keyboards. If the keyboard has a scroll wheel, that feature will be listed separately as another HID-compliant mouse (refer to Figure 7.20).

Listings for a USB wireless keyboard

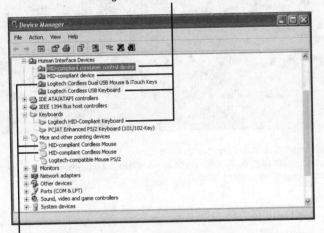

FIGURE 7.20

A wireless USB mouse and keyboard as listed in the Windows XP Device Manager.

Listings for a USB wireless mouse and keyboard's mouse features

Using the System BIOS to Solve Problems with USB Devices

System BIOS settings can affect USB input devices in two ways:

- If the USB ports are disabled, no USB devices, including input devices, will work.
- If the USB Legacy mode (also called *USB DOS mode*) is not enabled, a USB mouse and keyboard will work when the Windows desktop is displayed. However, the keyboard and mouse might not work within the system BIOS setup program or in a command-prompt mode such as the Windows XP Recovery Console. However, USB keyboards and pointing devices will work in Safe Mode on Windows XP.

Figure 7.21 shows a typical BIOS setup screen that contains the USB BIOS setup options.

FIGURE 7.21

A typical Integrated Peripherals (AMI BIOS) setup screen, which controls the USB functions.

```
            AMIBIOS NEW SETUP UTILITY - VERSION 3.31a
   Integrated Peripherals                       [ Setup Help ]

                                [ Options ]
   ▶ OnBoard PCI Controller
   Floppy Disk Controller        Disabled    ③
   Serial Port1                  No Mice
   Serial Port2                 All Device
      Port2 Mode
      IR Pin Select             [RRN/TRTX      ]
   Parallel Port                 Auto
      Port Mode                  ECP
      EPP Version                N/A
      Port IRQ                   Auto
      Port DMA                   Auto
   OnChip IDE Controller         Both
   OnChip USB Controller         6 USB Ports ①
      USB Legacy Support      ② All Device
      Port 64/60 Emulation       Enabled


   F1 :Help      ↑↓:Select Item     +/-:Change Values    F7 :Setup Defaults
   Esc:Previous Menu               Enter:Select ▶Sub-Menu  F6 :Hi-Performance
```

1. Enables/Disables/Sets number of USB ports
2. Enables/Disables use of USB keyboard and mouse outside Windows (Legacy mode)
3. Option screen for Legacy mode

Use the following tips to help troubleshoot your USB keyboard and pointing devices. Note that you might need to use a keyboard connected to the PS/2 keyboard jack to access your system BIOS to enable USB controllers or USB Legacy keyboard support on some systems:

- If the Device Manager doesn't list the Universal Serial Bus Controllers category, no USB devices will work. You need to enable the USB Controller option in the BIOS and restart the computer. Install drivers for USB devices as required.

- If the Device Manager doesn't list the Universal Serial Bus Controllers category, but the USB Controller option is enabled in the system BIOS, your USB controller is not supported by Windows. Contact the system or motherboard vendor for a BIOS upgrade and install it. If the controllers are still not recognized by Windows, disable the USB Controller setting in BIOS and install a USB 1.1 or USB 2.0 card if you want to use USB devices. We recommend a USB 2.0 (Hi-Speed USB) card because it supports faster USB 2.0 peripherals and works better with multiple USB 1.1 and USB 2.0 devices.

- If your USB keyboard or pointing device works within Windows, but not at a command prompt or within the BIOS setup program (a few BIOS setup programs are graphical and support a pointing device), you need to enable USB Legacy mode within the BIOS, as shown in Figure 7.21. Attach a PS/2 keyboard to the system to access the BIOS if you can't activate the BIOS setup program with your USB keyboard. If this mode is already enabled, contact your system or motherboard vendor for a BIOS update. On some systems, USB Legacy Keyboard and USB Legacy Mouse are separate options; enable either or both as desired.

Why It Pays to Keep an Old PS/2 Keyboard Around

Unless your computer is a so-called "legacy-free" model that has eliminated the venerable PS/2 keyboard and mouse connectors, it can be very useful to keep a PS/2 keyboard around even after you've switched over to a USB keyboard.

For example, as this section demonstrates, you may need to enter your system BIOS setup program to enable USB Legacy mode if you need to use your keyboard for the Windows XP Recovery Console or for other tasks outside the Windows GUI. If you don't have a PS/2 keyboard, you might not be able to enable the USB Legacy feature you need to use your USB keyboard at all times. Even if you've turned on the feature once, a battery failure or virus attack could require you to dive back into the BIOS again—but without a PS/2 keyboard, you're out of luck. On some systems running Windows XP, a USB keyboard can't display the troubleshooting startup menu, which is activated by pressing the F8 key, but a PS/2 keyboard will.

So, keep that old PS/2 keyboard around—or choose a USB keyboard that comes with a PS/2 adapter. You never know when you'll need it.

Troubleshooting Wireless Keyboards and Mice

Wireless mice and keyboards that have stopped working present a special troubleshooting challenge. The problem could be with any of the following:

- Their transceivers (which plug into the same connectors as normal input devices) can cause the devices to fail.

- The devices' transmission and reception of signals from the transceivers can also cause device failure.

- Problems with battery life will cause temporary device failure when the batteries are exhausted.

Most wireless input devices use radio signals, but a few low-cost devices from second-tier vendors use infrared (IR) signals instead.

Using Device Manager to Troubleshoot Wireless Mice and Keyboards

One major weakness of the Windows Device Manager is that it detects problems with the transceiver, not the device connected to the transceiver. For example, if the batteries in your wireless mouse or keyboard fail, the Device Manager will still report that the device works correctly. You can use the Device Manager to detect problems with how the transceiver is connected to your system. For transceivers that connect to the PS/2 port, see "Using Device Manager to Troubleshoot a PS/2 Mouse" and Table 7.3. For transceivers that connect to the USB port, see "Using Device Manager to Troubleshoot USB Input Devices."

To troubleshoot wireless-specific problems, see the next section, "Troubleshooting Problems with Wireless Input Devices."

Troubleshooting Problems with Wireless Input Devices

Even if the transceiver used by a wireless input device is working properly, the device itself might fail to work for one of the following reasons:

- Inability to exchange radio signals with the input device
- Loss of line-of-sight with an infrared (IR) input device
- Power failure due to dead batteries or dirty/corroded battery terminals
- Problems with Bluetooth (for Bluetooth-equipped wireless input devices)

If you are using a radio-controlled input device, the input device and the transceiver both need to use the same radio frequency. Depending upon the input device, you might need to select a frequency manually by pushing a button or rotating a dial, or the device might select a frequency for you. If you cannot select a frequency manually, you can reset the frequency used by removing the batteries from the input device and reinstalling them.

IR-based input devices need a clear line-of-sight established between the transceiver and the input device. This is relatively simple to do with an input device placed on the desktop, but it can be a lot harder if you use a wireless keyboard or keyboard/mouse combo on your lap.

Typical wireless devices that use alkaline batteries have a battery life of three to six months. Look for a battery-test light on the device to determine if the batteries are working, or remove them and use a separate battery tester. While most recent wireless input devices use a standard battery size such as AA or AAA, some older models might use less-common sizes. You should make sure you keep a spare set of batteries around to avoid running out of battery power at an inconvenient time. Some high-end wireless mice now use rechargeable batteries and a charging cradle to keep the batteries at full power all the time.

Some radio-frequency (RF) wireless keyboards have a control and troubleshooting properties sheet such as the one shown in Figure 7.22. Use this to check the RF channel in use, the battery life, connections, and for other tasks.

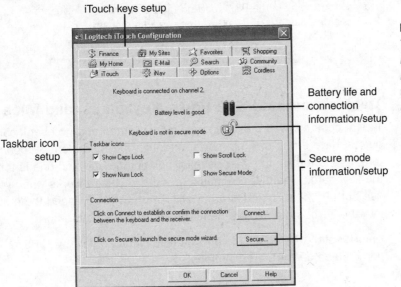

iTouch keys setup

Taskbar icon setup

Battery life and connection information/setup

Secure mode information/setup

FIGURE 7.22

The Wireless tab on Logitech's iTouch wireless keyboard is used to troubleshoot the connection and configure the connection type. Use the other tabs shown to configure the keyboard's special iTouch buttons.

If you use a Bluetooth-enabled keyboard or mouse, keep the following facts in mind:

- You must use a wired (PS/2 or USB) keyboard and mouse to install Windows XP Service Pack 2 and to configure Bluetooth support in SP2. Windows XP Service Pack 2 does not permit Bluetooth devices to work until they are configured. For more information, see Microsoft Knowledge Base article #873154.

- Microsoft Windows XP ships with support for many Bluetooth radios. If your Bluetooth radio is not on the list of supported devices, install the drivers provided by the mouse or keyboard vendor. For more information, see Microsoft Knowledge Base article #841803.

As you can see from the issues involved in wireless support, it's not time yet to throw out your wired keyboard and mouse!

Leo Says

The PS/2 Port's Not Dead Yet!

Many wireless transceivers used for both the mouse and keyboard have a PS/2 port and a USB port. If you have problems getting your wireless keyboard to work in BIOS setup when you use only the USB port, plug in the PS/2 port on the transceiver for keyboard functions and use the USB port for the wireless mouse functions.

Troubleshooting PS/2 Ports, Keyboards, and Mice

Typical desktop systems, and many recent laptop and notebook computers, have a pair of PS/2 ports. Although they use identical connectors, one is for the mouse or similar pointing device, and one is for the keyboard. If neither the mouse nor the keyboard works when you use both PS/2 ports, odds are really high that you plugged the mouse into the keyboard port and the keyboard into the mouse port.

Unfortunately, that's not the only problem you can have with PS/2 ports. Read on for more solutions!

Using Device Manager to Troubleshoot a PS/2 Mouse or Keyboard

Table 7.3 provides a quick reference to how problems with your PS/2 mouse or keyboard will be reflected in Device Manager, and how to resolve them. The solutions described in Table 7.3 are covered in greater detail following the table.

TABLE 7.3
THE PS/2 PORTS AND THE DEVICE MANAGER

Device Manager Display	Device Status	Problem	Solution
Mouse or keyboard displayed with (!) symbol.	Attached to port.	Problem with mouse, keyboard, or driver.	Open the properties sheet and follow the instructions for resolving the problem. See Table 2.4, Chapter 2, p. 104.
Mouse or keyboard displayed with red X.	Attached to port.	Mouse or keyboard disabled by Device Manager.	Open the properties sheet for the mouse or keyboard and enable the mouse or keyboard.
Mouse or keyboard displayed normally but doesn't work.	Attached to port.	Mouse not compatible with PS/2 port or wrong driver loaded; keyboard or keyboard adapter defective.	Check or replace the adapter. If you're using an adapter with a mouse not meant for use with a PS/2 port, it won't work. If the mouse is a PS/2 mouse, reload the driver. If you're using a 5-pin DIN keyboard with a PS/2 adapter, replace the adapter.
No mouse displayed.	Mouse attached to port.	PS/2 mouse port disabled.	Enable the port in BIOS or with the motherboard jumper (see system/motherboard manual for details).
		Mouse is defective.	Shut down the system and replace the mouse after verifying the PS/2 mouse port is enabled.
No mouse or keyboard displayed.	Mouse or keyboard not attached to port (or not plugged in properly).	Windows can't detect mouse or port.	Shut down the system and attach the mouse or keyboard to the correct PS/2 port. Then restart the system.

The PS/2 mouse port (also called the *6-pin mini-DIN port*) is designed for use with a PS/2 mouse. Other types of mice that include a PS/2 mouse port adapter can also be used with this port. Similarly, the PS/2 keyboard port, which has an identical physical connector but is not interchangeable with the mouse port, is designed for use with a PS/2 keyboard, or with an older 5-pin DIN keyboard equipped with a PS/2 adapter. Figure 7.23 shows examples of these adapters.

FIGURE 7.23
PS/2 keyboard and mouse port adapters.

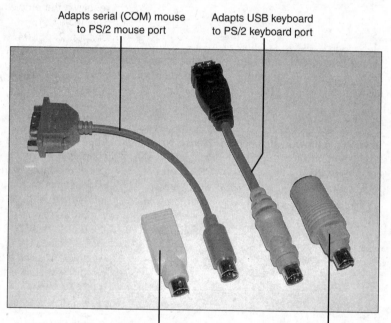

Adapts serial (COM) mouse to PS/2 mouse port

Adapts USB keyboard to PS/2 keyboard port

Adapts USB mouse to PS/2 mouse port

Adapts 5-pin DIN (IBM AT) keyboard to PS/2 keyboard port

Unlike some other types of input devices, which list the port separately from the device, the Windows Device Manager lists the PS/2 mouse as a mouse and the PS/2 keyboard as a keyboard (see Figure 7.24), but doesn't list the ports separately. If you have more than one mouse installed, such as a USB and a PS/2 mouse, you can tell which one is the PS/2 mouse because the Device Manager entry for the PS/2 mouse normally lists PS/2 as part of the description.

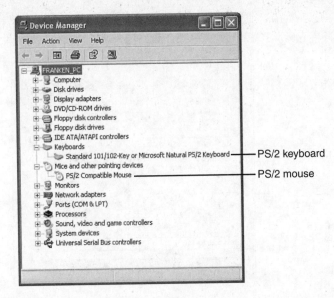

FIGURE 7.24
Standard PS/2 keyboard and mouse as shown in Windows Device Manager.

The integrated pointing devices built into notebook computers typically emulate the PS/2 mouse. If you use a USB mouse instead of a PS/2 mouse, you might prefer to disable the integrated pointing device so that you don't move the mouse pointer accidentally. You can disable the PS/2 mouse port or integrated pointing device on most computers in one of two ways:

- Through the system BIOS
- Through the Windows Device Manager

Note that some laptop and notebook computers automatically disable the integrated pointing device if you plug in a PS/2 mouse.

To disable the integrated pointing device with the Device Manager, open the properties sheet for the mouse or pointing device and select Do Not Use This Device (Disable), as shown in Figure 7.25.

If you disable the PS/2 mouse with the Device Manager, it will be displayed with a red X, as shown earlier in Figure 7.4. However, if your PS/2 mouse port is not enabled or if you plug the mouse into the wrong PS/2 port, it will not appear in Device Manager at all. In fact, the "Mice and Other Pointing Devices" or "Mouse" category in Device Manager will not appear at all if no mouse is connected to a valid port. Similarly, if the PS/2 keyboard is attached to the mouse port by mistake, or is not plugged into the system at all, it will not appear in Device Manager, and the "Keyboard" category will not be listed (unless another keyboard is connected via the USB port).

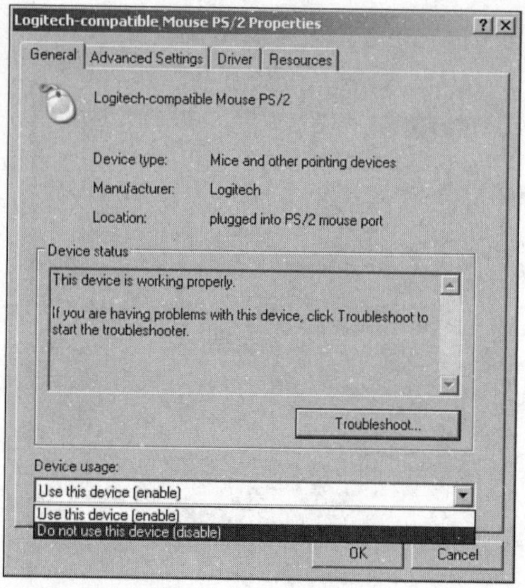

FIGURE 7.25

Disabling a PS/2 mouse or integrated pointing device with the Windows XP Device Manager.

Making PS/2 Ports Work for You

Regardless of the computer, if you have two PS/2 ports stacked on top of each other on the rear of the computer, as shown earlier in Figure 7.1, the *bottom* PS/2 port is for the keyboard, and the *top* one is for the mouse. Although some computers and input devices are color-coded to help you plug the correct device into each one, the physical connectors for the keyboard and mouse are identical. You won't hurt the ports or the devices if you mix up the ports, but the keyboard and pointing device won't work if they're plugged into the wrong ports.

If you attach a mouse to the PS/2 mouse port or a keyboard to the PS/2 keyboard port but they aren't displayed in Device Manager, they might not be connected tightly to the ports. If the port is disabled in the system BIOS, the PS/2 mouse port will not be displayed, even if the mouse is properly attached. If you need to enable the port, see "Using the System BIOS to Solve Problems with PS/2 Pointing Devices," later in this chapter.

However, a defective mouse or keyboard attached to the correct PS/2 port will not be visible either. To determine if the port or the device is at fault, perform this test:

1. Shut down Windows. If the mouse doesn't work, press Ctrl+Esc or the Windows key to open the Start button menu. You can use arrow keys to select Turn Off Computer and then press the Enter key.

2. If the PS/2 mouse isn't working, make sure the PS/2 mouse port is enabled. See "Using the System BIOS to Solve Problems with PS/2 Pointing Devices," later in this chapter. Keep in mind that some motherboards don't have provisions for disabling the PS/2 mouse port.

3. Plug a known-working keyboard or mouse into the correct PS/2 port; you can borrow one from another working computer at home or at the office (different brands are interchangeable). If you don't have a spare, buy a cheap mouse or keyboard for testing purposes (you'll spend all of $10 or $15 each to get them). If you have a USB mouse or keyboard with PS/2 adapters, use the adapter to convert the mouse or keyboard to PS/2, and use the adapted keyboard or mouse in the appropriate PS/2 port.

4. Restart the computer. If the original mouse or keyboard was defective, you should be able to use the replacement and see it displayed in the Device Manager. If the port is defective, the replacement won't work either.

5. Replace the defective component; if the PS/2 port on the motherboard is bad, you need to replace the motherboard if you want to use PS/2 devices. However, if the PS/2 mouse port has failed, you can use a USB mouse. If the PS/2 keyboard port has failed and your BIOS is configured to enable USB keyboards to function at all times (USB Legacy mode enabled), you can use a USB keyboard.

Leo Says

Be Careful with PS/2 Ports!

I've seen a fair number of computers with fried PS/2 mouse ports, and I think I've finally figured out why: People forget that PS/2 ports are *not* hot-swappable ports! Don't try to change PS/2 mice or keyboards while your system is running; you might fry the port. A second reason for PS/2 mouse port failures is the shape of the port; sure it's keyed, but because it's round, there are a lot of wrong ways to plug in the mouse cable and damage something. USB ports have a much more foolproof design and are designed for hot-swapping and hot-plugging.

Using the System BIOS to Solve Problems with PS/2 Pointing Devices

The PS/2 mouse port uses a hardware resource called an IRQ. It uses IRQ 12, to be specific. If your PS/2 mouse won't work when you attach it to the PS/2 port, boot your computer and ensure that you don't have any other devices using IRQ 12 (see "IRQs," Chapter 1, p. 59); if no other devices are using IRQ 12, the port might not be enabled.

→ *For more information about the system BIOS, see "Controlling Your PC's Operation with BIOS Setup," Chapter 1, p. 41.*

Most computers with a PS/2 mouse port control the port through a setting in the system BIOS, although some older systems may use a jumper block on the motherboard to enable or disable the port. To view the current setting, shut down your computer, restart it, and press the key or key combination that starts the system BIOS setup program; if the correct keys are not displayed onscreen, check your computer or motherboard reference manual for the correct ones to press. Depending on the system, you might need to look in the Advanced menu (shown in Figure 7.26), the Integrated Ports menu, or other places.

FIGURE 7.26

A typical Award BIOS Advanced setup screen that controls the PS/2 mouse and USB Legacy (keyboard/mouse) functions. The Auto setting enables the devices when they are attached.

PS/2 mouse control

```
                          AwardBIOS Setup Utility
      Main    Advanced   Power    Boot    Exit
    Operating Frequency Setting  [Standard]       Item Specific Help
    CPU Clock Multiplier         [11.0x]
    CPU Frequency                [ 100 MHz]     This item provide the
    DRAM Frequency               [ 100 MHz]     user options to set the
    System Performance Setting   [Optimal]      operating frequency of
    CPU Vcore Setting            [Auto]         FSB.
    CPU Level 1 Cache            [Enabled]
    CPU Level 2 Cache            [Enabled]      [NOTE]:The options show
    CPU Level 2 Cache ECC Check  [Disabled]     up depending on the
    BIOS Update                  [Enabled]      Jumperfree jumper
    PS/2 Mouse Function Control  [Auto]         setting.
    USB Legacy Support           [Auto]
    OS/2 Onboard Memory > 64M    [Disabled]
  ▶ CHIP Configuration
  ▶ I/O Device Configuration
  ▶ PCI Configuration
  ▶ Shadow Configuration

    F1   Help    ↑↓  Select Item   /    Change Values    F5   Setup Defaults
    ESC  Exit    ←→  Select Menu   Enter Select ▶ Sub-Menu  F10  Save and Exit
```

USB Legacy (keyboard/mouse) control

Depending on the system, there are two or three options available for configuring ports in the BIOS:

- **Enabled**—This setting enables the port and uses IRQ 12 for the mouse, even if no mouse is present.

- **Disabled**—This setting turns off the port and frees up IRQ 12 for other devices.

- **Auto**—This setting, shown in Figure 7.26, enables the mouse only if it is present. If it is not present, IRQ 12 can be used for other devices.

If the mouse pointer won't move when you use a PS/2 pointing device, check the following:

- Determine if the PS/2 Mouse BIOS option is configured as Enabled or Auto (either of which will enable a PS/2 pointing device to work). If the setting is Disabled, enable the device and then restart the computer. Retry the mouse.

- If the PS/2 mouse was already configured as Enabled or Auto, but the mouse pointer won't move, open the mouse and make sure the rollers and ball are clean and working. If they are dirty, clean them and retry. If they appear OK, replace the pointing device with a known-working PS/2 mouse and retry. If a replacement mouse works, the original pointing device is defective and should be replaced. If the replacement doesn't work, the PS/2 mouse port is defective.

- If you determine that your PS/2 mouse port is defective and you don't want to replace your motherboard, use a USB mouse instead.

- If the mouse is connected to the PS/2 port by an adapter, the adapter could be defective or the mouse might not be compatible with the adapter. Make sure the mouse and adapter are designed to work together, or use a mouse without an adapter for testing the PS/2 port.

When (and Why) Adapters Don't Always Work

Most pointing device manufacturers package their devices with an adapter that enables the device to work with two different port types. The most common option today is to package a USB device with a PS/2 mouse port adapter. Serial mice were sometimes packaged with a PS/2 port adapter, and PS/2 mice have sometimes been packaged with a serial or a USB adapter. These mice are sometimes called *combo mice* because they can work with more than one port type.

However, although retail stores sell serial-to-PS/2 or PS/2-to-serial adapters separately, trying to use an adapter with a pointing device that's not designed for an adapter just won't work. The firmware inside the mouse has to be designed to handle different types of connectors for an adapter to work. What if you lose the adapter for your pointing device? You *might* be able to use a third-party replacement, but you're probably better off contacting the pointing device manufacturer for a replacement, or just upgrading to a newer model with more features.

The situation is much different with keyboards. Because the old, large 5-pin DIN connector used by older PCs uses the same signals as the 6-pin mini-DIN PS/2 connector used by newer keyboards, you can adapt either type of keyboard to either type of system—no problem. However, keyboards designed for USB ports won't work with adapters unless the manufacturers design that capability into their keyboards—and if they do, they will supply the adapter.

The bottom line is that if the pointing or input device is an OEM unit bundled with a computer, it's not designed to work with other interfaces. On the other hand, if you buy the device retail *and* an adapter is included, the device will work with that adapter. Otherwise, you're probably out of luck.

Troubleshooting Pointing Device Problems with Control Panel

If your mouse or other pointing device works, but you are not satisfied with its performance, compatibility, appearance, or movements, use the Mouse properties sheet in the Windows Control Panel to adjust these settings. Figure 7.27 shows the properties sheet tabs for a standard wheel mouse using standard Windows XP drivers. If you use a mouse with vendor-specific drivers or additional hardware features, you might see additional options.

Table 7.4 shows you how to use the Mouse properties sheet for Windows XP to solve common pointing device problems.

FIGURE 7.27
*The Mouse properties
sheet in Control Panel
for a Windows XP
system.*

TABLE 7.4
USING THE POINTING DEVICE PROPERTIES SHEET

Problem	Properties Sheet Tab to Use	Solution
I need to set up the mouse for a left-handed user.	Buttons	Select the Switch Primary and Secondary Buttons box.

TABLE 7.4 (continued)

Problem	Properties Sheet Tab to Use	Solution
Double-click doesn't work consistently.	Buttons	Use the Double-Click Speed slider and test box to adjust the speed.
Items are dragged around the screen after I click them, even if I don't hold down the primary mouse button.	Buttons	Clear the ClickLock option box; if the ClickLock option isn't selected, the primary mouse button is probably broken and the mouse should be replaced.
I need different (larger, animated, high-contrast) mouse pointers.	Pointers	Select the desired mouse scheme from the menu; install the mouse software provided by the vendor for additional schemes.
The pointer moves too fast or too slow.	Pointer Options	Adjust the Motion slider to the desired speed.
The pointer is hard to move over short distances or hard to stop.	Pointer Options	Enable the Enhance Pointer Precision option.
I'm tired of moving the pointer to a dialog to click OK.	Pointer Options	Enable the Snap To option.
The pointer disappears when it's moved quickly (especially on LCD displays).	Pointer Options	Enable the Pointer Trails option and select the desired trail length.
The pointer covers up typed text.	Pointer Options	Enable the Hide Pointer While Typing option.
The pointer is hard to find on a cluttered screen.	Pointer Options	Enable the Show Location When I Press CTRL Key option.
The scroll wheel motion is too fast or too slow.	Wheel	Select the number of lines to scroll with each click of the wheel, or select one screen at a time.

TABLE 7.4 (continued)

Problem	Properties Sheet Tab to Use	Solution
I'm not sure which pointing devices are active.	Hardware	This properties sheet displays the current device(s) and provides shortcuts to Troubleshooter and Properties.
The mouse pointer disappears or only appears on parts of the screen.	Pointer Options	Enable the Show Location When I Press CTRL key option. Note: You might also want to minimize and maximize the active application to force Windows to redraw the screen.

Using Other Methods to Diagnose Problems with Input Devices

As you have seen, the Windows Device Manager and Mouse Control Panel can fix many problems with input devices, but a defective input device might still be reported as "OK" by the Device Manager or might be connected to a fully BIOS-enabled and functioning port. If the BIOS settings are correct for your device and the Device Manager reports it as having no problems, but it still doesn't work, the device itself may be to blame. How can you tell? You can physically inspect the device, clean the device, unplug and reattach the device, and swap the device with another to make sure the device itself is to blame, as detailed here:

- **Physical inspection**—Take a good look at the device. If the device's cabling is cracked, frayed, or has loose wires, replace the device. If one or more of the pins in the connector are bent or broken, replace the device. If the mouse uses a ball and the mouse's ball is missing or the rollers are missing or broken, repair or replace the mouse. Test the batteries on a wireless device; if they're weak or dead, replace them. If you're using an optical or laser mouse, make sure the LED or laser is working, and make sure that the mousing surface isn't reflective or has a repeating pattern (both of which can confuse the motion sensor in the mouse).

- **Cleaning**—Gunk and dirt on mouse or trackball rollers can cause erratic pointer movements, or in extreme cases, no pointer movement at all. Use a mouse cleaning kit or carefully clean the rollers with alcohol-dipped swabs. Keyboards with sticky keys should be vacuumed out or blown out with compressed air. Wipe dust or dirt away from the bottom of an optical or laser mouse.

- **Unplugging and reattaching the device cable**—In many cases, this simple process fixes the problem. If the device connects to a PS/2 port, you will need to shut down the computer first, but if the device plugs into the USB port, you can unplug it and reattach it while the power's on, thanks to the hot-swappable nature of USB connections.

- **Parts swapping**—Swap a suspicious keyboard, mouse, or pointing device with another (preferably one that's known to be working) and see if the new device works OK. If it does, replace the old device. If no device works on the port, the port itself is defective, regardless of what the Windows Device Manager says about it or how it is configured in the BIOS.

When In Doubt, Turn It Off!

If you've decided it's time to swap a balky keyboard or mouse for one that works to figure out why you can't type or use your mouse anymore, don't forget to shut down and turn off your system if you're swapping PS/2 devices. Unlike newer USB devices, which can be hot-swapped, PS/2 keyboards, mice, and pointing devices can only be recognized if they're attached while the system is turned off. Also, make sure you attach the cable correctly. If you push the keyboard, mouse, or pointing device cable in at an angle, you could break the solder joints that carry signals between the connector and the motherboard. The only cure for *that* problem is a new motherboard!

If known-working devices don't work with your system, you can replace onboard USB ports with a USB card, but defective PS/2 ports mean that you're in the market for either new USB peripherals or a new motherboard.

Troubleshooting Serial and Parallel Ports

Serial and parallel ports aren't as popular as they once were; most new peripherals use USB ports instead. However, if you still use these ports, you don't need a lecture about the virtues of USB ports; you want help!

Both serial and parallel ports are often called *legacy* ports. These ports are similar in two ways:

- Built-in serial and parallel ports are ISA (Industry Standard Architecture) devices. They cannot share IRQs with other devices, making system configuration potentially more difficult than with USB and IEEE-1394 ports.

- Serial and parallel ports have heavy cables that use thumb-screws to secure them to the back of your PC. If you don't secure these cables, they can become loose, causing erratic device performance or device failure.

However, serial and parallel ports also differ in some ways from each other. Use the following sections to keep your legacy ports and the devices that depend on them working properly.

Parallel Port Troubleshooting

The most common problems with parallel (LPT) ports include:

- The parallel cable is not connected properly to the computer or device.

- Incorrect mode setting for the device(s) connected to the parallel port.

- The parallel cable does not support the selected parallel port mode.

- The parallel port hardware resources conflict with another device.

Connecting the Parallel Cable to the Computer and Device

A loose parallel cable can cause the following problems:

- Gibberish printing

- Failure to receive status messages from a parallel printer

- Inability to communicate with other parallel port devices

To make sure your parallel cable stays connected, secure it in place. The DB25M connector used to connect the cable to the parallel port on the PC or onto devices such as scanners or removable-media drives is equipped with thumbscrews. Tighten them securely, as shown in Figure 7.28, to avoid problems with the cable.

Thumbscrews on parallel cable

FIGURE 7.28
Using thumbscrews to secure a parallel cable to the PC's parallel port.

A parallel cable used with a parallel printer has two different connectors: A 25-pin male connector (DB25M) connects the cable to the parallel port on the PC, and a 36-pin Centronics edge connector connects the cable to the printer's parallel port. Instead of using thumbscrews, the printer uses retaining clips to hold the cable in place, as shown in Figure 7.29.

Troubleshooting Parallel Port Mode Settings

Parallel ports can operate in several modes:

- **Compatible**—Slow operation, output only
- **Normal**—Slow operation, limited bi-directional capabilities
- **Enhanced Parallel Port (EPP)**—High-speed printing and full bi-directional capabilities for reporting error or other status messages such as ink or toner levels
- **Enhanced Capabilities Port (ECP)**—High-speed printing and data transfer to devices other than printers (such as scanners and removable-media drives)
- **EPP/ECP**—Supports devices that use EPP or ECP mode

EPP, ECP, and EPP/ECP modes require the printer port to have a dedicated IRQ (normally 7); ECP and EPP/ECP modes also require a direct memory access (DMA) channel for data transfer (normally 3).

Retaining clips on parallel printer

FIGURE 7.29

Parallel printers use retaining clips to hold the parallel cable in place.

EPP, ECP, and EPP/ECC modes cannot work if the port has any hardware resource conflicts with other devices.

To check or change the parallel port mode and hardware resource settings currently in use for a built-in parallel port, follow these steps:

1. Restart the computer.

2. Start the system BIOS setup program.

3. Display the menu that contains the parallel (LPT) port settings. This is often called Integrated Peripherals or Integrated Ports; see your system or motherboard manual for details.

4. Compare the current parallel port setting to the setting recommended for the drive. If the current parallel port setting is not configured properly for the drive, change it to a suitable setting (see Figure 7.30). This setting most likely should be EPP, ECP, or EPP/ECP, but check your drive's manual to be sure.

5. Save any changes you made to the BIOS configuration and then restart the computer.

→ *To learn how to use the Windows Device Manager to detect and solve conflicts, see "Using Device Manager," Chapter 2, p. 100.*

→ *For more details about accessing and using the system BIOS setup program, see "Controlling Your PC's Operation with BIOS Setup," Chapter 1, p. 41.*

FIGURE 7.30

Selecting a different parallel port mode in the system BIOS.

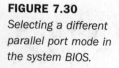

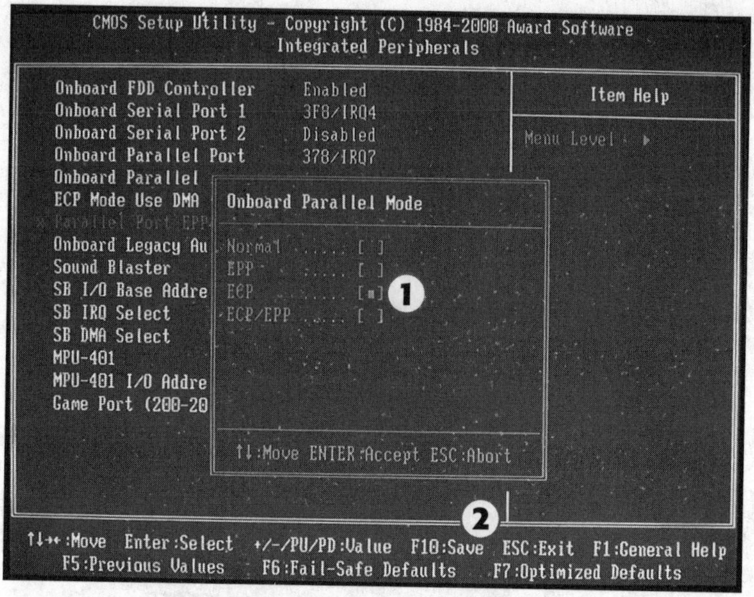

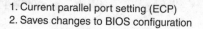

1. Current parallel port setting (ECP)
2. Saves changes to BIOS configuration

Troubleshooting a Disabled Parallel or Serial Port

If you need to connect a parallel or serial device to a PC that has not been used with a parallel device, you should make sure the port is not disabled. Some users prefer to disable the parallel and serial ports in the system BIOS to free up hardware resources for use by other devices.

To determine if the parallel or serial port is enabled, start Windows and open the Device Manager. Click the plus sign (+) next to the Ports (COM & LPT) category. If a parallel or serial port has been disabled in the system BIOS, it will not appear. If the port has been disabled in the Device Manager, it will appear with a red X across the port symbol. Figure 7.31 illustrates a system with a parallel port disabled in the system BIOS and a serial port disabled in Device Manager.

To enable a parallel or serial port disabled in the system BIOS, follow these steps:

→ *For more details about accessing and using the system BIOS setup program, see "Controlling Your PC's Operation with BIOS Setup," Chapter 1, p. 41.*

1. Restart the computer.

2. Start the system BIOS setup program.

3. Display the menu that contains the parallel (LPT) and serial (COM) port settings. This is often called Integrated Peripherals or Integrated Ports; see your system or motherboard manual for details.

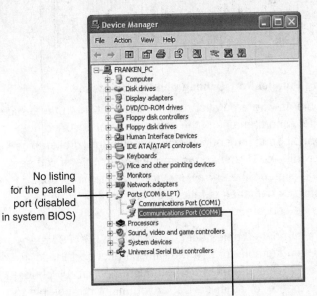

FIGURE 7.31
The Windows Device Manager's display of disabled parallel and serial ports.

No listing for the parallel port (disabled in system BIOS)

COM 4 disabled in Device Manager (red X)

4. Select the option to enable the port. Figure 7.32 compares the listing for parallel and serial ports when disabled and enabled.

FIGURE 7.32
Disabled (left) and enabled (right) parallel and serial ports.

5. If you are enabling both serial ports (COM 1 and COM 2), make sure that you set them to the defaults shown in Figure 7.32— IRQ4/3F8 (COM 1) and IRQ3/2F8 (COM 2)—or use Auto. If you use a graphics card with an ATI chipset, do not use IRQ3/2E8; this setting conflicts with an I/O port address on some ATI chipsets, and your system might not start.

6. Save changes and restart the system.

To enable a parallel or serial port disabled in Device Manager, follow these steps:

1. Open Device Manager.

2. Open the properties sheet for the port.

3. Select Enable.

4. Click OK.

Troubleshooting Parallel Port Cabling and Device Issues

If you have problems with a parallel port device, shut down the device, shut down the PC, and then check the cable (parallel ports do not support hot-swapping). If you notice cracked insulation, broken pins in the interface, or missing thumbscrews, replace the cable. If you see missing retaining clips on the printer, replace the retaining clips. However, defective or damaged parallel port cables aren't the only cable issues to be concerned about.

Virtually all parallel printer cables sold today meet IEEE-1284 standards, making them suitable for use with any parallel port mode. If you use an older parallel printer cable, you might not get full performance from your printer or other device, or you might not be able to receive status or error messages from your printer.

IEEE-1284 compatibility is also important if you need to replace or extend the cables included with other types of parallel devices. If you no longer have the packaging, check the cable itself; many 1284-compatible cables list IEEE-1284 compliance on the outer jacket of the cable.

Make sure you use a straight-through device cable. Don't use a file-transfer cable for connecting to a device, such as the cables made for Direct Parallel Connection, LapLink, or Direct Cable Connection. Parallel file-transfer cables feature crossover connections at one end of the cable and omit other wires needed for parallel devices.

Parallel port drives or scanners must be turned on before they can be recognized and used. If the drive's software was installed and the drive was turned on and connected to a properly configured parallel port without any resource conflicts, but the drive can't be recognized, you might need to update the drive's device drivers. Check with the vendor's website for updates and details.

Troubleshooting Parallel Port Daisy-Chaining Issues

Since parallel ports were not originally designed to connect to devices other than printers, daisy-chaining a drive and another device other than a printer to a parallel port might not work (normally, a drive plus a printer will work with little difficulty).

If you have the drive plugged into another device that is plugged into the parallel port, make sure the other device and the drive are turned on before you turn on the computer. If the drive still won't work, shut down the computer and all devices and plug your drive directly into the parallel port. If the drive works when it's plugged directly into the parallel port, but not when it's connected to the other device, you might not be able to use the two devices on the same port. Try adjusting the mode (EPP, ECP, EPP/ECP) and connecting the other device to the drive to see if reversing the order of devices in the daisy-chain will work correctly.

Serial Port Troubleshooting

The major causes of serial port problems include:

- Serial cable not connected properly to the computer or device
- Serial port disabled in the system BIOS or Device Manager
- Two serial ports set to the same IRQ
- Conflicts between a serial port configured as COM 4 and some video cards

The odds of serial port problems increase if your computer has more than one active serial port.

Connecting the Serial Cable to the Serial Port

The serial port on a PC uses a DB9M connector, so the serial cable uses a DB9F connector. Although serial cables are much lighter than parallel cables, you should use the thumbscrews provided to prevent the cable from being bumped or falling off (see Figure 7.33).

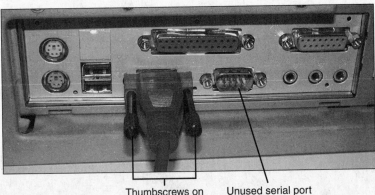

Thumbscrews on a serial cable

Unused serial port

FIGURE 7.33
Connecting a serial cable to a serial port.

Troubleshooting a Disabled Serial Port

To determine if the serial ports in your system have been disabled in the system BIOS or Device Manager, or to enable them, see "Troubleshooting a Disabled Parallel or Serial Port," this chapter, p. 456.

Preventing IRQ Conflicts Involving Serial Ports

Serial ports can be set to one of four combinations of IRQ and I/O port address:

- IRQ4/3F8 (COM1)
- IRQ3/2F8 (COM2)
- IRQ4/3E8 (COM3)
- IRQ3/2E8 (COM4)

If you need to use two serial ports, use the first two settings listed or configure your ports to use the Auto setting shown in Figure 7.32.

Don't use settings that use the same IRQ for both serial ports. This causes a hardware conflict if you need to use both ports at the same time.

If you use video cards that use older ATI chipsets, don't use the COM4 setting, because this can cause your system to fail to boot.

Troubleshooting Your Network and Internet Connections

TROUBLESHOOTING

FAST TRACK TO SOLUTIONS (SYMPTOM TABLE)

Symptom	Flowchart or Book Section	See Page
I can't connect to the Internet.	Can't Connect to Internet	**667**
Network users can't change or copy files to a shared folder.	Can't Access Shared Files	**672**
Some users on the network can't access shared resources.	Some Network Users Can't Access Shared Resouces	**673**
I can't download a file from a website.	File Download Problems	**671**
I can't open or view a particular web page, although other pages open properly.	Web Page Problems	**670**
I can't use email.	Email Problems	**669**
I can't view some types of web content.	Troubleshooting Missing or Outdated Software Components	**466**
I can't open a secured website.	Troubleshooting Problems with Secure Web Sites	**469**
How can I tell if my browser is connecting to a secured website?	Sidebar: Easy Ways to Determine Secured Sites	**470**
Some of my favorite websites use Java, but my copy of Internet Explorer doesn't include Java.	Sidebar: With IE, You'll Need to Add Java	**473**
The colors used on some web pages are hard to read.	Website Viewing Tips and Tricks	**475**
I don't understand the security warnings displayed when I try to download an ActiveX control.	Troubleshooting Problems with Viewing Certain Web Sites	**471**
What do the most common website error messages mean?	Dealing with Website Error Messages	**474**

TROUBLESHOOTING

FAST TRACK TO SOLUTIONS, *Continued*

Symptom	Flowchart or Book Section	See Page
I want to save a web page as a document so I can view it or email it at a later time.	Sidebar: Grabbing the Troubleshooting Information You Need the Easy Way	**477**
My browser keeps crashing	Sidebar: Stopping Browser Crashes without Deleting Vital Information	**478**
I've just moved, and I need to change the dial-up number I use to connect to the Internet.	The Dial-Up Networking General Tab	**480**
I use a dial-up Internet connection in various locations, and I don't want to keep entering the dial-up number every time.	The Dial-Up Networking General Tab	**480**
I'm having a hard time connecting to my dial-up provider, or the connection drops out when I'm reading my email	The Dial-Up Networking Options Tab	**482**
I need to configure my dial-up or PPPoE Internet connection to use a fixed IP address.	Using a Fixed IP Address with a Dial-Up or PPPoE Broadband Connection in Windows XP	**534**
I need to configure my cable modem, DSL modem or wireless Internet connection with a fixed IP address.	Using a Fixed IP Address with a LAN, Cable Modem or Fixed Wireless Connection in Windows XP	**535**
I need to configure a computer on the network with a fixed IP address.	Using a Fixed IP Address with a LAN, Cable Modem or Fixed Wireless Connection in Windows XP	**535**
When I try to connect to the Internet with my modem, there's no dial tone.	Modem Has No Dial Tone	**484**
My computer dials, but I never connect with the remote computer.	PC Can Dial but Does Not Connect	**485**

TROUBLESHOOTING

FAST TRACK TO SOLUTIONS, *Continued*

Symptom	Flowchart or Book Section	See Page
I get a "port already open" error when I try to connect to the Internet with my modem.	Port Already Open/Modem in Use by Another Application	**487**
I'm not sure my modem is working.	Troubleshooting Dial-Up Modem Hardware	**484**
I'm not sure my network cables are plugged in properly.	Troubleshooting a Broadband Internet Connection	**490**
I'm not sure the connections to my cable modem are working.	Troubleshooting a Cable Modem Connection	**490**
I'm having problems with my DSL connection to the Internet.	Troubleshooting a DSL Connection	**492**
I'm having problems with my DirecWAY, Starband, or other satellite Internet connection.	Troubleshooting a Satellite Connection	**494**
The signal lights on my broadband Internet modem don't look right.	Using Signal Lights to Troubleshoot Your Connection	**494**
I'm not sure what settings are needed for my home network.	Troubleshooting Network Software Configuration	**495**
I connect to the Internet through a router, and I've lost my connection.	Troubleshooting Routers and Gateways	**524**
I need to find out what Internet settings my computer is using.	Using IPCONFIG	**536**
How do I use PING to test my Internet connection?	Using PING	**538**
How can I find out if my network adapter is working?	Troubleshooting Network Adapter Installations	**506**
How can I check my cabling?	Troubleshooting Cabling	**510**
I connected my computer to the Uplink port on a switch or router and now I can't connect to the Internet.	Troubleshooting Cabling	**510**

TROUBLESHOOTING

FAST TRACK TO SOLUTIONS, *Continued*

Symptom	Flowchart or Book Section	See Page
I'm having problems adding a computer to my wireless network.	Troubleshooting Wi-Fi Networks	512
	Using the Windows XP SP2 Wireless Network Setup Wizard	521
Can I use an 802.11a wireless network adapter with an 801.11b or 802.11g network?	Sidebar: Wi-Fi Isn't Completely Standard	528
I can't get a CardBus or PC Card network adapter to work in my notebook computer.	Troubleshooting PC Card/CardBus Devices	531
I can access the Internet, but I can't see other computers or shared resources on the network.	I'm Not Sure My Network Settings Are Correct	499
I want a fast way to fix common problems with Windows XP's Internet and network connections.	Troubleshooting Your Network/Internet Connections	541
	Using Net Diagnostics	541
I can't use File and Printer Sharing when I enable the Windows XP Firewall.	SP2 Firewall Exceptions	543
I need to reset the Windows XP Firewall to its default settings.	SP2 Firewall Advanced Settings	545
How do I use PING to check my connection to the Internet?	Using TCP/IP Diagnostics to Troubleshoot Your Connection	536
	Using PING	538
How do I use IPCONFIG to check my network configuration?	Using TCP/IP Diagnostics to Troubleshoot Your Connection	536
	Using IPCONFIG	536

Once upon a time, the hardware, software, and methods used to connect computers were divided into two distinct categories:

- Dial-up connections
- Network connections

Today, that's no longer the case. Whether you use a dial-up modem, a broadband Internet connection, or a home network, Windows XP uses the same interface, My Network Connections, to store and configure your connections. The TCP/IP protocol has become universal for both Internet connections and network configuration. Also, as more and more of us move to broadband and away from dial-up, more computer users than ever before are using a wired or wireless network adapter as their connection both to other computers and to the Internet.

Although standardizing on TCP/IP as the common software for both Internet access and networking makes initial configuration a bit easier in some ways, networking and Internet access are far from "no-brainers," especially when things go wrong. In this chapter, we'll help you deal with the most common problems that can spoil your online and networking experience, including the following:

- Defective modem or network hardware
- Loose cables
- Problems with wireless network configuration
- Incorrect TCP/IP configuration settings
- Missing or outdated software components such as browsers, plug-ins, and ActiveX controls

Troubleshooting Missing or Outdated Software Components

Depending on the type of Internet access you have (dial-up or broadband) and the types of web content you plan to access, you need to install a variety of Windows components and programs to fully enjoy the Internet.

Use the checklist in Table 8.1 to determine whether your system has up-to-date components.

TABLE 8.1
SOFTWARE COMPONENTS NEEDED FOR INTERNET ACCESS

Task	Software Needed	Where to Get It	Where to Get Downloads/ Updates
Web browsing	Internet Explorer 6.x or above; Mozilla Firefox 1.x or above	Install IE from Windows CD-ROM; download Firefox.	Windows Update[1] or http://www.microsoft.com/windows/ie/default.mspx (Internet Explorer); http://www.mozilla.org (Firefox)
Reading Adobe Acrobat (.PDF) files	Adobe Reader 7.x or above	Download from Adobe.	http://www.adobe.com/products/acrobat
Connecting to the Internet (all types)	Windows TCP/IP components	Install from Windows CD-ROM.	Windows Update
Virtual Private Networking (VPN; used to create a secure connection between your remote computer and your office network)	Windows VPN components	Install from Windows CD-ROM.	Windows Update
Email	Email client such as Microsoft Outlook Express or Mozilla Thunderbird, Eudora, or others	Outlook Express is included in IE. MS Outlook needs to be purchased separately or as part of MS Office. Thunderbird, Eudora, and others must be downloaded from vendor.	Windows Update (Outlook Express); http://office.microsoft.com/en-us/officeupdate/default.aspx (Office Update); http://www.mozilla.org (Thunderbird); http://www.eudora.com (Eudora)
Viewing Flash animation (used for many website front ends)	Flash Player	Often comes preinstalled with browser.	http://www.macromedia.com

1. To access Windows Update, click the Windows Update icon on your Start menu, or set your Internet Explorer browser to http://windowsupdate.microsoft.com.

Installing New Windows Components

In some cases, even if your ISP provides you with a signup kit or a setup CD, you might need to install or reinstall some Windows components to configure your Internet connection or make it work better for you.

With any recent version of Windows, open the Add/Remove Programs icon in Control Panel to get started. Select Add/Remove Windows components and then select the Windows components you need from the list. Be sure to click the Details button to see the specific items in each category.

If you installed Windows yourself, insert the Windows CD-ROM when prompted. If Windows was pre-installed, a folder on your computer might have the Windows files you can install. If Windows asks you if you want to replace a newer component with an older file, either during the component installation process or at other times, answer No. You want the latest, freshest Windows components to keep Windows working properly.

Installing/Reinstalling ISP Setup Software

Most ISPs provide an installation kit on CD-ROM that installs at least Dial-Up Networking (if needed), TCP/IP components (TCP/IP is a computer language that must be used by all computers and devices on the Internet), and Internet Explorer/Outlook Express 6.x or above (some vendors might supply Mozilla Firefox instead of IE). You might need to provide the following information (assigned to you by your ISP) during the installation process:

- Telephone number to use for Dial-Up Networking access
- Username (for logging into the Internet)
- Password
- Email name (usually the same as the username)

Be sure to record this information in a safe place (*not* in a file stored on your PC, lest you lose it to a hard disk failure or a nosy hacker!) in case you need to reinstall your Internet access software.

If you damage your Internet software configuration through making changes to the Network Neighborhood/My Network Places properties sheets, rerun the installation software and provide the needed information to configure your connection again. Then, download and install updates as noted in Table 8.1.

After you've installed the software provided by your ISP, you should run Windows Update to install security or other updates for Internet Explorer, Outlook Express, or TCP/IP software.

Use the Windows Update icon on your Start menu to access Windows Update (or enter http://windowsupdate.microsoft.com into your IE address window), which will automatically detect the version of Windows and Internet Explorer installed on your system and will select the updates needed.

Stay Secure with Critical Updates

After you connect with Windows Update the first time, be sure to download and install the critical updates first. These help protect your system against various Internet threats. Then, select other updates listed according to your needs.

If you choose not to enable automatic critical updates, be sure to run Windows Update at least once a week as well as whenever you find out about security issues that require new critical updates.

If your ISP doesn't provide a setup program, see either "TCP/IP Configuration and Troubleshooting" (p. 533) to learn how a broadband Internet connection is configured, or "Configuring Dial-Up Networking" (p. 478) if you use an analog (dial-up) modem.

Troubleshooting Problems with Secure Websites

If you can browse the Web, but can't connect to secure websites such as online stores, e-banking, or stock trading sites, you are probably using a browser with incorrectly configured security settings.

Security in online transactions is based on the strength of the encryption used to scramble data in transit between your browser and the secured website. Encryption strength is commonly expressed in bits: the higher the bits, the greater the number of possible combinations of information that can be used to encrypt the data, and the greater the security. All current browsers, including Internet Explorer 5.5 or greater, Mozilla Firefox, Netscape 6.x or greater, and Opera version 3.5 or greater, support 128-bit encryption as standard in most world areas, enabling your web browser to connect to secure sites.

Easy Ways to Determine Secured Sites

To determine whether a website is secure, look for these clues:

- A website URL that begins with https:// instead of http:// is a secured site (the s stands for *secured*).
- IE and Mozilla Firefox use a padlock in the lower-right side of the browser window to indicate a secure site.
- Netscape displays a key in the lower-left side of the browser window to indicate a secure site.
- Opera displays a padlock symbol to the left of the URL address bar at all times: An open padlock means the site is not secure, and the number of squares next to a closed padlock indicate the level of security on the site. One square means low security, two squares means medium security, and three squares means high security. Recent versions also display a yellow security bar on secure sites; click this bar to learn more about the security certificate in use.

VeriSign and Website Security 101

VeriSign, a major provider of website security technologies, has an easy-to-understand FAQ about basic website security:

http://www.verisign.com.au/support/server/knowledgebase/technicalfaq.shtml

Even if a web browser is designed for 128-bit encryption, it's possible to disable its ability to connect to secure sites. The current security standard is SSL (Secure Sockets Layer). Another standard, TLS (Transport Layer Security), might replace SSL eventually, but should not be enabled at present unless you encounter a website that specifically supports it; TLS can interfere with SSL's operation. To make sure that SSL is enabled, follow these instructions:

- In Internet Explorer, click Tools, Internet Options, Advanced, and scroll down to Security (see Figure 8.1).
- In Mozilla Firefox, click Tools, Options, Advanced, click the plus sign (+) next to Security.
- In Netscape 6.x and above, click Tasks, Privacy and Security, Security Manager, Advanced, Options.
- In Opera, click Preferences/Security.

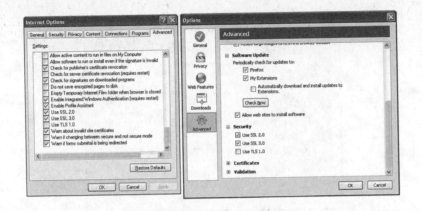

FIGURE 8.1

Viewing SSL and TLS security settings in Internet Explorer (left) and Mozilla Firefox (right).

Don't Forget to Take Your Favorites/Bookmarks with You

If you decide it's time to switch browsers, you don't need to lose your favorite sites. With IE, use the File, Import and Export menu to create an HTML file of your Favorites folder, which you can transfer to another browser such as Netscape or Opera. Firefox also allows you to import URLs from IE or Netscape 6 and above with the File, Import menu option. If you want to move your bookmarks out of another browser to IE, use the same menu. Follow the prompts, and it's easy to use your favorites or bookmarks in other places.

Troubleshooting Problems with Viewing Certain Websites

Although your web browser is designed to display pages written in the Internet's Hypertext Markup Language (HTML) and some types of graphics, many websites have content or features that require you to install additional software to view the content or use the website's special features. If you don't have this additional software, the site either won't load or will be missing content or features. To enable your browser to view active content, you need to grant the website permission to install the software. In the initial release of Windows XP and in Service Pack 1, the dialog used by Internet Explorer was similar to the one shown in Figure 8.2.

FIGURE 8.2

A typical security warning from the IE browser that prompts you to accept or reject the ActiveX or Java software that a website wants to install on your system.

Security Warning

Do you want to install and run "Crescendo version 5.0 Part 1 of 2" signed on 6/15/2000 8:02 AM and distributed by:

LiveUpdate

Publisher authenticity verified by VeriSign Commercial Software Publishers CA

Caution: LiveUpdate asserts that this content is safe. You should only install/view this content if you trust LiveUpdate to make that assertion.

☐ Always trust content from LiveUpdate

| Yes | No | More Info |

However, starting in Windows XP Service Pack 2, the dialog changed to make your system more secure. In many cases, you must right-click an Information Bar and select Install ActiveX Control to start the process.

Next, you see a new dialog similar to the one shown at the upper-left part of Figure 8.3. If you want to download only this particular control from the website, click Install. However, to have the option to automatically accept or block all downloads from this website, click More Options and choose the appropriate option. To view the digital signature used by the file, click the name of the provider. To learn about the risks of downloading an ActiveX control, click What's the Risk? Figure 8.3 also shows these optional dialogs.

Some websites will automatically offer you the control so that you can access the site's special features, such as live music, animations, or movies. In other cases, the website will offer links you must click to download the control.

When a security warning pops up, look carefully at the name of the program and its provider before you accept the program. Many advertising-sponsored websites have their own version of spam: They offer you unsolicited ActiveX controls, where the box offering the program pops up even though you didn't click anything to request the download. Many of these programs are known as *spyware*, because their primary function is to gather information about your web-surfing habits, or *adware*, because they display pop-up ads that might, or might not, be connected to your web-surfing habits. Typically, such programs offer to perform other services for you, and you must look closely at the user agreement to discover that they are spying on you, using your computer's idle time to perform tasks for the software provider, and so forth.

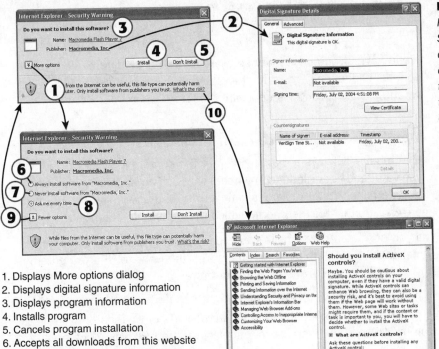

FIGURE 8.3

From the basic Security Warning dialog (top left), you can get details about the digital signature of the file (top right), choose how to handle future downloads from the same vendor (bottom left), or learn more about ActiveX controls (bottom right).

1. Displays More options dialog
2. Displays digital signature information
3. Displays program information
4. Installs program
5. Cancels program installation
6. Accepts all downloads from this website
7. Rejects any downloads from this website
8. Each download is prompted (default)
9. Switches back to basic dialog
10. Opens IE Help page on ActiveX controls

Leo Says

Just Because They Offer It Doesn't Mean I'll Take It

I've prevented a lot of spyware and adware from entering my system with a simple test: If I didn't ask for a website control, I think twice about installing it; I'll install it only if I really need the content the control provides. If the program has nothing to do with the site's purpose, I won't install it at all. Try these simple tests before you install an unsolicited website control, and I think you'll also reduce your problems with spyware and adware.

With IE, You'll Need to Add Java

Microsoft no longer includes its version of Java (Java VM) in recent versions of Internet Explorer. If you go to a website that uses Java and you don't have Java VM or Sun Microsystems's Java plug-in installed, you'll be prompted to install Sun's Java Runtime Environment (JRE). Because many website features won't work without Java, install it, although it could take several minutes (depending on the speed of your connection).

→ *To learn more about detecting and stopping spyware, see "Slamming Spyware," Chapter 2, p. 160.*

Get the latest version of Sun's Java Runtime Environment from http://java.sun.com/j2se/1.5.0/download.jsp.

If you have all the necessary software to view a website properly and you still experience problems, the source of your troubles is elsewhere. The next sections deal with those problems.

Dealing with Website Error Messages

If a website displays a blank screen or the content looks distorted and you've already downloaded any necessary add-on software, you need to determine if the problem is with your URL, the website, or with a browser that is not the one for which the website is optimized.

If you don't see the website you expected but you see a numeric error message instead, there's a problem with the website URL you entered or with the web page itself, not your browser.

The most common numerical error is a "404 – Not Found" error. This indicates the document you requested could not be found. If you typed in the URL yourself, check your spelling. If the URL was a link from another site, the link is out of date or misspelled. As more and more websites switch to database-driven or dynamic designs, expect to see more of these errors if you're using a list of website links that hasn't been updated lately. Some websites customize their 404 error message page to provide you with help in resolving the problem.

Leo Says

Beating the 404 Blues

If you get a 404 error the next time you follow a link, try these tips to help you find the page you want:

- Edit the URL so you go to the home page of the website; then search for the page by its title (if you know it) or an unusual word or phrase likely to be on the page. If the website doesn't have its own search engine, use Google or another search engine that permits you to specify a specific site to search. In Google, use site:*thesite.com* as part of your search (replace *thesite.com* with the actual name of your search).

- If the website was stored on a hosted site such as AOL, Tripod, or similar (these sites have URLs similar to http://*www.host.com/~mysite*), try searching for the name of the site or the name of the site creator using Google or another search engine. Popular websites often outgrow the limitations of bandwidth or size imposed by site hosts and move to their own URL.

Other errors you might encounter include the following:

- **401 – Unauthorized**—Your browser didn't supply the correct credentials for the web page (such as a username and password); if you are an authorized user, you need to log into the main website and then access the page. The 403 (Forbidden) error is similar.

- **500 – Internal Error**—The website server has a software error that prevents it from sending you the page.

- **502 – Service Temporarily Overloaded**—The website can't service your request because of too much traffic. If you go to a website featured in a blog or web article, you might see this for a few hours or a couple of days after the site was first listed. Bookmark it and check it again after the initial surge of traffic has quieted down.

The 400 series of errors indicates a problem with the URL address or with your credentials, whereas the 500 series of errors indicates a problem with the website server.

An error such as "Host Unavailable" or "Unable to Locate Host" could indicate either a temporary problem with the website host, a lost Internet connection, or a mistyped URL. Check your spelling or try again later. If you can't browse to any sites, your connection is down.

400s, 500s, and the Rest of the Error Message Gang

Of the numerous websites that list common website error messages, I recommend the Webopedia "Web Server Error Messages" page at http://www.webopedia.com/quick_ref/error.asp.

Website Viewing Tips and Tricks

An increasing number of users are tired of the frequent security updates necessary for Microsoft Internet Explorer and are switching to Mozilla's Firefox web browser. We like Firefox, which offers tabbed windows and many open source add-ons, but we're not ready to abandon Internet Explorer just yet.

Many websites are optimized for Internet Explorer's not-always-standard method of rendering web pages, and browsers such as Opera and Firefox (which actually follow the official rules for HTML more closely than IE) don't always display some pages properly. You also need to use Internet Explorer to use Windows Update to keep your system up to date.

In addition to viewing certain sites in the web browser the site was optimized for, here are some other tricks that can help you view sites that are hard to read:

- Highlight the text to reverse foreground and background colors. Many website designers have gone for "cool" instead of "readable." This can result in text that may be hard to read or even invisible, depending on your browser's settings. Click your mouse at the start of the text you want to read and hold down the left button as you highlight the text. This can make a lot of hard-to-read pages easier to read.

- Permanently force your browser to use your choice of colors rather than the designer's. See the following web page for details for various versions of both IE and Netscape:

  http://www.blind.org.uk/adjust_browser.html

  The directions listed for Internet Explorer 5/6 also work for Mozilla Firefox.

- If you're desperate for the information that's available on a "blank" page but you can't highlight the page with your mouse (and you understand HTML tags), use the View Source or Page Source option to display the contents of a "blank" page. Even if your browser is baffled by the HTML on a particular web page, you can click View, Source (IE) or View, Page Source (Netscape) to open a window that shows the actual HTML code used to create the page. If you're trying to find a link on the page, look for a URL inside the `<a href>` code, as in this example:

  ```
  <a href=http://www.mozilla.org/source.html>Source Code</a>
  ```

  Highlight the URL (in this example, the URL is http://www.mozilla.org/source.html), copy it, and paste it into your browser to go to the website.

- Use the Text Size option in your browser to shrink oversized text or enlarge tiny text to make it easier to read. In IE, click View, Text Size to display a list of choices. In Firefox, click View, Increase (or Decrease) Text Size.

Grabbing the Troubleshooting Information You Need the Easy Way

One of the best reasons to use the Internet is because it's the gateway to immense amounts of troubleshooting information. Instead of running your inkjet printer dry to print tutorials, FAQs, and articles, use your browser to capture the information you need to your hard disk.

If you want to save a picture or a file from a website where there's no specific "download" link, right-click the picture or file reference and select Save As or Save Target As from the menu. In some cases the link displayed is not the actual file, but it displays another page where the actual link is displayed.

If you want to save the entire page as displayed in your browser with IE, click File, Save As, Web Archive, which creates a file ending with .MHT. This single file stores all the text and graphics, and you can view it in any recent browser and print it if you want to. You can save web pages in other browsers, but they save the page and its graphics in separate files.

Please note, however, that images appearing on websites generally are copyrighted, meaning that although nothing is stopping you from copying them to your hard drive for reference, you are not free to distribute them or include them in your own documents.

Internet Options

The Internet Options icon doubles as the properties sheet for Internet Explorer (IE). It has seven tabs:

- **General**—Configures your home page, temporary files, history, screen colors, fonts, languages, and accessibility features.
- **Security**—Configures security zones.
- **Privacy**—Configures cookie settings.
- **Content**—Configures the Content Advisor (used to control access to sites based on content ratings or user selections), digital certificates, and personal information that is used to auto-complete forms or is provided to websites.
- **Connections**—Configures dial-up and LAN settings.
- **Programs**—Used to select the default programs to use for Web browsing, email, and other Internet tasks.
- **Advanced**—Custom settings for many IE features.

Stopping Browser Crashes Without Deleting Vital Information

If IE crashes frequently, you should click the General tab and select Delete Files to clear out the disk cache (stored web content). However, don't click Delete Cookies if you want easy access to websites that require registration; the cookie files that store your registration information will be lost if you click Delete Cookies. To delete certain files only, click Settings, View Files to display the contents of your Temporary Internet Files folder and select only the cookie or other files you want to remove.

With Mozilla Firefox, click Tools, Options, Privacy to open the dialog for clearing the cache and other information. Click the plus sign next to each listing for more information or more options.

Troubleshooting a Dial-Up (Analog Modem) Connection

Although dial-up (analog modem) connections are stored in the Network Connections folder in Windows XP, they differ in many ways from other types of network connections. Some typical problems include the following:

- Incorrect telephone number
- Incorrect username or password
- Loose or damaged RJ-11 telephone cable
- No dial tone
- Modem failure
- Driver corruption or incorrect driver installed
- Windows software component corruption
- Busy signal or server problems at the ISP

Configuring Dial-Up Networking

If you need to manually configure a dial-up networking connection for an analog modem connection to the Internet or for connecting to a remote computer, here's the information you need for any connection:

- The telephone number, including the area code for the ISP or remote computer
- Your username and password (if required)

You should write down this information (and keep it in a secure location) in case you need to re-create your dial-up network connection manually.

By default, a dial-up connection assumes that you are connecting to an ISP's server. If you cannot connect, contact the ISP for additional settings that may be required. In rare cases, you might need to specify a particular Internet Protocol (IP) address provided by the ISP for your machine, but most dial-up Internet connections automatically assign you a new IP address whenever you connect. See Figure 8.4 for a typical example of dial-up networking with Windows XP.

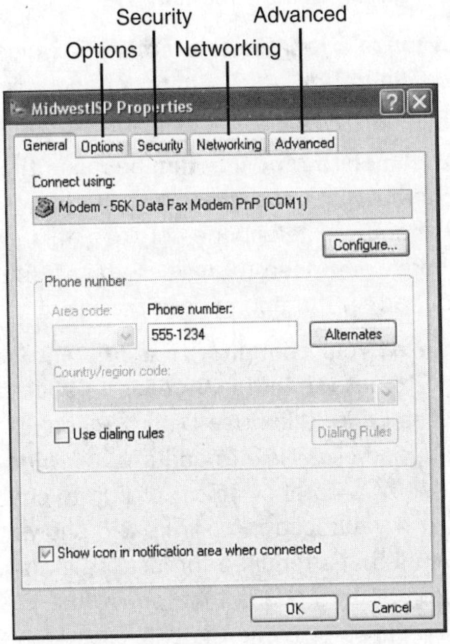

FIGURE 8.4
The properties sheet for a dial-up networking connection in Windows XP.

In most cases, you should never need to adjust the settings on these tabs if your ISP provided a configuration program to set up your connection. However, if your ISP changes how it handles Internet connections, if you change locations, or if your ISP provided you with manual Internet connection instructions instead of a setup program, you might need to work with these tabs to create a new connection or correct problems with an existing connection.

The Dial-Up Networking General Tab

The General tab (refer to Figure 8.4) lets you view and configure the following settings:

- The modem used for the connection
- The telephone number
- Any dialing rules needed to make the connection
- Status icon display in the system tray

Generally, you should not need to change these options from the settings originally supplied by your ISP or configured by the ISP's setup program except in the following circumstances:

- **You cannot make a reliable connection because of your modem's configuration.** Click Configure and adjust the settings as recommended by your ISP's help desk (see Figure 8.5).

- **You cannot complete a connection because the ISP's dial-up telephone number has changed.** With the explosion in new area codes and alternative telephone services, this might be the most common change you need to make. Enter the number and area code (if required) in the appropriate fields.

- **You have moved your computer to a different location that requires you to enter additional codes to access an outside line or an area code.** Click Use Dialing Rules, click the Dialing Rules button, and click New to add a location (recommended for temporary use at a hotel or office) or Edit to change the dialing rules for your default location. Figure 8.6 shows the General dialog, which is all that's required for local calls. If you will be calling from different area codes that require the area code plus number to be dialed to make the call, click Area Code Rules and specify how to handle calls using an area code. If you want to use a calling card, click Calling Card, select the calling card you use (or click New to create a new calling card setting), and enter the account and PIN number you use.

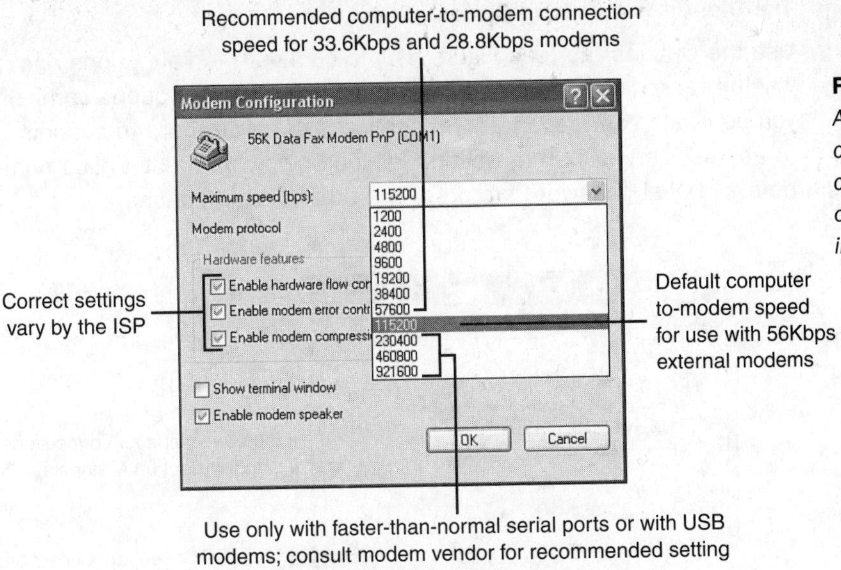

Recommended computer-to-modem connection
speed for 33.6Kbps and 28.8Kbps modems

FIGURE 8.5

Adjusting the computer-to-modem connection speed and other modem settings in Windows XP.

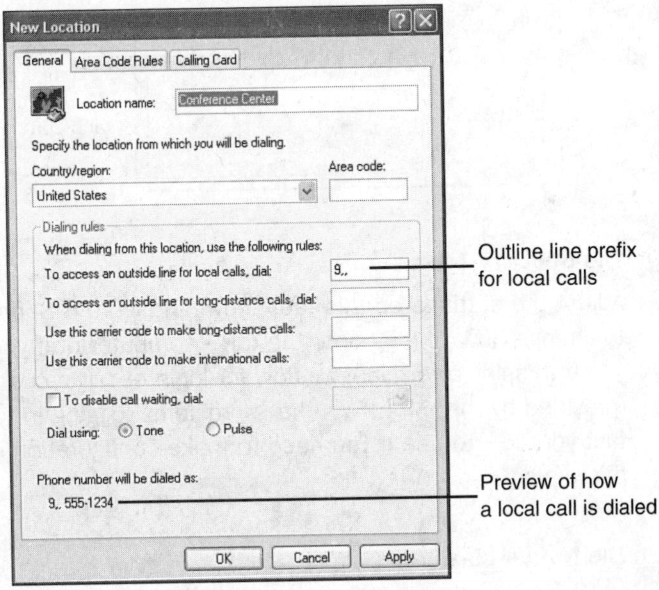

Correct settings
vary by the ISP

Default computer
to-modem speed
for use with 56Kbps
external modems

Use only with faster-than-normal serial ports or with USB
modems; consult modem vendor for recommended setting

FIGURE 8.6

Creating a new dialing rule for use when the modem is connected through a switchboard that requires the user to request an outside line.

Outline line prefix
for local calls

Preview of how
a local call is dialed

The Dial-Up Networking Options Tab

Use the Options tab (see Figure 8.7) to configure redial options and whether to redial if the connection is dropped. These options can help you deal with overloaded dial-up services, which are hard to connect to at peak periods. Other options let you specify different dial-up numbers, optional password prompts, and other dialing options.

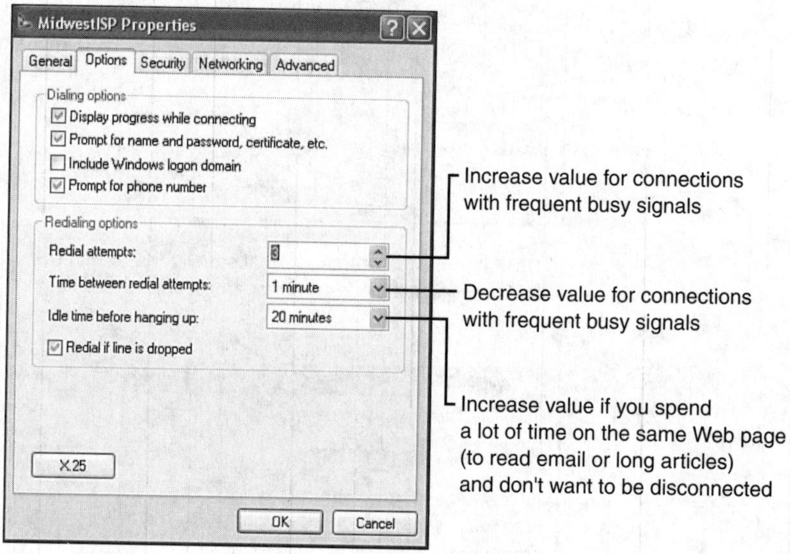

FIGURE 8.7

Adjusting redialing options in Windows XP.

Increase value for connections with frequent busy signals

Decrease value for connections with frequent busy signals

Increase value if you spend a lot of time on the same Web page (to read email or long articles) and don't want to be disconnected

The Security Tab

Adjust the settings on this tab, shown in Figure 8.8, only if you need to change how you log onto the ISP's computer or if your ISP requires you to display a terminal window for login or run a customized script (provided by the ISP). If you have problems logging in to your ISP, contact your ISP to see if you need to make configuration changes with this dialog.

The Networking Tab

Use the Networking tab (see Figure 8.9) if your ISP requires you to adjust how the dialup server connection is made or if you need to modify the default settings for network software components. For example, if your ISP requires you to specify a particular IP address for your computer, you would need to adjust the properties for Internet Protocol (TCP/IP) and add the IP address information provided by your ISP for your account.

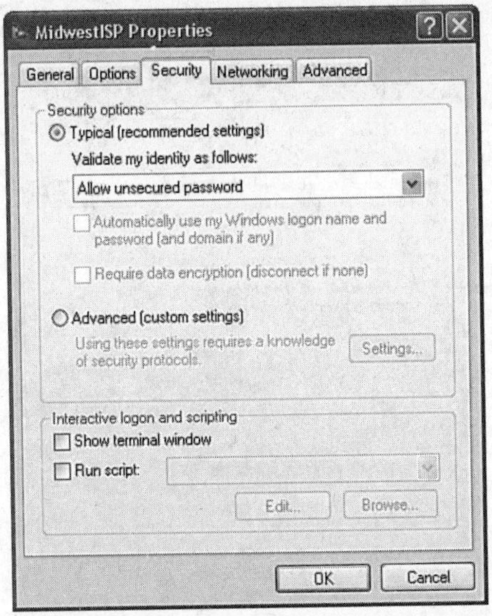

FIGURE 8.8
The Security dialog for a dial-up connection.

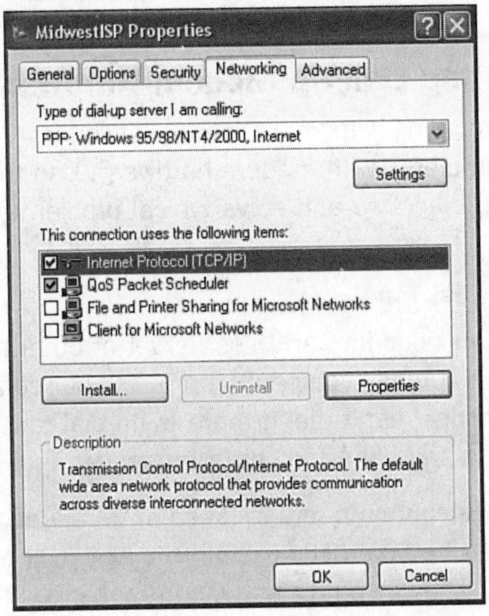

FIGURE 8.9
The Networking tab for Windows XP's Dial-Up Networking configuration.

The Advanced Tab

Open the Advanced tab (see Figure 8.10) to configure Windows XP's Windows Firewall (which prevents unsolicited access to your computer from the Internet) or to configure your computer to share its Internet connection with Internet Connection Sharing.

FIGURE 8.10
Use the Advanced tab to set up Internet Connection Sharing and the Windows Firewall.

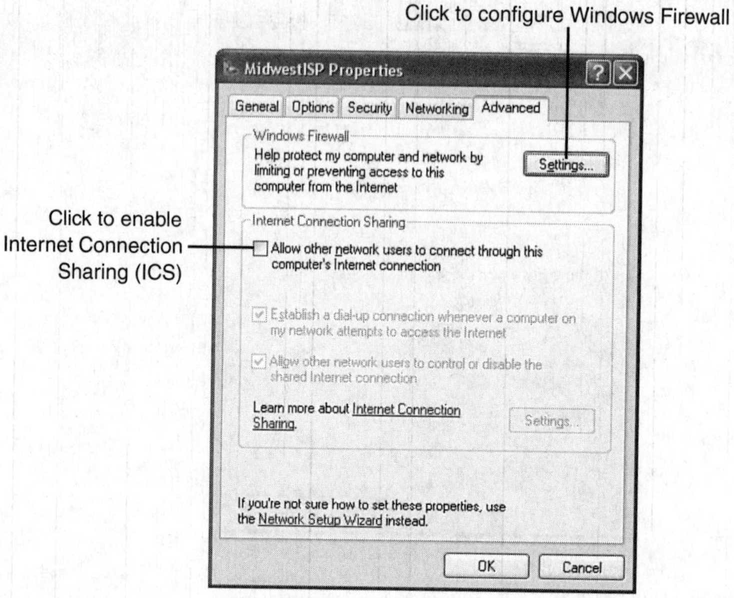

→ **For more about Internet Connection Sharing, see "Troubleshooting Network Software Configuration," this chapter, p. 495.**

→ **For details about configuring the Windows Firewall, see "Troubleshooting the Windows XP Firewall," this chapter, p. 542.**

Click to configure Windows Firewall

Click to enable Internet Connection Sharing (ICS)

MidwestISP Properties

General | Options | Security | Networking | Advanced

Windows Firewall
Help protect my computer and network by limiting or preventing access to this computer from the Internet   Settings...

Internet Connection Sharing
☐ Allow other network users to connect through this computer's Internet connection

☑ Establish a dial-up connection whenever a computer on my network attempts to access the Internet

☑ Allow other network users to control or disable the shared Internet connection

Learn more about Internet Connection Sharing.   Settings...

If you're not sure how to set these properties, use the Network Setup Wizard instead.

OK   Cancel

Troubleshooting Dial-Up Modem Hardware

In addition to problems with your Dial-Up Networking configuration, you can also have problems with modem hardware. Use the following sections to help you diagnose and solve typical problems.

Modem Has No Dial Tone

If your modem can't dial into an ISP's server or other remote computer's telephone number, you can't complete your connection. Modems, like phones, can't dial if there is no dial tone. Check the following if you get a "no dial tone" error message:

- **The RJ-11 telephone cable is loose or damaged.** Make sure the cable is attached correctly to both the wall jack and the modem. Figure 8.11 shows correct and incorrect connections. Try replacing the cable with one known to work. If it does, you have a damaged cable that you must replace.

- **The telephone cable is plugged into the wrong jack on the modem.** Some modems have two jacks, one for the phone line and one for sharing the line with a telephone. Use the jack marked "line" for the cable to the wall jack, and use the jack marked "phone" for an extension phone. Some modems can use either jack for either task.

Locking clip is loose   Locking clip is in place

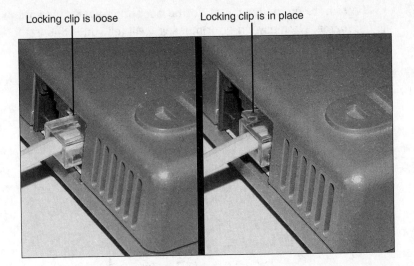

FIGURE 8.11
Incorrect (left) and correct (right) RJ-11 telephone cable connections.

- **A phone on the same circuit is off the hook.** Pick up your phone and listen for a dial tone. If you can't hear a dial tone, make sure all extension phones are properly hung up and try the connection again.

- **The phone service is dead.** If all phones are hung up but you still can't connect or make a voice call with your phone, your phone service is dead. Contact the phone company for repair assistance.

- **The modem is damaged or destroyed.** If you can't connect after a lightning strike or a power outage, your modem may have been damaged or destroyed. To see if it's still working, see "Using Analog Modem Diagnostics," this chapter, p. 488.

PC Can Dial But Does Not Connect

If you can dial the remote computer but can't complete the connection, check the following:

- **You may be dialing the wrong number.** Open the modem properties sheet and increase the speaker volume to maximum. Try the connection again and listen for the tones played by the remote device when it answers. If you hear a series of hisses, that's a modem at the other end. However, if you hear a repeated warble, that's a fax machine, not a modem—and that's a wrong number. If you hear a live human being or an answering machine, that's also a wrong number.

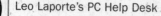

- **The remote computer might not be accepting your password or username.** Normally, an error message will tell you if this is the case. Reenter the correct username and password on the connection screen (see Figure 8.12) and retry your connection.

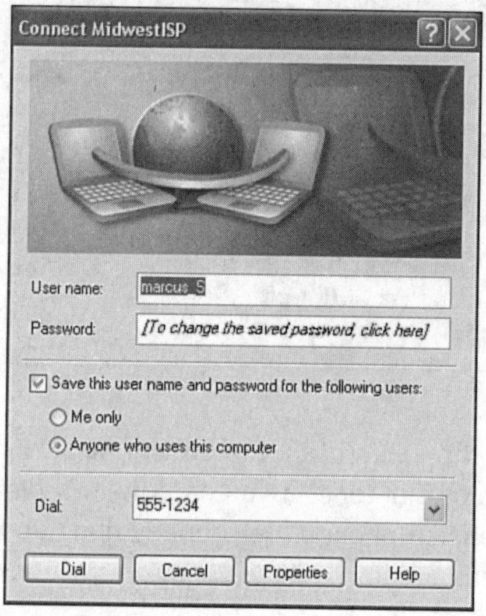

FIGURE 8.12
The dial-up connection dialog in Windows XP. Reenter the username and password if the remote computer doesn't recognize them.

- **The software configuration may be damaged.** Rerun the installation program provided by the ISP, or call the ISP for assistance and manually check the configuration as instructed by their help desk.

- **The ISP's telephone number might be busy.** If repeated attempts to connect result in a busy signal each time, contact the ISP by telephone to determine if there are alternate numbers you can call to connect. Adjust the redial options (see "The Options Tab," this chapter, p. 482) to redial more frequently to make your connection.

- **You might have problems with your TCP/IP configuration.** Call your ISP's tech support desk and ask them to walk you through the TCP/IP configuration for the service to make sure your system is properly configured.

If your computer locks up when you try to make the connection, your modem (or the port the modem is connected to) has a hardware conflict (probably an IRQ conflict) with another device. Restart your computer and open Device Manager to check for IRQ conflicts between the modem and another device (usually a COM port); you can also use the Conflicts/Sharing section of the Windows System Information utility to check for conflicts. Change the modem to another IRQ or disable the COM port if you don't use it; you might need to restart your computer and access the system BIOS setup program to change or disable the COM port on the computer.

➔ *See "Using Device Manager," Chapter 2, p. 100, "Using System Information," Chapter 2, p. 114, and "Integrated Peripherals (I/O Devices)," Chapter 1, p. 51.*

Port Already Open / Modem in Use by Another Application

If you see one of these error messages when you try to make a connection, another program, such as AOL or Quicken, is trying to use the modem. Try these solutions:

- Make sure you are not trying to send a fax with your modem at the same time. Complete the fax transmission and retry the connection.

- Close other programs with the Windows Task Manager if you cannot close them normally. Press Ctrl+Alt+Delete to bring up the Task Manager. Click Applications. Select each program you are no longer using and select End Task. Retry your connection.

- If you use an external modem, unplug it, wait a few moments, and try again. If this doesn't work, shut down the computer and restart it.

- If you use an internal modem, shut down your computer and restart it.

- If you formerly used America Online (AOL), but no longer use it, make sure you remove it from your system with the Add/Remove Programs icon in Control Panel.

  Here's how to remove AOL from your system if you no longer use it:

  1. Open the Add/Remove Programs icon in Control Panel.

  2. Select each program that mentions AOL or America Online (except AOL Instant Messenger) and click remove. If you use AOL Instant Messenger, you don't need to remove it, because it works with any Internet connection.

3. Open the Network icon in Control Panel and remove items such as AOL Adapter, Client for America Online, and other AOL/America Online references.

4. Restart your computer and retry your normal dial-up connection.

- Disable the Quicken Download Manager (Qagent) if you use Quicken. This utility is part of Quicken 2000, and it's used to download financial information into Quicken even when you are not using Quicken. Qagent might still be present on your system if you have upgraded to newer versions of Quicken.

  To prevent Qagent from running in the background, follow these steps:

  1. Start Quicken.

  2. Click Edit, Options, Internet Options.

  3. Click Connection on the Customize Quicken 2000 Download window.

  4. Select the Don't Use Background Downloading option.

  5. Click OK.

  6. Close Quicken.

  7. Restart your computer to use this new configuration.

  See the Intuit website at http://web.intuit.com/support/quicken/2004/win/6173.html to learn how to shut down background downloading with Quicken 2004.

If your modem won't respond when you try to open a connection, test it with Windows modem diagnostics. The next section, "Using Analog Modem Diagnostics," discusses these diagnostic tools in more detail.

Using Analog Modem Diagnostics

Windows contains a built-in modem diagnostics feature that you can use to determine if your modem is working, even if you cannot dial out to make an Internet connection.

To run the modem diagnostics with Windows XP, follow these steps:

1. Open the Phone and Modem Options icon in the Control Panel.

2. Click the Modems tab.

3. Select your modem and click Properties.

4. Click Query Modem.

Upon running the test, you should see various AT commands (AT commands are used by dial-up networking and other software to control the modem) and the modem's responses in the Command/Response window, as shown in Figure 8.13.

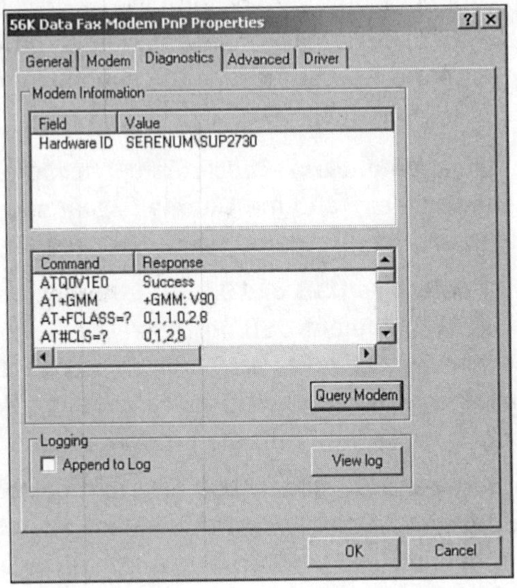

FIGURE 8.13

A successful modem test; the modem responds to the commands listed.

You can also open the Device Manager, select the modem from the list of hardware devices, and access its properties sheet to perform this test.

If the modem fails to respond, an error message will be displayed suggesting that you need to turn on the modem (for external modems) or check for hardware conflicts (for internal modems).

If an internal modem has no hardware conflicts with other devices or an external modem is connected to a working port and is turned on but doesn't respond during the modem diagnostics test, it is probably defective. Contact the modem vendor's tech support center for help.

External Modem Doesn't Work? Check the Port!

Before you assume that a modem plugged into a serial or USB port is defective, make sure the port is working. If your system's serial ports are disabled, for example, neither a modem nor any other device will work when plugged in. To check a USB port, connect another USB device such as a mouse or keychain drive to the port. To check a serial port, make sure the port is displayed in Windows Device Manager and that no problems are listed. If your computer has two serial ports but only one is enabled, you might have connected the modem to the wrong port.

Troubleshooting a Broadband Internet Connection

Because broadband Internet connections such as cable modems, fixed wireless, DSL, and satellite use either 10/100 Ethernet or USB connections to your computer, connection failures are caused by different problems than those afflicting analog modem Internet connections. Regardless of the type of broadband connection, these problems include the following:

- **Loose or damaged cables**—Check the connections between the computer, the modem, and the external signal source; tighten loose cables and replace damaged cables (see Figure 8.14).

- **Disabled or defective USB or 10/100 Ethernet ports**—Connect a USB cable to a different USB port; use the Device Manager to determine whether the ports are configured correctly (see "Using Device Manager," Chapter 2, p. 100, for details). Use any diagnostics software provided with the network adapter to test it.

- **Conflicts between USB or 10/100 Ethernet ports and other hardware devices**—See "Using Device Manager," Chapter 2, p. 100, for details.

- **Incorrect TCP/IP configuration**—See "TCP/IP Configuration and Troubleshooting," this chapter, p. 533, for details.

- **Router failure (a router lets you share a broadband Internet connection among multiple computers)**—See "Troubleshooting Routers and Gateways," this chapter, p. 524, for details.

In addition to these problems common to all types of broadband Internet connections, each type of broadband connection can have unique problems.

Troubleshooting a Cable Modem Connection

Cable modems, which use the same connection into your location as cable TV, are the most popular form of broadband Internet. Here are solutions to problems unique to cable modems:

- If you have cable TV and cable Internet, and you cannot see any cable TV channels or receive cable Internet service, contact the cable provider to report a service outage.

Loose Category 5 cable; not plugged into socket completely

Signal lights indicate a connection only for the properly connected cable

Category 5 cable completely plugged into socket

FIGURE 8.14

Loose (top) and properly connected (bottom) Category 5 Ethernet cables plugged into a typical 10/100 Ethernet card.

- If cable TV is working, but cable Internet service is not working, check the cable connections to your PC and cable modem (refer to Figures 8.14 and 8.15). Loose cables should be tightened; damaged cables should be replaced.

- If the connections between the cable modem and the computer appear to be correct, check the signal lights on the cable modem to see if they indicate problems. See "Using Signal Lights to Troubleshoot Your Connection," this chapter, p. 494, for details.

- If the cable modem doesn't report any problems, your computer's TCP/IP address may not be valid. To check your TCP/IP configuration, see "TCP/IP Configuration and Troubleshooting," this chapter, p. 533.

FIGURE 8.15
Loose (left) and properly-connected (right) coaxial cables on a typical cable modem.

Loose coaxial cable; note large amount of screw thread visible

Coaxial cable correctly screwed into place

Troubleshooting a DSL Connection

Digital Subscriber Line (DSL) connections also share a common connection into your location: your telephone line. However, unlike cable modem service, which is provided over an upgraded cable TV network, which also provides digital cable TV, DSL connections share your telephone line. Because DSL is carried over the telephone line (which wasn't originally designed to handle high-frequency, high-speed DSL traffic), telephone-related problems can cause havoc with your DSL connection.

- If you lose voice telephone service because of a problem with the telephone wiring outside your home, you've also lost DSL service, since both services are carried over the same lines. However, other types of DSL problems don't necessarily affect your phone lines.

- If your telephone service is working, but your DSL connection is not working at all, check the connections between the DSL modem, your computer, and the telephone wall jack.

- A slow DSL connection, or one that doesn't work at all, may be caused by interference from telephones, answering machines, or fax machines. Most DSL installations at home, especially self-installed installations, prevent interference through the use of small devices called microfilters (Figure 8.16). Microfilters are installed between telephony devices and telephone jacks. To determine if your microfilters are defective, disconnect all telephone-type devices from the telephone jacks and try your DSL connection again. If your connection starts working, or runs much faster than before, replace the microfilters. You can buy them at Radio Shack or other electronics stores.

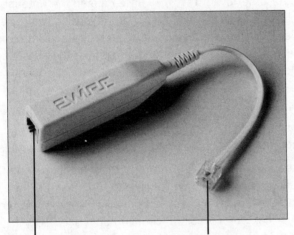

FIGURE 8.16
A typical DSL microfilter. Photo courtesy of 2Wire.

Connection for line from telephone
or telephone-type device

Connection to
telephone wall jack

- Check the signal lights on the DSL modem to see if they indicate problems with your connection. See "Using Signal Lights to Troubleshoot Your Connection," this chapter, p. 494, for details.

- If the DSL modem doesn't report any problems, your computer's TCP/IP address may not be valid. To diagnose problems with your computer's TCP/IP configuration, see "TCP/IP Configuration and Troubleshooting," this chapter, p. 533.

- Most DSL connections use a protocol known as PPPoE (Point-to-Point Protocol over Ethernet), which requires the user to log in during the connection process. You can store the username and password for convenience, or enter the username and password each time you want to make the connection. The dialog is the same as the login dialog for a dial-up connection (refer to Figure 8.12). If you are unable to connect, reenter your username and password and try again. If you are still unable to connect, call your ISP for help.

Troubleshooting a Satellite Connection

Satellite-based connections such as DirecWay (formerly DirecPC) and StarBand can be knocked off the air by antenna misalignment, cabling problems, and satellite modem problems. Here are some points to keep in mind:

- If you are unable to connect to the Internet after a storm, earthquake, or other event that may have caused the antenna to be misaligned, check the signal strength if your software installation includes this feature. If your signal strength is low or zero, or if you have no signal strength feature, contact the satellite Internet provider for assistance. Note that heavy rain or snow can also cause slow connections or interruptions, but this type of disruption will stop when the rain or snowstorm is over.

- If you see physical damage to the satellite dish with any type of satellite Internet service, contact the vendor for repair assistance.

- If the satellite modem doesn't report any problems and the signal strength appears to be within acceptable limits, your computer's TCP/IP address may not be valid. To diagnose problems with your computer's TCP/IP configuration, see "TCP/IP Configuration and Troubleshooting," this chapter, p. 533.

Using Signal Lights to Troubleshoot Your Connection

Most broadband Internet modems, particularly those used for DSL, cable modem, and fixed wireless connections, are external devices. The signal lights on the unit can be used to help you diagnose problems with your Internet connection (see Figure 8.17).

The following tips are general guidelines; to determine exactly what the signal lights are called and what they indicate on your broadband modem, consult your broadband modem's instruction manual:

- If the broadband modem is not receiving power, check the power cable and the connection to the wall outlet or surge protector.

- If the signal light for the connection to the computer indicates a problem with the modem's connection to the computer, check the USB or RJ-45 cable connection between the device and the computer. If the cable is attached correctly, check the USB or Ethernet port on the computer and make sure it's working correctly. See "Using Device Manager," Chapter 2, p. 100, for details.

- If the signal light for the connection to the broadband network indicates a problem, reset the broadband modem. If the modem still indicates a problem after about 30 minutes or so, contact the ISP; the ISP may have a problem.

- If the self-test light on the modem indicates a problem, reset the modem. If resetting the modem doesn't solve the problem, contact the ISP (if you leased the modem from them) or the modem vendor (if you purchased the modem outright).

- If the ready light on the modem indicates a problem, reset the modem. If the ready light still indicates a problem, check the cables and contact the ISP for help.

Troubleshooting Ethernet Networks

Ethernet networks are widely used in home and small businesses to share Internet connections, folders, and printers. Use the following sections to troubleshoot problems with your network configuration.

Troubleshooting Network Software Configuration

Each computer that uses shared Internet access needs the following software installed:

- **TCP/IP**—The protocol required for all computers on the Internet; this is normally installed automatically during the installation of a network adapter.

- **Client for Microsoft Networks**—Permits logging onto a Microsoft network to share resources.

- **File and Printer Sharing for Microsoft Networks (Optional)**— Required only for systems that need to share drives, folders, printers, or other resources with other computers.

The following settings are needed for each client:

- **A unique IP address**—Generally, the address is assigned by the device that acts as a gateway to other networks, such as a router. However, you can also assign an IP address manually if necessary for special situations, such as routing traffic for a web server or a game to a particular computer.

- **A workgroup name**—The same name must be used by all computers on the network.

- **A unique computer name**—Use a unique computer name for each computer on the network.

➜ *For more information about TCP/IP and DHCP, see "TCP/IP Configuration and Troubleshooting," this chapter, p. 533.*

The easiest way to add these components to most Windows networks is to use the Home Networking Wizard included with Windows XP.

Even though the latest Windows versions make configuring your network simpler than before, you still need the following information to configure your network with any version of Windows:

- **How will computers get an IP address?** Generally, you should use the default—server-assigned IP addresses—for the easiest configuration. Providing a fixed IP address to each computer on the network can lead to problems. For example, if you assign two computers the same IP address, neither computer will have Internet or network access.

- **What name will you use for the workgroup?** Every computer on the network must use the same workgroup name; otherwise, shared resources such as folders, drives, and printers won't be available to some users. Some ISPs require you to use a particular workgroup name, whereas others don't care.

Why "MSHome" Shouldn't Be Your Home Network's Name

When you run the Home Networking Wizard, Microsoft uses the "MSHome" network name by default. You should change this to a name you prefer. If you add wireless hardware to your network at a later time and don't enable security, it would be easy for a hacker to get on your network and access unsecured resources if you use the default network name.

- **Which name will you assign to each computer?** While the work-group name is common to all computers, each computer needs a unique computer name. If more than one computer has the same name, those computers won't be able to access shared resources.

- **What resources do you want to share?** You might want to share document folders or printers on some computers, but not others. The Home Networking Wizard shares the Shared Documents (Windows XP) folder by default, but you can skip this step on some computers if you don't want those folders shared. You can manually select other folders or printers for sharing later with Windows Explorer or the Printers folder.

Although several steps are involved in this process, you can complete the configuration task very simply by using the Windows Home Networking Wizard with Windows XP. If your network has computers running older versions of Windows, Windows 95, 98, or 98SE, as well as computers running Windows Me or XP, you can still use the Windows XP Home Networking Wizard to configure systems with older versions of Windows by creating a Home Network Setup floppy disk on the system(s) running Windows XP.

To start the Home Networking Wizard with Windows XP, follow these steps:

1. Click Start, All Programs, Accessories, Communications, Network Setup Wizard.

2. If you are configuring the computer as an ICS host, make sure you specify that this computer has a direct connection to the Internet and that you want to share the connection with others. Note that you must have two network connections to use ICS with a broadband modem: the first one connects the PC to the broadband modem, and a second one connects the PC to the network.

3. If you are configuring the computer as a client (connecting through an ICS host, a router, or a gateway), make sure you specify that the computer will access the Internet through another computer (a router or gateway is considered a computer by the wizard). In either case, you can select to share a document folder and a printer with other users on the network.

4. You must specify a workgroup name (the same for all computers) and specify a unique computer name for each computer.

5. At the end of the process, you can create a Home Networking Wizard floppy disk you can use to configure other Windows computers on the network. The Home Networking Wizard floppy disk you can create with Windows XP contains a program called NET-SETUP.EXE. Run NETSETUP.EXE to configure other Windows computers on the network; select The Computer Connects to the Internet Through Another Computer and specify whether you want to share a document folder or a printer.

If your network is not a wired Ethernet network, you might need to run special setup software provided by the network vendor in addition to, or instead of, using the Home Networking Wizard. See your network hardware's instruction manual for details. With Windows XP Service Pack 2, use the Wireless Network Setup Wizard to help configure your network wireless network. See "Using the Windows XP SP2 Wireless Network Setup Wizard," this chapter, p. 521, for details.

Once you have configured the network software on the host and each client computer and have then rebooted the host, followed by the client computers, each one should be able to access the Internet and shared resources on the network.

If your network isn't working after you have installed it, use the following sections to discover what's wrong and learn how to fix it.

I Can't Access Other Computers on the Network

If you can't see other computers on the network, one of the following could be the reason:

- The network hardware has failed.
- You don't have a working connection to the network.

Connecting to a shared Internet connection requires that your computer has the TCP/IP protocol installed and has a valid IP address. If you can connect to the Internet, your network hardware is working correctly. If you can't connect to the Internet or to other computers on your network, see "Troubleshooting Ethernet Networks," p. 495, if your computer uses wired Ethernet. See "Troubleshooting Wi-Fi Networks,"

p. 512, if you can't connect to the Internet or to other computers from a computer using wireless Ethernet. If you can connect to other computers, but not to the Internet, see "Troubleshooting a Broadband Internet Connection," p. 490.

If you still can't access network resources, check the other options listed in the following sections.

I'm Not Sure My Network Settings Are Correct

The following items might indicate a problem with your network software configuration:

- You can see other computers on the network, but you can't see any shared folders or printers.
- You can access the Internet, but you can't see other computers.
- You can't access the Internet or see other computers.

To solve the first problem (can't see shared folders or printers), make sure that the computers that have folders to be shared are running File and Printer Sharing and have specified folders to share. You can rerun the Home Networking Wizard on these computers or manually configure each computer's network settings to install File and Printer Sharing. The wizard will also permit you to share the My Documents folder on computers running versions of Windows other than Windows XP and to select shared printers. For Windows XP, the Shared Documents folder is shared by default.

You can also manually set up folder and printer shares. Open My Computer or Windows Explorer, right-click a folder you'd like to share, select Sharing from the menu, and specify a share name (a descriptive name for the shared resource that will be visible to other users on the network). To share a printer, open the Printers folder, right-click a printer, select Sharing, and specify a share name. Passwords are optional but recommended for security. If you share a printer on a Windows XP or Windows 2000 computer on a network that has other versions of Windows running on it, click the Additional Drivers button (see Figure 8.18) to install drivers that can be used by other versions of Windows. The drivers will be downloaded to the other computers when they browse to the shared printer on the network.

FIGURE 8.18

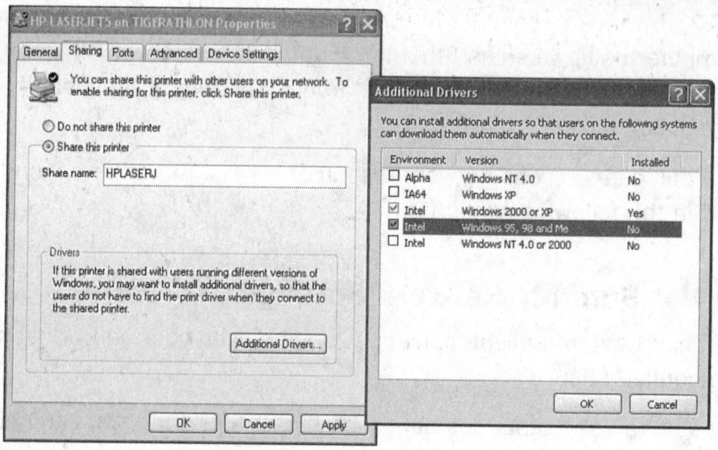

Using the Additional Drivers option in Windows XP to provide drivers for other Windows versions.

If you can access the Internet but not other computers on the network, your workgroup name doesn't match the workgroup name of the other computers on the network. You can rerun the Home Networking Wizard and enter a common workgroup name, or you can change the name manually.

To change the workgroup name in Windows XP, follow these steps:

1. Open the Start menu, right-click My Computer, and select Properties.

2. Click the Computer Name tab on the System properties sheet.

3. Click Change to open the Computer Name Changes dialog.

4. Click Workgroup (if necessary).

5. Enter the correct workgroup name (see Figure 8.19).

6. Click OK.

7. Reboot the computer.

Taking Work Home Means Changing Your Workgroup Name

Another reason you might not be able to connect with the home network is because you've moved a notebook computer from an office network to your home network. If your office network uses server-assigned IP addresses and you use 10/100 Ethernet, you should be able to get on the Internet at home just by connecting your computer to a network cable and powering it up. However, if you use a wireless network or you use a static IP address at the office, you could be in for a messy reconfiguring job when you want to bring your notebook computer home.

Check out Globesoft's Multinetwork manager, a low-cost solution for managing multiple network configurations on your computer. Learn more about it and download a trial version at http://www.globesoft.com/ mnm7_home.asp.

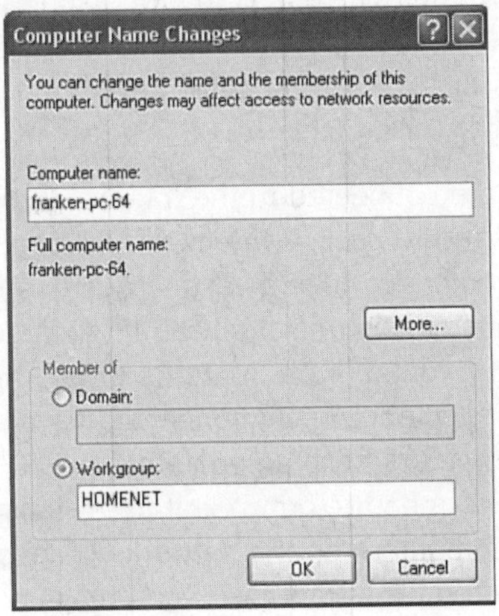

FIGURE 8.19

Changing the work-group name in Windows XP.

If you can't access the network or see other computers, the solution is usually pretty simple if you connect to the Internet through a routing device (router, gateway, or access point): Rerun the Home Networking Wizard, or make sure you have configured your network as discussed in "Troubleshooting Network Software Configuration," this chapter, p. 495.

If you use Internet Connection Sharing, make sure the computer with the shared Internet connection (also called the ICS host) can connect with the Internet. If it can't connect, nobody can. Restart this computer and then rerun its Home Networking Wizard if it still can't connect. If the ICS host can connect to the Internet, but other users can't, or if no users can connect to the Internet on an ICS or router-based network, check the options discussed next.

I'm Not Sure I Have a Valid IP Address

Whether you connect through a routing device or through an ICS host, your computer should have received a valid IP address from the DHCP server included in the routing device or the ICS host. Use IPCONFIG in Windows XP (similar to WINIPCFG in Windows 9x/Me) to check your IP address.

➔ *For details, see "Using IPCONFIG," this chapter, p. 536.*

If you use ICS or a third-party sharing program, the computer with the shared Internet connection must be turned on and completely booted before it can provide a valid IP address to other computers on the network. If not, all computers should be shut down, the host computer should be started and finish booting, and then the client computers should be started. If this process is followed and the client PCs still can't get a valid IP address (they have an IP address of 0.0.0.0. or an address starting with "169."), you could have problems with your network adapter, cabling, or switch.

If your computers are connected to the Internet through a router, any computer can be used to access the Internet independently of the others, because the router provides a valid IP address to each user. If one or more computers don't have a valid IP address (0.0.0.0 or 169.x.x.x), check the router. If the router is turned off, has its power supply cable disconnected, or isn't connected to the network cables running to your computers or to a separate network switch or hub used by the computers on the network, it can't provide valid IP addresses to the computers on the network. Recheck the cable connections, reset the router or turn it off and on again, shut down and restart the computers on the network, and then retry connecting to the Internet.

Updating Network Hardware Drivers

If you discover problems with your network hardware, a driver or firmware update might be necessary to solve the problem. Follow these guidelines to ensure success in your update:

- Switches and hubs made for home office and small office use (brands such as Linksys, D-Link, Netgear) don't use firmware and can't be updated. If they fail, replace them. If you're planning to share an Internet connection, you can use a router with an integrated switch as a replacement for a switch or hub.

- Some network adapters have upgradable firmware and some don't, but all of them use drivers that can be updated.

- If Windows Update doesn't have an updated driver for a network adapter, go to the vendor's website.

If your normal broadband Internet connection isn't working because of router or network adapter problems, here are some alternatives that can help you get the driver or firmware updates you need:

- **Connect a working PC directly to the broadband Internet modem.** If the routing device has a problem, bypass it until you can get a replacement. To avoid problems with ISPs that identify your connection by its MAC address, see "Troubleshooting a Router," this chapter, p. 528.

- **Use the USB connection instead of the 10/100 Ethernet connection on the broadband Internet modem if the Ethernet card needs a new driver.** Although the Ethernet connection is a bit faster in practice, USB will work well enough, especially if you plug it directly into your computer and not into a hub that's already handling other USB devices.

- **Use your computer's dial-up (analog) modem to connect to the Internet and get updates.** Some broadband ISPs offer a limited amount of dial-up service as a backup in case of failures, or you can use a free service offer (AOL, anyone?). If you decide to use AOL or some other Internet service that uses proprietary software, just remember that you will need to uninstall it and reinstall your normal Internet connection software after you are finished. If you have problems after you remove AOL or similar programs, run System Restore with Windows XP or Me and select a system restore point before the date you installed the proprietary online software.

- **Buy prepaid dial-up or broadband Internet access.** You can purchase prepaid dial-up or broadband Internet access from a company such as Slingshot Communications, Inc. (http://www.slingshot.com) or Maglobe (http://www.maglobe.com).

  → *For details on updating all types of drivers, see "Using Device Manager," Chapter 2, p. 100.*

- **Follow the instructions for updating the firmware on a routing device very carefully.** If you don't update the firmware correctly, you will ruin the device's BIOS chip and a trip to the repair shop will be required. Make sure you write down the current settings used by the routing device before you update its firmware.

Printing Routing Device Settings

If your network's routing device uses a web-based interface for configuration, you can use your web browser's Print option to record its settings before you update its firmware.

Troubleshooting Ethernet Network Hardware

If your network adapter, cables, or other hardware doesn't work, you can't connect to other computers, and if you depend on your network to reach the Internet, you won't have Internet access either. Use this section to help you troubleshoot problems with network hardware.

Network hardware can be divided into the following categories:

- **Network adapters**—A network adapter enables a computer to connect to other computers. Some computers have built-in network adapters, but you need to add a network adapter to many computers to enable them to join a network. Network adapters used for wireless networks have fixed or detachable antennas, whereas network adapters used for wired networks have jacks for network cable (see Figure 8.20).

- **Network switches or hubs**—10/100 and other wired Ethernet networks transfer data between computers through multiport devices such as hubs (which subdivide the total data transfer rate, or bandwidth, among connected devices) and switches (which provide full-speed connections to each device).

- **Routers and gateways**—A router enables computers on a local network to access another network such as the Internet. Access points are used by wireless networks to pass data between stations; they can also include routers for access to the Internet. Routers and access points can also incorporate switches.

- **Network cables**—Wired networks use cable to connect each computer to the rest of the network. 10/100 Ethernet networks use Category 5 cables, which use an RJ-45 connector. HomePNA networks use telephone cables to piggyback on your existing telephone network.

Problems with network adapters can be caused by the following:

- Loose or incorrectly installed network adapters
- Hardware conflicts between network adapters and other devices
- Incompatibilities between network adapters and routers or access devices
- Incorrect configuration of wireless network hardware

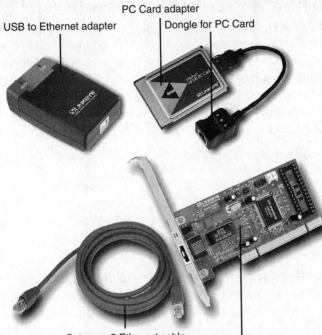

USB to Ethernet adapter

PC Card adapter

Dongle for PC Card

Category 5 Ethernet cable

PCI Network Interface Card (NIC)

FIGURE 8.20
Typical 10/100 Ethernet network adapters. (Photos courtesy Linksys.)

Problems with network cables can be caused by the following:

- Incorrectly wired network cables
- Loose or damaged network cables
- Connecting network cables to the wrong port on a router, switch, or hub

Problems communicating between computers on a network can be caused by the following:

- Incorrect configuration of wireless network access points
- Incorrect cabling
- Incorrect configuration of network software
- Switch or hub failure

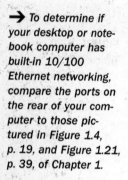

Troubleshooting Network Adapter Installations

The types of problems you can have with a network adapter vary by where it's installed and how it connects with other computers. Keep in mind that your computer might already have a 10/100 Ethernet network adapter built into the rear of the machine (a frequent feature on the latest desktop and notebook computers). Some notebook computers might also have a Wi-Fi Wireless Ethernet network adapter included; consult your computer documentation for details.

➜ To determine if your desktop or notebook computer has built-in 10/100 Ethernet networking, compare the ports on the rear of your computer to those pictured in Figure 1.4, p. 19, and Figure 1.21, p. 39, of Chapter 1.

If you need to add a network adapter, you can connect it to any of the following locations:

- USB port
- PCI expansion slot
- PC Card/CardBus expansion slot

If your computer has USB 2.0 ports, they're the easiest place to add a network adapter. However, I don't recommend using USB 1.1 ports because they slow down network traffic too much.

➜ For details about troubleshooting USB ports and determining whether a port is USB 1.1 or USB 2.0, see "Troubleshooting USB Ports and Hubs," Chapter 7, p. 418.

When you connect your network adapter to a USB port, it will work as long as the USB port is already working and can supply sufficient power for the adapter.

If you use PCI or PC Card/CardBus expansion slots, however, Windows and the system BIOS must detect the card and locate nonconflicting hardware resources to enable the network card to work properly. Windows and the system BIOS can do this only if the card is properly installed.

If a card plugged into a PCI slot is not inserted completely into the expansion slot and fastened tightly into place (see Figure 8.21), the card will not work.

FIGURE 8.21
Fastening a 10/100 Ethernet PCI card into place.

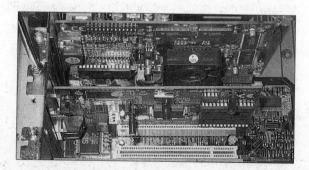

Similarly, if you don't slide a PC Card or CardBus card all the way into the slot on a notebook computer, the card will not work.

To determine if a PC Card or CardBus card is correctly connected to the slot, check the Windows system tray for an icon called Safely Remove Hardware. Double-click the icon to display a dialog. If your network card is displayed, it has been detected and installed.

What Is CardBus?

CardBus cards use a 32-bit internal design, instead of the original PC Card's 16-bit design; therefore, CardBus cards and slots can transmit or receive twice the data per operation and support much faster devices than normal PC Card cards and slots can. You can plug PC Card devices into CardBus slots. However, you cannot use CardBus devices in PC Card slots.

CardBus cards are recommended for 10/100 Ethernet and other high-speed tasks, but they do cost a little more than normal PC Card devices. CardBus cards have a gold grounding strip on the top of the card connector.

Once Windows has detected your network adapter (either upon rebooting your PC, inserting the PC Card or CardBus card, or attaching the USB adapter), follow these steps to complete the process:

1. Once Windows identifies your network adapter, it usually asks you to provide network drivers from the adapter's CD-ROM or floppy disk. These drivers are usually more up to date than those provided with Windows. However, for the most up-to-date drivers, visit the vendor's website.

2. Windows installs a default set of network protocols that vary by version whenever a network adapter is installed.

The Installer Might Pause

During the installation of the network card's drivers and Windows own network software, the Windows installer might pause and indicate it can't find a particular file. This usually takes place when the installer is switching back and forth between installing the network adapter's own files and Windows network files. Use the Browse button to redirect the installer to the correct drive and folder to finish the process.

→ See "Using Device Manager," Chapter 2, p. 100, to see how to troubleshoot installed hardware such as network adapters.

If Windows is unable to locate unique hardware resources for your network adapter, or if you don't provide the correct drivers, the network adapter will not function. To determine whether your network card is installed properly or has a problem, open the Device Manager.

To determine if your network adapter is working after you install it, you can use the following procedures:

- Check the Windows Device Manager listing for the network adapter to see if Windows has recognized it and doesn't report any problems.

- Check for signal lights on the rear of a 10/100 Ethernet or HomePNA network adapter after you attach a network cable to the card, attach the other end of the cable to a powered hub, switch, or router (Ethernet) or to the telephone jack (HomePNA), and turn on the computer.

→ See "Using Device Manager," Chapter 2, p. 100, to diagnose problems with your network adapter's drivers or configuration.

- Run the diagnostic software provided by the network adapter vendor.

Both 10/100 Ethernet and HomePNA network adapters have signal lights indicating proper operation. Normally, a signal light glows when the network adapter has a working connection to the rest of the network. Some network adapters have other signal lights to indicate network speed or other information. The signal lights on a PC Card or CardBus card that uses a dongle are located on the dongle rather than the card itself. See Figure 8.20 for an example of a network adapter that uses a dongle.

If your network adapter's connection signal light doesn't glow after you have connected the network adapter to its cable, connected the other end of the cable to the network, and turned on the computer, see "Troubleshooting Cabling," this chapter, p. 510.

Diagnostic software for your network adapter might be located on the network adapter driver floppy disk, or it can be downloaded from the vendor. You must start your computer with a boot disk to use diagnostic software.

To create a boot disk with MS-DOS files, follow these steps:

1. Insert a blank floppy disk into your computer's floppy drive.

2. Open My Computer.

3. Right-click the A: drive icon and select Format.

4. Click the box marked Create an MS-DOS Startup Disk.

5. Click Start.

6. After the format process is over, remove the disk until you want to use it to start your computer.

The Program Could Lock Up

If you try to run the network adapter diagnostic program from within a Windows command-prompt window, the program might lock up partway through or not be able to find the network adapter at all because the diagnostics program must have exclusive access to the adapter's hardware.

To run network adapter diagnostics from the driver floppy, follow these steps:

1. Insert the boot disk into drive A:.

2. Start your computer.

3. If the computer doesn't boot from the floppy disk, you need to change the boot sequence so that the floppy drive is listed first.

4. When the system completes booting (the screen will display an A:\> prompt), wait for the light on the floppy drive to go out, press the eject button to release the floppy disk from drive A:, and insert the floppy disk containing the diagnostics files.

5. Follow the instructions provided with the network adapter card for running diagnostics (the instructions might be found on a Readme.txt file on the disk). For example, the driver disk supplied with Linksys NICs contains a \DIAG folder that contains DIAG.EXE. To run a program in a folder, change to the folder (CD\DIAG) and enter the name of the program (DIAG). Figure 8.22 shows the output from the Linksys diagnostics program.

→ *For details about changing the boot order, see "Advanced BIOS and Chipset Features Menus," Chapter 1, p. 49, and "Troubleshooting Hard Disk or Optical Drive Bootup Problems," Chapter 3, p. 207.*

If a test such as internal loopback, I/O, or Interrupt fails, the card is defective and should be replaced. Some diagnostics programs will display a FAIL message for network function or other tests that involve sending and receiving data; disregard this error message unless you are running the diagnostics program on another computer and have configured both to send and receive data.

After you complete the tests, exit the program, remove the floppy disk from drive A:, and restart the computer.

FIGURE 8.22

The Linksys diagnostics program, DIAG.EXE, testing a properly working network card. To check network cabling, run the program on two different computers and enable the Network Function Test to send data between computers.

```
Linksys LNE100TX Fast Ethernet Adapter (LNE100TX v4) Diagnostic Program
   Ver 1.14   01-06-2000   (C) Linksys Group

                                      Node ID: [ 00 20 78 0D D5 BF ]
 #0LNE100TX   IRQ :255Port :8000    Tx Count    :              0 Packets
                                    Rx Count    :              0 Packets
 Configuration Test    : PASS
 I/O Test              : PASS       CRC Error   :          0
 ID Test               : PASS       ALG Error   :          0
 Internal Loopback Test: PASS       COLLISION   :          0
 Link Status Test      : PASS
 Interrupt Test        : PASS
 Network Function Test : OFF        Tx Perf.    :          0 Mbps
                                    Rx Perf.    :          0 Mbps
                                    Performance :          0 Mbps
 F10 -> Change Turbo Mode
 Turbo Mode :  ENABLE               Time        :          0 Seconds
                                    -->Burst  1  packets at most each time
 F3  -> [ACPI Test]                 ( PgUp, PgDn to change burst number)

      Press <F1> to Reset Counters, <F2> to Toggle ON/OFF, <ESC> to Exit
```

Troubleshooting Cabling

10/100 Ethernet networks depend on hubs or switches and twisted-pair cabling with RJ-45 connectors at each end to transfer data between computers. CAT5, CAT5e, and CAT6 cabling can all be used for 10/100 Ethernet networks.

A normally functioning hub has a signal light called Link or Link/Activity, whereas switches and routers with built-in switches have additional signal lights, as shown in Figure 8.23. The Link signal light will glow when a working network cable is plugged into the hub and the computer at the other end of the cable is running. If the signal light doesn't appear, make sure the hub or switch is turned on and that the computer at the other end of the cable is also turned on and make sure the hub or switch is turned on.

FIGURE 8.23

The front of a typical router with a built-in switch. (Photo courtesy of Linksys.)

Link/activity lights for the network ports

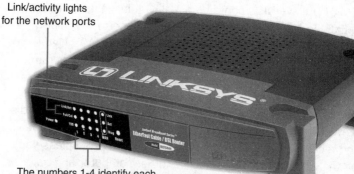

The numbers 1-4 identify each of the switch's network ports

If the link signal light still doesn't light up, check the following:

- **Is the cable tightly connected to the network adapter?** RJ-45 cables are designed to lock tightly into place. If the cable is loose, the network connection won't work and the signal light won't come on.

→ *See Figure 8.14, p. 491, for an example of correctly and incorrectly installed Category 5 (RJ-45) network cables.*

- **Are you using the correct type of cable on a 10/100 Ethernet network?** The only time a crossover Category 5/5e/6 cable should be used is to connect two computers together without using a hub or switch, or to connect a hub or switch to another hub or switch when an uplink port is not available. Use straight-through Category 5/5e/6 cabling between hubs, switches, or routers with built-in switches and network adapters.

Take a Quick Look to Determine Which Type of Network Cable You Have

A normal (straight-through) Category 5/5e/6 network cable used with 10/100 Ethernet connections has the wire pairs in the same order at both ends; you can see them through the transparent plastic connector. The most common wire pairing for standard cables is the TIA568B standard, though it's possible that you will come across the TIA568A standard as well.

Wire #	TIA568B Wire Color	TIA568A Wire Color
1	White/Orange	White/Green
2	Orange	Green
3	White/Green	White/Orange
4	Blue	Blue
5	White/Blue	White/Blue
6	Green	Orange
7	White/Brown	White/Brown
8	Brown	Brown

A crossover cable will have different wire pair matchups at each end. For example, if one end of the cable uses the TIA568B layout, and the other end uses the TIA568A layout, you have a crossover cable. A crossover cable can be used to connect two (and only two) computers directly, and it can be used to connect a switch or hub to another hub if an uplink port (a port with its connections switched) is not available. For normal network use, use a regular Category 5/5e/6 cable.

See illustrations of both cable types at the "Wiring & Cable Color Scheme" page at http://www.aptcommunications.com/ncode.htm.

➡ See Figure 8.40, p. 531, for an example of a router/switch combination with an uplink port.

- **Is the cable connected to the Uplink port or to the port next to the Uplink port on the hub, switch, or router?** If the Uplink port is used to connect the hub or switch to another hub or switch, the port next to the Uplink port can't be used for a network connection. The Uplink port itself is used only to connect to another hub or switch, never for connections to a computer.

- **Is the cable damaged?** If any part of the cable is cracked or broken, including the plastic connector at the ends of the cable or the cable jacket, replace the cable. A cable whose locking clip is broken can still be pushed into a jack and work, but the cable may work loose over time and create an unreliable connection.

- **Is the cable connected to a dongle?** If you use a PC Card or CardBus network adapter that uses a dongle (a small patch cable that runs between the PC Card and the regular network cable; refer to Figure 8.20), it might not properly attached to the PC Card. If the dongle isn't tightly connected, you won't see a connected signal from the signal lights on the dongle or on the routing device, switch, or hub.

- **Have you tried another port on the hub, switch, or router?** If one connection on a hub or switch isn't working, connect the cable from the computer to another port to see if the hub or switch is working properly.

➡ If your hub or switch is part of a router (a device that enables network users to connect to the Internet), see "Troubleshooting a Router," this chapter, p. 528.

A defective cable can cause both network adapters and hubs/switches to appear to be malfunctioning. If you suspect a defective cable, try another cable between the hub or switch and a computer. If the hub or switch is turned on, the network adapter appears to be working properly, and a replacement cable works, the original cable was defective. However, if every cable you attach between the hub or switch and the network adapter doesn't activate the signal lights (and the computer can't access the Internet), the hub or switch could be defective. Replace it and retry your network connection.

Troubleshooting Wi-Fi Networks

Wireless Ethernet networks, most commonly known as *Wi-Fi*, are the hottest home and small office networking trend. Instead of using cables, Wi-Fi networks use radio signals to transmit data. Wi-Fi networks are easiest to use when they're not secured against intruders, but making them more secure can also make them harder to use. The following sections help you deal with the most common problems, such as the following:

- Incorrect software and security configurations
- Incompatible standards

If some computers on a Wi-Fi (IEEE 802.11a/b/g) or other wireless network can't connect with each other or with the Internet, check the following:

- **The access point and device have different SSIDs.** The SSID is a unique name for the wireless network. Each device on a wireless network must be configured with the *same* SSID as the one used by the wireless router or access point. Keep in mind that different brands of hardware have different default SSIDs. For example, Linksys hardware uses "Linksys" as the default SSID, whereas a U.S. Robotics wireless router uses the model number as its default SSID. To prevent unauthorized users from accessing the network, the default value(s) for the SSID should be changed to the same name (a name you make up) for each device on the network. Figure 8.24 shows the default SSID setting for a Linksys wireless access point (WAP).

- **The settings for WEP (Wireless Equivalent Privacy) or WPA (Wi-Fi Protected Access) aren't configured correctly.** Because an unsecured wireless network can be accessed by anyone with compatible hardware, you should enable security features on your network to prevent unauthorized users from sneaking onto your network. The wireless access point or router and every computer must use the same settings to protect your network from snoopers and to enable every computer on the network to work correctly. If possible, use WPA security, because it is harder to penetrate than WEP. However, not all Wi-Fi hardware, particularly 802.11b hardware, supports WPA. You must use the same security standard and settings on all the devices on your wireless network. Figure 8.25 illustrates WEP settings on a Linksys wireless access point, whereas Figure 8.26 illustrates WPA settings on the same access point.

The default SSID (wireless network name) should be changed
to a user-defined value; use the same name for all devices

FIGURE 8.24
*The default wireless
network settings for a
Linksys wireless
access point.*

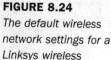

Enables wireless   Click to edit wireless
security   security settings

128-bit WEP encryption is the strongest mode supported
by most home and small-office wireless hardware
Selected security mode

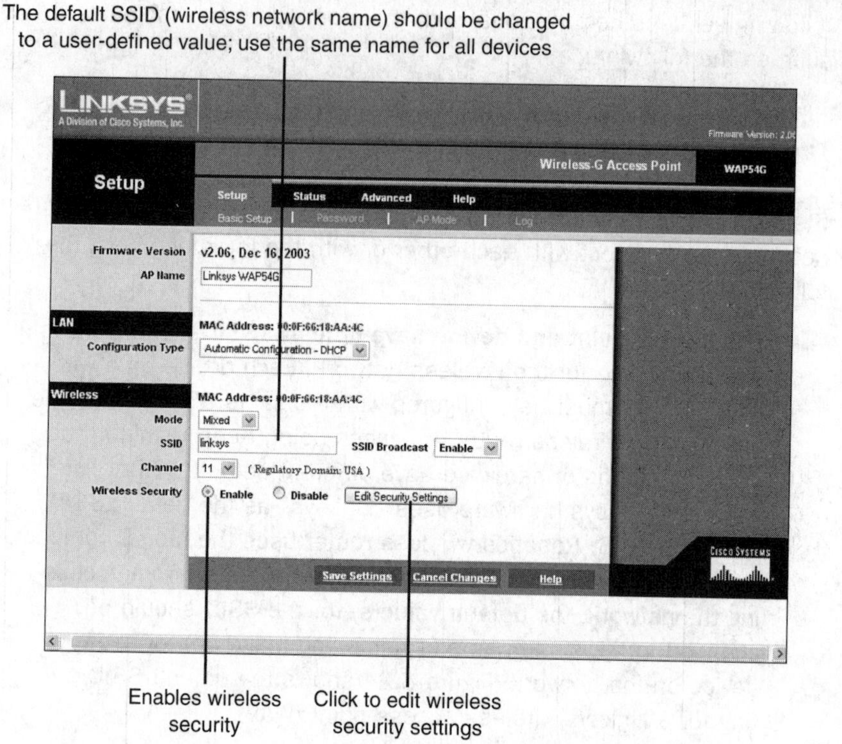

FIGURE 8.25
*A Linksys wireless
access point's WEP
security dialog with a
user-defined WEP key.*

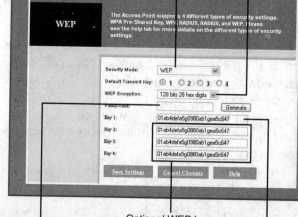

Optional WEP keys

Enter plain text here and click Generate   User-defined WEP key; use this key on all devices
to create a WEP key if you have only   which will connect to this WAP or wireless router
Linksys hardware on your network

TKIP is supported by all home and small-office
WPA-compatible wireless hardware

Selected security mode

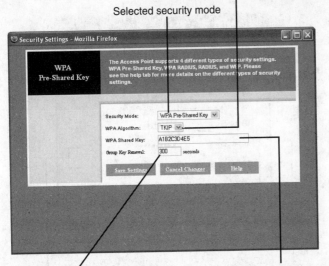

FIGURE 8.26
*A Linksys wireless
access point's WPA
security dialog.*

Specifies how often the key is
renewed; adjust this number higher if
you have problems with signal dropouts

Use this key on all devices which will
connect to this WAP or wireless router

When you configure your wireless access point to use WEP or
WPA security, you must enter the same settings on each device.
On a PC, you can use Windows XP's wireless network connection
properties sheet to enter this information. Figure 8.27 shows a
PC client being configured using the same security settings used
in Figure 8.26.

- **If you use WEP security, your wireless network hardware
  doesn't support the same levels of WEP encryption.** Encryption
  strengths (expressed as 40 bit, 56 bit, or 128 bit—larger is better) used by the WEP features of different types of hardware can
  vary. When you enable WEP, you need to select an encryption
  strength supported by all the equipment on the network. Note
  that 256-bit encryption is *not* supported by most hardware used
  in home or small office wireless networks.

- **The gateway, base station, or router is incorrectly positioned.** If
  the gateway, base station, or router can't be accessed by all the
  stations because of range issues or interference, those stations
  can't connect to the Internet or with each other. Follow the recommendations for device positioning very carefully. Use replacement antennas to improve the range or install a repeater to carry
  signals to some areas of your home or office.

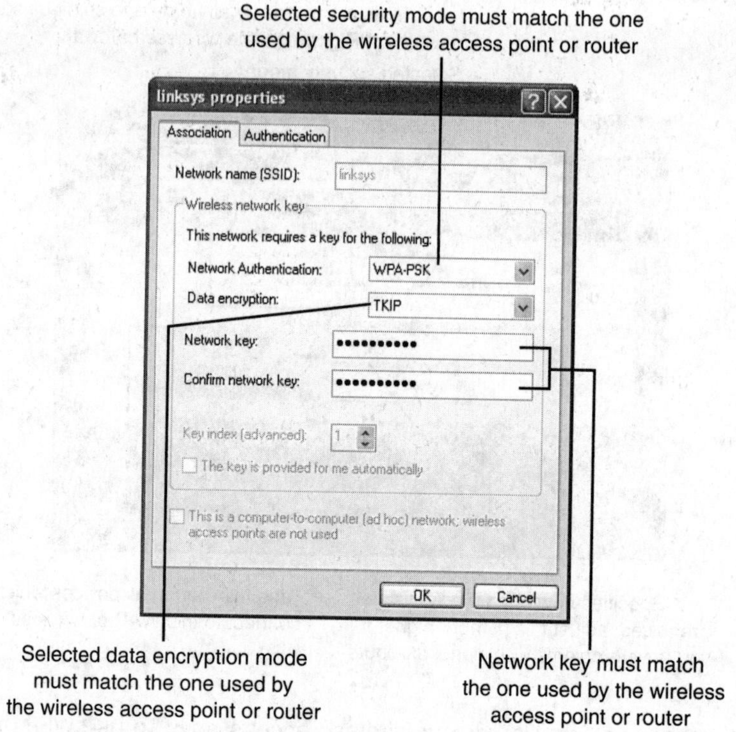

FIGURE 8.27

Using the Windows XP wireless network configuration properties sheet to connect to a wireless access point configured to use WPA security.

Selected security mode must match the one
used by the wireless access point or router

Selected data encryption mode
must match the one used by
the wireless access point or router

Network key must match
the one used by the wireless
access point or router

- **The connection to the wireless access point or router is poor.**
  The wireless access point or router is responsible for providing an IP address to each wireless client. To see the status of your connection with Windows XP, right-click the wireless icon in the system tray and select Status. The General tab (see Figure 8.28) shows the duration of your connection, signal strength, activity, and connection speed. Typically, if you see a very low speed (under 5Mbps with a 54Mbps wireless-G network), a low signal strength (one or two bars), and little or no activity with a connection that has been running for several minutes, you probably don't have a working connection. To see your computer's IP address, click the Support tab shown in Figure 8.28. If there's a problem with the connection, your client will have an invalid IP address (0.0.0.0) or will have a privately assigned IP address (169.254.x.x) rather than a DHCP-assigned IP address, as shown in Figure 8.29.

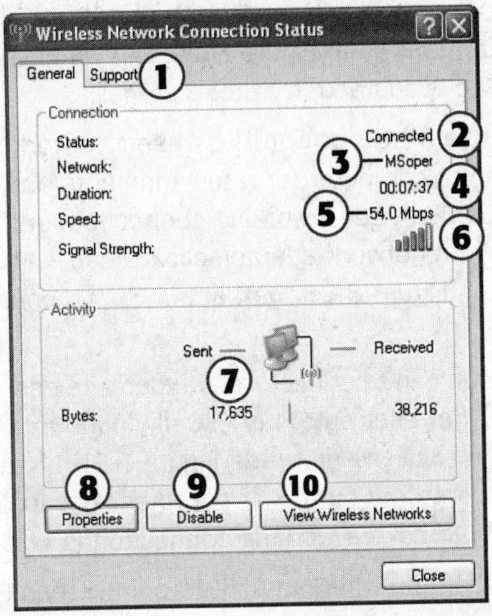

FIGURE 8.28
Displaying the status of a wireless connection using Windows XP SP2.

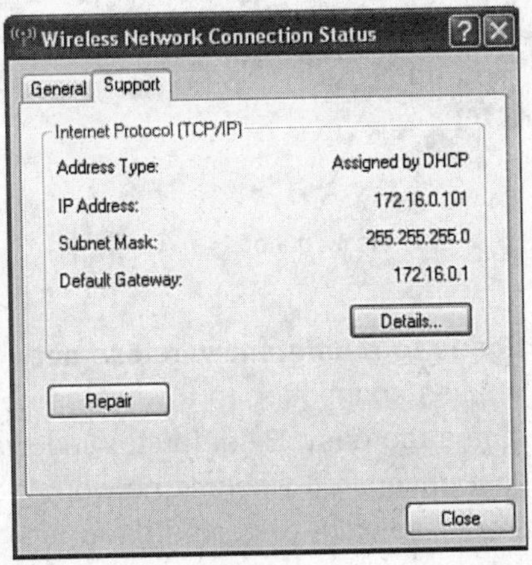

1. Click to view IP address
2. Connection status
3. Wireless network name (SSID) (not shown in earlier Windows XP releases)
4. How long current connection has been running
5. Connection speed
6. Signal strength (more bars = stronger signal)
7. Activity (little or no activity indicates a connection problem)
8. Displays network properties
9. Disables connection
10. Displays other wireless networks (not shown in earlier Windows XP releases)

FIGURE 8.29
A wireless client with a working IP address.

To correct a problem with an invalid IP address, you could try the Repair button shown in Figure 8.29, but we haven't had much success with it. Instead, try these steps:

1. If you use a USB or CardBus-based network adapter, remove it from the computer for a few moments and then reconnect it. If you don't get a working connection, or if you use a built-in wireless network adapter, click Disable on the dialog shown in Figure 8.28, wait about 30 seconds, and then click Enable.

2. If you still can't connect, reset your wireless access point or router. The reset button is usually found in a recessed hole on the rear of the unit (see Figure 8.30). Use a bent paper-clip to press the button. If the router is causing the problem, you should have a working connection in less than a minute.

3. If resetting the wireless access point doesn't help, restart your computer.

FIGURE 8.30
The reset button on the rear of a typical wireless access point.

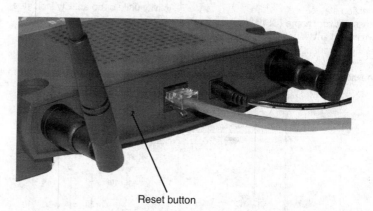

Reset button

- **The connection is to a different wireless network than yours.** Windows XP makes connecting to a wireless network very easy—sometimes too easy. By default, Windows XP will connect to the strongest unsecured wireless network it detects unless you configure your network to be the preferred network. To see the current list of wireless networks within range, click the View Wireless Networks button shown earlier in Figure 8.28. Windows XP Service Pack 2 displays a dialog similar to the one shown in Figure 8.31.

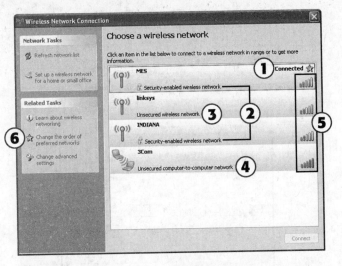

FIGURE 8.31
A typical list of wire-less networks within range of this Windows XP SP2 wireless client.

1. Network in use
2. Secured network (uses WEP or WPA key)
3. Unsecured (open) network
4. Ad-hoc network (can't be used for Internet access)
5. Signal strength
6. Click to specify the order of preferred networks

To specify your network as the preferred one if your system connects to a different network than yours, click the Change the Order of Preferred Networks button shown in Figure 8.31. This opens the Wireless Networks tab of the Wireless Networks Connection Properties dialog, shown in Figure 8.32. Use the Add button to add your wireless network if it is not shown in the list of preferred networks. Use the Remove button to remove any other networks listed. Click Move Up or Move Down to change the order of preferred networks. Click Properties to view or change security settings. Click Advanced to open a dialog in which you can specify whether to automatically connect to non-preferred networks. Note that if the Use Windows to Configure My Wireless Network Settings box is cleared, you must use the wireless network software provided by your network adapter vendor, not Windows, to configure your network.

FIGURE 8.32
Configuring available and preferred wireless networks.

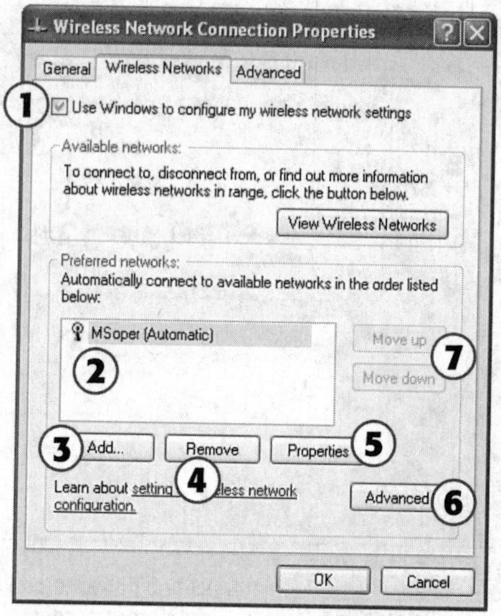

Wireless Network Connection Properties

General | Wireless Networks | Advanced

☑ Use Windows to configure my wireless network settings

Available networks:
To connect to, disconnect from, or find out more information about wireless networks in range, click the button below.

[View Wireless Networks]

Preferred networks:
Automatically connect to available networks in the order listed below:

📶 MSoper [Automatic]

[Move up] ⑦
[Move down]

③ [Add...] [Remove] [Properties] ⑤

Learn about setting ④ less network configuration.

[Advanced] ⑥

[OK] [Cancel]

① ②

1. Clear this checkmark if you prefer to use the wireless vendor's own configuration software
2. List of preferred networks
3. Adds a wireless network to the preferred list
4. Removes a wireless network from the preferred list
5. Displays security settings for the selected network
6. Displays advanced dialog
7. Changes order of preferred networks

- **You're using incompatible Wi-Fi standards.** 2.4GHz Wi-Fi network hardware running at 11Mbps (802.11b) and 54Mbps (802.11g) can coexist on the same network. However, 5GHz Wi-Fi network hardware uses the 802.11a standard; you cannot connect 802.11a-based network hardware to an 802.11b or 802.11g network unless the 802.11a hardware also supports 802.11b or 802.11g (so-called *dual-band hardware*). Note that you must configure an 802.11g wireless router or access point to run in mixed mode to support 802.11b and 802.11g hardware on the same network. If the router or access point is configured as a g-only device, 802.11b devices will not be able to connect to it.

Leo Says

Coping with a Mix-and-Match Wireless/Wired Network

Although this book has separate sections for wired and wireless networking, the reality is that many home and small office networks have "mix-and-match" networks with both wired and wireless components. A typical wireless router includes an Ethernet switch, enabling a single device to provide network and Internet access to wired and wireless clients. If your network has both types of hardware, keep these facts in mind:

- Both wired and wireless network clients need IP addresses; they can receive them from the router or can be configured manually.
- Both wired and wireless network clients need to use a common workgroup name to be on the same network.
- The workgroup name is *not* the same as the SSID (the name of the wireless network).
- You configure shared folders and printers the same way on both types of clients—either manually or with the Home Networking Wizard.

Essentially, both types of networks use the same configuration for TCP/IP networking and Internet, but wireless networks add a second layer of settings.

Using the Windows XP SP2 Wireless Network Setup Wizard

Starting with Windows XP Service Pack 2, Microsoft has added the Wireless Network Setup Wizard to help ease the difficulties of wireless network configuration.

Follow these steps to start the wizard:

1. Click Start, All Programs, Accessories, Communications, Wireless Networking Wizard. Then click Next.

2. In the Create a Name for Your Wireless Network dialog (see Figure 8.33), enter the SSID you want to use for your network.

3. Select whether you want to automatically assign a network key (default) or manually assign a network key. Use the manual option if you are adding your system to an existing network.

4. By default, the wizard uses WEP encryption; to use WPA encryption, click the Use WPA Encryption... check box. Click Next to continue. Note that you will see an error dialog onscreen if your network hardware does not support WPA. Click OK to continue.

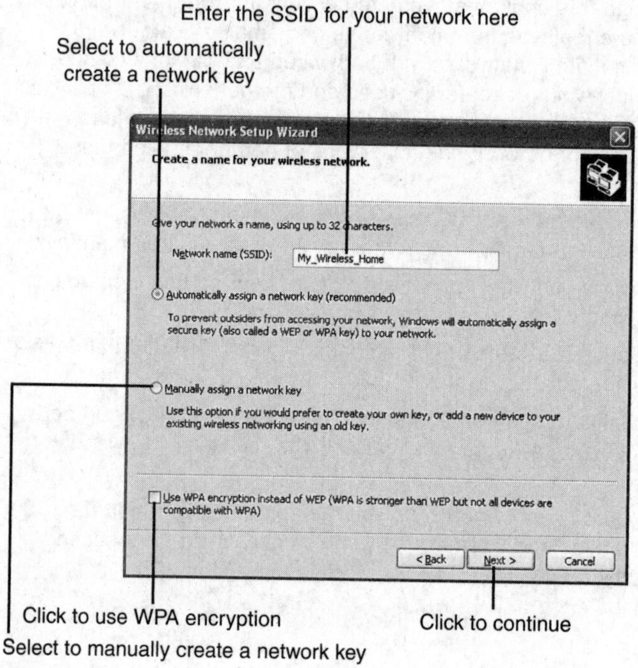

FIGURE 8.33

Creating an SSID and selecting network encryption with the Windows XP SP2 Wireless Network Setup Wizard.

Enter the SSID for your network here

Select to automatically create a network key

Click to use WPA encryption
Select to manually create a network key

Click to continue

5. If you select the default "automatic" option shown in Figure 8.33, you can select from two options to save your settings: a USB flash (keychain) drive or manual network setup. We recommend using the USB flash drive option. Insert the drive and click Next to continue.

6. If you select the option to enter a network key yourself, you will see the dialog shown in Figure 8.34. Enter the network key and then reenter it. Click Next to continue.

7. On the following screen, select the option to store the network settings to a USB flash drive or to configure the network manually.

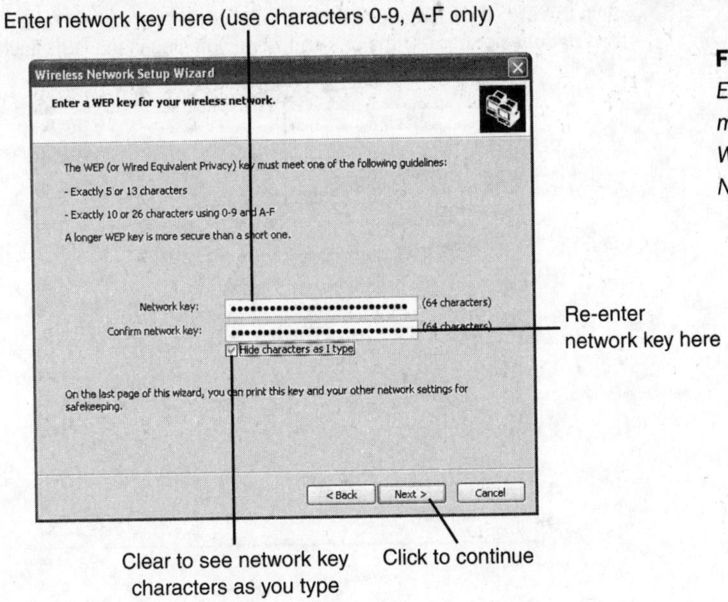

Enter network key here (use characters 0-9, A-F only)

FIGURE 8.34
Entering a WEP key manually with the Windows XP Wireless Network Setup Wizard.

Re-enter network key here

Clear to see network key characters as you type

Click to continue

8. If you selected the option to store the network settings on a USB flash drive, insert the drive when prompted. Click Next. A dialog displays the setup files as they are transferred to the flash drive.

9. Follow the instructions shown in Figure 8.35 to transfer the settings from the USB flash drive to your wireless access point (or router) and other network client PCs and devices. Click Next to continue.

10. At the end of the process, the wizard displays a "completed successfully" dialog.

11. Click the Print Network Settings button to open the settings in Notepad (see Figure 8.36).

12. Click File, Save As and name the file to create a backup of your settings, or click File, Print to make a printout that you can use to manually enter the settings on your wireless access point, router, or other network clients.

Skip this step if your wireless access point or router does not have a USB
port or does not transfer the settings when you plug in the USB flash drive

FIGURE 8.35
*How to transfer
settings to other
computers and
devices.*

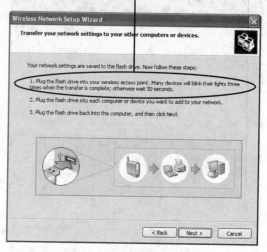

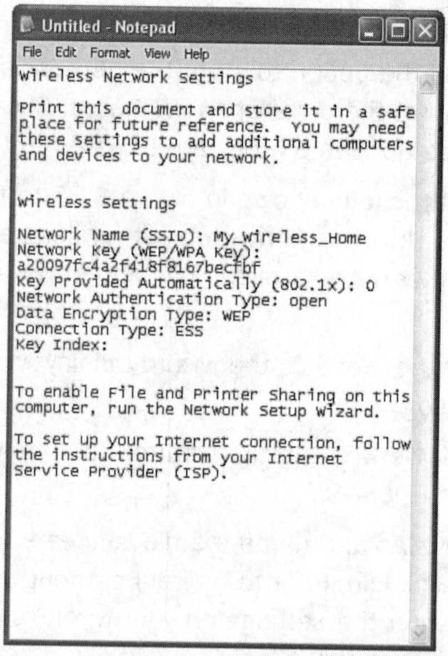

FIGURE 8.36
*Using Notepad to view,
save, or print your
settings.*

Troubleshooting Routers and Gateways

If you are using a router, gateway, or access point to share an Internet
connection with the network instead of using Windows ICS, you need
to configure it before you can configure the stations on the network.

Because the router, gateway, or access point replaces the original sin-gle-computer connection to the broadband Internet modem, it needs to use the same settings as you originally used for the computer that was attached directly to the broadband Internet modem. Run IPCON-FIG on the computer connected to the broadband Internet connection to display your current settings.

→ *See "Using IPCONFIG," this chapter, p. 536.*

Most routers are already configured to automatically obtain an IP address from the broadband modem (most broadband modems will work as DHCP servers). You will need to configure the router to pro-vide IP addresses for all the computers on your network. Otherwise, some or all of your computers might not be able to access the Internet.

Your routing device will need additional configuration settings if any of the following are true about your connection:

- If your Internet connection uses a static (fixed) IP address pro-vided by your broadband ISP, you will need to manually enter the computer's IP address and the IP addresses for DNS servers and your ISP's gateway into the routing device's configuration.

- If you must log into your broadband service using a username and password, this indicates that your service uses an option called PPPoE. You will need to select PPPoE in your router config-uration and specify your username and password.

- If you have an ISP that requires you to provide the hardware address (MAC address) of your network card when your system was first configured, you might want to use a feature known as "MAC address cloning." MAC address cloning enables the routing device to display the MAC address you specify (the one from your original network card) rather than its actual MAC address when it connects to the ISP's network. This option effectively hides your router from your ISP, making it look like your PC is connected directly to their network.

How can you determine if these special settings apply to your configu-ration?

- You can ask your ISP.

- You can examine your network configuration.

To examine your network configuration in Windows XP/2000, follow these steps:

1. Click Start, Control Panel, Network and Internet Connections, Network Connections.

2. If your connection is listed under LAN or High-Speed Internet, it doesn't use PPPoE. If your connection is listed under Broadband and includes PPPoE in its description, you will need to configure the router to use PPPoE in its login configuration and then enter the username and password you normally use to connect to the Internet.

3. To determine the IP address configuration of your connection, right-click the connection icon, select Properties, click Internet Protocol (TCP/IP), and click Properties.

If your connection uses a server-assigned IP address, the Obtain an IP Address Automatically and Obtain DNS Server Address Automatically options should be selected on the General tab. If you see specific IP addresses specified on the General tab for the computer's IP address and DNS servers, record the addresses for use with your router and click Advanced. Record the default gateway's IP address and other IP address and server name information provided so you can enter this information into the router's configuration screen.

➔ *For details, see "Using IPCONFIG," this chapter, p. 536.*

Because it's a good idea to clone the MAC address of your network adapter even if your ISP doesn't indicate they track this information, you should also record this information. To display the MAC address for your network adapter, use IPCONFIG with Windows XP.

Posting Your Findings

The easiest way to make sure you're recording the correct information you need to configure your routing device is to open the instruction manual included with the router, gateway, or access point, turn to the pages that discuss the configuration process, follow the instructions listed previously, and use the humble Post-It note from 3M to attach the correct values to the pages. You might even want to number each Post-It note to correspond with the figure numbers on the page.

If your instruction manual is electronic, print out the pages and use the Post-It note trick. It's better than writing on the pages themselves because you might discover you've made a mistake the first time you configure the device.

Follow the instructions provided with the routing device to configure it.
Depending on the router, you might use a web-based configuration utility that requires you to connect a computer to the routing device and
log into it through a web browser such as Internet Explorer; the
instruction manual for your routing device will provide the correct IP
address to access the routing device's setup program, or you might
use a wizard for initial configuration, then use a web-based configuration for changes later. Even if you're using a wireless routing device,
you might find it easier to connect a computer via an Ethernet cable
when it's time to configure it (if you have a choice). Figure 8.37 shows
an example of a wizard-based configuration for a U.S. Robotics
wireless router and switch.

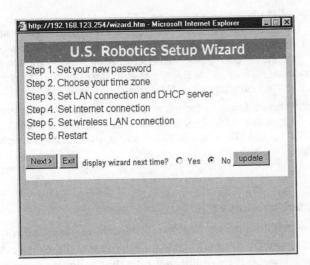

FIGURE 8.37
*A wizard-based
configuration utility for
a wireless router and
switch.*

In addition to configuring the connection between the routing device
and your broadband Internet modem (often referred to as the *WAN
connection*), you also need to configure the routing device to serve as
a DHCP server so it can provide IP address information to the computers on the network. Once you have completed the configuration of
the router, connect your computers to the routing device and configure
your network software. See "Troubleshooting Network Software
Configuration," this chapter, p. 495.

If you use a wireless network, you need to follow additional steps
before you can configure the computers on the network. You should
configure the access point to use WEP or WPA encryption and select

an encryption level compatible with both your access point and your network adapters. If you don't configure your wireless network to be secure, anyone with compatible wireless gear who's within range of your network could sneak onto your network and use your Internet connection for free. See "Troubleshooting Wi-Fi Networks," this chapter, p. 512, for more information.

Wi-Fi Isn't Completely Standard

A hallmark of 10/100 Ethernet is compatibility between different brands of hardware. I've mixed and matched two, three, or even four brands and models of NICs, routers, hubs, and switches (not to mention using both pre-made and bulk network cables) on a single network without any problems.

However, Wi-Fi (the popular name for IEEE-802.11-based wireless networks), isn't completely standardized, despite the multivendor testing the Wi-Fi trade organization performs. Because different vendors use different methods for configuring their access points and might add additional proprietary features to their hardware, you're better off if you get your access points/routers and NICs from the same vendor.

Also, don't be confused by the many IEEE-802.11-series wireless networks. Despite the similarities in name, IEEE 802.11a isn't compatible with 802.11b and 802.11g unless you use special multimode network hardware.

Troubleshooting a Router

Routers resemble a networking hub or switch, which is a device that allows multiple PCs to share data or peripherals. However, routers also have a special WAN or Internet port that connects them to broadband modems, providing a hardware method for sharing a single Internet connection among computers on a network. (Some routers only connect to one computer, but most can connect to four or more.) Like the modems themselves, routers can suffer from a number of problems that could interrupt your Internet service:

- If your ISP changes the type of IP address you have (the most common switch is from a static IP address, which never changes, to a dynamic IP address), you need to reprogram your router to use dynamic IP addressing; otherwise, your connection will fail (see Figure 8.38).

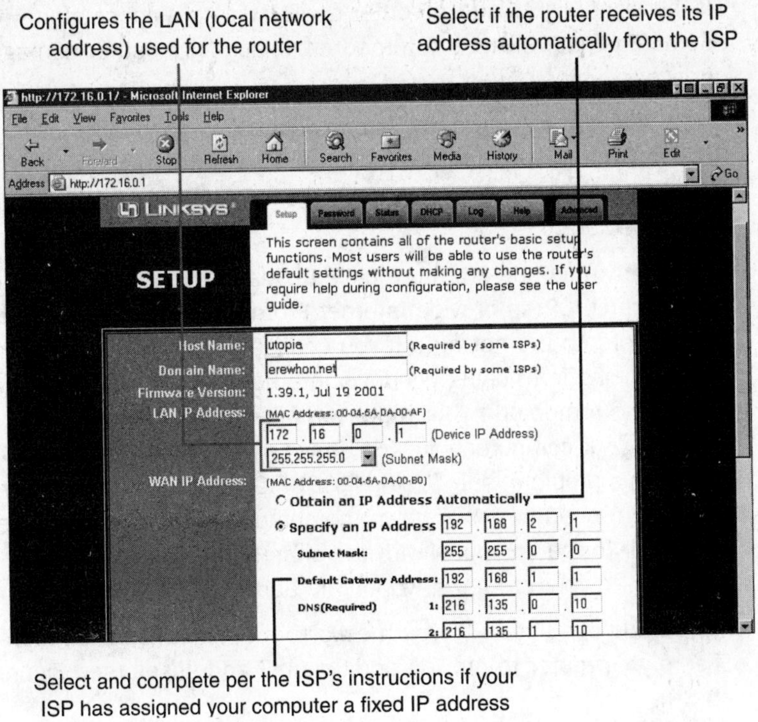

Configures the LAN (local network address) used for the router

Select if the router receives its IP address automatically from the ISP

FIGURE 8.38
The setup screen for a typical router (the Linksys BEFSR41); this screen controls the LAN (network) and WAN (Internet connection) IP addresses.

Select and complete per the ISP's instructions if your ISP has assigned your computer a fixed IP address

- Some ISPs dislike home networks and might shut off service to your computer if they determine that you are using a router to share your Internet connection. To avoid this problem, use the MAC address cloning feature in your router's setup to have the router report the same MAC address used by the network adapter originally connected to the cable modem to the ISP. To learn how to view your network adapter's MAC address, see "Using IPCONFIG," p. 536, this chapter. Note that some ISPs simply require you to register your new network hardware to continue your service.

- Your router or gateway has lost its connection to the broadband modem. Reset the router or gateway and retry your connection. If you still can't connect, contact the ISP and verify the settings for your account. Make sure your router configuration is using the correct settings for fixed or server-assigned IP addresses (fixed IP addresses also require settings for gateway and DNS servers) and any other configuration options used by your ISP.

- If the signal lights on the router don't indicate a connection with some computers that are turned on, check for loose or damaged network cables.

- No computers on the network can connect to each other or to the Internet if the router loses power. Check the power connections in the event of a power failure on the circuit that the router is connected to.

- Most networks use a feature called Dynamic Host Configuration Protocol (DHCP) to provide Internet Protocol (IP) addresses to the computers on the network. If you change sharing methods, such as switching from using Windows Internet Connection Sharing (ICS) to a router, or if your router wasn't powered on when you started your computer, you won't have a valid IP address. To solve this problem, see "Using IPCONFIG," p. 536, this chapter. You might need to power down the computers connected to the router or to the computer with the shared Internet connection and restart them to get a working IP address.

- If you add computers to your network, you might need to reconfigure your router to provide additional IP addresses (see Figure 8.39).

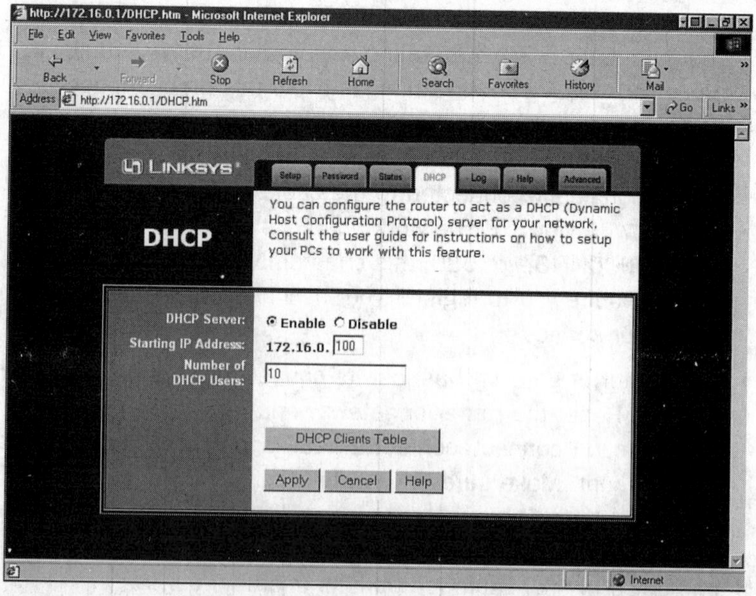

FIGURE 8.39

Configuring a typical router (the Linksys BEFSR41) to use DHCP to provide IP addresses for up to 10 computers. The router has a built-in web server that lets you use your web browser to configure it or view settings.

- If one computer on the network can't access the Internet, but others can, check the cabling between that computer and the router. Most routers incorporate what is called an *Uplink port*, which enables the router to be daisy-chained to another hub or switch to allow more computers to share data or Internet access across a network. If you plug a computer into the Uplink port (which has its connections reversed from a normal network cable) instead of into a normal port, the computer won't be able to "see" the Internet or the rest of the network. Also, if you use the Uplink port, the adjacent port is disabled (see Figure 3.40).

FIGURE 8.40
The ports on a typical four-port router with an integrated switch.

WAN port (connects to broadband modem)

LAN ports to computers (#4 on left to #1 on right)

Uplink port to another switch or hub. When this port is in use, LAN port #1 cannot be used

Troubleshooting PC Card/CardBus Devices

PC Cards (also called *PCMCIA cards*) provide a wide variety of I/O services to portable computers, including 10/100 Ethernet and wireless Ethernet (Wi-Fi) network adapters (CardBus cards are 32-bit versions of PC Cards). However, if any of the following are true, your PC Card–interfaced network adapters won't work properly:

- PC Card is not completely inserted.
- PC Card handlers are not installed in the operating system.
- Dongles attached to the PC Card have failed or are not attached properly.

If a PC Card is not completely inserted into the PC Card slot, you need to eject it and slide it in all the way. When it is installed, you should see a PC Card icon appear in the Windows system tray, by

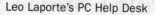
default, at the bottom of the screen (next to the clock). Windows XP refers to this icon as the Safely Remove Hardware icon.

If you have fully inserted a PC Card into the PC Card slot, and it is not recognized, there are three possible reasons:

- Windows cannot locate drivers for the PC Card.
- The PC Card configuration software used by Windows is not loaded.
- The PC Card configuration software used by Windows might have a problem.

Open the Device Manager and verify that the PC Card or CardBus (PCMCIA) controller is available and working properly (see Figure 8.41). If the controller is visible but doesn't report any problems, look for the icon for the device you installed. If it was recognized as a PC Card or CardBus device, it will be listed in the PCMCIA category in Device Manager. If you don't see the device listed in the PCMCIA category, it might be listed in the Other Devices category (see Figure 8.41); this category is used for devices that Windows cannot recognize until the appropriate device driver is installed. Open the device's properties sheet to verify that the device is installed in the PCMCIA slot. Follow the troubleshooting instructions listed; normally, you will need to install the correct driver for the device to enable Windows to recognize it.

FIGURE 8.41

An unrecognized device installed in a PCMCIA (PC Card or CardBus) slot.

→ *For more information on using the Solution button shown in Figure 8.41, see "Solving Resource Conflicts with Device Manager," Chapter 2, p. 100.*

Problem with device

Device is connected to the CardBus slot

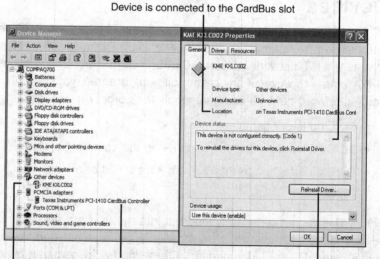

PC Card or CardBus host adapter

Unrecognized device

Solution button

If the controller is not visible, run Add New Hardware and install or troubleshoot it. A PC Card or CardBus controller is a very resource-hungry beast, using an IRQ, several memory ranges, and several I/O port address ranges. However, it should work correctly unless its drivers have been corrupted or another device is using one or more of the same memory or I/O port address ranges. If the controller is displayed, but has problems, use the status listed in the controller's properties sheet to determine the problem and solve it.

→ See "Using Device Manager," Chapter 2, p. 100, for details on troubleshooting hardware devices.

→ See "Hardware Resources," Chapter 1, p. 58, for details on how IRQs, I/O port addresses, and memory addresses are used by hardware.

If the PC Card or CardBus network adapter uses a dongle (refer to Figure 8.20) and you cannot connect to other network clients, make sure the network cable is tightly connected to the dongle. If the cable is tightly connected to the dongle, disconnect the dongle from the network adapter and reconnect it. If the cable works correctly with other network adapters, the dongle is defective. Replace the dongle or replace the card, preferably with a card that does not require a dongle. If the computer has USB 2.0 ports, use a USB 2.0/Ethernet adapter.

TCP/IP Configuration and Troubleshooting

TCP/IP, the Transport Control Protocol/Internet Protocol (often referred to in Windows as simply *Internet Protocol*), can be called the language of the Internet. It doesn't matter what type of computer you have; any computer or other device on the Internet needs to use TCP/IP to share information with the rest of the world's largest network.

Unfortunately, the flip side of the power of TCP/IP is that it can be very hard to configure. Every computer or other device on the Internet needs an IP address; computers and devices that are directly connected to the Internet need a public address unique to that machine. However, most Internet users don't connect directly to the Internet, but connect to an intermediate device or service that provides an IP address as needed. By default, Windows installs TCP/IP to receive an IP address from a Dynamic Host Control Protocol (DHCP) server, a feature of most ISPs as well as broadband modems, routers, and Internet sharing programs. A DHCP server automatically assigns an IP address when your computer makes the connection to the Internet.

However, if your ISP doesn't provide a setup CD for TCP/IP configuration, or if you need to make changes to your configuration because you are using Internet-sharing products such as a router, you might need to manually configure your computer's TCP/IP settings. This might include entering your computer's IP address, the IP addresses of the DNS servers the computer relies on to convert URLs into IP addresses, the IP address of the gateway to the Internet, and so forth. If you need to change these settings, open the properties sheet for the connection in Windows XP. Click the TCP/IP setting and select Properties. To learn how to view these settings in an easier-to-read list, see "Using IPCONFIG," this chapter, p. 536.

Using a Fixed IP Address with a Dial-Up or PPPoE Broadband Connection in Windows XP

To change the TCP/IP settings for a dial-up connection in Windows XP, follow these instructions:

1. Open the My Network Places folder.

2. Click View Network Connections.

3. Right-click the connection you need to change and select Properties.

4. Click Networking, click Internet Protocol (TCP/IP), and then click Properties (see Figure 8.42).

5. Click Use the Following IP Address and enter the IP address provided by the ISP for your computer.

6. Click Use the Following DNS Server Addresses and enter the IP addresses for the DNS servers used by the ISP.

7. If you need to make additional changes required by the ISP, such as WINS server IP addresses or additional DNS servers, click Advanced.

8. Click OK when you are finished.

If your broadband Internet connection requires you to log in and provide a username and password, the provider is using PPPoE (point-to-point protocol over Ethernet) for your account. DSL broadband accounts are the primary users of PPPoE, but other types of broadband might use it as well. Use the same procedure listed here to configure PPPoE broadband accounts with a fixed IP address.

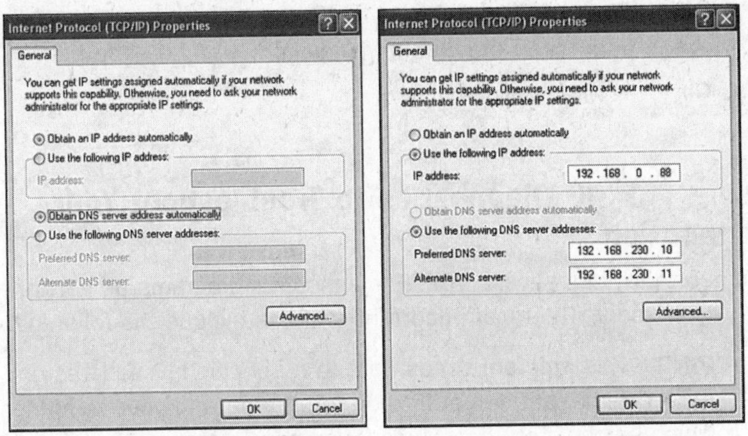

FIGURE 8.42

Configuring a Windows XP dial-up connection for the default server-assigned IP address (left) and for a fixed IP address (right).

Using a Fixed IP Address with a LAN, Cable Modem, or Fixed Wireless Connection in Windows XP

By default, Windows configures all types of Internet connections to use server-assigned IP addresses. In most cases, this is the correct setting because broadband Internet devices and routers (which are used to share a single Internet connection among multiple users) are normally configured to use DHCP to provide IP addresses to the devices connected to them. However, in some cases, an Internet connection using a LAN or a direct connection to a cable modem or other broadband device might need to use a fixed IP address.

To configure a LAN or broadband Internet connection with a fixed IP address in Windows XP, follow these steps:

1. Open the My Network Places folder.
2. Click View Network Connections.
3. Right-click the connection you need to change and select Properties.
4. Click Networking, click Internet Protocol (TCP/IP), and then click Properties.
5. Click Use the Following IP Address and enter the IP address provided by the ISP for your computer.
6. Click Use the Following DNS Server Addresses and enter the IP addresses for the DNS servers used by the ISP.

7. Click Advanced and click Add under the Gateway section; enter the IP address of the default gateway.

8. Click OK when finished.

Using TCP/IP Diagnostics to Troubleshoot Your Connection

Microsoft provides several TCP/IP diagnostics programs as part of the TCP/IP protocol. The most important of these include the following:

- **PING**—This program sends data to a specified IP address or server name. The target IP then returns data to your computer, which helps you to determine if you have a live connection and how fast it is. You can also use PING to make sure your computer has TCP/IP installed.

- **IPCONFIG**—This program displays the IP address and other details about your computer, and it can be used to release and renew IP addresses provided by a DHCP server (often built into a router or broadband modem). Note that if you still use Windows 9x/Me, WINIPCFG performs the same function.

These commands are covered in more detail in the upcoming sections.

To run PING and IPCONFIG, you need to open a command-prompt window. Within Windows XP, click Start, Run, type **CMD**, and then click OK. Then, type the command and options you want to use after the command prompt (>) and press Enter. After you are finished with command-line programs, type **EXIT** and press Enter to return to the Windows desktop.

Using IPCONFIG

If you're not a whiz at networking, digging around in the Networks icon in Control Panel probably isn't your idea of a good time. Fortunately, running IPCONFIG provides a fast way to see TCP/IP configuration information about your computer.

After opening a command prompt in Windows XP, type IPCONFIG and press Enter to display the name of the DNS server (the server that matches IP addresses to server names), the computer's IP address and subnet mask, and the default gateway (which connects your computer to the Internet). If you need more detailed information, type **IPCONFIG /ALL** and press Enter, as in Figure 8.43.

DHCP enabled; if yes, computer gets its
IP address from the DHCP server; if no,
the IP address is anually configured

Physical (MAC) address

FIGURE 8.43

IPCONFIG /ALL displays your MAC address (physical address), along with your computer's IP address, whether you use DHCP to get an IP address, and other information that tech support people might need to know about your system.

This computer's IP
address and subnet mask

Default gateway; PING this IP address to determine if you
have a connection to the device that can reach the Internet

If your computer has a wireless network adapter and an Ethernet port, you will see listings for both devices. If you use the wireless network adapter, the wireless network adapter entry lists information similar to the information shown in Figure 8.43, but the Ethernet adapter entry lists "media disconnected."

If you see an invalid IP address such as 0.0.0.0 and your computer uses dynamic IP addressing, type **IPCONFIG /RELEASE** and press Enter to release the current IP addresses. Then type **IPCONFIG /RENEW** and press Enter to get new IP address information for your system. If you still see 0.0.0.0 as the IP address, you need to do the following:

1. Make sure you have a working connection to the device that gives you your IP address (a router, a computer running a sharing program such as Internet Connection Sharing (ICS), or a broadband modem). If you use a separate switch and router, make sure both are turned on and that the switch is properly connected to the router and to all the computers.

2. Make sure the router, computer with shared Internet access, or modem is turned on. If you connect through a computer running ICS or a third-party sharing program, see if you can access the Internet from that computer. If not, you need to get that computer working first before others can use its connection.

3. Restart the router, computer with shared Internet access, or broadband modem. Wait for a computer that shares Internet access with others to complete booting.

4. Restart your computer and see if you can connect to the Internet.

If you see an IP address starting with 169, your computer has assigned itself a private IP address because it could not receive an IP address from the DHCP server on your network. Use the same checklist used to recover from an invalid IP address to solve this problem.

Using PING

PING must be used from a command prompt, as described in the previous section. It can be used to determine the following:

- Whether you have TCP/IP installed on your system

- Whether you have a connection to a specified IP address or server name

- The speed of your connection to a specified IP address or server name

To view the options you can use for PING, type **PING /?** and press Enter. Normally, you will use a command such as **PING *hostname*** (replace *hostname* with the IP address or server name). If PING can reach the specified hostname, it determines the host's IP address (a process called *resolving*), sends data to the host, and displays the roundtrip time (also called *site latency*), the host's IP address, and the time to live (TTL) value for that site (in milliseconds). Figure 8.44 shows a typical PING command and output.

FIGURE 8.44

Using PING to test the connection to a popular Internet news site. Note the average roundtrip time (also called the ping rate *or* latency *of the website).*

Checking Your TCP/IP Configuration with PING

To make sure that you have TCP/IP installed on your system, type
PING 127.0.0.1 (this IP address is called the *local loopback address*)
and press Enter. If you don't have TCP/IP installed, you will get an
"unknown host" error message instead of output similar to that shown
in Figure 8.44. Reinstall the TCP/IP protocol through the Network icon
in Control Panel.

Checking Your Connection to Your Broadband Modem or Router or ICS Host with PING

To determine the IP address of your broadband modem or router or
the computer that shares its Internet connection with the network, use
IPCONFIG. The value shown for the default gateway is the address to
use in your PING command. For example, if the default gateway is
listed as 192.168.0.1, use PING 192.168.0.1.

If you get a timeout error instead of a display similar to that shown in
Figure 8.44, you might have a cabling problem or the router or modem
might not be working. Restart your computer and try your connection
again. If it fails, then check the broadband modem or router to see if
the device is working correctly. If your computer uses another computer's Internet connection, restart the computer with the shared connection and make sure it's completely booted and is running the
sharing software before you try your Internet connection again.

If you can ping the IP address of your broadband modem, the router,
or the computer with the shared Internet connection, but you cannot
ping remote IP addresses or websites, there is a problem with your
Internet connection beyond your network. Restart the broadband
modem, router, or computer with the shared connection and try the
Internet connection again. If the connection still doesn't work, see
"Using Signal Lights to Troubleshoot Your Connection," this chapter,
p. 494, to troubleshoot your broadband modem, or see
"Troubleshooting a Router", this chapter, p. 528, to solve the router
problems.

If PING displays "Unknown Host" when you ping another computer or
IP address, make sure you specified the correct hostname and check
your TCP/IP settings to verify that you can reach a DNS server.

Using PING to Locate Fast Game Servers

Because PING can be used to measure the roundtrip speed between your computer and any other computer that responds to PING (some computers and websites block PING for security reasons), you can use PING to check your connection speed to a game server (PING *game-servername* or PING *Ipaddress of gameserver*). The lower the PING rate, the faster your connection.

Internet connections can be very complex, particularly if your ISP has provided you with a fixed IP address or if you use a network to provide shared Internet access. Using tools such as IPCONFIG and PING to determine your network configuration when it's working properly will make troubleshooting a broken system a lot easier to perform.

Network Connections

The Network Connections system folder displays the current network and Internet connections on your system. Right-click a connection to view its properties, repair it, enable or disable it, or use it as a bridge to another connection you specify (see Figure 8.45).

Click to configure the Windows Firewall

FIGURE 8.45

Using the Network Connections folder in Windows XP to repair a connection.

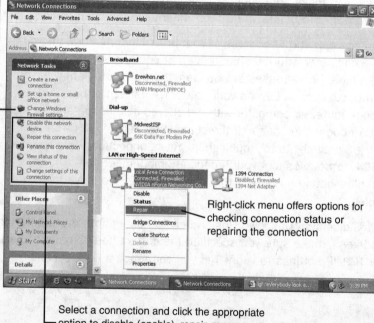

Right-click menu offers options for checking connection status or repairing the connection

Select a connection and click the appropriate option to disable (enable), repair, rename, view status or change connection settings

What Connections Do Which Task?

Figure 8.45 shows different types of connections. A broadband connection requires you to log in and supply a username and password when you connect. A dial-up connection uses a dial-up modem and your regular phone line. A LAN or high-speed Internet connection might use Internet Connection Sharing, a router, or a connection to a broadband device that's always on (no login or username/password required).

Troubleshooting Your Network/Internet Connections

The Network Connections display in Windows XP offers two different ways to fix a broken connection:

- Repair This Connection
- Change Settings of This Connection

Select the connection and click Repair This Connection or right-click the connection and select Repair to run a series of commands designed to fix common problems with connections that use dynamic IP addresses (as most Internet connections do). You can learn more about what Repair does from Microsoft Knowledge Base article 289256, available at http://support.microsoft.com/default.aspx?kbid=289256.

To fix other problems such as an incorrect user-set IP address, or to enable or disable the Internet Connection Firewall (Windows XP up through Service Pack 1) or Windows Firewall (Windows XP Service Pack 2 and beyond), select Properties from the right-click menu or Change Settings of This Connection from the left column. The General tab displays the network components installed. Authentication configures how your connection provides authenticated access to a network. Advanced lets you enable or disable the firewall. You can also click Change Windows Firewall Settings from the Network Tasks menu shown in Figure 8.45.

Using Net Diagnostics

Net Diagnostics runs a series of tests on your network, broadband, and dial-up Internet connections to determine whether they are working correctly. Net Diagnostics also checks software configurations for mail and news servers to see if they are properly configured (see Figure 8.46). You should start your dial-up or broadband Internet connection before you start Net Diagnostics.

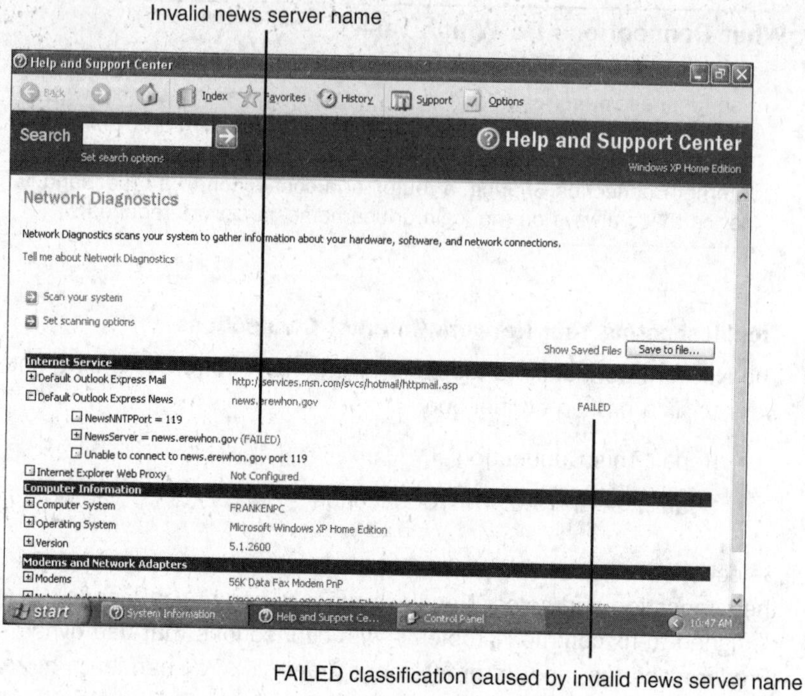

FIGURE 8.46

An incorrect setting for the news server causes this service to fail.

Invalid news server name

FAILED classification caused by invalid news server name

Click the plus sign (+) next to a category to expand it for more information, particularly if it's marked as FAILED. If a failed message appears next to a mail or news server, check the spelling of the name; if the name is incorrectly spelled, Windows can't find the resource. Open your default mail or news reader software (Outlook Express is used by most Windows users) and correct the spelling. If the spelling is correct, the remote server might not be responding.

If you see a FAILED message for hardware such as your network adapter or modem, use Device Manager to diagnose the problem.

Troubleshooting the Windows XP Firewall

A *firewall* is a device or program that stops unauthorized network traffic. Windows XP contains a built-in firewall that is configured through the Advanced tab of the properties sheet for any type of network or Internet connection, including dial-up (see Figure 8.47).

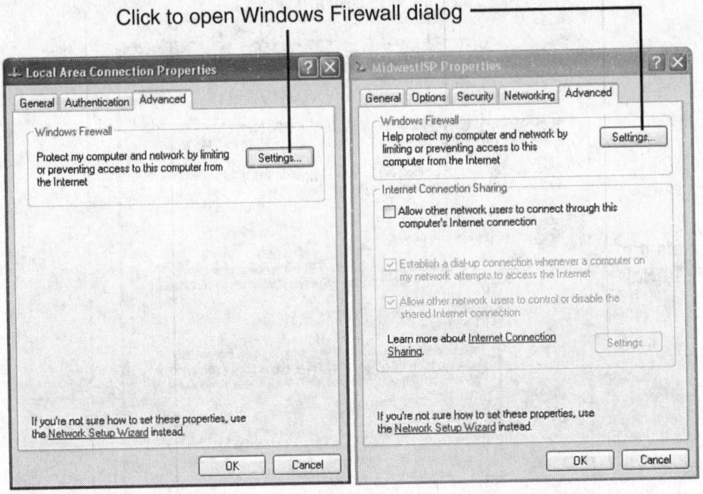

Click to open Windows Firewall dialog

FIGURE 8.47

Use the Advanced tab for a dial-up (left) or LAN connection (right) to access the Windows XP Firewall.

The original version of the Windows XP firewall was used in the initial release of Windows XP and Service Pack 1; it was designed primarily for direct connections to the Internet through a dial-up or broadband modem. If you enabled this version of the firewall on a system with shared resources such as printers or folders, other computers on the network could not access these resources. For this reason, many users of Windows XP used third-party firewalls instead.

Windows XP SP2 Firewall

Starting with Service Pack 2, the Windows Firewall was greatly improved; it now supports resource sharing on local area networks, while continuing to block unauthorized traffic from the Internet. Figure 8.48 shows the basic dialog for the SP2 version of the Windows Firewall.

SP2 Firewall Exceptions

When Windows Firewall is enabled, it blocks Internet access except for programs on the Exceptions tab (see Figure 8.49). The Exceptions tab contains a short list of programs you can select as exceptions to the "no unsolicited inbound traffic" rule used by Windows Firewall. To permit a program on the list to run, make sure the box is checked. By default, Remote Assistance is enabled. However, if you want to share resources, you must also check File and Printer Sharing. And, if you want your computer to automatically detect Internet gateways, check UPnP (Universal Plug and Play) Framework.

Current status of firewall (turned off)

FIGURE 8.48
This system's Windows Firewall is not enabled.

Click to enable the Windows Firewall

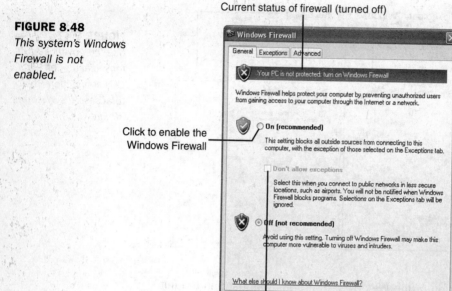

Click to block all unsolicited inbound traffic when Firewall
is enabled, including programs on the Exceptions list

Click to enable automatic detection of Internet gateways with UPnP
Click to enable File and Print Sharing

FIGURE 8.49
The only default exception is for Remote Assistance.

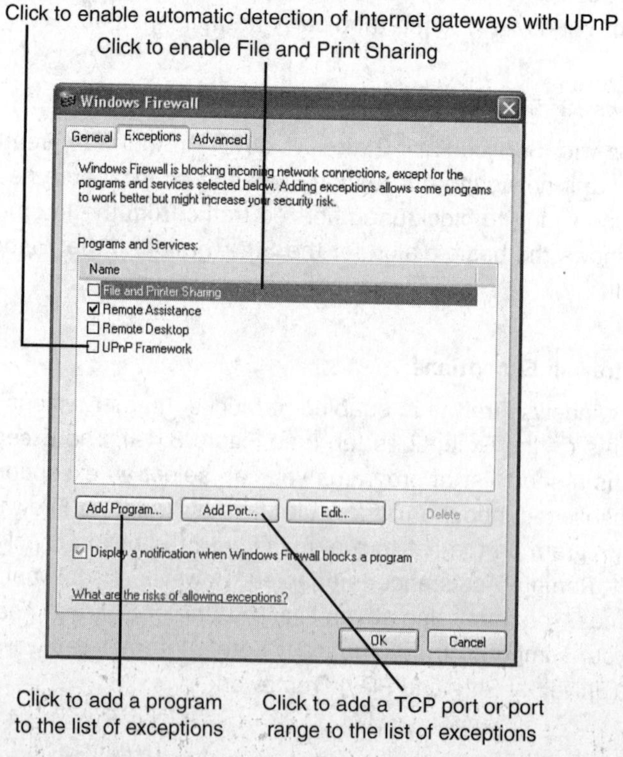

Click to add a program   Click to add a TCP port or port
to the list of exceptions   range to the list of exceptions

Protect Your Traveling PC: Make No Exceptions!

If you take your PC on the road and use unsecured "hot spots" in libraries, hotels, and airport terminals, make sure you're protected against unauthorized traffic. Open the Windows Firewall dialog as soon as you boot up your PC in such situations and click the Don't Allow Exceptions check box shown in Figure 8.48. This disables the Exceptions list, preventing your system from unauthorized file sharing and other risks. When you return to your home or office, uncheck this box and your normal Exceptions list takes effect again.

If Windows Firewall prevents you from using network or Internet-enabled programs, click Add Program and choose the program that needs Internet access from the list of installed programs. If your program needs access to specified TCP port numbers (often the case with online games), click Add Port and specify the TCP port numbers your program requires.

SP2 Firewall Advanced Settings

By default, the settings in Windows Firewall are the same for all network and Internet connections. To specify exceptions for a particular connection, click the Advanced tab and click Settings in the Network Connection Settings portion of the dialog (see Figure 8.50). The Advanced tab is also used to configure the network activity log created by Windows Firewall, to configure error and status message sharing, and to reset the firewall to its defaults.

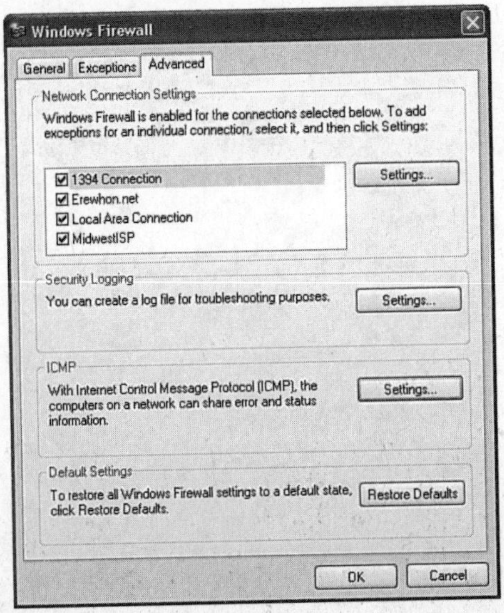

FIGURE 8.50

Use the Advanced tab to customize exceptions for a particular connection, to configure security logging or error and status information, or to reset the firewall to its defaults.

Troubleshooting Memory, Processor, and System Performance Problems

TROUBLESHOOTING

FAST TRACK TO SOLUTIONS (SYMPTOM TABLE)

Symptom	Flowchart or Book Section	See Page
My computer slows down when two or more programs are open.	Troubleshooting Slow System Performance	549
I want to defragment my drive, but Windows says there's not enough free disk space.	Sidebar: Freeing Up Space For Better Defragging	556
I want to install more memory in my system, but there aren't any empty memory sockets left.	Freeing Up Sockets for Additional Memory	574
I installed new memory, but the system didn't detect it.	Troubleshooting Memory Upgrade Problems	575
Some of my installed memory doesn't seem to be working.	Troubleshooting Defective Memory or Memory Sockets	578
My computer started beeping after I installed new memory.	Troubleshooting Memory with POST Beep Codes	581
I'm not sure if my processor fan is running properly.	Detecting Overheating and Incorrect Voltage Levels	583
I'm not sure if my system can use a faster processor.	Discovering Your Current Processor and BIOS Version	589
My computer is slow. What should I upgrade first?	Sidebar: What to Upgrade First	593
Where should I plug in the fan on the processor's heatsink?	I'm Having a Hard Time Installing My New Processor	594
I just installed a new processor and now my system won't start.	My System Won't Start After I Installed a New Processor	599
My processor is not running at its marked speed.	My New Processor Isn't Running as Fast as It Should	600
I don't know what sizes of motherboards will fit in my case.	Making Sure Your New Motherboard Will Fit Into Your Case	603
After I replaced the motherboard, my system started beeping.	My System Beeps Abnormally After I Restart It with the New Motherboard in Place	609
My system keeps overheating.	Troubleshooting Cooling Problems	610
The heatsink on my motherboard's North Bridge chip has failed. How do I replace it?	Preventing Overheating Damage to the Motherboard	611

Troubleshooting Slow System Performance

Although many different components affect system performance, such as the graphics card and hard disk, perhaps the two most important components affecting system performance are the memory and the processor (CPU). Although processor upgrades often require mother-board changes on desktop computers and can't be performed on note-book computers, virtually every computer can benefit from added memory. Also, even if you can't add more physical memory right now, you can also optimize your computer's use of virtual memory (a part of your computer's hard disk that handles overflow data from main memory).

Adding memory is not only one of the best ways to boost performance, but it is also one of the least expensive. How can you tell if you need to add memory? Here are some signs that your system may have a memory shortage:

- You see the Windows "I'm busy" hourglass appear frequently when you have multiple program windows open.
- The hard disk activity light is blinking furiously as you work.
- Switching between programs takes measurable time instead of being instantaneous.
- When you open a new folder, Windows takes several seconds to display the icons inside.

Is a lack of RAM really the problem? Use the following methods to determine if the performance bottleneck is caused by a lack of system memory:

- Determine the amount of memory you currently have installed on your system.
- Determine how many programs you run at the same time (on average).
- Check the performance of your system.

To find out how much physical memory is available to Windows (and how fast your processor is, too), right-click My Computer in Windows XP and select Properties. This displays the General tab of the System Properties dialog, as shown in Figure 9.1.

FIGURE 9.1

The General tab of the System Properties dialog in Windows XP.

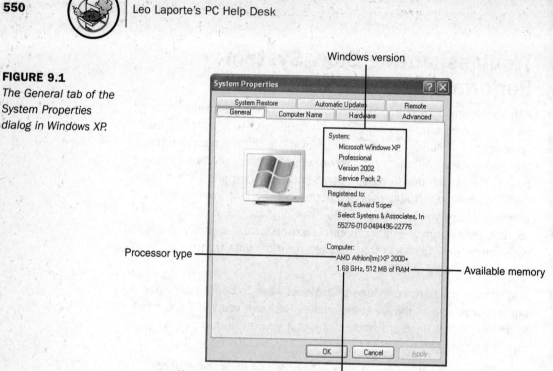

Compare the amount of available memory in your system to the figures in Table 9.1 to determine if adding memory could speed up your system.

TABLE 9.1
RECOMMENDED MEMORY SIZES FOR APPLICATIONS YOU USE

Number of Programs You Have Open at One Time (on Average)	Types of Programs	Recommended Minimum RAM
1 to 2	Word processing and email, card and board games, web browsing	256MB
1	3D games	768MB
2	Office suites, web browsing	256MB

TABLE 9.1 (continued)

Number of Programs You Have Open at One Time (on Average)	Types of Programs	Recommended Minimum RAM
3	Office suites, games, web browsing	384MB
3 or more	Office suites, photo and graphics editors, web browsing	512MB
3 or more	Office suites, photo and graphics editors, CAD, multimedia, web browsing	768MB
3 or more	3D CAD or modeling software, web browsing	2GB (motherboard might limit maximum memory size)

As you can see from Table 9.1, it makes sense to upgrade your system to at least 512MB of RAM, particularly if you work with multimedia or digital imaging or play 3D games. Keep in mind that if your computer runs out of actual RAM, it will use its *virtual* memory, which is stored in a file called the *page file* (also called the *swapfile*). The page file is an area of free space on your hard disk that the computer treats like additional RAM. Unfortunately, the difference between accessing data from system RAM and your hard drive is like the difference between making photocopies in your office or driving across town to a Kinko's. It's a very slow substitute.

If your system has less than 400MB of RAM, upgrade it to at least 512MB. If you can upgrade it to 1GB or more, you're even better off. Windows XP shatters the memory limits imposed by the old Windows 9x/Me versions, so you should add as much memory as your motherboard permits.

Tracking Down "Missing" Memory

If you use a low-cost computer with video integrated into the motherboard, or a notebook computer, you might see an unusual memory size such as 240MB (instead of 256MB) when you view your system properties (refer to Figure 9.1). This is because Windows cannot "see" memory that is set aside for use by your integrated video. Video integrated into the motherboard can use up to 64MB of RAM, depending on the computer and the amount of system memory installed.

When you add memory, I recommend you keep this factor in mind. If you are planning to upgrade to 512MB of RAM and your system uses 16MB or more of main memory for video, add an extra 256MB to the amount you were planning to add to make sure you have plenty of RAM after video takes its cut.

The figures in Table 9.1 are estimates based on typical usage. But who's typical? If you want a custom-tailored solution to the question, "Do I need more RAM?," you can use the Task Manager in Windows XP to display real-time statistics for memory usage:

1. Press the Ctrl+Alt+Delete keys to display Task Manager.
2. Click the Performance tab (see Figure 9.2).
3. Open the programs you plan to run at the same time.
4. Open typical data files within these programs.

Let's cut to the chase. Assuming you've opened up a typical mix of programs and data files, *if* Commit Charge (Total) is consistently larger than Physical Memory (Total), as in Figure 9.2, *then* you should shop for a memory upgrade.

What happens until you upgrade memory? Well, Windows doesn't go on strike. However, it uses the slowpoke virtual memory paging file on the hard disk to make up the difference. Thus, it's a good idea to fine-tune how well the paging file works.

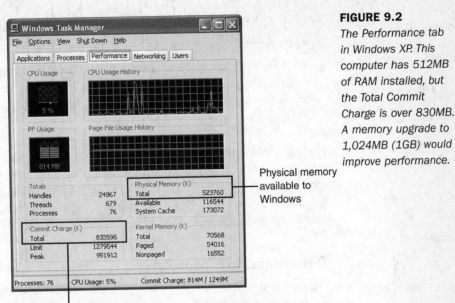

FIGURE 9.2
The Performance tab in Windows XP. This computer has 512MB of RAM installed, but the Total Commit Charge is over 830MB. A memory upgrade to 1,024MB (1GB) would improve performance.

Physical memory available to Windows

Memory currently used by Windows

For 64-bit Windows, More RAM Is Better RAM

If you're using Windows XP Professional x64 Edition, dig a little deeper in your couch cushions to find the money to bump up your system to 1GB of RAM. With the larger programs and datafile sizes that 64-bit computing can handle, more RAM is better RAM. Even if you're running mostly 32-bit apps, you can run more apps in memory at one time without using virtual memory.

Troubleshooting Virtual Memory

Even if you add more memory, working with large data files or running many programs at once might still force your system to make occasional use of its page file. The real goal is to minimize its use. After all, unless you have a big bank account (to buy more memory), you probably can't eliminate the use of virtual memory. So, if you have to use virtual memory, you should make sure your PC is using it effectively.

You can improve how quickly virtual memory works in these ways:

- Defragment the drive containing the page file frequently.
- Move the paging file to a separate hard drive that your commonly used programs and data don't use much; this drive letter should contain least 1GB or larger of free space before you move the page file to it.

Normally, Windows uses a variable-sized page file to save disk space. However, when Windows adjusts the size of this file, the system can slow down, particularly if the drive containing the paging file is badly fragmented (has many files whose sectors are scattered around the drive) and has less than 1GB of free space.

Defragmenting Your Drive

Defragmenting your hard disk realigns the sectors in each file with each other and puts the empty space on the hard disk together. The result is that the hard disk can locate all the parts of a file faster, improving performance for virtual memory and for other disk activity such as saving and opening files.

Defragment Isn't Perfect, but Still Very Useful

The Windows Defragment program can't move some types of files, so it's normal to see a few files still in a fragmented state after the program is finished. However, most data files and program files will be defragmented, resulting in a performance boost for your system.

For better performance, try a third-party defragger such as Perfect Disk (http://www.raxco.com/) or Vopt XP (http://www.vopt.com).

To start the Windows XP Defragment program, follow these steps:

1. Open My Computer or Windows Explorer.
2. Right-click your hard disk and select Properties.
3. Click Tools.
4. Click Defragment Now.

Wouldn't it be handy to know if you need to run Defragment before you start the process? With Windows XP you can. Just select a drive and click Analyze to determine the fragmentation status of the drive.

Windows will suggest that you defragment the drive if it determines that the drive contains many file fragments. For details, click View Report and scroll through the Volume information and Most Fragmented Files windows. Some files might be stored in hundreds of fragments (see Figure 9.3).

Percentage of free space on current drive

Drive analyzed and recommendation to defragment

Percentage of free space on other hard drive

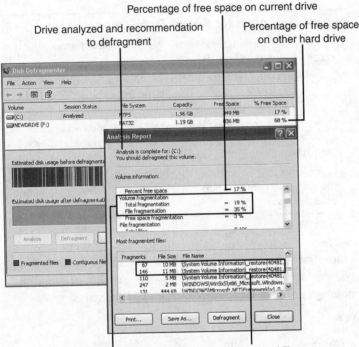

FIGURE 9.3
Displaying the fragmentation analysis on a Windows XP system with two hard disk drive letters.

Volume information indicating high total and file fragmentation   Most fragmented files

Click Defragment to begin the process if you have more than 15% free space on the drive, as in Figure 9.3. Depending on the size of the drive, the speed of the drive, and the amount of fragmentation on the drive, the operation could take anywhere from a few minutes to several hours.

Check for Errors First, Then Defragment

There's a reason that the Tools menu lists Error Checking above Defragmentation: You shouldn't defragment a drive that has errors! The system might move data from a good area of the disk surface to an area with problems. For more information on using error checking, see Chapter 2, "Troubleshooting Windows and Windows Applications."

Note that if Windows XP finds less than 15% free space on the drive, it might not be able to run properly and displays an onscreen warning. Free up space and try again if your system has less than 15% free space on the drive you want to defragment. Note that third-party defraggers might not need as much free space to run, although more free space helps any defragger run faster.

Freeing Up Space for Better Defragging

If you need to free up some disk space to allow Defragment to work properly with Windows XP, try the following:

- Run Disk Cleanup to delete temporary files (including temporary Internet files), delete files in the Recycle Bin, and compress old files. See "Using Disk Cleanup," this chapter, p. 557.

- Disable the paging file on the current drive and place the paging file on another drive. See "Viewing and Adjusting Page File (Swapfile) Configuration," this chapter, p. 558.

I recommend you run Disk Cleanup first, restart Defragment, and adjust the page file configuration if you're still below the recommended amount of disk space free.

Because Windows creates temporary files for printing and other program functions and resizes its swapfile as needed, I recommend that you defragment your drive about twice a month or more often if you notice a definite slowdown in system performance.

Leo Says

First-time Defragging Is Painful, but It Gets Better

If you've never defragmented your Windows drive before, don't expect to finish the task in a few minutes unless your hard disk is relatively empty. If you're a digital packrat like me and more than 75% of your hard disk is in use, it could take hours the first time you run it. Run it overnight, or else start watching that full-season DVD set you just bought. If you run Defragment regularly from now on, you'll only have time to watch an episode or two before it's time to get back to work (or play!).

There's a simple solution, by the way, to minimizing the "pain" of defragmenting your hard disk: Get a bigger one! I usually suggest doubling or tripling the size of your current drive when you upgrade. With more space to work with, defragging will be faster, at least until you fill up the new drive with digital pix, digital music tracks, and digital video!

Using Disk Cleanup

Because defragmentation uses empty space on your drive as a temporary location for files before it places them in their correct sequence, having enough empty space on your drive is critical to the correct operation of Defragment.

Disk Cleanup reclaims space by removing downloaded Internet temporary files and other types of Internet files as well as compressing old files you want to keep. To start Disk Cleanup, follow these steps:

1. Click Start.
2. Click (All) Programs.
3. Click Accessories.
4. Click System Tools.
5. Click Disk Cleanup.
6. Select the drive you want to clean up, and Disk Cleanup will scan the drive for files to process.
7. Disk Cleanup displays the file types it can process. Select each type of file you want to process, and Disk Cleanup will display the disk space you can gain (see Figure 9.4).
8. Click OK to process the files; files in the Compress Old Files category will be compressed to save space and can still be used afterwards, but files in all other selected categories will be discarded.
9. Disk Cleanup closes automatically after processing the selected file categories.

Controlling the Compression of Old Files

Windows defines an "old" file as one that hasn't been accessed for a specified time period. Click the Options button displayed when you select Compress Old Files to select the amount of days Windows waits before compressing a file.

Click the More Options tab to free up more space by uninstalling Windows components or third-party programs you don't use, or by discarding older System Restore checkpoints. Select the option you want to use and follow the wizard's prompts to perform the selected action.

FIGURE 9.4

Selecting file types for deletion or compression by Disk Cleanup in Windows XP.

Displays dialog box for uninstalling unused Windows components, unused programs, and to display other options to free up disk space

Total amount of disk space Disk Cleanup can free up

Selected file types and disk space used by each type

Nonselected file type; will not be processed by Disk Cleanup

Total of selected file types

Description of current category

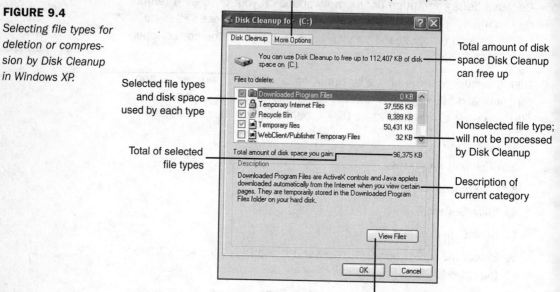

Displays files to be processed in current category

Viewing and Adjusting Page File (Swapfile) Configuration

If your default Windows system drive (normally C:) has less than 15% of free space left on it and you have other hard disk drive letters, consider changing the location of your page file to another drive with more space, particularly if you've already used Disk Cleanup to free up space and you still haven't been able to free up at least 15% of your hard disk drive. Moving your paging file to a drive with more space will make it easier to defragment your default Windows drive and can provide faster system performance.

To see how much of your hard disk is available, you can run Defragment in Windows XP (refer to Figure 9.3) or use the following procedure:

1. Open My Computer or Windows Explorer.

2. Right-click your hard disk.

3. Select Properties; a pie chart displays the free and used space (see Figure 9.5).

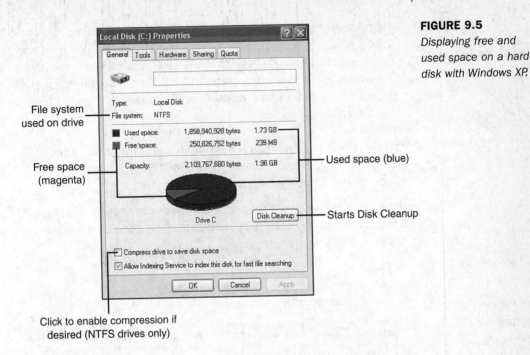

FIGURE 9.5

Displaying free and used space on a hard disk with Windows XP.

File system used on drive

Free space (magenta)

Used space (blue)

Starts Disk Cleanup

Click to enable compression if desired (NTFS drives only)

The drive shown in Figure 9.5 has about 11% of its total capacity free; this is not enough free space to run Defragment effectively. By default, Windows puts the page file on the Windows system drive (normally C:, as in this case). To free up enough space to run Defragment, you could disable the paging file temporarily (not recommended), remove some unused Windows components or programs, or configure this system to place its paging file on another drive.

To view or adjust the size or location of the paging file in Windows XP, follow these steps:

1. Right-click My Computer and select Properties.

2. Click Advanced.

3. In the Performance section, click Settings.

4. Click the Advanced tab and then click Change (Virtual Memory). Windows displays the recommended and current size for the paging file, and displays how much space is available on the drive used for the paging file (see Figure 9.6). To see the amount of space that could be used on another drive, click the drive.

5. To adjust the values for the paging file size and its location, click the drive letter and select System Managed Size (Windows will

manage the swapfile), No Paging File (the drive will not be used for a paging file), or Custom Size (you select the minimum and maximum). I recommend that you configure each of your hard drives to use a system-managed paging file to avoid running out of space on your default drive. Click Set and then click OK to save the changes.

You can place paging files on more than one drive or place the entire paging file on a different drive than the default if you are short of space on the default drive.

Because Windows must reboot, if you make changes to the page file, it requests that you restart the computer (you should heed this request).

FIGURE 9.6

Viewing the paging file size and location in Windows XP after configuring each hard disk drive letter with a system-managed paging file.

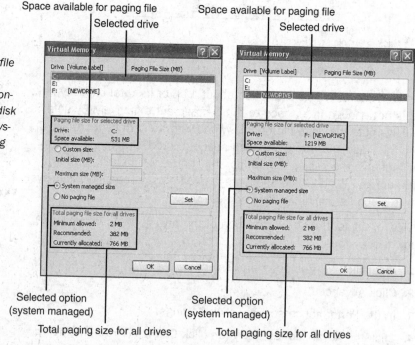

Don't Use a Removable-Media Drive for Your Page File

Windows XP can store all or part of its paging file on removable-media drives. What were they thinking? This is a potentially dangerous feature, because if you remove the disk containing part of the paging file, you could crash the system. If Windows XP displays multiple drive letters you can use for the paging file, as in Figure 9.6, make sure you choose only hard disk drive letters for your paging file locations. You can determine what type of drive each drive letter refers to by opening My Computer and viewing the list of drives.

Test Your Drive Before You Move Your Paging File or Swapfile

You should periodically check your drives for errors with the error-checking feature on the Tools menu for your drives. It's especially important to perform this test before you adjust the size or location of your page file or swapfile. For more information, see "Using Error-Checking (CHKDSK) and Defrag," Chapter 2, **p. 123**.

You should see improvements in the performance of disk-intensive activities (such as virtual memory, print spooling, and data file retrieval) after you defragment your hard disk and adjust the location of your paging file (if necessary). However, adding physical memory will provide a much bigger boost in performance, especially if your system has less than 400MB of RAM.

Troubleshooting Memory Upgrades

If you decide that you need to add memory to your system, your next question should be, What kind of memory can I add? Prepare to bone up on memory form factors, speeds, and sizes. Figure 9.7 shows some of the most common memory module form factors used in desktop computers.

Note that high-performance DDR SDRAM DIMMs often feature metal heat spreaders or finned heatsinks surrounding the memory chips.

Early Pentium 4 computers used a memory module based on RAMBUS RDRAM memory known as a RIMM. This type of memory had an integral heat spreader. See Figure 9.8 for an example.

A notebook computer might use the following:

- SDRAM SO-DIMM or DDR SO-DIMM (see Figure 9.9)
- Proprietary memory (designed specifically for your brand and model of notebook)

Each type of memory uses a different type of socket.

FIGURE 9.7

An SDRAM DIMM module (top) compared to a DDR SDRAM DIMM module (bottom).

SDRAM DIMMs use a three-section connector

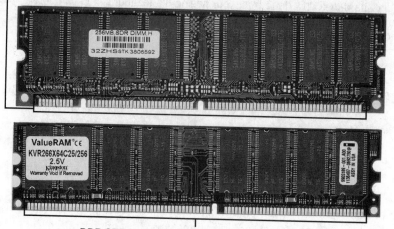

DDR SDRAM DIMMs use a two-section connector

FIGURE 9.8

An angled view of an RDRAM RIMM module. (Photo courtesy Kingston Technology.)

Heat spreader over memory chips

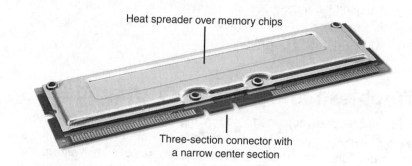

Three-section connector with a narrow center section

The newest type of memory modules for desktop and portable computers are based on DDR2 memory. These modules resemble DDR modules, but have more connectors.

With so many form factors, sizes, and speeds, it's easier than ever to make a mistake when you try to perform a memory upgrade. If you install a memory module that uses the wrong type of memory chips, you could have system lockups. If you install a memory module that's a size larger than your system is designed to handle, the computer might not recognize it, or might incorrectly identify it.

Although your system or motherboard manual will tell you what sizes and types of RAM you can install, it can't tell you what's already installed. There are several ways to determine what memory is already installed in your system:

FIGURE 9.9

Two types of SO-DIMM (Small Outline DIMM) memory modules used with notebook computers; the SDRAM SO-DIMM (top) has been replaced on recent systems by the DDR SDRAM SO-DIMM (bottom). (Photos courtesy Micron Technology.)

- To see the overall memory size, view the General tab of the system properties sheet in Windows (refer to Figure 9.1).

- Some computers display the specific memory size (and sometimes speed) of each module when the computer is started (see Figure 9.10).

- You can run a system analysis program such as SiSoftware Sandra to identify the memory modules in your system by brand, speed, and size.

How Large Is Each Memory Module?

It can be tricky to determine the size of each module if your system doesn't display this information at startup and if you don't use a system analysis program. However, the following rules of thumb can help you determine this information:

- The most common sizes of memory modules are 128MB, 256MB, 512MB and 1,024MB (1GB).

- If the computer has one memory module installed, the total amount of memory is the same as the size of the memory module installed.

- If the computer has two memory modules installed *and* the total size of memory equals the common sizes listed previously, each module is one-half that size. For example, in Figure 9.10, the total memory size is 512MB on a system with two modules. Divide 512MB by two, and each module is 256MB.

- If the computer has two memory modules installed *and* the total size of memory does *not* equal the common sizes listed previously, or if the computer has three or more memory modules installed, use system analysis software to determine the size of each module.

FIGURE 9.10

This computer has two DDR memory modules installed, providing 512MB (511MB + base memory) total RAM.

Used memory sockets and memory type   Total memory size

```
Main Processor    : AMD Athlon(tm) XP 2000+

Math Processor    : Built-In        Base Memory Size : 640KB
Floppy Drive A:   : 1.44 MB 3½"     Ext. Memory Size : 511MB
Floppy Drive B:   : None            Serial Port(s)   : None
Display Type      : VGA/EGA         Parallel Port(s) : 378
AMIBIOS Date      : 04/18/2003      Processor Clock  : 1692MHz
CPU Cache         : 384KB,Enabled   Power Management : Enabled
DDR at DIMM(s)    : 1,2

Hard Disk(s)      Cyl   Head Sector Size    LBA   32Bit Block PIO  UDMA
                                            Mode  Mode  Mode  Mode Mode
Primary Master   : 38309 16   255   80.0GB  LBA   Off   16Sec  4   5
Secondary Master : DVD-ROM                                      4   2

PCI Devices:
Slot 3 Ethernet, IRQ10            Onboard Multimedia Device, IRQ11
Onboard USB Controller, IRQ10    Onboard USB Controller, IRQ5
Onboard USB Controller, IRQ3     Onboard USB Controller, IRQ11
Onboard IDE, IRQ14,15            AGP Display Controller
AGP VGA, IRQ11

Searching for Boot Record from Floppy..
```

Determining the Right Memory for Your System

To determine what memory you can add to your system, you need to know the following:

- How many memory sockets are open?
- What size or sizes of memory modules are already installed?
- What type and sizes of memory modules can you install in your system?

Why are all three questions important? You need to know how many memory sockets are open to determine if you can add memory to your system or if you must remove low-capacity memory to make room for larger memory modules. You need to know the sizes of the memory modules to determine which module(s) you should remove to make room for larger modules if you don't have any memory sockets remaining. You need to know what type and sizes of memory modules your system uses to be sure of buying the right memory for your system.

If you know the motherboard or system brand and model (it might be displayed on the system properties sheet shown in Figure 9.1, at startup, or on a sticker on the side or rear of your computer), you can use interactive buying guides available online from various memory vendors to choose the right memory for your system. Most "white box" systems built from generic motherboards use standard memory modules, but many name-brand systems require proprietary modules that might be more expensive.

Selecting the Right Memory for Your System or Motherboard

Here are some of the major memory vendor websites that offer interactive memory selection guides:

- **Crucial.com**—http://www.crucial.com
- **Kingston**—http://www.kingston.com
- **PNY**—http://www.pny.com
- **Viking Components**—http://www.vikingcomponents.com

You can use a system analysis program such as SiSoftware Sandra or Belarc Advisor to help you determine more information about your system's memory and motherboard, which is very helpful if your system doesn't report these details when you start it and you can't locate the information in your documentation.

Discovering Your Memory Size and More

SiSoftware Sandra is available from SiSoftware online at http://www.sisoftware.net.

The Lite version of Sandra is free; the Professional version, with added features, is about $30.

Belarc Advisor is available from http://www.belarc.com/free_download.html; it is free for personal use.

To determine motherboard and memory information on your system with SiSoftware Sandra, start Sandra and open the Mainboard Information icon. The System section is displayed first. It lists the manufacturer and model number of your system or your motherboard (see Figure 9.11).

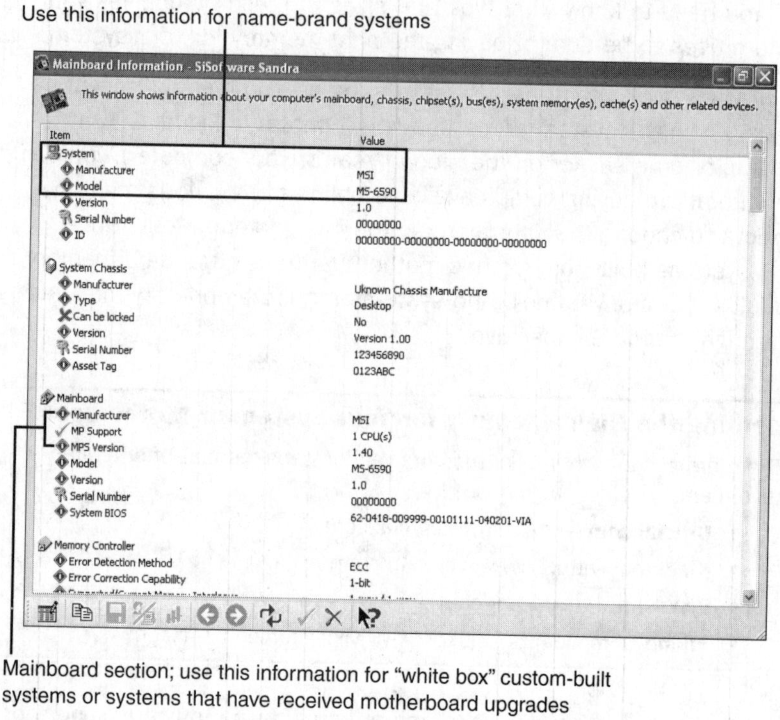

Use this information for name-brand systems

FIGURE 9.11

SiSoftware Sandra Lite determines that this computer is using an MSI MS-6590 motherboard.

Mainboard section; use this information for "white box" custom-built systems or systems that have received motherboard upgrades

To determine how many memory sockets you have and the details of the memory already installed, scroll down to the Physical/BIOS Memory Banks section. The number of memory sockets and their current contents are listed (see Figure 9.12).

This information is sufficient to purchase a memory upgrade for your system. However, if you want to determine the speed of your memory or other details, scroll down to the Memory Module sections (see Figure 9.13). The manufacturer, model number, speed, and other technical details are provided.

Empty memory socket

Memory size   Memory sockets in use

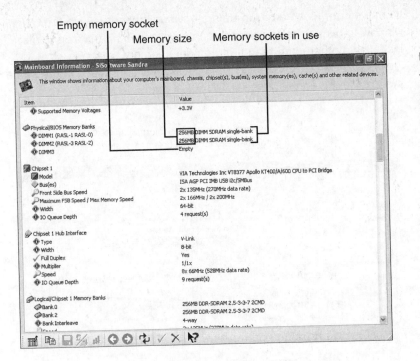

FIGURE 9.12

SiSoftware Sandra indicates this system has two of its three memory sockets in use; the third can be used to upgrade the system.

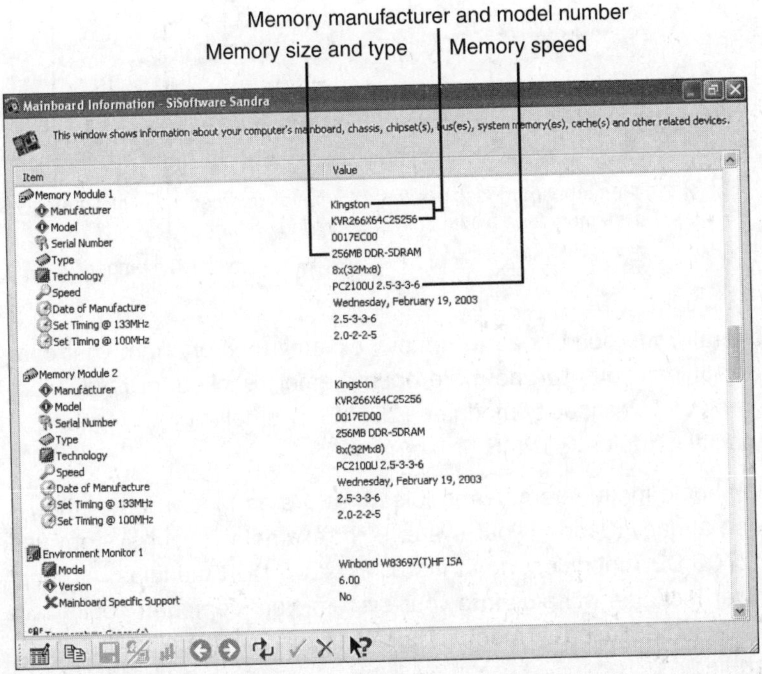

Memory manufacturer and model number

Memory size and type   Memory speed

FIGURE 9.13

This system is using PC2100 memory, which is relatively slow DDR memory. Faster system performance can result from upgrading to PC2700 or PC3200 modules.

When you download and run Belarc Advisor, it opens a web browser window to display its text-based report of your computer's contents, including motherboard brand and model, memory type, and size. Figure 9.14 shows a portion of the Belarc Advisor report on the same system illustrated in Figures 9.11, 9.12, and 9.13.

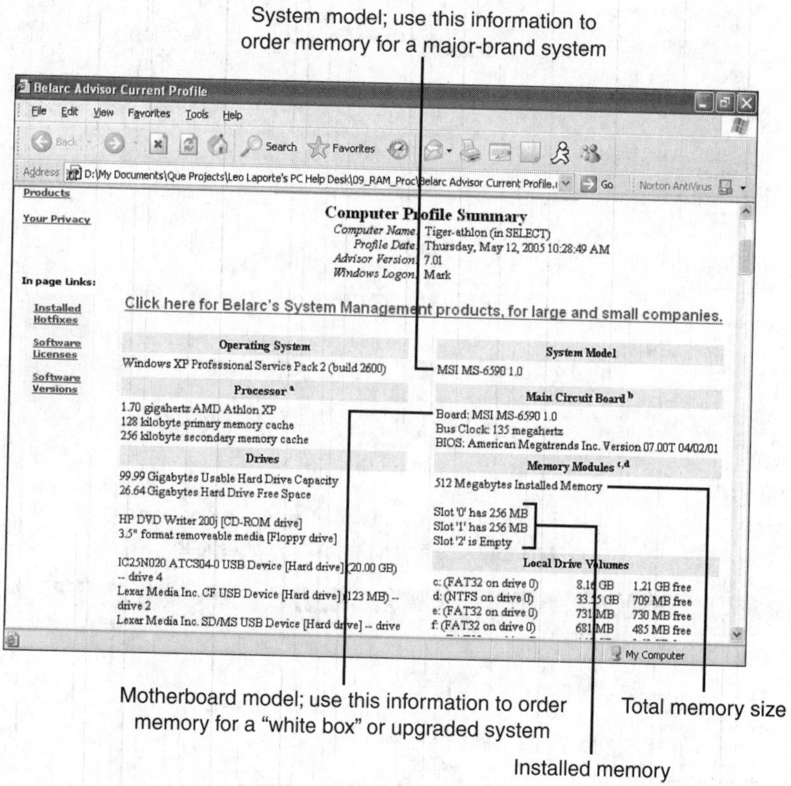

FIGURE 9.14

Belarc Advisor identifies the system, motherboard, total installed memory, and memory slots usage.

System model; use this information to order memory for a major-brand system

Motherboard model; use this information to order memory for a "white box" or upgraded system

Total memory size

Installed memory

Generally, you don't need to remove existing memory from your computer unless you have no more open memory sockets or if you want to replace low-capacity modules (256MB or smaller) with higher-capacity modules (512MB or larger).

You should install memory modules that are as fast or faster than those already found in your system. For example, if your system uses PC2700 DDR modules, don't install PC2100 DDR modules. Although slower modules will plug into your system, your computer could have problems because the memory is slower than what's already installed.

Faster, Larger Memory Makes Future Upgrades Easier

If you're thinking about upgrading to a faster processor on the same motherboard now or later, consider buying memory that's faster than your existing memory. For example, if you're running an Athlon XP 2000+ with PC2100 memory, you'd want to move to PC3200 memory if you're planning an upgrade to an Athlon XP 3200+ in the future. However, if you're planning to change motherboards and processor types, research your upgrade carefully if you want to reuse your existing memory.

Larger memory (such as 512MB or 1GB modules) also helps make your system "future-proof." Believe me, there's never going to be a new operating system or full-power application with a significantly smaller appetite for RAM!

Installing Desktop Computer Memory

Once you've determined that you need a memory upgrade and have purchased memory of the speed and type designed for your system, it's time to get it installed. Follow this procedure for installing new memory:

1. Shut down Windows and the computer.
2. Turn off the power supply if it is equipped with its own on/off switch.
3. Wait about 10 seconds for the system to completely shut down.
4. Unplug the power cord to the computer.
5. Take ESD precautions (see Chapter 1, "PC Anatomy 101," for details). If you don't have a wrist strap, touch metal parts on the computer to equalize electrical potential before you open the case.
6. Open the case. The procedure for opening a PC case varies from PC to PC. You may have to remove screws on the back of the system. On other cases, you may have to remove the front bezel (face plate) and then one or two screws on the front of your case. Most current cases allow you to remove just one side panel or the other. In this situation, you need only remove the left side of the PC as viewed from the front.

7. Touch metal parts on the computer to equalize electrical potential before you open the package containing the memory module.

8. Locate the memory sockets. If you cannot see the memory sockets (see Figure 9.15), move the cables out of the way. If you still cannot see the memory socket, you might need to remove the motherboard from your system before you can upgrade the memory.

FIGURE 9.15

Typical DDR DIMM memory sockets; the one on the left already contains a module, whereas the center and right sockets are empty.

Memory module locked into place

Locking tabs in closed position

Empty sockets

9. If the locking tabs at the ends of empty sockets are closed (as shown in Figure 9.15), they must be opened before additional memory modules can be installed. Open them (see Figure 9.16).

10. Install the memory module into the correct slot. Line up the connectors on the module with the connectors on the socket. Push the memory module straight down into the socket until the locking tabs flip into position (see Figure 9.16).

Locking tabs open; memory slot ready for upgrade

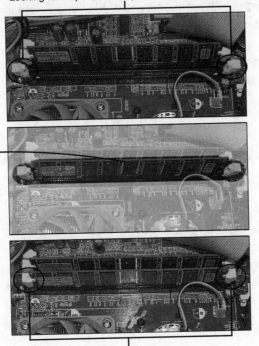

Memory inserted into slot; locking tabs open

Locking tabs engaged; installation complete

FIGURE 9.16
Installing DDR DIMM memory in a typical system.

11. If you removed the motherboard to install the memory, secure the motherboard back into the case.

12. Plug the power cord back into the computer.

13. Restart the computer and watch for startup messages or open the System Properties dialog after Windows boots to verify that the new memory has been detected.

14. Shut down running programs, Windows, and the computer.

15. Close the case and secure it.

Installing Notebook Computer Memory

Notebook computer memory upgrades offer the same performance benefits that desktop memory upgrades do, along with some hidden benefits:

- Longer battery life, because the computer uses the hard disk for virtual memory less often.

➜ *If the system doesn't boot or reports a memory error, see "Troubleshooting Memory Upgrade Problems," this chapter, p. 575.*

➜ *If you need to remove the motherboard to perform the memory upgrade, see "I'm Having a Hard Time Fitting My New Motherboard into My Case," this chapter, p. 604.*

- Larger video memory size on some systems if integrated graphics shares system memory and adjusts as memory size increases.

- Easier installation. You usually need to open just a small access panel on the underside of the computer rather than remove the entire case.

Notebook memory upgrades also have some challenges compared to desktop memory upgrades:

- There's usually only one memory socket that you can use for an upgrade, so you'd better install the largest memory module you can.

- Notebook memory is more expensive than desktop memory of the same size in MB.

As with desktop memory, you should use an online memory configurator along with the exact brand and model number of your system to find the right memory module for your system.

Leo Says

Flip It Over to Get the Real Model Number

Don't pay much attention to the model number on the top of your notebook computer; the real model number is on a sticker on the bottom of the system. Some notebook computer makers use the same general "family" name for systems with many variations on processor, motherboard, available memory upgrades, and so on.

If your notebook computer uses a typical SO-DIMM module (refer to Figure 9.9), it's usually installed this way (see the manual that came with your notebook, as some manufacturers do include specific instructions for upgrading):

1. Shut down Windows and your notebook.
2. Unplug the power cord.
3. Close the lid to protect the LCD display.
4. Turn the unit over.

5. Locate the access panel over the memory upgrade slot.

6. Remove any screws holding the panel in place.

7. If you need to remove the existing memory, pull the locking tabs on each side of the memory away from the module and lift up the top of the module. Slip the module out of the socket and place it on antistatic material.

8. Insert the new memory into the socket until the connector is inserted all the way into the slot (see Figure 9.17).

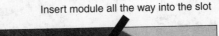
Insert module all the way into the slot

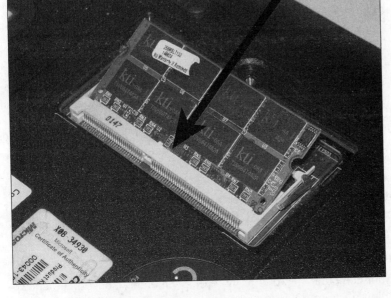

FIGURE 9.17

Inserting a typical SO-DIMM into a notebook computer.

9. Push the top of the module down until the locking tabs on each side of the module snap into place (see Figure 9.18).

10. Replace the access panel.

11. Fasten the access panel into place with the screws you removed in step 6.

12. Turn the machine upright.

13. Open the lid.

14. Reattach the power cord.

15. Restart the computer.

FIGURE 9.18

Completing the SO-DIMM installation.

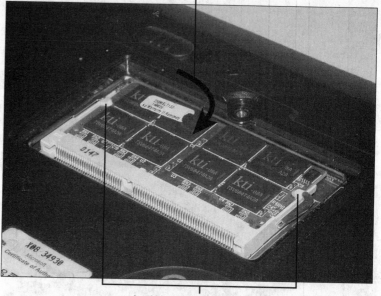

Push the top of the module down

Locking tabs snap into place

16. If the system starts normally, check the System Properties dialog to verify that the new memory has been recognized (refer to Figure 9.1).

Refer to your system documentation or to the third-party memory vendor for specific details that apply to your system.

Freeing Up Sockets for Additional Memory

If your computer has one or more empty memory sockets, as shown earlier in Figures 9.15 and 9.16, you can install the additional memory you need in the empty socket. However, if your motherboard's memory sockets are already full, you will need to remove one or more modules to make room to add memory. In such a case, consider installing just one large memory module rather than two smaller modules—for example, a single 512MB module rather than two 256MB modules. This strategy allows you to add additional memory in the future. This is a virtual must when you install memory in a notebook computer because most of them are designed to handle only one additional module.

If your total memory is a nonstandard size, such as 192MB (128MB+64MB) or 384MB (256MB or 128MB), look at the labeling on the module to determine which module is smaller if you want to remove only one of your existing modules. If the markings are hard to read, keep in mind that the memory module with memory chips on both sides is usually the larger one, and the smaller one usually has chips on only one side. If you used SiSoftware Sandra, Belarc Advisor or another memory identification program to examine your system, refer to the report and to your motherboard or system manual to determine which module is smaller.

Don't Break Up a Happy Couple (of Modules)

Although most systems let you remove or install one memory module at a time, there are some exceptions. Quite a few high-performance systems now use dual-channel memory; dual-channel systems treat a pair of identical memory modules as a single unit, which improves memory performance.

If your computer can support dual-channel memory, make sure you install matched pairs of modules (usually sold as a kit) when you upgrade or replace existing memory. If you're not sure if your system falls into this category, check with your system or motherboard maker.

Programs such as SiSoftware Sandra and Belarc Advisor will inform you of the motherboard chipset on your system, enabling you to look up the chipset vendor to get more information about memory usage and other features.

Keep in mind that a system designed for dual-channel memory can run in single-channel mode, but the memory performance will be lower.

Troubleshooting Memory Upgrade Problems

Memory upgrades are normally very easy to perform, but you can run into problems, particularly if you haven't upgraded a system before. Table 9.2 provides a quick reference to the problems you might encounter and their solutions. More details for each solution are provided in the following sections.

TABLE 9.2
MEMORY UPGRADE PROBLEMS AND SOLUTIONS

Symptom	Cause	Solution	Tips
Memory sockets are not accessible after the case is opened.	Components inside the case, such as the power supply or drives, are blocking access to memory.	Remove the motherboard from the case, if possible, or temporarily remove the component that's blocking access to the memory.	Take a look at your system documentation before you plan to perform the memory upgrade to determine if you need to remove the motherboard (it's necessary on some of the smaller retail-store systems). If you're not comfortable performing this job, ask a friend for help or pay the store's service department to perform the memory installation.
New memory was not detected after it was installed.	The new memory is not fully inserted into the socket.	Make sure the memory is locked into place (refer to Figure 9.16).	The memory socket is keyed to accept the memory the correct way only; if the memory won't go into the socket, you might be inserting it backwards.
	The memory is not inserted into the correct socket.	Install the memory into the socket next to the currently used socket(s).	Check your system manual to determine if the order in which you populate memory sockets can cause problems.
	The new memory is the wrong size or type.	Install the correct size and type of memory.	Use the interactive memory configurators and software tools discussed earlier to make sure you order the correct memory for your system.

TABLE 9.2 (continued)

Symptom	Cause	Solution	Tips
	The new memory is defective.	Test the new memory in a socket you've already used successfully with your older memory modules.	Be sure to keep your fingers away from the contacts on the bottom of the module during instal-lation to avoid static damage to the module.
	The memory socket is defective.	Test the socket by installing existing memory that works when used in a different socket.	If the memory socket is defective, you should replace the motherboard or use larger memory in the other sockets.
Computer reports memory errors after the installation of new memory.	The new memory may be defective.	Remove and reinstall the new memory and retry. If the computer still reports memory errors, replace the memory.	Many systems lock up if memory is defective, but lock-ups can also happen for other reasons. Ask the vendor to test the memory for you, or try a memory test program.

The most likely cause for new memory not being detected after instal-lation is that the memory is not properly installed. Refer to Figures 9.16 and 9.18 and note that not only must you insert the memory into its socket, but you must also ensure it is firmly pushed into place so that the locking clips can engage. Until the locking clips engage, proper contact between the motherboard and the memory module will not take place and the new memory will not work.

All modern types of desktop memory modules (SDRAM and DDR SDRAM DIMMs and RDRAM RIMMs) must be inserted straight down into the memory sockets and are keyed so that they can only be inserted one way. Memory for notebook computers must be inserted at an angle. If you cannot push the memory into place, you might not have the module lined up correctly with the guides incorporated into the locking clips, you might be trying to install the memory facing the wrong direction, or you might be trying to install the wrong type of memory into the socket.

Referring back to Figures 9.7, 9.8, and 9.9, note that each type of memory has a keyed notch on the bottom of the memory connector to prevent improper installation.

Because motherboards and systems are designed to use only specific types, sizes, and speeds of memory, installing incorrect memory sizes and speeds, even if the module physically attaches to the system, can also prevent the system from detecting and using the new memory. For example, if you install a 1,024MB (1GB) memory module into a system designed to work with 128MB, 256MB, or 512MB memory modules only, it won't work.

Troubleshooting Defective Memory or Memory Sockets

To determine if a defective memory module or a defective memory socket is preventing your computer from detecting the newly installed memory, first open the case using the steps described for installing a memory module. To determine whether a memory module or socket is defective if you have two or more modules installed, follow these steps:

1. Verify that the newly installed memory is the correct type, speed, and size; check the markings on the package with the system or motherboard manufacturer's requirements.

2. Remove the newly installed memory module.

3. Restart the computer and note the size of memory reported; it should be the size of the remaining module(s). Shut down the computer.

4. Remove one of the existing memory modules.

5. Insert the newly installed memory module into the socket used by the existing memory module you removed in step 4.

6. Restart the computer. The memory size displayed should be the size of the new memory module plus the size of any other module still in the system. If the memory size displayed doesn't reflect the size of the new memory module, the module might be defective or might be the wrong size or speed for the motherboard. Return it to the vendor for replacement.

7. If the memory size displayed does reflect the size of the new memory module, shut down the computer and reinsert the existing memory module into the empty socket. Restart the computer. If the memory size displayed doesn't reflect the size of the additional memory module (which you already know is working from step 3), the memory socket is defective and the motherboard should be replaced.

For example, assume that your motherboard has three memory sockets—one with a 128MB module, one with a 256MB module, and a third that is empty, for a total of 384MB. If you add another 256MB module, the memory should add up to 640MB if the memory module and the socket are okay.

If you remove the 256MB module that was installed before upgrading memory and install the new 256MB module in its place, you should still have 384MB of memory if the new module is working correctly. If you have only 128MB of RAM, the module is defective.

If the new module works correctly in slot 2, but is not recognized when you install it in slot 3, the slot itself is defective or you cannot use it with the combination of memory you are using. Check the documentation for your system. If the slot proves to be defective, you must either replace the motherboard or avoid using that slot for memory.

Troubleshooting Installed Memory

Troubleshooting memory problems after it has been installed in a system for a while can be more difficult than discovering a module that's failed directly out of the package. Early PC systems displayed memory parity errors when the contents of memory were corrupted, but this type of memory went out of fashion about a decade ago. Today, although many servers and some high-performance workstations use memory and motherboard chipsets that can detect and correct memory errors using a technology called ECC, this feature is extremely rare on typical home, home office, and corporate computers.

When a system locks up during operation, the problem could be memory related, but it could also be attributable to problems with other hardware or with Windows. The contents of memory can be corrupted by excessive heat or by problems with the system power supply.

→ *To learn more about detecting problems with your system's power supply, see "Troubleshooting System Lockups," Chapter 10, p. 628.*

→ *To learn more about reducing heat buildup inside your system, see "Troubleshooting Cooling Problems," this chapter, p. 610.*

You can test installed memory with a memory-testing program; your computer also tests memory during its Power-On Self-Test (POST) process.

Testing Installed Memory

Although today's memory modules are generally very reliable, it's still possible to have occasional memory errors after your memory is installed and working. To track down memory problems that might manifest themselves only after your computer has been running for a while, you can use memory-testing programs to provide a much more thorough test than what your computer's Power-On Self-Test (POST) performs when you turn on your computer.

Some memory-testing programs require you to boot your computer with a DOS or Windows 9x/Me floppy disk; if you use Windows XP, you can create a DOS-compatible boot disk from the Format menu; select Create an MS-DOS Startup Disk (see Figure 9.19). Make sure the disk is blank or contains no important files; all existing files will be deleted.

FIGURE 9.19

Creating an MS-DOS startup disk in Windows XP.

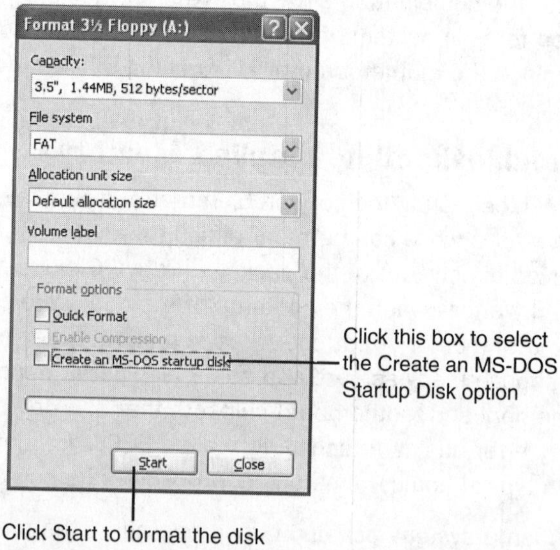

Click this box to select the Create an MS-DOS Startup Disk option

Click Start to format the disk

Although memory-testing programs are limited by the features of your motherboard and aren't as thorough as the dedicated memory testers used by some computer service shops, they can still help you determine if you have marginal memory modules that need to be replaced.

Memory-testing programs work by writing various patterns into memory and reading back the patterns; if the pattern of data written into memory doesn't match what the program reads back, the memory module is probably defective. For the most thorough test, set memory-testing programs to run their most thorough testing processes over a several hour period; this is sometimes referred to as "burning in the system."

Tracking Down Memory-Testing Programs

SIMMTester.com offers its free DocMemory testing program on its website: http://www.simmtester.com/PAGE/products/doc/docinfo.asp.

#1-PC Diagnostics Company (http://www.tufftest.com) has a free limited-feature version of its system and memory diagnostics software, #1 TuffTEST-Lite, available for download; it checks the first 8MB of RAM; more powerful versions are available for about $10 and $30 each.

Qualitas RAMexam is available for about $24 as a download; a free demo that checks only the first 640KB of RAM is also available at http://www.qualitas.com.

Troubleshooting Memory with POST Beep Codes

If your system beeps when you turn it on and doesn't finish the normal power-on process, your system BIOS is reporting a significant hardware error.

Memory is one of the parts of the computer that your BIOS checks during its Power-On Self-Test (POST) process. BIOS beep codes are designed to report memory problems when you start the computer. Beep codes vary by BIOS brand and version; you can use the methods described earlier in this chapter to determine the BIOS vendor your system or motherboard uses.

→ *For more information about how the BIOS reports errors, see "Power-On Self Test," Chapter 1, p. 57.*

If your computer has an AMI BIOS, the following beep codes are used to report memory problems

- **One beep**—Memory refresh failure
- **Two beeps**—Memory parity failure
- **Three beeps**—Memory failure in base (first 64KB) memory
- **Continuous beeping**—Memory failure (could also indicate video memory failure)

The Award BIOS uses one long beep or a continuous beep to indicate memory failure.

Phoenix BIOS version 4.0 release 6 also has several beep codes used to indicate memory failures:

- One beep, followed by three beeps, four beeps, one beep
- One beep, followed by three beeps, four beeps, three beeps
- One beep, followed by four beeps, one beep, one beep

If your computer is beeping at you during power-on but the beep pattern doesn't match any of these, your computer might use a different BIOS or the problem might be with some other part of your computer. Contact your system or motherboard vendor for help.

Troubleshooting Processor Failures

Adding more memory makes your computer run faster, but if your processor (CPU) isn't working, nothing will be happening until you replace it. The major reasons for processor failure include the following:

- Overheating
- Power surges
- Heatsink failure
- Heatsink detached from the processor
- Incorrect heatsink installation
- Wrong heatsink for the processor
- Incorrect insertion into the motherboard

The first four causes can affect any user, even if you never open your system to install a new processor. The last three are concerns for users who have replaced their older processor with a new processor or for users who have built their own system from components.

Getting Deeper into Processors and Motherboards

Because processors and motherboards are two of the most technically complex issues you will encounter, I recommend the following books for a deeper look at these technologies:

- *Upgrading and Repairing PCs, 16th Edition*, by Scott Mueller (Que, 2005)
- *Tech TV's Upgrading Your PC, Second Edition*, by Mark Edward Soper (New Riders, 2004)

Playing It Safe with Processor Upgrades

Increasingly, many processor upgrades also require motherboard and memory upgrades. For example, the Pentium 4 family includes processors that use three (!) different processor sockets; motherboards made for the various versions of this processor could use any of four (!!) memory technologies. The AMD Athlon 64 and 64FX family also uses three different processor sockets. Also, the newest motherboards support new technologies such as PCI-Express graphics and Serial ATA drive interfaces.

Even if you're moving up within the same socket type (for example, from an AMD Duron to an AMD Athlon XP), you might benefit from a memory upgrade.

In such cases, it's safer to install the new processor and memory on the motherboard before you install them in the case. If you don't install these components until after the motherboard is mounted in the case, you risk damaging the motherboard because of excessive flexing caused by the force needed to clip a heavy heatsink to the processor and lock it into place and the force needed to push memory modules into the locked position.

Even if your existing motherboard can handle a faster processor, you're better off to remove the motherboard from the case before you remove the old processor and heatsink and then mount the new processor and heatsink. Because you need to place the correct amount of thermal grease between the processor core and the heatsink to guarantee proper heat transfer and properly attach the heatsink to the processor, it's essential that you be able to work without the restrictions of a case while you perform the installation.

Detecting Overheating and Incorrect Voltage Levels

Anybody *want* to destroy a processor? We didn't think so. Nevertheless, every year many computer users lose their processors to problems with overheating and incorrect voltage levels. The sad fact is that many recent PCs include hardware monitoring features. They measure system temperature, voltage levels, and fan operation. Some computers display this information in the BIOS setup program, but you can also install and run a hardware monitoring program viewable in Windows. Some vendors include such a monitoring program with their systems or motherboards, whereas you might need to use a third-party program to view this information with other programs.

Figure 9.20 illustrates a typical vendor-supplied hardware monitoring program supplied with an Athlon-based motherboard.

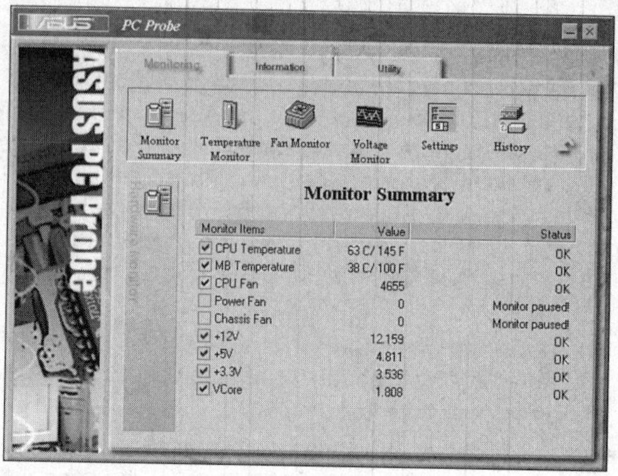

FIGURE 9.20

The Asus PC Probe hardware monitoring program. The power fan and chassis fan are not selected for monitoring because they aren't connected to the motherboard.

Detailed screens for each item monitored display the current values and the threshold value. To change the threshold value (the value that triggers an alarm), open the Settings dialog.

Getting Your Hands on a Hardware Monitoring Program

Some motherboard and system makers might offer a hardware monitoring program for your system, even though they didn't package it with the motherboard or computer. Contact your motherboard or system vendor for details.

If your vendor can't help you, try Hmonitor, which works with notebooks, desktop PCs, and also supports the new x64 version of Windows XP. Download Hmonitor from http://www.hmonitor.com and try it for a week; see the website for home and commercial pricing.

Hardware monitoring programs alert you when voltage levels, fan speeds, or temperature levels exceed threshold limits; a few can be configured to shut down your system if limits are exceeded for a protracted period of time.

You should pay attention to fan or temperature warnings you receive from your hardware monitor. Although some systems can throttle down the processor to a lower speed when it overheats or shut down the computer, this doesn't always work properly and can be disabled in the system BIOS or Power Management dialogs in Windows. A processor with a failed fan can be destroyed in just a few seconds.

VCore Settings and Overclocking

The VCore (core voltage setting) displayed in Figure 9.20 indicates the voltage used by the processor core. This is set automatically by the processor.

Because the processor automatically sets the correct voltage, how is it possible to damage the processor by using an incorrect voltage?

Even though the processor has a default setting for voltages, the motherboard is actually what controls how much power the processor receives. Some users attempt to "overclock" their processors. That is, they configure their processors to run faster than their rated speed. Doing this often requires small voltage increases to provide the CPU with more power, but this can also damage the processor. Overclocking is a popular hobby with many computer users, particular gamers, but it can be dangerous to your processor and your system. In some cases, certain unscrupulous vendors will "remark" an over-clocked CPU and sell it as if it were originally rated to run at the higher speed. This is, of course, highly illegal.

Because overclocking increases heat, extra cooling beyond what the normal case fans and the stock heatsink fan provide is necessary. To achieve higher speeds with stability, you might need to increase the default VCore voltage, but if the voltage is set too high without adequate cooling, you can fry your processor as surely as if you didn't use a powered heatsink at all.

If you want to overclock, follow these guidelines to stay out of trouble:

- Buy an OEM version of the processor you want to use (OEM processors are sold in bulk to vendors primarily for sales to computer makers, but are also sold by component vendors) and buy the best third-party heatsink fan you can afford that will fit on your motherboard. An OEM processor has a very short manufacturer's warranty (often just 30 days), but some sellers will provide a year or longer warranty for processors sold with a heatsink or assembled with heatsink fan on a motherboard sold by the same vendor. It's essential that you choose a heatsink fan that matches the speed of your processor as well as your processor model. Make sure a third-party heatsink will not bump into components around the processor socket such as the motherboard's voltage regulator. Check with the heatsink and motherboard vendors to determine if a particular heatsink has been used with a given motherboard.

- You shouldn't combine a retail boxed processor with a third-party heatsink unless you don't care about warranty coverage; removing the stock heatsink from a retail boxed processor voids the processor warranty. However, if it's a choice between your system working or not working while you wait for a replacement, replace the heatsink.

- Add extra case fans to the front and rear of the case. Front-mounted fans should be installed to blow cool air into the unit, whereas rear-mounted fans should be installed to blow hot air out of the unit.

- You should adjust the clock frequencies and voltages very cautiously if you want to overclock. Whereas some systems use jumper blocks on the motherboard to vary these settings from the factory specification, most overclocker-friendly motherboards use BIOS configuration screens to set these values.

- Add a large passive heatsink or fan to the North Bridge chip on the motherboard if it doesn't have a fan or a passive heatsink. See "Preventing Overheating Damage to the Motherboard," this chapter, p. 611, for details.

Overclocking Resources You Can't Afford to Overlook

The Overclockers.com website (http://www.overclockers.com) is a true one-stop shop for overclocking and system cooling tips, products, guides, and reviews. Find out what works and what needs work.

You can find a more detailed explanation of overclocking at

http://www.basichardware.com/overclocking.html

and how to overclock your system at

http://www.basichardware.com/how_to_overclock.html.

Note that most Intel-made motherboards don't provide any means to overclock either the clock multiplier or the FSB speed. Most third-party boards do, but check the specifications for the board.

Troubleshooting Voltage Problems

→ *For details on power supply testing, see "Troubleshooting System Lockups," Chapter 10, p. 628.*

If the hardware monitor indicates problems with your motherboard voltages, your best course of action is to test the power supply with a digital multimeter. If the power supply provides out-of-range readings on one or more voltage lines, replace the power supply.

Troubleshooting Processor Upgrades

Processor upgrades offer desktop computer users the promise of speed, speed, and more speed. However, processor upgrades can sometimes be more trouble than they're worth. In the following sections, we'll help you overcome some of the biggest challenges in performing a processor upgrade that works in your system and brings you truly better performance.

Fried Processor? Find Out Why Before You Do It Again!

If you're reading this chapter because your old processor has bit the dust, you'd better figure out why—and solve the underlying problem—before you pop a new processor in the system. If it's something as simple as a worn-out active heatsink (heatsink with a fan), go ahead and install a new processor and active heatsink, but make sure you install a reliable hardware monitoring program in Windows to warn you of problems in the future. However, if the fan seems fine but the processor just "woke up dead," you might have a problem with a bad power supply or motherboard. See Chapter 10, "Troubleshooting Power Problems," for testing methods. Don't install a new CPU until you know why the old one failed!

Understanding Processor Brands, Models, and Sockets

Why do processors with the same name use different socket types? We have no idea. The industry has oscillated between using a single socket type for a processor model and using the same processor name for processors that are so different they should have had different names. Table 9.3 lists upgrade paths for processors made by Intel and AMD from 2000 to 2004. Processors such as the Intel Pentium 4 Socket 775 and the AMD Athlon 64 and 64FX families are not listed; they are too recent to require a processor upgrade. Note that processors that do not offer an upgrade path to one running at least 2GHz are marked as "None."

TABLE 9.3
SUGGESTED PROCESSOR UPGRADE PATHS

Vendor	Processor Model	Form Factor	Upgrade Options
Intel	Pentium III, Celeron	Slot 1, Socket 370	None
Intel	Pentium 4	Socket 423	Third-party upgrades are available[1]
Intel	Pentium 4, Celeron	Socket 478	Socket 478 Pentium 4 up to 3.40GHz[2]
Intel	Celeron D	Socket 775	Socket 775 Pentium 4 up to 3.80GHz[2] or Pentium 4 Extreme Edition
AMD	Athlon, Duron, Athlon XP	Socket A (Socket 462)	Athlon XP up to 3200+ (2.2GHz)[2]
AMD	Athlon	Slot A	None

1. Third-party vendors such as PowerLeap (http://www.powerleap.com) and Evergreen Technologies (http://www.evertech.com) produce Socket 423/Socket 478 adapters, enabling you to run Socket 478 Pentium 4 or Celeron processors in your Socket 423 system.

2. Maximum processor speeds and models compatible with a particular system depend on the motherboard, BIOS, and memory speeds in use.

The socket names in Table 9.3 come from the number of pins in the processor socket.

Note that knowing the name of your processor isn't much help in determining if you can upgrade the processor without changing out the motherboard. For example, Intel has used the name "Celeron" for its low-cost processors in three different form factors, and AMD has used the name Athlon for processors in both slot and socketed varieties.

Your best bet if you're thinking about a processor upgrade is to do the following:

1. Determine what processor your system is currently using.

2. Determine what motherboard your system is using.

3. Check with the system or motherboard vendor to determine what processors work with the system.

4. Determine if a BIOS upgrade is required to use the processor you want to try.

5. Consider only processors that offer better features than your current processor, such as the following:

   - Larger L2 cache size
   - Significantly higher clock speeds (at least 20% faster)
   - Faster front side bus (the connection between CPU and memory)

These features will make a processor upgrade worthwhile.

Discovering Your Current Processor and BIOS Version

As indicated earlier in this chapter, we recommend using the latest version of SiSoftware Sandra Lite to dig up the information you need if you're considering a processor upgrade. After starting the program, click the CPU & BIOS Information icon. The processor information is given first. Note in particular the processor model number, actual clock speed, package (socket type), L2 cache size, and upgradeability information. See Figure 9.21 for a typical example.

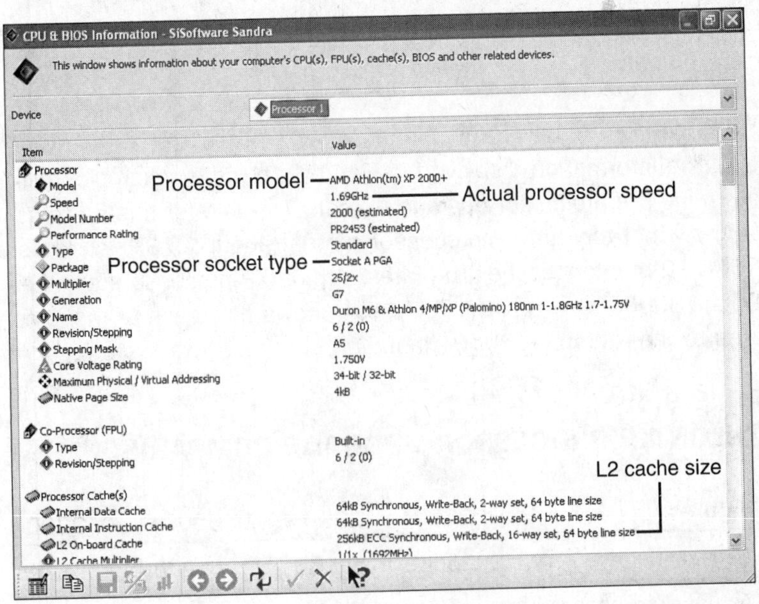

FIGURE 9.21

Checking CPU information with SiSoftware Sandra Lite.

To determine the upgradeability of the system, scroll down to the Upgradeability section (not shown). The motherboard shown in Figure 9.21 can use a processor up to 3GHz, which means it could use any Athlon XP processor up to the 3200+ (actual clock speed 2.2GHz).

Leo Says

"Appealing" SiSoftware Sandra's Upgrade Ruling

If SiSoftware Sandra doesn't think you can upgrade your motherboard with a faster processor, you might be able to "appeal" the decision. Check with your system or motherboard vendor to see if a BIOS upgrade is available for your system. Read the description of the BIOS upgrade to determine if it adds support for faster processors. Note that if your system BIOS is more than one revision behind that, you should read the features of all BIOS revisions more recent than yours (revisions are cumulative, so the latest version has all the previous fixes as well). Although SiSoftware Sandra Lite is designed to check for BIOS dates, this feature is not always accurate. Follow your system or motherboard maker's recommendations to determine the actual date and revision of your current BIOS. And follow the BIOS upgrade instructions carefully!

Evaluating Upgrade Options

Using the information displayed in Figure 9.21 as an example, let's determine if a processor upgrade is really feasible for this system. We know that the current processor runs at about 1.7GHz and has a 256KB L2 memory cache. The latest Athlon XP processors are the 2800+, 3000+, and 3200+. Table 9.4 shows how each of these compares to the Athlon XP 2000+ installed in our sample system.

TABLE 9.4
ATHLON XP PROCESSOR UPGRADE COMPARISON

Features	2000+	2800+	3000+[2]	3200+
L2 cache size	256KB	512KB	512KB	512KB
Actual clock speed	1.7GHz	2.083GHz	2.167GHz	2.200GHz
Clock speed comparison[1]	–	23% faster	27% faster	29% faster

TABLE 9.4 (continued)

Features	2000+	2800+	3000+[2]	3200+
Front side bus speed	266MHz	333MHz	333MHz	400MHz
DDR memory speed recommended	PC2100	PC2700	PC2700	PC3200

1. The actual performance increase will be less than the difference in clock speed, due to other factors such as graphics and hard disk performance.

2. The Athlon XP 3000+ is also available in a 400MHz front side bus model running at a clock speed of 2.1GHz. This processor would be 24% faster than the Athlon XP 2000+.

Any of the processors compared to the Athlon XP 2000+ in our sample system would be a worthwhile upgrade for these reasons:

- Double the size of L2 memory cache, which improves memory performance.
- Faster clock speed.
- Faster front side bus enables these processors to use faster memory to its fullest extent. However, even if you use the same memory, your system would be faster.

If you have an Intel Celeron or Pentium 4–based system using Socket 478, you'll find a couple sample comparisons in Tables 9.5 and 9.6.

TABLE 9.5
CELERON TO PENTIUM 4 PROCESSOR UPGRADE COMPARISONS

Features	2 GHz Celeron	2.80GHz Pentium 4	3.20GHz Pentium 4
L2 cache size	128KB	512KB	512KB
Actual clock speed	2.00GHz	2.80GHz	3.20GHz
Clock speed comparison[1]	–	40% faster	60% faster
Front side bus speed	400MHz	533MHz	800MHz
DDR memory speed recommended	PC2100	PC2700	PC2700

1. The actual performance increase will be less than the difference in clock speed, due to other factors such as graphics and hard disk performance.

TABLE 9.6

PENTIUM 4 PROCESSOR UPGRADE COMPARISONS

Features	2.4 GHz Pentium 4	3.00GHz Pentium 4	3.20GHz Pentium 4
L2 cache size	512KB	512KB	512KB
Actual clock speed	2.40GHz	3.00GHz	3.20GHz
Clock speed comparison[1]	–	25% faster	33% faster
Front side bus speed	400MHz	800MHz	800MHz
DDR memory speed recommended	PC2100	PC2700/ PC3200	PC2700/ PC3200

1. The actual performance increase will be less than the difference in clock speed, due to other factors such as graphics and hard disk performance.

In the first example, an upgrade will produce better performance because of the combination of faster clock speed and larger L2 cache size. However, in the second example, the differences are less clear-cut, except that the newer processors are designed to use faster memory.

Digging Up Processor Upgrade Options

The easiest way to find out which processor upgrades will work in your computer is to check with your computer maker (if you have a major "name brand" PC) or with your motherboard maker (if you have a "white box" or upgraded system that no longer contains the original motherboard). Vendor websites usually list the processors supported on a particular motherboard. If your system vendor acts as if it has never heard of a processor upgrade, use a program such as SiSoftware Sandra Lite or Professional to determine the brand and model number of the motherboard and do your own sleuthing online.

Who Gets the Best "Bang for the Buck" from a CPU Upgrade?

Who will benefit the most from a processor upgrade? Anybody who's running a computer with an "economy" processor from Intel or AMD, such as the following:

- Intel Celeron
- Intel Celeron D

- AMD Duron
- AMD Sempron

These processors have smaller memory caches onboard (often referred to as "L2" or "Level 2" cache), slower connections to system memory (often referred to as "front side bus"), and slower internal clock speeds than the top-level processors using the same processor socket.

This assumes, of course, that your system can handle significantly faster processors such as the ones shown in Tables 9.4, 9.5, and 9.6. Typically, name-brand computers don't offer the flexibility in processor upgrades that "white box" computers built using third-party motherboards do. However, every situation is different.

Keep in mind that we're taking about upgrading only the processor in your existing PC. If you upgrade the motherboard (and RAM, if necessary), you can install any processor that is compatible with your motherboard. Of course, you might prefer to buy a new computer instead!

Leo Says

What to Upgrade First

Just because this part of the chapter concerns processor upgrades, don't think this should be your first upgrade if you're frustrated by your system's performance. Instead, perform these upgrades first:

- Memory (512MB or larger)
- Hard disk (7200 rpm, 8MB buffer, 200MB or larger)
- Graphics card (mid-range or better AGP or PCI-Express from NVIDIA or ATI), especially if you're a gamer

If you're still not happy with your system performance, then look at a processor upgrade.

I'm Not Sure What Type of Processor I Can Use in My Motherboard

Motherboards are designed to use certain types of processors running at certain speed ranges only. Some of the reasons a particular processor might not work in your motherboard include the following:

- **Wrong form factor**—Consult Table 9.3 to learn what the general processor upgrade paths are for a particular processor socket. If you don't like your options (or lack of options, to be more precise), consider a motherboard swap to support the processor you want, or go shopping for a new computer.

- **Wrong voltage**—Although current processors can automatically adjust the voltage of the motherboard as needed, this feature depends on the motherboard being designed to handle the voltage range used by the processor. Many older motherboards lack the correct voltages to handle newer processors. Some motherboards can handle the voltage requirements of newer processors if you install a BIOS upgrade.

- **BIOS limitations**—Faster processors might require BIOS features and options not present on an older system. For example, Hyper-Threading Technology is available on newer Intel Pentium 4 processors (making the processor emulate two processors in certain tasks); a BIOS upgrade might be needed to add support for that feature to some systems. BIOS upgrades (which are usually available from the system or motherboard vendor) can sometimes allow an older system to handle a newer processor.

I'm Having a Hard Time Installing My New Processor

Whether you are installing a new processor into an existing motherboard or you are upgrading both components, getting your new processor properly installed is essential to your computer's proper operation.

Here are some of the most common problems you might encounter:

- **Failing to use proper thermal interface material between the processor and the bottom of the heatsink**—Boxed processors that include a heatsink normally use a preinstalled thermal pad (also known as "phase change material"), whereas the third-party heatsinks made for OEM processors might not always include a thermal pad or thermal paste. If you install an OEM processor and third-party heatsink, be sure to find out if thermal paste is included. If you need to order it, the most efficient thermal paste is a product called Arctic Silver, which is, as the name suggests, a liquid silver thermal paste. Most companies that stock third-party heatsinks also sell Arctic Silver (note the spelling; a very poor counterfeit product called Artic Silver is sold by some stores).

You *must* use either a thermal pad or thermal paste between the heatsink and the processor; otherwise, the heatsink is useless. If you replace your heatsink, make sure you remove the old thermal pad or thermal paste residue from the surface of your processor and apply new thermal material before you install the new heatsink. If you reuse an existing heatsink with a new processor, make sure you verify that the old heatsink will work with the new processor. Also, be sure to clean its surface before you install the heatsink on the new processor.

Figure 9.22 shows a typical installation of thermal paste on the processor core (the rectangular section in the middle of the processor) of a Socket A processor. If you use thermal paste on a Pentium 4, Celeron, or Athlon 64 processor, you should note that these processors have a metal heat spreader across their top.

Thermal paste

FIGURE 9.22
A typical Socket A processor after thermal paste has been applied.

Where and How to Install Thermal Paste

For a detailed tutorial on the entire thermal paste application and surface cleaning process for various types of processors, see the Arctic Silver website:

http://www.arcticsilver.com/arctic_silver_instructions.htm

Arctic Silver also offers ArctiClean, a two-step cleaning process for removing old thermal material from a processor. Learn more at http://www.arcticsilver.com/arcticlean.htm.

- **Difficulty in locking the heatsink in place**—Socket A processors use a spring-loaded heatsink that attaches to both sides of the processor socket (see Figure 9.23). If the heatsink is installed incorrectly or the wrong heatsink is used, the processor is ruined. If you buy an OEM processor and separate heatsink, make sure you verify that the heatsink you buy is designed for your CPU type and speed (retail boxed processors come with a matching heatsink, although third-party heatsinks often provide superior cooling).

FIGURE 9.23

A typical Socket A processor heatsink being locked into place on the processor socket.

Heatsink clip

Lug on processor socket

Fortunately, Intel Pentium 4 and AMD Athlon 64 processors use various types of external supports for the heatsink, enabling an easier installation. Figure 9.24 shows a typical installation of an AMD Athlon 64 Socket 754 processor and standard active heatsink.

FIGURE 9.24

A Socket 754 processor before heatsink installation (left) and after heatsink installation (right).

1. Athlon 64 Socket 754 processor
2. External support for heatsink
3. Socket locking arm
4. Connector for processor heatsink fan
5. Active heatsink installed on processor
6. Locking lever on heatsink
7. Power/monitoring lead from heatsink fan
8. Voltage regulator

Installing the Heatsink the AMD Way

AMD provides the "Socket A AMD Processor and Heatsink Installation Guide," a very detailed instruction manual for installing these processors with typical heatsinks on its website:

http://www.amd.com/us-en/assets/content_type/white_papers_and_tech_docs/23986.pdf

See the document "Builder's Guide for AMD Athlon 64 Processor-Based Desktops and Workstations" to learn how to install these processors:

http://www.amd.com/us-en/assets/content_type/white_papers_and_tech_docs/31684.pdf

(Note that these documents require the free Adobe Reader, available from http://www.adobe.com.)

...and the Intel Way

Intel's technical paper "Thermal Management for Systems Based on Boxed Pentium 4 Processors" includes detailed instructions on installing the processor's heatsink for Socket 478 and Socket 423 processors:

http://support.intel.com/support/processors/pentium4/sb/CS-007999.htm

If you're installing a Socket 775 processor, go to http://www.intel.com/go/integration and click the following link Thermal Management for Boxed Intel® Pentium® 4 Processor in the 775-land Package-Based Systems.

- **Not using a monitored fan connection for the processor's heatsink fan**—Look at the motherboard documentation carefully to determine which connection is designed to power the CPU fan and monitor its performance. Some motherboards might have two or three fan connections near the processor socket. Figure 9.24 shows a typical processor fan connection.

Protecting Your Motherboard and Processor from Installation Damage

It's all too easy to let your screwdriver slip during heatsink or motherboard installation, especially when you are locking a Socket A heatsink clip into place. A scratched motherboard might stop working because some of the wire traces that carry power and signals are on the surface of the motherboard. To minimize the risk, try these tips:

- Use a hexagonal driver rather than a screwdriver to secure the hex screws used to hold most motherboards in place. Phillips-head screwdrivers can slip fairly easily, but hex drivers rarely do.

- Instead of pushing the heatsink mounting clip into place with a flat-bladed screwdriver, as recommended by AMD for Socket A processors, you might try using a hex driver if you have one that is about the same diameter as the clip's locking lever. As with fastening the motherboard into place, there's less chance of a slip with the hex driver for this task. Be sure to practice using the hex driver or screwdriver to position the lever before you attach the heatsink to the processor to determine which tool you prefer.

- Before you order a high-performance third-party heatsink for a particular processor, find out if there's enough clearance between the components on the motherboard and the heatsink. The voltage regulator is located very close to the processor socket on some motherboards (refer to Figure 9.24), and if you damage its capacitors or other components with an oversized heatsink, say goodbye to your motherboard. Consult reviews of your motherboard at sources such as Tom's Hardware (http://www.tomshardware.com) and Anandtech (http://www.anandtech.com) to see which heatsinks have been tried with the board.

Protecting Your Athlon XP Processor

Because Athlon XP processors don't use a metal heat spreader over the CPU core (the small rectangular area in the middle of the processor) the way that Intel Pentium 4 and Athlon 64 processors do, they can be easily damaged by improper heatsink installation.

You can buy low-cost shims from various vendors to protect the processor from damage:

- **Tweakmonster**—http://www.tweakmonster.com/products/spacerpage.htm
- **UltraProducts**—http://www.ultraproducts.com
- **CaseCooler**—http://www.casecooler.com/nonconshim.html

My System Won't Start After I Installed a New Processor

If your system won't start after you installed a new processor, check the following:

- **Make sure you're using the correct fan connector for the type of processor heatsink fan you have.** One motherboard vendor has a "Guardian" feature built into its motherboard (it's enabled with a jumper) that, when enabled, prevents the system from starting if you don't have your processor fan plugged into the processor fan connector. Before he discovered this setting, Mark's son Jeremy spent six frustrating weeks trying to figure out why the vendor could make his motherboard work and he couldn't. Disable this feature if you don't use a compatible processor fan; for example, if you attach the fan to a drive power connector instead of the motherboard.

- **Double-check the processor connection to the motherboard.** You usually can't lock the heatsink on a socketed processor unless it's properly inserted into the processor socket and the socket-locking lever is closed, but a slot-mounted processor might appear to be in place, although not be locked into position.

- **Close the lever on the processor socket.** The system can't do anything until the processor is properly secured (refer to Figure 9.24).

- **Check whether the wire from the case switch is properly attached to the motherboard.** Unlike older systems, ATX and Micro-ATX systems are turned on and off via the motherboard.

My New Processor Isn't Running as Fast as It Should

If you install a fast processor and find out through speed measurements from SiSoftware Sandra or by watching bootup messages that it's not running at top speed, here are some possible solutions:

- **Your system has reverted back to a failsafe setting.** Some motherboards use a low clock multiplier and slow FSB setting if the system didn't boot properly on the previous attempt. So, if you shut off the system just a few seconds after you turned on the power, the system might have reverted to this state. Reset the correct values and try it again.

- **You used the wrong clock multiplier and memory speed settings if your motherboard doesn't automatically set these for you.** Consult your processor and system documentation to determine the correct settings for your memory speed and processor speed/type. If the reported clock speed is wildly faster or slower than what it's supposed to be, you have probably entered the wrong values.

- **You might have a re-marked processor.** Component counterfeiting, including the marking of low-speed processors as faster processors, has been an epidemic in recent years. If you buy OEM processors (which are shipped to computer vendors in large trays rather than factory-sealed boxes), be sure you buy from a reputable vendor.

- **The processor has been slowed down by power management settings.** Recent processors can throttle back to lower speeds when power management is configured for Portable/Laptop rather than Home Office/Desk and a suitable driver is installed. Some processors will slow down when they overheat. To solve this problem, use Home Office/Desk as the Power Scheme setting, and make sure your fans and system cooling are working properly.

How to Avoid Getting Ripped Off by a Re-marked Processor

Because there are subtle differences in the appearance of different versions and speeds of processors, you might find it useful to visit a site such as Tom's Hardware (http://www.tomshardware.com) and print out a picture of the processor you plan to buy. If the actual processor doesn't match the photo, you might be getting scammed. The technical information available at the AMD and Intel websites can also help you avoid getting ripped off.

Before you buy a processor at a computer show (a frequent target for counterfeit goods), check out the vendor with other attendees or by calling the Better Business Bureau.

Troubleshooting Motherboard Failures

Motherboard failures are exceptionally serious to your system because a damaged motherboard can damage every component connected to it, including your processor, memory, add-on cards, and even external devices connected to motherboard-based ports.

Motherboards can fail for the following reasons:

- Electrostatic discharge
- Power spikes, surges, or other power problems
- Physical damage (tool marks or impact damage) during motherboard or processor installation
- Excessive flexing during processor or memory upgrades or board installation
- Damage to components near the processor socket during processor installation
- Loose components inside the system causing impact damage when the system is moved
- Overheating of the North Bridge chip
- Shorting out of components after installation

Although some of these topics are a greater concern to you if you install internal system upgrades yourself or have someone else install them for you, some of these can affect any system even if you never open the computer.

Preventing Electrostatic Discharge Damage to Your Motherboard

If you are planning to perform a motherboard upgrade yourself, be sure to guard against electrostatic discharge (ESD). Touch the inside of the case before you remove the old motherboard, keep the new motherboard inside its antistatic packaging until it's time to install it, and hold the new motherboard by its edges. Keep your fingers away from the solder traces on the underside and the chips on the topside of the board, because these can conduct electricity and can carry ESD to ESD-sensitive components on the motherboard.

➡ *For more details, see "Stop ESD— Don't Fry Your PC!," Chapter 1, p. 22.*

Although motherboards are less likely to be damaged by ESD once they are installed, you should still avoid touching chips on the motherboard surface when you install memory, processor, or add-on card upgrades unless you are properly grounded to the system.

Preventing Powerline Damage to Your Motherboard

The first line of defense against power spike or surge damage to your motherboard is a true surge suppressor that has a UL-1449 approval, has a let-through voltage rating of no more than 330V, and provides features such as signal lights to indicate that protection is active and to warn you of wiring faults.

➡ *For more details, see "Selecting Powerline Protection," Chapter 10, p. 638.*

If your area suffers frequent blackout or brownout conditions, you should also consider connecting your computer to a battery backup unit. Most battery backup units have surge-suppression features built in. Typical models can provide power for up to 15 minutes of computer operation.

By keeping high-quality power flowing into your system, you help prevent motherboard and component damage.

Troubleshooting Motherboard Upgrades

Whether you're shopping for a new motherboard so you can enjoy 64-bit computing with a new EM64T-compatible Pentium 4 or Athlon 64 processor or because your old motherboard died, upgrading your motherboard can be challenging. You need to make sure of the following:

- The motherboard you choose fits in your existing case.
- Your power supply can work with the motherboard.
- The motherboard will work with the processor and memory of your choice.
- You don't damage the motherboard during installation.
- You have a working copy of Windows you can use for a repair installation after the upgrade.

We've performed a number of motherboard upgrades over the years, so let us guide you though the process.

Making Sure Your New Motherboard Will Fit into Your Case

Motherboards have been supplied in various form factors over the years. These form factors follow, for the most part, established guidelines for shape, size, and features. Most desktop computers built since the late 1990s correspond to the ATX or microATX form factor.

To determine if your system uses some type of ATX motherboard, you don't need to open the system...yet. Just look at the rear of your system and compare it to Figure 9.25. All ATX motherboards have port clusters similar to the one shown in Figure 9.25, although the exact location and types of ports in the cluster vary from system to system. The number of expansion slots shown at the back of the system indicate what size of ATX motherboard your system can use:

- Zero to three slots: flexATX
- Two to four slots: microATX or flexATX
- Five slots or more: ATX, microATX, or flexATX

The system shown in Figure 9.25 has seven expansion slots, indicating it can use any ATX-family motherboard.

→ *To learn about performing a repair installation of Windows after a motherboard upgrade, see "Repair Installations," Chapter 2, p. 134.*

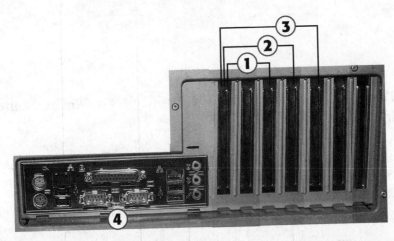

FIGURE 9.25
The design of the port cluster and the number of expansion slots in a case are useful in determining motherboard compatibility.

1. Zero to three slots indicates that the case is compatible with the flexATX motherboard
2. Two to four slots indicates that the case is compatible with the microATX motherboard
3. Five or more slots indicates that the case is compatible with the ATX motherboard
4. A typical ATX port cluster

→ *For details on power supply sizing, see "Right-Sizing a New Power Supply," Chapter 10, p. 637.*

A few systems support the new BTX standard, which uses a different port cluster and places the expansion slots to the left of the port cluster. These systems are too new to warrant motherboard upgrades. ATX variants are the overwhelming favorite for motherboard designs since the late 1990s. If you have an ATX system, you can install virtually any motherboard you like into the case, assuming your power supply is capable enough to handle the requirements of your new processor.

A microATX motherboard, the form factor used in many retail stores for low-cost smaller PCs, can also be upgraded, although the choices available aren't nearly as extensive as they are for full-size ATX systems (unless you replace the case with one designed for a full-size ATX motherboard). You can, however, use a microATX board in an ATX case. Theoretically, you can upgrade a system that uses a flexATX motherboard as well, but most of these systems use small-form-factor cases, which are extremely difficult to work with.

Figure 9.26 compares these motherboard designs to each other. Compare these drawings (which have been simplified to show only major components) to the motherboard in your current system to determine which motherboard type you can use for upgrades.

FIGURE 9.26

Top views of ATX (left), microATX (center), and flexATX (right) motherboards.

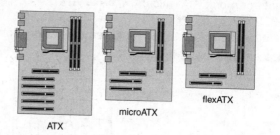

I'm Having a Hard Time Fitting My New Motherboard into My Case

After you determine what type of motherboard you can use for upgrades and install your processor and memory on the new motherboard, you need to remove the old motherboard so you can install the new one.

To avoid problems with this process, follow these suggestions:

- **Compare the current locations for screws in your current motherboard with the screw holes in your new motherboard.** If your old motherboard has screw holes in locations where your new motherboard doesn't, you should move the brass spacers visible after you unscrew and remove the old motherboard to mounting holes that correspond to the screw holes in your new motherboard (see Figure 9.27).

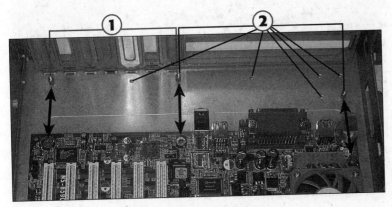

FIGURE 9.27
Brass standoff spacers in the correct position for the new motherboard.

1. Spacer and matching screw hole
2. Alternative position for spacer

- **When you slide the new motherboard into the case, you need to slide the I/O shield in first.** The I/O shield is the metal shield at the rear of the system that has the cutouts and markings for the USB, audio, network, and other ports on your motherboard (see Figure 9.28). It has small metal fingers that press against the ports on your motherboard, so you need to use some force to push the board into place. After you push the motherboard into place against the I/O shield, attach one or two of the screws to hold the motherboard in place.

During motherboard installation, you need to push the motherboard into place so that you can line up the holes in the motherboard with the standoffs attached to the case. The process of attaching the motherboard to the case can lead to physical damage that's not covered by the manufacturer's warranty if you're not careful.

You can prevent motherboard damage by follow these tips:

- Use hex-head screws and a hex driver to install your motherboard instead of a Phillips-head screwdriver. Hex drivers are less likely to slip and thus scratch the wire traces on the surface of the motherboard.

→ *Depending on the electrical requirements of your new motherboard, you might need to install a higher-wattage power supply that has suitable connectors for your new hardware. For details, see* "Troubleshooting a Power Supply Upgrade," Chapter 10, p. 635.

FIGURE 9.28

The I/O shield on a typical ATX motherboard as seen from the inside of the case. The holes to the right of the brass standoff can be used for additional standoffs if the motherboard needs them.

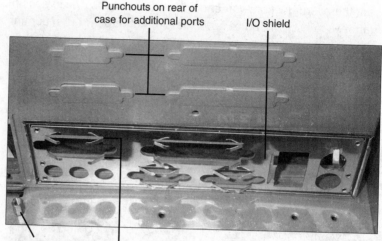

Punchouts on rear of case for additional ports

I/O shield

Brass spacer for fastening motherboard in place

Spring-loaded fingers on inside of I/O shield

- If your case has a removable motherboard tray, take the tray out of the system and attach the motherboard to the tray.

- Before you insert the new motherboard into the case, make sure the brass standoffs in the case line up with the screw holes (holes with metal rims) in your motherboard. If they don't, or if a brass standoff would line up with a hole that doesn't have a metal rim (see Figure 9.29), move the brass standoff (refer to Figure 9.27) to a different location.

For additional tips on proper motherboard installation, see "I'm Having a Hard Time Fitting My New Motherboard into My Case," this chapter, p. 604.

Preventing Damage to Your Motherboard During Memory and Add-in Card Installations

Your motherboard is not very thick, but within its layers are power, data, and signaling lines that carry vital information to every component built into or connected to your computer. If you put too much downward pressure on the motherboard when you install your memory, or add-in cards, you can crack the wire traces on the surface or inside your motherboard and ruin it.

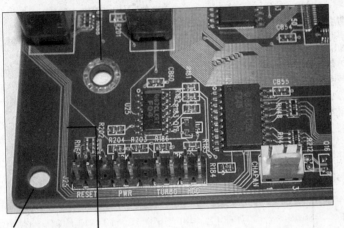

Screw hole (metal rim);
use with brass standoffs

Mounting hole; do not
use with brass standoffs

Wire traces; must not be scratched
or otherwise damaged

FIGURE 9.29
A typical motherboard has two types of holes; use only metal-rimmed holes to fasten the motherboard into place.

To avoid damaging your motherboard during component installation, try these tips:

- If you are performing a motherboard installation, add the memory to the motherboard before you install it inside your system. If the memory sockets are not visible when you open the case, you might need to remove the motherboard to perform a memory upgrade at a later date.

- When you install memory or add-on cards, make sure you line up the memory with the socket or the add-on card connector with the expansion slot before you push it into place. If you put downward pressure on the wrong part of the expansion slot or memory socket, you could damage it and cause it to short out. You might also damage nearby components when you attempt to slide the card into place if you don't have the card lined up correctly.

➔ *For more details about memory module installation, see "Installing Desktop Computer Memory," this chapter, p. 569.*

Beware the AGP Slot!

If you are installing an AGP video card, be very careful in particular that you don't damage nearby components such as the memory socket locking levers or the voltage regulator used to send the correct voltage to the processor. Some motherboards have very little clearance between the AGP slot and other components.

Also, some AGP slots are designed for AGP Pro cards (which use longer connectors than normal AGP cards) as well as normal AGP cards; if you accidentally connect a normal AGP card into the AGP Pro section of the connector, you'll fry your card. Many of these slots have a protective cover over the AGP Pro section of the slot; remove this cover only if you install an AGP Pro card.

Most recent AGP 4x/8x slots have locking mechanisms designed to hold the AGP card in place. Make sure that the locking mechanism is open before you insert the card and that it's closed after the card is inserted.

After the processor is installed into its socket, you will need to attach a heatsink fan to the processor. To learn how to avoid damage during this process, see "Protecting Your Motherboard and Processor from Installation Damage," this chapter, p. 598.

Preventing Damage from Loose Components Inside the Case

If you hear a rattle, bang, or ding inside your case when you move your computer, put it down immediately, pull out your toolkit, and open up your system to find the cause. Any loose component inside a system, from a misplaced screw to a heatsink, can cause a short circuit or impact damage to your system.

To minimize the chances of system damage due to loose components, use the following tips:

- Make sure you retrieve any loose screws or other parts you might drop inside a system whenever the case is open. Because the motherboard "floats" above the case on standoffs, it's easy for loose screws to get under the motherboard, touch some of the solder points, and cause the system to short out.

- Secure loose cables inside the case with cable ties. Don't over-tighten the cable tie because you might damage your cables, but take up enough slack to prevent the cables from blocking airflow to the fans.

- Make sure the memory modules, processor, and heatsink are locked into place whenever you open the system. A loose heatsink, in particular, is heavy enough to cause damage if it comes loose from the processor and could cause processor damage if it's not securely in place. For details, see "I'm Having a Hard Time Installing My New Processor," this chapter, p. 594.

Diagnosing Other Motherboard Problems

Because motherboards have so many onboard components, many problems with various devices can be traced back to motherboard problems:

- If you can't get your computer to recognize any type of add-on card inserted into a particular slot, the slot connector could be bad. Try inserting the card into another open slot.

- If your computer turns on but won't start the POST (Power-On Self-Test), you might have a loose socketed BIOS chip or a damaged flash BIOS. A socketed BIOS can become loose through chip creep (chips working loose from their sockets as a result of the motherboard heating up during use and cooling off when turned off), whereas a flash BIOS could be damaged by a computer virus, a power surge, or by an unsuccessful attempt to upgrade the BIOS.

   A socketed BIOS chip can be pushed into place, but a damaged flash BIOS needs to be reprogrammed or replaced. Contact your system or motherboard vendor for assistance.

- If you smell an unusual odor inside your computer, a resistor, capacitor, or other component may have shorted out or burned up. Resistors look like small light-colored Christmas lights on two-wire connectors, and they can be found on motherboards and add-on cards. Capacitors look like miniature soft drink cans and are part of the motherboard's voltage regulator (refer to Figure 9.23). If a resistor or a capacitor fails (look for discoloration on the component), test the power supply to make sure it is working correctly (replace it if it has failed or is out of specification). Then, replace the device containing the defective component.

→ A BIOS failure is one of the less likely reasons for a system to fail to start. See "Troubleshooting Hard Disk or Optical Drive Bootup Problems," Chapter 3, p. 207, and "Troubleshooting a Computer That Won't Turn On," Chapter 10, p. 623.

→ For details about power supply testing, see "Troubleshooting System Lockups," Chapter 10, p. 628.

My System Beeps Abnormally After I Restart It with the New Motherboard in Place

The system BIOS uses beep codes to report problems with your system, such as processor, memory, or other types of problems. The beep codes vary by BIOS brand and version.

➜ *For a listing of beep codes and their meanings, see "POST Codes," Chapter 1, p. 58.*

Some of the most common reasons for a computer to beep after you upgrade the motherboard include the following:

- The processor isn't plugged in correctly.
- The memory isn't installed or isn't locked into place.
- The video card isn't installed or isn't connected properly to the AGP, PCI-Express, or PCI slot.

If you know the BIOS type and count the beeps, you can determine the exact problem with your system.

Before you check any of these items or other problems that could be indicated by beep codes, be sure you shut down the computer and unplug it.

Troubleshooting Cooling Problems

If your hardware monitor warns you of excessively high processor or motherboard temperatures but the fan monitor doesn't indicate failures, check the following:

- Make sure the air intakes and fans on the front, sides, and rear of the computer are free of dust and grime. Use a computer vacuum cleaner or an antistatic spray cleaner such as Endust for Electronics to clean them.

Spray the Cloth, Not the Component!

If you use a spray cleaner to remove dust and gunk, be sure to spray your cleaning cloth and then wipe the component with the cloth. Spraying computer equipment directly, even if the equipment is turned off, can ruin it if the components are still damp when the power is turned back on.

- Replace heatsink and case fans that are noisy or don't spin fast enough with high-quality fans that use ball-bearing mechanisms. Sleeve-bearing fans are less expensive but will fail when their lubricant dries out.
- Clean the air intakes going into the power supply with a soft dry cloth or computer vacuum cleaner. You should unplug the power supply before you wipe it off or attempt to clean its internal or external fans.

- Add large passive heatsinks or active heatsinks (heatsink and fan) to the North Bridge chip.

- Check fans already present on video cards or motherboard chipsets for proper operation, and replace them if they are noisy or don't spin fast enough.

- Add additional fans to the front and rear of the case.

If the hardware monitor indicates that one or more fans have failed (very low or no RPMs for more than 10 seconds), shut down the system *immediately* and replace the fan that failed. If the fan on the power supply stops turning, shut down the system *immediately* and replace the power supply with a higher-rated unit.

→ *For more details about replacing the power supply, see "Troubleshooting a Power Supply Upgrade," Chapter 10, p. 635.*

Preventing Overheating Damage to the Motherboard

Most motherboards have two surface-mounted, nonremovable chips that handle data transfers between the processor and other components:

- **The North Bridge chip**—Also called the *memory controller hub* or *system controller*, this chip is responsible for handling high-speed traffic such as processor-to-memory or processor-to-video traffic. Because of the speeds at which this chip operates, it can become very warm.

- **The South Bridge chip**—Also called the *I/O controller hub* or *peripheral bus controller*, this chip is responsible for handling lower-speed traffic passed from the North Bridge to the hard disk, network and modem interfaces, USB ports, and similar devices.

The North Bridge chip is larger than the South Bridge chip and is usually located near the processor socket. On many recent systems and motherboards, the North Bridge chip is covered with a heatsink. Some systems use a passive-cooling heatsink that uses metal fins to dissipate heat away from the chip, whereas other systems use a heatsink fan (an active heatsink). See Figure 9.30 for an example of both types.

FIGURE 9.30

Typical factory-installed passive (top) and active (bottom) North Bridge heatsinks. Note the close proximity of the North Bridge chips to the processors.

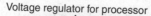
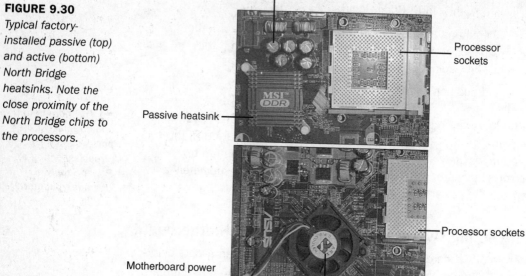

Voltage regulator for processor

Processor sockets

Passive heatsink

Processor sockets

Motherboard power connector for active heatsink

Active heatsink

If your motherboard or system uses a heatsink fan that draws its power from the motherboard (as in Figure 9.30), it might be monitored by the PC Health or Hardware Monitor feature built into many recent systems. Use the monitoring software provided with your system to verify the fan is working properly.

If your North Bridge chip doesn't have a heatsink, I recommend you add one. You have two options for mounting the heatsink:

- Plastic pegs that attach to holes on either side of the North Bridge chip

- Thermal tape that attaches the heatsink to the top of the North Bridge chip

Figure 9.31 shows a typical aftermarket kit containing both types of North Bridge heatsinks.

Passive heatsink

3-wire to 4-wire power adapter

Installation overview

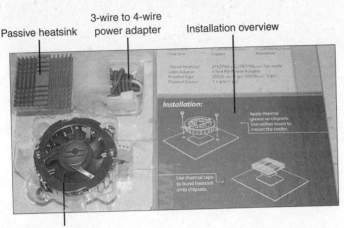

Active heatsink

FIGURE 9.31

A typical North Bridge chipset heatsink kit. This kit features both passive and active heatsinks, but only the active heatsink can be attached with mounting pins; the passive heatsink uses thermal tape.

If your heatsink is equipped with mounting pegs, use them if the motherboard has mounting holes near the North Bridge chip. Be sure to apply the recommended amount of thermal paste between the heatsink and the North Bridge chip. Although some North Bridge heatsinks are supplied with double-stick adhesive thermal tape, as in Figure 9.31, we don't recommend this mounting method if mounting holes are available on the motherboard and heatsink. If the thermal tape adhesive dries out, the heatsink could fall off the North Bridge chip and possibly cause this chip to overheat and fail. Because the North Bridge chip can't be removed from the system, you must replace the motherboard if its North Bridge chip fails.

On the Web

Zalman Tech Co, Ltd, a popular maker of heatsink and other cooling solutions, offers animated tutorials showing how to install passive North Bridge coolers. See the tutorial at http://www.zalman.co.kr.

Scott Mueller's article, "Improving System Cooling Part 2—Keeping the North Bridge Cool," features an illustrated tutorial of a typical North Bridge active heatsink installation. See it at http://www.quepublishing. com/articles/article.asp?p=339028.

If you prefer an active heatsink, for additional safety, connect the power lead on the heatsink to a monitored power connector on the motherboard so you can be notified of any problems with fan performance. Use the three-pin-to-four-pin (drive power connector) adapter only if you can't plug the heatsink power lead into the motherboard.

For more information about system monitoring, see "Detecting Overheating and Incorrect Voltage Levels," this chapter, p. 583.

10

Troubleshooting
Power Problems

TROUBLESHOOTING

FAST TRACK TO SOLUTIONS (SYMPTOM TABLE)

Symptom	Flowchart or Book Section	See Page
The power supply is very warm to the touch.	Troubleshooting an Overheated Power Supply	619
My computer restarts itself, even though I didn't do anything.	Troubleshooting a Power Supply That Reboots the Computer	622
My computer works well in one room, but if I move it to another room, it crashes frequently.	Checking Wall Outlets	639
When I plug in a bus-powered USB device, the computer doesn't always recognize it.	Troubleshooting an Overloaded Power Supply	633
When I plug in an additional drive or add-on card, either the computer can't start or it crashes, but the same device works correctly in another PC.	Troubleshooting an Overloaded Power Supply	633
My computer locks up frequently.	Troubleshooting System Lockups	628
I'm not sure if my power supply is putting out the right voltage levels.	Troubleshooting System Lockups	628
I have a Dell computer that needs a new power supply. How can I tell if it needs a standard or a special Dell model?	Sidebar: Watch Out for the Difference in Older Dells	631
How can I avoid buying a power supply that's too small?	Right-Sizing a New Power Supply	637
How can I make sure I'm getting a big enough battery backup unit (UPS)?	Battery Backup Systems	643

Why Power Supplies Fail

If power supplies could talk, they'd probably sound a lot like the late Rodney Dangerfield: "I don't get no respect!" If you're planning a system upgrade, it's likely that your power supply is not on the list. After all, it doesn't *appear* to affect a system's performance or features. But appearances can be deceiving. As a quick review of the Hardware forum at Leoville Town Square (my online home) shows, bad power supplies can cause a lot of grief. A lot of the problems PC users experience that get blamed on memory, Windows, and so on can all be traced to a faulty or poor-quality power supply. Sadly, the power supply is often the first component most PC vendors attempt to skimp on.

What can a bad power supply do to your system? It prevents your computer from running reliably, can cause bus-powered USB and IEEE-1394 devices to be unreliable, and can even cause the computer to reboot spontaneously or fail to boot at all. The trouble is, a bad power supply isn't the only PC component that can cause these kinds of problems. In this chapter, we'll put on our deerstalker caps, grab our magnifying glasses, and turn amateur detectives to determine if you have a defective power supply. You'll learn how to protect your power supply and how to replace your power supply with the right model for your needs.

Keep in mind that a "power supply" doesn't contain a small atomic reactor or any other true source of power. Instead, power supplies convert potentially deadly high-voltage AC wall current into safe low-voltage DC power. A byproduct of the transforming process is heat; hence, a desktop PC's power supply contains a built-in fan, which pulls air through the power supply to dissipate heat. This also helps to cool the system. Laptop computers work a little differently—they typically use an external "briquette" transformer to turn AC into DC power. Consequently, the laptop's power supply is responsible for fiddling the DC power coming into the unit into the various voltage levels needed for drive motors, cooling fans, and chips.

Now that you understand what a power supply is—and what it does—it's time to find out what makes one conk out:

- **Excessive wattage demand by the system**—If your power supply doesn't have a high enough wattage rating (larger is better) to handle the power needs of your computer and the components plugged into it, the power supply will wear out prematurely. (Remember, any time you add to the components in your PC, you increase the load on your power supply.) Connecting bus-powered IEEE-1394 and USB devices or installing additional internal drives and cards can cause a marginal power supply to become completely unreliable because the computer provides power to these devices.

→ **For details about cleaning your computer, see "Troubleshooting Cooling Problems," Chapter 9, p. 610.**

- **Overheating**—Overheating can be caused by dirty power supply air intakes or by excessive power demands. Both can cause the power supply to fail.

- **AC power quality problems**—Although power supplies can handle moderate surges (up to 600 volts AC) by themselves, much larger surges can take place as a result of lightning strikes or other power disturbances. In addition to power surges and spikes, excessive electrical "noise" (interference from other devices on a circuit) or frequent periods of lower-than-normal voltage can also lead to power supply failure. If the lights often dim at your home or office (sometimes called a "brownout"), you have AC power quality problems—and your PC's power supply doesn't appreciate it!

- **Poor airflow**—Most power supplies cool your system by acting like vacuum cleaners, pulling air through the system to the power supply's air intakes and out the rear of the system. Dirty air intakes on the case or the power supply or a lack of free space behind the system can block airflow and lead to overheating and eventual power supply failure.

- **Higher-than-normal input voltage**—Two major voltage standards are supported by personal computers: the 115-volt/60-cycle standard used in North America and the 230-volt/50-cycle standard used in most of the rest of the world. Whereas most notebook computer power supplies automatically adjust to the incoming voltage, most desktop computer power supplies must be manually set, using a switch on the back of the power supply, to use the correct voltage level.

In the following sections you will learn how to determine which of these is causing problems for your power supply and find out how to solve or prevent these problems.

Determining You Have a Power Supply Problem

Someday we might have talking computers that tell us when trouble's a-brewing—but until then, you'll just need to recognize the symptoms. When you notice one or more of the following problems, your power supply's trying to tell you, "Help me!"

- The rear of the power supply is too hot to touch while the computer is running. Ouch!

- You're working away at something, hands well away from the reset switch on the front of the case, but the next thing you see is the power-on screen because the computer has rebooted itself.

- You cannot turn on the computer.

- The computer locks up or generates Windows errors (like the blue screen of death) at random intervals.

- As soon as you plug in a bus-powered USB or IEEE-1394 device or install an additional hard disk, DVD drive, or add-on card, your computer starts crashing.

- You must unplug and reattach a USB device repeatedly before the computer recognizes it.

Before you whip out your wallet to buy a replacement power supply, stop for a moment. The power supply might not be damaged, but you'd better figure out *why* you're seeing these problems—and solve them first.

Troubleshooting an Overheated Power Supply

Sooner or later, an overheated power supply's going to quit on you—and chances are that will happen when you have a screenful of unsaved data. Try the following to help your power supply to keep running reliably:

- Make sure the air intakes on the computer case, the air intakes into the power supply, the power supply fan, and the exhaust are clean and free of obstructions.

- Make sure the power supply fan is turning at full speed; if the power supply has a fan facing inside the system, make sure it is turning as well. If the power supply fan has failed, replace the power supply. If the power supply has a monitoring lead that connects to the motherboard, you can check the system BIOS's hardware monitor or run software supplied by the motherboard or system maker to see if the fan is running at the proper speed.

- Fold or cable-tie drive ribbon cables inside the case to prevent them from blocking airflow. You can also replace flat cables with pre-rounded cables available from many vendors. Another option is to purchase split-loom or braided cable sleeving and then fit your IDE and floppy cables into them. This will both increase airflow inside the case and give your case a custom look. Use cable ties to secure the split-loom sleeves. Various kinds of cable sleeves can be purchased at computer mod websites or at automotive websites.

- Using Serial ATA (SATA) drives instead of ATA/IDE drives gets rid of most ribbon cables inside the system. SATA cables are much smaller and don't block airflow.

- Check the wattage rating of the power supply and compare it to the wattage requirements of your computer's onboard and connected equipment. To see the wattage rating of your current power supply, open your system and look for a printed label on the unit (you might need to remove the power supply from your computer to see this information).

Figure 10.1 shows you a typical power supply label.

It's never too early—or never too late—to take a close look at the information label on your power supply. Here are some ways the label can help you determine if your power supply is just not adequate for the task:

- You should *never* use a power supply that doesn't have safety ratings from an authority such as CSA (Canada), UL (USA—the backwards UR is the UL marking for components), TÜV (Germany), or CE (European Union). Believe it or not, you can buy power supplies that have no safety ratings. They're cheap—until you figure out the cost of lost data and downtime.

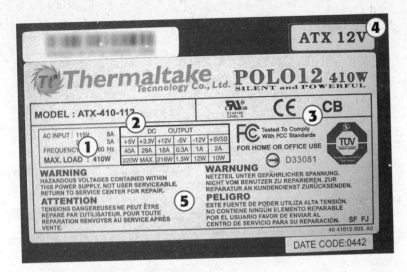

FIGURE 10.1
The label from a typical 410-watt power supply.

1. Power supply wattage rating
2. Maximum amperage available per voltage level
3. Safety approvals
4. Unit supports the ATX 12V standard
5. Safety warnings

- If you're planning to upgrade an old Pentium III or Athlon (non-XP) system with a new motherboard and processor, look for the ATX 12V rating (or the ATX 12V connector shown later in Figure 10.7). Motherboards made for the Pentium 4, Athlon XP, and Athlon 64 require this connector to provide adequate power. If your power supply doesn't include this connector, add the price of a power supply to your upgrade budget. If you want to upgrade to a Socket 775–based motherboard and processor (the "Prescott" Pentium 4), you need a power supply that supports ATX 12V Version 2.0.

- If you have components that require a high amperage level on some voltage lines, knowing the amount of amperage available on each of the four voltage lines (+5V, –5V, +12V, and –12V) is useful to help you determine if your power supply is adequate. For example, some generic 400 watt power supplies only provide 12A on the +12V rail, but the latest Pentium 4 "Prescott" processor design requires 18A. Motherboard vendors also list the power requirements for each model, so dig out your manual or visit your vendor's website to see if your power supply is up to snuff.

Electric Shock Hazard!

Figure 10.1 also warns you not to open the power supply cover under any circumstances. Even when the computer is turned off and unplugged, the wire coils inside the power supply retain potentially lethal levels of electricity. When a power supply fails, don't even think about repairing it; throw it away.

If the power supply continues to overheat even after you have improved airflow to and through the unit, you should replace it with a unit that has a higher wattage rating—at least 400 watts for a mid-tower or more for a full tower.

Power Supply Sizing the Easy Way

PC Power and Cooling's interactive power supply selector can help you find out if the current size of power supply you have is adequate or if you need a larger unit. (They also sell great power supplies!) Try it out for yourself at

http://www.pcpowercooling.com/products/power_supplies/selector/index.htm.

Troubleshooting a Power Supply That Reboots the Computer

What causes a computer to reboot itself? The power supply! One of the pins on the power supply connector is known as the Power Good line; when voltage drops below or exceeds the range established for Power Good (nominally +5V with an acceptable range from +3V to +6V), the computer is sent a reset signal by the power supply. In essence, the power supply reboots the computer.

Although a rare spontaneous reboot is nothing to worry about (glitches happen!), frequent reboots might indicate your computer has an over-loaded power supply that needs to be replaced with a unit with a higher wattage rating. Before you assume the power supply is at fault, though, try plugging the system into a different wall outlet. Wiring faults can also cause the computer to reboot spontaneously. However, if the computer reboots on its own no matter what wall outlet you use, it's safe to assume that the power supply needs to be replaced.

Troubleshooting a Computer That Won't Turn On

If you can't even get your computer to start up, don't panic! Before you assume that your power supply is pushing up the daisies, check the following:

- The computer might not be plugged in.

- The surge suppressor the computer is plugged into might be turned off.

- The power switch on the rear the power supply might be turned off (not all power supplies have this switch).

- You might have the wrong input voltage selected on the rear of the power supply.

- The wiring from the case's on/off switch might not be properly connected to the correct jumpers on the motherboard.

- The power connectors to the motherboard might not be properly connected; some motherboards require you to connect the ATXAux or ATX12V connector as well as the primary connector to the motherboard for adequate power.

- You might have an internal short that shuts down the power supply as soon as you start the system.

- The motherboard has a "Guardian" function that prevents you from starting the computer unless a working processor fan is plugged into a particular jack.

→ *See "My System Won't Start After I Installed a New Processor," Chapter 9, p. 599.*

Leo Says

Don't Assume Your Computer Is Plugged In— Check It!

We're not the only ones to have assumed that a PC, a vacuum cleaner, a printer, or a TV was dead because they weren't connected to a working AC power source. Check the simple stuff first! Remember that even if the device is plugged in, that doesn't necessarily mean the power jack is getting juice. Try testing the outlet by plugging in some other electric device that you know works (or plugging your PC into a different outlet that you know functions). And, don't forget to make sure that the computer's AC cord is firmly plugged into the power supply.

➜ *For more about troubleshooting philosophy and methods, see "The Troubleshooting Process," Appendix A, p. 646.*

You're probably using a surge suppressor between your computer and the wall outlet, so don't ignore the possibility that the surge suppressor is turned off or has failed. If the computer runs when you plug it into a wall outlet, but won't work when you plug it into a surge suppressor that's turned on, look for a reset button on the surge suppressor and press it. If the surge suppressor doesn't have a reset button, or still doesn't work after you try it, the suppressor is dead and needs to be replaced.

If you're wondering if the third and fourth possibilities apply to you, take a look at the back of your system. If your computer's power supply has an external on/off switch, make sure it's turned on. Some vendors don't include this switch (it's handy for turning off your PC if the front switch doesn't work), but almost all power supplies have a selector switch that is used to select 115V or 230V as the input voltage.

It's a harmless (but annoying) prank to set the switch to 230 volts if you are using the computer in North America. The keyboard light might flash before the computer shuts down completely because the input voltage setting is too high. However, don't try the reverse trick if your location uses 230 volts; setting the input voltage to 115 volts and starting the computer will destroy the power supply and might also destroy the motherboard and other components!

Take a look at Figure 10.2 to see the on/off switch and voltage selection switch on the rear of a typical power supply.

If you can't turn on your system after you opened it to perform an internal upgrade, to clean it out, or just because you're curious, you might have accidentally disconnected the wire that connects the case's on/off switch to the motherboard. Before you reconnect this wire, unplug the computer from the power. Figure 10.3 shows a typical power switch cable and motherboard connector.

Your system probably has an internal short if it turns on for a couple of seconds, then stops. Internal shorts can be caused by any of the following:

- Loose screws inside the computer case
- Defective components in the power supply
- Bare wires on the power supply cables or splitter/extensions (which extend or split one 4-pin drive connector to service two devices)
- Damaged components plugged into the power supply, such as drives or fans

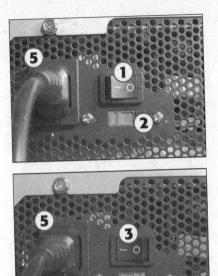

FIGURE 10.2
Switch settings on the rear of a typical desktop computer's power supply.

1. Power switch set to Off
2. Input voltage set to 230V
   (Outside North America)
3. Power switch set to On
4. Input voltage set to 115V
   (North America)
5. AC cord connected to power supply

Power switch wires from
PC's front panel

Motherboard legend

FIGURE 10.3
The cable from the computer's power switch must be properly connected to the motherboard; otherwise, you can't start the PC.

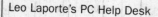
To check for loose screws, use this procedure:

1. Turn off the power supply if it has an external switch (refer to Figure 10.2).

2. Unplug the AC power cord.

3. Open the system.

4. Pick up and shake the system gently while you listen for loose screws.

5. Remove any loose screws.

6. Plug the power supply back in.

7. Turn the power supply on.

8. Try to restart your computer.

If it restarts, hooray! Turn it off, close it up, and get back to business.

To check for shorts caused by bare wires or bad power splitters, follow a similar procedure, but at step 4, look for bare wires or poorly constructed Y-splitters (used to split one power source into two). Disconnect any of these you find in step 5, and proceed. *Don't disconnect a power splitter that runs your CPU fan—you can (depending on the kind of CPU) fry your CPU in seconds if it's not cooled!* If disconnecting a Y-splitter or device with a bare wire solves the problem, replace the splitter or device. If a replacement is not available, use electrical tape to cover the bare wire and see if the computer will start. Get a replacement as soon as you can.

To check for shorts caused by bad drives, select a drive that is not using a Y-splitter in step 4 and disconnect it from the power supply in step 5 (you can leave the drive connected to its data cable). If the drive uses a Y-splitter, connect it directly to the power supply. If the system works when you bypass the Y-splitter, replace the Y-splitter. If the system will not start with a particular drive connected to the power, replace the drive.

One hidden benefit of upgrading to a large-wattage power supply is the greater number of drive connectors built into the new power supply.

Because a defective motherboard or other component can cause your power supply to appear to be defective, it's a really good idea to test the power supply in isolation from the motherboard, fans, and drives. Several power supply vendors, including Antec and PC Power and Cooling, sell self-contained power supply testers like the one shown in Figure 10.4. Check component stores to find this type of tester.

Signal LED lights up when system is turned on if power supply is working

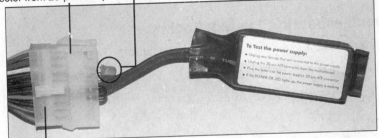

Connector from 20-pin ATX power supply

Connects to
power supply

FIGURE 10.4

A self-contained power supply tester in use.

Here's how to use the tester:

1. Unplug the computer from AC power.

2. Open the computer case.

3. Disconnect the power supply from the motherboard, drives, and fans.

4. Plug the computer into AC power.

5. Connect the motherboard power connector from the power supply to the tester.

6. Turn on the power supply and computer.

7. If the green LED on the tester lights up, the power supply is working.

If the power supply is dead, replace it.

However, even if the power supply is working, it might not be providing correct power levels. The tests in the next section will help you determine if your power supply is providing correct power levels and a valid Power Good signal to the motherboard.

Power Supply Vendors You Can Trust

In the opinion of many users, the very best power supplies, testing, and cooling accessories around are sold by PC Power and Cooling:

http://www.pcpowerandcooling.com

Antec is another high-quality vendor, which is also famous for its cases:

http://www.antec.com

If you have eliminated all these possibilities and the computer still won't start up, you probably need a new power supply.

Troubleshooting System Lockups

System lockups can be caused by many factors:

- Defective or overheated memory modules
- Hardware resource conflicts, particularly IRQ conflicts (although these are very rare today)
- Incorrect voltage levels on the motherboard

→ *See "Using Device Manager," Chapter 2, p. 100, to learn how to detect hardware resources.*

Generally, defective memory modules trigger a beep code when the computer is turned on, and overheated memory modules will cause problems only after the system has been running for a long time. You can detect hardware resource conflicts with the Windows Device Manager or with System Information.

Voltage problems can also cause reliability problems such as lockups, although it sometimes takes more effort to track them down.

There are two ways to check the voltage levels coming out of the power supply:

- **Test the power supply with a multimeter, which can be set to DC voltage.** This option requires you to have a pinout of the power supply connectors.
- **Use the PC Health or Hardware Monitor feature built into the system BIOS.** If you want to see voltage levels after the system has been running for a while, install a monitoring program.

→ *See "Controlling Your PC's Operation with BIOS Setup," Chapter 1, p. 41, for details about accessing the system BIOS.*

On recent desktop systems, it's easier to use the Hardware Monitor option in the system BIOS at startup (see Figure 10.5). While the computer is running, you can use the Windows-based hardware monitor provided by many system and motherboard makers (see Figure 10.6).

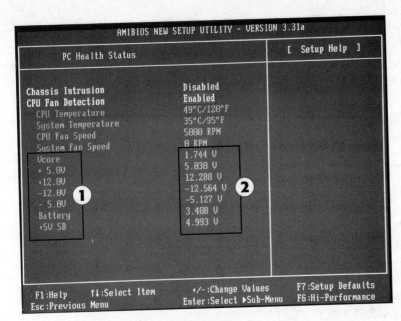

FIGURE 10.5
*The PC Health
(Hardware Monitor)
BIOS screen displays
processor core and
motherboard voltage
levels.*

1. System components
2. Voltage levels for listed components

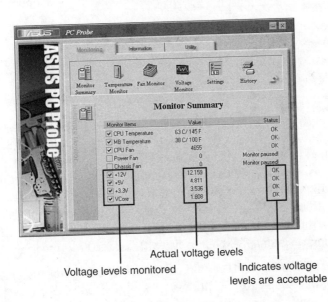

FIGURE 10.6
*The Asus PC Probe
hardware monitoring
program displays tem-
perature, voltage, and
fan performance infor-
mation detected by the
system BIOS within
Windows.*

Actual voltage levels

Voltage levels monitored

Indicates voltage
levels are acceptable

Getting Your Hands on a Hardware Monitor Program

Some motherboard and system makers might offer a hardware monitor program for your system, although you might not have received it with your motherboard or computer. Contact your motherboard or system vendor for details.

If you need an alternative, try Hmonitor. You can download it from http://www.hmonitor.com or http://www.hmonitor.net. The current version works with both the 32-bit and 64-bit versions of Windows XP as well as with many notebook computers.

If your hardware monitoring solution doesn't indicate if voltages are within limits, compare the voltages reported to those in Table 10.1. Table 10.1 lists the acceptable voltage ranges for all types of power supplies, including Power Good. If your power supply doesn't provide power within these limits, replace it.

TABLE 10.1
ACCEPTABLE VOLTAGE RANGES

Rated Voltage	Minimum	Maximum
+5V	+4.8V	+5.2V
–5V	–4.5V	–5.4V
+12V	+11.5V	+12.6V
–12V	–10.8V	–12.9V
Power Good	+2.4V	+6.0V

Note that Power Good (which reboots your system if it is not within the specified values) is not displayed by BIOS or software-based system monitors. If you're trying to figure out why your system keeps rebooting itself, you need to open it up and use a digital multimeter to check Power Good. You can use a multimeter for lots of different tasks, including testing AC wall outlet voltage, checking cable continuity, and checking resistance; expect to pay at least $20 for a typical unit.

As you saw in Figure 10.4, the power supply connector running from your power supply to your PC has a lot of wires. You need to check the correct wires to make sure your power supply is providing proper voltage. Most desktop PCs built since the late 1990s use a 20-pin ATX power supply connector. However, if you have a new system with PCI-Express slots or a system using the new BTX motherboard form factor (look for lots of these in 2006), you might have a 24-pin power connector. Some high-performance (400-watt or greater) power supplies are equipped with a 20-pin-to-24-pin adapter, enabling them to work with both types of motherboards. Most recent motherboards, especially those for the Pentium 4 or AMD Athlon 64, also use the 4-pin ATX12V power connector. All three power leads are shown in Figure 10.7.

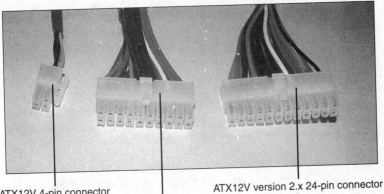

ATX12V 4-pin connector

ATX 20-pin connector

ATX12V version 2.x 24-pin connector

FIGURE 10.7

The standard 20-pin ATX power connector compared to the 24-pin connector used by some recent systems and the 4-pin ATX12V connector.

Some Dell computers built in the late 1990s through about 2000 used a proprietary version of this connector. The connector has completely different wiring, although it looks physically the same. If you have an older Dell PC, read the sidebar "Watch Out for the Difference in Older Dells" to learn about the dangers in mixing standard ATX and Dell's short-lived alternative ATX power supplies and motherboards.

Watch Out for the Difference in Older Dells

Dell Computers used motherboards and power supplies with a proprietary pinout in Dell Dimension models sold starting in September 1998 and continuing through 2000. These systems were prior to the Dimension 2200, Dimension 4300, and Dimension 8200 and newer series, which have reverted to the ATX standard shown in Figure 10.7. How can you tell if you have a nonstandard power supply? Watch for differences in color-coding: The Dell version has only one orange wire in the middle of the 20-pin connector, whereas ATX standard has three orange wires at one end of the connector. Also, Dell's three +3.3V wires are coded blue/white and are built into a 6-pin auxiliary connector along with three black ground wires.

Although the physical connectors mimic the ATX standard, the wiring and voltage levels are completely different. If you connect a standard power supply to a Dell computer using the nonstandard design, or install a standard motherboard in a Dell computer using the nonstandard design, call the fire department or at least have a fire extinguisher handy. At the very least, you'll destroy either the motherboard or power supply, and it is possible one of these components will catch fire as soon as you turn on the power!

Hardware superstar Scott Mueller (author of the classic *Upgrading and Repairing PCs* series) has placed a detailed report about this problem on his website. The article includes the pinouts you need if you want to test a Dell motherboard that uses the nonstandard ATX pinout. You can read it at

http://www.quepublishing.com/articles/article.asp?p=339053

If you need to replace the power supply in your older Dell computer but don't want to replace the motherboard at the same time, some vendors sell Dell-specific power supplies. You can also select your Dell model to determine whether it uses a standard ATX or Dell-specific power supply.

Figure 10.8 shows the pinouts used by the 20-pin and 24-pin ATX power supply connectors. The 24-pin ATX power supply pinout is also used by the new CFX12V and TFX12V power supplies used by new models of small-form factor and thin PCs.

How can you test your power supply while the system is running? Follow this procedure:

1. Shut down the computer and unplug it.

2. Open the computer case and locate the power connector.

3. Turn on your multimeter and set it for DC power.

4. Plug in the computer.

5. Turn on the computer.

6. Check Power Good, +5V, –5V, +12V, and –12V voltage levels; insert the red lead into the top of the power connector to touch the metal connector inside, and touch the black lead to a ground such as the case frame or power supply case (see Figure 10.9).

7. Check the readings against those shown in Table 10.1. If you see a rating that falls outside the range listed, the power supply is defective and should be replaced.

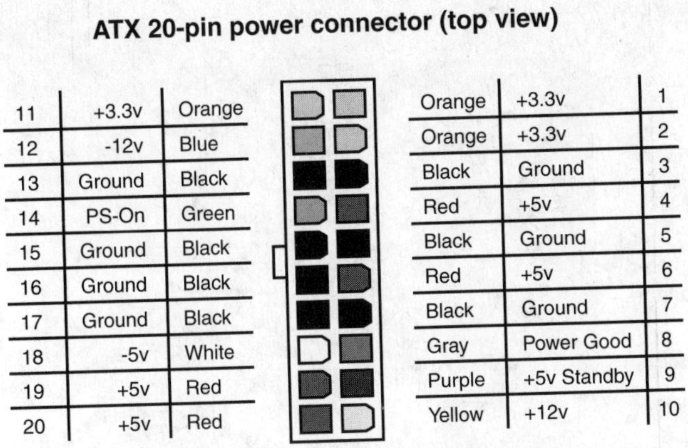

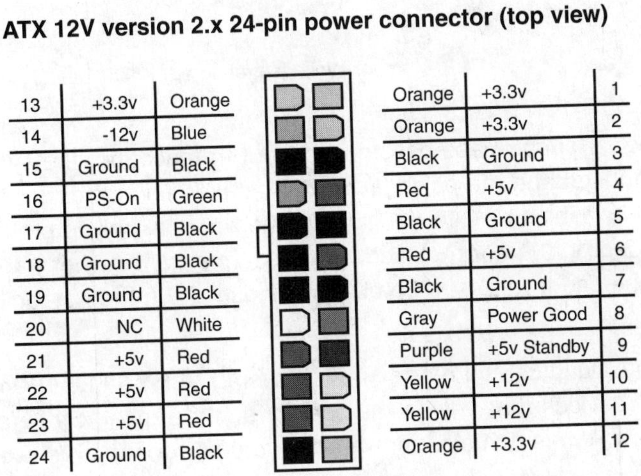

ATX 20-pin power connector (top view)

FIGURE 10.8
The 24-pin ATX12V v2.x power supply pinout (bottom) is based on the 20-pin ATX power supply pinout (top). This pinout shows the top view of the connectors as they attach to the motherboard.

11	+3.3v	Orange
12	-12v	Blue
13	Ground	Black
14	PS-On	Green
15	Ground	Black
16	Ground	Black
17	Ground	Black
18	-5v	White
19	+5v	Red
20	+5v	Red

Orange	+3.3v	1
Orange	+3.3v	2
Black	Ground	3
Red	+5v	4
Black	Ground	5
Red	+5v	6
Black	Ground	7
Gray	Power Good	8
Purple	+5v Standby	9
Yellow	+12v	10

ATX 12V version 2.x 24-pin power connector (top view)

13	+3.3v	Orange
14	-12v	Blue
15	Ground	Black
16	PS-On	Green
17	Ground	Black
18	Ground	Black
19	Ground	Black
20	NC	White
21	+5v	Red
22	+5v	Red
23	+5v	Red
24	Ground	Black

Orange	+3.3v	1
Orange	+3.3v	2
Black	Ground	3
Red	+5v	4
Black	Ground	5
Red	+5v	6
Black	Ground	7
Gray	Power Good	8
Purple	+5v Standby	9
Yellow	+12v	10
Yellow	+12v	11
Orange	+3.3v	12

Troubleshooting an Overloaded Power Supply

As you have already learned, a power supply is really a power converter whose capacity is measured in two ways:

- Watts
- Amperage levels available for each voltage level

A power supply is overloaded if it is powering devices that draw more wattage or a higher amperage level for a given voltage level than the power supply can produce.

FIGURE 10.9

Testing a +12V line on a standard ATX motherboard. The actual voltage (+11.92V) is well within specifications.

DC voltage readout

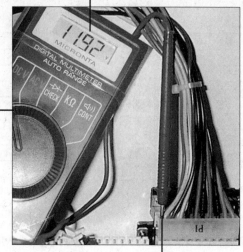

Digital multimeter set to DC voltage

Voltage probe (red)

If the power supply case becomes too hot to touch, but the system is well-ventilated and the power supply air intakes are not dirty or blocked by cables or external objects, the power supply is probably overloaded. If it is not replaced with a unit providing higher wattage and amperage levels, it will probably fail outright in the not-too-distant future.

If you must unplug and reattach bus-powered USB or IEEE-1394 devices (devices that rely on the port for power) repeatedly before they can function, this can also indicate that the power supply is overloaded.

If you have upgraded your system from a slower to a faster processor and the system will no longer run properly, the power supply is probably overloaded. Current processors such as the Pentium 4, Athlon XP, and Athlon 64 use much more +12V DC power than their predecessors.

Whether your power supply is overloaded, has failed outright, or is not powerful enough to handle a major upgrade such as a new motherboard and processor or a high-end AGP or PCI-Express graphics card (many of which require you to connect power cables in addition to receiving power through the expansion slot), you're going to need a power supply upgrade to get back to work. The next section covers that process.

Troubleshooting a Power Supply Upgrade

The process of replacing your power supply involves the following steps:

1. Determining the correct form factor, wattage rating, and special features you need in a new power supply.

2. Disconnecting drives and fans from the old power supply.

3. Removing the old power supply from your system.

4. Installing the new power supply in your system.

5. Reconnecting drives and fans to your new power supply.

6. Restarting the computer and verifying proper operation with a multimeter or the PC's hardware monitor.

Leo Says

Replace Your Power Supply? Time to Fix Your Software

If your power supply caused a lot of system crashes before you replaced it, you might need to reinstall some of your applications and possibly even your operating system after you install a new power supply. A bad power supply can cause files to be corrupted if the power supply fails or restarts the computer during disk access.

So, if you see program or Windows errors after you install a new power supply, reinstall the program or perform a repair installation of Windows (see Chapter 1, "PC Anatomy 101," for details); the error messages are telling you that your old power supply corrupted some files during its death throes.

If you're replacing your motherboard to enable yourself to move to a new processor, check the new motherboard's requirements and make sure the appropriate connectors are available on your existing power supply. Refer back to Figure 10.7 to see how the 4-pin ATX12V connector (used by Pentium 4 and Athlon 64 motherboards) and the new 24-pin ATX12V V2.x connector (used by motherboards equipped with PCI-Express x16 graphics card expansion slots) compares with the standard 20-pin ATX power connector. If your motherboard uses a 24-pin or 4-pin connector, your power supply needs to as well. Note that some new 20-pin ATX power supplies rated at 400 watts and above include a 20-pin-to-24-pin adapter to make them compatible with both types of motherboards.

Follow these suggestions to help ensure a trouble-free upgrade to a new power supply:

- Take a careful look at your current power supply before you order a new one. The interactive buying guide available at the PC Power and Cooling website provides sketches that will help you determine which form factor you need for your system. Compare the sketches to your actual power supply. Note that current systems in a micro-tower configuration and other small form-factor systems use smaller power supplies known as SFX.

- When you disconnect your drives from the old power supply, wriggle the connectors before you pull them apart to loosen the connection.

- If you are using Y-splitters or extenders, remove them and examine them carefully to see if they're in good enough condition to reuse. Reinstall them only if the new power supply doesn't have enough leads or if they can't reach the power connectors on your drives. If your power supply is under 300 watts, note that using too many Y-splitters could overload your power supply.

→ See "Troubleshooting Serial ATA Hard Disk Drives," Chapter 3, p. 182, for details about Serial ATA power and data cables,.

- If you are planning to install Serial ATA (SATA) drives in your computer, make sure your new power supply has at least two SATA power leads. Although you can adapt the standard 5-pin Molex power connector to the SATA standard, the fewer the power adapters you use, the more reliable your installation is likely to be.

- Don't mix up the case and power supply screws when you open the case and remove the power supply. Some vendors use different screw types.

→ See "Preventing ESD," Chapter 1, p. 22, for details about preventing ESD.

- If you need to remove components from your system to gain access to the power supply, carefully remove them and place them on antistatic material to avoid damage from ESD.

- Look carefully at your case design before you remove the existing power supply. Some case designs require you to remove the top plate, whereas others allow you to remove the side panel over the expansion slots and slide the power supply out and through the open side.

- When you insert the new power supply, make sure the mounting holes line up correctly with the corresponding holes in the rear of the case.

- Use the drive cables to connect to your drives before you reinstall extenders or Y-splitters. Because extenders and Y-splitters can cause shorts, you're better off without them if you don't need them.

- If a case fan needs to use a drive connector for power, use a power connector that's not being shared with another device, if possible, or choose a connector that is not used much, such as the power connector to the floppy drive.

Right-Sizing a New Power Supply

When you replace your existing power supply, you should always opt for a model with a higher wattage rating than your existing power supply, even if an interactive buying guide suggests that your current wattage rating is sufficient. A larger (in watts) power supply doesn't require any more electricity than your existing power supply, but provides a greater safety margin (the difference between the actual power required and the power supply's maximum output) and more power for additional devices you might install later.

For example, if you are switching from serial and parallel devices (these are self-powered) to USB or IEEE-1394 devices that are bus-powered (powered by your computer), such as keyboards, mice, scanners, web cams, and drives, you need a power supply with a larger wattage rating. Adding internal upgrades such as additional memory, hard drives, or optical drives also adds to the demand on your power supply.

A good rule of thumb for full-size ATX computers is to replace an existing power supply with one that is at least 400 watts in size if your current power supply is 300 watts or less. Keep in mind that the actual efficiency of typical high-quality power supplies without active power factor correction is 70% at operating temperature. This means that you lose about 30% of the theoretical wattage possible (the wattage rating on the label) at typical operating temperatures. Power supplies with active power factor correction (PFC) are able to convert virtually all input power into usable DC power.

If you're replacing a power supply in a retail store computer that uses a Micro-ATX motherboard (these systems use SFX power supplies), your options are more limited. The largest SFX power supply on the market is 180 watts, compared to the standard 145-watt model. Although Micro-ATX systems have more limited expansion capabilities compared to full-size ATX systems, the 180-watt models are recommended as replacements to provide additional power and a wide safety margin.

If you are upgrading to a dual-processor motherboard or a motherboard that supports the new SLI dual PCI-Express x16 expansion slots, make sure you get a power supply that is designed for your system. Different types of dual-processor motherboards require different connectors on the power supply. Vendors that specialize in these types of power supplies often offer compatibility charts. You can also check with your motherboard vendor for recommendations.

Selecting Powerline Protection

You probably don't connect your computer, monitor, printers, scanners, and external drives directly to your AC wall outlets—and that's good! Most homes and offices don't have nearly enough electrical outlets for the increasing number of PC-related hardware connected to modern systems. You probably use a multiple-outlet device called a *surge suppressor* or *surge protector*. When was the last time you changed it, or even thought about it?

Some so-called surge suppressors aren't very good, and most of the models you can buy at retail stores can wear out over time. If you depend on a worn-out surge suppressor to protect your computer, you might get an unpleasant surprise the next time a power surge happens.

Your computer needs reliable, high-quality power. To make sure you achieve that goal, a complete powerline-protection strategy should include the following:

- Checking wall outlets for proper wiring
- Using surge suppressors with filtering, wiring-fault warning, and high levels of protection against surges and spikes for all AC-connected equipment

- Isolating electrically noisy devices such as laser printers from computers or other devices by using surge suppressors with separate filter banks or separate surge suppressors for the printer and other devices

- Using a battery backup system for your computer and monitor if your area is subject to frequent electrical blackouts (complete loss of power) or brownouts (voltage sags below 100V AC).

Now that you have an overview, let's cover the details.

Checking Wall Outlets

The polarized and grounded design used by wall outlets today is intended to provide high-quality power to your computer and peripherals and other devices in your home or office. However, all too often, incorrect wiring is present, regardless of whether the wiring was performed by professional or do-it-yourself electricians. If you don't determine that the wiring is correct, you could damage your computer or, at least, decrease its reliability by plugging it into an improperly wired outlet.

Fortunately, it's not difficult or expensive to test your electrical outlets for problems such as incorrect grounding and reversed hot/neutral polarity. You can purchase an outlet tester similar to the one shown in Figure 10.10 from many electronics and home-improvement stores for around $5 or so. The signal lights on the tester indicate whether the outlet is wired properly, or if it's wired incorrectly, what type of wiring fault is present. Testers include a chart (often attached to the unit as in Figure 10.10) indicating the meaning of the signal lights.

Leo Says

Surge Suppressor Signal Lights Are No Substitute for a True Outlet Test

Many mid-range and high-end surge suppressors feature a single signal light to indicate if your wiring has a fault or is correct. Although this is a useful feature to warn you of an incorrectly wired outlet, such units don't provide enough information to help you fix the problem. If your surge suppressor indicates you have a wiring problem, get a tester similar to the one in Figure 10.10 and find out the exact problem.

FIGURE 10.10
A typical receptacle/outlet tester in use; the signal lights indicate the outlet is correctly wired.

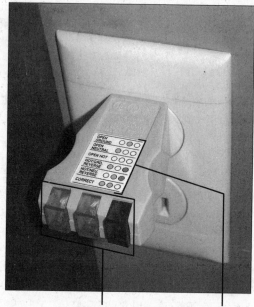

Signal lights   Legend indicates wiring is correct

If you live in an older home without three-wire grounded electrical outlets, you're just asking for trouble with your computer. Using three-prong to two-prong adapters is definitely not recommended, even if you attach a ground wire to a good earth ground (such as a metal water pipe). Have your home office rewired with modern electrical cable attached to ground and put in three-prong outlets.

Choosing the Right Surge Suppressor for Your Equipment

The two types of power problems a properly designed surge suppressor can handle are spikes and surges.

Both spikes and surges are overvoltage events: voltage levels higher than the normal voltage levels that come out of the wall socket. Spikes are momentary overvoltages, whereas surges last longer. Both can damage or destroy equipment.

Surge suppressors seem to multiply like rabbits; every store that carries computer equipment offers a huge number of models from different vendors. It's tempting to go with the cheapest model to save a few bucks or buy the most expensive model—after all, don't you get what you pay for? However, getting the right surge suppressor isn't that easy.

You can make sure you get the right surge suppressor by looking for the following features:

- Make sure you're looking at a true surge suppressor, which has a UL-1449 rating, and not a multiple-outlet strip (UL-1363 transient voltage tap rating). Some stores and product vendors don't adequately mark their products, so it can be easy to mix up these different types of devices.

- The surge suppressor should have a low UL-1449 let-through voltage level (400V AC or less; 330V AC is the lowest available). This might seem high compared to the standard line voltages (115V or 230V), but computer power supplies have been tested to handle up to 500V AC without damage.

UL-1449 Second Edition: The Sequel Is Better, but Tougher

In 1998, Underwriter's Laboratory made significant revisions to its UL-1449 certification tests for surge suppressors. UL-1449 Second Edition tests are much more rigorous than the original tests, but you can't always tell from the packaging or unit markings whether a particular surge suppressor was approved under the original or revised testing procedure. Contact the manufacturer before you buy to make sure you're getting a model that has passed the revised tests.

- A fast response (under 1 nanosecond) to surges helps prevent damage to equipment.

- A covered-equipment warranty that includes lightning strikes (one of the biggest causes of surges and spikes).

- A fuse or failsafe feature that will prevent fatal surges from getting through and will shut down the unit permanently when the unit can no longer provide protection.

- Telephone, fax, and modem protection if your system has a modem or is connected to a telephone or fax. Many users forget that their telephone lines can act as a "back door" to fatal surges, wiping out their modem and sometimes the entire computer.

- Coaxial cable protection if your system is attached to a cable modem. Just as telephone lines can carry damaging surges, so can coaxial cable lines.

- RJ-45/Ethernet cable protection if your system is attached to a network. Network cables can also carry damaging surges.

- EMI/RFI noise filtration (a form of line conditioning). This helps prevent electrically "noisy" equipment such as printers from interfering with computers, but it's best to plug laser printers and copiers into a separate outlet (or separate circuit) from your computer if possible.

- Site fault wiring indicator (no ground, reversed polarity warnings). This can prevent you from using a bad electrical outlet, but it's not a substitute for a true outlet tester.

- Most low-cost (under $50) surge suppressors are based on MOV (metal-oxide varistor) technology; MOVs will wear out over time and will self-destruct when exposed to a very high surge. A surge suppressor that uses MOVs should be replaced every two years. MOVs also present a potential fire hazard, because they have been known to catch fire when exposed to a high-voltage surge. Better-quality surge suppressors supplement MOVs with other components, but the best (and most expensive) models use non-MOV series designs.

- Metal cases are recommended because the metal case helps minimize the risk of fire if the unit fails and also helps minimize the odds of electrical interference with other devices.

- If you use devices powered by AC/DC converter "bricks," be sure to use surge suppressors with extra-wide spacing between the plugs to provide adequate clearance.

Power-Protection Vendors Online

- **American Power Conversion (APC)**—http://www.apc.com
- **EFI**—http://www.efinet.com
- **Panamax**—http://www.panamax.com
- **Tripp-Lite**—http://www.tripplite.com

The following vendors sell the more-expensive series-type surge suppressors:

- **Zero Surge, Inc.**—http://www.zerosurge.com
- **Price Wheeler Corp.**—http://brickwall.com

If you use surge suppressors with these features and attach your system to a properly wired outlet, you will minimize system problems caused by power issues.

Battery Backup Systems

Although high-quality surge suppressors stop damaging overvoltages, undervoltages and electrical blackouts can also damage your system, and they pose even greater risks to your data. If you live or work in an area that is subject to frequent brownouts (voltage under 100V AC compared to normal 115V AC) or blackouts (complete power failure), or if you just don't like surprise power failures, you need to add a battery backup system (also called a *uninterruptible power supply* or *UPS*) to your power protection lineup.

Most so-called UPS systems actually provide battery power only when AC power fails and should be called *standby power supplies (SPS)*. However, the term UPS is used for both SPS-type and so-called "true UPS" systems, which power the computer from a battery at all times.

Most UPS systems contain integrated surge suppression technology, but vary greatly in how long they'll run your computer. Because a UPS is designed to run your computer only long enough to shut it down without data loss, a runtime of 10 to 15 minutes is long enough to provide adequate protection.

Right-Sizing Your Battery Backup System the Easy Way

If you know the wattage or amp requirements of your computer, its peripherals, and your monitor, you can manually calculate the appropriate VA (volt-amp) rating to look for in a battery backup system:

- Multiply the total amps by voltage (120 in North America, 230 in Europe and Asia)
- Multiply the total wattage by 1.4.

However, because it can be difficult to calculate the actual power consumption of your computer and its peripherals, the most convenient (and often more accurate) way to determine the battery backup size you need is to use the vendors' interactive selection tools, available on most UPS vendor websites.

The essential features of a battery backup system include the following:

- **High-quality integrated surge suppression**—In most cases, you should not use a separate surge suppressor with a battery backup unit.

- **Appropriate sizing for your system and runtime**—The price of a battery backup system goes up significantly as the volt-amp (VA) rating climbs. Buying more than 10 minutes of runtime is usually not necessary unless you frequently run programs you can't shut down until the current process is complete.

- **Automatic system shutdown after a power failure has been detected**—This requires that your UPS supports the version of Windows you're using and that you connect the battery backup system to your computer with a compatible serial or USB cable. Windows XP has native support for several popular brands. (Note that some low-cost UPS systems omit this feature.)

- **Fast battery recharge, particularly if your area suffers frequent blackouts**—Look for systems that recharge in less than 12 hours if you rarely have blackouts, and expect to pay more for recharge times of 6 hours or less.

UPS Vendors

Major vendors of battery backup systems include the following:

- **American Power Conversion (APC)**—http://www.apc.com
- **Tripp-Lite**—http://www.tripplite.com
- **Invensys (Best Power)**—http://www.powerware.com
- **Liebert**—http://www.liebert.com

Basic or Enhanced Protection? Your Choice, Your Money

All battery backup (UPS) systems will power your system for several minutes during a blackout, most will also protect you against power surges, and many will also shut down your system. However, some are designed to protect you against additional power problems, including the following:

- Undervoltage (brownout)
- EMI/RFI interference (line noise)
- Other power quality distortions

More expensive battery backup systems typically provide these types of power-conditioning features as well as basic power-outage protection, but you should carefully review the vendors' datasheets to see the differences in features between battery backup systems with similar VA ratings but wide differences in price.

Troubleshooting Methods and Flowcharts

The Troubleshooting Process

If you don't service computers for a living, it might seem scary to talk about the troubleshooting process. But, believe us, it's worth the effort to follow a process that can find problems in a hurry, whether you earn your living at it or just want to save a few bucks and be the hero of your office or home.

To become a successful troubleshooter, you need to do the following:

- Learn as much as you can about what went wrong.
- Evaluate the environment where the computer problem took place.
- Use testing and reporting software to gather information about the system.
- Form a hypothesis about the nature of the problem and how to resolve it (a theory you will try to prove or disprove).
- Use the troubleshooting cycle to isolate and solve the problem.

The First Step—Finding Out What Happened

Whether you're troubleshooting your own computers or helping out a co-worker, a friend, your spouse, your kids, or your parents with a computer problem, the first task is to find out *what happened*. Unless you know what was happening when the problem first showed up, you're going to have a very hard time finding and solving the problem.

Here's what you need to find out—or remember:

- What software was being used
- What hardware was being used
- What error messages were displayed
- What the computer user was working on
- What type of environment (electrical and otherwise) was in the work area at the time of the problem
- Whether any new hardware, software, operating system updates were installed recently

The last item is designed to help you determine the answer to the question, "What changed since the last time it worked?" This question has been recommended for years by PC enthusiast Jerry Pournelle, a long-time columnist for *Byte* magazine (you can read his columns at http://www.jerrypournelle.com/ and http://www.byte.com), and it's been endlessly helpful over the years in tracking down the cause of a particular computer problem.

Let's look at the first item, what software was being used. You want to find out the following:

- **The name of the program and the version**—Restart the program and click Help, About to see this information.

- **The version of Windows being used**—Open the Windows System properties sheet and click the General tab to see this information or use Microsoft System Information (msinfo32.exe).

- **System configuration information**—Physical and virtual memory (page file) sizes, page file location, default system drive, processor and chipset, and other information can be useful in tracking down performance and memory problems. Use Microsoft System Information and SiSoftware Sandra to display and print this information.

- **Installed hotfixes**—Although the System properties sheet's General tab lists the latest service pack installed as well as the major version of Windows in use, hotfixes that have been installed since the service pack was installed can also affect the operation of your system. To get a listing of installed hotfixes, use Belarc Advisor.

- **Any other programs that were also in use at the time**— Programs and the device drivers they use can contribute to system problems such as STOP errors, lockups, and slow system performance.

→ *For more information about Windows System Information, see "Using System Information," Chapter 2, p. 114. For more information about SiSoftware Sandra or Belarc Advisor, see "Determining the Right Memory for Your System," Chapter 9, p. 564.*

The second item, what hardware was being used, should reveal what add-on hardware (printer, scanner, CD burner, Internet/network connection) was in use.

The third item is simple: What error messages were displayed? You might need to try to reproduce the problem to display a complex error message such as a Blue Screen of Death or Fatal Exception Error.

The fourth item, what was the user working on, is designed to determine the specifics of the task. For example, trying to print a multipage document with lots of graphics to a laser printer is a different task

→ *For more details about software and Windows errors, see Chapter 2, "Troubleshooting Windows XP and Windows Applications."*

➜ *For more details about software conflicts, see "Fixing Programs That Won't Run," Chapter 2, p. 136, and "Troubleshooting STOP Errors with Windows XP," Chapter 2, p. 153.*

than printing a single-page letter to the same printer, or to a different printer. You should also find out what programs the user was running, because some programs might conflict with others running at the same time.

The amount of time and the types of programs the user was running on the computer since it was last started can also be useful, particularly if you suspect that the system might be overheating or that some programs are conflicting with other programs.

Sometimes, after you learn the answers to these questions, the solution to the problem will jump out at you. But, sometimes, you'll need to look around your computer space (if it's your problem) or go to the problem's central location and put on your deerstalker cap and play detective.

How to Check Out the Computing Environment

Even if you're trying to solve a problem with your own computer, and especially if you're assisting somebody else, you need to find out some facts about the environment where the computer is located.

What kinds of information are you looking for? Use Table A.1 to provide a quick checklist of what to take with you or what you'll need access to, depending on what you learned from your initial questions.

TABLE A.1
TROUBLESHOOTING TESTS AND REQUIREMENTS

Test	Requires
Power	Multimeter, circuit tester
BIOS beep and error codes	List of BIOS codes
Printer self-test	Printer and paper
Windows bootlog	Starting Windows with the correct option
Hardware resources (IRQ, and so on) System Information	Windows Device Manager; Windows
Installed software and Windows configuration	Windows System Information, Add/Remove Programs (Control Panel); Windows System Information
System hardware configuration	SiSoftware Sandra Lite; Windows System Information

Which test or diagnostic routine is the best one to start with? Before you perform any specific tests, review the clues you received when you asked the initial questions. For example, if you found out that you could print simple documents to a laser printer with Microsoft Word, but you had problems printing graphics-rich publications with Adobe InDesign, the problem isn't with Windows (which controls the printer), and probably not with the printer, but it could be with the documents themselves. To learn more about the printer, you should use the printer's self-test.

A laser printer's self-test usually indicates the amount of RAM onboard, the emulation (HP or PostScript), and firmware revisions. The amount of RAM onboard is critical, because, as discussed in Chapter 4, "Troubleshooting Your Printer," laser printers are page printers; the whole page must fit into the laser printer's RAM to be printed.

Therefore, there are two variables to this printing problem: the amount of RAM in the printer, and the size of the InDesign document. If, for example, the self-test reveals the printer has only 2MB installed, then the amount of RAM is adequate for text, but an elaborate page can overload it. If a look at the InDesign document reveals that it has a large amount of graphic content or many different fonts, then you're likely to have problems.

You have three possible solutions to this type of problem:

- Add more memory to the printer.
- Reduce the graphics resolution.
- Reduce the number of fonts in the document.

It's easier (and cheaper!) to reduce the graphics resolution to see if the InDesign documents will print. If this works, you can check with a memory vendor for a printer memory upgrade if you need the full graphics quality, or you can keep using the printer with the lower graphics quality setting.

→ *For details about adjusting graphics print quality, see "Accessing the Properties Sheets for Your Printer," Chapter 4, p. 276.*

On the other hand, if the problem you're experiencing centers on the computer locking up frequently (and randomly), you'd want to check the electrical power. The first step here is to see if the power the computer uses is good. A low-cost wall outlet analyzer (available from Radio Shack and similar stores) is a useful tool. This device has signal lights indicating whether the wiring is correct or if there are faults with grounding, reversed polarity, and the like. Random lockups,

➜ *For details, see "Detecting Overheating and Incorrect Voltage Levels," Chapter 9, p. 583.*

crashes, and other types of mysterious computer problems can be traced to bad power. If the problem happens only after the computer's been on for a while, it's time to look at the computer's hardware monitor to check the internal temperature or voltage settings. The system could be overheating.

Conversely, if the system only locks up when you're using a specific application, then it's more than likely there's a problem with the application and not the computer. In that case, you should check the application vendor's website to see if it's a common problem and if there's a patch available to fix it.

Your Diagnostics Toolbox

If you like to be prepared for any computing disaster, it's helpful to have the tools you need ready at all times. Here are the tools we recommend:

- Hex drivers
- Phillips and straight-blade screwdrivers
- Torx drivers
- Three-claw parts retrieval tool
- Hemostat clamps
- Needle-nose pliers
- Eyebrow tweezers
- Penlight and magnifier

For diagnosing power issues and working safely with equipment, we recommend you have the following:

- An AC/DC multimeter with Ohm and Continuity options
- A grounded AC circuit tester
- An anti-static mat and wrist strap

Any set of cleaning and maintenance tools should include these items:

- Compressed air
- Keyboard key puller (you can use a DIP chip puller for this job)
- Computer-rated mini-vacuum cleaner

- Wire cutter and stripper
- Extra case, card, and drive screws (salvaged or new)
- Extra card slot covers (salvaged or new)
- Extra hard disk and motherboard/card jumper blocks (salvaged or new)
- Endust for Electronics or similar anti-static cleaning wipes and spray

If you think you might need to reinstall Windows, you'll need the following items:

- The original operating system CD. Keep in mind that many recent brand-name systems use a restore CD or a hidden disk partition that contains restore files instead of a bootable CD.
- The emergency boot floppy disk(s) for a Windows 9x/Me installation or for a Windows 2000/XP installation on a system without a bootable CD or DVD drive.
- A USB-based 10/100 Ethernet network adapter and drivers (so you can download the latest patches and service packs after the installation is complete).

For hard disk testing, especially if you can't start Windows, we recommend Gibson Research SpinRite 6 (http://www.grc.com). It comes on a self-booting CD and is compatible with any PC file system (including Linux!).

A Live Demonstration of SpinRite 6

See a live demonstration of SpinRite 6 and Leo's interview with Steve Gibson at http://www.grc.com/sr/themovie.htm.

Use these tools to help you perform the steps you need to follow during the troubleshooting cycle.

The Troubleshooting Cycle

The troubleshooting cycle is a method you can use to determine exactly what part of a complex system, such as a computer, is causing the problem.

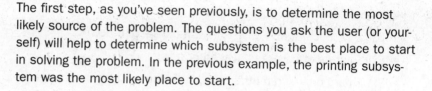

The first step, as you've seen previously, is to determine the most likely source of the problem. The questions you ask the user (or yourself) will help to determine which subsystem is the best place to start in solving the problem. In the previous example, the printing subsystem was the most likely place to start.

To help you focus on the likely cause for a computer problem, use the Symptoms Table at the front of each chapter to look up the most likely solutions for the symptoms of the computer problem. Follow the flow-chart or write-up suggested for the symptom, and you're on the road to the solution.

Sometimes, you might discover that a particular symptom seems ambiguous: It points to more than one possible solution. In cases like this, it's helpful to realize that any computer is a collection of subsystems. What's a subsystem?

A *subsystem* is the combination of components designed for a particular task, and it can include both hardware and software components. Use Table A.2 to better understand the nature of the subsystems found in any computer.

TABLE A.2
COMPUTER AND PERIPHERAL SUBSYSTEMS AND THEIR COMPONENTS

	Components		
Subsystem	**Hardware**	**Software**	**Firmware**
Printing	Printer, cable, parallel or serial port	Printer driver in Windows, Application	BIOS configuration of the port
Display	Graphics card, monitor, cables, port type, cables, motherboard (integrated video)	Video drivers in Windows	Video BIOS, BIOS configuration of the video type, AGP/PCI BIOS boot priority
Audio	Sound card, speakers, cables, motherboard (integrated audio)	Audio drivers in Windows	BIOS configuration of the integrated audio

Components

Subsystem	Hardware	Software	Firmware
Mouse and Pointing Device	Mouse or pointing device, serial or mouse port, USB port	Mouse driver in Windows	BIOS port config uration, USB Legacy config-uration
Keyboard	Keyboard, PS/2 or USB port	Keyboard driver in Windows	BIOS keyboard configuration, USB Legacy con-figuration
Storage	Drives, data cables, power connectors, USB, IEEE-1394 or SCSI cards or built-in ports	Storage drivers in Windows	BIOS drive config-uration, BIOS configuration of the built-in USB or other ports
Power	Power supply, splitters, fans	Power-management software (Windows)	BIOS power-management configuration
CPU	CPU, motherboard	System devices	BIOS cache and CPU configuration
RAM	RAM, motherboard	(None)	BIOS RAM config-uration
Network	NIC, motherboard, USB port (for USB devices)	Network config-uration files and drivers	BIOS PnP and power manage-ment, BIOS con-figuration of the integrated net-work port or USB port
Modem	Modem, mother-board or serial port, or USB port	Modem drivers and the application	BIOS PnP, power management, BIOS port configuration

You can see from this list that virtually every subsystem in the computer has hardware, software, and firmware components. A thorough troubleshooting process will take into account both the subsystem and all its components.

As you use the Symptoms Table at the front of each chapter and the flowcharts that follow this text, keep the subsystems inside your computer in mind. The flowcharts and chapter write-ups are designed to cover the different components of each subsystem. However, in some cases, you might need to check more than one subsystem to find the solutions you're looking for.

Testing a Subsystem

Whether you troubleshoot to save money or to make money, and whether you're operating on your own computer or a friend's, you should take the computer user's version of the Hippocratic oath: "First, do no harm (to the computer)."

Before you change anything, record the current configuration. Depending on the item, this may include one or more of the following steps:

- Recording jumper or DIP switch settings on the motherboard or an add-in card
- Printing the complete report from the Windows Device Manager
- Saving or printing a complete report from Windows System Information (msinfo32.exe)
- Printing a complete report from a third-party diagnostic or reporting program such as SiSoftware Sandra
- Recording current BIOS settings (use a digital camera with a close-up lens setting to grab these easily)

Once you have recorded the configuration you are going to change, follow this procedure:

1. Change one hardware component or hardware/software/firmware setting at a time.

2. Try the task the user was performing after a single change and evaluate the results.

3. If the same or similar problem reoccurs, reinstall the original component or reset the hardware/software/firmware to the original settings and continue with the next item.

4. Repeat until the subsystem performs normally. The last item changed is the problem; repair, replace, or reload it as appropriate to solve the problem.

Best Sources for Replacement Parts

To perform parts exchanges for troubleshooting, you need replacement parts. If you don't have spare parts, it's very tempting to go to the computer store and buy some new components. Instead, if you have one available, take a spare system that's similar to the "sick" computer, make sure that it works, and then use it for parts. Why? Because *new* doesn't mean it works.

A while back, Mark replaced an alternator with a brand-new, lifetime-warranty alternator that failed in less than a week. Whether it's a cable, a video card, a monitor, or some other component, try using a known-working item as a temporary replacement rather than first forking over good money for a brand-new part. If you have the means, borrow parts from a spare system (check with your kids or their friends, or check out the office's junk room) rather than opening up a working system and taking it out of action. However, it's easy to borrow parts such as keyboards, mice, and monitors from a working system and put them back when you're done. Just be sure to turn off the computer or monitor before you unplug components, and leave it off until you reattach the components.

Upgrading? Save Those Old Parts!

If you're planning to upgrade your hard drive, optical drive, add-on cards, or other components, save the old parts for use as temporary replacements if they're still working. Make sure you put the old parts into anti-static bags for ESD protection, and protect them from damage (try bubble wrap or the box a new component came in). As time passes, you'll have a collection of spares you can use for troubleshooting.

Where to Start?

As the preceding subsystem list indicates, there's no shortage of places to start in virtually any subsystem. What's the best way to decide whether a hardware, software, or firmware problem is the most likely cause?

Typically, hardware problems come and go, whereas software and firmware problems are consistent. Why is that? A hardware problem is often the result of a damaged or loose wire or connection; when the connection is closed, the component works, but when the connection opens, the component fails.

On the other hand, a software or firmware problem will cause a failure under the same circumstances every time.

Another rule of thumb that's useful is known as Occam's Razor, or the least hypothesis. English Philosopher William of Occam suggested centuries ago that the simplest (or least complex) explanation that fits the known facts is usually the accurate one. Although TV shows such as the late lamented *X-Files* are enjoyable to watch, their "trust no one" paranoia and incredibly complicated explanations for everything are exactly the wrong approach to take when you're trying to fix a computer problem. Instead, look at the least expensive, easiest-to-replace item first. In most cases, the cable connected to a subsystem is the first place to look for problems. Whether the cable is internal or external, it is almost always the least-expensive part of the subsystem, can easily come loose, and can easily be damaged.

If a cable is loose; has bent pins; or has a dry, brittle, or cracked exterior, replace it. Although it may sound overly simplistic, good cables usually look good, and bad cables often look bad.

When new software or new hardware has been introduced to the system and a problem results immediately afterward, that change is often the most likely cause of the problem.

Hardware problems caused by incorrect or buggy drivers are typical causes of failure when new hardware is introduced. New software can also cause problems with hardware, because of incompatibilities between software and hardware, or because new software has replaced drivers required by the hardware.

➜ *For more information about System Restore, see "Using System Restore," Chapter 2, p. 114.*

To confirm whether new hardware or software is at the root of a PC problem, you should remove it and reboot your PC or use System Restore to return your system to its condition before the hardware or software was installed. If all functions normally again, you have your answer (or at least part of it).

Where to Go for More Information

Once you've gathered as much information as possible, you may find that you still need more help. User manuals for components often are discarded, software drivers need to be updated, and some conflicts don't have easy answers. There's one "place" to go to find the information you need: the World Wide Web. Fire up your browser and check out the websites suggested in the On the Web sidebars in this book, use search engines such as Google (http://www.google.com) or Teoma (http://www.teoma.com) to search for solutions, and also try the following:

- The various manufacturers' websites
- C|net's Download.com (http://www.download.com) for drivers and applications
- Online computer magazines such as *PCMagazine* (http://www.pcmag.com), *PCWorld* (http://www.pcworld.com), and others
- The numerous technology-related blogs created with Blogger (http://www.blogger.com), Movable Type (http://www.sixapart.com/movabletype), and other platforms

Keeping Track of Your Solutions

If you hate solving the same problems over and over again (and who wouldn't?), keep detailed notes about the problems you solve. Be sure to note symptoms, underlying problems, workarounds, and final resolutions. Use the Copy and Paste feature in Windows to store website URLs, and use File, Save as Web Archive in Internet Explorer to save useful web pages and their graphics in the documents you write up.

Summarizing the Troubleshooter's Philosophy

The troubleshooter's philosophy can be summarized as follows:

- Discover what really was happening when trouble happened.
- Find out what changed.
- Use the troubleshooting cycle to reproduce the problem and discover a solution.
- Record the solution in case you need it again.

Use this philosophy and the rest of this book to become a troubleshooting hero to your family, friends, and co-workers.

Flowcharts

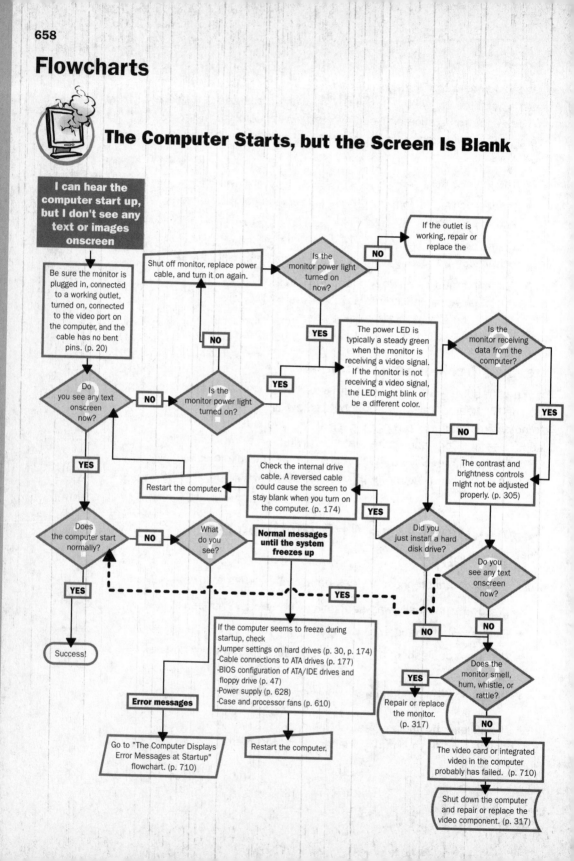

The Computer Starts, but the Screen Is Blank

I can hear the computer start up, but I don't see any text or images onscreen

Be sure the monitor is plugged in, connected to a working outlet, turned on, connected to the video port on the computer, and the cable has no bent pins. (p. 20)

Shut off monitor, replace power cable, and turn it on again.

Is the monitor power light turned on now?

NO → If the outlet is working, repair or replace the

YES

The power LED is typically a steady green when the monitor is receiving a video signal. If the monitor is not receiving a video signal, the LED might blink or be a different color.

Is the monitor receiving data from the computer?

NO

Do you see any text onscreen now?

NO ← Is the monitor power light turned on?

YES →

YES

YES

The contrast and brightness controls might not be adjusted properly. (p. 305)

Check the internal drive cable. A reversed cable could cause the screen to stay blank when you turn on the computer. (p. 174)

Restart the computer. ←

YES

Does the computer start normally?

NO → What do you see?

Normal messages until the system freezes up

Did you just install a hard disk drive?

Do you see any text onscreen now?

YES

YES

Success!

If the computer seems to freeze during startup, check
-Jumper settings on hard drives (p. 30, p. 174)
-Cable connections to ATA drives (p. 177)
-BIOS configuration of ATA/IDE drives and floppy drive (p. 47)
-Power supply (p. 628)
-Case and processor fans (p. 610)

NO

NO

Error messages

YES → Repair or replace the monitor. (p. 317)

Does the monitor smell, hum, whistle, or rattle?

NO

Go to "The Computer Displays Error Messages at Startup" flowchart. (p. 710)

Restart the computer.

The video card or integrated video in the computer probably has failed. (p. 710)

Shut down the computer and repair or replace the video component. (p. 317)

Part of the Screen Image Is Missing

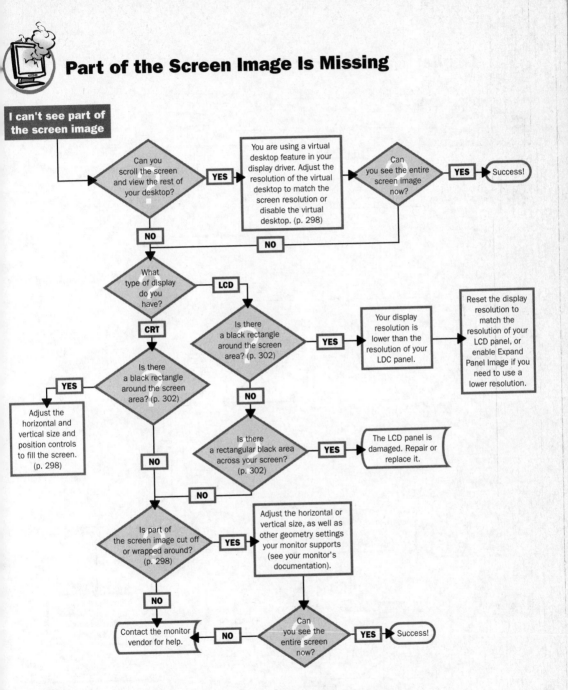

I can't see part of the screen image

Can you scroll the screen and view the rest of your desktop?

YES → You are using a virtual desktop feature in your display driver. Adjust the resolution of the virtual desktop to match the screen resolution or disable the virtual desktop. (p. 298)

Can you see the entire screen image now?

YES → Success!

NO (from "Can you scroll the screen")

NO (from "Can you see the entire screen image now?")

What type of display do you have?

LCD →

CRT ↓

Is there a black rectangle around the screen area? (p. 302)

YES → Your display resolution is lower than the resolution of your LDC panel. → Reset the display resolution to match the resolution of your LCD panel, or enable Expand Panel Image if you need to use a lower resolution.

NO ↓

Is there a black rectangle around the screen area? (p. 302)

YES → Adjust the horizontal and vertical size and position controls to fill the screen. (p. 298)

NO ↓

Is there a rectangular black area across your screen? (p. 302)

YES → The LCD panel is damaged. Repair or replace it.

NO →

Is part of the screen image cut off or wrapped around? (p. 298)

YES → Adjust the horizontal or vertical size, as well as other geometry settings your monitor supports (see your monitor's documentation).

NO ↓

Contact the monitor vendor for help. ← **NO** — Can you see the entire screen now?

YES → Success!

Display Has Too Few Colors

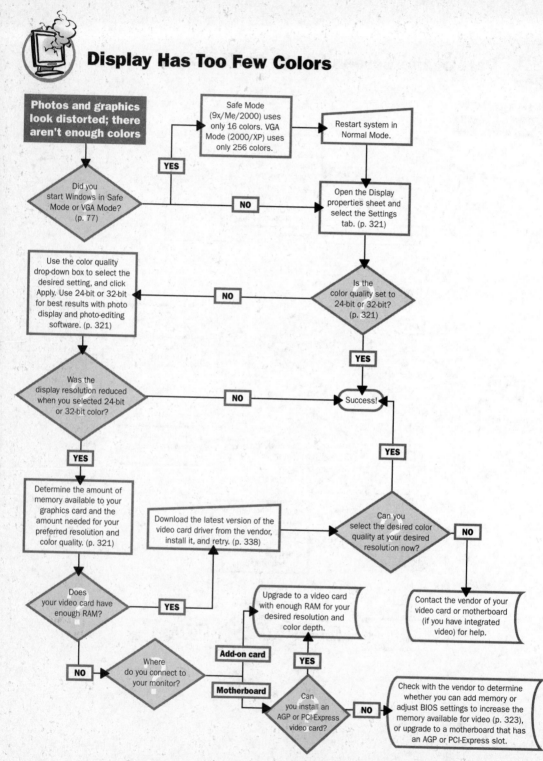

Photos and graphics look distorted; there aren't enough colors

Safe Mode (9x/Me/2000) uses only 16 colors. VGA Mode (2000/XP) uses only 256 colors.

Restart system in Normal Mode.

Did you start Windows in Safe Mode or VGA Mode? (p. 77)

YES

NO

Open the Display properties sheet and select the Settings tab. (p. 321)

Use the color quality drop-down box to select the desired setting, and click Apply. Use 24-bit or 32-bit for best results with photo display and photo-editing software. (p. 321)

NO

Is the color quality set to 24-bit or 32-bit? (p. 321)

YES

Was the display resolution reduced when you selected 24-bit or 32-bit color?

NO

Success!

YES

YES

Determine the amount of memory available to your graphics card and the amount needed for your preferred resolution and color quality. (p. 321)

Download the latest version of the video card driver from the vendor, install it, and retry. (p. 338)

Can you select the desired color quality at your desired resolution now?

NO

Contact the vendor of your video card or motherboard (if you have integrated video) for help.

Does your video card have enough RAM?

YES

Upgrade to a video card with enough RAM for your desired resolution and color depth.

Where do you connect to your monitor?

Add-on card

Motherboard

YES

Can you install an AGP or PCI-Express video card?

NO

NO

Check with the vendor to determine whether you can add memory or adjust BIOS settings to increase the memory available for video (p. 323), or upgrade to a motherboard that has an AGP or PCI-Express slot.

Display Has Wavy Lines

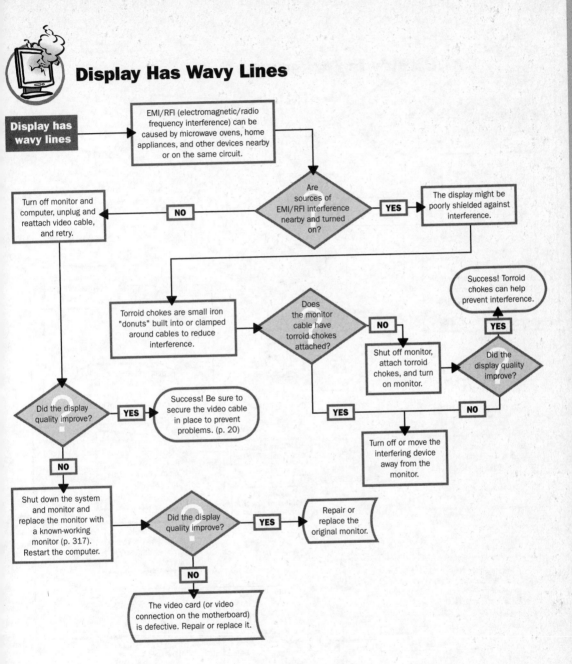

Display has wavy lines

EMI/RFI (electromagnetic/radio frequency interference) can be caused by microwave ovens, home appliances, and other devices nearby or on the same circuit.

Are sources of EMI/RFI interference nearby and turned on?

YES → The display might be poorly shielded against interference.

NO → Turn off monitor and computer, unplug and reattach video cable, and retry.

Torroid chokes are small iron "donuts" built into or clamped around cables to reduce interference.

Does the monitor cable have torroid chokes attached?

NO → Shut off monitor, attach torroid chokes, and turn on monitor.

Did the display quality improve?

YES → Success! Torroid chokes can help prevent interference.

NO → Turn off or move the interfering device away from the monitor.

YES (from torroid chokes question) → Turn off or move the interfering device away from the monitor.

Did the display quality improve?

YES → Success! Be sure to secure the video cable in place to prevent problems. (p. 20)

NO → Shut down the system and monitor and replace the monitor with a known-working monitor (p. 317). Restart the computer.

Did the display quality improve?

YES → Repair or replace the original monitor.

NO → The video card (or video connection on the motherboard) is defective. Repair or replace it.

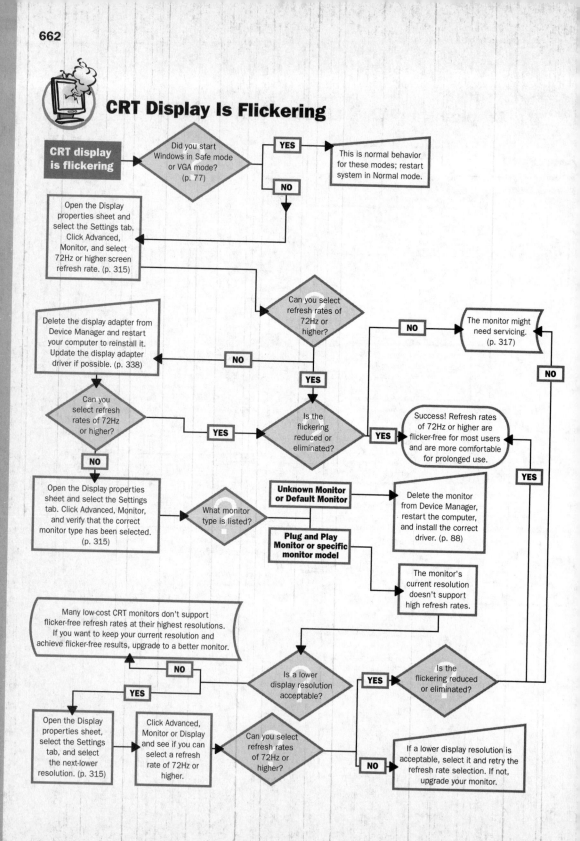

CRT Display Is Flickering

CRT display is flickering

Did you start Windows in Safe mode or VGA mode? (p. 77)

YES → This is normal behavior for these modes; restart system in Normal mode.

NO ↓

Open the Display properties sheet and select the Settings tab. Click Advanced, Monitor, and select 72Hz or higher screen refresh rate. (p. 315)

Can you select refresh rates of 72Hz or higher?

NO → The monitor might need servicing. (p. 317)

YES ↓

Delete the display adapter from Device Manager and restart your computer to reinstall it. Update the display adapter driver if possible. (p. 338)

NO

Can you select refresh rates of 72Hz or higher?

YES →

Is the flickering reduced or eliminated?

YES → Success! Refresh rates of 72Hz or higher are flicker-free for most users and are more comfortable for prolonged use.

NO ↓

Open the Display properties sheet and select the Settings tab. Click Advanced, Monitor, and verify that the correct monitor type has been selected. (p. 315)

What monitor type is listed?

Unknown Monitor or Default Monitor → Delete the monitor from Device Manager, restart the computer, and install the correct driver. (p. 88)

Plug and Play Monitor or specific monitor model

The monitor's current resolution doesn't support high refresh rates.

Many low-cost CRT monitors don't support flicker-free refresh rates at their highest resolutions. If you want to keep your current resolution and achieve flicker-free results, upgrade to a better monitor.

NO

Is a lower display resolution acceptable?

YES →

Is the flickering reduced or eliminated?

YES

YES ↓

Open the Display properties sheet, select the Settings tab, and select the next-lower resolution. (p. 315)

Click Advanced, Monitor or Display and see if you can select a refresh rate of 72Hz or higher.

Can you select refresh rates of 72Hz or higher?

NO → If a lower display resolution is acceptable, select it and retry the refresh rate selection. If not, upgrade your monitor.

3D Gaming Display Quality Problems

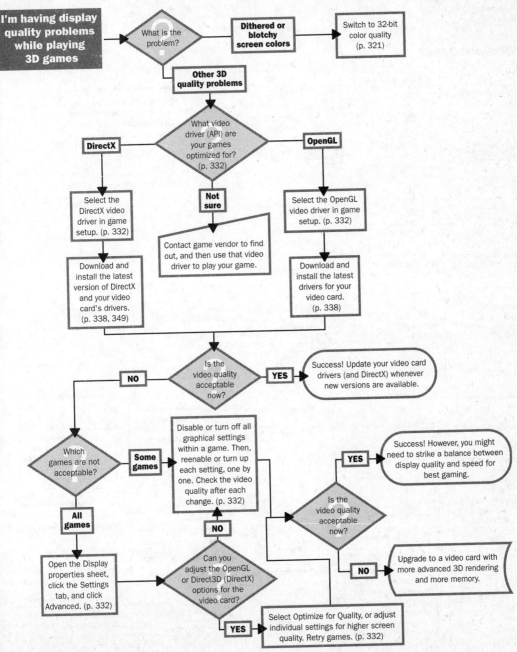

I'm having display quality problems while playing 3D games

What is the problem?

Dithered or blotchy screen colors → Switch to 32-bit color quality (p. 321)

Other 3D quality problems

What video driver (API) are your games optimized for? (p. 332)

DirectX / **Not sure** / **OpenGL**

Select the DirectX video driver in game setup. (p. 332)

Contact game vendor to find out, and then use that video driver to play your game.

Select the OpenGL video driver in game setup. (p. 332)

Download and install the latest version of DirectX and your video card's drivers. (p. 338, 349)

Download and install the latest drivers for your video card. (p. 338)

Is the video quality acceptable now?

NO / **YES**

Success! Update your video card drivers (and DirectX) whenever new versions are available.

Which games are not acceptable?

Some games

Disable or turn off all graphical settings within a game. Then, reenable or turn up each setting, one by one. Check the video quality after each change. (p. 332)

YES

Success! However, you might need to strike a balance between display quality and speed for best gaming.

All games

NO

Is the video quality acceptable now?

Open the Display properties sheet, click the Settings tab, and click Advanced. (p. 332)

Can you adjust the OpenGL or Direct3D (DirectX) options for the video card?

NO → Upgrade to a video card with more advanced 3D rendering and more memory.

YES → Select Optimize for Quality, or adjust individual settings for higher screen quality. Retry games. (p. 332)

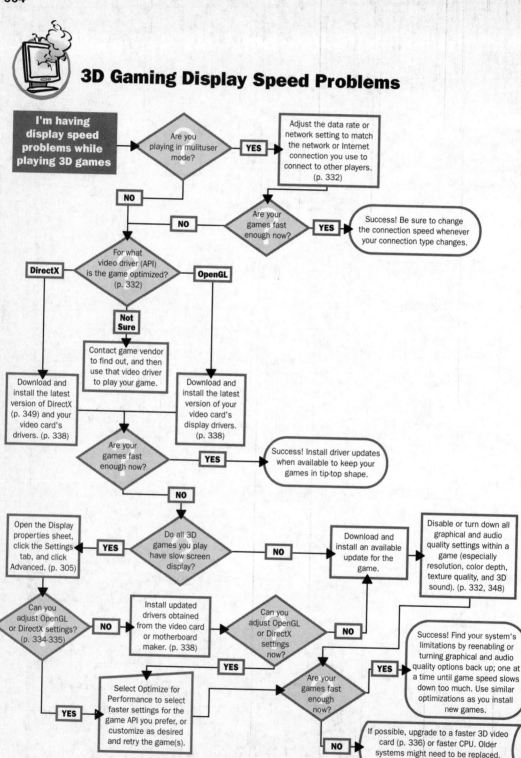

3D Gaming Display Speed Problems

I'm having display speed problems while playing 3D games

Are you playing in mulituser mode? — **YES** → Adjust the data rate or network setting to match the network or Internet connection you use to connect to other players. (p. 332)

NO

Are your games fast enough now? — **YES** → Success! Be sure to change the connection speed whenever your connection type changes.

NO

For what video driver (API) is the game optimized? (p. 332) — **DirectX** / **OpenGL** / **Not Sure**

Not Sure → Contact game vendor to find out, and then use that video driver to play your game.

DirectX → Download and install the latest version of DirectX (p. 349) and your video card's drivers. (p. 338)

OpenGL → Download and install the latest version of your video card's display drivers. (p. 338)

Are your games fast enough now? — **YES** → Success! Install driver updates when available to keep your games in tip-top shape.

NO

Do all 3D games you play have slow screen display? — **YES** → Open the Display properties sheet, click the Settings tab, and click Advanced. (p. 305)

Do all 3D games you play have slow screen display? — **NO** → Download and install an available update for the game. → Disable or turn down all graphical and audio quality settings within a game (especially resolution, color depth, texture quality, and 3D sound). (p. 332, 348)

Can you adjust OpenGL or DirectX settings? (p. 334-335) — **NO** → Install updated drivers obtained from the video card or motherboard maker. (p. 338)

Can you adjust OpenGL or DirectX settings now? — **NO**

YES → Select Optimize for Performance to select faster settings for the game API you prefer, or customize as desired and retry the game(s).

Are your games fast enough now? — **YES** → Success! Find your system's limitations by reenabling or turning graphical and audio quality options back up; one at a time until game speed slows down too much. Use similar optimizations as you install new games.

Are your games fast enough now? — **NO** → If possible, upgrade to a faster 3D video card (p. 336) or faster CPU. Older systems might need to be replaced. Adjust AGP options. (p. 336)

Audio Hardware Problems

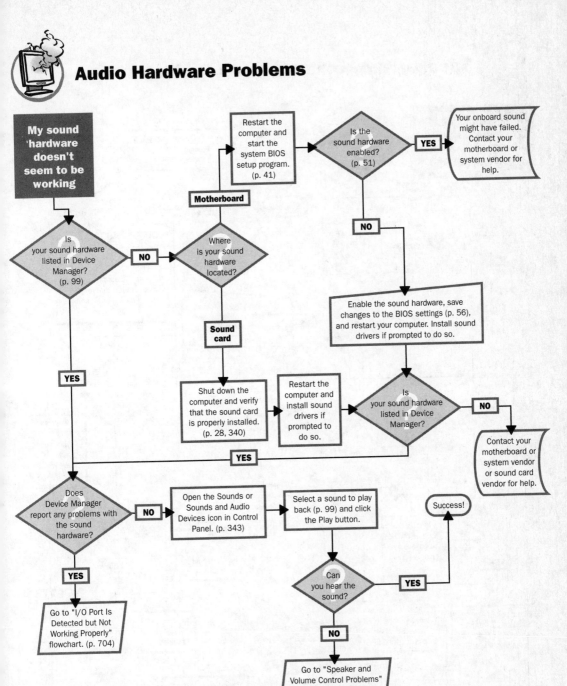

Speaker and Volume Control Problems

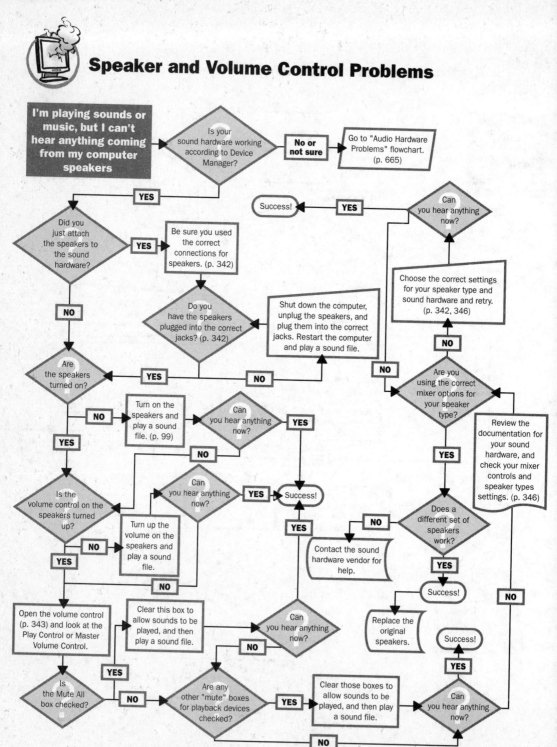

Can't Connect to the Internet via a Dial-Up Connection

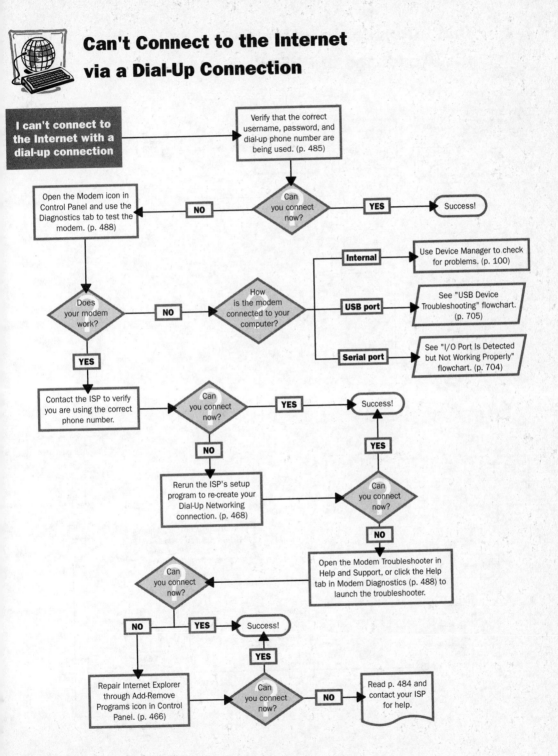

I can't connect to the Internet with a dial-up connection

Verify that the correct username, password, and dial-up phone number are being used. (p. 485)

Can you connect now? — **YES** → Success!

NO → Open the Modem icon in Control Panel and use the Diagnostics tab to test the modem. (p. 488)

Does your modem work? — **NO** → How is the modem connected to your computer?

- **Internal** → Use Device Manager to check for problems. (p. 100)
- **USB port** → See "USB Device Troubleshooting" flowchart. (p. 705)
- **Serial port** → See "I/O Port Is Detected but Not Working Properly" flowchart. (p. 704)

Does your modem work? — **YES** → Contact the ISP to verify you are using the correct phone number.

Can you connect now? — **YES** → Success!

NO → Rerun the ISP's setup program to re-create your Dial-Up Networking connection. (p. 468)

Can you connect now? — **YES** → Success!

NO → Open the Modem Troubleshooter in Help and Support, or click the Help tab in Modem Diagnostics (p. 488) to launch the troubleshooter.

Can you connect now? — **YES** → Success!

NO → Repair Internet Explorer through Add-Remove Programs icon in Control Panel. (p. 466)

Can you connect now? — **YES** → Success!

NO → Read p. 484 and contact your ISP for help.

Can't Connect to Internet via Broadband or PPPoE

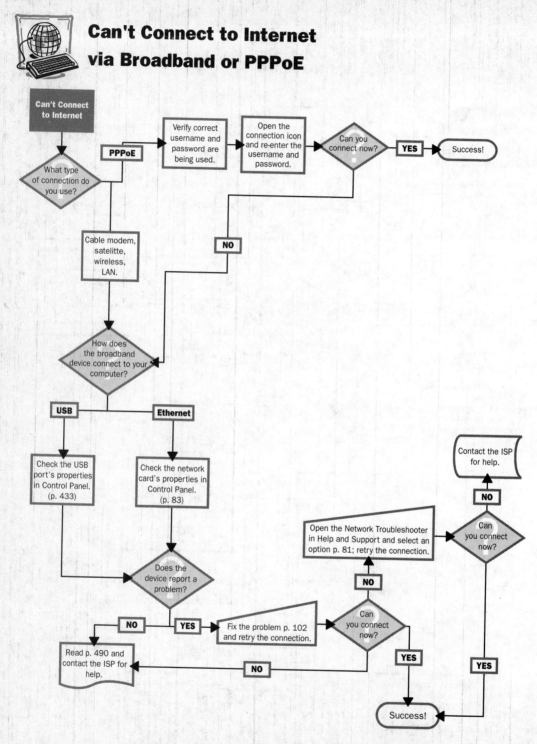

Can't Connect to Internet

What type of connection do you use?

PPPoE → Verify correct username and password are being used. → Open the connection icon and re-enter the username and password. → Can you connect now? → **YES** → Success!

Cable modem, satelitte, wireless, LAN.

NO

How does the broadband device connect to your computer?

USB → Check the USB port's properties in Control Panel. (p. 433)

Ethernet → Check the network card's properties in Control Panel. (p. 83)

Contact the ISP for help.

NO

Open the Network Troubleshooter in Help and Support and select an option p. 81; retry the connection.

Can you connect now?

Does the device report a problem?

NO

NO | **YES** → Fix the problem p. 102 and retry the connection. → Can you connect now?

Read p. 490 and contact the ISP for help.

NO

YES

YES

Success!

Email Problems

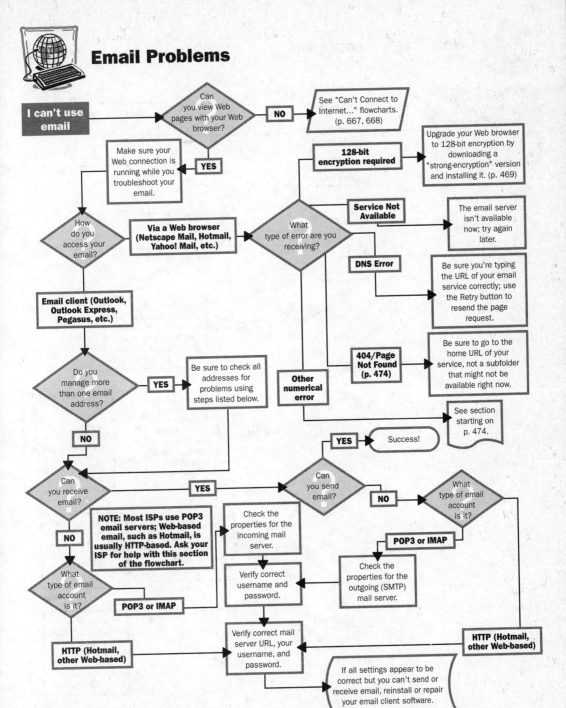

I can't use email

Can you view Web pages with your Web browser? → **NO** → See "Can't Connect to Internet..." flowcharts. (p. 667, 668)

YES

Make sure your Web connection is running while you troubleshoot your email.

How do you access your email?

→ **Via a Web browser (Netscape Mail, Hotmail, Yahoo! Mail, etc.)** → What type of error are you receiving?

→ **128-bit encryption required** → Upgrade your Web browser to 128-bit encryption by downloading a "strong-encryption" version and installing it. (p. 469)

→ **Service Not Available** → The email server isn't available now; try again later.

→ **DNS Error** → Be sure you're typing the URL of your email service correctly; use the Retry button to resend the page request.

→ **404/Page Not Found (p. 474)** → Be sure to go to the home URL of your service, not a subfolder that might not be available right now.

→ **Other numerical error** → See section starting on p. 474.

Email client (Outlook, Outlook Express, Pegasus, etc.)

Do you manage more than one email address? → **YES** → Be sure to check all addresses for problems using steps listed below.

NO

Can you receive email? → **YES** → Can you send email? → **YES** → Success!

NO → What type of email account is it?

Can you send email? → **NO** → What type of email account is it?

→ **POP3 or IMAP** → Check the properties for the outgoing (SMTP) mail server.

→ **HTTP (Hotmail, other Web-based)**

NOTE: Most ISPs use POP3 email servers; Web-based email, such as Hotmail, is usually HTTP-based. Ask your ISP for help with this section of the flowchart.

Can you receive email? **NO** → What type of email account is it?

→ **POP3 or IMAP** → Check the properties for the incoming mail server.

→ Verify correct username and password.

→ **HTTP (Hotmail, other Web-based)** → Verify correct mail server URL, your username, and password.

If all settings appear to be correct but you can't send or receive email, reinstall or repair your email client software.

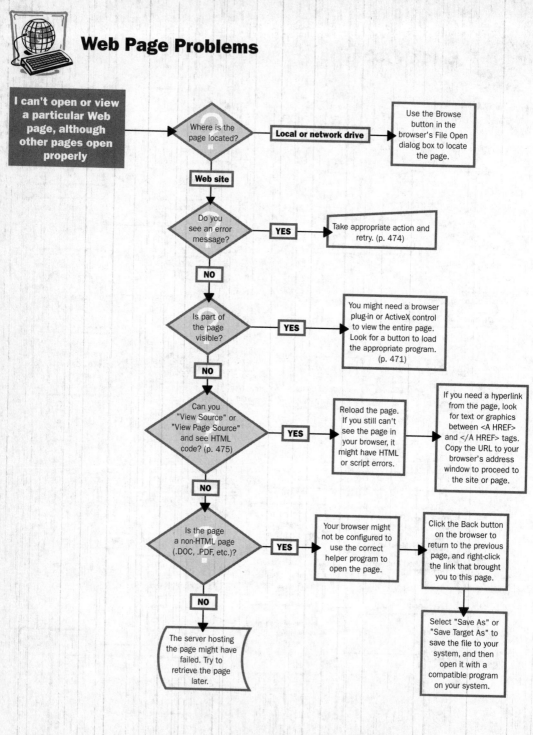

Web Page Problems

I can't open or view a particular Web page, although other pages open properly

Where is the page located?

Local or network drive → Use the Browse button in the browser's File Open dialog box to locate the page.

Web site

Do you see an error message? — **YES** → Take appropriate action and retry. (p. 474)

NO

Is part of the page visible? — **YES** → You might need a browser plug-in or ActiveX control to view the entire page. Look for a button to load the appropriate program. (p. 471)

NO

Can you "View Source" or "View Page Source" and see HTML code? (p. 475) — **YES** → Reload the page. If you still can't see the page in your browser, it might have HTML or script errors. → If you need a hyperlink from the page, look for text or graphics between <A HREF> and </A HREF> tags. Copy the URL to your browser's address window to proceed to the site or page.

NO

Is the page a non-HTML page (.DOC, .PDF, etc.)? — **YES** → Your browser might not be configured to use the correct helper program to open the page. → Click the Back button on the browser to return to the previous page, and right-click the link that brought you to this page. → Select "Save As" or "Save Target As" to save the file to your system, and then open it with a compatible program on your system.

NO

The server hosting the page might have failed. Try to retrieve the page later.

File Download Problems

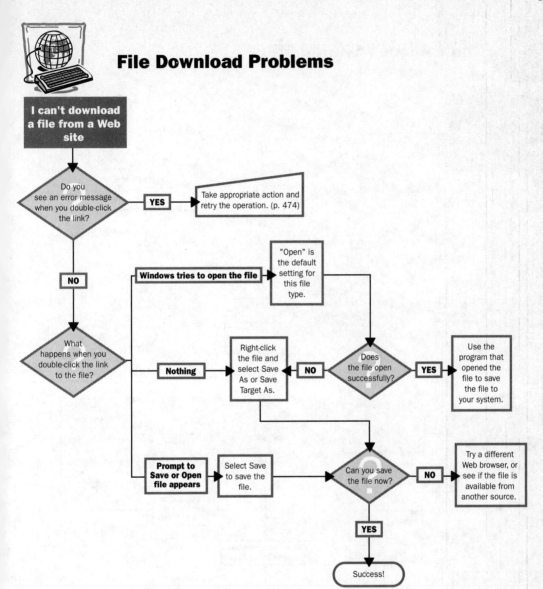

Can't Access Shared Files

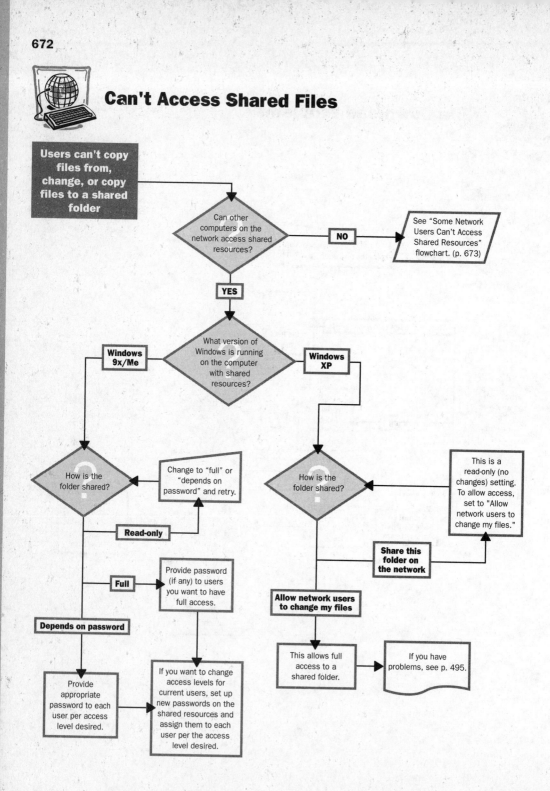

Users can't copy files from, change, or copy files to a shared folder

Can other computers on the network access shared resources?

NO → See "Some Network Users Can't Access Shared Resources" flowchart. (p. 673)

YES

What version of Windows is running on the computer with shared resources?

Windows 9x/Me / **Windows XP**

Windows 9x/Me

How is the folder shared?

Change to "full" or "depends on password" and retry.

Read-only

Full → Provide password (if any) to users you want to have full access.

Depends on password

Provide appropriate password to each user per access level desired. → If you want to change access levels for current users, set up new passwords on the shared resources and assign them to each user per the access level desired.

Windows XP

How is the folder shared?

This is a read-only (no changes) setting. To allow access, set to "Allow network users to change my files."

Share this folder on the network

Allow network users to change my files

This allows full access to a shared folder. → If you have problems, see p. 495.

Some Network Users Can't Access Shared Resources

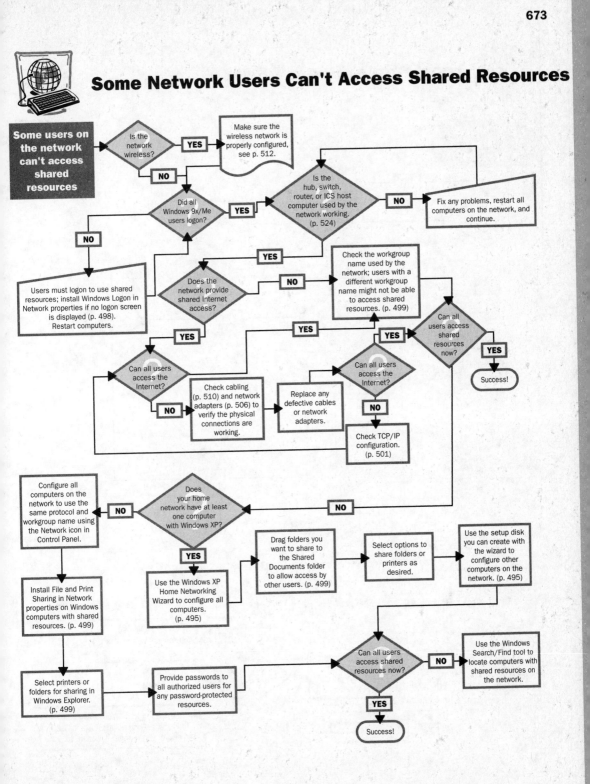

Local Printer Doesn't Print

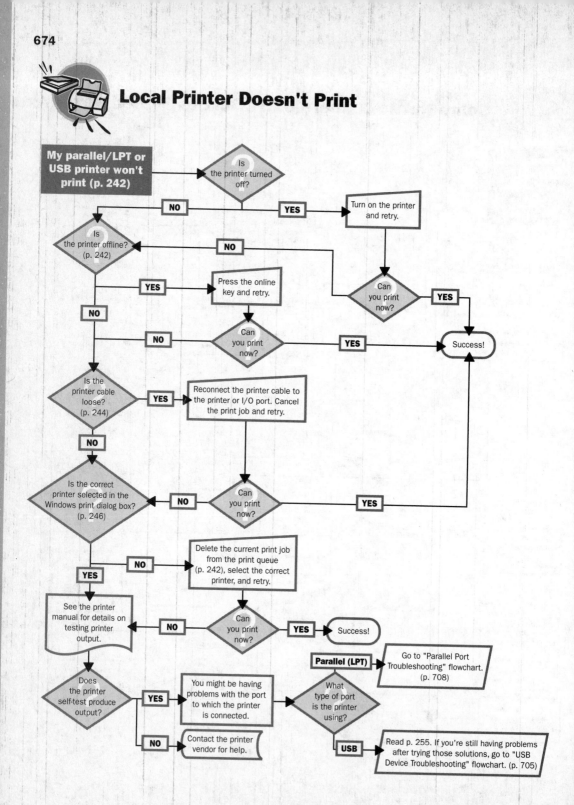

My parallel/LPT or USB printer won't print (p. 242)

Is the printer turned off?

NO

YES → Turn on the printer and retry.

Is the printer offline? (p. 242)

NO

YES → Press the online key and retry.

Can you print now?

NO

YES → Success!

Can you print now? **YES** → Success!

Is the printer cable loose? (p. 244)

YES → Reconnect the printer cable to the printer or I/O port. Cancel the print job and retry.

NO

Can you print now?

NO

YES

Is the correct printer selected in the Windows print dialog box? (p. 246)

NO → Delete the current print job from the print queue (p. 242), select the correct printer, and retry.

YES

Can you print now?

YES → Success!

NO → See the printer manual for details on testing printer output.

Does the printer self-test produce output?

YES → You might be having problems with the port to which the printer is connected.

NO → Contact the printer vendor for help.

What type of port is the printer using?

Parallel (LPT) → Go to "Parallel Port Troubleshooting" flowchart. (p. 708)

USB → Read p. 255. If you're still having problems after trying those solutions, go to "USB Device Troubleshooting" flowchart. (p. 705)

Network Printer Doesn't Print

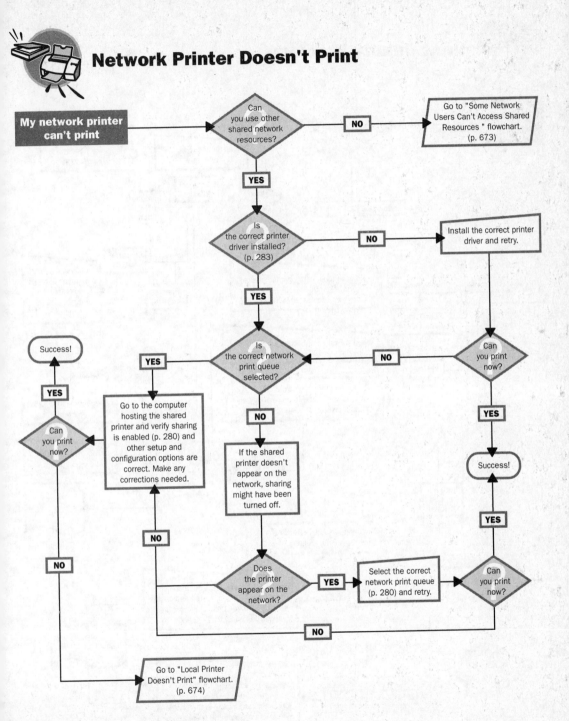

My network printer can't print

Can you use other shared network resources?

→ **NO** → Go to "Some Network Users Can't Access Shared Resources " flowchart. (p. 673)

YES ↓

Is the correct printer driver installed? (p. 283)

→ **NO** → Install the correct printer driver and retry.

YES ↓

Is the correct network print queue selected?

← **NO** ← Can you print now?

YES → Go to the computer hosting the shared printer and verify sharing is enabled (p. 280) and other setup and configuration options are correct. Make any corrections needed.

Can you print now? → **YES** → Success!

Can you print now? — **YES** → Success!

NO (from "Is the correct network print queue selected?") ↓

If the shared printer doesn't appear on the network, sharing might have been turned off.

↓

Does the printer appear on the network?

→ **YES** → Select the correct network print queue (p. 280) and retry.

→ Can you print now? — **YES** → Success!

NO → Go to the computer hosting the shared printer...

NO (from "Does the printer appear on the network?") → Go to "Local Printer Doesn't Print" flowchart. (p. 674)

Can you print now? **NO** → Go to "Local Printer Doesn't Print" flowchart. (p. 674)

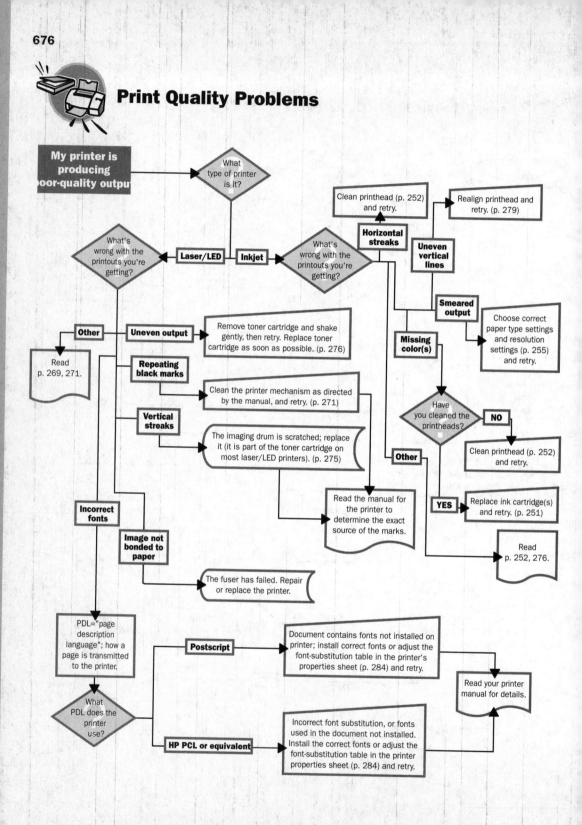

Print Quality Problems

My printer is producing poor-quality output

What type of printer is it?

Laser/LED **Inkjet**

What's wrong with the printouts you're getting?

What's wrong with the printouts you're getting?

Horizontal streaks — Clean printhead (p. 252) and retry.

Uneven vertical lines — Realign printhead and retry. (p. 279)

Smeared output — Choose correct paper type settings and resolution settings (p. 255) and retry.

Other — Read p. 269, 271.

Uneven output — Remove toner cartridge and shake gently, then retry. Replace toner cartridge as soon as possible. (p. 276)

Repeating black marks — Clean the printer mechanism as directed by the manual, and retry. (p. 271)

Vertical streaks — The imaging drum is scratched; replace it (it is part of the toner cartridge on most laser/LED printers). (p. 275)

Missing color(s)

Have you cleaned the printheads?

NO — Clean printhead (p. 252) and retry.

Other — Read the manual for the printer to determine the exact source of the marks.

YES — Replace ink cartridge(s) and retry. (p. 251)

Read p. 252, 276.

Incorrect fonts

Image not bonded to paper — The fuser has failed. Repair or replace the printer.

PDL="page description language"; how a page is transmitted to the printer.

What PDL does the printer use?

Postscript — Document contains fonts not installed on printer; install correct fonts or adjust the font-substitution table in the printer's properties sheet (p. 284) and retry.

HP PCL or equivalent — Incorrect font substitution, or fonts used in the document not installed. Install the correct fonts or adjust the font-substitution table in the printer properties sheet (p. 284) and retry.

Read your printer manual for details.

Scanner Problems

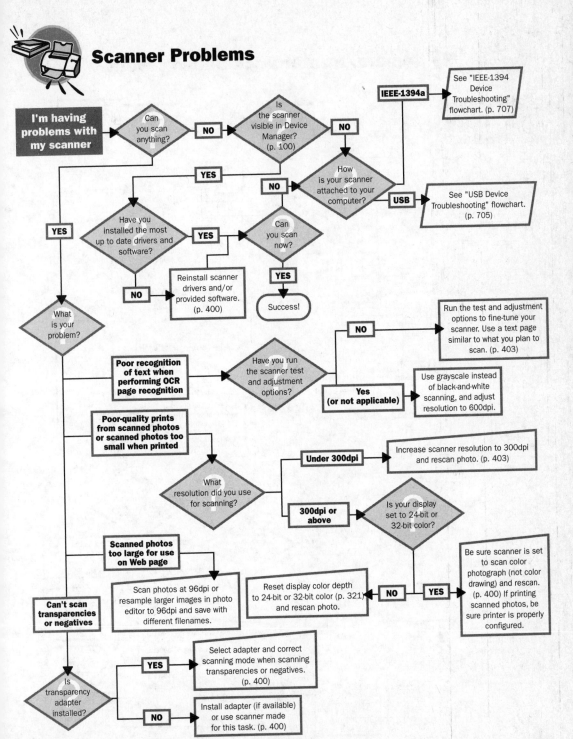

I'm having problems with my scanner

Can you scan anything?

NO → Is the scanner visible in Device Manager? (p. 100)

NO → IEEE-1394a → See "IEEE-1394 Device Troubleshooting" flowchart. (p. 707)

YES → **NO** → How is your scanner attached to your computer?

USB → See "USB Device Troubleshooting" flowchart. (p. 705)

Have you installed the most up to date drivers and software?

YES → Can you scan now?

YES → Success!

NO → Reinstall scanner drivers and/or provided software. (p. 400)

YES → What is your problem?

Poor recognition of text when performing OCR page recognition

→ Have you run the scanner test and adjustment options?

NO → Run the test and adjustment options to fine-tune your scanner. Use a text page similar to what you plan to scan. (p. 403)

Yes (or not applicable) → Use grayscale instead of black-and-white scanning, and adjust resolution to 600dpi.

Poor-quality prints from scanned photos or scanned photos too small when printed

→ What resolution did you use for scanning?

Under 300dpi → Increase scanner resolution to 300dpi and rescan photo. (p. 403)

300dpi or above → Is your display set to 24-bit or 32-bit color?

NO → Reset display color depth to 24-bit or 32-bit color (p. 321) and rescan photo.

YES → Be sure scanner is set to scan color photograph (not color drawing) and rescan. (p. 400) If printing scanned photos, be sure printer is properly configured.

Scanned photos too large for use on Web page

→ Scan photos at 96dpi or resample larger images in photo editor to 96dpi and save with different filenames.

Can't scan transparencies or negatives

→ Is transparency adapter installed?

YES → Select adapter and correct scanning mode when scanning transparencies or negatives. (p. 400)

NO → Install adapter (if available) or use scanner made for this task. (p. 400)

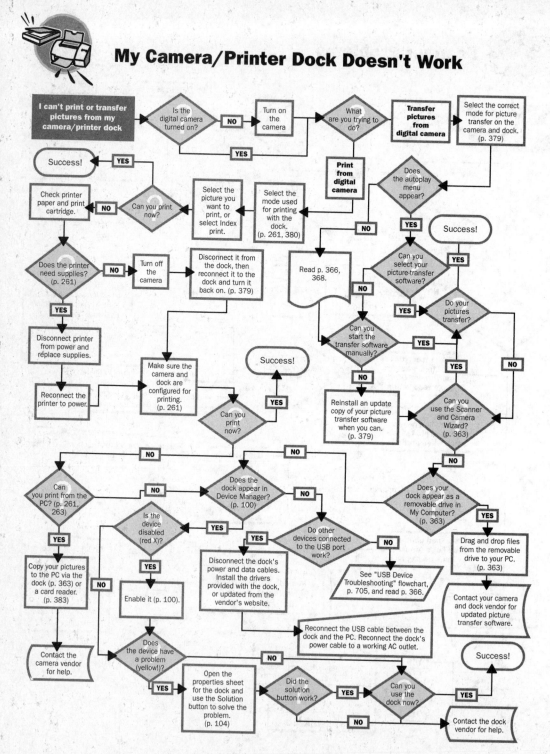

My Camera/Printer Dock Doesn't Work

I can't print or transfer pictures from my camera/printer dock

Is the digital camera turned on? → **NO** → Turn on the camera

YES →

What are you trying to do? → **Transfer pictures from digital camera** → Select the correct mode for picture transfer on the camera and dock. (p. 379)

Print from digital camera

Success! ← **YES** ←

Check printer paper and print cartridge. ← **NO** ← Can you print now? ← Select the picture you want to print, or select Index print. ← Select the mode used for printing with the dock. (p. 261, 380)

Does the autoplay menu appear? → **NO** → Read p. 366, 368.

YES → Success!

Does the printer need supplies? (p. 261) → **NO** → Turn off the camera → Disconnect it from the dock, then reconnect it to the dock and turn it back on. (p. 379)

Can you select your picture-transfer software? → **YES** →

NO →

Do your pictures transfer? → **YES**

YES

Disconnect printer from power and replace supplies.

Can you start the transfer software manually? → **YES** → Do your pictures transfer?

NO →

Reconnect the printer to power.

Make sure the camera and dock are configured for printing. (p. 261)

Success!

Can you print now? → **YES** → Success!

Reinstall an update copy of your picture transfer software when you can. (p. 379)

Can you use the Scanner and Camera Wizard? (p. 363) → **NO**

YES ← → **NO**

NO ↓

Can you print from the PC? (p. 261, 263) → **NO** → Does the dock appear in Device Manager? (p. 100) → **NO**

NO ←

Does your dock appear as a removable drive in My Computer? (p. 363) → **YES** → Drag and drop files from the removable drive to your PC. (p. 363)

YES ↓

Copy your pictures to the PC via the dock (p. 363) or a card reader. (p. 383)

Is the device disabled (red X)? → **YES** →

Do other devices connected to the USB port work? → **NO** → See "USB Device Troubleshooting" flowchart, p. 705, and read p. 366.

YES → Disconnect the dock's power and data cables. Install the drivers provided with the dock, or updated from the vendor's website.

YES ↓

Enable it (p. 100).

NO →

Contact your camera and dock vendor for updated picture transfer software.

Contact the camera vendor for help.

Reconnect the USB cable between the dock and the PC. Reconnect the dock's power cable to a working AC outlet.

Does the device have a problem (yellow!)? → **NO** →

Success!

YES → Open the properties sheet for the dock and use the Solution button to solve the problem. (p. 104) → Did the solution button work? → **YES** → Can you use the dock now? → **YES** → Success!

NO → Contact the dock vendor for help.

ATA/IDE Disk Drive Installation Troubleshooting

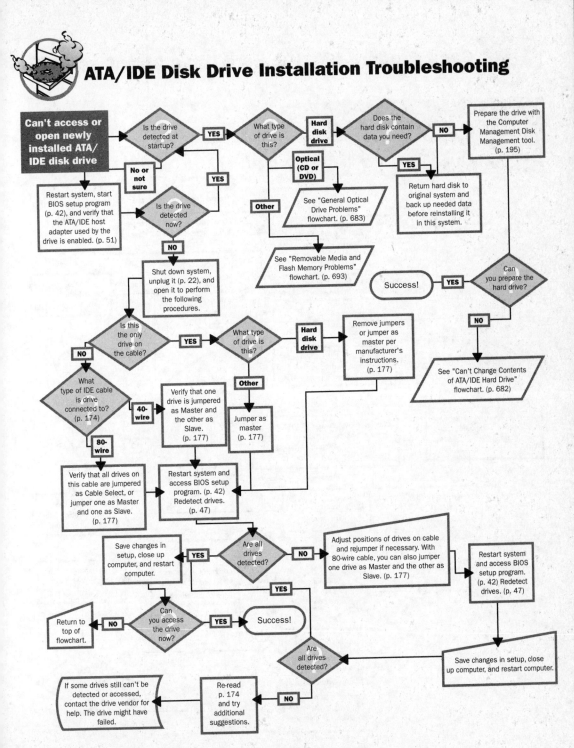

Can't access or open newly installed ATA/IDE disk drive

Is the drive detected at startup?

→ YES → What type of drive is this?

- **Hard disk drive** → Does the hard disk contain data you need?
  - NO → Prepare the drive with the Computer Management Disk Management tool. (p. 195)
  - YES → Return hard disk to original system and back up needed data before reinstalling it in this system.
- **Optical (CD or DVD)** → See "General Optical Drive Problems" flowchart. (p. 683)
- **Other** → See "Removable Media and Flash Memory Problems" flowchart. (p. 693)

No or not sure → Restart system, start BIOS setup program (p. 42), and verify that the ATA/IDE host adapter used by the drive is enabled. (p. 51)

Is the drive detected now?

- YES (→ toward top)
- NO → Shut down system, unplug it (p. 22), and open it to perform the following procedures.

Is this the only drive on the cable?

- YES → What type of drive is this?
  - **Hard disk drive** → Remove jumpers or jumper as master per manufacturer's instructions. (p. 177)
  - **Other** → Jumper as master (p. 177)
- NO → What type of IDE cable is drive connected to? (p. 174)
  - **40-wire** → Verify that one drive is jumpered as Master and the other as Slave. (p. 177)
  - **80-wire** → Verify that all drives on this cable are jumpered as Cable Select, or jumper one as Master and one as Slave. (p. 177)

Prepare the drive with the Computer Management Disk Management tool. (p. 195) → Can you prepare the hard drive?
- YES → Success!
- NO → See "Can't Change Contents of ATA/IDE Hard Drive" flowchart. (p. 682)

Restart system and access BIOS setup program. (p. 42) Redetect drives. (p. 47)

Are all drives detected?

- YES → Save changes in setup, close up computer, and restart computer.
- NO → Adjust positions of drives on cable and rejumper if necessary. With 80-wire cable, you can also jumper one drive as Master and the other as Slave. (p. 177) → Restart system and access BIOS setup program. (p. 42) Redetect drives. (p. 47)

Can you access the drive now?

- YES → Success!
- NO → Return to top of flowchart.

Are all drives detected?

- YES (→ Success!)
- NO → Save changes in setup, close up computer, and restart computer.

Are all drives detected?

- NO → Re-read p. 174 and try additional suggestions. → If some drives still can't be detected or accessed, contact the drive vendor for help. The drive might have failed.

Can't Prepare ATA/IDE Hard Drive After Installation

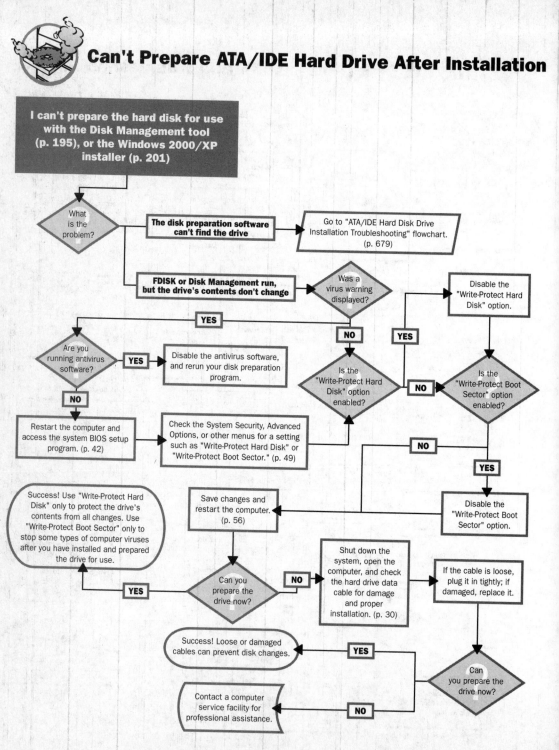

I can't prepare the hard disk for use with the Disk Management tool (p. 195), or the Windows 2000/XP installer (p. 201)

What is the problem?

The disk preparation software can't find the drive → Go to "ATA/IDE Hard Disk Drive Installation Troubleshooting" flowchart. (p. 679)

FDISK or Disk Management run, but the drive's contents don't change

Was a virus warning displayed?

Disable the "Write-Protect Hard Disk" option.

Are you running antivirus software? — YES → Disable the antivirus software, and rerun your disk preparation program.

Is the "Write-Protect Hard Disk" option enabled?

Is the "Write-Protect Boot Sector" option enabled?

Restart the computer and access the system BIOS setup program. (p. 42)

Check the System Security, Advanced Options, or other menus for a setting such as "Write-Protect Hard Disk" or "Write-Protect Boot Sector." (p. 49)

Success! Use "Write-Protect Hard Disk" only to protect the drive's contents from all changes. Use "Write-Protect Boot Sector" only to stop some types of computer viruses after you have installed and prepared the drive for use.

Save changes and restart the computer. (p. 56)

Disable the "Write-Protect Boot Sector" option.

Can you prepare the drive now?

Shut down the system, open the computer, and check the hard drive data cable for damage and proper installation. (p. 30)

If the cable is loose, plug it in tightly; if damaged, replace it.

Success! Loose or damaged cables can prevent disk changes.

Can you prepare the drive now?

Contact a computer service facility for professional assistance.

Hard Drive Doesn't Boot

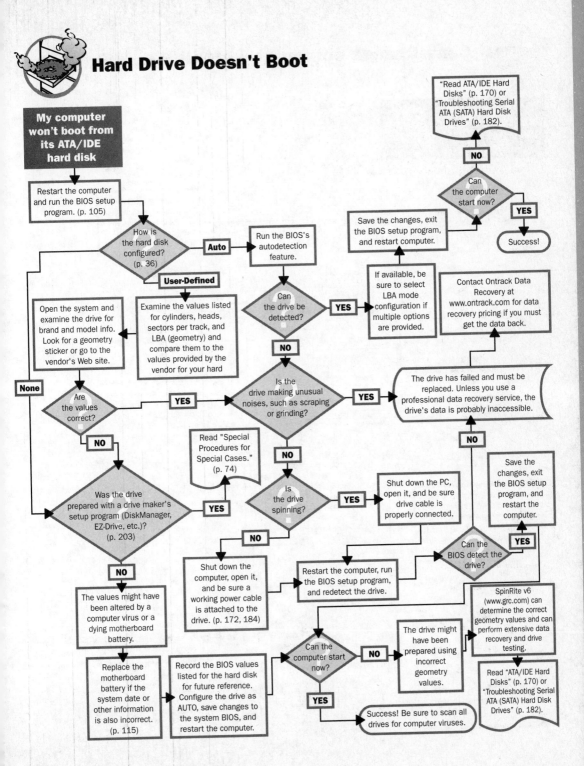

My computer won't boot from its ATA/IDE hard disk

Restart the computer and run the BIOS setup program. (p. 105)

How is the hard disk configured? (p. 36)

Auto → Run the BIOS's autodetection feature.

Can the drive be detected?

YES → If available, be sure to select LBA mode configuration if multiple options are provided.

Save the changes, exit the BIOS setup program, and restart computer.

Can the computer start now?

YES → Success!

NO → "Read ATA/IDE Hard Disks" (p. 170) or "Troubleshooting Serial ATA (SATA) Hard Disk Drives" (p. 182).

User-Defined → Examine the values listed for cylinders, heads, sectors per track, and LBA (geometry) and compare them to the values provided by the vendor for your hard

Open the system and examine the drive for brand and model info. Look for a geometry sticker or go to the vendor's Web site.

None

Are the values correct?

YES → Is the drive making unusual noises, such as scraping or grinding?

YES → The drive has failed and must be replaced. Unless you use a professional data recovery service, the drive's data is probably inaccessible.

Contact Ontrack Data Recovery at www.ontrack.com for data recovery pricing if you must get the data back.

NO (from drive detected) → Is the drive making unusual noises...

NO → Was the drive prepared with a drive maker's setup program (DiskManager, EZ-Drive, etc.)? (p. 203)

YES → Read "Special Procedures for Special Cases." (p. 74)

NO → The values might have been altered by a computer virus or a dying motherboard battery.

Replace the motherboard battery if the system date or other information is also incorrect. (p. 115)

Record the BIOS values listed for the hard disk for future reference. Configure the drive as AUTO, save changes to the system BIOS, and restart the computer.

Is the drive spinning?

YES → Shut down the PC, open it, and be sure drive cable is properly connected.

NO → Shut down the computer, open it, and be sure a working power cable is attached to the drive. (p. 172, 184)

Restart the computer, run the BIOS setup program, and redetect the drive.

Can the BIOS detect the drive?

YES → Save the changes, exit the BIOS setup program, and restart the computer.

NO → The drive has failed and must be replaced...

SpinRite v6 (www.grc.com) can determine the correct geometry values and can perform extensive data recovery and drive testing.

Can the computer start now?

NO → The drive might have been prepared using incorrect geometry values.

Read "ATA/IDE Hard Disks" (p. 170) or "Troubleshooting Serial ATA (SATA) Hard Disk Drives" (p. 182).

YES → Success! Be sure to scan all drives for computer viruses.

Can't Change Contents of ATA/IDE Hard Drive

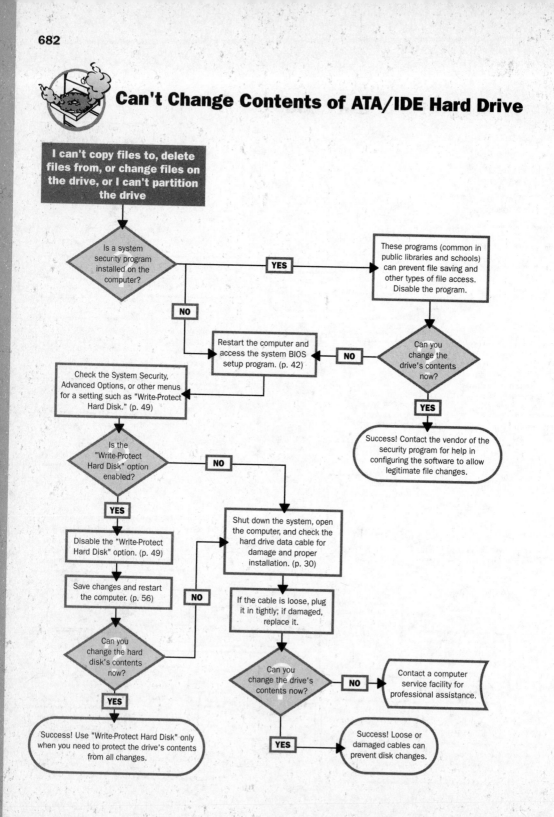

I can't copy files to, delete files from, or change files on the drive, or I can't partition the drive

Is a system security program installed on the computer?

YES → These programs (common in public libraries and schools) can prevent file saving and other types of file access. Disable the program.

NO

Can you change the drive's contents now?

NO → Restart the computer and access the system BIOS setup program. (p. 42)

YES

Success! Contact the vendor of the security program for help in configuring the software to allow legitimate file changes.

Check the System Security, Advanced Options, or other menus for a setting such as "Write-Protect Hard Disk." (p. 49)

Is the "Write-Protect Hard Disk" option enabled?

NO → Shut down the system, open the computer, and check the hard drive data cable for damage and proper installation. (p. 30)

YES

Disable the "Write-Protect Hard Disk" option. (p. 49)

Save changes and restart the computer. (p. 56)

If the cable is loose, plug it in tightly; if damaged, replace it.

Can you change the hard disk's contents now?

NO →

YES

Success! Use "Write-Protect Hard Disk" only when you need to protect the drive's contents from all changes.

Can you change the drive's contents now?

NO → Contact a computer service facility for professional assistance.

YES → Success! Loose or damaged cables can prevent disk changes.

General Optical Drive Problems

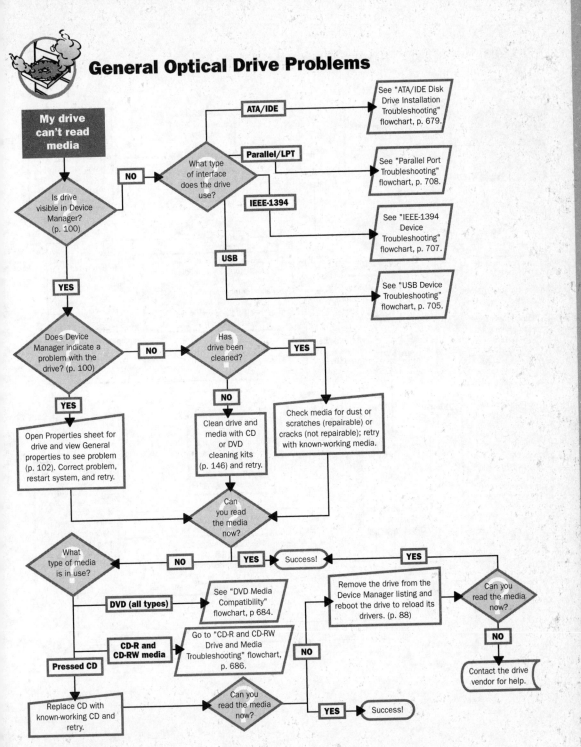

DVD Media Compatibility

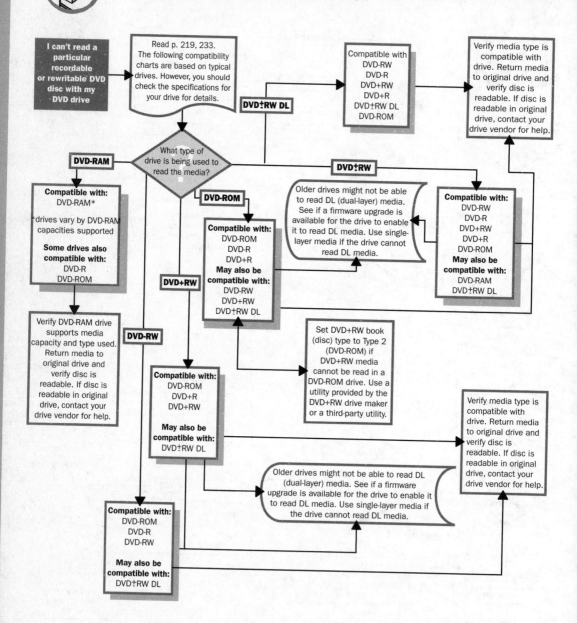

I can't read a particular recordable or rewritable DVD disc with my DVD drive

Read p. 219, 233. The following compatibility charts are based on typical drives. However, you should check the specifications for your drive for details.

DVD±RW DL

Compatible with
DVD-RW
DVD-R
DVD+RW
DVD+R
DVD±RW DL
DVD-ROM

Verify media type is compatible with drive. Return media to original drive and verify disc is readable. If disc is readable in original drive, contact your drive vendor for help.

What type of drive is being used to read the media?

DVD-RAM

Compatible with:
DVD-RAM*

*drives vary by DVD-RAM capacities supported

Some drives also compatible with:
DVD-R
DVD-ROM

Verify DVD-RAM drive supports media capacity and type used. Return media to original drive and verify disc is readable. If disc is readable in original drive, contact your drive vendor for help.

DVD-ROM

Compatible with:
DVD-ROM
DVD-R
DVD+R
May also be compatible with:
DVD-RW
DVD+RW
DVD±RW DL

DVD±RW

Older drives might not be able to read DL (dual-layer) media. See if a firmware upgrade is available for the drive to enable it to read DL media. Use single-layer media if the drive cannot read DL media.

Compatible with:
DVD-RW
DVD-R
DVD+RW
DVD+R
DVD-ROM
May also be compatible with:
DVD-RAM
DVD±RW DL

DVD+RW

DVD-RW

Compatible with:
DVD-ROM
DVD+R
DVD+RW

May also be compatible with:
DVD±RW DL

Set DVD+RW book (disc) type to Type 2 (DVD-ROM) if DVD+RW media cannot be read in a DVD-ROM drive. Use a utility provided by the DVD+RW drive maker or a third-party utility.

Verify media type is compatible with drive. Return media to original drive and verify disc is readable. If disc is readable in original drive, contact your drive vendor for help.

Older drives might not be able to read DL (dual-layer) media. See if a firmware upgrade is available for the drive to enable it to read DL media. Use single-layer media if the drive cannot read DL media.

Compatible with:
DVD-ROM
DVD-R
DVD-RW

May also be compatible with:
DVD±RW DL

Buffer Underrun Problems on Drives without Underrun Protection

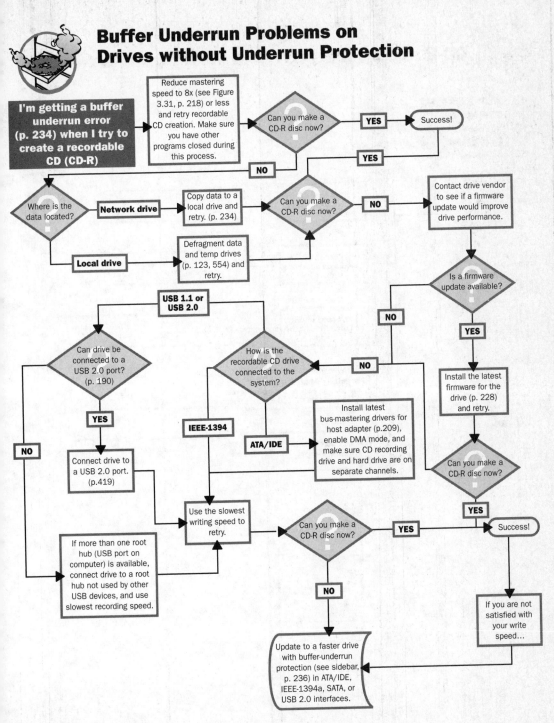

I'm getting a buffer underrun error (p. 234) when I try to create a recordable CD (CD-R)

Reduce mastering speed to 8x (see Figure 3.31, p. 218) or less and retry recordable CD creation. Make sure you have other programs closed during this process.

Can you make a CD-R disc now? — YES → Success!

YES

NO

Where is the data located? — Network drive → Copy data to a local drive and retry. (p. 234) → Can you make a CD-R disc now? — NO → Contact drive vendor to see if a firmware update would improve drive performance.

Local drive → Defragment data and temp drives (p. 123, 554) and retry.

Is a firmware update available?

NO

YES

USB 1.1 or USB 2.0

Can drive be connected to a USB 2.0 port? (p. 190)

How is the recordable CD drive connected to the system? — NO

Install the latest firmware for the drive (p. 228) and retry.

YES

IEEE-1394

ATA/IDE → Install latest bus-mastering drivers for host adapter (p.209), enable DMA mode, and make sure CD recording drive and hard drive are on separate channels.

NO

Connect drive to a USB 2.0 port. (p.419)

Can you make a CD-R disc now?

YES

Use the slowest writing speed to retry.

Can you make a CD-R disc now? — YES → Success!

If more than one root hub (USB port on computer) is available, connect drive to a root hub not used by other USB devices, and use slowest recording speed.

NO

Update to a faster drive with buffer-underrun protection (see sidebar, p. 236) in ATA/IDE, IEEE-1394a, SATA, or USB 2.0 interfaces.

If you are not satisfied with your write speed...

CD-R and CD-RW Drive and Media Troubleshooting

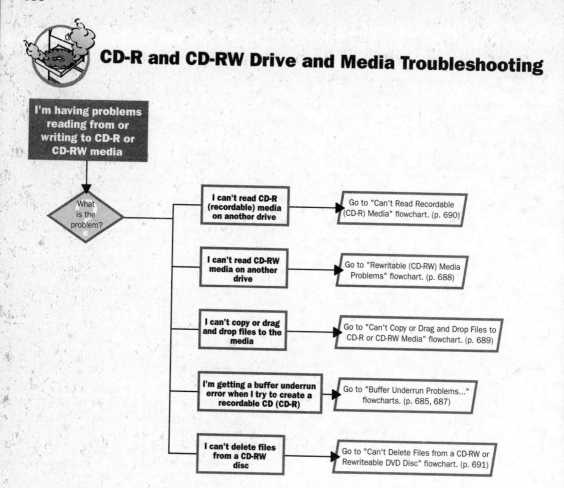

I'm having problems reading from or writing to CD-R or CD-RW media

What is the problem?

I can't read CD-R (recordable) media on another drive
→ Go to "Can't Read Recordable (CD-R) Media" flowchart. (p. 690)

I can't read CD-RW media on another drive
→ Go to "Rewritable (CD-RW) Media Problems" flowchart. (p. 688)

I can't copy or drag and drop files to the media
→ Go to "Can't Copy or Drag and Drop Files to CD-R or CD-RW Media" flowchart. (p. 689)

I'm getting a buffer underrun error when I try to create a recordable CD (CD-R)
→ Go to "Buffer Underrun Problems..." flowcharts. (p. 685, 687)

I can't delete files from a CD-RW disc
→ Go to "Can't Delete Files from a CD-RW or Rewriteable DVD Disc" flowchart. (p. 691)

Buffer Underrun Problems on Drives with Underrun Protection

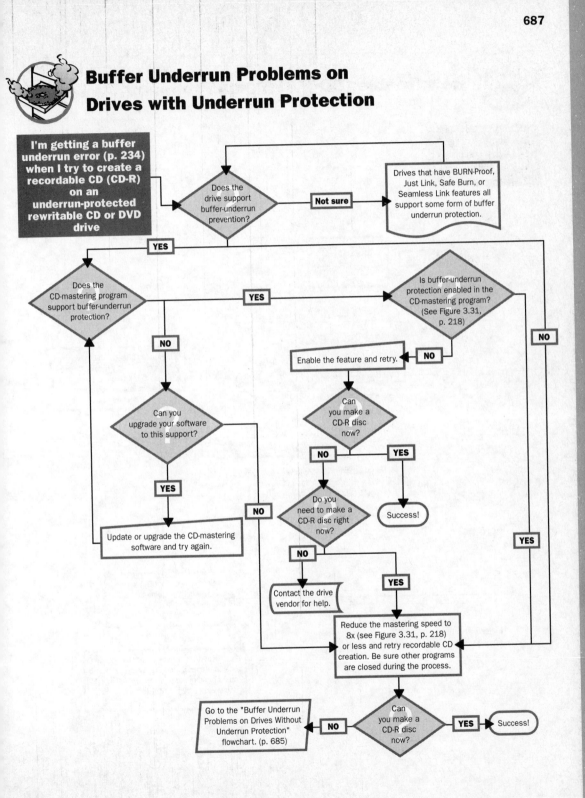

I'm getting a buffer underrun error (p. 234) when I try to create a recordable CD (CD-R) on an underrun-protected rewritable CD or DVD drive

Does the drive support buffer-underrun prevention?

Not sure → Drives that have BURN-Proof, Just Link, Safe Burn, or Seamless Link features all support some form of buffer underrun protection.

YES

Does the CD-mastering program support buffer-underrun protection?

YES → Is buffer-underrun protection enabled in the CD-mastering program? (See Figure 3.31, p. 218)

NO → Can you upgrade your software to this support?

NO → Enable the feature and retry.

YES → Update or upgrade the CD-mastering software and try again.

Can you make a CD-R disc now?

NO → Do you need to make a CD-R disc right now?

YES → Success!

NO → Contact the drive vendor for help.

YES → Reduce the mastering speed to 8x (see Figure 3.31, p. 218) or less and retry recordable CD creation. Be sure other programs are closed during the process.

NO

Can you make a CD-R disc now?

NO → Go to the "Buffer Underrun Problems on Drives Without Underrun Protection" flowchart. (p. 685)

YES → Success!

Rewriteable (CD-RW) Media Problems

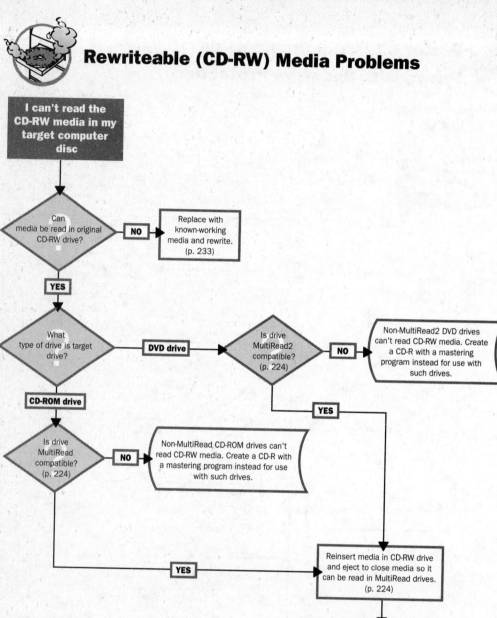

I can't read the CD-RW media in my target computer disc

↓

Can media be read in original CD-RW drive?

→ **NO** → Replace with known-working media and rewrite. (p. 233)

↓ **YES**

What type of drive is target drive?

→ **DVD drive** → **Is drive MultiRead2 compatible? (p. 224)** → **NO** → Non-MultiRead2 DVD drives can't read CD-RW media. Create a CD-R with a mastering program instead for use with such drives.

↓ **CD-ROM drive**

Is drive MultiRead compatible? (p. 224)

→ **NO** → Non-MultiRead CD-ROM drives can't read CD-RW media. Create a CD-R with a mastering program instead for use with such drives.

YES (from MultiRead2 compatible) →

YES (from MultiRead compatible) →

Reinsert media in CD-RW drive and eject to close media so it can be read in MultiRead drives. (p. 224)

↓

If the UDF (packet-writing) software doesn't install a reader on the CD-RW media for use on other computers, download and install one provided by the UDF software vendor. (See sidebar p. 227)

Can't Copy or Drag and Drop Files to CD-R or CD-RW Media

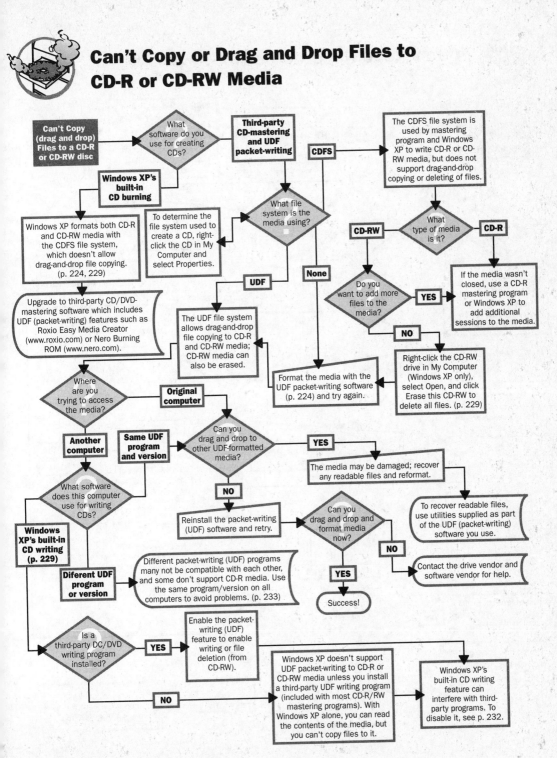

Can't Copy (drag and drop) Files to a CD-R or CD-RW disc

What software do you use for creating CDs?

Third-party CD-mastering and UDF packet-writing

CDFS → The CDFS file system is used by mastering program and Windows XP to write CD-R or CD-RW media, but does not support drag-and-drop copying or deleting of files.

Windows XP's built-in CD burning

Windows XP formats both CD-R and CD-RW media with the CDFS file system, which doesn't allow drag-and-drop file copying. (p. 224, 229)

To determine the file system used to create a CD, right-click the CD in My Computer and select Properties.

What file system is the media using?

What type of media is it?

CD-RW / **CD-R**

If the media wasn't closed, use a CD-R mastering program or Windows XP to add additional sessions to the media.

Upgrade to third-party CD/DVD-mastering software which includes UDF (packet-writing) features such as Roxio Easy Media Creator (www.roxio.com) or Nero Burning ROM (www.nero.com).

UDF

The UDF file system allows drag-and-drop file copying to CD-R and CD-RW media; CD-RW media can also be erased.

None

Do you want to add more files to the media? → **YES**

NO

Format the media with the UDF packet-writing software (p. 224) and try again.

Right-click the CD-RW drive in My Computer (Windows XP only), select Open, and click Erase this CD-RW to delete all files. (p. 229)

Where are you trying to access the media?

Original computer

Another computer

Same UDF program and version

Can you drag and drop to other UDF-formatted media? → **YES**

The media may be damaged; recover any readable files and reformat.

NO

Reinstall the packet-writing (UDF) software and retry.

What software does this computer use for writing CDs?

Windows XP's built-in CD writing (p. 229)

Diferent UDF program or version

Different packet-writing (UDF) programs many not be compatible with each other, and some don't support CD-R media. Use the same program/version on all computers to avoid problems. (p. 233)

Can you drag and drop and format media now? → **NO**

To recover readable files, use utilities supplied as part of the UDF (packet-writing) software you use.

Contact the drive vendor and software vendor for help.

YES

Success!

Is a third-party DC/DVD writing program installed? → **YES**

Enable the packet-writing (UDF) feature to enable writing or file deletion (from CD-RW).

NO

Windows XP doesn't support UDF packet-writing to CD-R or CD-RW media unless you install a third-party UDF writing program (included with most CD-R/RW mastering programs). With Windows XP alone, you can read the contents of the media, but you can't copy files to it.

Windows XP's built-in CD writing feature can interfere with third-party programs. To disable it, see p. 232.

Can't Read Recordable (CD-R) Media

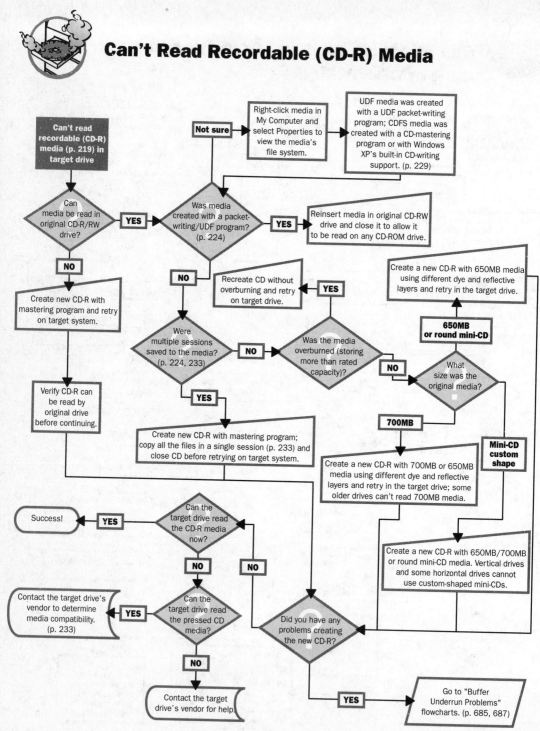

Can't read recordable (CD-R) media (p. 219) in target drive

Can media be read in original CD-R/RW drive?

Not sure → Right-click media in My Computer and select Properties to view the media's file system. → UDF media was created with a UDF packet-writing program; CDFS media was created with a CD-mastering program or with Windows XP's built-in CD-writing support. (p. 229)

YES → Was media created with a packet-writing/UDF program? (p. 224)

YES → Reinsert media in original CD-RW drive and close it to allow it to be read on any CD-ROM drive.

NO → Create new CD-R with mastering program and retry on target system.

Verify CD-R can be read by original drive before continuing.

NO → Were multiple sessions saved to the media? (p. 224, 233)

Recreate CD without overburning and retry on target drive. ← **YES** ← Was the media overburned (storing more than rated capacity)?

Create a new CD-R with 650MB media using different dye and reflective layers and retry in the target drive.

650MB or round mini-CD

NO → Was the media overburned (storing more than rated capacity)? **NO** → What size was the original media?

YES → Create new CD-R with mastering program; copy all the files in a single session (p. 233) and close CD before retrying on target system.

700MB

Mini-CD custom shape

Create a new CD-R with 700MB or 650MB media using different dye and reflective layers and retry in the target drive; some older drives can't read 700MB media.

Success! ← **YES** ← Can the target drive read the CD-R media now?

Create a new CD-R with 650MB/700MB or round mini-CD media. Vertical drives and some horizontal drives cannot use custom-shaped mini-CDs.

NO ... **NO**

Contact the target drive's vendor to determine media compatibility. (p. 233) ← **YES** ← Can the target drive read the pressed CD media?

Did you have any problems creating the new CD-R?

NO

Contact the target drive's vendor for help. → **YES** → Go to "Buffer Underrun Problems" flowcharts. (p. 685, 687)

Can't Delete Files from a CD-RW or Rewriteable DVD Disc

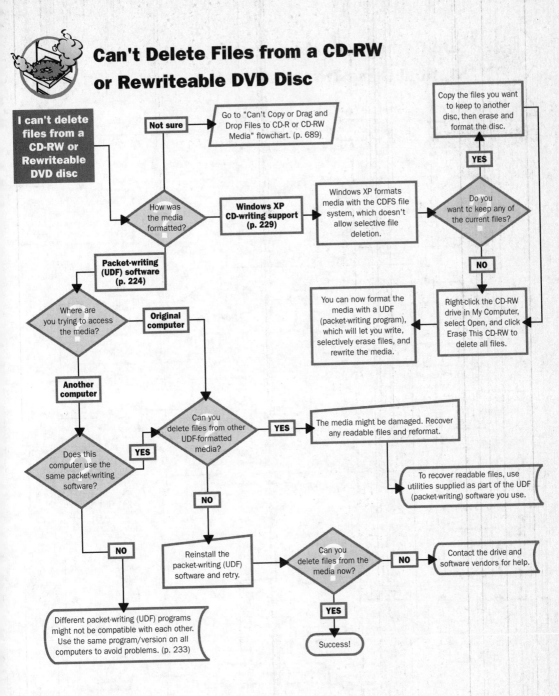

I can't delete files from a CD-RW or Rewriteable DVD disc

Not sure → Go to "Can't Copy or Drag and Drop Files to CD-R or CD-RW Media" flowchart. (p. 689)

How was the media formatted? → **Windows XP CD-writing support (p. 229)** → Windows XP formats media with the CDFS file system, which doesn't allow selective file deletion.

Do you want to keep any of the current files?

YES → Copy the files you want to keep to another disc, then erase and format the disc.

NO → Right-click the CD-RW drive in My Computer, select Open, and click Erase This CD-RW to delete all files.

You can now format the media with a UDF (packet-writing program), which will let you write, selectively erase files, and rewrite the media.

Packet-writing (UDF) software (p. 224)

Where are you trying to access the media?

Original computer →

Another computer ↓

Does this computer use the same packet-writing software?

YES → **Can you delete files from other UDF-formatted media?**

YES → The media might be damaged. Recover any readable files and reformat.

To recover readable files, use utilities supplied as part of the UDF (packet-writing) software you use.

NO → Reinstall the packet-writing (UDF) software and retry.

NO → Different packet-writing (UDF) programs might not be compatible with each other. Use the same program/version on all computers to avoid problems. (p. 233)

Can you delete files from the media now?

NO → Contact the drive and software vendors for help.

YES → Success!

IDE Removable Media and Optical Drive Troubleshooting

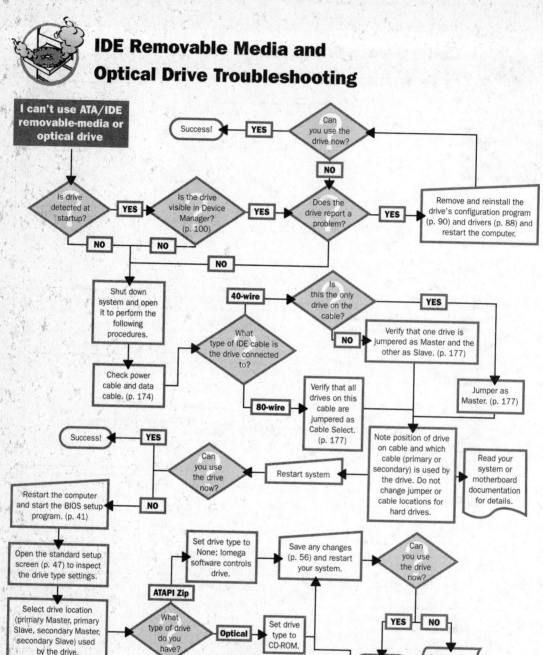

I can't use ATA/IDE removable-media or optical drive

Is drive detected at startup? → YES → Is the drive visible in Device Manager? (p. 100) → YES → Does the drive report a problem? → YES → Remove and reinstall the drive's configuration program (p. 90) and drivers (p. 88) and restart the computer.

Can you use the drive now? → YES → Success!

Can you use the drive now? → NO

Is drive detected at startup? → NO

Is the drive visible in Device Manager? → NO

Does the drive report a problem? → NO

Shut down system and open it to perform the following procedures.

Check power cable and data cable. (p. 174)

What type of IDE cable is the drive connected to?

40-wire → Is this the only drive on the cable? → YES → Jumper as Master. (p. 177)

Is this the only drive on the cable? → NO → Verify that one drive is jumpered as Master and the other as Slave. (p. 177)

80-wire → Verify that all drives on this cable are jumpered as Cable Select. (p. 177)

Note position of drive on cable and which cable (primary or secondary) is used by the drive. Do not change jumper or cable locations for hard drives. → Read your system or motherboard documentation for details.

Restart system

Can you use the drive now? → YES → Success!

Can you use the drive now? → NO → Restart the computer and start the BIOS setup program. (p. 41)

Open the standard setup screen (p. 47) to inspect the drive type settings.

Select drive location (primary Master, primary Slave, secondary Master, secondary Slave) used by the drive.

What type of drive do you have?

ATAPI Zip → Set drive type to None; Iomega software controls drive.

Optical → Set drive type to CD-ROM.

Other → Read the documentation for your drive and follow those instructions.

Save any changes (p. 56) and restart your system. → Can you use the drive now? → YES → Success!

Can you use the drive now? → NO → Contact the drive vendor for help.

Removable Media and Flash Memory Problems

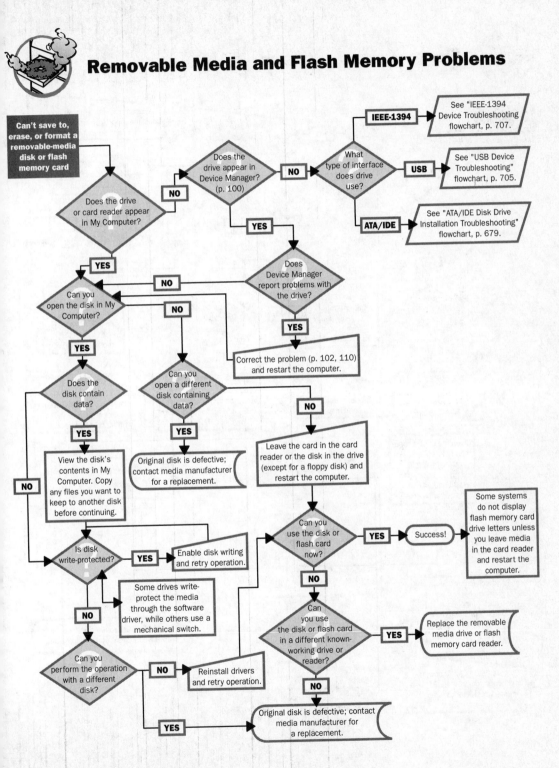

Can't save to, erase, or format a removable-media disk or flash memory card

Does the drive or card reader appear in My Computer?

— **NO** → Does the drive appear in Device Manager? (p. 100)

— **NO** → What type of interface does drive use?
- **IEEE-1394** → See "IEEE-1394 Device Troubleshooting flowchart, p. 707.
- **USB** → See "USB Device Troubleshooting" flowchart, p. 705.
- **ATA/IDE** → See "ATA/IDE Disk Drive Installation Troubleshooting" flowchart, p. 679.

— **YES** → Does Device Manager report problems with the drive?

— **YES** → Correct the problem (p. 102, 110) and restart the computer.

— **NO** → Can you open the disk in My Computer?

YES (from Does the drive or card reader appear in My Computer?) → Can you open the disk in My Computer?

YES → Does the disk contain data?

NO → Can you open a different disk containing data?

Does the disk contain data?
- **YES** → View the disk's contents in My Computer. Copy any files you want to keep to another disk before continuing.
- **NO** →

Can you open a different disk containing data?
- **YES** → Original disk is defective; contact media manufacturer for a replacement.
- **NO** → Leave the card in the card reader or the disk in the drive (except for a floppy disk) and restart the computer.

Is disk write-protected?
- **YES** → Enable disk writing and retry operation.
- **NO** →

Some drives write-protect the media through the software driver, while others use a mechanical switch.

Can you perform the operation with a different disk?
- **NO** → Reinstall drivers and retry operation.
- **YES** → Original disk is defective; contact media manufacturer for a replacement.

Can you use the disk or flash card now?
- **YES** → Success!
- **NO** → Can you use the disk or flash card in a different known-working drive or reader?

Some systems do not display flash memory card drive letters unless you leave media in the card reader and restart the computer.

Can you use the disk or flash card in a different known-working drive or reader?
- **YES** → Replace the removable media drive or flash memory card reader.
- **NO** → Original disk is defective; contact media manufacturer for a replacement.

Floppy Drive Problems

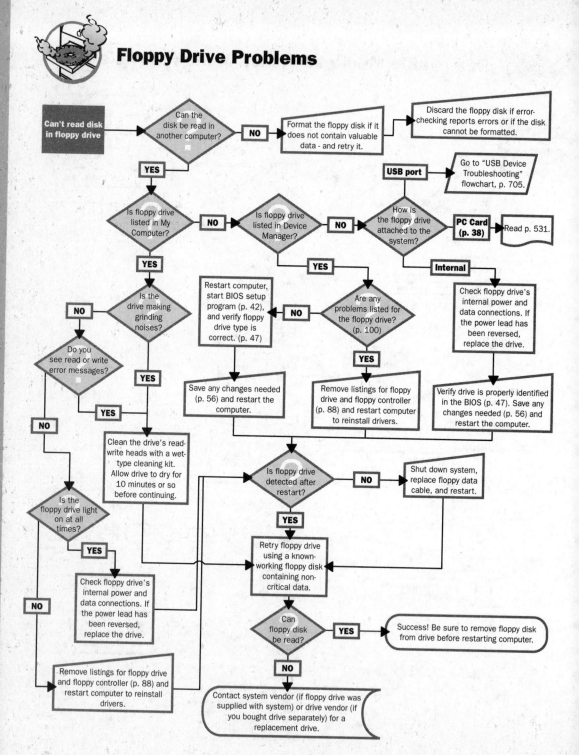

Can't read disk in floppy drive → Can the disk be read in another computer?

NO → Format the floppy disk if it does not contain valuable data - and retry it. → Discard the floppy disk if error-checking reports errors or if the disk cannot be formatted.

YES ↓

Is floppy drive listed in My Computer?

NO → Is floppy drive listed in Device Manager?

NO → How is the floppy drive attached to the system?

USB port → Go to "USB Device Troubleshooting" flowchart, p. 705.

PC Card (p. 38) → Read p. 531.

YES ↓ (My Computer)

Is the drive making grinding noises?

NO → Do you see read or write error messages?

YES (Device Manager) → Restart computer, start BIOS setup program (p. 42), and verify floppy drive type is correct. (p. 47)

NO → Are any problems listed for the floppy drive? (p. 100)

Internal → Check floppy drive's internal power and data connections. If the power lead has been reversed, replace the drive.

YES (Is the drive making grinding noises) ↓

YES (read or write error messages) ↓

Save any changes needed (p. 56) and restart the computer.

YES (problems listed) ↓ Remove listings for floppy drive and floppy controller (p. 88) and restart computer to reinstall drivers.

Verify drive is properly identified in the BIOS (p. 47). Save any changes needed (p. 56) and restart the computer.

NO (read or write error messages) ↓

Clean the drive's read-write heads with a wet-type cleaning kit. Allow drive to dry for 10 minutes or so before continuing.

Is the floppy drive light on at all times?

Is floppy drive detected after restart?

NO → Shut down system, replace floppy data cable, and restart.

YES ↓

Retry floppy drive using a known-working floppy disk containing non-critical data.

YES (floppy drive light) → Check floppy drive's internal power and data connections. If the power lead has been reversed, replace the drive.

NO (floppy drive light) ↓

Remove listings for floppy drive and floppy controller (p. 88) and restart computer to reinstall drivers.

Can floppy disk be read?

YES → Success! Be sure to remove floppy disk from drive before restarting computer.

NO ↓

Contact system vendor (if floppy drive was supplied with system) or drive vendor (if you bought drive separately) for a replacement drive.

Can't Change Contents of a Floppy Disk

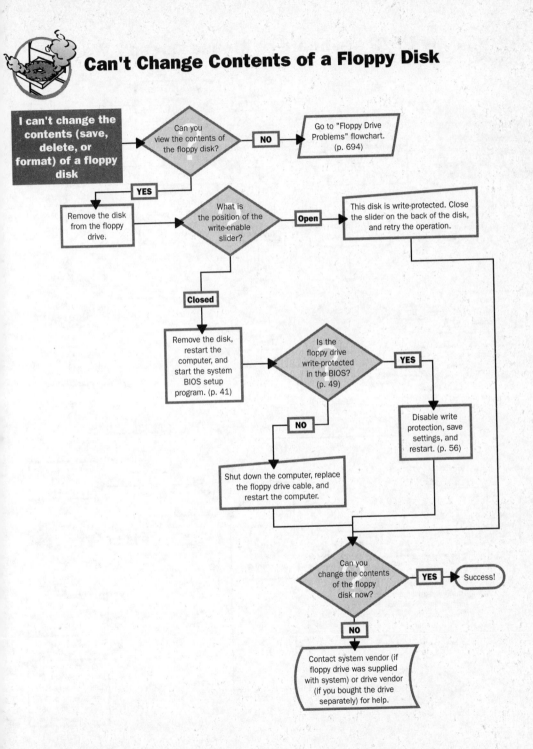

I can't change the contents (save, delete, or format) of a floppy disk

Can you view the contents of the floppy disk?

NO → Go to "Floppy Drive Problems" flowchart. (p. 694)

YES → Remove the disk from the floppy drive.

What is the position of the write-enable slider?

Open → This disk is write-protected. Close the slider on the back of the disk, and retry the operation.

Closed → Remove the disk, restart the computer, and start the system BIOS setup program. (p. 41)

Is the floppy drive write-protected in the BIOS? (p. 49)

YES → Disable write protection, save settings, and restart. (p. 56)

NO → Shut down the computer, replace the floppy drive cable, and restart the computer.

Can you change the contents of the floppy disk now?

YES → Success!

NO → Contact system vendor (if floppy drive was supplied with system) or drive vendor (if you bought the drive separately) for help.

My PS/2 Keyboard or Mouse Doesn't Work

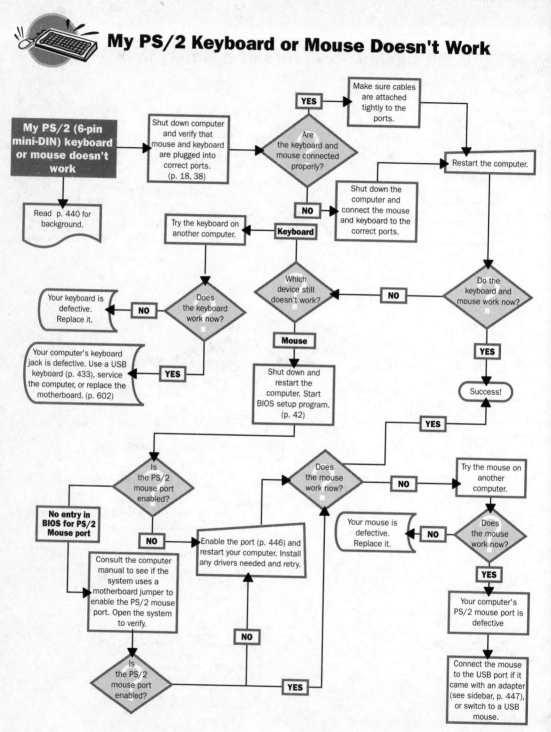

My PS/2 (6-pin mini-DIN) keyboard or mouse doesn't work

Read p. 440 for background.

Shut down computer and verify that mouse and keyboard are plugged into correct ports. (p. 18, 38)

Are the keyboard and mouse connected properly?

YES → Make sure cables are attached tightly to the ports.

NO → Shut down the computer and connect the mouse and keyboard to the correct ports.

Restart the computer.

Do the keyboard and mouse work now?

NO → Which device still doesn't work?

YES → Success!

Keyboard → Try the keyboard on another computer.

Does the keyboard work now?

NO → Your keyboard is defective. Replace it.

YES → Your computer's keyboard jack is defective. Use a USB keyboard (p. 433), service the computer, or replace the motherboard. (p. 602)

Mouse → Shut down and restart the computer. Start BIOS setup program. (p. 42)

Is the PS/2 mouse port enabled?

No entry in BIOS for PS/2 Mouse port

NO → Consult the computer manual to see if the system uses a motherboard jumper to enable the PS/2 mouse port. Open the system to verify.

Is the PS/2 mouse port enabled?

YES →

Enable the port (p. 446) and restart your computer. Install any drivers needed and retry.

NO →

Does the mouse work now?

NO → Try the mouse on another computer.

YES →

Does the mouse work now?

NO → Your mouse is defective. Replace it.

YES → Your computer's PS/2 mouse port is defective

Connect the mouse to the USB port if it came with an adapter (see sidebar, p. 447), or switch to a USB mouse.

Some Keys on the Keyboard Don't Work

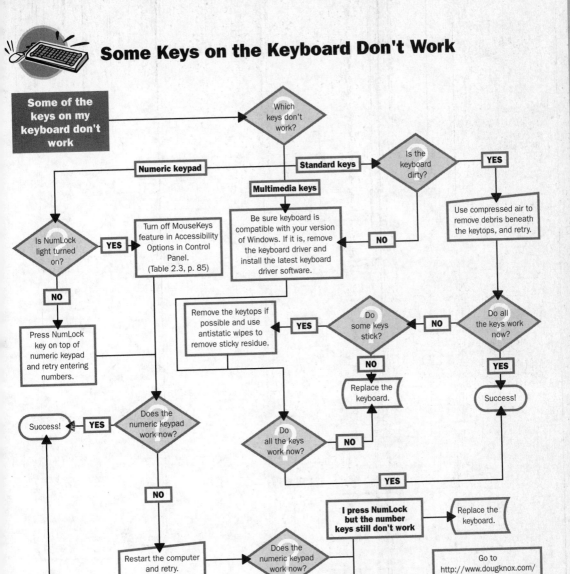

Some of the keys on my keyboard don't work

Which keys don't work?

Numeric keypad

Standard keys

Is the keyboard dirty?

YES

NO

Multimedia keys

Be sure keyboard is compatible with your version of Windows. If it is, remove the keyboard driver and install the latest keyboard driver software.

Use compressed air to remove debris beneath the keytops, and retry.

Is NumLock light turned on?

YES

Turn off MouseKeys feature in Accessibility Options in Control Panel. (Table 2.3, p. 85)

NO

Press NumLock key on top of numeric keypad and retry entering numbers.

Remove the keytops if possible and use antistatic wipes to remove sticky residue.

YES

Do some keys stick?

NO

Do all the keys work now?

NO

Replace the keyboard.

NO

Do all the keys work now?

YES

Success!

Does the numeric keypad work now?

YES

Success!

NO

YES

Restart the computer and retry.

Does the numeric keypad work now?

I press NumLock but the number keys still don't work

Replace the keyboard.

Only after I press the NumLock key

Go to http://www.dougknox.com/xp/utils/xp_numlock.htm to learn to dowload a program that can turn on NulLock at startup.

YES

No Keys on the Keyboard Work

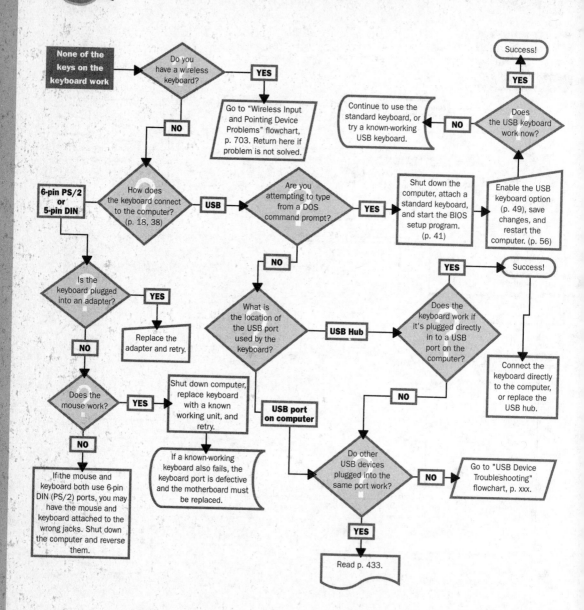

None of the keys on the keyboard work → Do you have a wireless keyboard? → **YES** → Go to "Wireless Input and Pointing Device Problems" flowchart, p. 703. Return here if problem is not solved.

NO ↓

How does the keyboard connect to the computer? (p. 18, 38) → **6-pin PS/2 or 5-pin DIN** / **USB**

USB → Are you attempting to type from a DOS command prompt? → **YES** → Shut down the computer, attach a standard keyboard, and start the BIOS setup program. (p. 41) → Enable the USB keyboard option (p. 49), save changes, and restart the computer. (p. 56)

Enable the USB keyboard option → **YES** → Does the USB keyboard work now? → **YES** → Success!

Does the USB keyboard work now? → **NO** → Continue to use the standard keyboard, or try a known-working USB keyboard.

NO (from DOS prompt) ↓ What is the location of the USB port used by the keyboard? → **USB Hub** → Does the keyboard work if it's plugged directly in to a USB port on the computer? → **YES** → Success!

Does the keyboard work if it's plugged directly in to a USB port on the computer? → **NO** → Connect the keyboard directly to the computer, or replace the USB hub.

What is the location of the USB port used by the keyboard? → **USB port on computer** → Do other USB devices plugged into the same port work? → **NO** → Go to "USB Device Troubleshooting" flowchart, p. xxx.

Do other USB devices plugged into the same port work? → **YES** → Read p. 433.

6-pin PS/2 or 5-pin DIN ↓ Is the keyboard plugged into an adapter? → **YES** → Replace the adapter and retry.

NO ↓ Does the mouse work? → **YES** → Shut down computer, replace keyboard with a known working unit, and retry. → If a known-working keyboard also fails, the keyboard port is defective and the motherboard must be replaced.

NO ↓ If the mouse and keyboard both use 6-pin DIN (PS/2) ports, you may have the mouse and keyboard attached to the wrong jacks. Shut down the computer and reverse them.

General Pointing Device Problems

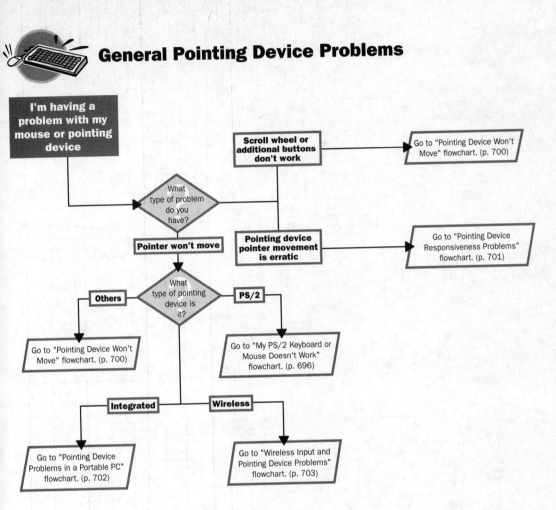

I'm having a problem with my mouse or pointing device

What type of problem do you have?

Scroll wheel or additional buttons don't work → Go to "Pointing Device Won't Move" flowchart. (p. 700)

Pointing device pointer movement is erratic → Go to "Pointing Device Responsiveness Problems" flowchart. (p. 701)

Pointer won't move

What type of pointing device is it?

Others → Go to "Pointing Device Won't Move" flowchart. (p. 700)

PS/2 → Go to "My PS/2 Keyboard or Mouse Doesn't Work" flowchart. (p. 696)

Integrated → Go to "Pointing Device Problems in a Portable PC" flowchart. (p. 702)

Wireless → Go to "Wireless Input and Pointing Device Problems" flowchart. (p. 703)

Pointing Device Won't Move

My pointing device pointer won't move

Go to "Wireless Input and Pointing Device Problems" flowchart. (p. 703)

How is the device connected to the computer?

- **Wireless**
- **Wired**
- **Integrated into portable computer**

Restart the computer and start the system BIOS setup program. (p. 42)

Is the pointing device enabled? (p. 440, 446)

NO → Enable the device, save the changes to the system configuration, and restart the computer.

YES

See www.microsoft.com/enable/products/keyboard.aspx for keyboard shortcuts for your version of Windows.

YES → Disconnect the other device and restart the computer.

Is another pointing device connected to the computer?

NO → Service the computer.

Does the pointing device work now?

NO → Service the computer.

YES

Is the pointing device listed as working in Device Manager? (p. 416)

YES → **Does the driver appear to be the correct one?**

NO

YES → **What type of pointing device is it?**

Success! Your system might allow only one pointing device at a time.

Install an updated driver from the vendor's Web site (p. 416) or Windows Update (p. 132) and retry.

NO

Is the device listed at all?

YES

Open the device's properties sheet, correct the reported problem, and retry.

- **Optical mouse**: Verify that the sensors are free of dust and that the mousing surface is not mirrored or printed with a repeating pattern. (p. 451)
- **Ball-type mouse or trackball**: Verify that the ball is in place and that the ball and rollers are clean. (p. 451)
- **Touchpad**: Verify that the touch surface is clean and that your fingers are clean. (p. 451)

If you have a USB mouse, reconnect it to a USB port on the PC, not an external hub. If you have a PS/2 mouse, shut down the PC, reconnect it to the PS/2 mouse port and restart.

Does the pointing device work now?

NO → **Do other devices on the same port work correctly?**

NO → Contact the computer or add-on card vendor for help.

Yes, or only device on port → Replace the pointing device and retry. (p. 440, 451)

YES → Success!

Pointing Device Responsiveness Problems

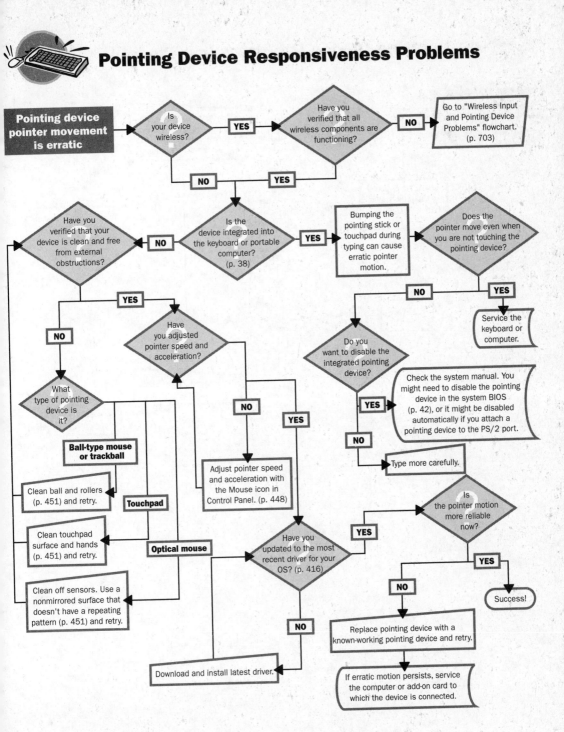

Pointing Device Problems in a Portable PC

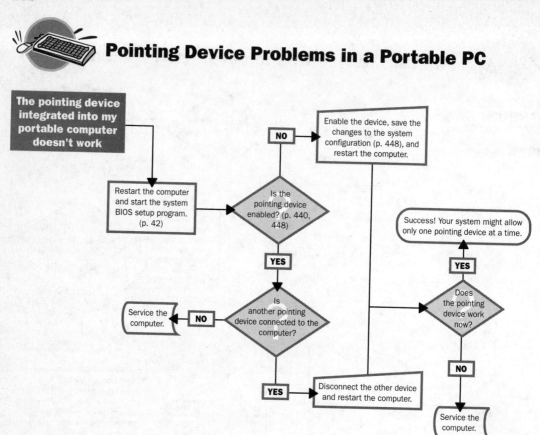

The pointing device integrated into my portable computer doesn't work

Restart the computer and start the system BIOS setup program. (p. 42)

Is the pointing device enabled? (p. 440, 448)

NO → Enable the device, save the changes to the system configuration (p. 448), and restart the computer.

YES

Is another pointing device connected to the computer?

NO → Service the computer.

YES → Disconnect the other device and restart the computer.

Does the pointing device work now?

YES → Success! Your system might allow only one pointing device at a time.

NO → Service the computer.

Wireless Input and Pointing Device Problems

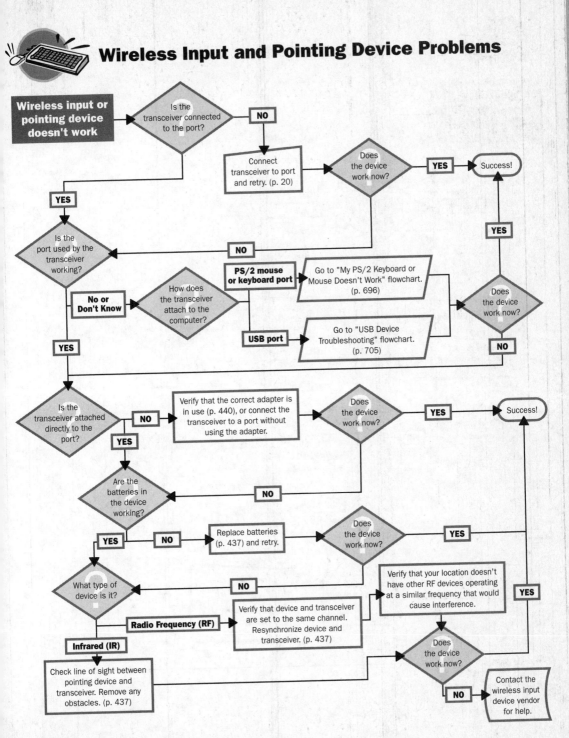

Wireless input or pointing device doesn't work

Is the transceiver connected to the port?
— **NO** → Connect transceiver to port and retry. (p. 20) → Does the device work now? — **YES** → Success!

Does the device work now? — **YES** → Success!

YES ↓

Is the port used by the transceiver working?
— **NO** →

How does the transceiver attach to the computer?
— **PS/2 mouse or keyboard port** → Go to "My PS/2 Keyboard or Mouse Doesn't Work" flowchart. (p. 696)
— **USB port** → Go to "USB Device Troubleshooting" flowchart. (p. 705)

Does the device work now? — **NO**

No or Don't Know ↑

YES ↓

Is the transceiver attached directly to the port?
— **NO** → Verify that the correct adapter is in use (p. 440), or connect the transceiver to a port without using the adapter. → Does the device work now? — **YES** → Success!

YES ↓

Are the batteries in the device working?
— **NO** → Replace batteries (p. 437) and retry. → Does the device work now? — **YES**

YES ↓ **NO**

What type of device is it?
— **Radio Frequency (RF)** → Verify that device and transceiver are set to the same channel. Resynchronize device and transceiver. (p. 437)
— **Infrared (IR)** → Check line of sight between pointing device and transceiver. Remove any obstacles. (p. 437)

Does the device work now? — **NO** → Verify that your location doesn't have other RF devices operating at a similar frequency that would cause interference.

Does the device work now? — **YES**
— **NO** → Contact the wireless input device vendor for help.

I/O Port Is Detected but Not Working Properly

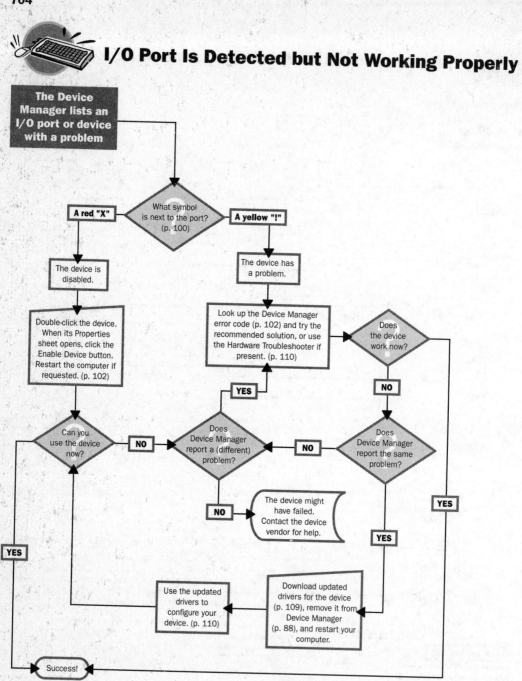

The Device Manager lists an I/O port or device with a problem

What symbol is next to the port? (p. 100)

A red "X"

The device is disabled.

Double-click the device. When its Properties sheet opens, click the Enable Device button. Restart the computer if requested. (p. 102)

Can you use the device now?

A yellow "!"

The device has a problem.

Look up the Device Manager error code (p. 102) and try the recommended solution, or use the Hardware Troubleshooter if present. (p. 110)

YES

Does the device work now?

NO

Does Device Manager report a (different) problem?

NO

Does Device Manager report the same problem?

NO

YES

The device might have failed. Contact the device vendor for help.

YES

YES

Use the updated drivers to configure your device. (p. 110)

Download updated drivers for the device (p. 109), remove it from Device Manager (p. 88), and restart your computer.

YES

Success!

USB Device Troubleshooting

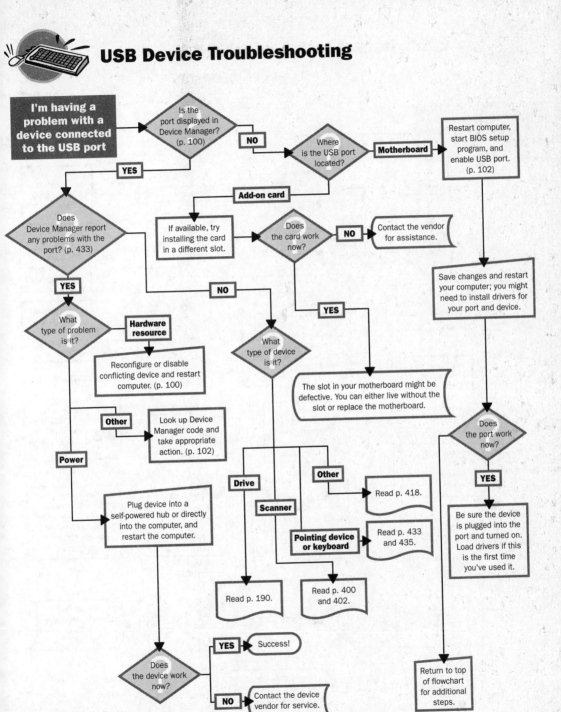

I'm having a problem with a device connected to the USB port

Is the port displayed in Device Manager? (p. 100)

NO → Where is the USB port located?

Motherboard → Restart computer, start BIOS setup program, and enable USB port. (p. 102)

Add-on card → If available, try installing the card in a different slot. → Does the card work now? — **NO** → Contact the vendor for assistance.

YES → Does Device Manager report any problems with the port? (p. 433)

YES → What type of problem is it?

Hardware resource → Reconfigure or disable conflicting device and restart computer. (p. 100)

Other → Look up Device Manager code and take appropriate action. (p. 102)

Power → Plug device into a self-powered hub or directly into the computer, and restart the computer.

NO → What type of device is it?

YES → The slot in your motherboard might be defective. You can either live without the slot or replace the motherboard.

Save changes and restart your computer; you might need to install drivers for your port and device.

Does the port work now?

YES → Be sure the device is plugged into the port and turned on. Load drivers if this is the first time you've used it.

Drive → Read p. 190.

Scanner → Read p. 400 and 402.

Pointing device or keyboard → Read p. 433 and 435.

Other → Read p. 418.

Does the device work now?

YES → Success!

NO → Contact the device vendor for service.

Return to top of flowchart for additional steps.

706

Can't Detect Installed IEEE-1394 Port

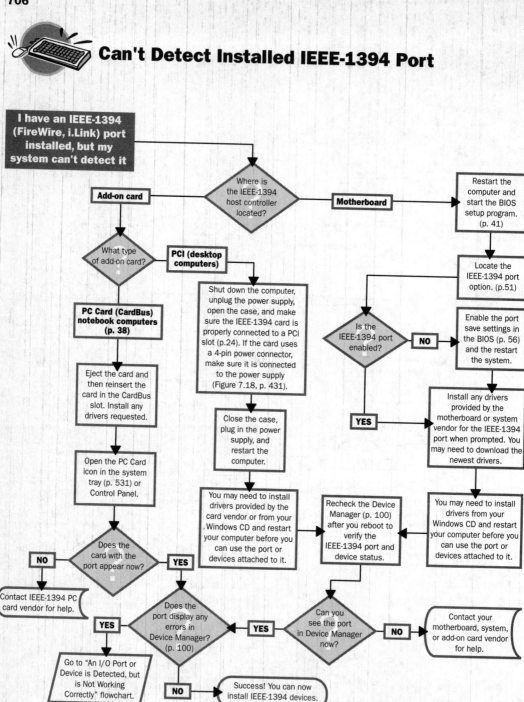

IEEE-1394 Device Troubleshooting

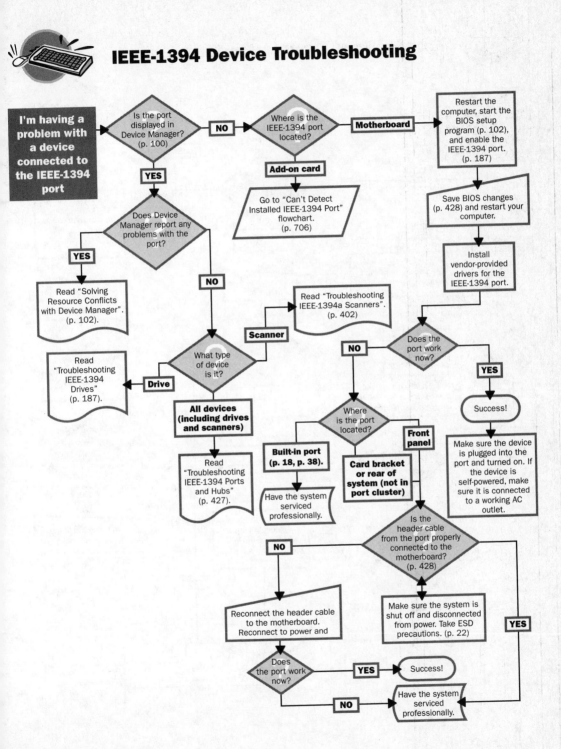

Parallel Port Troubleshooting

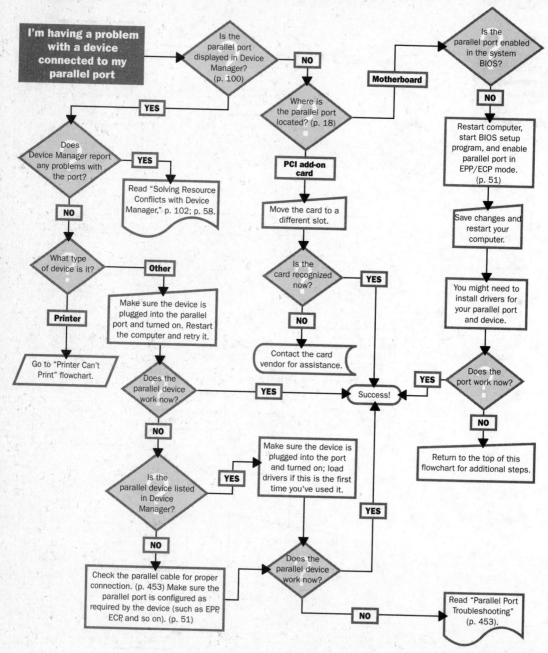

I'm having a problem with a device connected to my parallel port

Is the parallel port displayed in Device Manager? (p. 100)

NO

Where is the parallel port located? (p. 18)

Motherboard

Is the parallel port enabled in the system BIOS?

NO

Restart computer, start BIOS setup program, and enable parallel port in EPP/ECP mode. (p. 51)

Save changes and restart your computer.

You might need to install drivers for your parallel port and device.

Does the port work now?

YES

Return to the top of this flowchart for additional steps.

NO

YES

Does Device Manager report any problems with the port?

YES

Read "Solving Resource Conflicts with Device Manager," p. 102; p. 58.

PCI add-on card

Move the card to a different slot.

Is the card recognized now?

YES

NO

Contact the card vendor for assistance.

NO

What type of device is it?

Other

Make sure the device is plugged into the parallel port and turned on. Restart the computer and retry it.

Printer

Go to "Printer Can't Print" flowchart.

Does the parallel device work now?

YES

Success!

NO

Is the parallel device listed in Device Manager?

YES

Make sure the device is plugged into the port and turned on; load drivers if this is the first time you've used it.

YES

NO

Check the parallel cable for proper connection. (p. 453) Make sure the parallel port is configured as required by the device (such as EPP, ECP, and so on). (p. 51)

Does the parallel device work now?

NO

Read "Parallel Port Troubleshooting" (p. 453).

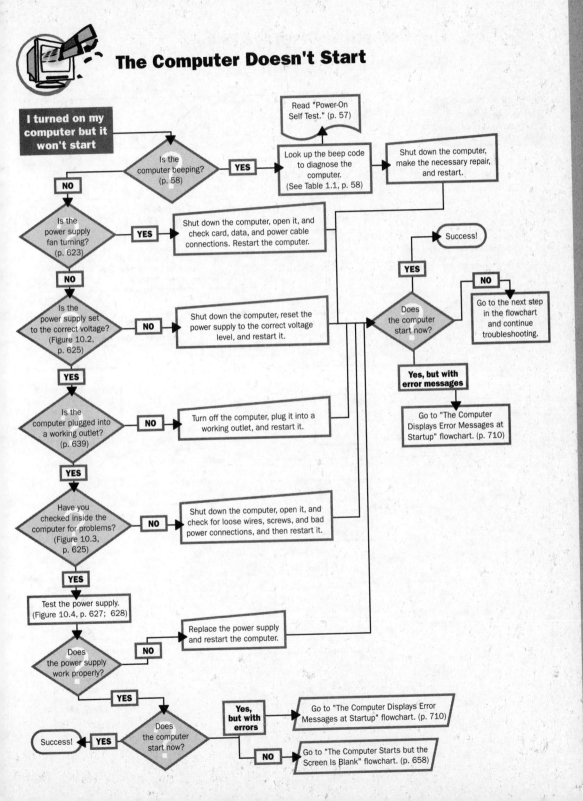

The Computer Doesn't Start

I turned on my computer but it won't start

Is the computer beeping? (p. 58)

YES → Look up the beep code to diagnose the computer. (See Table 1.1, p. 58)

Read "Power-On Self Test." (p. 57)

→ Shut down the computer, make the necessary repair, and restart.

NO

Is the power supply fan turning? (p. 623)

YES → Shut down the computer, open it, and check card, data, and power cable connections. Restart the computer.

NO

Is the power supply set to the correct voltage? (Figure 10.2, p. 625)

NO → Shut down the computer, reset the power supply to the correct voltage level, and restart it.

YES

Is the computer plugged into a working outlet? (p. 639)

NO → Turn off the computer, plug it into a working outlet, and restart it.

YES

Have you checked inside the computer for problems? (Figure 10.3, p. 625)

NO → Shut down the computer, open it, and check for loose wires, screws, and bad power connections, and then restart it.

YES

Test the power supply. (Figure 10.4, p. 627; 628)

Does the power supply work properly?

NO → Replace the power supply and restart the computer.

YES

Does the computer start now?

YES → Success!

NO → Go to the next step in the flowchart and continue troubleshooting.

Yes, but with error messages → Go to "The Computer Displays Error Messages at Startup" flowchart. (p. 710)

Does the computer start now?

Yes, but with errors → Go to "The Computer Displays Error Messages at Startup" flowchart. (p. 710)

Success! ← **YES**

NO → Go to "The Computer Starts but the Screen Is Blank" flowchart. (p. 658)

The Computer Displays Error Messages at Startup

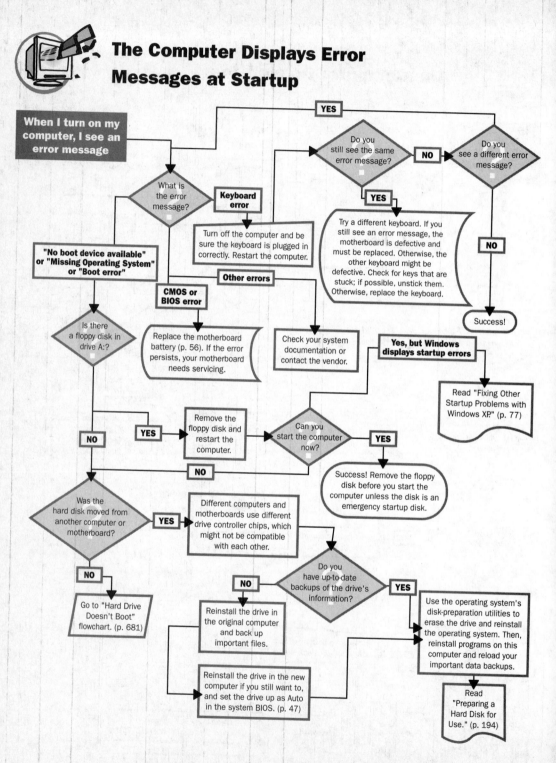

When I turn on my computer, I see an error message

What is the error message?

Keyboard error

Turn off the computer and be sure the keyboard is plugged in correctly. Restart the computer.

Other errors

CMOS or BIOS error

"No boot device available" or "Missing Operating System" or "Boot error"

Is there a floppy disk in drive A:?

Replace the motherboard battery (p. 56). If the error persists, your motherboard needs servicing.

Check your system documentation or contact the vendor.

Do you still see the same error message?

YES

Try a different keyboard. If you still see an error message, the motherboard is defective and must be replaced. Otherwise, the other keyboard might be defective. Check for keys that are stuck; if possible, unstick them. Otherwise, replace the keyboard.

NO

Do you see a different error message?

YES

NO

Success!

Yes, but Windows displays startup errors

Read "Fixing Other Startup Problems with Windows XP." (p. 77)

NO — **YES**

Remove the floppy disk and restart the computer.

Can you start the computer now?

YES

NO

Success! Remove the floppy disk before you start the computer unless the disk is an emergency startup disk.

Was the hard disk moved from another computer or motherboard?

YES

Different computers and motherboards use different drive controller chips, which might not be compatible with each other.

NO

Go to "Hard Drive Doesn't Boot" flowchart. (p. 681)

NO

Reinstall the drive in the original computer and back up important files.

Do you have up-to-date backups of the drive's information?

YES

Use the operating system's disk-preparation utilities to erase the drive and reinstall the operating system. Then, reinstall programs on this computer and reload your important data backups.

Reinstall the drive in the new computer if you still want to, and set the drive up as Auto in the system BIOS. (p. 47)

Read "Preparing a Hard Disk for Use." (p. 194)

Windows Starts only in Safe Mode

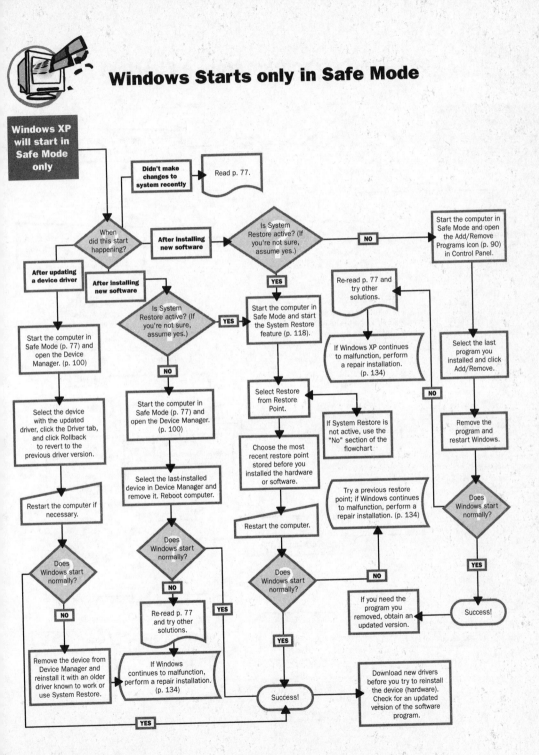

Can't Start a Program from a Shortcut

I can't start a program from its Start menu or Desktop shortcut

Did you boot in Safe Mode? (p. 77)

YES → Some programs and devices aren't available in Safe Mode. Reboot normally and retry.

NO

Is the program located on a network drive?

YES → Can you access other network resources?

NO → Log off and log on to the system again so you can reconnect with network resources.

YES

Right-click on the shortcut, select Properties, and view the path to the program or file.

YES ← Can you access the network now?

NO →

NO (Is the program located on a network drive? → Right-click...)

Can you access the network now? **NO** → Go to "Some Network Users Can't Acess Shared Resources" flowchart. (p. 673)

Does the shortcut point to the correct file?

YES → Click Find Target (Windows will attempt to locate the file referenced in the shortcut).

NO → Shortcuts can be altered by installing or removing a drive or by other means. → Create a new shortcut to the file; see p. 141 for an example.

YES ↑

What is the result of Find Target?

Folder opens → Windows opens the folder containing the file and highlights the file. → Double-click the file to open it. → Can you open the file?

Can you open the file? **YES**

Can you open the file? **NO** →

"Missing Shortcut" error → The file to which the shortcut points has been deleted or moved. → Reinstall the file referred to in the shortcut from a backup or by reinstalling the program. ← **NO**

Do you see an error message? **YES** → Go to "A Program Displays an Error When I Use It" flowchart. (p. 713)

Do you see an error message? **NO**

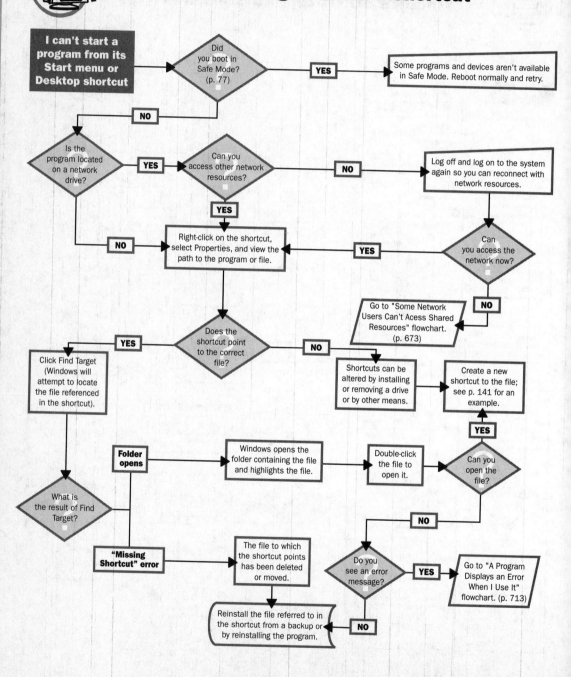

A Program Displays an Error When I Use It

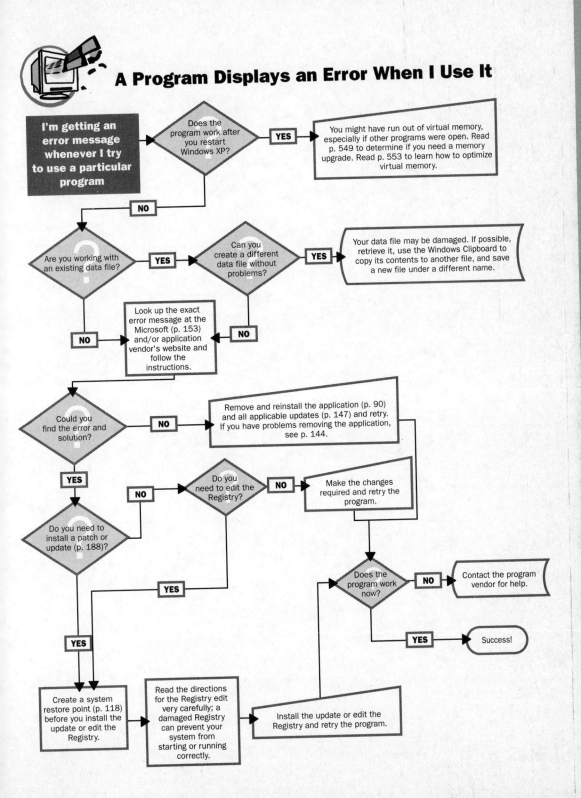

I'm getting an error message whenever I try to use a particular program

Does the program work after you restart Windows XP?

YES → You might have run out of virtual memory, especially if other programs were open. Read p. 549 to determine if you need a memory upgrade. Read p. 553 to learn how to optimize virtual memory.

NO

Are you working with an existing data file?

YES → Can you create a different data file without problems?

YES → Your data file may be damaged. If possible, retrieve it, use the Windows Clipboard to copy its contents to another file, and save a new file under a different name.

NO → Look up the exact error message at the Microsoft (p. 153) and/or application vendor's website and follow the instructions. ← **NO**

Could you find the error and solution?

NO → Remove and reinstall the application (p. 90) and all applicable updates (p. 147) and retry. If you have problems removing the application, see p. 144.

YES

Do you need to edit the Registry?

NO → Make the changes required and retry the program.

Do you need to install a patch or update (p. 188)?

NO

YES

Does the program work now?

NO → Contact the program vendor for help.

YES → Success!

YES

Create a system restore point (p. 118) before you install the update or edit the Registry.

Read the directions for the Registry edit very carefully; a damaged Registry can prevent your system from starting or running correctly.

Install the update or edit the Registry and retry the program.

Index

Numbers

A

F

faded printouts (laser/LED printers), 275-276

failure, points of
definition of, 14
front-mounted ports, 17-18
interior of computer, 27, 30
notebook computers, 40-41
peripheral cabling, 20-22
power supply, 22

fans, 598

FAT32, 196

field service kits, 24

File and Printer Sharing for Microsoft Networks, 496

File Signature Verification, 113, 120

file systems, 196

files
file-format compatibility, 149-150
ntbtlog.txt bootlog file, 79-81
page files, 551, 558-561
saving from websites, 477

firewalls, 159, 542-543
Advanced settings, 545
exceptions, 543-545

FireWire drives. See IEEE-1394 drives

firmware, updating, 502-503

FIXBOOT, 76

fixed IP addresses, 534

flash memory cards
printing from, 265-266
readers, 383-384

Flash Player, 467

flexATX motherboards, upgrading, 604

flicker (displays), 315-316

floppy disks, non-bootable floppy disks in drive A:, 169-170

Folder Options, 96

folders, configuring applications to use, 149

Forced Hardware, 116

formatting hard drives, 194-200

front-mounted header cables, connecting, 429

front-mounted ports, 15-16

front panel connectors, 35-36

front panel failures, 30

Fulton, Wayne, 404

G

gaming
3D gaming
3D sound, 348-350
AGP chipset drivers, 337-338
audio acceleration settings, 350
speeding up, 332-336
website resources, 336
troubleshooting, 151-152

gamma controls, 307-308

gateways, 504, 524-528

General settings (Internet Options), 477

General tab
Dial-Up Networking, 480
printer properties, 277

generic USB hubs, 425

geometry settings (desktop), 304

gibberish output (printers), 290-291

Gibson Research SpinRite 6, 651

graphics
3D gaming
AGP chipset drivers, 337-338
speeding up, 332-336
website resources, 336
acceleration settings, 320-321
diagnosing problems, 294-295
displays
adjusting brightness of, 305-308
common problems, 296-297
damaged/defective displays, 317
high-contrast option, 311-313
icon size, adjusting, 308-310
integrated graphics, 323
memory, increasing, 323
refresh rates, 315-316
resolution, 308-310
screen flicker, 315-316
text size, adjusting, 308-310
icons
resizing, 308-310
spacing between, 313-314
multiple monitors
3D graphics, 330
configuring, 324-325
drivers, 331
enabling, 325-331
troubleshooting, 328-331
photos
recovering from digital cameras, 374-377
speeding access to, 384
viewing, 377-379
saving from websites, 477

X-Y-Z